D1223647

The Cambridge History of American Theatre

This is an authoritative and wide-ranging history of American theatre in all its dimensions, from theatre building to playwriting, directors, performers, and designers. Engaging the theatre as a performance art, a cultural institution, and a fact of American social and political life, the History addresses the economic context that conditioned the drama presented. The history approaches its subject with a full awareness of relevant developments in literary criticism, cultural analysis, and performance theory. At the same time, it is designed to be an accessible, challenging narrative. All volumes include an extensive overview and timeline, followed by chapters on specific aspects of theatre.

Volume Three examines the development of the theatre after World War II, through the productions of Broadway and beyond and into regional theatre across the country. Contributors also analyze new directions in theatre design, directing, and acting, as well as key plays and playwrights through the 1990s.

The Cambridge History
of American Theatre

Volume Three

The Cambridge History of American Theatre

Volume Three:
Post-World War II to the 1990s

Edited by

Don B. Wilmeth
Brown University

Christopher Bigsby
University of East Anglia

JENKS L.R.C.
GORDON COLLEGE
255 GRAPEVINE RD.
WENHAM, MA 01984-1895

CAMBRIDGE
UNIVERSITY PRESS

PUBLISHED BY THE PRESS SYNDICATE OF THE UNIVERSITY OF CAMBRIDGE
The Pitt Building, Trumpington Street, Cambridge, United Kingdom

CAMBRIDGE UNIVERSITY PRESS
The Edinburgh Building, Cambridge CB2 2RU, UK   http://www.cup.cam.ac.uk
40 West 20th Street, New York NY 10011-4211, USA   http://www.cup.org
10 Stamford Road, Oakleigh, Melbourne 3166, Australia

First published 2000

Printed in the United Kingdom at the University Press, Cambridge

Typeset in ITC Cheltenham Book 10/13   [SE]

A catalogue record for this book is available from the British Library

ISBN 0 521 66959 6 hardback

Volume 1: *Beginnings to 1870*
ISBN: 0521 47204 0
Volume 2: *1870–1945*
ISBN: 0521 65179 4
Three volume set
ISBN: 0521 78092 6

Contents

List of Illustrations

(credits appear with each photo)

Contributors

The Editors

CHRISTOPHER BIGSBY is Professor of American Studies at the University of East Anglia in Norwich, England, and has published more than twenty books on British and American culture, including *Confrontation and Commitment: A Study of Contemporary American Drama 1959–1966* (1967); *The Black American Writer,* two volumes (1969); *The Second Black Renaissance* (1980); *Joe Orton* (1982); *A Critical Introduction to Twentieth Century American Drama,* three volumes (1982–85); *David Mamet* (1985); *Modern American Drama 1940–1990* (1992); *Contemporary American Playwrights* (1999). He is the editor of *Contemporary English Drama* (1991); *Arthur Miller and Company* (1990); *The Portable Arthur Miller* (1995); and *The Cambridge Companion to Arthur Miller* (1997). He is also the author of radio and television plays and of three novels: *Hester* (1994), *Pearl* (1995), and *Still Lives* (1996).

DON B. WILMETH is The Asa Messer Distinguished Professor and Professor of Theatre and English at Brown University, Providence, Rhode Island. He is the author, editor, or co-editor of more than a dozen books, including *The American Stage to World War I: A Guide to Information Sources* (1978); the award-winning *George Frederick Cooke: Machiavel of the Stage* (1980); *American and English Popular Entertainment* (1980); *The Language of American Popular Entertainment* (1981); *Variety Entertainment and Outdoor Amusements* (1982); the *Cambridge Guide to American Theatre* (co-editor 1993 edition with Tice L. Miller; editor 1996 paperback edition); and *Staging the Nation: Plays from the American Theatre 1787–1909* (1998). With Rosemary Cullen he co-edited plays by Augustin Daly and William Gillette, and currently he edits for Cambridge University Press a series, Studies in American Theatre and Drama. He is a frequent contributor to reference works and sits on editorial boards of six journals. A past Guggenheim Fellow and President of the American Society for Theatre Research, he was Dean of the College of Fellows of the American

Theatre, 1996–98. In November 1998 he was presented a special achievement award by the New England Theatre Conference for his contribution to the theatrical profession with an impact on the national level.

The Contributors

ARNOLD ARONSON teaches in the Theatre Division of the Columbia University School of the Arts (where he served as Chair, 1991–98). Author of *American Set Design* (1985) and *The History and Theory of Environmental Scenography* (1981), he served as editor of *Theatre Design & Technology* from 1978 to 1988 and has contributed articles on theatre design and avant-garde theatre to a wide range of publications. He is Chair of the History and Theory Commission of the International Organization of Scenographers, Theatre Architects, and Technicians, and he curated the American exhibit of scenic and costume design and theatre architecture at the 1995 Prague Quadrennial. In addition to Columbia he has chaired programs at Hunter College and the University of Michigan and taught at Virginia, Cornell, and Delaware.

MARVIN CARLSON is the Sidney E. Cohn Distinguished Professor of Theatre and Comparative Literature at the Graduate Center of the City University of New York. He has received the ATHE Career Achievement Award, the George Freedley Award for contribution to the literature of the theatre, the George Jean Nathan Award for dramatic criticism, and is a Fellow of the American Theatre. He is the founding editor of the journal *Western European Stages* and the author of many books and essays on American and European theatre history and theory. His most recent books are *Performance: A Critical Introduction* (1996) and *Voltaire and the Theatre of His Age* (1998).

JONATHAN CURLEY, a graduate of Brown University, is a former Fulbright recipient to Ireland and currently a doctoral student in English at New York University.

JOHN DEGEN is a frequent director of musicals at Florida State University and teaches in this area. He contributed numerous entries on musical theatre for the *Cambridge Guide to American Theatre* (1993) and has published articles in the *Theatre Journal, Theatre Survey, Theatre History Studies, Victorian Poetry*, and the *Kurt Weill Newsletter.*

MEL GUSSOW, a critic and author, writes about theatre and other arts for the *New York Times.* He is the author of *Conversations with Pinter* (1994) and *Conversations with Stoppard* (1995), both published by Grove Press, and of *Don't Say Yes Until I Finish Talking: A Biography of Darryl F. Zanuck* (1971). He is the author of profiles for *The New Yorker* and other magazines. Winner of the George Jean Nathan Award for Dramatic Criticism, his reviews and essays were collected in *Theater on the Edge: New Visions, New Voices* (1988). A recipient of a Guggenheim Fellowship, Gussow for three years served as President of the New York Drama Critics' Circle. Prior to coming to the *New York Times,* he was a critic and cultural writer on *Newsweek* magazine. He is a graduate of Middlebury College (and recipient of its Alumni Achievement Award) and of Columbia University's Graduate School of Journalism.

FOSTER HIRSCH is Professor of Film at Brooklyn College, City University of New York, and the author of fifteen books on theatre and film. His most recent is *The Boys From Syracuse* (1998), a study of the Shuberts' theatrical empire. He has written studies of The Actors Studio, Harold Prince, Hollywood acting, film noir, and of the film work of Laurence Olivier, Joseph Losey, and Woody Allen. Current projects include a book on Joseph Papp and the New York Shakespeare Festival. Among publications that have featured his essays and reviews are *American Theatre, The Nation, The New York Times, Film Comment,* and *Film Quarterly.*

SAMUEL L. LEITER is Professor of Theatre at Brooklyn College, City University of New York, and the Graduate Center, CUNY. He has been editor of *Asian Theatre Journal* since 1992 and has published articles in such publications as *Literature East and West, Educational Theatre Journal, Drama Survey, Theatre History Studies, Players, Theatre Crafts,* and *Asian Theatre Journal.* His numerous books include the three-volume *Encyclopedia of the New York Stage, 1920–1930* (1985), *1930–1940* (1989), and *1940–1950* (1992); *From Belasco to Brook: Representative Directors of the English-Speaking Stage* (1991); and *From Stanislavsky to Barrault: Representative Directors of the European Stage* (1991). He is also an actor and director.

MARTHA LOMONACO is Associate Professor and Director of the Theatre Program for the Department of Visual & Performing Arts at Fairfield University in Connecticut. She is an active director, having premiered new works in New York City, throughout New England, and at the Edinburgh Festival Fringe, and writer, who has published articles on American theatre and popular entertainments. She is author of *Every Week, A Broadway Revue: The Tamiment Playhouse, 1921–1960* (1992) and is at work on a history of American summer theatre.

LAURENCE MASLON is on the faculty of the Graduate Acting Program at New York University's Tisch School of the Arts, where he also teaches for the Musical Theater Program. A graduate of Brown and Stanford, he worked for seven years at Washington D.C.'s Arena Stage, where he was the Associate Artistic Director. At Arena he directed, wrote, or adapted many productions. He has contributed to the *Cambridge Guide to American Theatre* (1993),

American National Biography (1999), and *Dramaturgy in America* (1996), and has written articles and drawn caricatures in *American Theatre* magazine. He wrote the "Mr. Gershwin Goes to Washington" concert for Carnegie Hall and is currently working on a musical version of Kaufman and Hart's *Once in a Lifetime.*

MATTHEW ROUDANÉ is Professor of English at Georgia State University in Atlanta, where he specializes in American drama. Among his publications are: *Understanding Edward Albee* (1987); *Conversations with Arthur Miller* (1987); *American Dramatists* (1989); *"Who's Afraid of Virginia Woolf?": Necessary Fictions, Terrifying Realities* (1990); *Public Issues, Private Tensions: Contemporary American Drama* (1993); *American Drama Since 1960: A Critical History* (1996). He is the editor of *Approaches to Teaching Miller's "Death of a Salesman"* (1995) and *The Cambridge Companion to Tennessee Williams* (1997). He is also editor of the *South Atlantic Review.*

JUNE SCHLUETER is the Charles A. Dana Professor of English at Lafayette College. Her numerous publications include *Metafictional Characters in Modern Drama* (1979); *The Plays and Novels of Peter Handke* (1981); *Arthur Miller* (1987) with James K. Flanagan; *Reading Shakespeare in Performance: "King Lear"* (1991) with James Lusardi; and *Dramatic Closure: Reading the End* (1995). She has edited six books, including *Feminist Rereadings of Modern American Drama* (1989) and *Modern American Drama: The Female Canon* (1990). She has also published essays and reviews on modern drama and Shakespeare and is co-editor of *Shakespeare Bulletin.*

RONN SMITH has written about theatre, film, and television design for a variety of magazines, including *American Theatre* and *Theatre Crafts.* He is the author of *American Set Design 2* (1991) and *Nothing But the Truth: A Play* (1997). He is also a frequent director.

Preface and Acknowledgments

As was demonstrated in Volume One of this study, the American theatre has a history going back to the first encounter of Europeans with what, to them, was a new continent and, in the form of Native American rituals and ceremonies, a prehistory. In Volume Two the contributors explained that the theatre, the most public of the arts, has always been a sensitive gauge of social pressures and public issues; the actor has been a central icon of a society which, from its inception, has seen itself as performing, on a national stage, a destiny of international significance. As articulated in the introduction to this volume, the period since World War II has led to even greater variegated theatre with worldwide influence.

For the purposes of this History we have chosen to use the word "theatre" to include all aspects of the dramatic experience, including major popular and paratheatrical forms. Contributors have been asked to address a particular aspect of that experience – whether it be theatre architecture, stage design, acting, playwriting, directing, and so forth – but they have also been invited to stress the wider context of those subjects. Indeed, they have been encouraged to engage the context within which theatre itself operates. Hence, we have set out to produce a history which will be authoritative and wide-ranging, which will offer a critical insight into plays and playwrights, but which will also engage the theatre as a performance art, a cultural institution, and a fact of American social and political life. We have sought to recognize changing styles of presentation and performance and to address the economic context which conditions the drama presented. This may lead, on occasion, to a certain recrossing of tracks as, for example, in the case of a chapter on playwrights which invokes the career of particular actors and a chapter on actors which describes the plays in which they appeared, but this is both inevitable and desirable, stressing, as it does, the interdependence of all aspects of this craft.

The theatre has reflected the diversity of America and the special circumstances in which it has operated in an expanding country moving toward a sense of national identity. The history of the American stage and the making of America have been coterminous, often self-consciously so, and to that end each volume begins with a timeline followed by a wide-ranging essay which attempts to locate the theatre in the context of a developing society. Both timeline and overview also allow individual authors to avoid any urge to offer inclusiveness and to provide, when appropriate, more detailed coverage of important individuals or events, so that, for example, Arnold Aronson offers a unique perspective in his introductory overview chapter, while other authors, such as Marvin Carlson in chapter 2, focus attention on one particular aspect of this history, such as alternative theatre.

The History could have run to many more volumes but the economics of publication finally determined its length, together with the number of illustrations that were possible. In the case of this present volume, this has meant both that certain choices of emphasis have been necessary, with the result that more attention has been paid to some topics rather than others, and that we have not been able to include as many illustrations as we would have liked. The precise division between the three volumes and the strategies involved in structuring this History, however (especially since from the outset it was agreed that this would be a collective history), was a matter of serious debate, a debate in which the editors were assisted by others in meetings which took place in 1994 at Brown University, in the United States, and the following year at York University, in Canada. It is proper, in fact, to pause here and, as we did in Volumes One and Two, to gratefully acknowledge the financial assistance for the Brown meeting given by Brown University, the curators of its special collections, and Cambridge University Press. For the York meeting we are indebted to Christopher Innes, who served as an advisor to the editors, and the Social Sciences and Humanities Research Council of Canada, who helped fund the expenses. In Providence we were able to gather a notable group of experts: Arnold Aronson, the late Frances Bzowski, T. Susan Chang, Rosemary Cullen, Spencer Golub, James V. Hatch, Warren Kliewer, Brooks McNamara, Brenda Murphy, Tom Postlewait, Vera Mowry Roberts, Matthew Roudané, David Savran, Ronn Smith, Susan Harris Smith, and Sarah Stanton. In Canada the editors were joined by Christopher Innes and the authors of overview essays for each volume (Arnold Aronson, Tom Postlewait, and Bruce McConachie). We are indebted to these experts for their thoughtful and challenging ideas and recommendations.

Ultimately, of course, the editors accept responsibility for the present format, but without the preliminary discussions we would have doubtlessly floundered. In the final analysis, the fact that we have chosen roughly 1870 and 1945 as defining chronological parameters is, in part, an expression of our desire to relate the theatre to a wider public history but in part also a recognition of certain developments internal to theatre itself. Any such divisions have an element of the arbitrary, however, chronological periods doing damage to the continuity of individual careers and stylistic modes. But, division there must be and those we have chosen seem more cogent than any of the others we considered, despite our strong suspicion that any periodization can be misleading. In truth, Volume One extends to the post-Civil War period, and Volume Two, in order to establish some sense of continuity, dovetails the time frame of that volume, as this volume overlaps World War II, though its major emphasis is post-World War II.

The organization of the three volumes does, however, reveal a bias in favor of the modern, which previous prefaces in this series of volumes deplored. Yet it does not presume that theatrical history began with Eugene O'Neill, as often implied, but simply recognizes that the story of the American theatre is one of a momentum which gathers pace with time, while acknowledging the rich heritage and accomplishments of American theatre during its earlier periods.

As suggested above, the History does not offer itself as encyclopedic. Given restrictions of space this could never have been an objective, nor was such a strategy deemed appropriate. Those wishing to research details not found in these pages should consult the *Cambridge Guide to American Theatre* (1993, 1996), edited by Don B. Wilmeth and Tice L. Miller, and *Theatre in the United States: A Documentary History* (vol. I, 1750–1915), edited by Barry Witham (vol. II is well underway). Both works were published by Cambridge University Press, and this History was planned with those volumes in mind, as a complementary effort. The *Guide* is an especially important supplement to this volume. Rather than offer comprehensive detail, what this History does aim to do is to demonstrate that this nation is constructed of more than a set of principles enforced by a common will. It builds itself out of more than contradictions denied by rhetoric or shared experience. The theatre first played its part in shaping the society it served; later it reflected the diversity which was always at odds with a supposed homogeneity. Inevitably derivative, in time it accommodated itself to the new world, and, in creating new forms, in identifying and staging new concerns, was itself a part of the process which it observed and dramatized.

Theatre is international. Today, an American play or prominent production is as likely to open in London as in New York and to find its primary audience outside the country of its birth. The 1997–98 Broadway season was a good example of this, with a revival of *Cabaret* that began its life in England, a blockbuster hit musical *Ragtime* that developed in Canada, and major prizes going to a play which originated in France (*Art* by Yasmina Reza) and one that was Anglo-Irish in origin (*The Beauty Queen of Leenane*). Despite the restrictions imposed by Actors' Equity, actors move between countries, as do directors and designers. Film and television carry drama across national frontiers. Yet, the American playwright still addresses realities, myths, concerns born out of national experiences; the American theatre still stages the private and public anxieties of a people who are what they are because of history. The accomplishments of the American theatre are clear. This is an account of those accomplishments as it is, in part, of that history.

We are extremely grateful for financial support from our institutions – Brown University and the University of East Anglia – and we are pleased to acknowledge the editorial assistance of Diana Beck, funded by the Brown Graduate School, who made many chores less arduous in the early preparation of this volume. The initial idea for this History came from Cambridge editors Sarah Stanton and Victoria Cooper, who not only brought the editors together but have also been a constant source of support and encouragement; Anne Sanow, formerly with Cambridge University Press, and Victoria Cooper, in the British Office of the Press, have helped to shepherd this volume through its various stages, and Audrey Cotterell has served us well in the copy-editing process. The thirteen authors of chapters in this volume are clearly indebted to the scholarship of those who have gone before, as well as to colleagues still active in the field. The specific debts of each author are suggested in notes and, most significantly, in the bibliographical essays that conclude each chapter. Credits for illustrations are indicated with each photograph. Though not successful in every instance, every possible effort has been made to obtain photographic permission. We have nonetheless given credit to all photographers when known and would be delighted to seek formal permission for subsequent editions should contact finally be made. We are grateful to individual authors who furnished or suggested illustrations and the staffs of the collections identified who helped to locate or provide illustrations. In particular, we are pleased to single out the assistance of Melissa Miller of the Humanities Research Center's Theatre Collection at the University of Texas; Ian Rand of the Publicity Department of Livent, Inc.; Christine Nicholson of Davis, California; Oskar Eustis of the Trinity Repertory Theatre; designers Eugene Lee, Harry Matheu, Tony Walton, and John Lee Beatty; Levi D. Phillips of Special Collections, University of California–Davis; John Degen, Martha LoMonaco, and Marvin Carlson; photographer Bill Rice; Peggy Shaw of Split Britches; Carol Bixler of En Garde Arts; Michael B. Dixon and Jennifer McMaster of Actors Theatre of Louisville; Ruth Maleczech of Mabou Mines; Richard Foreman of the Ontological-Hysteric Theatre Company; Anne Reiss of The Wooster Group; Jennifer Garza of the Alley Theatre; and Anna Strasberg and Ivana Ruzak of the Lee Strasberg Theatre Institute. We are especially grateful to Laurence Maslon for the three wonderful caricature composites that he drew expressly for this History and which grace his section on Broadway.

Introduction

Christopher Bigsby

The previous volume of this History told the story of the growth of Broadway theatre, the emergence of major playwrights, the shift from melodrama to a new realism and from that realism to a self-conscious experimentalism. It identified the extent to which the theatre reflected social change, as America moved from a rural to an urban economy, engaged a modernity which both delighted and appalled, and found in social inequity the source of dramatic energy. It charted the continuing influence, on actor training and design no less than dramaturgy, of the European theatre but also identified the extent to which America now exercised a powerful role. Through boom and Depression, the theatre in all its guises – from the Little Theatre movement, to the Federal Theatre, Broadway comedies and musicals, to powerful dramas of social and psychological experience – proved a public art with public appeal.

Yet already that role was threatened by the emergence of Hollywood. Ahead lay television. By the turn of the twenty-first century hundreds of channels would be available while cyberspace would exert its own seductive allure. Meanwhile, the economics of an art which required the collaborative efforts of a large number of people, used its plant inefficiently, and was often inconveniently situated, made it potentially less attractive than other arts or forms of entertainment.

This volume, though, is not an account of decline. Indeed, in some respects it covers a period in which the achievements of the American theatre were acknowledged worldwide as never before. For much of the second half of the century its playwrights were dominant, its musicals defined the genre, its actors, directors, and designers proved uniquely talented and internationally influential. But it did change in radical ways, which, unsurprisingly, mirrored transformations in society.

After a decade or so Broadway declined, a decline balanced by the emergence, in New York, of Off- and Off-Off Broadway. A similar development was to occur in Chicago and elsewhere. Indeed, the dominance of New York itself

1

came to an end as regional theatres spread throughout the country, generating plays that then fed back to Broadway, reversing the flow of the prewar world. And if audiences diversified on a regional basis, so they did on that of race, gender, national origin, and sexual preference. In other words, as the ruling metaphor of American society changed, from melting pot to rainbow, the theatre acknowledged this. The presumed homogeneity of the audience no longer prevailed. Just as television and publishing began to adopt a strategy of niche marketing, the theatre sought out a variety of different audiences, though often the concerns of such groups proved paradigmatic.

There were parallels with previous periods. The annual accounts of New York theatre offered by Otis L. Guernsey, Jr. itemized the continuing impact of British theatre, a thread which runs through all three of these volumes. It was responsible for just under half the Tony Awards for Best Play between 1964 and 1989 and rather more than half of the New York Drama Critics' Circle Best Play awards for the same period. By the 1970s, indeed, the British, previously believed to be genetically incapable of writing musicals, began to displace the homegrown product, until that time rightly regarded as one of the major accomplishments of the American theatre. Indeed in June 1997, *Cats*, by the ubiquitous Andrew Lloyd Webber, became the longest running musical in American theatrical history, displacing *A Chorus Line* (1975). Meanwhile, the experimental theatre of the teens and twenties had its corollary in the fifties and sixties, modernism was revisited, and where the Depression had radicalized the theatre in the thirties, the war in Vietnam did the same in the sixties and early seventies.

For the first time, though, the Federal Theatre aside, public subsidy was granted and though it was modest – occasionally to the point of near invisibility (in the 1970–71 season the American government's support for the arts amounted to seven and a half cents per head; the figure for West Germany was two dollars and forty-two cents; that for England, one dollar and twenty-three cents) – it was a sign that theatre was at last acknowledged as an art which made legitimate demands on the public purse as well as on public attention. Nonetheless it was an embattled art, constantly struggling to survive. But it was an art which accurately registered the shifting mood and concerns of a nation which stepped from Depression into war and from war into the uncertainties of a post-nuclear age. And as such it told the story, in the words of Philip Roth's Nathan Zuckerman, of the "disruption of the anticipated American future that was simply to have unrolled out of the solid American past, out of each generation's getting smarter . . . out of each generation's breaking away from the parochialism a little further" (*American Pastoral*, 85). In part, as the decades passed, that involved acknowledging what Roth calls "the indigenous American beserk," and in part recognizing that the centripetal project implied in the motto *E Pluribus Unum* could be seen as a false rather than simply a utopian model, as radically divergent experiences were presented on America's stages.

The war marked another kind of divide. Some of those who had helped define the 1920s and 1930s did not survive to do the same for the postwar world. In the novel, Theodore Dreiser, Sherwood Anderson, F. Scott Fitzgerald, Nathanael West, and Gertrude Stein died between 1940 and 1946, while Ernest Hemingway, William Faulkner, and John Steinbeck no longer seemed to have a purchase on their society, despite their international recognition in the form of the Nobel Prize. In the theatre, likewise, Susan Glaspell, Sidney Howard, Jerome Kern, Lorenz Hart, and, within a few years, Philip Barry and Robert Sherwood were dead, while Maxwell Anderson and Lillian Hellman produced little to rival their earlier work.

Eugene O'Neill, meanwhile, had succumbed to a Parkinson-like disease which frustrated his efforts to write. He had, however, stored up works of great accomplishment, which, for over a decade after the war, would light up a Broadway season, works which plundered his life for the raw materials of plays that confronted his characters with their failure to realize the hopes that had once energized and now ironized them, plays whose very bleakness he had judged too great for wartime audiences.

A further irony awaited, however, in that the two not so very young men who appeared on the scene in the mid-1940s – Tennessee Williams and Arthur Miller, both in their thirties at the time of their first Broadway successes – were in fact shaped by the previous decade in which they had written, and indeed staged, radical dramas. They certainly reflected the mood of their own time – Miller, in particular, taking pride in his sensitivity to the contemporary – but both were marked by a decade in which the solitary individual was obliged to acknowledge a social obligation or be excluded alike from history and the moral world. Miller, as was signaled by the title of his first success, *All My Sons*, opted for a drama which staged the individual's struggle to negotiate personal meaning in a social context. Williams, as is indicated by the title of one of his plays, *Fugitive Kind*, explored the plight of the self in recoil from the public world.

Stylistically, O'Neill moved from a lyric celebration of the outsider, to an exuberant expressionism, to a strained realism, a naturalism which mocked its own assumptions. Williams and Miller both sought a more fluid, or, to use Williams's own word, plastic staging in which dramatic metaphor found a correlative in visual symbol. O'Neill's appeal lay in a relentless quality, as characters were driven beyond the point at which they could negotiate the terms of their existence. Miller's lay in the strenuous demands made of those required suddenly to confront the nature and extent of their own moral failings. Williams took his audience in a wholly different direction. His plays often threatened and, indeed, delivered, violence or displayed sexual need. Their

southern settings and lyrically expressive language offered a seductive exot-
icism not wholly unrelated to that being explored by Jack Kerouac, for whom
the improvisatory free spirit lay, if not at the heart of meaning, then at the
heart of the search for such.

Writing of the 1950s, Daniel Bell observed that: "America in mid-century is in
many respects a turbulent country. Oddly enough, it is a turbulence born, not
of depression, but of prosperity. Contrary to the somewhat simple notion that
prosperity dissolves all social problems, the American experience demonstrates that prosperity brings in its wake new anxieties, new strains, new
urgencies" (*The End of Ideology*, 103). Prosperity, indeed, was in part the
problem. As Kenneth Keniston and Paul Goodman, psychologist and philosopher respectively, were to observe, materialism was not an ideal in itself; on
the contrary, it provoked a desire for transcendence, for a personal economy
independent of that generated by a mechanistic civilization. The very
success of America gave economic power to a generation that in time found
the ritual of earning and spending inadequate to their needs. They, or at least
a number of them, became rebels without knowing the faith in whose name
they rebelled. America, immediately after the war, may have celebrated its
renewed status as a city on the hill and many of its citizens begun to dream
a familiar dream, but there were others, and many writers among them, for
whom the logic of history had other lessons to teach than America's steady
rise toward the empyrean.

Looking back from the distance of the mid-seventies, Bell, or, rather, the
writers whose views he summarized, and who had themselves emerged as
commentators and primary movers (Norman O. Brown, Michel Foucault, R. D.
Laing, and, in another sense, Charles Reich and Theodore Roszak), saw a generation which, in the late fifties and through the sixties, had chosen as their
field of revolt "consciousness: a new polymorphous sensuality, the lifting of
repression, the permeability of madness and normality, a new psychedelic
awareness, the exploration of pleasure" (Bell, *The Coming of Post-Industrial
Society*, 476). But this is not how the world seemed in 1945 when the war
ended and Americans celebrated the return of what they took to be normalcy.

As ever, wars both mark a social and psychological divide and provoke a
desire for continuities. Philip Roth, or his fictional alter ego Nathan
Zuckerman, in *American Pastoral*, speaks of "the clock of history" being
"reset" as Americans celebrated the end of the Second World War. "Everything
was in motion," he insists. Men were back from Europe and Japan. America
was the sole possessor of the Bomb. What could resist the newly unleashed
energy of a nation politically secure and economically booming? Admittedly,
the Depression was only a few years in the past and a tremor of anxiety could
still pass through those who had lived through that time, but the rallying cry,

as he recalls it, was "*Make something of yourselves.*" His generation, he insists, "were steered relentlessly in the direction of success" (41).

But Roth's novel is a story not just of paradise remembered (the title of its first section) but of paradise lost. For if ahead lay a materialism to be celebrated and deplored, ahead also lay assassinations, racial conflict, riots, corruptions, and another war which scarred a generation, and his novel is an account of the loss of innocence, the crumbling of assurance, a deepening anxiety about personal and public meaning, the "disruption of the anticipated American future... the ritual postimmigrant struggle for success turning pathological" (85–86).

But that lay far ahead. For the moment, the response was euphoria, followed by a desire to reach back not to Depression but the world which that disruption of the dream had seemed to invalidate, a world of material well-being and a confident faith in American principles. Consumerism was the new god while Manifest Destiny seemed reinstalled and legitimated. People picked up their lives and elected first a haberdasher from Missouri and then a general from Denison, Texas (who described his policy as one of "dynamic conservatism") as President, content to view the past only as processed through the calculated nostalgia of *Saturday Evening Post* covers. Meanwhile, a pediatrician, Dr. Benjamin Spock, was on hand to tell mothers that a new day had dawned, that they should trust themselves. He reassured them that the rigors of discipline need no longer prevail; desires could be satisfied without guilt.

The one-car family became the two-car family. Television plugged Americans into a common cerebral cortex. The consumer society consumed. As John Updike's narrator observed, in a short story called "When Everyone Was Pregnant," "Guiltlessness. Our fat Fifties cars, how we loved them, revved them: no thought of pollution. . . Romance of consumption at its height. Shopping for baby food in the gaudy trash of the supermarkets. Purchasing power: young, newly powerful, born to consume." And yet, as he pointed out, this coexisted with a "smug conviction that the world was doomed. Beyond the sparkling horizon, an absolute enemy. Above us, bombs whose flash would fill the scene like a cup to overflowing" (in *Museums and Women*, 92–93). And, indeed, the world had changed profoundly. The sky had been lit up by the twin suns of Hiroshima and Nagasaki, and when the Soviet Union broke the American monopoly on nuclear destruction and China was "lost," for the first time a country previously invulnerable to attack felt deeply vulnerable. And since its military and scientific preeminence had been an article of faith, such catastrophes could only be a result of treachery and subversion. When had that subversion begun? Was it, perhaps, in the days of the New Deal or the brief period of U.S.–Soviet cooperation? If so, then it was necessary to rewrite history in such a way as to show that the thirties had been an aberration.

But the war itself had already sent a shock wave through those who could not regard the allied victory as a vindication of the human spirit, and that tremor, as ever, was registered by the writer. Thus, in Europe, the bleakly comic ironies of the absurd had their roots in a very precisely definable political and social reality, while the *nouveau roman*, which marginalized the human figure, was, Alain Robbe-Grillet explained, no more than an expression of what he had observed in a war which relegated the individual human being quite literally to the ash heap. The Jewish writer in particular was unlikely to regard the Holocaust as no more than a brief interruption in the ascent of man.

The Jewish American writer, indeed, took from the war either a sense that the individual was a victim, trying to understand the ironies in which he was apparently trapped, or a desperate desire to reconstitute values apparently so profoundly denied as to negate the very idea of social or metaphysical purpose. Either way there was a sense of deep dismay, often rendered comically. The irony, however, was that by degrees such writers found themselves speaking for those for whom an old world – essentially rural, untroubled – no longer seemed accessible. Nor were Jewish writers the only ones to flirt with black humor (James Purdy, John Hawkes, Kurt Vonnegut, Joseph Heller), or the deracinated or alienated individual (J.D. Salinger, Carson McCullers, Truman Capote). The new world was urban or, at best, suburban and, beyond the glitter of consumer products, was increasingly perceived as charged with tensions, infected with deep insecurities – sexual, financial, racial. What was at stake was a sense of identity and purpose, and unsurprisingly this was felt most acutely by those whose grip on national myths and realities was most tenuous: the Jewish and African American writer. No wonder Sartrean Existentialism hovered in the wings. They might acknowledge their victim status but they also resisted it in the name of an existential drive which was sometimes acknowledged and sometimes not. The irony is that the protagonists of such books as Norman Mailer's *The Naked and the Dead* (1948), Saul Bellow's *Dangling Man* (1944) and *The Victim* (1947), Bernard Malamud's *The Assistant* (1957), Philip Roth's *Goodbye Columbus* (1959), Ralph Ellison's *Invisible Man* (1952), and James Baldwin's essays *Nobody Knows My Name* (1957) came to seem expressions of a more general sense of alienation and anxiety. They might be marginalized by WASP society but such marginalization came increasingly to seem a common, and even celebrated, experience (see Jack Kerouac, Allen Ginsberg, Gregory Corso). In the words of the protagonist of *Invisible Man*, "Who knows but that, on the lower frequencies, I speak for you?"

For Professor of Psychology Kenneth Keniston at Yale University, drawing on his own work and that of others in the fifties and sixties,

> The prevailing images of our culture are images of disintegration, decay, and despair; our highest art involves the fragmentation and distortion of traditional realities; our best drama depicts suffering, misunderstanding, and

breakdown; our worthiest novels are narratives of loneliness, searching, and unfulfillment . . . Judged by the values of past generations, our culture seems obsessed with breakdown, splintering, disintegration, and destruction. Ours is not an age of synthesis but of analysis, not of constructive hopes but of awful destructive potentials, not of commitment but alienation. (*The Uncommitted*, 2)

The argument may have been overstated and the comparison with the past suspect, but this language did, indeed, have currency, not least in literature.

And what was true in the novel and poetry was true also in drama. Neil Simon presented comically what Arthur Miller presented tragically, namely the dilemma of the individual who no longer feels he has a connection with his own life or with the community in which he finds himself. Miller in particular set himself very consciously to reconstitute the moral world denied equally by the Holocaust, which made its way into more than one of his plays, and by a particularly American penchant for denying the past. Those Americans who wanted to believe in business as usual, selling America back to itself as the best product on the market, were, in his plays, made to face the fact of their own fallibility as well as the falseness of the promises which elevated the future over the present and which denied the moral logic which linked that present to the past. He wrote plays which were as centrally concerned with moral identity as the novels of Bellow and Ellison. Indeed, in 1945 he himself wrote a very successful novel, *Focus*, which explored both the nature of American anti-Semitism and the existential dilemma of a man who struggles toward a sense of his own identity and of his responsibility toward others. In his plays his characters cry out their names precisely because identity has been placed under such pressure. The American dream, meanwhile, becomes an evasion, merely the expression of a need for coherence and meaning, a project whose indefinite deferral is a judgment equally of the individual and his society. When Willy Loman, in *Death of a Salesman*, tries to offer his false dreams as an inheritance to his sons he acknowledges a failure which touches very directly on his sense of himself. As Erich Fromm observed:

When a person feels that he has not been able to make sense of his own life, he tries to make sense of it in terms of the life of his children. But one is bound to fail within oneself *and* for the children. The former because the problem of existence can only be solved by each one only for himself, and not by proxy; the latter because one lacks in the very qualities which one needs to guide the children in their own search for an answer. (*The Art of Loving*, 86)

By the same token Tennessee Williams's characters spoke of their sense of paranoia as power and money assumed an implacable authority, and the natural processes of mortality denied the very promises that life seemed to offer. His fragile characters, menaced in their sexuality and their social roles, desperate for a love which simultaneously terrified them, registered something more than his intensely personal sense of oppression as homosexual and artist. Throughout his life he insisted on his radicalism, a radicalism literal enough in the works which he wrote in the thirties, but evident, too, in the subversive drive of plays which constantly celebrated the marginal, the dispossessed, the disregarded. In interviews and public statements he denounced a society which literally and legally proscribed his sexuality but that also, from time to time, menaced the freedom which his plays celebrated even in the moment that that freedom was being withdrawn. What some took for his southern gothicism, his melodramatic imagination, he regarded as a staging of the conflict between an implacable materialism and a redeeming, though ultimately defeated, human spirit.

Despite the fact that decades are little more than convenient means of organizing experience, rarely beginning and ending with any precision, they do, on occasion, have a persuasive shape. It was true of the twenties, heralded by Prohibition, as it was of the thirties, bracketed by the Crash and World War II. The sixties, likewise, obligingly began with what seemed like a clear shift in values, style, and priorities, though the election of John F. Kennedy was perhaps of greater symbolic than actual significance, not least because the drama of his assassination brought an abrupt end to his administration (and it is hard not to think of the events of those days, played out as they were on television, as a kind of theatre). Certainly little was accomplished in his brief presidency either domestically or in terms of foreign policy, beyond a somewhat grudging moral commitment to racial justice at home and a near lethal engagement with the Soviet Union over Cuba and a growing involvement in Vietnam. But everything about him signaled change. He was young, Catholic, sexually active (just how much so only becoming apparent later). He valued the arts, invited writers to the White House, and went to the theatre. His successor, too, invited writers to the White House. The difference was that some of them refused to go because by then, and despite his genuine commitment to social justice, Lyndon Johnson had committed America more completely to the war in Vietnam and this had distorted national politics and radicalized a generation. Robert Lowell and Arthur Miller both declined invitations, Miller, ironically, to Johnson's signing of a bill setting up the National Endowment for the Arts, itself a significant change in attitudes toward support for the arts in America. The impact both of social change and of that war was clear on all aspects of American life.

Not the least important aspect of that change was the emergence, essentially from the mid-fifties onward, of teenagers. With money in their pockets they provoked and responded to a new market in popular music, while finding images of their youthful disaffection in the movies – James Dean's drive to oblivion merely reinforcing his role as social rebel. A decade later they were tuning in, turning on, and dropping out at the behest of Timothy Leary or marching against the war. The contraceptive pill had released them from biological discipline and hence, to a large degree, from moral constraint. Dr. Spock, who had been responsible for their nurturing, now found himself attacked for creating a permissive generation and himself followed what seemed to him to be the logic of his profession, as pediatrician, by protesting the war and even running for the presidency as a way of protecting future generations of babies. In short, within the course of a decade old authorities had lost their power: economic, social, moral.

Kenneth Keniston spoke of an "unprogrammatic alienation," a "rebellion without a cause" (*The Uncommitted*, 67). In his book on alienated youth in America he observed the degree to which the vocabulary of social commentary increasingly stressed the distance between people and between people and the objects of their concern.

> Alienation, estrangement, disaffection, anomie, withdrawal, disengagement, separation, non-involvement, apathy, indifference, and neutralism – all of these terms point to a sense of loss, a growing gap between men and their social world. The drift of our time is away from connection, relation, communion and dialogue, and our intellectual concerns reflect this conviction. Alienation, once seen as imposed *on* men by an unjust economic system, is increasingly chosen *by* men as their basic stance toward society. (*The Uncommitted*, 1)

It is hard not to see this as a description of the mood of Edward Albee's first success, *The Zoo Story* (1959), produced on the cusp of the sixties, in which the protagonist, withdrawn, disaffected, acutely aware of the gap between himself and others, has, indeed, chosen alienation; nor hard either to see in it a reflection of those concerns voiced by another psychologist, Erich Fromm, who, in his fifties book *The Art of Loving*, reflected both Keniston's views and those to be found in Albee's *The American Dream* when he oberved that: "Modern man has transformed himself into a commodity. . . He is alienated from himself, from his fellow men and from nature" (88), consoled by the "strict routine of bureaucratised, mechanical work" (74). The paramount need, Fromm insisted, was "to leave the prison of his aloneness." The mechanism whereby this was to be attained was love: "a power which breaks through the walls which separate man from his fellow men, which unites him with others" (24). The imagery was specifically that taken up by Albee, the potentially religious overtones being preserved in the symbolism of his early plays, as it was by Tennessee Williams, for whom love was indeed an active principle capable of neutralizing the alienation felt by so many of his characters. As the fifties slid into the sixties, love, counterpoised to the mechanistic drive of materialism or, more specifically, of the military, was celebrated as a secular virtue or a spiritual principle, by a counterculture celebrating the body and frequently exhibiting a fascination with Zen Buddhism, a direction taken by Paul Goodman (an admirer, more accurately, of Taoism), whose interests spanned those of academic analysis and theatre.

By the sixties the novel seemed to be flying in all directions. Gore Vidal wrote a patrician version of history, John Updike and John Cheever a middle-class and suburban one respectively. John Barth, meanwhile, blended history with fiction, as E. L. Doctorow, William Styron, and Robert Coover were to do. There were parallels in the theatre as Miller revisited the Holocaust in *After the Fall* and *Incident at Vichy*, O'Neill plunged further back in the posthumous *More Stately Mansions* (1962), and Howard Sackler explored a version of the African American past in *The Great White Hope* (1968).

There were parallels, too, to the non-fiction novel of Truman Capote, the new journalism of Tom Wolfe, and the explorations of contemporary reality by Norman Mailer, though several of these came from abroad, most notably Rolf Hochuth's *The Investigation* (1965) and Heinar Kipphardt's *In the Matter of J. Robert Oppenheimer* (1964). Martin Duberman's *In White America* (1963) deployed documentary material, as did Daniel Berrigan's and Saul Levitt's *The Trial of the Catonsville Nine* (1969), which began Off-Off Broadway and transferred to Broadway, but the documentary play proved of limited appeal.

Perhaps a closer parallel is that between a new spirit of experimentalism in the novel, which included such diverse talents as William Burroughs, Ken Kesey, Thomas Pynchon, William Gass, Richard Brautigan, Donald Barthelme, and Kurt Vonnegut, and the neo-Surrealist and Dadaist concerns of the creators of Happenings, the Artaud-influenced performances of the Living Theatre, the Grotowski-inspired work of the Performance Group, the early plays of Sam Shepard, and the work of Jean-Claude Van Itallie, Rochelle Owens, Megan Terry, and Ronald Tavel. The fact is that increasingly there seemed to be no orthodoxy either to enforce or rebel against. Certainly, in 1961 Philip Roth spoke of the difficulty for the writer of making American reality credible. However, what seemed difficult in 1961 must have appeared all but impossible as assassination piled on assassination, Americans were invited to join the drug culture, cities burned, and young men were returned from a foreign war in body bags. Revolt, pressing toward revolution, spread around the globe. Authority was challenged, no less in the arts than in any other area of life.

The counterculture gave primacy to the Pleasure Principle over the Reality Principle; resisted the idea of distinctions, divisions, categories, hierarchies. It distrusted rationality as self-limiting and located an essentially Romantic exploration of the self in the context of a new communalism. Much the same had been true of the early decades of the century when Modernism was born out of a loss of confidence in old forms and structures, political and social no less than aesthetic. The bohemian elite, then as now, extended experimental life styles in the direction of art, the Provincetown Players, for example, being the product of those equally committed to anarchism, free love, communitarian politics, anything, in short, which marked them out as different from those who preceded them. They established their New York center in Greenwich Village. So, too, did many of those who in the fifties and sixties reacted against normative values and conventional theatre. Off-Broadway and Off-Off Broadway were born.

This move from the large scale to the small, from the presumed homogeneity of the audience to self-selecting coteries, from spaces which separated performers from observers to those which brought them into immediate proximity, itself reflected changing values. If Off- and Off-Off Broadway were not physical locations they did imply a shift in priorities. Money was not a primary determinant, at least not at first (though Off-Broadway saw a rapid increase in costs and therefore ticket prices). Experiment became possible. In one direction the theatre theorized itself, self-consciously exploring its component elements, opening itself to European and other influences. In another, it examined the politics of its own existence. After all, this was a theatre which appealed not to the expense-account executive or those bussing in from New Jersey, but to a largely student audience whose own growing radicalism – aesthetic and political – it partly reflected, as later it appealed to those who for the first time saw their own lives dramatized on a stage.

The immediate precursor to sixties experimentation in the theatre was the Living Theatre, established in the fifties, whose directors, Julian Beck and Judith Malina, saw themselves as anarchists, whose company lived as well as performed together, and whose productions were, more often than not, explorations of the equivocal nature of art and reality – which is to say they were a late flowering of Modernism; and the theatre, and other arts, did show a renewed interest in Dada and Surrealism, for example. One of the Living Theatre's productions was of a play by Paul Goodman, a psychiatrist, who, in *Growing Up Absurd*, argued that the individual was now cut off from the natural world by a machine culture. And another aspect of sixties counterculture was, indeed, a renewed interest in the physical being, a desire to reinstate the body – both as sensual and political fact. Thus the overt sexuality, the nudity, the stress on physical movement to be found both in the counterculture at large and the theatre in particular, was matched by a conviction that physical presence – at demonstrations, marches, rock concerts – was itself crucial. Being there was what counted. There was a ritualized, a ceremonial and symbolic content to experience, and to the theatre, which required participation. And if that was evidenced by love-ins, teach-ins, Woodstock and the March on Washington, it was also evident in that erosion of the distinction between actor and audience which became a central tenet of belief, if also frequently a naive objective, for certain theatre groups. The Living Theatre and the Performance Group, in particular, appeared to revel in and indeed demand audience participation, though a certain totalitarianism revealed itself from time to time. Attending the theatre itself was now seen as an event sometimes with almost quasi-religious overtones.

The removal of clothing was in part designed to *épater le bourgeois*, though many of those participating were card-carrying members of the bourgeoisie themselves. Beyond that, it was offered as a sign of authenticity as if, like King Lear, they were getting down to the simple, unaccommodated man and woman. At such events the drama critic found himself (and more than 90 percent of critics were male) awkwardly placed, such authenticity being ambiguously related to theatrical truth. Thus the Living Theatre's Julian Beck attacked Walter Kerr, the *New York Times* Sunday critic, for his failure to accept the invitation to audience members, in *Paradise Now*, to join the cast on the stage and remove his clothes. He was, Beck asserted, obviously a lonely man in a decade in which solitariness was, if not a crime, then at least tangential to a celebratory and politically confident communalism.

Unsurprisingly, an ever vigilant capitalist Broadway (and Hollywood) quickly moved to transform the pursuit of truth into the pursuit of titillation. When the Off-Broadway *Hair*, in which the drafting of a young man for the Vietnam War provided part of the plot, was moved to Broadway, nudity was added. There were, however, limits to which the authorities were not prepared to go, the police arresting cast and producers of the Off-Off Broadway *Che!* on charges of obscenity and consensual sodomy, thereby inadvertently raising the issue at the heart of Diderot's paradox, which debated the question of whether the best actor is one who simulates or feels the emotions portrayed, though in ways that Diderot is unlikely to have imagined. It was not, however, a tactic which could redeem the unredeemable. Despite the success of *Oh! Calcutta!*, *Grin and Bare It!* (the exclamation point being, it seems, a required and highly charged signifier) folded after twelve performances on Broadway in the 1969–70 season while *The Way It Is*, despite an admirable number of previews, never actually succeeded in opening.

If the sixties were characterized by the experiments and exuberance of the counterculture, they were also marked by a growing politicization that contrasted sharply with the largely unfocused discontents of the previous decade. As Daniel Bell had pointed out, in the fifties the disenchanted were not the workers, who were more than happy to lay claim to the new materialism, but the intellectuals whose disaffection had lost its ideological basis. Not the least of the ironies of the McCarthy period, indeed, was that those summoned before the House Committee on Un-American Activities (a wonderfully Orwellian newspeak title) had long since been disenchanted with the doctrines of Marx. The disaffection of intellectuals now was less rooted, more diffuse. It had elements of nostalgia, as mass society and mass culture began to erode those qualities which they presumed to have distinguished cultural life hitherto. It also related to their own lack of a role. In the thirties the artist was a standard bearer for revolution. At a time of crisis the intellectual, vaguely in concert with an even more vaguely perceived working class, had a seemingly central function, if not in fact then at least in rhetorical and symbolic terms. In the fifties he was not only marginal but a subject of suspicion, whether as teacher, artist, or writer. The intellectual had not only lost status but a place to stand. America was working again. In the thirties left-leaning writers (and, from their own point of view, what other kind were there?) had seemingly been driven by passion. Even Ernest Hemingway had abandoned the mannered ironies of *A Farewell to Arms* to write *To Have and Have Not*, with its insistence that "a man alone ain't got no bloody fucking chance" (though the penultimate word was rendered by an asterisk, being seen as more subversive than the thought itself). The whimsies of early Steinbeck were transformed into a blend of Karl Marx and Ralph Waldo Emerson in *In Dubious Battle* and *The Grapes of Wrath*. In the fifties, by contrast, the energy came from guilt, self-doubt, liberal angst, alienation. Marx had been displaced by Freud. But the sixties were to offer the intellectual a role once again. An essayist, James Baldwin, mediated with government; a poet, Robert Lowell, challenged attempts to coopt culture to the side of authority; a novelist, Norman Mailer, turned into the biographer and autobiographer of revolt; academics, such as Herbert Marcuse and Noam Chomsky, challenged national priorities and values. And the theatre found itself, briefly, at the center, though the center proved remarkably unstable.

The revolt was an international one, as powerful in Europe as in America. In France, where a government was nearly toppled from power, Jean-Louis Barrault's theatre, the Odéon, became for a while a focal point for student revolt and, by chance, members of the Living Theatre were present for the debates that were conducted there (Barrault was subsequently sacked by France's Minister of Culture, André Malraux). They returned to America fired with enthusiasm, believing that theatre had a key role to play and, indeed, theatre, if not their own somewhat gnomic and romantically self-regarding version of it, did prove part of that complex of cultural and political forces which together formed the political, spiritual, and social rebellion of that overheated decade. They took their theatre onto the street, seeking confrontation with authority, an action which proved paradigmatic. On the West Coast, the San Francisco Mime Troupe performed in a park and fought municipal authorities for the right to do so, becoming quickly radicalized, as did the Bread and Puppet Theatre (participants in many anti-Vietnam marches). California's El Teatro Campesino was radical from the start, performing for striking grape pickers. Universities from Berkeley to Princeton, University of California–Davis to Buffalo, staged events, sketches, agit prop dramas. Still other theatrical rebels interrupted performances in Broadway theatres, becoming, in their own minds, theatrical guerillas, infiltrating the bland products of an art which had settled for mere entertainment, thereby becoming complicit with those who would distract the citizenry from the crimes of the state. In Harlem, LeRoi Jones turned his back on a promising dramatic career, staged his plays on the street, thereby losing a federal grant, and changed his name to Amiri Baraka prior to lending his talents to the black cause by writing agit prop plays designed for all-black audiences.

Collective work, reflecting the communitarian politics of its creators, tended to replace plays which were the product of an individual sensibility. Indeed, the writer was frequently marginalized as the source of a suspect authority or embraced as merely part of a collective whose collectivity was itself a statement of priorities and values. Few of these groups were, at least initially, as concerned with craft as with ideological convictions, or they adapted their craft to the necessities of communicating in public spaces beyond the confines of a purpose-built building. Theatre was a means, its transformations a key to those other transformations – social, economic, political – that it was designed to provoke.

There were other groups, however, for whom craft was central, and though these, too, were radicalized by Vietnam, the Open Theatre and the Performance Group, in particular, were governed, at least initially, by a concern for intellectual and artistic rigor.

All of these experiments, concerned with the erosion of the supposedly clear distinction between audience and performer, served as a reminder, on the one hand, of the performative content of social behavior and, on the other, of the communal nature of experience and the power generated by a shared perception of reality – social and political no less than artistic. In other words, the theatre offered itself as paradigmatic and, indeed, was seen as such by sociologists (Erving Goffman), literary critics (Richard Poirier), and psychotherapists, no less than by those who in staging their public rites sought to exorcise what they saw as the rationalist, positivist, racist, imperialist, and capitalist thrust of their society. And that reaction against authority was, to some degree, evident within the theatre as the playwright was invited to become no more than a participant in the creation of a text and even the authority of the director was disputed or willingly surrendered. As Jerzy Grotowski insisted, "In our productions next to nothing is dictated by the director" (quoted in Guernsey, *Curtain Times*, 171). The productions were designed to express the communal conditions of their construction and hence to offer a corrective to the abuse of power and authority in society.

But this fact alone should signal a warning, for though American policy did change, and the pressure of public opinion (shaped in part by those who staged the great demonstrations, marches, and paratheatrical events of the decade) played its part in this, theatre no more wholly gave itself over to such activities than were the public motivated by the communitarian ideals, radical politics, and vague romanticism of the counterculture. The riots of 1965, 1967, and 1968 left many Americans bemused after what they had taken to be a settling of accounts with the Civil Rights Act of 1964 and the Voter Registration Act of 1965. With casualties rapidly growing toward what would eventually become 55,000 young Americans dead, America simply ceased to believe what its leaders said. In 1968 the Tet Offensive convinced many that the war was lost and that American lives were being sacrificed for no purpose. The white middle class itself became increasingly alarmed at the thought that their own children might be required to sacrifice themselves to a cause they found increasingly difficult to understand in a country remote from their own, where it was hard to believe that national security was genuinely at risk. The President resigned and America elected Richard Nixon, who promised to end the war, though for some time his promises proved no more reliable in this area than in others.

The theatre, meanwhile, had not given itself over wholly to politicized groups or even radical experimentation, though the theories of Antonin Artaud and Jerzy Grotowski proved deeply influential on the avant-garde, the one stressing the multiple resources of theatre – its power to create images not necessarily dependent on language – the other focusing on the actor and his or her relationship with an audience inducted into theatre as they might be into a religion. The fact is that some of the most powerful and successful plays of the 1960s were products of Broadway, if not typical Broadway fare. Edward Albee's *Who's Afraid of Virginia Woolf?* (1962), brilliantly funny and articulate, like his earlier one-act play *The Zoo Story*, expressed a sense of the collapse of relationships, itself a key to a failure of nerve and commitment which had social and even political dimensions. It expressed an optimism which quickly disappeared from his later work, a closing down of possibilities already apparent in his Pulitzer Prize-winning play, *A Delicate Balance* (1968). By the end of the decade the apocalyptic tone of his plays was undeniable, *Box* and *Quotations from Chairman Mao Tse-Tung* (1968) offering a lament for a world in which communication had proved impossible and annihilation something more than a present possibility.

Another powerful and successful play, Arthur Miller's *The Price*, was staged in that *annus mirabilis*, 1968. A play which looked back toward the thirties, and whose set was that of a realist drama, it nonetheless managed to engage a question which in some ways was antecedent to that raised or implied by the self-consciously public art of the decade: what is one's responsibility for one's own life and therefore for the lives of others? His earlier sixties plays, *After the*

Fall (1964) and *Incident at Vichy* (1964) had also engaged history but in such a way as to raise questions about a contemporary world in which racism was a dominant fact and personal commitment a necessity.

The decade ended with Arthur Kopit's *Indians* (1969), which, like Miller's plays, used the past as a means of commenting on the present. It was, however, a product of Arena Stage in Washington and as such anticipated a process that became a commonplace thereafter, as plays reached Broadway either from regional theatre, which expanded rapidly in the seventies, or from Europe. Costs, union intransigency, a deteriorating Broadway environment, the loss of informed reviewers (New York lost most of the newspapers which had guaranteed a wide spread of opinion: the *World, Telegram, Sun, Journal, American, Herald,* and *Tribune* had gone, effectively leaving one voice to decide on the future of a production and, through occasional forays across the Atlantic, even to decide which British shows would transfer), the star system, all contributed to a theatre unwilling to take the initiative in terms of productions or to stage work which could not be guaranteed a sufficiently long run to recoup investment.

New plays did continue to be produced on Broadway but often they made their way from Britain, from Off-Broadway, and from the regional theatres. It remained true, however, that Broadway was still seen as an ultimate destination, no matter how perilous and costly productions there might be, no matter that its audience was increasingly defined by price and not always receptive to work which challenged their assumptions.

By the mid-seventies Vietnam was finally over, though the plays which registered its effects continued. Students, intellectuals, and radical artists could no longer convince themselves that they spoke for or to an America attracted by the slogans of revolt. The barricades came down and America ceased to live its politics on the street, except in so far as the appearance of the homeless spoke of another kind of politics. A decade of rebellion gave way to what was dubbed the "me" generation, which in turn led to a decade in which the denial of social responsibility became an article of faith for government. Watergate seemed to slam the door on the notion that government might be the source of renewal, while the later election of Ronald Reagan was an explicit assertion that government should have little role in the lives of citizens who were seen as being effectively in competition with one another for resources and success, coming together only to celebrate national myths of unity and national superiority. Nor did having an actor in the White House imply that the arts had a friend at court. On the contrary, he was no believer in funding organizations that might be seen as supporting unexamined national values.

It is tempting to see this turn from a public to a private world as symbolized in the theatre by a series of plays which explored illness, from cancer and deafness to stroke. Robert Wilson's work with an autistic boy, and the emphasis on aphasia and brain damage in several of Sam Shepard's plays, seemed to imply a similar withdrawal from the public world and from social engagement. The experimental theatre, meanwhile, which in the sixties had concerned itself with the interplay between the private and public self, an exploration of the social no less than the aesthetic implications of the verb to act, became primarily concerned with the nature of consciousness, with the manner in which the real is constituted, involving the audience, not, like the Living Theatre, as fellow actors, but as fellow playwrights, creating the world to which they then responded. This was a theatre which resisted the literary (unless it be the Modernism of Gertrude Stein), its aesthetic being derived in part from art (and, indeed, there were lines which connected what became known as the Theatre of Images with the late fifties neo-Surrealist experiments, Happenings, and events). There were also those – Richard Foreman and Ping Chong – who were fascinated by the uses of video in the context of their performances.

In the eighties and nineties a group of performance artists began to generate work out of their own autobiographies, work which reinstated language as they told stories, elaborated accounts of personal events, and presented one-person shows that made the self the subject and object of concern. Such events, of course, served to raise questions about the nature of that self, how it is composed and presented, whether it be Spalding Gray in *Swimming to Cambodia*, or Linda Montano in *The Story of My Life*. In other words, like the Theatre of Images, this work theorized the nature of dramatic presentation, not only raising questions about the constructed self (questions that for some performers had political implications, since that self had been appropriated by others) but also challenging presumptions about the communal nature of theatrical performance, though Laurie Anderson has insisted that what interests her is less the uniqueness of her experiences than the similarity which audiences detect between their own privacies and the performer's. Thus, though Spalding Gray, who began working with the Wooster Group in the seventies, has spoken of the narrative of his stories being shaped by events in his own life, and being, at the same time, "the next chapter of my life" and a "public confessional," he does not see this as narcissism, because, as he insisted in 1997, "a narcissist is not conscious of their narcissism." His work, therefore, he regards as "already reflexive." But, like Anderson, he also asserts that "I try to go through myself out to all other selves because, if I'm talking about neurotic behavior, I think we all share that in common . . . all I can do is look in – in order to look out."[1] And that line out of privacy was important to some performance artists for whom a motivating force in such a focused self-expression lies in the freedom it offers to express gender, race, nationality, and sexual preference, unmediated by playwright or the conventions of actorly presentation.

There was something equally ambivalent on this score about the concerns of those women playwrights who emerged in the seventies and eighties, winning three Pulitzer Prizes in the latter decade. Long marginalized or, indeed, excluded, such dramatists tended to focus on interpersonal relationships, the psychological fall-out of inhabiting a society which saw men as primary actors in the social drama. For a number of them, too, illness – mental and physical – became a principal subject, as it did of gay playwrights who had barely made their presence felt before AIDS gave them a subject which was all but unavoidable. And this is where assumptions about a turn from public to private prove difficult to sustain, for the fact is that public and private are intimately connected, a truth felt equally by Hispanic, Asian, Chicano, and, indeed, African American playwrights. August Wilson's plays may quite consciously have concerned themselves with the private lives of his characters but his plays were also a deliberate attempt to construct an alternative history of America as seen through the eyes of those presumed to be no more than the victims of that history. And what was true of his work was true, too, of that produced by others for whom the theatre became an agency of cultural reinforcement, a mechanism for dramatizing the tensions which defined an American experience that could no longer be plausibly presented as homogeneous.

However, in so far as there was a tendency toward the single performer (and, under the pressure of economics, the single-set, small-cast play), at the other extreme was the musical, which by century's end often required the kind of budget more usually associated with film (with, sometimes, returns to match), though in the late nineties the British composer of hit musicals, Andrew Lloyd Webber, predicted the end of the large-scale musical. But the fact remained that in order to compete with the cinema's computer-generated special effects, its power to overwhelm the sensibility of audiences not as Artaud had wished, but with digitalized images and enhanced sound systems, the musical had turned either to pastiche and nostalgia, presenting revivals, musical compilations from past successes, or movie musicals transposed to the stage, or to what in the nineteenth century might have been called extravaganzas, in which the mechanics of stage construction vied with the actor/singers, and sound was under the control of engineers (the miking of shows, incidentally, even spreading from musicals to straight plays). Thus, audiences responded to an onstage train in *On the Twentieth Century* (1978) as they did to the helicopter in *Miss Saigon* (1991) or the sinking ship in *Titanic* (1998), just as they had a century and more before to similar gestures of technical accomplishment. It is not, however, necessarily a good sign when audiences applaud the scenery. But by this time theatre competed not only with movies but also with rock shows that were very consciously staged as theatrical events, deploying the full resources of technology and with the musicians often presenting themselves as a series of characters, as a blend of self and role in which the distinction was not always easy to make (Alice Cooper, Madonna, David Bowie, Michael Jackson, and so on).

As the turn of the century and millennium arrived, no single style, no dominant ideology, no ruling orthodoxy, no theatrical center predominated. Just as the desperate desire to pull together a heterogeneous society deferred to a different model of society, so theatre reflected this. In the late nineties a fierce dispute broke out over the legitimacy of what was coyly called non-traditional casting, the casting of parts with no particular attention to race and even gender. In 1986 the Non-Traditional Casting Project established a database of minority actors available for work in theatre, film, and television. Tony Kushner called for cross-gender casting in *Angels in America* (1993). But in 1997 a debate was staged between two significant figures in contemporary American theatre. By what seemed something of an irony to some, the Professor of Drama at Harvard University (and artistic director of the American Repertory Theatre), Robert Brustein, argued in favor of such a practice, and the multiple Pulitzer Prize-winner, August Wilson, against, on the grounds that, since theatre remained institutionally white, special funding, and the task of developing black talent, should go to the relatively few African American theatres.

Beyond what might seem a parochial cultural debate lay a continuing disagreement as to the definition of America and the function of theatre. America was, after all, abandoning affirmative action programs and, in the process, according to President Clinton, of reinventing segregation, with whites closing doors previously left ajar and African Americans withdrawing into their own communities, even segregating themselves in college dorms and cafeterias. A mid-nineties march on Washington, in stark contrast to Martin Luther King's in the sixties, was all-black and all-male. In 1991 America may have seen its first African American drama critic on a mainstream newspaper (the *Denver Post*), but it was still a noteworthy event, as was the first major play, also in Denver, to employ a cast consisting entirely of Native Americans and Hispanics. Robert Brustein spoke out of a liberal conviction that the United States would only fulfill its promise when its inhabitants realized that "we are citizens first, Americans second, and tribalists third." For Wilson, this was to deny the reality of the America he saw, an America in which racism flourished, as it was to deny the legitimacy of a cultural identity which lay outside equally of liberal individualism and a supposed national identity: "inside all blacks," he insisted, "is at least one heartbeat that is fueled by Africa."

For Brustein, "art does not change consciousness," while for Wilson, "Art changes individuals, and individuals change society."[2] If he thereby reinvented the individualism whose substance he doubted, he also reaffirmed his belief in the power of theatre to propose its transformations as paradigmatic. It was not that he wrote avowedly political plays – in a simple form these had all but disappeared from the American theatre – but that he saw in the theatre a form with the power both to reflect society and, in the process, to change our sense of it and thus, incrementally, to change the thing itself.

Those who turned to the theatre in the early days of the new republic did so because they wished to capture a world which was changing before their eyes. Beyond that, they wanted to be part of those changes, staging the real but also what might become the real, in terms of an emerging national identity. At the turn of the twenty-first century those drawn to the creation of theatre in America have, as ever, mixed motives. But among their objectives is to offer their own interpretation of the American experience in the knowledge that to do so is to contribute to a definition that can only ever be provisional, for this is a society dedicated to the proposition that all men can be other than they are created.

Theatre remains what it ever was: entertainment, distraction, amusement, polemic, private confession, public assertion, communal rite, a shared apprehension of the nature of experience, and a challenge to our notions of what might constitute that experience. It is deeply implicated in the economics and politics of its day, as it is in the shifting aesthetic values of its own culture and the wider international culture of which it is a part.

American drama continues to invent, to speak, to imagine America. It is as various as the society which generates it. Design flaws in software may have sent many computers spinning back to the turn of the last century with the arrival of the new millennium, but the theatre, whose condition of being and whose primary justification depends upon the cooperative endeavors of artists – writers, actors, directors, designers – and the coming together of artists and public in a living art, continues to assert a gravitational pull for those who will never be entirely satisfied with the privacies of some other arts or the ironic community of those who meet only as glowing pixels on a screen lit by nothing but electricity and their own desire to connect.

Notes

1 Gray quoted in Tom Dewe Matthews, "Gray Area," *The Independent* (26 June 1997): 6–7.
2 See Stephen Nunns's analysis of the Brustein–Wilson debate in "Wilson, Brustein and the Press," *American Theatre* 14 (March 1997): 17–19.

Timeline: Post-World War II to 1998

Compiled by Don B. Wilmeth with Jonathan Curley

This chronological chart by years (only major events are ordered chronologically within each year) provides a quick overview of major events during the time period covered by this volume (through June 1998). Briefly noted in the timeline are the following: in column one, major theatrical events in the history of the theatre in the United States; in column two, other U.S. cultural and his- torical events of significance, or representative data; and in column three, key historical and cultural events from other parts of the world, included in order to provide points of reference in a wider context. Unless otherwise indicated specific theatrical events in column one occurred in New York City and dates refer to production.

DATES	THEATRICAL EVENTS IN AMERICA	SELECTED HISTORICAL/CULTURAL EVENTS IN AMERICA	SELECTED HISTORICAL/CULTURAL EVENTS THROUGHOUT THE WORLD
1946	Eugene O'Neill's *The Iceman Cometh* premieres.	U.S. birthrate soars to 3,411,000 births, up from 2,858,000 the previous year.	Fulbright scholarships established for U.S. teachers, researchers, and students to encourage exchange programs with other nations.
	Irving Berlin musical *Annie Get Your Gun* is directed by Joshua Logan and stars Ethel Merman.	U.S. GI Bill passed.	J.-P. Sartre publishes *Existentialism and Humanism*.
	State of the Union by Howard Lindsay and Russel Crouse.	U.S. military branches united under Department of Defense.	Violent protests against British rule in several Indian cities (21–22 Feb.).
	Maxwell Anderson's *Joan of Lorraine*.	Atomic Energy Commission founded.	Verdicts reached in Nuremberg war trials.
	Lillian Hellman's *Another Part of the Forest*.	U.S. scientist creates first artificial snowstorm by seeding cloud with dry ice.	Riots over bread shortages in Paris and Rouen (4 Jan.).
	Garson Kanin's *Born Yesterday* opens with Judy Holliday, who takes over at last minute and achieves stardom.	U.S. scholars complete "Revised Standard Version" of the Bible.	German novelist Herman Hesse awarded Nobel Prize for Literature.
	Call Me Mister, with sketches by Arnold Aurebach and Arnold B. Hewitt, premieres, showing the difficult transition of World War II veterans from war to the labor force.	Robert Penn Warren's *All the King's Men*.	Juan Perón elected President of Argentina.

21

DATES	THEATRICAL EVENTS IN AMERICA	SELECTED HISTORICAL/CULTURAL EVENTS IN AMERICA	SELECTED HISTORICAL/CULTURAL EVENTS THROUGHOUT THE WORLD
	Anita Loos's *Happy Birthday*.	Hans Morgenthau's *Scientific Man vs. Power Politics*.	Soviet government withdraws artistic subsidies and imposes strict theatrical censorship.
	Eva Le Gallienne's American Repertory Theatre founded; defunct by 1948.	John Hersey's *Hiroshima*.	United Nations holds first session.
		James B. Conant's *Understanding Science*.	Italy becomes a republic.
		Willem De Kooning begins series of black and white paintings which establish him as a leading Abstract Expressionist.	French playwright Jean Anouilh's *Medea*.
		Mark Rothko's painting *Prehistoric Memories*.	Christopher Fry's play *A Phoenix Too Frequent*.
		William Wyler's film *The Best Years of Our Life* released.	Terence Rattigan's play *The Winslow Boy*.
		Bikini swimsuits introduced.	
		President Truman establishes Committee on Civil Rights.	
1947	Actors Studio opens.	22nd Amendment proposed by Congress to limit presidential services to two terms in office (21 March). It is ratified 26 February 1951.	Truman warns USSR that U.S. "would support free peoples who are resisting subjugation by armed minorities or by outside pressure." The policy is known as the Truman Doctrine.
	Poet Robinson Jeffers adapts *Medea* for the stage.	Jackie Robinson becomes first black man to sign on to a professional ball club, the Brooklyn Dodgers (11 April).	Marshall Plan implemented as coordinated program to help European nations recover from World War II.
	Bertolt Brecht summoned to testify before House Un-American Activities Committee.	Christian Dior introduces the "New Look" into women's fashion clothes; ultra-feminine and full-skirted, it differs greatly from wartime wear and fashion (3 June).	Pandit Nehru and Muhammad Ali Jinnah, leaders of two major Indian political parties, Congress and Muslim League, endorse Britain's plan for partition of India (June).

Margo Jones founds theatre (as Theater '47) in Dallas; Alley Theatre opens in Houston.

Tennessee Williams's *A Streetcar Named Desire* opens on Broadway with Marlon Brando (4 Dec.).

Arthur Miller's *All My Sons.*

Brigadoon, a Jay Lerner and Frederick Loewe production, hits the stage.

Burton Lane and E.Y. Harburg's *Finian's Rainbow* introduces choreographer Michael Kidd.

First Tony Awards dinner held at Waldorf Astoria.

The Heiress by Ruth and Augustus Goetz. William Haines's *Command Decision.*

First production of O'Neill's *A Moon for the Misbegotten* (written 1943) in Ohio; did not play New York.

Congress passes antilabor-union Taft-Hartley Act over Truman's veto (23 June).

Rocket-powered research plane flown by Charles Yeager breaks the sound barrier at 650 m.p.h. (14 Oct.).

Polaroid camera developed.

U.S. congressional committee claims there are Communists in movie industry, leading to blacklisting of suspect writers and actors.

Lionel Trilling's *Middle of the Journey.*

Paul Samuelson's *Foundations of Economic Analysis.*

Willem De Kooning's painting *Pink Angels.* Goodyear introduces tubeless tire.

First microwave cooker sold in United States.

Henry Ford dies.

Great Books Program started.

Sculptures by Albert Giacometti and Henry Moore exhibited.

American physicist William Shockley invents the transistor.

CORE stages "Journey of Reconciliation," first freedom ride to challenge segregation on interstate transit.

The "Dead Sea Scrolls" discovered in cave in Jordan.

Marc Chagall's painting *Madonna of the Sleigh.*

Albert Camus's novel *The Plague.*

India gains independence.

Anne Frank's diary published.

Jean Genet's play *The Maids.*

DATES	THEATRICAL EVENTS IN AMERICA	SELECTED HISTORICAL/CULTURAL EVENTS IN AMERICA	SELECTED HISTORICAL/CULTURAL EVENTS THROUGHOUT THE WORLD
1948	Living Theater founded by Judith Malina and Julian Beck.	Organization of American States Charter provides for regional security and economic development.	A Universal Declaration of Human Rights approved by UN General Assembly. It declares essential human rights for all people.
	Thomas Heggen's and Joshua Logan's World War II comedy *Mr. Roberts,* starring Henry Fonda, opens in February.	Harry S. Truman elected thirty-third President.	
	World premiere of Bertolt Brecht's *The Caucasian Chalk Circle* at Carlton College.	Controversial, pseudo-scientific Kinsey report on male sexual behavior published.	George Orwell's novel *Nineteen Eighty-Four.*
	A Streetcar Named Desire wins Pulitzer and Drama Critics' Award (film, 1951).	First self-service McDonald's hamburgers restaurants open in California. The franchise will spread across the nation and around the world by end of twentieth century.	Gandhi assassinated (30 Jan.).
	Cole Porter's *Kiss Me, Kate* premieres, with Alfred Drake and Patricia Morison.	Norman Mailer's *The Naked and the Dead.*	State of Israel proclaimed, with David Ben-Gurion as head of provisional government (14–15 May).
	Moss Hart's *Light Up the Sky.*	B.F. Skinner's *Walden Two.*	Somali people appeal to UN for united Somalia after Ethiopia takes control of Somalia's Reserved Areas (23 Sept.).
	Maxwell Anderson's *Anne of the Thousand Days.*	Alger Hiss accused of spying.	First Arab–Israeli War.
	Lindsay and Crouse's *Life With Mother.* First New York production of Williams's *Summer and Smoke* (premiered in Dallas preceding year; film 1961).	James Gould Cozzen's *Guard of Honor.* Jackson Pollock exhibits controversial "action painting" in New York for first time.	T.S. Eliot wins Nobel Prize for Literature. Laurence Olivier's film *Hamlet* opens.
		Robert Motherwell, William Baziotes, Barnett Newman, and Mark Rothko found school of art to encourage Abstract Expressionism.	Giorgio de Chirico's painting *Antique Era.*

1949			
Clifford Odets writes *The Big Knife*. Arthur Miller's *Death of a Salesman*, directed by Elia Kazan, is brought to stage and wins Pulitzer. The Rodgers and Hammerstein musical *South Pacific*, with Mary Martin and Ezio Pinza, wins Pulitzer in 1950 (second musical to do so). The Falmouth Playhouse, a summer stock repertory theatre, is founded by Richard Aldrich. Maxwell Anderson's musical dramatization of Alan Paton's novel *Cry, the Beloved Country*, called *Lost in the Stars*, produced.	Andrew Wyeth paints *Christina's World* in American Realist style. James Michener's *Tales of the South Pacific*. Baseball slugger Babe Ruth dies. LP (long-playing record) introduced. Armed forces desegregated per order of the President. Robert Motherwell's painting *At Five in the Afternoon*. Jackson Pollock's painting *Number 10*. Robert Merton's *Social Theory and Social Justice*. Morton White's *Social Thought in America*. Joseph Campbell's *The Hero with a Thousand Faces*. Mary McLeod Bethune founds National Council of Negro Women, which opposes poll tax and racial discrimination, and promotes teaching of black history in public schools. William Faulkner wins Nobel Prize for Literature.	Term "Cold War" coined by Bernard Baruch. The North Atlantic Treaty is signed in Washington, DC by Britain, Belgium, Italy, the Netherlands, Denmark, Luxembourg, Portugal, Iceland, Norway, Canada, and the United States. It promises mutual assistance against the Soviet Union in a defensive pact under the guidance of the North Atlantic Council (4 April). Revolution in China under Mao Tse-Tung. Beijing falls to Communists; the Siege of Peking a crucial military success as well (22 Jan.). French Existentialist Simone de Beauvoir's *The Second Sex*. Pandit Nehru becomes Prime Minister of India. Eire leaves Commonwealth and becomes Republic of Ireland (18 April).	

DATES	THEATRICAL EVENTS IN AMERICA	SELECTED HISTORICAL/CULTURAL EVENTS IN AMERICA	SELECTED HISTORICAL/CULTURAL EVENTS THROUGHOUT THE WORLD
	Anita Loos's book *Gentlemen Prefer Blondes* is adapted for the stage as a musical by Jule Styne; makes Carol Channing a Broadway star.		T.S. Eliot's drama *The Cocktail Party*.
	Sidney Kingsley's *Detective Story*.		Apartheid established in South Africa. Bertolt Brecht founds The Berliner Ensemble.
1950	During 1949–50 season, only fifty-nine new plays debut on Broadway.	The Brink's Bank Robbery breaks all previous records for losses to armed robbers: $1,218,211 in cash and $1,557,000 in money orders is taken (17 Jan.). U.S. Atomic Energy Commission is ordered by President Truman to construct a hydrogen bomb.	
	The New York Commissioner of Licenses requires *Michael Todd's Peep Show*, a burlesque revue, to tone down its strip tease routine and make costumes less revealing.	Minimum wage of $.75 goes into effect under amendment to the Fair Labor and Standards Act.	UN Security Council establishes unified command under the United States to send aid to South Korea (7 July).
	The Arena Stage is founded by a group associated with George Washington University, in Washington, D.C.	Color television broadcasts begin.	George Bernard Shaw dies (b. 1852).
	Shirley Booth opens in William Inge's *Come Back, Little Sheba*.	Diners' Club introduces the charge card, the first example of a credit card.	Ezra Pound's *Cantos* published.
	Frank Loesser's and Abe Burrows's *Guys and Dolls* opens 24 November at The 46th Street Theatre in New York and runs for 1,200 performances.	Lionel Trilling's *Liberal Imagination*. Henry Steele Commager's *The American Mind.* T.W. Adorno et al., *The Authoritarian Personality.*	Korean War begins.

Chiang Kai-Shek resumes presidency of Nationalist China.

So-called "Theatre of the Absurd" appears in France (e.g., Eugène Ionesco's The Bald Soprano).

Christopher Fry's play Venus Observed.

Winston Churchill becomes Prime Minister of Britain.

Eugene Ionesco's play The Lesson. Christopher Fry's play A Sleep of Prisoners. Jean Anouilh's play Colombe.

Salvador Dali's painting Christ of St. John on the Cross.

Benjamin Britten's opera Billy Budd and Ralph Vaughan Williams's opera The Pilgrim's Progress premiere in London.

David Riesman et al., The Lonely Crowd. Erik Erikson's Childhood and Society.

Ralph Bunche wins Nobel Peace Prize for negotiating armistice between Israelis and Arabs.

Jackson Pollock's painting Lavender Mist.

National Council of Churches is established.
Over 100 million tons of steel manufactured annually by this year.

Direct long-distance dialing service begins.

Scandal erupts in college basketball when revelations of game-fixing for gambling emerge.

William Styron's Lie Down in Darkness. Rachel Carson's The Sea Around Us. Robert Frost's Complete Poems.

James Jones's From Here to Eternity. J.D. Salinger's The Catcher in the Rye.

C. Wright Mills's White Collar. Talcott Parsons's The Social System. Hannah Arendt's Origins of Totalitarianism. W.V.O. Quine's "Two Dogmas of Empiricism."

Clifford Odets's The Country Girl, directed by the author.

Novelist Carson McCullers adapts her book The Member of the Wedding to the stage.

Broadway theatre begins tradition of the Gypsy Robe when a dancer presents a dressing robe adorned with momentos to a friend in the cast of the next show to open.

Arthur Miller's version of Ibsen's An Enemy of the People.

1951

The American Shakespeare Theatre is founded in Stratford, Connecticut, by Lawrence Langner.

Actors' Equity appoints Frederick O'Neal to head committee to investigate declining employment of black actors on Broadway. O'Neal finds that only thirteen blacks had parts in Broadway plays between 1 September 1951 and 15 March 1952.

John Van Druten's I Am a Camera. Tennessee Williams's The Rose Tattoo (film 1955).

Maxwell Anderson's Barefoot in Athens.

Rodgers–Hammerstein production of The King and I, with Yul Brynner and Gertrude Lawrence (in her final stage role), opens 29 March.

DATES	THEATRICAL EVENTS IN AMERICA	SELECTED HISTORICAL/CULTURAL EVENTS IN AMERICA	SELECTED HISTORICAL/CULTURAL EVENTS THROUGHOUT THE WORLD
		George Kennan's *American Diplomacy, 1900–1950.*	
		Hans Reichenbach's *The Rise of Scientific Philosophy.*	
		Kenneth Arrow's *Rational Choice and Individual Value.*	
	Donald Bevan's and Edmund Trzcinski's *Stalag 17.*	Release of Huston's film *The African Queen* and Minelli's *An American in Paris.*	
	Lillian Hellman's *The Autumn Garden.*	Gian Carlo Menotti composes *Amahl and the Night Visitors* for NBC Television.	
	Sidney Kingsley's stage version of Arthur Koestler's novel *Darkness at Noon* produced.	C. Vann Woodward's *Origins of the New South.*	
	Jan de Hartog's *The Fourposter.*	*I Love Lucy* begins its long television run.	
1952	Off-Broadway records first major success with José Quintero's revival of Tennessee Williams's *Summer and Smoke* at the Circle in the Square.	Dwight D. Eisenhower elected President.	U.S. explodes first hydrogen bomb at Eniwetok Atoll in the Pacific.
	The American Mime Theatre founded in New York by Paul Curtis.	Rocky Marciano wins heavyweight boxing championship from "Jersey" Joe Walcott in Philadelphia, knocking him out in the thirteenth round.	Batista seizes power in Cuba (10 March).
	Joseph Kramm's *The Shrike* wins Pulitzer.	Some 17 million U.S. homes have TV sets at year's end, up from 5 to 8 million in 1950.	Dr. Kwame Nkrumah becomes first African prime minister south of the Sahara (21 March).
	The Climate of Eden by Moss Hart opens.	In Dennis et al. v. U.S., Supreme Court rules in favor of 1946 Smith Act, a law against the advocacy of overthrow of government by force.	U.S. occupation of Japan ends (28 April).

1953

George Axelford's *The Seven Year Itch* begins a 1,141-show run on Broadway.

Arthur Laurents's *The Time of the Cuckoo.*

Phoenix Theater founded by T. Edward Hambleton and Norris Houghton.

Arthur Miller's *The Crucible* uses Salem witch hunts as parable for McCarthyism.

Tennessee Williams's *Camino Real.*

"American Bandstand" premieres on television.

A polio epidemic strikes 47,500 Americans.

Invisible Man by Ralph Ellison published. Whitaker Chambers's *Witness.*

Paul Tillich's *The Courage to Be.*

Edmund Wilson's *The Shores of Light.*

Herman Wouk's *The Caine Mutiny.*

Ernest Hemingway's *The Old Man and the Sea.*

Reinhold Niebuhr's *The Irony of American History.*

Humphrey Bogart wins Best Actor Oscar for *The African Queen.*

John Cage's notorious musical composition "4' 33''," in which no sound is recorded.

Willem De Kooning's *Woman I* painting. Film *High Noon* released.

The Rosenbergs, first sentenced as atomic spies in 1951, are executed.

Playboy magazine, the first large-circulation magazine in America featuring photos of scantily clad and nude women, debuts in December.

Wide-screen projection (Cinemascope) is introduced.

Irish expatriate Samuel Beckett's play *Waiting for Godot.*

Agatha Christie's play *The Mousetrap* opens at London's Ambassador Theatre (still running in 1999).

Dr. Albert Schweitzer wins Nobel Peace Prize.

Contraceptive pill introduced.

Jean Anouilh's play *Waltz of the Toreadors.*

Ionesco's play *The Chairs.*

George VI dies; Elizabeth II becomes Queen of England.

U.S. biologist James Watson and British physicist Francis Crick describe their famous model of the DNA molecule, showing its structure to be a double helix.

Polish emigré C. Milosz's *The Captive Mind.*

Jorge Luis Borges's *Labyrinths.*

Ludwig Wittgenstein's posthumously published *Philosophical Investigations.*

DATES	THEATRICAL EVENTS IN AMERICA	SELECTED HISTORICAL/CULTURAL EVENTS IN AMERICA	SELECTED HISTORICAL/CULTURAL EVENTS THROUGHOUT THE WORLD
	William Inge's *Picnic* (wins Pulitzer).	Robert Oppenheimer, father of atomic bomb, has security permit withdrawn by President Eisenhower, having been accused of being a Communist and holding up development of hydrogen bomb (23 Dec.).	French semiotician Roland Barthes's *Writing Degree Zero*.
	Robert Anderson's *Tea and Sympathy*. John Patrick's *Teahouse of the August Moon*. Howard Teichmann's and George Kaufman's *The Solid Gold Cadillac*. Eugene O'Neill dies (b. 1888).	Saul Bellow's *The Adventures of Augie March*. James Baldwin's *Go Tell It on the Mountain*.	Stalin dies (b. 1879); Nikita Khrushchev appointed First Secretary of the Communist Party.
		Daniel Boorstin's *The Genius of American Politics*. Leo Strauss's *Natural Right and History*. Alfred Kinsey's *Sexual Behavior in the Human Female*.	Ceasefire in Korea. Korean War ends soon after.
	Musical *Wonderful Town* reunites composer Leonard Bernstein with lyricists Betty Comden and Adolphe Green.	Dylan Thomas dies in New York.	Martial law imposed in East Berlin.
		Buckminster Fuller designs geodesic dome. Federal budget deficit hits high to date for peacetime: $9.4 billion.	Fidel Castro leads abortive coup against Batista in Cuba (26 July). Elizabeth II crowned Queen of England. Anouilh's play *The Lark*.
1954	Joseph Papp founds New York Shakepeare Festival, considered the most significant of the Off-Broadway movements.	U.S. Supreme Court rules in Brown v. Board of Education of Topeka that segregation in public schools violates the fourteenth amendment.	William Golding's novel *Lord of the Flies*. British poet John Betjeman's *A Few Late Chrysanthemums*. J.R.R. Tolkein's *The Lord of the Rings*. Kingsley Amis's first novel, *Lucky Jim*.

1955

Milwaukee Repertory Theater formed.

George Abbott's musical *Pajama Game* introduces composing team of Richard Adler and Jerry Ross, choreographer Bob Fosse, and producer Harold Prince to Broadway.

Thornton Wilder's *The Matchmaker* with Ruth Gordon.

Gian Carlo Menotti's opera *The Saint of Bleecker Street* wins Pulitzer (1955).

Tennessee Williams's *Cat on a Hot Tin Roof* directed by Elia Kazan wins both Critics' Circle Award and Pulitzer.

Twenty-six comic book publishers voluntarily adopt censorship code to eliminate vulgar or obscene comics.

Jonas Salk invents an injectible vaccine for infantile paralysis. After school-children are vaccinated in Pittsburgh, a nationwide program begins.

Senator Joseph McCarthy forms a Permanent Investigating Subcommittee for hearings on Communist activities in the government.

Elvis Presley makes first professional recording at nineteen and achieves some success with "That's All Right, Mama" and "Blue Moon of Kentucky."

First "TV dinners" are sold by Swanson Co.

Hemingway wins Pulitzer for literature.

Marlon Brando wears denim jeans and leather jacket in *The Wild One*, setting new fashion.

Wallace Stevens's *Collected Poems*. David Potter's *People of Plenty*. Newport Jazz Festival founded. Veterans Day (11 Nov.) proclaimed holiday to honor all who fought for nation.

Jasper John's painting *Flag*.

Disneyland, America's most popular amusement/theme park, is founded in Anaheim, California.

French sociologist Jacques Ellul's *Technological Society*.

U.S. ratifies mutual security treaty with South Korea (26 Jan.).

French defeat at Dien Bien Phu ends Indochinese War.

Rebellion breaks out against French control in Algeria.

Death of Spanish playwright Jacinto Benavente (b. 1866).

Terence Rattigan's play *Separate Tables*.

Enid Bagnold's play *The Chalk Garden*. Death of artist Henri Matisse (b. 1869). Federico Fellini's film *La Strada*.

U.S. begins economic aid to Laos, Cambodia, and South Vietnam.

DATES	THEATRICAL EVENTS IN AMERICA	SELECTED HISTORICAL/CULTURAL EVENTS IN AMERICA	SELECTED HISTORICAL/CULTURAL EVENTS THROUGHOUT THE WORLD
	Williamstown Theatre Festival founded.	A bus boycott of black citizens led by Martin Luther King, begins in Montgomery, Alabama (1 Dec.).	French anthropologist Claude Lévi-Strauss's *Tristes Tropiques*.
	Arthur Miller's *A View from the Bridge* and *A Memory of Two Mondays*.	Albert Einstein dies in Princeton, New Jersey, aged 76.	Graham Greene's novel *The Quiet American*.
	William Inge's *Bus Stop* with Kim Stanley, directed by Harold Clurman.	The American Federation of Labor and the Congress of Industrial Organizations unify under George Meaney, ending their rivalry.	UN report reveals that slavery persists in some countries in South America, the Middle East and Southeast Asia.
	Jerome Lawrence's and Robert E. Lee's *Inherit the Wind* (premiered in Dallas), based on Scopes Monkey Trial and with Paul Muni and Ed Begley, becomes popular court drama.	First electrical synthesizer built in Princeton, New Jersey.	Agatha Christie's play *Witness for the Prosecution*.
	George Abbott's, Richard Adler's and Jerry Ross's *Damn Yankees*.	Davy Crockett craze results in $100 million industry, which includes sales of Crockett caps, raccoon coats, and even ladies' panties.	
	S. N. Behrman and Harold Rome musical, *Fanny*.	Film *Marty* with Ernest Borgnine opens.	Vladimir Nabokov's novel *Lolita*.
	Death of Robert E. Sherwood (b. 1896).	*The Village Voice*, an alternative New York newspaper, appears.	Salvador Dali's painting *Last Supper*.
	Cole Porter's *Silk Stockings*.	Walter Lippmann's *The Public Philosophy*. Louis Hartz's *The Liberal Tradition in America*. James Baldwin's *Notes of a Native Son*. Herbert Mancuse's *Eros and Civilization*. C. Vann Woodward's *The Strange Career of Jim Crow*. Will Herberg's *Protestant–Catholic–Jew*.	

1956			
Long Day's Journey Into Night, which O'Neill ordered to be withheld until 25 years after his death or until all of the models for his characters had died, is performed for the first time. It garners a Pulitzer the following year.	Richard Hofstadter's *Age of Reform*. Norman Vincent Peale's *The Power of Positive Thinking*.		Atomic Energy Commission develop atomic powered rockets.
Alan Jay Lerner's and Frederick Loewe's *My Fair Lady*, based on Shaw's *Pygmalion*, is produced with Rex Harrison and Julie Andrews.	An oral vaccine against polio is developed by Arthur Sabin.		
	Elvis Presley releases *Heartbreak Hotel*, the first of his string of more than 170 hit singles and 80 hit albums.		Khrushchev's "secret speech."
Philadelphia Drama Guild founded.	World heavyweight boxing champ Rocky Marciano retires, having won all forty-nine bouts of his career (April).		Soviets crush rebellion in Hungary.
The Diary of Anne Frank, by Frances Goodrich and Albert Hackett, wins Pulitzer.	Allen Ginsberg's long experimental poem, *Howl*, decribed as an elegy of the American dream, is the first major work of the Beatnik cultural/literary movement.		Biggest anti-Communist uprising since 1953 when Polish workers riot at industrial fair in Poznan (28 June).
Ringling Bros., Barnum & Bailey give last circus performance under canvas big top.	By mid-50s bust lines are accentuated in figure-hugging evening wear. Suits and dresses are the fashion in women's daily wear.		Egyptian President Nasser seizes Suez Canal (26 July).
Samuel Beckett's *Waiting for Godot* with Bert Lahr and E.G. Marshall stuns audiences and alters course of modern theatre.	C. Wright Mills's *Power Elite*. William H. Whyte's *The Organization of Man*. Walter Kaufman, ed., *Existentialism from Dostoevsky to Sartre*.		Ingmar Bergman's film *The Seventh Seal* released. Swiss playwright Friedrich Durrenmatt's *The Visit*. Irish pundit and playwright Brendan Behan's *The Quare Fellow*.
Frank Loesser's musical *The Most Happy Fella* is milestone with blending of opera and musical comedy style.	John F. Kennedy's *Profiles in Courage*.		Bertolt Brecht dies (b. 1898).

DATES	THEATRICAL EVENTS IN AMERICA	SELECTED HISTORICAL/CULTURAL EVENTS IN AMERICA	SELECTED HISTORICAL/CULTURAL EVENTS THROUGHOUT THE WORLD
		Martin Luther King emerges as civil rights leader.	
		Edwin O'Connor's novel *The Last Hurrah*, based on the life of Boston Mayor James Michael Curley.	John Osborne's play *Look Back in Anger* is described by critics as "an angry young man piece".
			French thief and playwright Jean Genet's *The Balcony*.
1957	*West Side Story*, a collaboration of Leonard Bernstein, Arthur Laurents, and Stephen Sondheim, opens.	Grace Metalious's bestseller *Peyton Place*.	
		Congress enacts Civil Rights Act, the first civil rights legislation since Reconstruction. It prohibits discrimination in public places based on race, color, religion, or national origin.	Sputnik launched by Russians.
	The Burlesque Artists Association has license revoked.	Southern Christian Leadership Conference (SCLC) forms, led by Martin Luther King and dedicated to non-violent protest of racial discrimination.	Milovan Dijilas's *New Class* published.
	William Inge's *The Dark at the Top of the Stairs*.	Labor leader James "Jimmy" Hoffa becomes head of the Teamsters' Union.	Harold Pinter's *The Dumb Waiter*, his first play.
	William Saroyan's *The Cave Dwellers*.	First plastic Frisbee is introduced.	French send in military to combat ALN (Armeé de Liberation), fighting for Algerian independence (31 Jan.).
	Detroit Repertory Theatre founded.	Althea Gibson becomes the first black player to win the Wimbledon tennis title (6 July).	Samuel Beckett's *Endgame*.
	Jujamcyn Theatre chain begins with purchase of New York's St. James Theatre.	Jack Kerouac's *On the Road*, a semi-autobiographical novel and the most popular contribution to the Beat Generation, is published.	Harold Macmillan becomes Great Britain's Prime Minister.

1958			
Meredith Willson's *The Music Man* with Robert Preston and Barbara Cook.	James Gould Cozzen's *By Love Possessed.*	Israel withdraws from Sinai Peninsula and hands over Gaza Strip to United Nations.
Tennessee Williams's *Orpheus Descending.*	Dwight MacDonald's *Memoirs of a Revolutionist.*	Albert Camus wins Nobel Prize for Literature.
Look Homeward, Angel, adapted by Ketti Frings (opened Nov. 1957).	Mary McCarthy's *Memories of a Catholic Childhood.*	Russian modernist Boris Pasternak's novel *Doctor Zhivago* published.
Eugene O'Neill's *A Touch of the Poet* first produced (with Eric Porter, Helen Hayes, Kim Stanley).	Leon Festinger's *A Theory of Cognitive Dissonance.*	Harold Pinter's *The Birthday Party.* Max Frisch's *Biedermann and the Firebugs.*
Elmer Rice's adaptation of *Hamlet, Cue for Passion*, is produced.	Art Linkletter's *Kids Say the Darndest Things.*	Shelagh Delaney's play *A Taste of Honey.*
Dore Schary's *Sunrise at Campobello.*	Richard Starkweather begins his murderous rampage across the Midwest (Jan.). He will kill eleven before apprehension by police on 30 January.	Edmund Hillary reaches South Pole with New Zealand expedition, beating rival British group by seventeen days (3 Jan.).
The Pleasure of His Company by Samuel Taylor and Cornelia Otis Skinner.	The U.S. Supreme Court orders Little Rock High School in Arkansas to admit blacks (12 Sept.).	Campaign for Nuclear Disarmament forms in Britain (17 Feb.).
	The U.S. nuclear submarine, *Nautilus*, passes under ice cap at the North Pole, showing efficacy of shortening commercial sea routes.	Nikita Khrushchev succeeds Bulganin as premier while retaining position of First Secretary of Communist Party, thereby taking full control of USSR in first return to one-man rule since Stalin's death in 1953 (27 March).
	U.S. unemployment reaches a postwar high of more than 5.1 million, and the Department of Labor reports that a record 3.1 million receive unemployment insurance benefits.	
	U.S. announces start of manned space program, Mercury. U.S. government establishes National Aeronautics and Space Administration (NASA) to compete with Soviet Union on space exploration.	

DATES	THEATRICAL EVENTS IN AMERICA	SELECTED HISTORICAL/CULTURAL EVENTS IN AMERICA	SELECTED HISTORICAL/CULTURAL EVENTS THROUGHOUT THE WORLD
	Williams's *The Garden District* (retitled *Suddenly Last Summer*, film 1959).	The hula hoop, the biggest toy fad in history, is introduced.	King Faisel of Iraq, his heir and premier Nuri-es-Said are assassinated (14 July).
	William Gibson's *Two for the Seesaw* with Henry Fonda and Anne Bancroft.	The Guggenheim Museum, designed by Frank Lloyd Wright, opens in New York City.	Racial tensions erupt in violence when black and white youths battle in Nottingham, England (23 Aug.).
	Critic George Jean Nathan dies (b. 1882).	Daniel Lerner's *The Passing of Traditional Society*.	Pope Pius XII dies and is succeeded by Cardinal Angelo Giuseppe Roncalli, who takes the name Pope John XXIII (9 Oct.).
		John Kenneth Galbraith's *The Affluent Society*.	
		Martin Luther King's *Stride Toward Freedom*.	
		John Rawls's "Justice as Fairness."	
		William Lederer and Eugene Burdick's *The Ugly American*.	
		Film of Tennessee Williams's *Cat on a Hot Tin Roof*, directed by Richard Brooks.	Beginning of Great Leap Forward in China (until 1960). A period of radical change to cultivate modernization, it proves disastrous.
		Truman Capote's novel *Breakfast at Tiffany's*.	Graham Greene's novel *Our Man in Havana*.
			Alan Sillitoe's novel *Saturday Night and Sunday Morning*.
			Chinua Achebe's novel *Things Fall Apart*.
			Max Ernst's painting *Après Moi le Sommeil*.
			European Common Market established.
			Irishman Brendan Behan writes *The Hostage*.
			Beckett's *Krapp's Last Tape*.
			Peter Shaffer's play *Five Finger Exercise*.

1959			
Lorraine Hansberry's *A Raisin in the Sun*, showing the tribulations of a struggling black family, opens to boisterous critical and popular praise (with Sidney Poitier, Ruby Dee, Diana Sands).	Launching in the U.S. of the first atomic submarine (9 June), and the first atomic-powered cargo ship, *Savannah* (21 July). First Barbie doll introduced in California.		C.P. Snow's *The Two Cultures*.
The San Francisco Mime Troupe, founded by R.G. Davis and using techniques from the commedia dell'arte, is started. Mixing radical politics with farce and invective, they stage crude parables and in later years Vietnam protest plays.	Alaska and Hawaii, under U.S. territorial control since 1912 and 1898 respectively, achieve state status.		After Batista flees, Castro takes control and becomes premier of Cuba (2 Jan.).
Dallas Theater Center founded.	Xerox introduces its first copier.		Mrs. Indira Gandhi, only daughter of India's Prime Minister Jawaharlal Nehru, elected President of ruling Congress Party (2 Feb.).
Edward Albee's *The Zoo Story* premieres in Berlin.	The "Twist" dance is introduced.		Resistance to Chinese rule in Tibet leads to revolt. Chinese forces crush rebellion, and the Dalai Lama flees to India (13–27 March).
Jack Gelber's *The Connection* staged by Living Theatre.	Singer and teen idol Buddy Holly dies in a plane crash at age twenty-two (3 Feb.). Blues singer Billie Holiday dies at age forty-four.		Eamon De Valera resigns as premier and becomes President of Eire. Charles De Gaulle becomes President of France (17 June).
Poet Archibald Macleish wins Pulitzer for his verse play *J.B.* (opened 1958 with Christopher Plummer, Raymond Massey, Pat Hingle).	Harold Rosenberg's *Tradition of the New.* Norman O. Brown's *Life Against Death.* William A. Williams's *The Tragedy of American Diplomacy.* C. Wright Mills's *The Sociological Imagination.*		Eugène Ionesco's *The Rhinoceros*. Jean Genet's *The Blacks*.
Lindsay's and Crouse's, Rodgers's and Hammerstein's *The Sound of Music* (with Mary Martin). Mary Rodger's and Marshall Barer's Off-Broadway musical *Once Upon a Mattress* with Carol Burnett.	William Burroughs's underground novel *The Naked Lunch.* Robert Lowell's poetry collection *Life Studies.*		
Gypsy created by team of Jerome Robbins, Jule Styne, Stephen Sondheim, and Arthur Laurents (with Ethel Merman).	William Faulkner's novel *The Mansion.* Philip Roth's novel *Goodbye, Columbus.*		
Fiorello! (Jerome Weidman, George Abbott, Jerry Bock, and Sheldon Harnick) with Tom Bosley as La Guardia (wins 1960 Pulitzer).			

DATES	THEATRICAL EVENTS IN AMERICA	SELECTED HISTORICAL/CULTURAL EVENTS IN AMERICA	SELECTED HISTORICAL/CULTURAL EVENTS THROUGHOUT THE WORLD
	Williams's *Sweet Bird of Youth* directed by Kazan with Paul Newman and Geraldine Page (a work in progress had been seen in Florida in 1956; film 1962).	Jasper Johns's painting *Numbers in Color*.	John Arden's play *Serjeant Musgrave's Dance*.
	William Gibson's *The Miracle Worker* (with Anne Bancroft and Patty Duke).	Hawaii becomes 50th state.	Films *Hiroshima, Mon Amour* (Alain Resnais) and *La Dolce Vita* (Fellini) released.
	Paddy Chayefsky's *The Tenth Man*.		Pope John XXIII calls Ecumenical Council, first since 1870.
1960		John F. Kennedy elected thirty-fifth (and youngest) President.	
	Association of Producing Artists founded.	D.H. Lawrence's *Lady Chatterley's Lover* is ruled not obscene, and therefore mailable, by the U.S. Court of Appeals in New York (25 March).	American U-2 spy plane, piloted by Francis Gary Powers, shot down over Russia.
	Asolo Center for the Performing Arts established.	Alan Freed, coiner of the term "rock'n'roll" and one of the most famous early disc jockeys, is arrested in "Payola scam." It is a charge of commercial bribery, which accuses Freed of accepting money from record companies in exchange for playing their releases on air (19 May).	Austrian-born British art historian E.H. Gombrich's *Art and Illusion* published. Hans Gadamer's *Truth and Method* appears.
	Cincinnati Playhouse in the Park opens.	Charles Van Doren, star contestant of TV quiz show "21," arrested for perjury, based on statements that quiz shows provided answers to contestants prior to competition (17 July).	Start of civil disobedience campaign against pass laws in South Africa. Sixty-seven blacks are killed at Sharpeville (21 March).
	Albee's *The Zoo Story* has its American premiere in New York (14 Jan.). Also, his *Fam and Yam* and *The Sandbox*.	The 23rd Amendment proposed by Congress to grant rights of voting and representation to the District of Columbia. It is ratified in 1961.	Nigeria achieves independence within Commonwealth (1 Oct.).

After an Actors' Equity Strike, twenty-two legitimate Broadway theatres close, the first time since 1919 (12–13 June).

Williams's *Period of Adjustment*.

Lillian Hellman's *Toys in the Attic*.

Tom Jones's and Harvey Schmidt's *The Fantasticks* opens (3 May) at Off-Broadway's Sullivan St. Playhouse; still playing there in 1999.
The rock'n'roll phenomenon quickly sweeps Broadway with the production of Michael Stewart, Charles Strouse, and Lee Adams's *Bye Bye Birdie*, featuring TV personality Dick Van Dyke.
Meredith Willson's *The Unsinkable Molly Brown* with Tammy Grimes.

Richard Burton, Julie Andrews, and Robert Goulet star in *Camelot* at The Majestic Theatre. The musical, based on T.H. White's *The Once and Future King*, later becomes a successful film.

Student Nonviolent Coordinating Committee (SNCC) forms during lunch-counter sit-in in Greensboro, North Carolina.

Congress passes Civil Rights Act of 1960, addressing voter-registration practices. Because it is not enforced, it is virtually ineffective.

Soft drink manufacturers introduce aluminum cans. Pop-top cans follow in 1963.

1960s. The use of birth control pills by women grows widespread.

W.W. Rostow's *Stages of Economic Growth*.

Paul Goodman's *Growing Up Absurd*.

Daniel Bell's *The End of Ideology*.
Bruno Bettelheim's *The Informed Heart*.
Sheldon Wolin's *Politics and Wisdom*.
Angus Campbell et al., *The American Voter*.
S.M. Lipset's *Political Man*.
John Courtney Murray's *We Hold These Truths*.
Bobby Fischer, aged sixteen, defends U.S. chess title.

Harold Pinter's *The Caretaker* and *The Dumb Waiter*.

Terence Rattigan's *Ross*.

Lionel Bart's *Oliver* at London's New Theatre.

DATES	THEATRICAL EVENTS IN AMERICA	SELECTED HISTORICAL/CULTURAL EVENTS IN AMERICA	SELECTED HISTORICAL/CULTURAL EVENTS THROUGHOUT THE WORLD
		The film *Ben Hur* wins record ten Oscars. Completion of Robert Motherwell's huge sequence of paintings, *Elegy to the Spanish Republic*. Alfred Hitchcock's *Psycho* premieres. Pacemaker to regulate heartbeat developed. Edward Hopper's painting *Second-Story Sunlight*.	
1961	Theatre clubs and coffeehouses like Caffe Cino and La MaMa Experimental Theater Club open, providing an alternative outlet for avant-garde artists and dramatists.	The Peace Corps initiated by President Kennedy (1 March).	Bloodless coup overthrows junta in El Salvador (25 January).
	Records reveal that Special Services Division of U.S. Army in Europe had censored, cut, or rewritten Broadway plays "to keep them clean," without notification to the authors of the Dramatists Guild.	Hemingway kills himself with his own gun (2 July).	A campaign of civil disobedience in Ceylon (30 Jan.).
	The Children's Theatre Company, a Minneapolis-based children's theatre, is created by John Clark Donahue; New York based Theatreworks/USA also established as touring children's theatre company.	New York Yankee Roger Maris breaks Babe Ruth's 1927 record of sixty home runs, with sixty-one (1 Oct.).	Trial of Nazi Adolph Eichmann begins in Jerusalem. He is convicted and sentenced to death (11 April).
	The Theatre Communications Group (TCG) founded in New York City as umbrella organization for not-for-profit theatres.	JFK reaffirms commitment to South Vietnam (14 Dec.).	Anti-Castro Cuban activists, trained by U.S. Central Intelligence Agency, land in failed invasion at Bay of Pigs, Cuba, with U.S. military supplies and support facilities (17 April).

Tad Mosel's *All the Way Home.*

Neil Simon's *Come Blow Your Horn* opens, beginning his reign as Broadway's top playwright.
Robert Bolt's *A Man for All Seasons,* a biography of martyred saint Sir Thomas More, is imported from London, and stars Paul Scofield in the lead role.
Williams's *The Night of the Iguana* wins Drama Critics' Award (film 1964).

First U.S. spaceman Alan Shephard rockets 116.5 miles up in a 302-mile trip. Kennedy publicly commits U.S. to sending man to the moon by end of decade.

Pinter introduced to Broadway with *The Caretaker.*

How to Succeed in Business Without Really Trying, by Abe Burrows, Willie Gilbert, Jack Weinstock, and Frank Loesser (wins Pulitzer).

Ossie Davis's *Purlie Victorious,* with Davis, Ruby Dee, Godfrey Cambridge, and Alan Alda.

Peter Schumann's Bread and Puppet Theater founded. It utilizes politics and puppets for trenchant social commentary and anti-war polemic.

The Zoo Story by Albee and *Call Me By My Rightful Name* by Michael Shurtleff are banned from performance at a high school in Rockport, Massachusetts, for undercurrents of homosexuality in the former, racial triangles in the latter.

Freedom Riders come to the South to help expose segregation in bus terminals.

First Lady Jacqueline Kennedy popularizes the short, tailored 2-piece suit and pillbox hat created by Oleg Cassini.
Joseph Heller's *Catch-22.*
Erving Goffman's *Asylums.*

Lionel Trilling's "On the Teaching of Modern Literature."
Ernest Nagel's *The Structure of Science.*
Robert Dahl's *Who Governs?*
William Shirer's *The Rise and Fall of the Third Reich.*

Premiere of Robert Rossen's film *The Hustler* with Jackie Gleason and Paul Newman.

"Century 21 Exposition," a world's fair for the space age, is held in Seattle, Washington (21 April).

The 24th Amendment is proposed by Congress to eliminate the poll tax. It is ratified 23 January 1964.

Construction of Berlin Wall begins (17–18 April). Two U.S. army helicopter companies with 400 men arrive in Saigon (11 Dec.).

Samuel Beckett's *Happy Days.*
John Osborne's *Luther.*
South African playwright Athol Fugard's *The Blood Knot.*
Harold Pinter's *The Collection.*
Arnold Wesker's *The Kitchen.*
John Whiting's *The Devils.*

Russian Yuri Gagarin becomes first man in space, orbiting the Earth for 108 minutes in Vostok 1 (April).

European film openings include François Truffaut's *Jules and Jim;* Vittorio De Sica's *Two Women;* Tony Richardson's *A Taste of Honey;* Luis Buñuel's *Viridiana.*

John Glenn becomes first American to orbit earth.

During Cuban Missile Crisis, President Kennedy demands withdrawal of Soviet missiles from Cuba. An air and naval quarantine is ordered. Khrushchev later agrees to dismantle and remove Soviet rockets, and Kennedy agrees not to invade Cuba.

1962

DATES	THEATRICAL EVENTS IN AMERICA	SELECTED HISTORICAL/CULTURAL EVENTS IN AMERICA	SELECTED HISTORICAL/CULTURAL EVENTS THROUGHOUT THE WORLD
	Lincoln Center for the Performing Arts is built in New York City.	Federal troops sent to University of Mississippi to force school to enroll African American James Meredith.	U.S. loans $100 million to UN to help resolve its financial crisis.
	The 400th birthday of Shakespeare is celebrated across the country. Thirty of his thirty-seven plays are performed nationwide (23 April).	American labor leader Cesar Chavez organizes California grape pickers. He forms the farm workers' association (UFW).	Irish Republican Army announces suspension of campaign of violence begun in 1956 against Northern Ireland government (26 Feb.).
	Great Lakes Theater Festival begins (14 Aug.).	Thomas Kuhn's *The Structure of Scientific Revolutions.*	Jamaica gains independence in Commonwealth (6 Aug.).
		Michael Harrington's *The Other America.*	
		Milton Friedman's *Capitalism and Freedom.* Marshall McLuhan's *The Gutenberg Galaxy.*	Uganda gains independence in Commonwealth (9 Oct.).
		Rachel Carson's *Silent Spring.*	
		Ken Kesey's *One Flew Over the Cuckoo's Nest.*	Doris Lessing's novel *The Golden Notebook.*
		Katherine Ann Porter's *Ship of Fools.*	Anthony Burgess's novel *A Clockwork Orange.*
	Arthur Kopit's *Oh, Dad, Poor Dad, Mamma's Hung You in the Closet and I'm Feelin' So Sad* (Off-Broadway).	Students for a Democratic Society (SDS) publish Port Huron Statement.	First James Bond film, *Dr. No*, premieres.
	Albee's *Who's Afraid of Virginia Woolf*, with Arthur Hill and Uta Hagen.	Robert Rauschenberg's painting *Barge.* Andy Warhol's silkscreen *Marilyn Monroe* and painting *Green Coca Cola Bottles.*	Algeria is granted independence, ending Algerian War.
	Herb Gardner's *A Thousand Clowns*, with Jason Robards, Jr. and Sandy Dennis.		Second Vatican Council, 1962–65, produces sixteen documents outlining reforms and modernization of Roman Catholic practice.
	Thornton Wilder's *Plays for Bleecker Street.*		Friedrich Dürrenmatt's *The Physicists.* Ann Jellicoe's *The Knack.*
	A Funny Thing Happened on the Way to the Forum stars Zero Mostel and features		

songs by Stephen Sondheim, his first composed musical.

Arnold Wesker's *Chips with Everything*. Peter Shaffer's *The Private Ear and the Public Eye*. Eugène Ionesco's *Exit the King*. Arabs in Iraq resume civil war with Kurds (10 June).

Medgar Evers, Field Secretary for the NAACP, is shot and killed in Jackson, Mississippi. His assailant will not be convicted until 1993. Black civil rights demonstration; Reverend Martin Luther King delivers the "I Have a Dream" speech (29 Aug.).

1963

The Minnesota Theater Company founded as alternative to New York commercial theatre.

President Kennedy makes attack on Communism during visit to West Berlin (26 June).

The Free Southern Theatre, inspired by the Civil Rights Movement, founded by John O'Neal, Gilbert Moses, and Doris Derby. Open Theatre, an experimental Off-Off Broadway acting company, created by Joseph Chaikin.

President Kennedy shot to death in motorcade in Dallas, Texas by Lee Harvey Oswald (22 Nov.).

Scandal over security by involvement of Secretary of State for War John Profumo with model Christine Keeler brings about British Prime Minister Harold Macmillan's resignation (10 October). Black nationalist leader Nelson Mandela brought from jail to stand trial for treason (3 Dec.). German playwright Rolf Hochhuth's controversial *The Deputy* premieres in Berlin.

Goodspeed Opera House (Connecticut) opens as home of American musicals.

March for racial equality by 200,000 in Detroit, Michigan.

The Guthrie Theater founded in Minneapolis.

The characteristic 60s clothes emerge, featuring miniskirts, stretch pants, hip-hugger bell-bottomed trousers, and collarless jackets.

Tony Richardson's film *Tom Jones*. Ingmar Bergman's *The Silence*. Lindsay Anderson's *This Sporting Life*.

Seattle Repertory Theatre founded.

Author Betty Friedan publishes *The Feminine Mystique*, a seminal work in the continuing women's movement. Mary McCarthy's *The Group*. Nathan Glazer and Daniel Moynihan's *Beyond the Melting Pot*. Martin Luther King's "Letter from the Birmingham Jail." Jessica Mitford's *The American Way of Death*.

The Beatles score first hit with "I Want to Hold Your Hand."

Trinity [Square] Repertory Company of Providence, Rhode Island, founded.

Williams's *The Milk Train Doesn't Stop Here Anymore*. This and subsequent Williams plays produced (some ten) are largely unsuccessful.

DATES	THEATRICAL EVENTS IN AMERICA	SELECTED HISTORICAL/CULTURAL EVENTS IN AMERICA	SELECTED HISTORICAL/CULTURAL EVENTS THROUGHOUT THE WORLD
	Langston Hughes's *Tambourines to Glory*.	Poet Adrienne Rich's *Snapshots of a Daughter-in-Law*.	
	Harnick's and Bock's musical *She Loves Me*.	Poet Sylvia Plath publishes a semi-autobiographical novel *The Bell Jar*.	
	Neil Simon's *Barefoot in the Park* (over 1,500 performances).	First push-button telephones introduced.	
	Proletarian dramatist Clifford Odets dies at age fifty-seven.	Eastman Kodak introduces Instamatic camera.	
1964	Imamu Amiri Baraka's (né LeRoi Jones) *The Dutchman*, called the "best one-act play in America" by Norman Mailer, receives the Off-Broadway Award for Best American Play of 1963–64.	Comedian Lenny Bruce arrested for indecency and for using foul language at Greenwich Village café.	Clashes erupt over disputed rights in Panama Canal (9 Jan.).
	The Black Arts Repertory founded.	Beatlemania sweeps U.S. as their albums sell 2,000,000 copies in a month and they embark on national tour.	Palestinian Liberation Organization (PLO) founded (June).
	Living Theater proprietors Julian Beck and his wife Judith Malina are convicted of impeding federal officers from closing the theatre down.	Three civil rights activists – Michael Schwerner, Andrew Goodman, and James Chaney – murdered in Mississippi.	After North Vietnamese gunboats fire on U.S. ships in Gulf of Tonka, U.S. Senate passes resolution authorizing President Johnson to repel armed attacks and prevent further aggression (7 June).
	Actors Theatre of Louisville, Hartford Stage Company, Missouri Repertory Theatre, and South Coast Repertory – all founded.	Martin Luther King awarded Nobel Peace Prize. At age thirty-five, he is youngest recipient of all time.	Iris Murdoch and J.P. Priestley adapt Murdoch's novel, *A Severed Head*, for the stage.
	Funny Girl (Jule Styne and Bob Merrill) makes star of Barbra Streisand with her portrayal of Fanny Brice.	Joe Orton's *Entertaining Mr. Sloan*. Free Speech Movement begins among Berkeley students under Mario Savio, Jack Weinberg, and others.	Peter Weiss's play *Marat/Sade*. John Osborne's *Inadmissable Evidence* at London's Royal Court.
	Bock/Harnick musical *Fiddler on the Roof* stars Zero Mostel with scenery by Boris Aronson.	The Beatles arrive in New York to ecstatic reception (8 Feb.).	Peter Shaffer's *The Royal Hunt of the Sun*.

O'Neill Theater Center founded in Connecticut.

Arthur Miller's *After the Fall* at ANTA Theatre-Washington Square. Muriel Resnik's *Any Wednesday.* Frank D. Gilroy's *The Subject Was Roses.* Murray Schisgal's *Luv.*

James Baldwin's *Blues for Mr. Charlie.*

Hello, Dolly! by Jerry Herman and Michael Stewart, based on Wilder play, opens with Carol Channing, who will tour successfully with the musical in the 1990s. A gigantic flop, *Kelly,* lasts only one performance in New York and costs $650,000.

Robert Lowell's *The Old Glory* produced at St. Clement's Church, New York.

New Codes of Ethics of the League of New York Theatres dealing with fiscal details of producing created. Sidney Kingsley named new President of The Dramatists Guild, Inc. Actors' Equity stages a one-day strike.

Miller's *Incident at Vichy,* William Hanley's *Slow Dance on the Killing Ground,* Simon's *The Odd Couple,* and *Fiddler on the Roof,* all designated Best Plays for 1964–65.

Cassius Clay beats Sonny Liston to become heavyweight champion of the world (25 Feb.).

Kitty Genovese murdered in Queens, New York, while thirty-seven witnesses do nothing to prevent crime. Case becomes searing indictment of city residents' fear of becoming involved in such attacks (13 March).

Verrazano-Narrows Bridge, possibly most expensive structure ever built at $325 million, constructed in New York City. U.S. Office of Criminal Justice established to study and improve criminal justice process.

Saul Bellow's *Herzog.* Ken Kesey's *Sometimes a Great Notion.* Ralph Ellison's *Shadow and Act.*

Clifford Geertz's "Ideology as a Cultural System." Clark Kerr's *The Uses of the University.* Philip E. Converse's "The Nature of Belief Systems in Mass Publics." Hannah Arendt's *Eichmann in Jerusalem.*

Martin Luther King's *Why We Can't Wait.*

World's first discotheque, the "Whiskey-a-Go-Go," opens in Los Angeles. Riots in Harlem.

Roger Sessions's opera *Montezuma* premieres in West Berlin.

Marshall McLuhan's *Understanding Media.*

DATES	THEATRICAL EVENTS IN AMERICA	SELECTED HISTORICAL/CULTURAL EVENTS IN AMERICA	SELECTED HISTORICAL/CULTURAL EVENTS THROUGHOUT THE WORLD
	Plan to export *Hello, Dolly!* to South Africa vetoed after NAACP expresses its disapproval. Sam Shepard's *Cowboy* and *The Rock Garden* receive Off-Broadway Obies.	Robert Lowell's *For the Union Dead.* Poet Marianne Moore writes *The Arctic Ox.* Sidney Poitier becomes first black actor to win Oscar for Best Actor, for his role in *Lilies of the Field.* Jimmy Hoffa brings all truckers under a single Teamsters' Union contract.	
1965	The American Conservatory Theatre (now Theater) founded by William Ball at Pittsburgh Playhouse. It relocates to San Francisco in 1967.	Lyndon Johnson, elected in 1964, unveils his Great Society Program.	President Lyndon Johnson commits troops to Vietnam.
	With the purchase and renovation of the Palace Theatre, the Nederlander family from Detroit bring new theatrical dynasty to Broadway.	Black leader Malcolm X shot dead in Harlem (21 Feb.).	Rolling Stones gain great popularity with "Satisfaction."
	Jon Jory and Harlan Kleiman open Long Wharf Theatre, a non-profit resident theatre in New Haven, Conn. National Playwrights Conference established by George C. White.	More than fifty blacks injured during brutal attack by sheriff's posse and state troopers in Selma, Alabama (7–9 March). Blacks riot for six days in Watts section of Los Angeles. National Guard called in to restore order.	Winston Churchill dies at age ninety-one.
	Neil Simon's highly successful *The Odd Couple* opens with Art Carney and Walter Matthau.	Martin Luther King heads procession of 4,000 civil rights demonstrators from Selma to Montgomery, Alabama, to deliver petition on racial grievances (21 March).	U.S. begins retaliatory bombing raids on North Vietnam (7 Feb.). On 2 March U.S. declares combatant status.
	El Teatro Campesino, an agit prop troupe, emerges with activist Luis Valdez. Situated in San Juan Bautiste, group devises new theatrical form, the	Mass anti-war demonstrations (15–18 Oct.).	Nigerian author Wole Soyinka's novel *The Interpreters.*

acto, combining elements of Aztec mythology and contemporary social life in the barrio. Concerned with working-class politics and factory disputes, some dramas are staged directly on picket lines.

Baraka's *The Toilet* faces censorship problems in Boston and Los Angeles. James Baldwin's *The Amen Corner* has brief run on Broadway. Ed Bullins's *Clara's Old Man.*

Congress establishes National Endowment for the Arts to make grants to theatrical groups and projects.

Peter Brook's production of *Marat/Sade* imported to New York; becomes influential theatre piece.
Roundabout Theatre Company forms. A Contemporary Theatre founded.

Studio Arena Theatre forms.

Abe Burrows's *Cactus Flower* with Lauren Bacall.
The annual gross for the 1964–65 season on Broadway is $50,462,765.

Major Edward White leaves Gemini 4 capsule for twenty minutes, becoming first American to walk in space.

25th Amendment proposed to establish system for succession for presidency and for replacement of the vice president. It is ratified 10 February 1967.

Congress passes Voting Rights Act in August, outlawing literacy tests and other voter-registration tests.
Some 240 million radios and 61.8 million TV sets are in use in U.S.
Jim Brown sets record for most lifetime touchdowns (126).
Herbert Marcuse's "Repressive Tolerance."
Lionel Trilling's *Beyond Culture.*
Noam Chomsky's *Aspects of the Theory of Syntax.*
Malcolm X's *Autobiography.*
Harvey Cox's *The Secular City.*
Tom Wolfe's *The Kandy-Kolored Tangerine-Flake Streamline Baby.*
Singer Nat King Cole dies at age forty-five.

Harold Pinter's *The Homecoming.*
Frank Marcus's *The Killing of Sister George.*
Peter Shaffer's *Black Comedy.*
Edward Bond's *Saved.*
Joe Orton's *Loot.*
Czech dramatist and future Prime Minister Vaclav Havel's *The Memorandum.*

DATES	THEATRICAL EVENTS IN AMERICA	SELECTED HISTORICAL/CULTURAL EVENTS IN AMERICA	SELECTED HISTORICAL/CULTURAL EVENTS THROUGHOUT THE WORLD
	William Alfred's *Hogan's Goat* at the American Place Theatre. Producer David Merrick brings Irish writer Brian Friel's *Philadelphia, Here I Come!* to Broadway.	Sylvia Plath's *Ariel*, published posthumously. Norman Mailer's *American Dream.*	
	Man of La Mancha, a vehicle for Richard Kiley, opens 22 November and runs for 2,238 performances.	Swami Pradhupada founds International Society of Krishna Consciousness, Vaisnava devotional movement, in Los Angeles.	Louis Althusser's *For Marx.*
	Vivian Beaumont Theatre in Lincoln Center opens 21 October. Sam Shepard's *Chicago.* Lanford Wilson's *Balm in Gilead.* Paul Zindel's *The Effect of Gamma Rays on Man-in-the-Moon Marigolds* premieres in Houston.	Walter Piston's Symphony No. 8 premieres at Boston's Symphony Hall.	
	A Delicate Balance, Generation, Cactus Flower, The Lion in Winter, and *Man of La Mancha* designated Best Plays of 1965–66.		
1966	Robert Wilson starts Byrd Hoffman School for Byrds, an institution to help children with learning disabilities and other brain disorders. This work leads to *Deafman Glance* (1970), an "opera of images."	The Motion Picture Association replaces 1930 Hayes code with new, concise guidelines for clarifying films as to suitability for audiences (20 Sept.).	French philospher Michel Foucault's *The Order of Things* and psychoanalyst Jacques Lacan's *Ecrits.*
		U.S. Supreme Court overturns conviction of confessed rapist, establishing requirements for so-called Miranda warnings in Miranda v. Arizona.	U.S. resumes bombing of North Vietnam after thirty-seven-day pause (31 Jan.).
	Yale Repertory Theatre established.	Chicago race riots take 4,200 National Guardsmen and 533 arrests to quell.	President Kwame Nkrumah's government overthrown in miliatry coup in Ghana (24 Feb.).

1967			
INTAR Hispanic American Arts Center founded in New York. John Kander/Fred Ebb/Joe Masteroff musical *Cabaret*, based on *Berlin Stories* by Christopher Isherwood and *I Am a Camera* by John Van Druten, opens at the Broadhurst Theatre on 20 November, produced by Hal Prince and with Joel Grey as decadent master of ceremonies. James Goldman's *The Lion in Winter* with Robert Preston and Rosemary Harris. Jean-Claude Van Itallie's *America Hurrah* opens at Off-Broadway Pocket Theatre. Nightclub comic Lennie Bruce found dead of a drug overdose. Death of showman Billy Rose (b. 1899). *A Delicate Balance, You Know I Can't Hear You When the Water's Running,* and *The Apple Tree* named Best Plays of 1966–67. Season musicals include *Sweet Charity, Mame, The Apple Tree,* and *I Do! I Do!* Ron Tavel's *The Gorilla Queen* premieres at Theatre of the Ridiculous. Jules Feiffer's *Little Murders* at the Broadhurst Theatre.	National Organization of Women (NOW) founded by Betty Friedan. Women's fashion geared toward youth and features the "boy look" popularized by model Twiggy. Bill Russell becomes first black head coach of any professional sport team when he is named head coach of the Boston Celtics. Peter Berger and Thomas Luckerman's *The Social Construction of Reality.* Robert Lane's "The Decline of Politics and Ideology in a Knowledgeable Society." Bernard Malamud's *The Fixer.* Truman Capote's *In Cold Blood.* Roy Lichtenstein's painting *Yellow and Red Brushstrokes.* TV science fiction serial *Star Trek* begins. Screen version of Albee's *Who's Afraid of Virginia Woolf,* directed by Mike Nichols with Richard Burton and Elizabeth Taylor. Civil rights rally in Jackson, Mississippi, marred by violence when James Meredith – the first black to attend University of Mississippi – is shot and wounded (26 June). The Monterey Pop Festival, the first large rock gathering, held at Monterey, California.	Clashes between police and students at Barcelona University (27 April). Israel attacks Jordan in the Hebron area (13 Nov.). *Pravda* ("Truth," founded 1912) has 6 million readers in Soviet Union. Floods ravage Northern Italy, destroying art treasures in Venice and Florence.	French deconstructionist Jacques Derrida's *On Grammatology* and *Writing and Difference.*

DATES	THEATRICAL EVENTS IN AMERICA	SELECTED HISTORICAL/CULTURAL EVENTS IN AMERICA	SELECTED HISTORICAL/CULTURAL EVENTS THROUGHOUT THE WORLD
	Hair (the "American Tribal Love-Rock Musical") opens Off-Broadway at Joseph Papp's New York Shakespeare Festival Theater (29 Oct.). It closes 10 December after forty-nine performances but reopens 29 April 1968, on Broadway with house lights dimmed to make cast's nudity less conspicuous.	U.S. Antarctic Mountaineering Expedition scales Vinsear Massif, a 16,864-foot peak, on Sentinel Range of the Ellsworth Highland.	The number of U.S. troops in Vietnam reaches 380,000 (1 Jan.).
	Broadway set designer David Hays founds National Theatre for the Deaf.	The radical, revolutionary Black Panther Party organized in Oakland, California, by Huey Newton and Bobby Seale.	Beijing put under military rule (11 Feb.).
	The Negro Ensemble Company established.	Harold Cruse's *The Crisis of the Negro Intellectual.* John Kenneth Galbraith's *The New Industrial State.*	Ibo eastern region of Nigeria secedes as Biafra (30 May).
	Albee's *Everything in the Garden.* Robert Anderson's *You Know I Can't Hear You When the Water's Running.*	*Rolling Stone* magazine begins publication in November.	Alan Ayckbourn's *Relatively Speaking.* Peter Nichols's *A Day in the Death of Joe Egg.* Tom Stoppard's *Rosencrantz and Guildenstern are Dead.* Brendan Behan's *Borstal Boy.*
	New York's Classic Stage Company (CSC) founded. Magic Theatre founded in San Francisco. Mark Taper Forum created (Los Angeles). Theatre Development Fund established to assist "meritorious but risky plays" on Broadway.	Over 100,000 march through New York and assemble at UN headquarters to protest Vietnam War (15 April).	Six-Day War begins between United Arab Republic (UAR) and Israel (5 June).
	Barbara Garson's *Macbird!*, satire on Lyndon Johnson and Kennedy's assassination, opens Off-Broadway before moving to Garrick Theatre.	William Styron's novel *The Confessions of Nat Turner.*	Colombian author Gabriel García Márquez's *One Hundred Years of Solitude.*
		Summer riots (Detroit, Newark) in over 100 cities leave forty-one dead, 4,000 arrested, and 5,000 homeless.	Revolutionary Che Guevara killed by government troops in Bolivia. David Hockney's painting *A Bigger Splash.*

1968		
Albee's *A Delicate Balance* wins Pulitzer. *I Never Sang for My Father*, *The Price*, and *Plaza Suite* among best plays of 1967–68. Richard Foreman creates Ontological-Hysteric Theatre that eschews plot conventions, characters, or themes for an intimate representation of the psyche and unconsciousness. Mart Crowley's *The Boys in the Band*, the first mainstream drama to deal with homosexuality, runs for 1,000 performances Off-Broadway. The Negro Ensemble created. Ed Bullins's *Goin' a Buffalo* and *The Electronic Nigger*. The New York Street Theater Caravan founded by Marketa Kimball and Richard Levy, a troupe oriented to working-class audiences. Jay Presson Allen's adaption of Muriel Spark's *The Prime of Miss Jean Brodie* with Zoe Caldwell. Howard Sackler's *The Great White Hope*, with James Earl Jones and Jane Alexander, opens at Arena Stage prior to Broadway, setting a new trend for play development. Arthur Kopit's *Indians* opens in London and then has U.S. premiere at Arena.	Mike Nichol's film *The Graduate*, starring Dustin Hoffman, released. Crimes of violence up 57% since 1960. Major civil rights legislation prohibits racial discrimination in sale or rental of about 80% of U.S. housing (11 March). Martin Luther King shot to death in Memphis (4 April); presidential hopeful Robert Kennedy assassinated at Ambassador Hotel in Los Angeles (5 June). The Poor People's March, a demonstration with its final destination in Washington, D.C. and led by the Reverend Ralph Abernathy, begins (2 May). James Watson's *The Double Helix*.	British playwright Joe Orton hammered to death by his jealous lover. Death of artist René Magritte at age sixty-eight. Stage censorship dating back to 1737 abolished in England. Abortive revolution in France (2 May). Violent protests by militant left-wing Sorbonne students spreads to civilian population. German philosopher Jürgen Habermas's *Knowledge and Human Interests*. Swiss psychologist Jean Piaget's *Structuralism*. The Vietcong's Tet Offensive gains ground (Jan.). Demonstrators in Warsaw, protesting government interference in cultural affairs, fight with police and armed militia men (11 March). Alan Ayckbourn's *How the Other Half Loves*. Peter Barnes's *The Ruling Class*. Edward Bond's *Narrow Road to the Deep North*. John Osborne's *A Hotel in Amsterdam*.

DATES	THEATRICAL EVENTS IN AMERICA	SELECTED HISTORICAL/CULTURAL EVENTS IN AMERICA	SELECTED HISTORICAL/CULTURAL EVENTS THROUGHOUT THE WORLD
	Alliance Theatre Company, largest resident professional theatre in the southeast, founded in Atlanta.	John Updike's *Couples*.	U.S. troops massacre village of My Lai, South Vietnam (16 March).
	The National Black Theatre established by actress/play director Barbara Ann Teer.	Richard Nixon elected U.S. President after Lyndon Johnson decides not to run again (5 Nov.).	Peace talks between U.S. and North Vietnam in Paris (13 May).
	Arthur Miller's *The Price*.	Stanley Kubrick's film *2001: A Space Odyssey* premieres.	Czech intellectuals produce their "2,000 words," an appeal to speed up democratization (27 June).
	Omaha Magic Theatre founded in Nebraska.		Catholics clash with police in Northern Ireland, protesting discrimination by Protestant majority (5–6 Oct.).
	Repertorio Español formed. Israel Horwitz's *The Indian Wants the Bronx*. S. N. Behrman's final play *The Burning Glass* produced. Tennessee Williams's *In the Bar of a Tokyo Hotel*.		Soviet invasion of Czechoslovakia.
1969	Richard Schechner's *Dionysus in '69*, improvisational piece based on Euripides' *The Bacchae*, in which actors remove clothing and mingle with audience, staged at Performing Garage in New York.	A Federal Grand Jury indicts eight anti-war protesters for conspiracy to start a riot at 1968 Democratic National Convention in Chicago.	Neil Armstrong is first man to set foot on moon (21 July).
	After opening performance of *Che!* at Free Store Theater, criminal court justice signs warrant for cast, producers, and crew, on charges of public lewdness, obscenity, consensual sodomy, and impairing the morals of minors (24 March).	Berkeley students and members of neighboring community attacked as they try to claim ownership of People's Park, built on property owned by university (15 May).	Incursion into Cambodia.

Organic Theatre Company, known for its ribald humor and nostalgia for 1950s sci-fi, founded by Stuart Gordon in Chicago.

Circle Repertory Company founded.

Shakespeare Theatre, Washington, D.C., founded.
In the late 1960s Miriam Colon's Puerto Rican Traveling Theatre brings bilingual productions to Spanish-speaking neighborhoods of New York City.

Frank MacMahon's adaptation of Brendan Behan's *The Hostage* hits Broadway, winning the New York Drama Critics' Circle and Tony Awards.
Kenneth Tynan's *Oh! Calcutta!*, an amalgam of theatrical pastiches, with the cast fully nude, opens in New York. Plays of the year include Lonne Elder III's *Ceremonies in Dark Old Men*, Lorraine Hansberry's posthumous *To Be Young, Gifted, and Black*, Leonard Gersh's *Butterflies are Free*, Neil Simon's *Last of the Red Hot Lovers*, Terrence McNally's *Next*, and Sam Shepard's *The Unseen Hand*.

Rioting follows police raid on the Stonewall Inn, a New York City gay bar; it mobilizes gay community and signals start of gay liberation movement (27 June).

The Woodstock Music and Arts Festival held in Bethel, New York. Crowd estimated at 300,000 to 400,000 (15–18 Aug.).
Congressional Black Caucus forms.

DDT, widely used pesticide, banned in U.S. because of adverse effects on environment.
U.S. surgeons implant first artificial heart in human.

Actress Sharon Tate and four others are murdered by the Manson cult (9 Aug.).

The Saturday Evening Post publishes final issue (until later reborn).

John Schlesinger's *Midnight Cowboy*, starring Dustin Hoffman and John Voight, wins Oscar. It is the first X-rated film to do so.

Theodore Roszak's *Making of a Counterculture*.
Kate Millett's *Sexual Politics*.

Michel Foucault's *Archaeology of Knowledge*.

Yasir Arafat elected chairman of PLO (3 Feb.).

Catholic/Protestant riots in Belfast and Londonderry (12 Aug.).
North Vietnamese President Ho Chi Minh dies aged seventy-nine (3 Sept.).

Nixon announces withdrawal of additional 35,000 men from South Vietnam by 15 December (16 Sept.).

Willy Brandt becomes Chancellor of West Germany (21 Oct.).

"Soccer War," fought between Honduras and El Salvador.

Athol Fugard's *Boesman and Lena*.
Peter Nichols's *The National Health*.
Joe Orton's (posthumous) *What the Butler Saw*.
Harold Pinter's *Landscape and Silence*.

DATES	THEATRICAL EVENTS IN AMERICA	SELECTED HISTORICAL/CULTURAL EVENTS IN AMERICA	SELECTED HISTORICAL/CULTURAL EVENTS THROUGHOUT THE WORLD
1970	Charles Gordone's *No Place to be Somebody* (opened in 1969) wins Pulitzer. Experimental theatre Mabou Mines created. Manhattan Theatre Club established. New York season includes Robert Marasco's *Child's Play*, Paul Zindel's *The Effect of Gamma Rays on Man-in-the-Moon Marigolds* (wins Pulitzer in 1971), Neil Simon's *The Gingerbread Lady*, Bruce Jay Friedman's *Steambath*, Lanford Wilson's *Lemon Sky*, and Sam Shepard's *Operation Sidewinder*. New Federal Theatre founded. A proposed Middle and Far East tour of avant-garde playlets produced under the supervision of Gordon Davidson in Mark Taper's Forum "New Theater for Now" series is canceled by U.S. State Department because of "unstable and changing political conditions in the host countries."	Kurt Vonnegut's *Slaughterhouse Five.* Philip Roth's *Portnoy's Complaint.* U.S. Army panel casts blame on fourteen officers for My Lai Massacre in 1968. Observation of "Earth Day" (22 April). Four anti-Vietnam student protesters are killed by National Guard at Kent State University in Ohio (4 May). Voting age lowered from 21 to 18. The first "Jumbo" jet, the Boeing 747, begins passenger service. Robin Morgan, ed., *Sisterhood Is Powerful.* Richard Macksey and Eugenio Donato, eds., *The Structuralist Controversy.*	Trinidadian playwright and poet Derek Walcott's *The Dream on Monkey Mountain and Other Plays.* General Ojukwu's flight to Ivory Coast ends Biafran secession from Nigeria and the civil war (12 Jan.). The Nuclear Nonproliferation Treaty of 24 November 1969 goes into effect, ratified by forty-five countries (5 March). Heads of East and West Germany, Willy Brandt and Willi Stoph, meet in Erfurt, East Germany – first meeting of the heads of the two governments since Germany's division (19 March). British Prime Minister Wilson pledges to keep troops in Northern Ireland as long as necessary (7 April). Death of Portuguese premier Antonio Salazar, aged eighty-one (27 July).

The Gingerbread Lady and Follies garner Best Plays awards for 1970–71. Broadway musicals include The Last Sweet Days of Isaac, Purlie, Applause, Company, The Rothschilds, and Two by Two.

Rock stars Jimi Hendrix and Janis Joplin die of drug overdoses.
Clean Air Act passed, further restricting emission of pollutants.

Cambodia becomes Khmer Republic under Lon Nol (9 Oct.).
Death of wartime resistance leader and later President of France, Charles de Gaulle, aged eighty (9 Nov.).

Nobel Prize for Literature won by Russian author Alexander Solzhenitsyn.
David Storey's play Home, a starring vehicle for Ralph Richardson and John Gielgud.
Christopher Hampton's The Philanthropist, Anthony Shaffer's Sleuth, and Alan Ayckbourn's How the Other Half Loves also part of English season.
Antonio Gramsci's Prison Notebooks (posthumous).

1971 Tom O'Horgan's staging of the musical Jesus Christ Superstar helps the rising star of British composer Andrew Lloyd Webber.
Jorge Huerta founds Teatro de la Esperanza (Theatre of Hope) in Santa Barbara, California.

Theatre for the New City and Playwrights Horizons founded in New York.

John Guare scores first true critical notice with House of Blue Leaves when staged Off-Broadway.
David Rabe's The Basic Training of Pavlo Hummel and Sticks and Bones establish him as major new playwright.

Melvin Van Peebles's highly succesful film, Sweet Sweetback's BaaDAsssss starts "blaxploitation" film trend of early 1970s.
26th Amendment approved by Congress and ratified (30 June), changing legal voting age from twenty-one to eighteen.

200,000 protesters march in Washington against Vietnam War (24 April).

Riot at Attica, a New York prison, ends in forty-three deaths, marking increased unrest in U.S.
John Rawls's Theory of Justice.
B. F. Skinner's Beyond Freedom and Dignity.

Army officers led by Major-General Idi Amin oust President Milton Obote in military coup in Uganda (25 Jan.). Amin proclaims himself President on 20 February.
Northern Ireland First Minister Faulkner invokes emergency powers of preventive detention without trial and begins arrests of suspected leaders of Irish Republican Army (IRA) (9 Aug.).
Harold Pinter's Old Times.

Simon Gray's Butley stars Alan Bates.
David Storey's The Changing Room.

DATES	THEATRICAL EVENTS IN AMERICA	SELECTED HISTORICAL/CULTURAL EVENTS IN AMERICA	SELECTED HISTORICAL/CULTURAL EVENTS THROUGHOUT THE WORLD
	Playwright and anti-war activist Father Daniel Berrigan is jailed for anti-war protest "crimes" described in his dramatization entitled *The Trial of the Catonsville Nine*.	E. O. Wilson's *Insect Societies*. Wallace Stegner's *Angle of Repose.* Paul de Man's *Blindness and Insight.* Deaths of musicians Louis Armstrong and Jim Morrison.	Punishing students by caning banned in London schools.
	South African playwright Athol Fugard is denied a passport to the U.S. by his country.	Alexander Solzhenitsyn's *August 1914.*	
	The going rate for best seat at a Broadway musical is $15.	Apollo 13 and 14 launched.	
	Kurt Vonnegut, Jr.'s dramatic debut, *Happy Birthday, Wanda June.*	Openings of films include Woody Allen's *Bananas*, William Friedkin's *The French Connection*, Peter Bogdanovich's *The Last Picture Show*, Alan J. Pakula's *Klute*, Stanley Kubrick's *Clockwork Orange.*	Non-U.S. films include: Federico Fellini's *The Clowns*, Bernardo Bertolucci's *The Conformist*, Luchino Visconti's *Death in Venice*, Peter Brook's *King Lear* (with Paul Scofield).
	Musicals include: *Follies, Godspell, Two Gentlemen of Verona.*	Erich Segal's novel *Love Story.*	
	Steven Tesich's *The Carpenters* opens at Wynn Handman's American Place Theater.	John Updike's *Rabbit Redux.*	
	Irv Bauer's *A Dream Out of Time.* Sam Shepard's *Back Bog Beast Bait.* Joyce Carol Oates's *Sunday Dinner.* Zindel's *And Miss Reardon Drinks a Little.* George Tabori's *Pinkville.* Ed Bullin's *The Duplex.* A.R. Gurney's *Scenes from an American Life.*		

56

1972

Neil Simon's *The Prisoner of Second Avenue*, Michael Weller's *Moonchildren* (opens Feb. 1972), Rabe's *Sticks and Bones*, and the musical *Ain't Supposed to Die a Natural Death*, win Best Play awards for 1971–72 season.

Duck Variations, one-act by David Mamet, brings attention to the Chicago playwright.

Off-Off Broadway links theatre companies through Alliance.

Hanay Geiogamah founds first all-Indian repertory company, the American Indian Theatre Ensemble (later changed to the Native American Theatre Ensemble). *Pippin* the first Broadway show advertised on television.

The Creation of the World, The Sunshine Boys, Finishing Touches, The River Niger, and *A Little Night Music* win Best Play awards for 1972–73 season.

TOSOS (The Other Side of the Stage), a gay producing company, founded by Doric Wilson. It disbands five years later.

A plaque is attached to space probe Pioneer 10 to communicate with other possible intelligent life forms beyond solar system.

Equal Rights Amendment specifying equal rights for women approved by Congress. Ratified by thirty-five states, but despite three-year deadline extension in 1979, it falls three states short of passage in 1982.

Congress passes Equal Opportunity Act, allowing for preferential hiring and promotion of women and minorities. Lionel Trilling's *Sincerity and Authenticity*.

Nixon re-elected President.

Five men seized while trying to install eavesdropping equipment in Democratic National Committee's Headquarters in Washington: Watergate break-in (17 June). Beginning of Watergate scandal.

U.S. announces $2,047 million trade deficit, first since 1888.

Nixon anounces 70,000 U.S. troops will be withdrawn from Vietnam (13 Jan.).

"Bloody Sunday" in Londonderry, Northern Ireland. Thirteen civilians killed during riots against 1971 internment laws (30 Jan.).

Nixon vists Beijing, first visit of U.S. president (21–28 Feb.) to China. Nixon arrives in Moscow, first U.S. president to visit USSR (22 May).

DATES	THEATRICAL EVENTS IN AMERICA	SELECTED HISTORICAL/CULTURAL EVENTS IN AMERICA	SELECTED HISTORICAL/CULTURAL EVENTS THROUGHOUT THE WORLD
	The Acting Company forms.	Release of blockbuster film *The Godfather*, directed by Francis Ford Coppola.	Irish poet Seamus Heaney's collection *Wintering Out*.
	Indiana Repertory Theatre established.	Two feminist magazines appear: *MS* in the U.S. and *Spare Rib* in the UK.	Tom Stoppard's *Jumpers*. Athol Fugard's *Sizwe Banzi Is Dead*.
	McCarter Theatre Center for the Performing Arts is founded.	Military draft ended; beginning of all-volunteer army.	Managua, Nicaragua, devastated by earthquake measuring 6.2; about 10,000 perish.
	Musical *Fiddler on the Roof* hits record 3,225 performances in single run (17 June).		
	Plays of the year include Williams's *Small Craft Warnings*, Miller's *The Creation of the World and Other Business*, Jason Miller's *That Championship Season* (wins Pulitzer in 1973), Simon's *The Sunshine Boys*, and Shepard's *The Tooth of Crime*.		
	Gerald Schoenfeld and Bernard B. Jacobs become Chair and President, respectively, of The Shubert Organization.		
	The Irish Rebel Theater of New York City's Hell's Kitchen created to reflect sensibility of "Irish immigrants and blue-collar American Irish."		
	Grease, with book, music, and lyrics by Jim Jacobs and Warren Casey, opens at the Eden Theatre on St. Valentine's Day, transfers to Broadway, and plays for 3,388 performances, one of longest runs in history (later revived in 1994 and still running in 1997).		

1973	Michael Bennett's *A Chorus Line*, the longest running show on Broadway until 1997, opens. Tennessee Williams's *Out Cry*. Mark Medoff's *When You Comin' Back, Red Ryder?* Robert Patrick's *Kennedy's Children*. The Rhode Island Feminist Theatre founded. Lanford Wilson's *The Hot l Baltimore*. Alvin Ailey's ballet, *The Lark Ascending*. Simon's *The Good Doctor*, Miguel Piñero's *Short Eyes* (opens 1974), and McNally's *Bad Habits* (also 1974) win Best Play awards for 1973–74 season. Musicals include *A Little Night Music*, *Seesaw*, and *Raisin*.	Vice-President Spiro Agnew pleads *nolo contendere* to charges of income tax evasion, and resigns from office. Daniel Bell's *The Coming of Post-Industrial Society*. Hayden White's *Metahistory*. William Friedkin's box-office smash *The Exorcist* is released. Thomas Pynchon's novel *Gravity's Rainbow*. Erica Jong's *Fear of Flying*. Neither the Pulitzer Prize for literature, nor the one for drama, awarded this year.	U.S. population is 210.1 million, increase of 1.6 million since 1972. Arab oil embargo (1973–74) creates gasoline shortages and increases prices. Long lines and rationing occur at gas stations in several regions of country. U.S. Skylab, 120-foot long orbiting work station, launched into orbit (14 May). Members of American Indian Movement (AIM) make grievances known during seventy-day siege of trading post and church at Wounded Knee, South Dakota. Watergate trial opens in Washington, D.C. Supreme Court, in controversial landmark decision Roe v. Wade, uphold woman's right to privacy in opting for abortion before sixth month of life.	U.S. and South Vietnam sign a ceasefire with North Vietnam and Viet Cong, ending Vietnam War. Jürgen Habermas's *Legitimation Crisis*. Marxist Chilean President Salvador Allende and 2,700 others are killed by General Pinochet and a CIA-backed military junta (11 Sept.). U.S. and Egypt restore diplomatic relations (7 Nov.). Pablo Picasso dies at age ninety-one. Wole Soyinka's *Season of Anomy*. Peter Shaffer's *Equus*. Alan Ayckbourn's *Absurd Person Singular*. Christopher Hampton's *Savages*. U.S. skylab, 120-foot long orbiting work station, launched into earth's orbit.	
1974	The American Jewish Theatre founded by Stanley Brechner, to deal with Jewish ideas and culture.			Alexander Solzhenitsyn deported from USSR and stripped of citizenship (13 Feb.).	

DATES	THEATRICAL EVENTS IN AMERICA	SELECTED HISTORICAL/CULTURAL EVENTS IN AMERICA	SELECTED HISTORICAL/CULTURAL EVENTS THROUGHOUT THE WORLD
	Oakland Ensemble Theatre founded.	American newspaper heiress Patty Hearst kidnapped by Sybionese Liberation Army (SLA). In 1976, she is convicted of collaborating and aiding in robbery.	Death of Juan Perón (1 July).
		Nixon resigns (9 Aug.), succeeded by Gerald Ford.	
	Roadside Theater founded in Kentucky.	Atlanta Braves' Hank Aaron hits 715th career homerun, to break Babe Ruth's career record (8 April).	Turkey invades Cyprus (20 July).
	Syracuse Stage founded.	President Ford pardons Nixon for Watergate crimes.	
	Victory Gardens and Wisdom Bridge theatres founded in Chicago.	U.S. grants amnesty to those who evaded draft during Vietnam War years.	Emperor Haile Selassie of Ethiopia deposed in bloodless coup (12 September).
	Anthony Hopkins introduced to Broadway as Dysart in *Equus*.	Streaking – running naked at parties, ceremonies, sporting events, etc. – enjoys a short-lived fad.	Britain outlaws the IRA (29 November).
		Joseph Beuys's performance art-piece, *Coyote: I Like America and America Likes Me*, takes place in a New York City.	
	Ntozake Shange's *For Colored Girls Who Have Considered Suicide When the Rainbow is Enuf*/is developed at the Bacchanal, a bar in Berkeley.	The Sears Tower in Chicago becomes the world's tallest building at 1,454 feet.	Tom Stoppard's *Travesties*. Alan Ayckbourn's *The Norman Conquests*. Howard Brenton's *The Churchill Play*.
	Dinner theatre emerges as a new fad in theatregoing.		Turkish DC-10 crashes after takeoff near Paris, France; 346 are killed in worst crash to date.
	The Rocky Horror Show, imported from England and later a cult film, premieres in New York.		

1975	The Wooster Group forms, with Spalding Gray and Willem Dafoe as members. The troupe is known for their experimental, often farcical productions. Pittsburgh Public Theater founded. The Road Company founded in Tennessee. *A Chorus Line* transfers from Off-Broadway to Broadway. Ed Bullins's *The Taking of Miss Janie* has brief run at Lincoln Center's Mitzi E. Newhouse Theatre.	U.S. Equal Credit Opportunity Act prohibits discrimination against women in granting loans or credit. Disco becomes current dance craze. Viking spacecraft lands on Mars. Assassination attempt on President Ford (5 Sept.).	The Druid Theatre Company is founded by Garry Hynes in Galway, Ireland. Margaret Thatcher elected leader of Conservative Party in Britain (11 Feb.). U.S. increases airlift of arms and ammunition to Phnom Penh (12 Feb.), but Cambodian government surrenders to Khmer Rouge on 17 April. The Khmer Rouge forcibly removes entire city to countryside, where estimated 1 million to 3 million die. Turkish Cypriots proclaim northern part of Cyprus a separate state (13 Feb.).
	Edward Albee wins another Pulitzer for *Seascape*. David Merrick's production of Williams's *The Red Devil Battery Sign* fails miserably. Musicals include: *The Wiz, Shenandoah,* and *Chicago* (Chita Rivera and Gwen Verdon).	Work begins on Alaskan oil pipeline, largest private construction project to date in U.S. Arthur Ashe becomes first black player to win men's singles at Wimbledon (5 July). Saul Bellow's novel *Humboldt's Gift.*	South Vietnam surrenders to North Vietnamese Communists (30 April). Six men, known as the "Birmingham Six," are sentenced to life imprisonment after being convicted of planting bombs that killed twenty-one people in Britain (15 Aug.). They are acquitted and released in 1989.
	Murray Schisgal's *All Over Town,* Bernard Slade's *Same Time, Next Year,* and Terrence McNally's *The Ritz* win Best Play awards. The latter one of the first Broadway comedies with a gay milieu.	Steven Spielberg's blockbuster *Jaws* released.	Seamus Heaney's *North.* Wole Soyinka's *Death and the King's Horseman.*
		U.S. scientists warn of danger of chlorofluorocarbons.	Harold Pinter's *No Man's Land.* Vaclav Havel's *Audience.* Simon Gray's *Otherwise Engaged.*

DATES	THEATRICAL EVENTS IN AMERICA	SELECTED HISTORICAL/CULTURAL EVENTS IN AMERICA	SELECTED HISTORICAL/CULTURAL EVENTS THROUGHOUT THE WORLD
1976	The Roadside Theater (Kentucky) begins touring Appalachian working-class communities.	Former Teamsters boss Jimmy Hoffa disappears and is presumed murdered.	South American writer Carlos Fuentes's *Terra Nostra*. A rebellion by Kurds in northern Iraq is crushed.
	The Iron Clad Agreement founded in Pittsburgh by Julia Swoyer and Wilson Hutton to bring plays about labor and industrial history to working-class audiences.	Outbreak of Legionnaire's Disease occurs at Philadelphia convention of American Legion.	Deaths of Chinese Prime Minister Zhou Enlai and Mao Zedong.
		Jimmy Carter succeeds Ford as President.	Civil war between Muslim and Christian forces intensifies in Lebanon (13–19 May).
	San Diego Repertory Theatre founded.	Nobel Prize for Literature won by Saul Bellow.	Mystery writer Agatha Christie dies at age eighty-five.
	Steppenwolf Theatre Company forms in Chicago.	Blockbusters *Rocky, One Flew Over the Cuckoo's Nest,* and *All the President's Men* released.	Race riots in Soweto, South Africa, in protest against legislation to force use of Afrikaans in some teaching. By June 25, 176 are dead and over 1,000 injured (16 June).
	Julia Heyward's *Shake! Daddy! Shake!* performance piece.	Alex Haley's *Roots,* an ancestral novel dealing with U.S. history and the black experience.	Idi Amin of Uganda is made President for life (25 June).
	A Chorus Line, by Michael Bennett, James Kirkwood, Nicholas Dante, Marvin Hamlisch, and Edward Kleban, garners Pulitzer.	Bicentennial celebrated; American population at 215 million.	25,000 Protestants and Catholics take part in peace march in Londonderry, Northern Ireland (4 Sept.).
	Sam Shepard's *The Curse of the Starving Class.*		Argentine writer Manuel Puig's *The Kiss of the Spider Woman.*
	Julie Harris wins unprecedented fifth Tony for solo performance in *The Belle of Amherst.*		"Punk" music and style emerges on streets of London.

1977

Jules Feiffer's *Knock Knock*, Milan Stitt's *The Runner Stumbles*, and the Stephen Sondheim/John Weidman musical *Pacific Overtures* designated Best Plays. Other plays and musicals of the year include: Simon's *California Suite*, Preston Jones's *A Texas Trilogy*, Mamet's *A Life in the Theater*, Shepard's *Angel City*, *Bubblin' Brown Sugar*.

Two former members of San Francisco Mime Troupe, Denny Patridge and Steve Friedman, found Modern Times Theater at School for Marxist Education.

The Dakota Theater Caravan founded in South Dakota to deal with regionalist histories and themes.

Pan Asian Repertory Theatre founded.

Plays of the year include: Mamet's *The Water Engine*, Miller's *The Archbishop's Ceiling*, Marsha Norman's *Getting Out*, Simon's *Chapter Two*, Wendy Wasserstein's *Uncommon Women and Others*, Williams's *Vieux Carré*, Albert Innaurato's *Gemini*, D. L. Coburn's *The Gin Game* (with Hume Cronyn and Jessica Tandy; directed by Mike Nichols), Ronald Ribman's *Cold Storage*.

Beatlemania, an odd mixture of Broadway musical, social documentary, and rock concert, opens.

Dracula, with Frank Langella as the Count, comes to the Broadway stage for 925 performances.

Second widespread gasoline shortage in U.S.

Gary Gilmore asks for and receives death penalty, the first person executed in the U.S. in ten years.

The King of rock'n'roll Elvis Presley dies at age forty-two (16 Aug.).

Toni Morrison's novel *Song of Solomon*.

Soundtrack album for *Saturday Night Fever* becomes worldwide bestseller.

Woody Allen's film *Annie Hall* sets off fashion craze.

Australia's Perth Entertainment Centre built with seating capacity of 8,003, making it world's largest theatre in regular operation.

Violent student riots in Italy (14 March).

President Mgoubi of the Congo shot and killed (18 March).

Leonid Brezhnev named USSR President and Communist Party leader (16 June). "Gang of Four" expelled from Chinese Communist Party (22 July).

Charlie Chaplin dies at Swiss estate at age eighty-eight.

Civilian government in Thailand ousted in bloodless coup (20 Oct.).

Tom Stoppard's play *Every Good Boy Deserves Favour*.

DATES	THEATRICAL EVENTS IN AMERICA	SELECTED HISTORICAL/CULTURAL EVENTS IN AMERICA	SELECTED HISTORICAL/CULTURAL EVENTS THROUGHOUT THE WORLD
	David Mamet's *American Buffalo* introduces the playwright to Broadway. *Annie* by Charles Strouse, Martin Charnin, and Thomas Meehan the musical hit of the year.	George Lucas's *Star Wars* a blockbuster hit.	Djibouti, last European colony in Africa, granted independence. The punk group Sex Pistols hit headlines for their foul language and bad behavior, and are banned from the BBC.
1978	Susan Eisenberg founds Word of Mouth Productions, an all-women political theatre collective established to reach working-class women audiences.	Supreme Court issues Bakke decision, in which it is ruled that a white medical student applicant was illegally discriminated against, and principle of affirmative action upheld.	Pope Paul VI dies (6 Aug.), is succeeded by John Paul I, who dies suddenly. On 16 October, Cardinal Karol Wojtyla of Poland becomes first non-Italian Pope since 1523.
	The Crossroads Theatre, an African American theatre, founded in New Brunswick, New Jersey.	Polish émigré Czeslaw Milosz's *Bells in Winter.*	President Jimmy Carter hosts talks between Egypt and Israel, resulting in the Camp David Accords, which fix schedule for peace negotiations (5–17 Sept.).
	Theatre de la Jeune Lune founded in Minneapolis.	Alexander Solzhenitsyn completes *The Gulag Archipelago.*	911 members from the People's Temple in San Francisco commit suicide at Jonestown, Guyana, with their leader, Rev. Jim Jones (18 Nov.).
	Women's Project and Productions founded in New York.	Isaac Bashevis Singer wins Nobel Prize for Literature.	Egyptian Premier Anwar Sadat and Israeli Prime Minister Menachem Begin share Nobel Peace Prize.
		Philip Guston's painting, *The Ladder.*	Iris Murdoch's *The Sea, The Sea* wins Booker Prize.
	Plays of year include: Lanford Wilson's *Fifth of July*, Ira Levin's *Deathtrap*, Sam Shepard's *Buried Child, Curse of the Starving Class* (written 1976) and *Seduced,* Luis Valdez's *Zoot Suit* (Los Angeles), Arthur Kopit's *Wings* (Yale Rep), and Christopher Durang's *A History of the American Film* (written in 1976).	*The Deer Hunter*, starring Robert De Niro, wins five Oscars.	U.S. agrees to return full control of Panama Canal to Panama in 1999.

1979			
Musicals: *On the 20th Century*, *Ain't Misbehavin'*, *The Best Little Whorehouse in Texas*, *Evita*, *Ballroom*.	Three Mile Island nuclear plant near Middleton, Penn., damaged. A state of emergency declared pending investigation.	Iranian revolution opposing governmental reforms Westernizing the country begins.	
The Harold Clurman Theater established in New York City.	In U.S. v. Weber, U.S. Supreme Court ruling supports affirmative action.	Irish playwright Hugh Leonard's *Da*.	
The Everyday Theater of Washington, D.C. founded to play to working-class tenants. The nine members are directly involved in struggles as activists in tenants' rights movement.	Ex-Sex Pistol Sid Vicious dies of a drug overdose.	Test-tube fertilization success with birth of Louise Brown in England.	
The American Repertory Theatre founded in Cambridge, Massachusetts.	*Apocalypse Now*, directed by Francis Ford Coppola, released.	David Hare's *Plenty*.	
Perseverance Theatre formed in Alaska.	American Airlines plane crashes at Chicago's O'Hare Airport; 275 die in worst U.S. air crash to date.	Pinter's *Betrayal*.	
New York Second Stage and Theatre for a New Audience founded in New York.	Sony Walkman introduced.	Stoppard's *Night and Day*.	
Plays of the year include: Ernest Thompson's *On Golden Pond*, Michael Weller's *Loose Ends*, Vernel Bagners's *One Mo' Time*, Bernard Slade's *Romantic Comedy*, Christopher Durang's *Sister Mary Ignatius Explains It All for You*, Beth Henley's *Crimes of the Heart* (Actors Theatre of Louisville).		Strategic Arms Limitation Treaty (SALT II) between U.S. and USSR sets maximum number of long-range missiles and bombers for each nation.	
Virginia State Company formed.		Diplomatic relations established between China and U.S. for the first time since creation of People's Republic (1 Jan.).	
		Ayatollah Khomeini returns to Iran after fifteen-year exile (15 Feb.).	
		President Sadat and Prime Minister Begin sign peace treaty, ending thirty-one years of war (26 March).	
		Margaret Thatcher becomes first female prime minister in Europe, after UK general election (3 May).	
		Earl Mountbatten of Burma, last British Viceroy of India, killed by IRA bomb (27 Aug.).	

DATES	THEATRICAL EVENTS IN AMERICA	SELECTED HISTORICAL/CULTURAL EVENTS IN AMERICA	SELECTED HISTORICAL/CULTURAL EVENTS THROUGHOUT THE WORLD
	Sam Shepard wins Pulitzer for *Buried Child*.		Nobel Peace Prize awarded to Mother Teresa.
			The Gay Men's Press founded in London.
	Stephen Sondheim's *Sweeney Todd, The Demon Barber of Fleet Street* with Angela Lansbury and Len Cariou premieres.		Soviet Union invades Afghanistan.
			In war in El Salvador, government fights leftist rebels and rightist death squads.
	First Monday in October, Wings, On Golden Pond, and *Sweeney Todd* designated Best Plays for 1978–79.		Peter Shaffer's *Amadeus*.
			Caryl Churchill's *Cloud Nine*.
			American-born English playwright Bernard Pomerance writes *The Elephant Man*.
			American writer Martin Sherman's *Bent* premieres at London's Royal Court.
1980	Workers' Stage of New York City founded.	Race riots in Miami after all-white jury acquits four white policemen charged with fatal beating of black man (17–19 May).	Dissident physicist Andrei Sakharov stripped of honors and exiled from Moscow (22 Jan.).
	The Denver Center Theatre Company founded.	Sioux Indian nation wins $122.5 million in compensation and interest for federal government's illegal seizure of their Black Hill land in 1877 (30 June).	Catholic archbishop Oscar Romero shot dead, while celebrating mass in San Salvador (24 March).
	The Portland Repertory Theater founded.		President Carter breaks all diplomatic relations with Iran and announces a ban on trade with Iran because of continued detention of U.S. hostages. U.S. negotiates through other countries for Americans held hostage by Iranians in Tehran (7 April).
		Ronald Reagan elected President.	

Lanford Wilson's *Talley's Folly* with Judd Hirsch wins Pulitzer.

Plays of the year include: Albee's *The Lady from Dubuque,* William Mastrosimone's *The Woodgatherers,* Miller's *The American Clock,* Shepard's *True West,* Mark Medoff's *Children of a Lesser God* (Tony award for deaf actress Phyllis Frelich), Samm-Art Williams's *Home,* Wilson's *The Fifth of July* (on Broadway).

Philip Glass's opera, *Satyagraha.*

Musicals of the season: *Barnum, Sugar Babies,* and *42nd Street,* the latter opening hours after director Gower Champion dies.

Peter Hall's production of Shaffer's *Amadeus* stars Ian McKellen and Tim Curry on Broadway.

Former Beatle John Lennon is shot and killed outside his New York City hotel by jealous fan (8 Dec.).

Severe summer drought and heatwave roasts U.S. Midwest, Southwest, and South. Over 1,200 perish and livestock and crops are heavily damaged.

Russian émigré poet Joseph Brodsky's *A Part of Speech.*

Nobel Prize for Literature awarded to Polish émigré Czeslaw Milosz.

Jack Beal's painting *The Harvest.*

Mount St. Helens erupts, kills eight and sends up 60,000-foot plume of ash.

Louis Malle film *Atlantic City* with script by John Guare.

David Lynch's *The Elephant Man* with Anthony Hopkins and John Hurt.

Death of Jean-Paul Sartre, aged seventy-four (15 April).
Death of Josip Broz Tito, ruler of Yugoslavia for thirty-five years, at age eighty-seven (4 May).
Death of actor Peter Sellers at age fifty-four (24 July).
Vietnam invades Thailand by way of Cambodia (23 June).

Olympic Games held in Moscow, but boycotted by over forty-five nations, for Soviet invasion of Afghanistan (19 July–3 Aug.).
Lech Walesa forms unprecedented independent trade union in Poland, Solidarnosc (31 Aug.).

War breaks out in Persian Gulf as Iraq invades Iran (22 Sept.).

Howard Brenton's *The Romans in Britain.*
Ayckbourn's *Season's Greetings.*
Pam Gems's *Piaf.*
David Edgar's adaptation of *Nicholas Nickleby,* produced by RSC.
Willy Russell's *Educating Rita.*

DATES	THEATRICAL EVENTS IN AMERICA	SELECTED HISTORICAL/CULTURAL EVENTS IN AMERICA	SELECTED HISTORICAL/CULTURAL EVENTS THROUGHOUT THE WORLD
1981	Lena Horne: The Lady and Her Music and the New York Shakespeare Festival production of The Pirates of Penzance garner special citations of New York Drama Critics Award.

Plays include: Beth Henley's Crimes of the Heart, Kevin Wade's Key Exchange, Harvey Fierstein's Torch Song Trilogy, Charles Fuller's A Soldier's Play, Bill C. Davis's Mass Appeal.
Frank Rich replaces Walter Kerr as drama critic for the New York Times.

Musicals: Sophisticated Ladies, Woman of the Year, Dreamgirls. March of the Falsettos introduces work of William Finn. Tennessee Williams's final New York production, Something Cloudy, Something Clear, fails.
Nickolas Nickleby imported to Broadway. This eight-hour marathon is first collaboration between Shubert and Nederlander organizations. | President Reagan and three aides shot in assassination attempt (30 March).

Sandra Day O'Connor becomes first woman member of Supreme Court.

Exclusion of women from draft upheld by U.S. Supreme Court. It is considered a setback by women's movement.

Music Television (MTV) premieres on Cable Network, featuring video renditions of pop music.
John Updike's novel Rabbit Is Rich, the third in a series of four.
Toni Morrison's Tar Baby.
President Reagan orders firing of some 12,000 federal air-traffic controllers after they refuse to end illegal strike. | U.S.–Iran agreement frees fifty-two hostages held in Teheran since November, 1979.

Bobby Sands is first of ten IRA hunger strikers to die in Maze Prison in Belfast. Riots erupt in Northern Ireland after his death (5 May).
Death of Jamaican reggae singer/activist Bob Marley, aged thirty-six (11 May).

Wedding of Prince Charles of Britain and Lady Diana Spencer of Britain (29 July).

Researchers identify acquired immuno-deficiency syndrome (AIDS), whose symptoms first appeared in late 1970s.
President Anwar Sadat of Egypt assassinated by Muslim extremists (6 Oct.).

Simon Gray's Quartermaine's Terms.
Beckett's Catastrophe and Rockaby.
Edward Bond's Restoration. |

1982	The Gay Meridian Theatre founded by Terry Miller and Terry Helling. The Huntington Theatre Company of Boston, Massachusetts, founded. Plays of the year include: A.R. Gurney's *The Dining Room*, John Pielmeier's *Agnes of God*, *"Master Harold"... And the Boys* (Fugard's Broadway debut), revival of Shepard's *True West* (with John Malkovich and Gary Sinese in New York debuts), William Mastrosimone's *Extremities*. Musicals include: *Forbidden Broadway*, *Nine*, and Andrew Lloyd Webber's *Cats* (7 Oct.), the latter produced by Cameron Mackintosh and the symbolic start of the "British invasion" of musicals. Harvey Fierstein's *Torch Song Trilogy* transfers 10 June to the Little Theatre on Broadway and lasts 1,222 performances.	Jarvik 7 artificial heart implanted. Recipient Barney Clark survives 112 days. *USA Today*, first national newspaper, launched by Gannet. Michael Jackson releases *Thriller* (LP), which outsells all previous solo records. Sales for record reach $40 million by 1988. "Rap" music becomes popular in the U.S. and UK. Worldwide glut in oil supply leads to declining gasoline and home-heating oil prices in U.S.	Hungarian architect Erno Rubik introduces Rubik's Cube, with 42.3 quintillion possible configurations. Poet Derek Walcott's collection *The Unfortunate Traveller*. Argentinian forces invade Falkland Islands (2 April). President-elect of Lebanon, Bashir Gemayel, killed in bomb explosion in Beirut (14 Sept.). Soviet President Leonid Brezhnev dies of heart attack at seventy-five (10 Nov.). Australian novelist Thomas Keneally writes *Schindler's Ark*, of which a movie version in 1994 becomes a blockbuster. Bruce Chatwin's *On the Black Hill*. Gabriel García Márquez's *Chronicle of a Death Foretold*. Márquez wins Nobel Prize for Literature. Caryl Churchill's *Top Girls*. David Hare's *A Map of the World*. Michael Frayn's *Noises Off*. C.P. Taylor's *Good* (posthumous). Tom Stoppard's *The Real Thing*.
1983	Howard Ashman's and Alan Menken's *The Little Shop of Horrors* opens at the Orpheum Theatre, Off-Broadway. The Cleveland Public Theatre founded.	Compact disc (CD) technology introduced in U.S. President Reagan announces beginning of Strategic Defense Initiative (23 March).	U.S. and Caribbean allies invade Granada.

DATES	THEATRICAL EVENTS IN AMERICA	SELECTED HISTORICAL/CULTURAL EVENTS IN AMERICA	SELECTED HISTORICAL/CULTURAL EVENTS THROUGHOUT THE WORLD
	Marsha Norman's 'night, Mother wins Pulitzer. Other new plays include: Tina Howe's Painting Churches, Simon's Brighton Beach Memoirs, Mamet's Glengarry Glen Ross (premieres in London), and Shepard's Fool for Love. Tennessee Williams dies in New York City.	Sally Ride, first female astronaut, launched into orbit (18–24 June). NutraSweet introduced as synthetic sugar substitute.	Nazi war criminal Klaus Barbie imprisoned in Lyons (5 Feb.). U.S. embassy in Beirut bombed, killing more than thirty (18 April).
	Musicals: My One and Only, La Cage Aux Folles, Baby, and The Tap.	Australia II becomes first boat to take Americas Cup from New York Yacht Club (26 Sept.).	Yuri Andropov elected President of Soviet Presidium (16 June).
	British director Peter Brook brings La Tragédie de Carmen to Lincoln Center.	Nearly 100 million watch TV film The Day After about nuclear holocaust (28 Nov.).	Rebels from Sri Lanka's Tamil minority kill thirteen government soldiers, sparking off ethnic riots (23 July).
		Alice Walker's novel The Color Purple wins Pulitzer.	Thirty-eight prisoners, members of IRA, escape in massive breakout of Maze Prison in Northern Ireland (25 July).
		Brad Davis's painting Evening Shore.	Soviet fighter plane shoots down South Korean airliner, off course in Soviet airspace; 269 are killed. Caryl Churchill's Fen. Hugh Williams's Pack of Lies.
1984	Mamet's Glengarry Glen Ross wins Pulitzer and New York Drama Critics' Circle Award for best American play. Samuel Beckett receives special citation from New York Drama Critics' Circle for life achievement. James Lapine directs Sondheim's Sunday in the Park with George, which wins Pulitzer.	Martin Luther King Day becomes U.S. national holiday. Subway passenger Bernhard Goetz shoots and wounds four black youths after they allegedly try to mug him (24 Jan.). New rating category, PG-13, adopted by film industry. 70mm and Dolby sound introduced. Baboon heart implanted into human baby.	George Orwell's Nineteen-Eighty-Four, a novel expressing a grim future of totalitarianism, is thirty-six years old. Mine workers stage coal strike in over 100 pits in UK (12 March). Hundreds die when Indian troops storm the holiest Sikh shrine, the Golden Temple of Amritsar (5–7 June).

Plays of the season include: Beth Henley's *The Miss Firecracker Contest*, David Rabe's *Hurlyburly*, Lanford Wilson's *Balm in Gilead*, and Larry Shue's *The Foreigner*.

August Wilson's *Ma Rainey's Black Bottom* is his first play seen on Broadway.

Gunman opens fire in McDonald's hamburger restaurant in San Diego, California, killing twenty-one (18 July).

Geraldine Ferraro first woman on major party ticket to run for vice president.

In South Africa, fourteen are killed at Sharpeville and black townships near Johannesburg (3 Sept.).

IRA launch bomb attack at Grand Hotel in Brighton where most of British cabinet is staying (12 Oct.).
Indian Prime Minister Indira Gandhi assassinated (Oct. 31).
Nobel Peace Prize awarded to South African bishop Desmond Tutu.
Toxic leakage at U.S.-owned Union Carbide in Bhopal, India causes 2,500 deaths (Dec.).
Sarah Kirsch's play *Katzenleben*.
Alan Ayckbourn's *A Chorus of Disapproval*.
Michael Frayn's *Benefactors*.
Czech writer Milan Kundera publishes *The Unbearable Lightness of Being*.
Soviet premier Chernenko dies; Mikhail Gorbachev succeeds him as General Secretary of the Communist Party (10 March).
New round of nuclear limitation talks in Geneva between U.S. and USSR.
Gorbachev announces policy of *perestroika* (June).
Palestinian guerillas hijack Italian liner and murder U.S. hostage (7 Oct.).

1985

William Hoffman's *As Is*, the first AIDS play on commercial stage, opens (10 March).

U.S. becomes net debtor nation for first time since early 1900s, as result of continuing trade deficits.

Sagging ticket sales and higher costs of production in New York City's theatre district lead to cutbacks of shows staged. 1985 has lowest number of plays staged since 1900.

Coca-Cola introduces new formula Coke. Public outcry results in return to old formula a year later.

Bookstores in U.S. and Canada number 23,749.

DATES	THEATRICAL EVENTS IN AMERICA	SELECTED HISTORICAL/CULTURAL EVENTS IN AMERICA	SELECTED HISTORICAL/CULTURAL EVENTS THROUGHOUT THE WORLD
	League of New York Theatres and Producers changes name to League of American Theatres and Producers to reflect nationwide scope of industry. Yul Brynner, who dies this year, gives 4,625th and last performance in *The King and I*.

Plays of year include: Simon's *Biloxi Blues*, Herb Gardner's *I'm Not Rappaport*, Shepard's *A Lie of the Mind*, Christopher Durang's *The Marriage of Bette and Boo* (revised), Larry Kramer's *The Normal Heart*, and Lyle Kessler's *Orphans*.

Musicals: *Big River* and *The Mystery of Edwin Drood*. | President Reagan sworn in for second term in office (20 Jan.).

Actor Rock Hudson dies of AIDS at age fifty-nine.

Amy Clampitt's novel *What the Light Was Like*.
Alison Lurie wins Pulitzer for *Foreign Affairs*.

Retired naval officer Arthur James Walker is convicted by a federal judge of participating in a Soviet spy ring (1 July).

Marathon rock concert in Philadelphia, Live Aid, raises $70 million for starving Africans. | Vaclav Havel's play *Temptation*.
Irish dramatist Tom Murphy's *Bailegangaire*.
Peter Barnes's *Red Noses*.
Gabriel García Márquez's *Love in the Time of Cholera*.
Anita Brookner wins Booker Prize for *Hotel Du Luc*.
Columbian leftist terrorist group M-19 seizes Palace of Justice and executes 100 people.
Drug trade increases sharply in Columbia, Peru, Bolivia, and Ecuador.
Almost 700 terrorist attacks worldwide.

Claude-Michel Schonberg's, Alain Boubil's, and Herbert Kretzmer's musical *Les Misérables* opens in London. It will play around the world to well over 35 million people. |
| *1986* | 1985–86 is a financially and critically disastrous New York season. Slim offerings include A. R. Gurney's *The Perfect Party*, Simon's *Broadway Bound*, Ken Ludwig's *Lend Me a Tenor*, Tina Howe's *Coastal Disturbances*. | Space Shuttle Challenger explodes after launch at Cape Canaveral, Florida, killing all seven on board (28 Jan.). | President Jean-Claude Duvalier flees Haiti (7 Feb.).
President Marcos flees the Philippines (26 Feb.) after twenty years with U.S. assistance, as Corazon Aquino is elected President. |

1987

Lincoln Center Theatre Company launched with revival of *The Front Page*.

London import *Me and My Girl* opens Marquis Theatre in Marriott Marquis Hotel, the prior site of the Helen Hayes and Morosco theatres.

August Wilson's *Fences*, starring James Earl Jones, wins Pulitzer and New York Drama Critics' Circle Awards for Best Play, regardless of category.

Les Liaisons Dangereuses and *Les Misérables* (opens 12 March at Broadway Theatre) win New York Drama Critics' Circle Awards for best foreign play and best musical, respectively.

Two scientific teams report finding AIDS viruses. U.S. officials predict AIDS cases will increase tenfold over next five years.

President Ronald Reagan denies exchanging hostages and halts arms sales (19 Nov.); diversion of funds from arms sales to Nicaraguan contras revealed (25 Nov.).

U.S. Supreme Court upholds affirmative action hiring quotas, which promote hiring of women and minorities as remedy for past discrimination.

Paul Simon releases *Graceland* album, with black South African musicians performing on it.

Author Paul Auster's *The New York Trilogy*.

First wave of baby-boomers born after World War II turn forty.

The FDA approves of the experimental drug *AZT* for treatment of AIDS sufferers (20 March).

Tom Wolfe's bestselling tale of corporate greed, *The Bonfire of the Vanities*.

Kurt Waldheim's Nazi past is revealed (3 March).

U.S. aircraft attack targets in Libya after alleged Libyan attacks on U.S. aircraft participating in exercises in Gulf of Sirtre (24 March).

Desmond Tutu is elected head of the Anglican Church, South Africa (14 April).

Chernobyl nuclear plant explodes in Ukraine, near Kiev (26 April).

Jonathan Jay Pollard is found guilty of being a spy for Israel (4 June).

Nobel Prize for Literature is awarded to Nigerian poet and playwright Wole Soyinka.

Andrew Lloyd Webber musical, *Phantom of the Opera*, directed by Hal Prince, premieres at London's Her Majesty's Theatre.

Intermediate Nuclear Forces Treaty (INF) provides for dismantling of all Soviet and U.S. intermediate-range nuclear weapons.

U.S. and Soviet Union work toward coordinating future Mars missions and exchanging space data.

Christie's auction rooms in London sells Van Gogh's *Sunflowers* for $39.9 million (30 March).

DATES	THEATRICAL EVENTS IN AMERICA	SELECTED HISTORICAL/CULTURAL EVENTS IN AMERICA	SELECTED HISTORICAL/CULTURAL EVENTS THROUGHOUT THE WORLD
	Plays of the year include: Alfred Uhry's *Driving Miss Daisy* (wins 1988 Pulitzer), Lanford Wilson's *Burn This*, Robert Harling's *Steel Magnolias*, McNally's *Frankie and Johnny in the Clair de Lune.* Sondheim's and James Lapine's musical *Into the Woods* opens at the Martin Beck.	The Crash of 1987, in which stock prices plummet 508 points, occurs (19 Oct.). Elementary and secondary school teachers in U.S. earn annual salary of $26,700. Joseph Brodsky wins the Nobel Prize for Literature. Robert Bork is rejected as Supreme Court Justice (23 Oct.). 40% of American households own a VCR.	Klaus Barbie, Gestapo wartime chief in Lyons, is sentenced to life imprisonment (4 July). UN implements resolution calling on Iran and Iraq to agree on ceasefire (20 July). Peace accord signed with India to stop bloodshed in Sri Lanka, between Tamils and Sinhalese (29 July). Nazi Rudolph Hess commits suicide in Spandau Prison, Berlin (17 Aug.). South African musical *Serafina!* premieres at Johannesburg's Market Theatre. Peter Shaffer's *Lettice and Lovage* a major hit in London for Maggie Smith. Intifada in Israel begins. Worldwide stock exchange crash on 19 Oct.
1988	*The Phantom of the Opera*, with music by Andrew Lloyd Webber and starring Michael Crawford, opens on Broadway (26 Jan.) with biggest advance to date. Still running in 1999. Premiere of Philip Glass's opera *The Making of the Representative for Planet 8.*	U.S. produces 13 million cars and trucks this year. Bernardo Bertolucci's *The Last Emperor* wins nine Oscars. Toni Morrison's novel *Beloved.*	USSR premier Gorbachev announces Soviet troops will begin withdrawal from Afghanistan (8 Feb.). Three IRA soldiers shot dead by British SAS forces in Gibraltar under controversial "shoot to kill" policy (6 March). U.S. warship *Vicennes* shoots down Iranian civilian airliner, killing all 290 aboard (3 July).

1989	Plays include: A. R. Gurney's *The Cocktail Hour* and *Love Letters*, David Henry Hwang's *M. Butterfly* (commissioned specifically for Broadway), Wendy Wasserstein's *Heidi Chronicles* (wins 1989 Pulitzer), David Mamet's *Speed-the-Plow*, Simon's *Rumors*, August Wilson's *Joe Turner's Come and Gone* (1984 premiere at Yale Rep). New York Landmarks Preservation Commission designates most Broadway theatres as historic sites. Number and quality of productions on Broadway reach all-time low during first six months of year, followed by a spurt of activity between September and end of year.	Robots are used for fruit-picking in U.S. experiments. Sculptor Louise Nevelson dies at age eighty-eight. George Bush elected President.	25 million left homeless in Bangladesh due to widespread flooding (31 July). 50,000 killed in earthquake in Armenia (7 July). Pan Am Boeing 747 crashes at Lockerbie, Scotland, killing all 259 aboard (21 Dec.). Investigations reveal crash was due to terrorist bomb. Salman Rushdie's *Satanic Verses* sparks religious controversy; Ayatollah Khomeini calls for the author's death on 14 February 1989. Italian semiotician and fiction writer Umberto Eco's *Foucault's Pendulum*. U.S. sends troops to Honduras following border incursion by Nicaraguan troops. Agatha Christie's *The Mousetrap* is longest running play to date. First performed in 1952, it tops 14,500 performances in 1988. American-born playwright Timberlake Wertenbaker's *Our Country's Good* (based on Thomas Keneally's *The Playmaker*) opens at London's Royal Court. Estonian and Lithuanian legislatures pass laws making Estonian and Lithuanian official languages of republics (Jan.).

DATES	THEATRICAL EVENTS IN AMERICA	SELECTED HISTORICAL/CULTURAL EVENTS IN AMERICA	SELECTED HISTORICAL/CULTURAL EVENTS THROUGHOUT THE WORLD
	In controversial move, National Endowment for Arts refuses to fund performance artists Holly Hughes, John Fleck, Karen Finley, and Tim Miller.	An upturned tanker Exxon Valdez sends 11 million gallons of crude oil into Alaska's Prince William Sound (24 March).	Death of Hirohito, Emperor of Japan since 1926 (7 Jan.).
		The Corcoran Art Gallery cancels exhibition of Robert Mapplethorpe's homoerotic photographs (12 June); Senator Jesse Helms introduces legislation that would ban National Endowment of the Arts from funding "obscene works."	The first democratic Soviet elections (26 March).
	Plays include: Aaron Sorkin's *A Few Good Men*, Fugard's *My Children, My Africa*, and McNally's *Lisbon Traviata*.	Colin Powell is first African American to be named Chairman of the Joint Chiefs of Staff (9 Aug.).	3,000 students demanding greater democratic freedom begin hunger strike in Tiananmen Square in Beijing (13 May). Government imposes martial law on May 20. The student rising is crushed on 4 June.
	Jerome Robbins' Broadway wins Tony for best musical, suggesting the low ebb of the Broadway musical. Only original musicals of note are *Grand Hotel* and *City of Angels*, though revival of *Gypsy* is successful (as are *Anything Goes* at Lincoln Center and *Sweeney Todd* at Circle in the Square).	Legal status of abortion challenged by ProLife groups, following reinterpretation of Roe v. Wade. The Supreme Court in Webster v. Reproductive Health Services upholds Missouri law banning abortion by public employees unless life of mother is in danger.	Mikhail Gorbachev elected President of USSR (25 May).
	Vanessa Redgrave appears in revival of *Orpheus Descending*; Dustin Hoffman essays Shylock (both directed by Peter Hall).	New studies comparing math abilities of students in six countries show U.S. students last and South Korean students first.	Death of Ayatollah Khomeini (3 June).
		U.S. space probe Magellan launched from earth orbiting shuttle, *Atlantis*. It will reach Venus fifteen months later. U.S. launches space probe *Galileo*, which will rendezvous with Jupiter in 1995.	P. W. Botha resigns as President of South Africa (14 Aug.). F.W. de Klerk assumes acting presidency.

France celebrates bicentennial of Revolution (13 July).

Deng Xiaoping resigns from China's leadership (9 Nov.).
The Berlin Wall comes down (10 Nov.).

U.S. begins military assault on Panama to capture General Manuel Noriega (20 Dec.).

Japanese-born writer Kazuo Ishiguro's *The Remains of the Day.*
Irish filmmaker Jim Sheridan's adaptation of Christy Brown's life story, *My Left Foot.*
The Dalai Lama of Tibet wins Nobel Peace Prize.

Miss Saigon by Alain Boubil, Claude-Michel Schonberg, and Richard Maltby, Jr. opens with Jonathan Pryce at London's Drury Lane.

Serial killer Theodore "Ted" Bundy executed in Florida for 1978 murder of twelve-year-old Kimberly Leach. He is convicted of two others, and confesses to sixteen more.
First flight of the stealth bomber.

Hurricane Hugo devastates east coast, causing extensive property damage and virtually leveling Charlestown, South Carolina.
Thomas Pynchon's *Vineland.*

Amy Tan's *The Joy Luck Club.*
Peter Halley's painting *Red Cell.*

Bruce Beresford's film *Driving Miss Daisy* wins four Oscars and Academy Award for Best Picture.
USX workers end longest strike in U.S. history (1 Aug. 1988–2 Feb. 1989).
American steel companies report earnings of some $2 billion, marking strongest recovery from 1982–86 lows.
Junk Bond King Michael Milken is indicted on securities laws violations. He pleads guilty and agrees to pay record $600 million in penalties.
Stock market plunges 190 points, second largest drop in one day in history of NYSE.
Activist Abbie Hoffman dies.
Willem De Kooning's *Interchange* sells for $20.7 million.

DATES	THEATRICAL EVENTS IN AMERICA	SELECTED HISTORICAL/CULTURAL EVENTS IN AMERICA	SELECTED HISTORICAL/CULTURAL EVENTS THROUGHOUT THE WORLD
1990	*A Chorus Line* closes in April to capacity crowd of 1,500 at New York's Shubert Theatre; record of 6,137 performances.	During 1990s Germany and Japan join U.S. as leading economic forces, while many U.S. companies start or strengthen operations abroad.	Cuba joins UN Security Council after thirty-year break (1 Jan.).
	Actor Rex Harrison dies at age eighty-two. Film actress Irene Dunne dies at age ninety-one.		Protesters riot in Soviet Republic of Azerbaijan (3 Jan.).
	Actress and singer Pearl Bailey dies at age seventy-two.	The Hubble Space Telescope deployed in Earth orbit.	General Manuel Noriega surrenders in Panama (3 Jan.).
		Composers Leonard Bernstein, Aaron Copland, and Doc Pomus all pass away.	President F.W. De Klerk lifts thirty-year ban on ANC and South African Communist Party (2 Feb.).
	Broadway Alliance created to stimulate production and develop new audiences. Plays of year include Craig Lucas's *Prelude to a Kiss*, about AIDS.		Nelson Mandela released from Victor Verster prison near Cape Town (11 Feb.). First genuine multiparty elections since 1917 held in USSR (24 Feb.).
	August Wilson receives second Pulitzer for *The Piano Lesson* (premiered at Yale Rep in 1988).		Augusto Pinochet, President of Chile, hands power over to Patricio Aylwin, ending dictatorship (11 March).
	Chicago continues to be a major hub of America's theatrical activity.		Violent protests across Britain and Wales as councils set poll tax rates (March).
			Iraq invades Kuwait (2 Aug.). The Republic of Armenia declares independence from USSR (23 Aug.). Cold War officially ends, with signing of Treaty on Conventional Armed Forces in Europe (19 Nov.).
			Thatcher announces she will not fight for Tory party leadership; John Major becomes Prime Minister of Britain (22 Nov.).

1991

John Guare's *Six Degrees of Separation* (opened 1990) wins New York Drama Critics' Circle Award for Best American Play; English actress Eileen Atkins receives special citation for her portrayal of Virginia Woolf in *A Room of One's Own*. *Lost in Yonkers* by Neil Simon wins Tony Award and Putlitzer, Simon's first. Other plays include McNally's *Teeth Together, Lips Apart* and Jon Robin Baitz's *The Substance of Fire*. Robert Lewis, Pearl Bailey, Leland Hayward, Tony Walton, Paddy Chayefsky, Earl Blackwell, Tommy Tune, Chita Rivera, John Kander, and Fred Ebb are elected to Theater Hall of Fame by American Theater Critics Association. Edward Albee wins tenth annual William Inge Award for lifetime achievement in American theatre.

During the controversial Supreme Court hearings of nominee Clarence Thomas alleged sexual harassment involving aide Anita Hill emerges (Oct.).

First digital high-definition television developed.

A.S. Byatt's novel *Possession* wins Booker Prize.
Landmark agreement between Soviet President Gorbachev and West German Chancellor Helmut Kohl, in which Gorbachev drops opposition to membership of united Germany in NATO.
Soviet troops based in Czechoslovakia since 1968 begin phased withdrawal to be completed by 1 July 1991.
British plays: David Hare's *Racing Demons*, Ayckbourn's *Man of the Moment*. Irish play: Brian Friel's *Dancing at Lughnasa*.
War (Operation Desert Storm) breaks out in Persian Gulf (16 Jan.).
President Bush announces allies have won war to liberate Kuwait (28 Feb.).

Warfare breaks out in Slovenia as Yugoslav tanks arrive to curb rebellion (27 June).
Tensions grow between Serbs and Croats in Croatia (9 July).
Gorbachev resigns as head of Communist Party (25 Aug.). Boris Yeltsin takes over.
Communism ends in Eastern Europe and, later, Soviet Union. Cold War ends.

Writer Graham Greene dies, aged eighty-six.
Nobel Prize for Literature awarded to South African writer Nadine Gordimer.

DATES	THEATRICAL EVENTS IN AMERICA	SELECTED HISTORICAL/CULTURAL EVENTS IN AMERICA	SELECTED HISTORICAL/CULTURAL EVENTS THROUGHOUT THE WORLD
	Ulysses Dove, Eiko and Koma, Karen Finley, Margarita Guergue and Hahn Rowe, Robbie McCauley, Mark Morris, and Wim Vandekeybus win the choreographer/creator award for seventh annual New York Dance and Performance (Bessie) Awards. Jonathan Pryce and Lea Salonga, stars of *Miss Saigon*, win Tony Awards for best acting in musical. Biggest box office advance in theatrical history. Broadway musical *The Secret Garden* boasts of its predominately female creative team. Lillian Hellman dies, aged eighty-three. Joseph Papp dies (b. 1921), leaving the New York Shakespeare Festival in disarray. After much promise, the musical *Nick and Nora* closes after nine performances. *The Will Rogers Follies* opens at the newly renovated Palace, with book by Peter Stone, music by Cy Coleman, and lyrics by Betty Comden and Adolph Green; wins six Tony Awards. Broadway Cares and Broadway Fights AIDS introduce the red "AIDS ribbon" at Tony Awards.		German-Swiss playwright Max Frisch dies.
1992	David Mamet and Patricia Wolff found Boston's Back Bay Theater Company, though other than premiering *Oleanna* it fails to develop.	Riots in Los Angeles after four white police officers acquitted on assault charges on black motorist, Rodney King (29 April). Fifty-eight people killed in next six days of unrest.	President Bush and President Yeltsin sign statement of general principles to bring East–West rivalry and the Cold War to an end (1 Feb.).

The Pope admits the Catholic Church was wrong in condemning Galileo (31 Oct.).

Czech and Slovak regional parliaments adopt joint resolutions authorizing the separation of Czechoslovakia into two separate independent republics (17 Nov.).
UN authorizes the blockade of Yugoslavia (Nov.).

California struck by two severe earthquakes which injure 170 and kill two (28 June). Thirty-five people killed when Hurricane Andrew sweeps across southern Florida and Louisiana (25–26 Aug.). It is the most expensive natural disaster in U.S. history, with thousands left homeless and damage in Florida alone in excess of $20 million.

The Catholic Church issues new catechism, voicing disdain for drunkenness, embezzlement, and speeding (16 Nov.).

Ten women accuse Republican Senator Robert Packwood of sexual harassment (22 Nov.).
U.S. jobless rate is at a five-year high.

In TV address President George Bush announces commitment of U.S. forces to help UN relief effort in Somalia, "Operation Restore Hope." 28,000 U.S. military personnel scheduled to be dispatched. On 9 December U.S. troops land in Somalia.

The Broadway commercial theatre experiences a surfeit of film stars, including Richard Dreyfuss, Gene Hackman, Glenn Close, Alan Alda, Ben Gazzara, Joan Collins, Judd Hirsch, Jessica Lange, and Alec Baldwin. Their presence creates the illusion of prosperity.

Tony for Best Play goes to Irish playwright Brian Friel's *Dancing at Lughnasa*.

Biggest musical hit on Broadway is a revival of *Guys and Dolls* directed by Jerry Zaks.
Clown Lou Jacobs dies at age eighty-nine. Pioneer choreographer Hanya Holm dies.
Mamet's *Oleanna* creates controversy Off-Broadway and later around the country.
Tony Randall establishes National Actors Theatre (actually debuts with *The Crucible*, December 1991) but fails to produce any notable stagings (as will be the case for most of the next several seasons).
Director/playwright George C. Wolfe makes Broadway debut with *Jelly's Last Jam* and wins Tony.

DATES	THEATRICAL EVENTS IN AMERICA	SELECTED HISTORICAL/CULTURAL EVENTS IN AMERICA	SELECTED HISTORICAL/CULTURAL EVENTS THROUGHOUT THE WORLD
1993	Tony Kushner's *Angels in America* (part one, *Millennium Approaches*), opens 4 May and wins Tony.	Bill Clinton becomes President.	Canadian Prime Minister Brian Mulroney steps down, resigning as leader of the Progressive Conservative Party (24 February).
	The Kentucky Cycle (winner of 1992 Pulitzer) has brief run on Broadway.	A bomb set by Islamic fundamentalists explodes beneath World Trade Center in New York City, killing 6 people (26 February).	Apartheid rule ends in South Africa.
	A revival of The Who's 1969 rock opera *Tommy* opens to gigantic ticket sales and critical success.	Four federal agents killed in confrontation with Branch Davidian cult led by David Koresh (28 Feb.). Seventy-two succumb during an inferno in compound in April.	Chris Hani, Secretary General of the South African Communist Party and leader of the African National Congress, is assassinated (10 April).
	Irish playwright Frank McGuinness's *Someone Who'll Watch Over Me* is a hit on Broadway.	A mysterious illness kills ten in the Southwest (29 May).	President of Sri Lanka Ranasingha Premadasa is assassinated (23 April).
	Broadway officially celebrates its 100th birthday.	*Jurassic Park* opens, setting the record for largest opening day box office earnings, with $18.2 million in first day gross ticket sales (11 June).	The IRA explodes a bomb in London's financial district, razing buildings, killing one, and injuring forty-five (24 April). The military ousts President Serrano Elias of Guatemala (25 May).
	As in recent years, New York's institutional theatres offer most of the serious dramatic fare.	The Chicago Bulls led by Michael Jordan win their third straight NBA title (20 June).	Germany restricts access to immigrants seeking asylum (28 May).
	Broadway openings include Wasserstein's *The Sisters Rosensweig*, Simon's *Laughter on the 23rd Floor*, and *Kiss of the Spider Woman*, book by McNally, music and lyrics by Kander and Ebb (Tony for Best Musical).	Midwest suffers disaster when Mississippi River floods. Fifty die, 70,000 left homeless and without drinking water, and eight million acres inundated (July).	Moderate Yugoslavian President Dobrica Cosic is ousted (1 June).

1994		
Actress Helen Hayes dies in March at age ninety-two.	U.S. military issues its "Don't ask, don't tell" policy on homosexuals for their admissibility in armed forces (19 July).	The PLO and Israel exchange letters of mutual recognition and sign an agreement on Palestinian autonomy in Israeli-occupied territory (Sept.). Yeltsin routs foes in a bloody confrontation, which leaves 187 dead (Oct.).
AIDS is a major topic in both serious and comic plays (such as Paul Rudnick's *Jeffrey*).	Deputy White House counsel Vincent Foster is found shot to death in a park in Washington, D.C., an apparent suicide (20 July).	Irish actor Cyril Cusack dies at age eighty-two.
In an attempt to bolster business, Las Vegas entertainment establishments cater more to family patrons.	The Pope attends a Youth Festival in Colorado (11 Sept.).	Civil war in Rwanda results in massacre. 30,000 are expected to die from cholera alone. A UN relief mission is announced by President Clinton to be readying supplies and first aid for country. Tom Stoppard's *Arcadia* opens in London and ranks among his better efforts.
Adrian Mitchell's adaptation of Gogol's *The Government Inspector* bombs on Broadway (6 Jan.).	Vietnam-era radical Kathleen Ann Power surrenders, having been on the run for thirteen years from a robbery charge (Sept.). Basketball star Michael Jordan retires (6 Oct.); returns in 1995. Toni Morrison wins the Nobel Prize for Literature.	
Edward Albee's *Three Tall Women* opens Off-Broadway, the first New York opening for the playwright in eleven years (13 Feb.). Wins Pulitzer.	Clinton approves of a naval blockade around Haiti to prevent immigrants into the country.	As produced by the Royal National Theatre, Arthur Miller's *Broken Glass* is far more successful in London than on Broadway. In general, Miller has fared well in the UK during the 1980s and 1990s, while being virtually ignored in the U.S.
	On 19 August President Clinton revises U.S. immigration asylum policies, turning away thousands of Cubans attempting to flee the economic hardships of their homeland.	
David Richards replaces Frank Rich for a short tenure as *New York Times* drama critic (March).	Republican party wins majority of seats in both the U.S. Senate and House of Representatives.	

DATES	THEATRICAL EVENTS IN AMERICA	SELECTED HISTORICAL/CULTURAL EVENTS IN AMERICA	SELECTED HISTORICAL/CULTURAL EVENTS THROUGHOUT THE WORLD
	A revival of Clifford Odets's *The Flowering Peach* (1954) opens at Lyceum Theatre in New York (20 March).	Republican "Contract With America" threatens to eliminate or drastically to cut funding for NEA, NEH, and PBS. Battles continues into 1997.	
	Kushner's *Perestroika*, part two (joined part one in fall 1993) of *Angels in America*, wins Tony for Best Play.	Movie attendance in the U.S. reaches 1,291,700, a record in thirty-five years of tracking attendance.	
	New musical productions, many revivals, including Lloyd Webber's *Sunset Boulevard* (cost $13 million), Sondheim's *Passion*, stage version of film *Beauty and the Beast*, Hal Prince's production of *Show Boat*, and revivals of *Damn Yankees*, *Grease*, and *Carousel*.		
	Michael John LaChiusa emerges as new musical talent with *Hello Again* (based on Arthur Schnitzler's *La Ronde*) at Lincoln Center.		
	Composer Jule Styne dies at age eighty-eight.		
1995	Neil Simon ignores Broadway and has *London Suite* produced Off-Broadway.	Football-media star O.J. Simpson accused of brutally murdering his wife and Ron Goldman, his wife's friend, but is later acquitted.	15 million people around the world communicate on the Internet.
	Broadway's output during the 1994–95 season is anemic. Some of the most critically acclaimed productions are imports or revivals: Stoppard's *Arcadia*, Cocteau's *Indiscretion (Les Parents Terribles)*, *Hamlet* (with Ralph Fiennes), Ruth and Augustus Goetz's *The Heiress*, Turgenev's *A Month in the Country*.	Death of former Chief Justice of the Supreme Court, Warren Burger, 25 June, at age eighty-seven.	During the spring Europe, Russia, and U.S. commemorate the 50th anniversary of victory in Europe; 6 August, 50th anniversary of A-bombing of Japan.

	Cult blamed for 20 March nerve gas attack on Tokyo's subway which kills twelve and sickened more than 5,500.	168 lives lost in bombing of federal building in Oklahoma City (April).	McNally's *Love! Valour! Compassion!* transfers successfully from Off-Broadway to Broadway.
	Jacques Chirac becomes President of France, replacing François Mitterrand.		Ringling Bros. and Barnum & Bailey Circus celebrates 125th anniversary; plans made to add new international touring units by 1997.
	50th anniversary of United Nations (June).		Revival of *How to Succeed in Business Without Really Trying* among few musical hits of spring 1995.
	HIV infections increased by a record 4.7 million; epicenter for AIDS cases shifts from Africa to Asia.		Broadway ticket prices rise to top of $75.
1996	David Hare's *Skylight* premieres at Royal National Theatre; critical success in New York in 1996 with Michael Gambon.	100th running of the Boston Marathon.	Fall 1995, Carol Channing and Julie Andrews return to the Broadway stage.
	Assassination of Israel Prime Minister Yitzhak Rabin (Nov.).		*Rent*, hit musical by Jonathan Larson, receives Pulitzer and Tony.
	Benjamin "Bibi" Netanyahu defeats Shimon Peres to become Prime Minister of Israel.		Opening of New Victory Theatre, first major step in reclaiming of Forty-second Street.
	Boris Yeltsin elected to second term as President of Russia (July).		Broadway productions number thirty-nine for 1995–96 season (up from preceding season's twenty-eight), with the highest grossing season ever (c. $430 million).
	UK's worst ever mass shooting, at a primary school in Dunblane, Scotland (March).		
1997	China's Deng Xiaoping dies at age ninety-two (Feb.).	Abstract expressionist Willem De Kooning dies in March at age ninety-two.	Broadway gross receipts set new record; attendance second highest in history.

DATES	THEATRICAL EVENTS IN AMERICA	SELECTED HISTORICAL/CULTURAL EVENTS IN AMERICA	SELECTED HISTORICAL/CULTURAL EVENTS THROUGHOUT THE WORLD
	Four new musicals open in time for Tony Award consideration; the big winner among them is the $10 million *Titanic*, while even more successful is the revival of *Chicago*. Surprise play hit of the season is the Off-Broadway production of Paula Vogel's *How I Learned to Drive*, while the revival of *A Doll's House* is big Tony winner. Renovated Amsterdam Theatre reopens on Forty-second Street. *Cats* becomes Broadway's longest running musical.	Beat poet Allen Ginsberg dies in April at age seventy. Timothy McVeigh found guilty of Oklahoma City bombing in June. William Burroughs, author of *The Naked Lunch*, dies at age eighty-three (August).	Labour Party assumes control in Great Britain, as John Major is defeated in election, and Tony Blair becomes Prime Minister. Hong Kong returns to Chinese control at midnight, 30 June. Britain's Princess Diana killed in car accident (31 Aug.) while evading pursuit of paparazzi. A week later (5 Sept.), Mother Teresa (b. 1910), dies of heart failure.
1998	Film actors Robert Mitchum and Jimmy Stewart die early summer. Dramaturge's attempt to be legally designated as co-author of *Rent* fails in court. *Ragtime* and *The Lion King* major musical hits, the latter winning the Tony for Best Musical. Its director, Julie Taymor, wins Best Director for a Musical Award and Irish director Garry Hynes wins Best Director for a Play Award (the first women in history to win these awards). Paula Vogel's *How I Learned to Drive* wins Pulitzer.	Frank Sinatra dies in May (b. 1915).	

1

American Theatre in Context: 1945–Present

Arnold Aronson

Introduction

The history of the United States, more than that of most nations, has been depicted as a grand and heroic narrative – a great epic of the triumph of the human spirit over adversity, the victory of good over evil, and the success of the individual in the face of enormous odds. From colonial times well into the twentieth century, the theatre was not only a reflection of this mythology, it was a crucial instrument for the molding of public perceptions. Prior to the birth of the movies – which did not really become a mass medium until the 1910s – theatre, especially in its popular incarnations, such as circus, vaude-ville, and minstrel shows, was the closest thing to a national forum that the country had. Ideas were debated, public opinion was formulated, and national consciousness was achieved on the stages of American playhouses. In this context, the melodrama – the dominant form of the nineteenth century – was something close to American classicism. It created such quintessential figures as Mose the Bowery B'hoy, Nimrod Wildfire, Jonathan, and their kin – all symbols of the young, energetic, and fundamentally good American society, and all players in the grand story. As long as the American narrative was unfolding, the popular drama was a critical tool for the dissemination of ideas and the creation of a national sense of unity and purpose. But World War I began to reshape American consciousness as the country was no longer one player among many on the world stage but a protagonist; World War II contin-ued the transformation of global politics and economics while permanently altering America's international position and fundamentally transforming American life and sensibility. The "story of America" was seen as entering a new phase, possibly a final chapter in which Manifest Destiny was to be achieved. In such a situation theatre, indeed all the arts, would play a new role.

The aftermath of World War II complicated the narrative. The designation of that conflagration as the "last good war" was a reflection of the war as melo-drama. The U.S. and the Allies were the "good guys" beset by the evil Axis

87

powers. Hitler and Hirohito were, on some levels, Simon Legree-type characters – villains to be vanquished – and their defeat was the inevitable end of a
real cliffhanger. (Stalin, it should be remembered, was transformed into
"Uncle Joe" for the war years to make him into the friend of the "good guy.")
In the immediate afterglow of victory, many Americans saw the war in those
simple terms (and many continue to do so). Yet upon closer examination, not
all aspects of the conduct of the war fit the dramatic archetype. The use of
atomic weapons on Japan and the failure to take action against the concentration camps, for instance, called into question the moral purity and motives of
the United States – the putative protagonist in this melodrama. In the twenty-
five years or so following the war the emergence of the Cold War, the rising
tensions of race relations, the growing awareness of poverty, the wars in
Korea and Vietnam, and even a discomfort with the materialism of the
"affluent society" all contributed to a re-evaluation of American society and
erosion of the archetype. In the postwar era, the melodrama lost its validity
as a paradigm for society. Melodramatic heroes were replaced by so-called
anti-heroes, action was replaced by introspection, clear-cut morality was
replaced by ambiguity, and the traditional dramatic model was replaced by
free-form structures or structures devoid of meaningful content. With theatre
no longer providing the superstructure for the understanding of the society
at large, it lost its role as a primary outlet for cultural expression and exploration.

It is difficult at the end of the twentieth century to imagine how central the
theatre once was to the social and cultural life of the United States. The years
between the two world wars are now seen as a golden age in American theatre
and drama. In the first half of the century, the musical achieved its mature
form, a large number of significant playwrights emerged for the first time in
American history, comedy became both exuberant and sophisticated, a com-
paratively strong African American theatre began to develop, popular entertainments thrived, and an American avant-garde began to emerge. This was
also the period in which the Art Theatre or Little Theatre movement swept
over the country, introducing American audiences to the dramas, ideas, and
techniques of the European avant-garde in the teens and twenties and to the
politically engaged agit props and social dramas of the thirties.

Despite the diversity and variety of this theatre it was contained under one
roof, as it were; all the component pieces were perceived and experienced as
different aspects of a single entity known simply as theatre or entertainment.
Because of this unity a sense of nationhood was visible and an identifiably
American voice began to emerge from this lively conglomeration of theatrical
expression. Out of the theatrical cauldron came a distinctly American style in
acting, language, and design. The Group Theatre in the 1930s began to explore
the psychological realism of Stanislavsky and other offshoots of the Moscow

Art Theatre, while, at the same time, the ongoing love affair with British theatre and actors actually paved the way for the ideas of French innovators in a line of influence from Jacques Copeau through Michel Saint-Denis by way of London's Old Vic. Poetic diction could be found in the plays of Eugene O'Neill, Elmer Rice, Clifford Odets, and most especially William Saroyan, while Maxwell Anderson plunged into neo-Elizabethan verse drama. The New Stagecraft of Robert Edmond Jones, Norman Bel Geddes, and Lee Simonson supplanted the naturalism of David Belasco with symbolism and simplification, creating a scenographic equivalent to the abstraction of contemporary art. The dominant American style on the eve of World War II was characterized by psychological realism in acting, poetic diction in playwriting (applied to dark, gritty explorations of society that derived from the melodrama and the well-made play), and a semi-abstract, emblematic stage design. All in all, it was a seemingly incongruous pastiche of nineteenth-century American traditions dominated by melodrama, and early twentieth-century European avant-gardism that somehow coalesced into a fertile theatre.

The end of World War II brought unprecedented wealth and power to the United States and historical precedents suggest that such hegemony might have presaged a vigorous and energetic theatre as in Elizabethan England, the France of Louis XIV, or fifth-century Athens. But this was not to be. A certain confidence, sense of well-being, and exuberance, of course, did manifest itself in American culture, but more often in consumer goods than in art. Cars, for example, began to sprout tailfins – futuristic icons of useless excess – with the 1948 Cadillac; homes began to fill with gleaming white appliances; sleek "entertainment centers" disguised as furniture became the centerpieces of living rooms, and movies increasingly abandoned the "noir" tones of black and white for the saturated colors of Technicolor. Economist John Kenneth Galbraith popularized the term "affluent society" in a 1958 book to describe the sated, consumerist culture. Because the term implied a general material prosperity, it suggested a more democratic form of wealth than that of earlier generations. This was a whole society that shared in the riches, not a small sect of robber barons. The truth was, of course, that while the general standards of living were raised significantly for most people, and the middle class had a heretofore unheard-of purchasing power, there were still significant disparities within the society and disturbingly large segments of poverty. Galbraith also made the point that private affluence was being acquired at the expense of public service and civic needs. Nonetheless, this affluence, too, seemed the logical denouement for the American melodrama. A muscular and ebullient sense of triumph and joy was tangible in some movies – *Singin' in the Rain* is an excellent example – though a darker, more troubled genre also began to emerge, particularly in the filmed versions of several of the plays of Tennessee Williams and William Inge. To be sure, the American theatre in the second half of the twentieth century witnessed its share of significant dramas and playwrights – many of which now constitute the American canon – the birth (and ultimate mainstreaming) of an American avant-garde, a period of spirited and innovative musical theatre, the transformation of design into an art, and the spread of resident professional theatres across the country. But the combined forces of economics, politics, technology, and demographic upheavals conspired to remove the theatre from its position of centrality in American culture and transform it into peripheral entertainment divorced from the community at large. As American society became increasingly fragmented in the postwar years it was mirrored in a fragmented theatre by an increasingly introspective and highly ambiguous drama. Film, television, popular music, and new technologies combined to eviscerate the traditional theatregoing audience. Insofar as the theatre retained any relevance to a national discourse it was as a tool for localized political and social debate. Insofar as it retained a role in popular culture it was primarily as leisure-time spectacle typified by the extravaganzas of Las Vegas, the circus, and theme parks.

The Emerging Postwar Consciousness

Less than a year before the United States joined the combatants of World War II, Henry Luce, head of the Time-Life Corporation, famously declared this the "American Century" in a *Life* magazine essay. Primarily an appeal to join the Allies in the escalating war in Europe, Luce's essay argued that the unique position, history, and wealth of the United States created a moral obligation for it to be the guarantor of freedom around the globe and to establish international free trade, feed the world's population, and send forth its distinctly twentieth-century technology and culture. "We know how lucky we are compared to all the rest of mankind," he wrote. "At least two-thirds of us are just plain rich compared to all the rest of the human family – rich in food, rich in clothes, rich in entertainment and amusement, rich in leisure, rich" (quoted in Luce, *Ideas*, 107). At the end of the war, as if following Luce's exhortations, the United States was indeed the wealthiest, most powerful, most technologically advanced nation on earth. It imprinted itself indelibly upon the twentieth century, essentially shaping the world for years to come. Paradoxically for a nation historically in the cultural shadow of Europe, the most long-lasting and pervasive export has been American culture spread primarily through the machinery of movies, television, and popular music. But this new-found power was accompanied from the start by underlying American discomfort with such dominance and a constant questioning of our moral obligations in the world. This uneasiness has informed postwar art in both form and content.

The American century also meant that the visual and performing arts were transforming from absorbing international influences to a position of generating influence. A growing class of wealthy art patrons and the presence of a sizable body of European émigré artists between the wars fostered a creative ferment, invigorated the American art scene, and inspired a generation of young American artists. When World War II effectively ended European dominance of the art world, American culture was able to rush in and fill the vacuum. New York City in particular emerged not only as the cultural capital of the United States but of the world; all strands of the grand narrative seemed headed for triumphant conclusion. Sounding a bit like Luce, writer Clifton Fadiman could state in a 1940 radio discussion, "We have reached a critical point in the life of our nation. We are through as a pioneer nation; we are now ready to develop as a civilization" (quoted in Guilbaut, *How New York Stole the Idea of Modern Art*, 57). But it was critic Clement Greenberg, the primary articulator of the new formalist American aesthetic, who astutely perceived the inextricable connections between the development of a new art and international supremacy. "The main premises of Western art," he wrote, "have at last migrated to the United States along with the center of gravity of production and political power" (quoted in Guilbaut, *How New York Stole the Idea of Modern Art*, 172).

Freed of its subservience to European art and ideas and supported by a growing network of galleries, a unique American voice emerged, embodied in artists such as Jackson Pollock, Franz Kline, Robert Motherwell, Mark Rothko, and Barnett Newman. Similarly, what was for all intents and purposes the first generation of American composers and conductors appeared, including Leonard Bernstein, Milton Babbitt, and Lukas Foss. And the center of the dance world followed the other arts to New York – modern dance had European origins but found its mature expression in American choreographers and companies while postmodern dance was an almost purely American phenomenon. Theatre, too, began to explore new avenues of expression and by the sixties and seventies the American avant-garde was in the forefront of international theatre. Yet, unlike the situation in art or dance, this avant-garde movement did not supplant the established or traditional theatre that preceded it.

There are many possible explanations for the failure of theatre to evolve as the other arts did, the most immediate and compelling being the profound demographic changes that radically altered the constituency and attendance habits of theatre audiences. Another factor is the nature of the arts themselves. The primarily non-objective, emblematic, and symbolic vocabularies of music, visual art, and even dance allowed those forms to change more rapidly than theatre in response to shifting aesthetics and sensibilities, whereas the nature of Western theatre, with its narrative explorations of human interactions and emotions, has historically kept it in an essentially realistic framework. But in the aftermath of the atrocities of World War II, and faced with the overwhelming fear of nuclear Armageddon that pervaded consciousness during the Cold War, a realistic drama seemed feeble and impotent. "Naturalism is no longer adequate, either aesthetically or morally, to cope with the modern horror," declared critic Dwight MacDonald (quoted by Guilbaut, "The New Adventures of the Avant-garde in America," in Frascina, *Pollock and After*, 160). Certainly a theatre in which characters could do little more than talk about "the bomb" seemed painfully useless. At the same time Clement Greenberg warned painters against a polemic art. "In the face of current events," he cautioned, in order for modern art to be successful it must emulate "the greatest painter of our time, Matisse" who "wanted his art to be an armchair for the tired businessman" (quoted in Guilbaut, "The New Adventures," 159).

The elements that comprised the underlying vocabulary of naturalism remained visible in the new forms of art and theatre; however they now functioned not as building blocks of a narrative but as independent aesthetic objects. "The vernacular repertoire," explained art historian William C. Seitz in a 1961 essay,

> includes beat Zen and hot rods, mescalin experiences and faded flowers, photo-graphic bumps and grinds, the *poubelle* (i.e., trash can), juke boxes, and hydrogen explosions. Such objects are often approached in a mystical, aesthetic, or "arty" way, but just as often they are fearfully dark, evoking horror or nausea: the anguish of the scrap heap; the images of charred bodies that keep Hiroshima and Nagasaki before our eyes; the confrontation of democratic platitudes with the Negro's disenfranchisement . . . (*The Art of Assemblage*, 88–89)

His catalogue of elements, of course, is a prosaic echo of Allen Ginsberg's classic Beat poem *Howl*, which chronicled the "best minds of my generation destroyed by madness, starving hysterical naked, / dragging themselves through the negro streets at dawn looking for an angry fix, /. . . . listening to the crack of doom on the hydrogen jukebox" (*Howl*, 9–10). The theatre and art that emerged in the forties and fifties drew inspiration from the raw energy, form, and content of American pop culture and iconography, the wonder and fear of new technologies and media, and from the conflicting chaos of urban society.

If the artists of the postwar era expressed a degree of fear of nuclear annihilation and distrust of the establishment it was at least in part because the American government tended to situate everything in the context of national security – preparation for war against the Soviets. The interstate highway system, for instance, was initially the National Defense Highway system, designed to move military equipment and personnel efficiently around the country; the National Science Foundation was a response to the perceived advantage the Soviets had in military technology; support for schools came under the heading of the National Defense Education Act. It was, of course, harder to justify support for the arts as a factor in national security, but the emergence of a plethora of federal agencies which had a direct impact on daily life created an atmosphere in which support for the arts seemed plausible, and at the height of the Cold War, culture was a significant tool in international diplomacy. And it was, strangely enough, the identification of American Abstract Expressionism with democratic ideals that allowed modern art to move out of avant-garde fringes and into the mainstream, thereby making the funding of such art somehow patriotic.

The modern art movement in America captured the mantle of democratic righteousness after the war through a sort of "buy American" campaign, suggesting that supporting modern artists was virtually a patriotic duty. American artists were elevated to a level and prestige previously conferred only on European painters and sculptors. Not only serious critics, but the popular press such as *Life* magazine, began to pay attention to the new wave of artists and saw in them the new American spirit; they saw an art appropriate for the new postwar order. The process of acceptance was aided by the essentially apolitical nature of the new art, particularly Abstract Expressionism. This was in marked contrast to much art and especially theatre of the interwar years, which had been predominantly left-wing in its sympathies. At a symposium at the Museum of Modern Art in 1948 art critic Paul Burlin announced, "Modern painting is the bulwark of the individual creative expression, aloof from the political left and its blood brother, the right. Their common dictators, if effective, would destroy the artist" (quoted in Guilbaut, *How New York Stole the Idea of Modern Art*, 181). The practitioners of this new art became new American folk heroes in the tradition of the pioneers and so-called "modern art" became a *de facto* official art in the United States.

The theatre in 1945, weighted down with tradition, a formidable infrastructure, and an audience with no overt desire to overthrow the *status quo*, was ponderous and slow to change. But the changing aspects of American culture and society would serve to undermine theatre's function and audience. Mainstream theatre had served two primary roles in the prewar years: it was "entertainment for the tired business man" or it was a source of ideas and a forum for discussion. By the fifties, however, much of the entertainment function had been ceded to television, and the political atmosphere stifled the more open and visible forms of public debate.

America's entrance into the war had an immediate effect upon the content and style of drama. The whole genre of political drama as well as the social investigation that typified so much drama in the years following World War I seemed to evaporate overnight. Politics were now determined by military alliances, moral ambiguity gave way to fervent patriotism, and entertainment functioned in service to the war effort. It was important to see the nation as a unified whole; to focus on individual groups within society, to emphasize difference, or to question the fabric of American life was seen as counterproductive, even anti-patriotic. Thus, the rising tide of black theatre artists and companies dissipated, and the socially and politically oriented groups – from the Federal Theatre Project and Group Theatre, through the small workers' theatres, already on shaky economic and artistic legs – simply disappeared. But without the social, political, and intellectual ferment, the drama suffered. The American theatre during the war years produced an unusually mediocre crop of plays and musicals, perhaps the most uninteresting four or five Broadway seasons of the century. There were, to be sure, a few notable exceptions, and in these exceptions could be seen the seeds of what was to come.

The rising fascination with Freudianism, psychotherapy, and the mysterious workings of the mind was evident in Richard Rodgers's and Lorenz Hart's *Pal Joey* (1940). Just as the European Naturalistic movement of the 1870s was grounded in the belief that objective examination of the underside of society could lead to the healing of social ills, the contemporary popular understanding of Freudianism assumed that exploring the darker recesses of the psyche was the best way to understand human behavior. This musical put morally complex, even repugnant characters at the center of the story and created a dark and cynical atmosphere that repelled many critics and baffled some of the audience, though it demonstrated that the musical could be a vehicle for dark and disturbing themes. Freudianism on a somewhat lighter note was the basis of *Lady in the Dark* (1941) by Kurt Weill and Moss Hart. Weill also brought American jazz, via the filter of a European sensibility, to the American stage. Musical innovation of another kind arrived two years later, when the new team of Richard Rodgers and Oscar Hammerstein II created *Oklahoma!* While thematically this musical reverted to the sentimentality and lyricism of earlier American drama and musical comedy (it was based on Lynn Riggs's play of 1931, *Green Grow the Lilacs*) and possessed a certain earnestness of spirit associated with Americana plays of the twenties, structurally it would alter musical theatre for almost two decades (see discussion of *Oklahoma!* in Volume 2). Taking the integration of music, lyrics, and plot that had been bubbling beneath the surface at least since the Jerome Kern–Guy Bolton *Show Boat* (1927), *Oklahoma!* created a contemporary, American folk-pop-operetta style. And while George Balanchine had choreographed ballet sequences in the 1936 *On Your Toes*, Agnes de Mille's choreography for *Oklahoma!* used ballet as a motif for advancing the plot and created a genre of theatrical dance.

The one significant play of the war years was Thornton Wilder's *The Skin of Our Teeth* (1942). Its self-referential dialogue, breaking of the fourth wall, comic yet sometimes obscure symbolism, epic structure, and proto-Absurdist content served as a harbinger of a range of experimental theatre to come that vigorously and almost gleefully rejected the predominant American penchant for naturalism and sentimentality.

Of less quantifiable impact was the presence of refugee artists escaping the Nazis. Two who had significant influence on the development of the theatre were Bertolt Brecht and Erwin Piscator. While Brecht's residence in the US from 1941 to 1947 had few tangible manifestations – he worked on one film and several of his plays were translated and performed, but for very short runs that made almost no critical impression – it would have long-range effects by laying the groundwork for a new politically engaged theatre and the use of alienation or estrangement as a dramatic tool. Most of the translations of Brecht's work were done by scholar and playwright Eric Bentley, who almost single-handedly introduced Brecht's plays and theories to the U.S. after the war. Piscator, meanwhile, ran the Dramatic Workshop at the New School for Social Research in New York from 1939 to 1951, where he staged some 100 experimental works. These productions introduced a generation to the principles of epic theatre, and in his classes he influenced many of the practitioners of the postwar generation, including Judith Malina, a co-founder of the Living Theatre.

It was the arrival of Tennessee Williams on the theatrical scene, however, that signaled a genuine shift in American drama with *The Glass Menagerie*, which premiered a few months before the war's end in the spring of 1945. Williams stood at the nexus of melodrama and psychotherapy. His plays took the by-now classic American themes of home and family and, using an essentially melodramatic vocabulary of a lost past, unrequited love, and yearnings for a better future, explored the inner workings of societally marginal characters. Although Amanda and Laura are the focus of the play, it is in the characters of Jim, the gentleman caller who failed to fulfill his potential yet who sells himself as the epitome of the American striver (he is planning to take advantage of the newest technology, television), and especially Tom, the son straining against the stifling atmosphere of the home but with no plans other than unarticulated yearnings for excitement, that Williams has created the postwar American characters. Tom is the prototype of the anti-hero, the rebel without a cause. (Though recent criticism sees Tom as autobiographical and therefore gay, so his rebellion actually does have a cause – just one that could not be articulated in 1945.)

In terms of dramatic technique, Williams's significant contribution was to find a theatrical framework by which the audience was allowed into the inner workings of the minds and souls of the characters without reverting to the often contrived and self-conscious theatrical devices earlier employed by Eugene O'Neill. Though not a political or morality play, *The Glass Menagerie* worked as metaphor for the country on the verge of something new, yet filled with doubts and insecurities and unwilling to let go of a romanticized past. Stylistically, it drew upon the poetic atmosphere of the Symbolists, the associative world of the Surrealists, and the use of projections first exploited by Piscator, to create what Williams called a memory play. Following in the footsteps of William Saroyan, Williams created the genre of poetic realism or American symbolism, which is the closest thing the US had to a national style for the next fifteen years.

A contributing factor to the success of the play, and a significant element in establishing poetic realism as the dominant style, was the design by Jo Mielziner. Never before in American theatre had design and text been so fully integrated and so interdependent. Using scrims and painterly decor, Mielziner created an ethereal look, while facilitating the cinematic flow from scene to scene called for by Williams, and providing the ideal means for the depiction of memory. In fact, much of the postwar theatre was dependent for its success on a strong visual realization and an emotionally energetic acting style. The creative team of Mielziner and director Elia Kazan, formerly of the Group Theatre, together with Williams and later Arthur Miller, most notably in his play *Death of a Salesman*, would create a series of productions that typified the postwar style and that some would see as the pinnacle of American theatre. To a large degree, this was the result of the development of the art of lighting design. The effectiveness of the scrim, the creation of memory and dream, and the cinematic flow were dependent on the precise and fluid use of light. Jean Rosenthal, who worked with Orson Welles, and Abe Feder, both beginning in the thirties, virtually created the profession of lighting designer and went on to significant theatrical careers, while Mielziner, working with Ed Kook and building upon the aesthetics of Rosenthal, transformed lighting into an art.

As crucial to the success of the plays of Miller and Williams as the visual environment were the acting and directing. Once again, the American fascination with psychology informed the development of acting style and led to a major shift in the forties from a technical virtuosity to a more energetic emotionalism. Here, the influence of the Group Theatre of the thirties cannot be overstated. Lee Strasberg and Stella Adler had championed the ideas of Stanislavsky, though each drew upon a slightly different understanding of the Russian director's work. At root, they were interested in an emotionally truthful form of acting that emanated more from an internal and psychological understanding of character than from external techniques. As Group Theatre alumnus Elia Kazan emerged as the leading director of the late forties this Americanized naturalistic style was melded with the poetic realism of the new playwrights. Characterized by brooding portrayals, relaxed body language, and a verbal style that, in contrast to the contemporary stage diction, seemed to consist of mumbling and stuttering, the Kazan productions seethed with emotional turbulence and sexual tension that were revolutionary for the time. Marlon Brando, who played Stanley Kowalski in Williams's *A Streetcar Named Desire* (1949), was the quintessence of this new style that was a direct challenge to the artificiality of stage decorum. He embodied the anti-hero – the protagonist of the emotionally ambiguous postwar era. Kazan, with other Group alumni Robert Lewis and Cheryl Crawford, created the Actors Studio in 1947 as a workshop for Stanislavsky-inspired acting training. Lee Strasberg joined in 1949 and soon became the sole director of the Studio. Under his autocratic leadership until his death in 1982, Strasberg trained several generations of actors in what became known simply as "The Method." Ironically, the Strasberg approach became increasingly ineffective on the stage as Absurdism, the neo-Expressionistic ensemble theatre movement, and various avant-gardes transformed the American theatre from the late fifties onward, but the Studio became the training ground for virtually the entire postwar cadre of film actors. This group includes, aside from Brando, James Dean, Marilyn Monroe, Montgomery Clift, Paul Newman, Joanne Woodward, Anne Bancroft, Shelley Winters, Geraldine Page, Dustin Hoffman, Robert De Niro, and Al Pacino. In opposition to the rugged good looks or perfect beauty of prewar movie stars and their unambiguous identification as either "good guys" or villains, the postwar generation was idiosyncratic and flawed in their physicality, and possessed of a moral ambiguity. The Method, which thrived on personal quirks and emphasized the emotionality beneath the surface, was ideal for a post-Holocaust, atomic society that was no longer certain of truth, morality, or even beauty. (See Chapter 6 for additional commentary on "The Method.")

One might have expected the war itself to preoccupy playwrights in the late 1940s, but while it provided raw material for dozens of movies over several decades and much fiction, including Norman Mailer's debut novel *The Naked and the Dead*, it was surprisingly absent from the postwar theatre. The war as melodrama was fit for the entertainment needs of Hollywood, but playwrights seemed more interested in the postwar American society and its discontents. Arthur Miller's first hit play *All My Sons* (1947) used the war as a background for his moral exploration of individual responsibility, but it was set – as so many American plays were – in a home in a small midwestern community. The play was not about the war *per se*, but about the individual's responsibility to the larger society. The protagonist, Joe Keller, manufactured airplane parts during the war. Putting profit ahead of morality, he sold defective parts to the army, leading to the deaths of several fliers and ultimately the suicide of his son. With this play Miller established himself as the keeper of America's conscience, but it was not an investigation of war.

One of the only other theatre pieces to represent the war was Rodgers's and Hammerstein's *South Pacific*, which opened in the spring of 1949. The plot ostensibly dealt with fairly serious material. Set on an island in the South

Pacific during World War II, it involved a mission by the American servicemen to establish a secret base on a nearby enemy-held island. It also dealt with issues of interracial romance and marriage. Although the latter issue had been addressed in varying degrees in the twenties and thirties, it was starkly absent from the mainstream drama of the immediate postwar years and was something that only black playwrights seemed to confront until well into the sixties. Yet the issue was ultimately side-stepped in *South Pacific*. By placing it in an exotic location, the issue became not white and black, but white and Polynesian. The potential moral dilemma raised by the romance between the American serviceman Cable and the native woman Liat was avoided by having Cable killed during the mission, a ploy that provided a melodramatically moving emotional peak, but seemed narratively too contrived or convenient.

Despite the potentially profound themes of *South Pacific*, it is best remembered as a comic romance that produced such memorable songs as "Some Enchanted Evening," "I'm Gonna Wash That Man Right Outa My Hair," and "There Is Nothing Like a Dame." The popularity of the songs is, of course, a tribute to Rodgers's and Hammerstein's appealing score and lyrics, but it was also a factor of a happy coincidence – the development of the long-playing record. Although cast recordings, especially in England, date back to the beginning of the century, it was the ability to record a Broadway show's score on a single, lightweight record that created a recording goldmine. For some fifteen years, from *South Pacific* until 1964's *Hello, Dolly!*, Broadway cast recordings regularly topped the *Billboard* popular music charts. Since musicals were more widely known through cast recordings than the actual production, for many people the musical was tantamount to its score or, more precisely, its cast album; the book became secondary at best and a show's themes and ideas could become divorced from its music if the songs did not directly address them. So while most serious postwar drama virtually ignored World War II, the most devastating conflagration in human history, and virtually no drama dealt with the deep-seated American dilemma of racial conflict, *South Pacific*, a musical, at least, confronted them. Yet for those who knew only the cast album, the issues were hidden at best. The operetta form of the American musical comedy, in which romance, song and dance, and lavish scenography were the paramount issues, undermined the ability of musicals to be a locus for serious social debate. (See Maslon, Chapter 2, "Broadway," on cast recordings.)

Economics and Demographics

At the start of the nineteenth century New York City emerged as the commercial and theatrical capital of the nation and, by the late nineteenth century,

American theatre was essentially divided into New York and "the Road" – touring theatre that originated in or emanated from New York. The New York theatre had, from its earliest days, been physically centered around Broadway, but like a demographic barometer it followed the movement of New York's population center up Broadway as the wealthy citizenry moved uptown. A theatrical building boom during the first three decades of the twentieth century anchored the theatre district firmly around the Times Square area and "Broadway" became a catchall term for mainstream theatre.

The economic structure of Broadway prior to World War I was based on relatively inexpensive labor, materials, and real estate, and sizable income from "the Road." Low ticket prices meant that audiences from nearly all strata of society could afford to go to the theatre, creating a situation akin in some respects to that of Elizabethan London. There were seven or more widely read newspaper critics of more or less equal weight, thereby guaranteeing that no single critic or paper could determine the fate of a production. Accessible and affordable theatre meant that audiences would not wait for "blockbusters" but might venture to see a show simply because it had a popular actor, enchanting scenery, or an element of novelty. With live performance as the primary form of entertainment, theatregoing was a regular practice for much of the population. The Broadway of the interwar years was in some ways a monolithic theatre engine that spewed forth a multifaceted product consisting of a vast array of dramas, comedies, musicals, revues, variety shows, revivals, and even ice shows and operettas. (The *New York Times*, in its annual end-of-season wrap up, classified shows according to these categories, but tellingly included them under the single heading of the "New York theatre season"; it was all theatrical entertainment.) The idea of niche-productions, cult, or elitist theatre that would come to comprise a significant proportion of the productions by the nineties, was a barely visible component, apparent only in the labor theatres and ethnic and racial theatre companies of the thirties; and even these latter theatres were seen as a crucial part of the larger entertainment structure. Given the wide variety of theatre that was produced and the ability to take risks, Broadway contained, in a sense, its own research and development arm that could continuously revitalize the theatre.

The combined effects of the Depression and World War II, however, altered the economic and aesthetic structure, leading to the artistic fragmentation and geographic decentralization of the American theatre. Although theatre had withstood the early onslaught of film, the addition of television to the mix beginning about 1948, in combination with a significant shift in audience demographics, signaled an end to theatre as the epicenter of cultural and intellectual life.

There had been a steady decline in the number of productions since the mid-1920s. The season of 1925–26 was the peak for theatre weeks – a figure representing the number of shows playing each week times weeks in the season – with 2,852.[1] By contrast, the 1945–46 season recorded 1,420 theatre weeks while by 1960–61 it had diminished to 1,210. Measured another way, 1927–28 was the peak season for new productions with 264 openings, whereas the 1945–46 season witnessed only 76 and the 1960–61 season a then record low of 48. By 1989–90 the season total for new productions was a mere 40, but of that number only 10 were new American plays, 3 of which had been originated either Off-Broadway or in a regional theatre, and only 8 were new musicals; the remainder consisted of one-person shows, revivals, and Radio City Music Hall revues. The decline after the twenties was exacerbated, of course, by talkies and the Great Depression and, to some extent, radio, but live entertainment remained a staple of American culture. Furthermore, movies were perceived almost exclusively as entertainment, whereas theatre – at least a portion of it – remained the focal point of American intellectual life and, as such, was seen to fill a role that movies could not. In the thirties, especially, it seemed as if many of the great social, political, and moral debates of the time were rehearsed upon the stage and continued in late-night discussions in restaurants and bistros afterward.

Radio, whatever its immediate effects on attendance, had a more long-term impact on perceptions of entertainment. Radio was able to bring vaudeville performers, film stars, music, soap operas, and news directly into homes. Though it was a mass medium, it seemed to function on an intimate level: listeners felt as if broadcasts were directed only to them and developed personal relationships with, say, Rudy Vallee as he sang or Walter Winchell as he reported his gossip. Audiences began to have different expectations of its performers and to develop a different relationship with celebrities.

But if the changing mood of the country was a factor in the shifting fortunes of the theatre after World War II, the more critical shift in American theatre resulted from a seismic demographic transformation that began after the war and continued for the next quarter-century. Beneath the seeming calm of the 1950s lay radical changes in the American population that would have profound effects on all aspects of society. Between 1945 and 1960 the general population increased by 40.1 million to 180 million or by nearly 29 percent. The overwhelming majority of this increase was in the suburbs, where 11 million new houses were built between 1948–58 (out of 13 million overall). The large middle class that had lived in New York and other urban centers, the societal segment that had anchored the residential neighborhoods and fueled urban mercantilism, began moving out to the suburbs as the postwar economic boom bestowed its benefits upon them. During the sixties, some 900,000 whites moved out of New York. By 1960, one of three Americans lived in a suburb. Historian Todd Gitlin expressed this transformation eloquently:

The Puritan utopia of a "city on a hill" found its strange completion in the flatlands of the American suburb. For growing numbers, daily life was delivered from the cramp of the city, lifted out to the half-wide, half-open spaces, where the long-sought and long-feared American wilderness could be trimmed back and made habitable. The prairie became the lawn; the ranch, the ranch house; the saloon, the Formica bar. (*The Sixties*, 14)

Also by 1960 75 percent of families owned a car and 87 percent a television; and it was the first society in history to have more college graduates than farmers. The automobile culture replaced the urban culture, and roads and highways received funding while urban mass transit deteriorated and was dismantled. Suburban communities and highways served as magnets for shopping centers and later malls that replaced the downtown centers and the village greens. For those who had left the cities, there were fewer and fewer reasons to return.

As the white middle class left the cities they were replaced in large part by African Americans moving north from the rural south and Latino groups moving from the Caribbean and Latin America, all hoping to benefit from the perceived prosperity. From 1940 to 1960, 375,000 African Americans moved to New York and the Latino population quadrupled, although the total population of the city declined. Thus, the economic base of the theatre of the previous decades was being lost, and the intellectual and cultural face of the city was being altered. The new urban dwellers might have formed the basis of a new audience, but a variety of factors worked against this development. There was no voice representing the new populations and the potential new audiences within the theatre world. And because the recent arrivals, in many cases, lacked a theatregoing tradition, there was no compelling need to meet their demands nor was there much impetus from within the communities to create theatre. The production of theatre remained in the hands of the older generation or at least the same segment of society that was deserting the cities. The theatre had become so institutionalized that rather than attempting to change, it metaphorically dug in its heels.

The response by producers to the erosion of the audience was to try to lure back the same audience. The single greatest cost increase for producers in the fifties was advertising, which rose some 300 percent. Curtain time was adjusted to meet the needs of suburban commuters – from 8:40 to 7:30 in 1971 and then back to 8:00, where it remains. The new suburbanites continued to return to the city to attend the theatre for a while but such a journey was more complex and certainly more costly than a mere subway or taxi ride. The cost of a trip into the city, the demands of family, and the rise of suburban movie theatres combined with the effects of television to alter theatregoing habits.

Although there was a continuous and significant drop in the number of productions in the decades after the war, the total audience remained more or less constant. Attendance figures fluctuated from year to year by as much as 20 percent, but on average the Broadway audience from the end of the war through the 1960–61 season remained at about 7 million. And despite the continuing decline in new productions the overall attendance figures actually rose through the seventies, peaking at 11 million in 1981 and then leveling off at about 9 million ever since. But with theatre tickets three to ten times more expensive than movies (through the sixties, the cheapest seats were competitive with movies, but prices began to skyrocket thereafter, reaching a $75 top in 1996 against $9.00 for a movie, and, even so, the rise in ticket prices did not keep pace with the rise in production costs), the greater effort to get to the theatre, and the diminishing product, producers had to work harder to get the audience into the seats. Audiences were becoming increasingly selective in what they saw, willing to commit their time and dollars only to certified hits.

The unorthodox and iconoclastic shows that had once survived and even thrived on the periphery of the great theatre machine were now banished to increasingly obscure venues. The phenomenal salaries and fees that Hollywood offered, especially with the birth of the television industry, lured actors and, more significantly, writers away from the legitimate stage. The result was a steady erosion of the number of new productions and an increasing conservatism on the part of producers fearful of losing ever larger sums of money. Finally, the new technology of television had a staggering effect on the theatre to a degree that the movies never had.

The statistics alone are sobering. The number of televisions sold in the United States jumped from a mere 172,000 in 1948 to 5 million in 1950 to over 79 million in 1960, by which time 90 percent of American families were regular viewers and the average viewer was watching an astounding forty-four hours a week of programming – more time watching than working. So much time in front of the small screen meant little or no time for theatre, reading, hobbies, and a host of leisure-time activities. Even movie attendance dropped from 90 million a week in 1946 to 46 million a week in 1955.

Overshadowed by television, the theatre, once prestigious, ubiquitous, and a mirror of national identity had, by the sixties, become an elitist entertainment aimed at a narrow segment of the population. Movies had taken over the melodrama, the thesis drama, the well-made play, and the romantic comedy; television had taken over vaudeville and all forms of popular entertainment, including the domestic comedy that had held the stage since the time of Menander.

In previous generations, in fact for virtually the entire history of theatre, those aspects of performance that are lumped under the category of popular entertainment had always constituted the foundation of theatre and provided an ongoing thread. Whatever happened in the mainstream or elitist theatres, including the virtual elimination of such theatres periodically throughout history, popular entertainment – singing, dancing, circus skills, comedy, and domestic skits – remained almost unaltered. In any other time in history, such entertainments would have sprung up in response to the needs of a changing audience – they would have weathered the storms of debilitating economics in the commercial theatre – and thus created a foundation for a revitalized theatre. But television supplanted live popular performance. Everything that might have been found in vaudeville houses, and much of the drama and comedy that had been a staple of the popular Broadway stage for decades, could now be found on television – and viewers did not even have to venture out of the house. Even the circus was put on TV. In one sense, the transference of popular entertainment to television meant that almost everyone could now attend the "theatre"; mass entertainment had never been so "mass." But on the other hand, the possibility for local and ethnically focused entertainments was being crushed beneath the weight of universal acceptance. The television had become the primary tool for achieving the conformist society. The weekly *Ed Sullivan Show* entered homes with a wider variety of entertainment than most people had ever seen before, but now audiences from the industrial northeast or rural south or western ranch lands, the Jew, the African American, the Hispanic, the Asian, and the Anglican were all presented with a bill of fare that either homogenized or obliterated individual voices, depending on one's point of view.

By the early fifties, most people involved with the Broadway theatre began to sound a note of panic as they recognized the situation. The pessimism was plaintively expressed by critic John Chapman dispiritedly summing up the season for *The Best Plays of 1950–1951*: "We must not look toward the future with any great amount of confidence, for the American theatre . . . has been in a decline during all the recent years. This decline has been both economic and artistic. Inflation has caused the economic decline, and few people can afford to be regular theatre goers any more" (v). In a history of Broadway twenty years later, *New York Times* critic Brooks Atkinson noted that theatre "as an industry . . . was obsolete . . . After World War II, theater owners became acutely conscious of a pitiless fact of life: a theatre could earn an income for only twenty-two hours a week, making only meager use of the expensive land it occupied" (*Broadway*, 417). Theatre was recognized as a business – an industry – and it was measured accordingly.

The 1950s

The decade of the fifties was long perceived as a period of conformity and stasis, although recent re-evaluations are challenging that view. Poet Robert

Lowell, for instance, could write of "the tranquillized fifties" where "even the man / scavenging filth in the back alley trash cans, / has two children, a beach wagon, a helpmate, / and is 'a young Republican'" ("Memories of West Street," 85). Eisenhower was depicted by comics as a president who spent more time playing golf than running the country. It was the period of the "organization man," the corporate conformist described by social observer William Whyte. The organization man had become so totally accepted as part of society by the early sixties that even the humorless IBM Corporation could manage a smile at itself by dressing the guides at its 1964 New York World's Fair pavilion in gray flannel suits. Social philosopher C. Wright Mills wrote *White Collar* in 1951 attacking the sales mentality that had overtaken the nation and supplanted middle-class independence. He followed this up in 1956 with the more radical *The Power Elite,* which warned of the dangers of the corporate mentality and its power over all aspects of society as well as the dangers of the military–industrial complex. Vance Packard and David Riesman also warned of the dangers of the increasingly consumerist society. These were not the muckraking books of the Upton Sinclair variety, exposing harmful and exploitative business practices; these books warned of something more sinister – a kind of brainwashing and a loss of individual freedoms and national spirit. The dark side of Freudianism in the popular understanding was that if the mind were ultimately quantifiable it must therefore be controllable as well. Those with the right knowledge – and the wrong motives – be they corporations selling you their product or Communist operatives taking over your soul, had the ability to brainwash you, render you into a zombie-like agent of their desires. (This was the message behind the chilling 1962 movie *The Manchurian Candidate.*) These writings laid the groundwork for an "us vs. them" mentality that pervaded the counterculture movements of the sixties. "Us" was the everyday, everyman, individual; "them" was the "establishment" of the government, military, and corporations or, in some contexts, the Communists, who were depicted as melodramatically evil. Cartoonist Walt Kelly, whose comic strip *Pogo* often skewered politicians, played upon this perception of the world at the start of the environmental movement in the early seventies. "We have met the enemy," declared a character, "and he is us."

The paranoid view of the world was captured in science fiction films and comic books that became filled with menacing blobs, things, body-snatchers, aliens, resurrected prehistoric monsters, and mutated – by atomic radiation or science experiments gone wrong – creatures including rabbits, plants, and housewives. The messages were plain and simple: Communists will steal your soul as soon as you let down your guard; and whenever science tries to play God it leads to tragic results.

Theatre has often been a stimulus for change or a challenge to a complacent culture, but the anti-Communist hysteria of the early fifties led by Senator

Joseph McCarthy squelched a great deal of free expression – more through intimidation than by direct action. Anti-Communist sentiment had existed in the U.S. since the Russian revolution of 1917 and had led to the creation of the House Un-American Activities Committee. In the postwar years the belief that Communists were infiltrating every aspect of American society and government reached epidemic proportions. "Better Dead than Red" was the battle cry of the political right. A wide range of individuals was investigated by Congress for possible Communist activities or connections, but the McCarthy hearings were virulent and used smear, innuendo, and intimidation. His investigations spread well beyond political figures and focused on high-profile and sensational figures in theatre, film, and television. Mere accusation or association led to blacklisting, ruining the careers of many writers, directors, and actors in all media. And with few exceptions, it led to the end of a theatre of ideas. It was as if the war years were a kind of purgative for the theatre and McCarthyism the death blow to a generation of playwrights. Of all the playwrights who had been successful before the war and who continued to produce afterward, including Clifford Odets, Maxwell Anderson, Robert Sherwood, Lillian Hellman, Elmer Rice, S.N. Behrman, William Saroyan – almost all of whom were noted as intellectual and politically provocative writers – not one met with anywhere near his or her previous success; none produced a hit play or lasting contribution to dramatic literature in the postwar years. Only Eugene O'Neill among the prewar playwrights achieved postwar success and this came in posthumous premieres and revivals such as *Long Day's Journey into Night*, *A Touch of the Poet*, and *A Moon for the Misbegotten*, after years of artistic eclipse. In the musical theatre, only Cole Porter equaled his prewar success with the 1948 *Kiss Me, Kate*. The public seemed to demand fresh voices for what was intuitively understood as a new era.

Arthur Miller was the only new playwright to attempt a theatre of ideas – somewhat in the tradition of Ibsen – and to confront contemporary politics. *The Crucible* (1953), about the Salem witch trials, was a thinly veiled attack upon McCarthyism, and *A View from the Bridge* (1955), which dealt with the struggle between self-interest and self-sacrifice as well as codes of honor, could be seen as a reflection of the moral dilemma of the times. But the majority of serious theatre moved toward psychological explorations. So prevalent was Freudianism and to a lesser degree Jungian psychology, that a book entitled *Freud on Broadway* was published which provided Freudian underpinnings for much of the modern American theatre.[2] The fascination with Freudian psychology and psychotherapy in the postwar years might have pushed the theatre toward psychological explorations of the individual in any case, but the proscription against political theatre hastened the shift in emphasis.

Off-Broadway

One response to the decline of the theatre was the emergence of Off-Broadway. In *The Best Plays of 1934–1935*, critic–editor Burns Mantle inaugurated a new category for revivals, classics, new plays, and even puppet and children's theatre performed in New York but outside the mainstream theatres of the Broadway district. He termed this "Off Broadway." But the popular conception of Off-Broadway as an artistic alternative to the commercial theatre predates the thirties. In a sense its roots can be traced to the late-nineteenth-century art theatres of Europe such as Théâtre Libre, the Freie Bühne, and even the Moscow Art Theatre, and to the so-called "little theatres" in the United States from the teens and twenties, such as the Washington Square Players, Provincetown Players, the Neighborhood Playhouse, and Civic Repertory Theatre, to the Group Theatre and the Federal Theatre Project in the thirties. In most cases the founders of these companies were discontented with the aesthetics of the mainstream and wished to explore and develop foreign plays, new approaches to American playwriting, and even new styles of acting in the less restrictive contexts of experimental theatres, which invariably had more intimate physical surroundings, fewer formal demands on production, and far less economic risk. Still, while the participants in these ventures saw themselves as challenging accepted practices and mainstream preconceptions, they rarely saw themselves as oppositional outsiders. In most cases the alternative became absorbed into the mainstream. The Washington Square Players, for example, became the Theatre Guild, which became a major producing organization on Broadway; Eugene O'Neill, first produced by the Provincetown Players, did not remain on the fringes for long; and the Group Theatre of the thirties produced the actors and directors of both Hollywood and New York for the forties and fifties. (See Volume 2, Chapter 4 for more discussion of the groups mentioned above.)

In the late forties it seemed as if history would repeat itself as an alternative theatre emerged once again. This time, however, most of the members of this new Off-Broadway movement were not rebelling so much against the aesthetics of Broadway as against the restrictive nature of its economically driven production structure. In a world of diminished opportunities and economic high risk, serious drama, experimental theatre, and unknown and untried playwrights found little welcome in the mainstream. Off-Broadway arose to take up the slack. But instead of being absorbed into the mainstream after a decade or so as its predecessor movements had been, Off- Broadway became a shadow Broadway, as it were – a movement that ultimately replaced Broadway's function as a producer of serious drama. The result therefore was not so much an alteration of Broadway aesthetics as a permanent shift in the production landscape and geography of New York theatre. (See Gussow, Chapter 2, "Off- and Off-Off Broadway.")

The population of theatre practitioners in the late forties was being fed by servicemen returning from the war, and a new phenomenon: graduates of college-based theatre training programs. Though still a limited factor in the forties, the college and university theatre that had begun in the first decades of the century with courses at Harvard, Yale, Columbia, and the Carnegie Institute of Technology (now Carnegie–Mellon), grew at astounding rates in the postwar years. By the nineties there were over 1,500 full-fledged theatre departments, and over 2,500 colleges and universities offering courses and mounting productions. Some of the most elaborate physical structures at many colleges and universities are state-of-the-art theatres housing lavish productions of a wide range of classics, modern, and original plays; in some communities they provide the only live theatre. But the professional theatres cannot absorb the great numbers of students coming out of the academic training programs, even the relatively small percentage who are well-trained and talented, so the vast majority of university-trained theatre artists wind up teaching in the academic theatre, which, therefore, becomes a self-perpetuating training ground. Commentators on the state of the arts in the United States sometimes bemoan the paucity of theatres per capita and the low percentage of theatregoing within the general population in comparison to most other developed countries. But if one adds the academic theatres to the total, then there may be more theatrical production in the United States than anywhere else in the world. Yet the rift between academic and professional theatre in many instances is great and the crossover from one to the other is minimal.

Since Broadway could no longer absorb these newcomers as it once might have, Off-Broadway became a home for young artists seeking a means of entry into the mainstream. For many, Off-Broadway was a way station, a place to become known before moving on to Broadway or, increasingly, on to Hollywood.

Two theatres that had been active Off-Broadway spaces since the twenties, the Cherry Lane and the Provincetown, along with some recital halls and non-traditional spaces, became home for the new Off-Broadway movement, and by 1949 seven groups were operating on a regular basis. In the face of pressure from Actors' Equity Association, the union of professional actors, five companies banded together to form the Off-Broadway Theatre League, which negotiated a contract with Equity. Off-Broadway theatres were limited by this contract to no more than 300 seats (there were separate contracts for 200-to-299-seat houses and those 199 and less), and outside the area bounded by Fifth and Ninth Avenues on the east and west, and Thirty-fourth and Fifty-sixth

Streets on the south and north. Although a 1972 history of Off-Broadway could describe it as "a state of mind, a set of production conditions, a way of looking at theater at every point at odds with Broadway's patterns" (Little, *Off-Broadway*, 13–14), it was really none of those things. Off-Broadway was a contractual and economic institution. Theodore Mann, a co-founder of the Circle in the Square, said, "We had no great standards, no great ideas. We simply loved the stage and we wanted a place where we could work." Director José Quintero, another founder, said simply, "The main difference between Broadway and Off-Broadway is economical" (Mann and Quintero quoted in Poggi, *Theater in America*, 173–74).

The Circle in the Square, founded by Quintero and Mann in a defunct night-club in Greenwich Village, opened in 1951 with *Dark of the Moon*. The innovative thrust stage – a long narrow stage surrounded on three sides by the audience – was not a factor of scenographic choice but of necessity; the producers had to work with the existing space. Yet it established Off-Broadway as a place for alternative approaches to stagecraft. In 1952, Quintero directed a revival of Tennessee Williams's *Summer and Smoke* that had failed in its initial Broadway run in 1948. It became a huge success downtown and established Quintero's reputation as a director, made a star of Geraldine Page, and launched the Circle in the Square as the paradigm of the Off-Broadway theatre. Other similar groups followed. The repertoire was comprised largely of those shows overlooked or mishandled by Broadway, including plays of Williams and O'Neill, and the more recent wave of European authors such as Genet, Sartre, and Beckett. Broadway, especially a Broadway geared toward light entertainment and hit shows and the largest possible audience within a shrinking pool, was ill-equipped to tackle the darker, more intimate, structurally and stylistically more complex plays emerging in the postwar era. The fact that movies and television had usurped the psychological drama for themselves altered spectator perceptions; audiences had become accustomed to a certain intimacy in this genre – the facial closeup cannot be duplicated in a 1,000- or 1,500-seat theatre. The intimate surroundings of an Off-Broadway theatre proved ideal for the psychological and emotional intensity of many of the plays. Whatever factors had contributed to the failure of *Summer and Smoke* on Broadway, it was clear that the unique spatial arrangement of the Circle in the Square contributed significantly to its Off-Broadway success.

But the Off-Broadway plays were not fundamentally different from what had been produced on Broadway in previous generations and it quickly became economically and structurally like Broadway – a place for the production of individual shows with artistic personnel hired by a producer on a per show basis, that would run as long as there were ticket-buying patrons. The cheaper costs (in part because of lower rents and freedom from union stage crews) and the more exotic surroundings were all that separated it from Broadway. By way of comparison, the average cost for mounting a straight play Off-Broadway in 1965 was $15,000 to $20,000. On Broadway the cost was approximately $100,000 to $110,000. Weekly operating costs for the same period averaged $2,500 for Off-Broadway and $20,000 for Broadway. An Off-Broadway musical cost in the neighborhood of $40,000, while the Broadway equivalent was $500,000. By the late nineties a Broadway musical spectacle could cost anywhere from $10,000,000 to $20,000,000, requiring multiple producers and corporate sponsorship.

Nonetheless, the audiences and artists coming of age in the postwar era saw in the revivals, classics, European plays, and new works of Off-Broadway a challenge to the increasingly banal world of the Broadway stage. The fact that "serious art" was now presented predominantly in one class of theatres, while entertainment was reserved for another, began a precipitous slide toward the ghettoization of theatre. Instead of a more or less homogeneous audience, there were increasingly separate constituencies; a two-tiered system of art had emerged in which each side saw the other as irrelevant and a threat to societal sensibilities. By the seventies this rift had multiplied into a variety of discrete, often mutually exclusive types of theatres frequently based on identity politics. There were theatres for African Americans, gays, Latinos, women, and numerous others, and even these groups were subdivided into varying political and social points of view. (See Carlson, Chapter 2, "Alternative Theatre".) The audience for one theatre generally did not attend the others, and they often openly despised and berated the mainstream and occasionally each other, as demonstrated in this 1968 statement by Teatro Campesino founder Luis Valdez. Noting that the world of mainstream theatre had nothing to do with his life or the society he knew, he proclaimed: "Who responds to Tennessee Williams or Arthur Miller picking his liver apart? You can't respond to that shit" (quoted in Schevill, *Break Out!*, 12). Much of the function of prewar Broadway, that is, the production of new dramas and classical revivals for a largely white, middle-class audience, moved to the resident professional theatres around the country until, by the nineties, the so-called regional theatres had largely supplanted the older theatrical institution of "the Road." Broadway became a place for splashy musicals, theatrical "events," and a few dramas that had first proved themselves outside New York. New drama was virtually confined to Off-Broadway.

Despite the long-range implications, there was a vitality to the Off-Broadway theatre of the fifties and early sixties. The number of new productions peaked in 1961–62 at 125 plus 20 holdovers from the previous season. When added to the 73 productions that played on Broadway that year (53 new and 20 continuing) plus the beginnings of Off-Off Broadway, the figures begin to rival the best years of the twenties. But they did so under significantly different circumstances. Except for Broadway, of course, these were not productions playing in 1,000-seat theatres for long runs; the majority were productions in small venues playing to audiences of 299 or fewer for a limited time. (In fairness, it should be noted that the majority of the 264 productions that opened in the 1927–28 season closed after brief runs, though with less serious financial implications than today.) Commenting in early 1998 on the inability of much drama to attract a sustainable audience, playwright and librettist Peter Stone suggested, somewhat facetiously, that "there is no shortage of good plays; what Broadway is suffering from is a shortage of good audiences."[3] From a statistical point of view this is essentially true. The total number of new productions in New York – considering all venues – has not significantly changed since World War I; but the audience has shrunk greatly.

Disaffection and Loss

In the years after World War II, American drama seemed to become totally preoccupied with the individual's struggle against society, often played out in the microcosm of some domestic or familial setting. Through the fifties, the most remarkable playwright of personal angst continued to be Tennessee Williams. His characters were the outcasts of society, possessed by some internal demons, and searching for human contact and understanding. And while the locale and provenance of these characters were often exotic (frequently the gothic South), the inner spirituality of the characters nonetheless appealed to Broadway audiences of the time. But the playwright who best succeeded in melding poetic realism with gritty American naturalism was William Inge, whose four major works, *Come Back, Little Sheba*, *Picnic*, *Bus Stop*, and *The Dark at the Top of the Stairs*, virtually spanned the fifties. As *New York Times* theatre critic Brooks Atkinson described Inge's plays, they were "dramas about the private dilemmas of obscure people" (*Broadway*, 434).

Significantly, Inge set his plays in the small towns and waysides of middle America. Although theatre is a decidedly urban activity – both its creation and production are inextricably intertwined with the energetic creative ferment of the city, and its success as a commercial operation depends upon a critical mass of sophisticated theatregoers – playwrights in the postwar era looked to rural and middle America much as Rousseau looked to the exotic new world. In this land, away from the corrupting influence and inhumanity of the cities, could be found either a lost innocence from the American past or the fragile remnants of a simpler world that was in danger of disappearing.

The St. Louis of *The Glass Menagerie* was a decaying industrial city seen through the fire escapes of an alley. New Orleans, the site of Williams's next play, *A Streetcar Named Desire*, is the least American of all US cities, made even more ethereal in Williams's vision. His subsequent plays through the fifties were set in the rural South or in fantastic, theatrical landscapes. Even though Arthur Miller's *Death of a Salesman*, the most classic play of this genre, was set in Brooklyn, there is a literal dialectic between the pastoral environs of the house as seen in Willy Loman's memories and the intrusion of high-rise apartments symbolizing the faceless urban milieu. Willy Loman became a symbol of the forgotten little man who is a victim of the materialism of the society as well as a victim of his own personal mistakes and agonies. A barely suppressed sexuality seethed just beneath the surface in these plays – it was significant that Marilyn Monroe played in the movie version of *Bus Stop* – that was both a harbinger of and a catalyst for the sexual revolution of the next decade. Because many of these plays became successful movies the ideas spread well beyond Broadway.

Ironically, in the aftermath of victory in which the United States emerged as the richest and most powerful nation in history, there was an apparent sense of emptiness and loss gnawing at the hearts of these playwrights. The United States experienced none of the physical destruction of Europe and Asia, and the human loss, though significant, paled in comparison to that suffered by the other participants. What the playwrights experienced instead was a loss of an American sensibility and mythos. Characters in these plays seemed confused in an increasingly baffling world in which the rules, mores, and even material objects were no longer comprehensible or negotiable.

The ideas of Existentialism and in particular the writings of Albert Camus were not yet available in English when Williams began writing – he was mirroring an unnamed sense of disaffection in the society – but as Camus's work became known (*The Stranger* was published in English in 1946, *The Plague* in 1948, though two significant essays, *The Rebel* and *The Myth of Sisyphus* were not available in English until 1953 and 1955, respectively) they became touchstones for a generation coming of age and seeking direction in the postwar years. And if the philosophical implications were not always fully understood, the sense of the meaninglessness of the universe and the consequent alienation of the individual certainly sunk in. While Existential philosophy informed the development of Absurdist drama in France and elsewhere in Europe, Americans grasped onto the superficial form and style of alienation and recreated the Existential hero in the Hollywood image, first with Marlon Brando in *The Wild One* (1953) and then James Dean in *Rebel without a Cause* (1955).

In *The Wild One*, Brando and his motorcycle gang swarm over the countryside, descending upon and terrorizing a small town. It is the nightmare version of *Our Town*: idyllic tranquility is shattered not by the rhythms of life and death but by random and meaningless acts of "an ugly, debauched and frightening . . . element of modern youth." [4] When asked by a local teenage girl what he is rebelling against, Brando snarls back the classic answer, "Whadda ya got?" Enshrined as a poster, the representation of a black-leather-clad Brando sneering from his Harley became a classic image of the fifties. The mantle of alienated youth was then assumed by James Dean, who with the collar up on his leather jacket and slicked-back hair created the "look" for a generation of rebellious teenagers in the aptly titled *Rebel without a Cause*. Future cultural icons from Bob Dylan to Jean-Paul Belmondo imitated the Dean look and style. Unlike Brando's character, who is an outsider, the characters of this film are part of the affluent society – it is set in wealthy suburban Los Angeles, all the teens have cars, and material wealth is everywhere. Dean plays a rebel against parental and societal authority, though for no clearly articulated reason. It would be a mistake to read too deeply into the film by Nicholas Ray – societal power ultimately kills the outcast (Sal Mineo) and Dean seemingly welcomes the re-establishment of paternal authority in the household. Dean's death in a high-speed auto accident three weeks before the release of the film helped escalate him to cult status and secure his mythological place. It seemed all of a piece: rebellion for rebellion's sake, rejection of authority, and living fast were established as ideals for a younger generation seeking identity and purpose. Most significantly, this was achieved through image and form – content was secondary if it existed at all.

The other significant factor, of course, was that a generational identity and credo were being created on the screen. While the actors had theatrical training and sometimes, as with Brando, theatrical experience, the theatre was neither the source nor the locus for this sullen exploration of disaffection, although the attitude pervaded much of the serious drama of the fifties.

Along with the slouched stance, the hooded eyes, and the upper lip curled into a sneer, the youthful image of disaffection was also identified with a slurred and mumbling style of speech. First popularized by Brando, it became associated with The Actors Studio approach. It was in stark opposition to proper stage diction but it was also in opposition to the proscriptions of proper societal behavior. To speak badly was to defy authority – parents, teachers, etiquette arbiters. It also suggested a distrust of eloquence; leaders on both sides of World War II after all had been compelling, even mesmerizing orators. But monosyllabic inarticulateness was merely a surface manifestation of a decades-long dramatic development. Characters were losing control of language; language as a means of communication evaporated and characters were increasingly unable to express ideas effectively or to talk to each other in meaningful ways. Characters in these plays became trapped in semantics, in situations in which the language itself seemed more important than the ideas it conveyed, or the words took on a life independent of the objects they represented. The erosion of language as a means of communication can be traced to the avant-garde movements in Europe at the turn of the century and most notably to the Dadaists, who divorced words from their referents and objects from meaning. This sense of language as a game reached a peak in the Absurdist movement in the fifties, particularly in the plays of Eugène Ionesco and Samuel Beckett. Whereas Absurdism in Europe seemed a logical, almost inevitable response to the irrationality of war, the analogous elements that surfaced in American drama seemed more a response to a materialist society run amok. The American-style Absurdism seemed to spring full-blown out of television advertisements and situation comedies, which had become new myth-making machines.

This breakdown of language was already implicit in *Death of a Salesman* and some of Williams's plays; it became explicit in the plays of Edward Albee. Albee burst onto the scene in 1960 with Off-Broadway productions of four one-act plays, *The Zoo Story*, *The Death of Bessie Smith*, *The Sandbox*, and *An American Dream*. The latter two in particular seemed to be directly influenced by the French Absurdists with their archetypal characters, symbolic plots, and eerily simplistic language. While Albee denied any knowledge of, let alone influence from the movement at the time of writing them, and attacked those who attempted to pigeonhole his style of writing, he clearly had an appreciation for the work of Genet, Beckett, and Ionesco, as evidenced in a 1962 essay in the *New York Times Magazine*. In a wry stab at his critics he remarked that he had always assumed that the appellation "absurdist theatre" referred to Broadway where "a 'good' play is one that makes money; a 'bad' play . . . is one which does not" ("Which Theatre is the Absurd One?," 146). His one-acts were followed two years later with the landmark Broadway production of *Who's Afraid of Virginia Woolf?*, a devastating critique of the American family and, by implication, American society. In a long, emotionally brutal night the protagonists George and Martha verbally attack and destroy each other and their two guests while shattering the illusions that have allowed them to function for two decades. In the best of Albee's plays there is a sense of anger and alienation as he meticulously dissects and skewers societal institutions, especially marriage and the family. The dominant, though not always triumphant, characters are ones who possess the greatest command of language, not unlike characters in a Restoration comedy of manners. In *Zoo Story*, the character Jerry literally commandeers the stage with an assault of language. Martha, in *Virginia Woolf*, bursts upon the stage with a Bette Davis quote which leads to a long night's journey of etymological gamesmanship and the revelation of a child who exists only as a verbal construct. The losers in such games, such as Nick and Honey in *Virginia Woolf*, are those for whom language is literal and pedestrian and who cannot fathom the subtexts of speech or the illusions that language can create.

American Absurdism reached its peak in Arthur Kopit's *Oh Dad, Poor Dad, Mamma's Hung You in the Closet and I'm Feelin' So Sad*, that had its New York premiere in 1962, the same year as *Virginia Woolf*. The same dysfunctional familial relations and damaged psyches explored by Williams and Inge with a kind of poetic reverence are presented to the world in this play as something so bizarre and grotesque they can only be laughed at. With Kopit's play, postwar alienation crossed a line into a territory that announced a kind of emotional disengagement and an unwillingness or inability to come to terms with such deep-seated trauma.

The Beats, Avant-Garde, and Rock'n'Roll

Perhaps the deepest embodiment of the spirit of disaffection and one of the strongest forces in the shaping of an American aesthetic for the fifties were the Beat writers. Best known today for Allen Ginsberg's poetry and Jack Kerouac's *On the Road* (1957), the Beat poets and novelists transformed language into a musical force that in its very rhythms and structures were an attack upon the mainstream culture of the period. Turning to the everyday – often the gritty and vulgar – for their subject matter, they moved art, literature, and theatre out of cultural institutions and into the locales of real life. Of great importance for the theatre was the emphasis on the performative. Their poetry was meant to be read aloud and the use of body and voice in delivery was as significant as the words themselves. Anticipating the performance artists of the seventies and eighties, the Beats saw all aspects of life as a kind of theatre, and the routines of daily life melded with the creation and performance of their art. Their use of bars, coffeehouses, church basements, and apartments as galleries, recital halls, and performance spaces paved the way for the venues of Off- and Off-Off Broadway. Their willingness to abandon conventional dramatic structure and their demonstration of the potential power of the raw language of the post-Atomic age provided a way for a new generation of playwrights and theatre artists to re-envision theatre.

The Beats trace their origin to the early forties when William Burroughs, Allen Ginsberg, Jack Kerouac, and others met at Columbia University. The term itself was picked up from Times Square hustler Herbert Huncke, though its interpretation varied from artist to artist and evolved over time. Sometimes called American Existentialists, the Beats associated themselves with the new jazz of Charlie Parker, the action painting of Jackson Pollock, and even the acting of Marlon Brando. In all cases the creative process tended to take precedent over the final product, which was devoid of conventional structures. The closer the product was to life (and the further from the accepted conventions of art) the better. Their life style was inseparable from their writing and they rejected not only the strictures of artistic convention but the constrictions of polite society. They reveled in the low-life, living in peripheral neighborhoods, frequenting seedy bars, rejecting material possessions, hitch-hiking across the country, and descending in many cases into alcoholism and drug addiction. But though they preceded the causeless rebels and seemed to possess some of the gratuitous spirit of disaffection, they were actually committed to the creation of a more humane world. Their writings were rarely political in the sense of agit props, but they bemoaned the suburban, materialist society and the threat of nuclear holocaust. Ginsberg, looking back on the era from the vantage of the nineties, catalogued the effects and influences of the Beats:

> Spiritual liberation, sexual "revolution" or "liberation" . . . / Liberation of the word from censorship . . . / The evolution of rhythm and blues into rock and roll as a high art form . . . / The spread of ecological consciousness . . . / Opposition to the military-industrial machine . . . / Return to an appreciation of idiosyncrasy as against state regimentation. / Respect for land and indigenous peoples and creatures.[5]

The liberation of the word had a double meaning. On the one hand it meant freeing language so that no word could be censored. So-called "dirty" words were as usable – and "beautiful" – to the Beats in poetry and prose as those allowed in polite conversation. This transformation of language had an effect on the "Free Speech" movement that erupted at the University of California at Berkeley in 1964, which in turn led to a redefinition of what could be said on the stage, in films, and on television, and what could be printed in newspapers and magazines. Though the works of the Beats themselves were the subject of censorship, their attacks upon the restrictions of language and subject matter were a factor in the Supreme Court battles over the American publications of *Lady Chatterley's Lover, Ulysses,* and the novels of Henry Miller. Everything from *Who's Afraid of Virginia Woolf?* to *Hair* to "Saturday Night Live" to *Angels in America* was indebted in some degree to the Beats. The liberation of language also meant a freeing from the rules of grammar and usage. Some Beat poetry took the form of concrete poetry whose meaning was bound up in its graphic form on the page, but it also took the form of performance – poetry whose meaning was complete only in live readings that often expanded into theatrical performances. Poet Diane DiPrima and her husband Alan Marlowe created the New York Poets Theatre that produced works by several leading poets. Some of the writers of this period – Frank O'Hara, Kenneth Koch, Jackson MacLow, for example – turned out a small body of dramatic work (and Koch continues to write plays). The onomatopoeic and rhythmic language and the often whimsical or bizarre imagery of many of these works limited their appeal, although there were some minor Off- and Off-Off Broadway successes, the most notable being Michael McClure's *The Beard* (1967). This play, which was first performed in San Francisco, achieved notoriety not for its poetry but for its then scandalous outpouring of expletives and the simulated act of cunnilingus. Somewhat like the nineteenth-century Romantic poets who also wrote plays, the drama of the Beat poets remained poetry even though encased in a dramatic structure.

Many of the same forces and ideas that served as foundation for the Beats also led to the development of a true avant-garde theatre in the United States. The term avant-garde has often been applied colloquially to anything new or unusual, but in theatre it more accurately reflects a genre that energetically rejects what theorist Michael Kirby called an "information structure,"[6] that is a work of art in which logical bits of information are sequentially presented to an audience and the understanding of the work depends upon the accumulation and decoding of this information. Typically this involves narrative (Aristotle's privileging of plot), and such elements as theme and character bolstered by the performative components of theatre such as set design, costume, props, sound, et cetera. Such a structure requires of the audience Coleridge's "willing suspension of disbelief" because it establishes a substitutional world on the stage that exists separately from the world of the spectator. Whether as a result of the war or the ever present threat of nuclear annihilation, many artists were pushed to extremes and created innovative and original work. Only the Dada and Futurist painters and poets earlier in the century had so completely and so successfully broken out of classical and conventional forms and structures. Form and object, cause and effect were sundered; Aristotelian structure was abandoned. Allan Kaprow summed up the innovations of "action painting" in his posthumous appreciation of Jackson Pollock, but it applies equally to experiments in theatre:

> Form. In order to follow it, it is necessary to get rid of the usual idea of "Form," i.e. a beginning, middle and end, or any variant of this principle – such as fragmentation. You do not enter a painting of Pollock's in any one place (or hundred places). Anywhere is everywhere and you can dip in and out when and where you can. This has led to remarks that his art gives one the impression of going on forever – a true insight. It indicates that the confines of the rectangular field were ignored in lieu of an experience of a continuum going in all directions simultaneously, *beyond* the literal dimensions of any work. ("The Legacy of Jackson Pollock," 26)

The narrative structure and psychologically based characters that had dominated virtually all Western theatre would be abandoned in favor of a theatre of sound, movement, form, and object that could be seen, on various levels, as an extension of the everyday world, in which – to quote Kaprow on Pollock once more – "the artist, the spectator and the outer world are . . . interchangeably involved" (26). Decorum in language and diction was also abandoned and what Allen Ginsberg called the "vernacular, idiomatic, rhythmic . . . cadences of actual talk . . . the actual spontaneous mind of the moment,"[7] began to replace the carefully crafted dialogue of stage speech. This technique borrowed from jazz and opened the door for non-speech sounds and music-like speech within stage performance.

The avant-garde entered the world of theatre through the world of art and music. Composer John Cage, through his study of Zen Buddhism, became fascinated with chance and indeterminacy as methods of composition and performance. In this way, Cage could not impose a particular aesthetic viewpoint in composing music – he would not choose a note simply because he liked the sound of it. Cage also believed that an individual sound was neither musical nor non-musical; thus, anything that produced sound was music, and since there was no such thing as absolute silence (even in an anechoic chamber, he discovered, you could hear the sounds of your own body, such as the hum of the nervous system or the coursing of blood), music was potentially everywhere. Cage felt his function as a composer was to create structures whereby a listener could hear sounds in a new way. Not surprisingly, Cage's compositions were seldom "popular," but the impact of his ideas on the performing arts was profound. On the one hand, they led to the removal of barriers among the different art forms, such as theatre, dance, and music (barriers that were largely peculiar to Western performance), and on the other they provided alternative structures for composition in a range of performing and plastic arts that removed them from Aristotelian or narrative or informational constructs.

1952 might serve as a reasonable date for the emergence of an American avant-garde theatre. In that year, at the experimental Black Mountain College in North Carolina, John Cage, choreographer Merce Cunningham, and painter Robert Rauschenberg created "Theatre Piece," a performance that involved a series of discrete actions selected by chance methods and performed interdeterminately by the performers within a given time structure. It was music, dance, poetry, and theatre all at once, though unlike any of these genres in any conventional sense. Many see it as the prototype of the Happening. In 1956 Cage taught a course in composition at the New School for Social Research in New York, a class taken by Allan Kaprow and several artists who would be instrumental in the development of Happenings and other forms of avant-garde theatre.

18 Happenings in 6 Parts emerged from Kaprow's interests in environmental sculpture, action painting, collage, and performance. The performance took place in the Reuben Gallery, an art gallery on Fourth Avenue. Within the space three contiguous rooms had been constructed of translucent plastic. Folding chairs were arranged in differing configurations in each room, and the space was illuminated by rows of red and white bulbs. There were other objects and decorative elements within the spaces. Spectators were given cards which instructed them to move to different spaces at the sound of a bell signaling the end of each part. The performance consisted of sounds, lights, and various actions by six performers. There was no apparent logic or meaning behind the sounds, images, and activities; the performers did not assume "characters" in the standard theatrical sense; and there was no discernible plot. Yet despite the name "Happening," which Kaprow came to regret because of its implications of spontaneity and frivolousness, this event was carefully rehearsed and highly structured, yet enigmatic. Though Happenings were a short-lived phenomenon, they had the effect of stripping away all preconceptions of Western drama, crossing boundaries among theatre, plastic arts, music, and dance, and creating a performance based on formal structures rather than narrative information.

In his landmark book *Happenings*, Michael Kirby traced the historical roots of Happenings and came up with the most complete and useful definition of the form: "a purposefully composed form of theatre in which diverse alogical elements, including non-matrixed performing, are organized in a compartmented structure" (22). Kirby defined "non-matrixed" performances as those that are not contextualized by fictive elements such as place, time, or character; "compartmented structure" refers to one in which no information necessarily carries from segment to segment so that in this sense, at least, the elements could be rearranged without loss of information. While the term Happening grew into a popular epithet for any loosely structured and unusual event, with suggestions of anarchy and improvisation, in its original form it provided the roots of the formalist avant-garde in the theatre, bringing a modernist sensibility to the cultural scene and even laying the groundwork for the postmodernism of the eighties.

The avant-garde movement in the United States is inextricably bound up with the Living Theatre, founded by Julian Beck and Judith Malina in 1948 and whose first performance was in 1951 in the living room of their Upper West Side apartment. While their initial theatrical endeavors were inevitably based upon existing theatrical models, their increasing frustration with the aesthetics of mainstream American playwriting and theatrical production led them in new directions. In a 1962 diary entry, Beck lambasted the world of commercial theatre:

> I do not like the Broadway theatre because it does not know how to say hello. The tone of voice is false, the mannerisms are false, the sex is false, ideal, the Hollywood world of perfection, the clean image, the well pressed

clothes, the well scrubbed anus, odorless, inhuman, of the Hollywood actor, the Broadway star. And the terrible false dirt of Broadway, the lower depths in which the dirt is imitated, inaccurate. (*The Life of the Theatre*, 7)

Even within the alternative world of Off-Broadway the Living Theatre operated on the fringes. Closer in aesthetics to the Beat poets and the Abstract Expressionist painters than to their contemporaries in the theatre, they sought out texts that eschewed narrative and challenged traditional dramatic structures. In the first years their repertoire consisted of verse dramas and a veritable who's who of the anti-establishment European and American literary avant-garde: Paul Goodman, Gertrude Stein, Federico García Lorca, Bertolt Brecht, Kenneth Rexroth, Pablo Picasso, T.S. Eliot, John Ashbery, W.H. Auden, August Strindberg, Jean Cocteau, Luigi Pirandello, William Carlos Williams, Jack Gelber, Jackson MacLow, Ezra Pound, and Kenneth Brown. By moving out of traditional theatre spaces – they presented one season at the venerable Off-Broadway Cherry Lane Theatre but then worked in lofts – they thwarted the expectations of the audience; habitual viewing patterns were disrupted as the conventions of theatregoing were undermined. By abandoning the slickness of commercial production they shifted the focus onto the text through a spare and raw emotional and visual style. A new kind of realism emerged from the use of "real" spaces and a more prosaic, pedestrian style of acting that depended for its success on its connection with the emotions of the spectators.

In the work of the Living Theatre, in Happenings, and ultimately in much experimental theatre of the sixties and after, literary theatre was rejected in favor of theatre that depended as much on production as on text and whose meaning was complete only in the performance. The value of the Living Theatre, furthermore, was in its position at the cross-section of the Beat literature, modern art, and the prewar European avant-garde, particularly the ideas of Antonin Artaud. French composer and conductor Pierre Boulez had introduced John Cage to the writings of Artaud. Cage, in turn, gave these to a colleague at Black Mountain College, Mary Caroline Richards, who translated *The Theatre and Its Double*. While working on the manuscript she sent a draft to Malina and Beck, who saw in Artaud's work a similar spirit to their own.

The Living Theatre's 1959 production of Jack Gelber's *The Connection* was seen at the time as a startling breakthrough into new realms of theatre. The play centers about the activities of a group of junkies and musicians who await a delivery of heroin in the first act, and then get high in the second act. Gelber framed the action by the conceit of two filmmakers documenting the action – claiming that the characters were recruited for a documentary on the drug culture and the jazz world. Many in the audience accepted the ruse and saw the play not as drama but as "real" people simply placed on a stage. The actors addressed the audience directly at times; during intermission at least one of the actors was panhandling in the lobby; many of the performers were, in fact, real musicians who played a jazz score as part of the performance. Critic Robert Brustein defined the significance of the play at the time:

> Constantly tripping over the boundary between life and art, stripped of all significant form, antagonistic to any theory or morality which does not accord with practice, *The Connection* is probably not a "good" play by any standard we now possess to judge such things; but it forms the basis for a brilliant theatrical occasion and it lives in that pure, bright, thin air of reality which few of our "good" playwrights have ever dared to breathe.[8]

Despite its innovations, however, the play was in many respects the culmination of Naturalism. Finally, here was a production so realistic that many in the audience failed to identify it as a piece of theatre and mistook the actors and actions as "a slice of life." Consequently, the Living Theatre felt that it no longer wished to pursue this direction; tricking the audience was antithetical to its aims. Rather, theatre should make the audience confront the real world through conscious decision-making. This would set the Living Theatre performers on a more Brechtian path toward presenting themselves not as characters but as themselves, and the theatre not as illusion but as a frank and open theatrical event. It also meshed with their passionate commitment to social ideas and an anarchist philosophy for political revolution. In 1964, in the wake of convictions for violation of income tax regulations, the Living Theatre went into a self-imposed exile in Europe, where they were greeted with enthusiasm.

One other contributing factor to the development of the avant-garde was the debut of the *Tulane Drama Review* in 1955,[9] which provided the means for the dissemination of ideas. Edited at first by Robert Corrigan, and then by Richard Schechner, *TDR*, as it was known, quickly supplanted the moribund *Theatre Arts Monthly*, which had been the primary source of theatre news for over three decades. The journal became a magnet for almost all theatre practitioners and scholars searching for new approaches to theatre. In its first few years, *TDR* focused primarily on new plays and theoretical ideas from Europe, and virtually every major European playwright and theoretician of the postwar years was first introduced to American theatre artists in its pages. Over the years it acquainted American readers with de Ghelderode, Sartre, Dürrenmatt, the Absurdists, Artaud, Brecht, Grotowski, Happenings, Cage, the Living Theatre, the Open Theatre, and even a re-evaluation of Stanislavsky. Under the editorship of Michael Kirby in the seventies it was a significant force in the rediscovery of Futurism, Dadaism, Symbolism, and the Russian avant-garde. It would ultimately champion and influence the work of Richard Foreman, Robert Wilson, Meredith Monk, Post-Modern Dance, the Performance and Wooster Groups, and the early performance artists, among others. During the peak years of avant-garde and experimental theatre, in the sixties and seventies, *The Drama Review* was virtually alone in its reportage and analysis. By the eighties, as the avant-garde was inevitably losing much of its initial energy, a host of new journals was spawned which focused on new performance and performance theory. Thus, instead of one or two major journals fostering an exchange of information and ideas, there developed numerous small journals with circulations of a few hundred to a few thousand, catering to very narrow fields of interest or points of view. The possibilities for the cross-fertilization of ideas were, ironically, greatly diminished.

The disintegration and transformation of language also owed much to the development of rock'n'roll (whose effects upon the theatre would begin to be felt most strongly in the Off-Off Broadway of the mid-sixties when the generation raised on rock began to create theatre). Rock'n'roll exploded on the scene in 1956 (the same year as Ginsberg's *Howl*). The immediate roots of the music can be traced to the rhythm and blues of the forties, although the real roots go back to African call and response music brought over by slaves, minstrel songs, Irish and Scottish ballads and jigs, jazz, blues, and country and western. The term "rock'n'roll" was supposedly coined by Cleveland disk jockey Alan Freed in 1951, although it had been in African American slang for much longer. Bill Haley's "Rock Around the Clock" became the first big rock-'n'roll hit in 1955, popularized by the movie *The Blackboard Jungle*. In that same year, Elvis Presley topped the country and western charts, while Chuck Berry and Fats Domino reached the top of the rhythm and blues charts. In 1956, however, the major rock'n'roll artists would cross over to dominate the pop charts: Presley released "Heartbreak Hotel," "Hound Dog," and "Love Me Tender," Little Richard had "Tutti Frutti" and three other top forty hits, and Berry and Domino moved from the rhythm and blues charts to the more broadly based pop charts as well. The appearance of Presley on the *Ed Sullivan Show* in the fall of 1956 transformed American popular culture in one evening.

Almost overnight, the arbiters of popular taste had shifted from the middle-aged middle class, to rebellious white youth drawing on black-inspired music that was raucous, raw, and pulsating with a barely concealed sexual energy. The language of rock'n'roll was usually simplistic and, even with the the three-to three-and-a-half-minute format of most songs, repetitive. But the language of the songs relied on nonsensical syllables, grunts, half-articulated and distorted words, and sounds that functioned more as percussion and rhythm than as communicative vocabulary. The Brando *cum* Kowalski mumble had become attached to a new music to become the emotional cry of a generation. Rationalism became as irrelevant as a need for a specific agenda for rebellion. While historically, nonsensical choruses could be traced back to Aristophanes' *The Frogs* and were common in popular song from medieval madrigals to modern times, the use of rhythmic choruses in rock music were foregrounded and became the essence of the song. The message seemed to be that proper language was insufficient, it was incapable of communicating the pain, anger, heartbreak, or simple confusion of teenage angst. Any number of rock'n'roll lyrics from the fifties could serve as an example, but it reached a zenith of sorts with the opening lines of the 1957 "Get a Job" by the Silhouettes:

> Sha da da da
> Sha da da da da
> Ba do
> Sha da da da
> Sha da da da da
> Ba do
> Sha da da da
> Sha da da da da
> Ba do
> Sha da da da
> Sha da da da da
> Ba do
> Ba yip yip yip yip yip yip yip yip
> Mum mum mum mum mum mum
> Get a job.

For a generation for whom this was both poetic and meaningful, the conventional language of traditional drama was going to be boring at best and incomprehensible at worst.

The other significant aspect of rock'n'roll was that it created a bridge, however tenuous and complicated, between white and black. It gave black performers entry into a white-controlled entertainment world, opened up a young white generation to new ideas and experiences – all the more dangerous because it was expressed through music and rhythm and therefore could not be combated with rational dialogue.

Broadway's only real acknowledgment of the new music at the time was in the 1960 *Bye Bye Birdie*, which, despite some rock-inflected music, was a sweet-spirited sendup of teenage mania for Elvis Presley. Structurally, it was the standard Broadway book musical. It allowed a baffled generation to smile condescendingly on youthful passions without realizing that the very form of theatre it was watching was being completely undermined by the music being parodied. The musical theatre which for generations had been the fount of American popular music suddenly found itself on the sidelines as popular music was created outside theatrical contexts altogether. The old pop music was transformed into "mood music" – background sound for elevators, restaurants, and supermarkets. As critic Martin Gottfried has observed, "this wordless sound – usually in the form of castrated Kern, Rodgers, Berlin, and Loesser – spread like an antimusical cancer at the very time that rock'n'roll was becoming popular . . . The theater, forgetting it had created the vital popular song of which the 'mood music' was a mockery, now became the slave of such music" (*Broadway Musicals*, 287).

Technology ensured the widespread consumption of the new music. The transistor radio was a low-cost, battery-operated radio that could fit into a large pocket or be easily carried and which also allowed for an earphone. A whole generation was literally plugged into "top 40 radio" as a primary source of culture. Ironically, even the success of rock'n'roll on radio was abetted by television. Presley's first appearance on the *Ed Sullivan Show* attracted the largest television audience to date. In that pre-cable era, when there were only three networks, television still had the ability to set national tastes. Nowhere was this more true than with Sullivan's show, which was essentially a nationally broadcast vaudeville show with a weekly display of everything from classical ballet to pie-plate jugglers. Presley's appearance established the power of television as a mass marketing tool for the rock'n'roll era. Thereafter, every new band needed an appearance on Ed Sullivan for validation. Although Sullivan regularly presented excerpts from Broadway musicals on the show (Rodgers and Hammerstein were guests on the very first broadcast), which could boost ticket sales or guarantee an audience for a soon-to-be-launched road tour, the impact paled in comparison to the hundreds of thousands, even millions of record sales generated by a rock star's appearance. Teenagers with disposable cash in the most prosperous decade of American history became the new consumers of popular culture. The baby-boom generation rejected the music and lyrics of a dying Broadway musical theatre for rock'n'roll. (It is telling that the cast album of *Hello, Dolly!* was knocked out of the number one spot in 1964 by the Beatles' *A Hard Day's Night.*) Those with a talent for musical composition who might have gone into theatre in previous generations now turned to the new music. Rock'n'roll was loud, raucous, direct, energetic. It spoke directly to the desires, longings, hidden fears, and curiosities of the younger generation. It was fast and it came in three-minute segments and even within this limited framework the songs were often able to tell stories – minidramas – from the defeat of the British in the War of 1812 to James Dean-like car crashes. Rock was accessible and it was everywhere. Who needed theatre?

Mainstream Response

While the musical went through an auspicious two decades following the war, producing such landmarks as *South Pacific, Guys and Dolls, My Fair Lady, Gypsy, Candide, West Side Story, The Most Happy Fella, Fiddler on the Roof*, and the Off-Broadway revival of the Brecht–Weill *Threepenny Opera*, among many others, it would suffer even more severely from the upheavals that beset Broadway. Musicals took a three-pronged hit during this period. Most profound, of course, was the devastating effect of rock'n'roll and the concomitant radical restructuring of the recording industry that altered the way in which popular songs were generated and marketed. Second, the fortunes of the musical, more so than the drama, were tied to the producing structure of commercial theatre, so that the shifting economics of Broadway had a potent impact. The complexities of bringing together the book, the lyrics, and the music – often the work of three separate creators – the usual components of choreography and orchestration, and the generally more elaborate visual demands of musicals, require financial, technical, and production support well in excess of most straight plays. Finally, the musical, like the drama, was faced with a structural dilemma in response to changing aesthetics and sensibilities.

Like the drama of the interwar years, the musical had thrived on a narrative structure in which a collection of songs was carefully interwoven within the structure of a story (the "book"). These musicals were basically plays with songs and dances, except that no matter how compelling, the book worked only insofar as it meshed with the music; it could never work as a play on its own. The central role of the songs meant that the success of these shows was often tied to particular performers who could "sell" the songs to the public. Most notable among these, of course, was Ethel Merman, who is, years after her death, still inextricably linked with many of the greatest songs of the American musical theatre. The very nature of the musical involves a shifting of emotion into the medium of song and music; complex dialogue and intricate plotting are anathema to the musical theatre genre.

But the narrative structure was as inadequate for the postwar musical as for the drama. The same forces that contributed to new movements in poetry, dance, and jazz also moved the musical toward the thematically conceived and choreographically driven concept musical with its greater emphasis on complex ideas, darker emotions, and an effect achieved completely only in the process of performance. The dark and disturbing themes of *Pal Joey* and *Lady in the Dark* were early harbingers of the new form while the episodic structure of Kurt Weill's and Alan Jay Lerner's *Love Life* (1948) was a self-conscious move away from the traditional narrative structure. These works paved the way for the successful 1954 revival of *The Threepenny Opera*, and in a sense allowed for the disturbing subtext of *Gypsy* (1959), which packed a psychological and emotional punch that seemed more appropriate for the world of Tennessee Williams.

The new form would be brought to fruition by Leonard Bernstein. Bernstein, like Weill and George Gershwin before him, succeeded in blending pop music with classical structures; he was strongly influenced by Igor Stravinsky and Aaron Copland in both his classical and Broadway compositions. Choreographed by Jerome Robbins, Bernstein's first musical, *On the Town* (1944), was propelled not by the book or even the songs, but by a thorough musical score and sophisticated and athletic ballet and modern dance which supplanted lyrics and dialogue as a means of story-telling and emotional conveyance. Bernstein's revolutionary *West Side Story* (1957) transformed the emotional energy of Shakespeare's *Romeo and Juliet* into complex rhythms and counterpoint in one of the most musically sophisticated scores ever to grace Broadway, while the tensions and energies of the show were brought to life in Robbins's stunningly balletic choreography. *West Side Story* marked the end of an era on Broadway – the book musical as a vital form was virtually dead within a decade.

With the exception of composer-lyricist Stephen Sondheim, the next generation of musical theatre stars were not the composers or singers, but the choreographers and directors – Bob Fosse (who, like Robbins, had been trained by Broadway director George Abbott), Michael Bennett, and Harold Prince. In the musicals developed by these choreographers and directors, which included *Fiddler on the Roof, Cabaret, Pippin, Chicago, Follies, Company, A Chorus Line,* and *Dreamgirls,* the emphasis was increasingly on staging and choreography over music and lyrics. These productions, especially those of Harold Prince, also revitalized American design. From the mid-sixties to the mid-seventies Prince worked with the Russian-born Boris Aronson. Though always highly regarded among his colleagues as one of the finest designers of the time, he had only moderate successes until he teamed up with Prince and Robbins on *Fiddler on the Roof* (1964) with its Marc Chagall-inspired sets. Thereafter, his designs for Prince's productions blended Constructivist elements with contemporary technology and the occasional touch of American sentiment to create some of the most stunning designs of the era. After Aronson's death in 1980, Prince found another soulmate in Eugene Lee. (See Chapters 2 [Maslon, "Broadway"] and 4 for more detailed analysis of musical theatre.)

As Broadway declined there was a significant growth of theatre outside New York City. Although there had long been local professional theatres, stock companies, and touring shows, New York's position as the originator and focal point of theatre and entertainment was clear and dominant. Ultimately, a play or actor that did not perform in New York lacked credibility. As if the relationship were not clear enough, during the interwar years *Theatre Arts Monthly* had a regular feature entitled "The Tributary Theatre," which was a roundup of theatrical activity outside New York City. Some of the prewar theatres such as the Goodman Theatre of Chicago, the Cleveland Play House, and The Karamu Theatre of Cleveland continued to produce in the postwar years, but a new crop of theatres also emerged. Beginning with Margo Jones's theatre-in-the-round in Dallas known as Theatre '47 (then Theatre '48, and so on), others soon followed, notably the Alley Theatre in Houston, the Arena Stage in Washington, D.C., and the Milwaukee Repertory Theater. The most important factor in this development was a study by the Ford Foundation in 1957 that led to funding of what became known as resident professional theatres. The Rockefeller Foundation also began to support such theatres, and finally, the creation of the National Endowment for the Arts in 1965 led to more support. As a result there was an explosion of new theatres around the country presenting original productions. (See Chapter 2 [LoMonaco, "Regional/Resident Theatre"] for an expanded coverage of regional theatre.)

These theatres employed thousands of theatre professionals and created venues for classics, revivals, and, especially, new plays that the New York theatre could no longer produce or originate. With the virtual elimination of the "Road," the resident professional theatres allowed a broad spectrum of the population to see live theatre. Several of the early theatres were founded and run by women, suggesting that the regional theatres provided opportunities that might have been denied to many in New York.

After half a century, however, despite developing many new plays, actors, directors, and designers, it is not clear that the regional theatre movement has advanced the American theatre significantly. Virtually all these theatres are not-for-profit and, having been founded with subsidies, they remain dependent on subsidies. When the theatres were run by visionary directors, the lack of dependence on the box office sometimes allowed for daring and innovative productions. But as support from foundations, federal and state agencies, and private donors diminished, and as production costs rose, and as the first generation of visionary artists died or retired, the resident theatres became increasingly conservative, producing cookie-cutter theatre they hoped would appeal, or at least be inoffensive to a conservative subscription-based audience. With a few notable exceptions, these "regional" theatres had nothing to do with their location; they rarely produced plays of local interest; they employed few local artists; most still had one eye on New York City. And in a development since the eighties, the best theatres moved their successful productions to Broadway. Notable examples include La Jolla Playhouse's productions of the musicals *Big River* and *Tommy*, the plays of August Wilson first produced by the Yale Repertory Theatre, and *Angels in America* developed by the Mark Taper Forum. The out-of-town tryout which used to be Broadway's primary development tool was largely supplanted by the out-of-town creation. Plays were created and developed in a resident theatre and then brought to New York. If successful, the originating theatre would reap financial rewards, while the Broadway producer was spared at least part of the high cost of developing a risky property. Depending on one's point of view, this was either the decentralization and democratization of the American theatre, or it was a further refinement of the tributary theatre with all streams still flowing into the great reservoir of New York City.

In one regard, though, some of the regional theatres – the American Repertory Theatre in Cambridge, the Hartford Stage Company, the Arena, the Guthrie, La Jolla, American Conservatory Theatre in San Francisco, and the Mark Taper, as well as the New York Shakespeare Festival under the late Joseph Papp – provided an opportunity that commercial theatre did not. They allowed the more daring contemporary directors, including Andrei Serban, Robert Woodruff, Liviu Ciulei, Mark Lamos, Marcus Stern, François Rochaix, Anne Bogart, JoAnne Akalaitis, Robert Wilson, and Richard Foreman, to direct innovative productions of classics. Texts were re-examined, deconstructed, and abstracted in order to find contemporary resonances through theatrical means beyond the mere updating of sets and costumes. Meanwhile, many designers who worked internationally or were aware of international developments expanded the visual component of this development. These included John Conklin, Santo Loquasto, Eugene Lee, Michael Yeargan, Robert Israel, and George Tsypin.

Social Upheavals

One wonders what might have happened (or more accurately, not happened) had the country continued on the superficially benign course and prosperity of the Eisenhower years. But the near nuclear war caused by the Cuban missile crisis followed by the assassination of President Kennedy in 1963 scarred the nation in ways that were not readily apparent for years by undermining a sense of stability and security and challenging the overall belief structure of the country. The rapidly increasing involvement in Vietnam, just at the point that the baby-boom generation was coming of draft age, divided the country along not only political but generational and class lines. For many of the younger generation the conflict was not a clear-cut "good war" but rather a war that seemed to be controlled by political factors and suspect ideology. Faith in government and political leadership was thus subverted and part of the mortar that held society together seemed to crumble.

The issue of race has always been the Achilles' heel of American society. The first half of the twentieth century was dotted with sporadic attempts by African Americans to achieve justice and equality. The National Association for the Advancement of Colored People (NAACP) was founded in 1910 in response to lynchings in Illinois, there were race riots in several urban centers in the years after World War I, and a concerted legal effort to end segregation had begun by the mid-thirties. The presence of substantial numbers of black troops in World War II inevitably began to reshape the preconceptions and attitudes of many of the white soldiers who fought alongside them. 1954 saw the landmark Brown v. Board of Education of Topeka Supreme Court case that ended legal segregation of public schools – a ruling that had to be enforced in Little Rock in 1957 by the National Guard, raising specters of a military occupation. The Montgomery bus boycott of 1955 led by Martin Luther King began a period of Thoreau-inspired civil disobedience that would inform the anti-war protests of the following decade. From the earliest days of the Civil Rights Movement and the philosophical differences between Booker T. Washington and W.E.B. Du Bois, the struggle was between immediate action and slow progress; between integration and empowered separation.

The Civil Rights Movement had shown some faint signs of progress following the march on Washington led by Martin Luther King in 1963 and the passage of the Civil Rights Act in 1964. But the Vietnam War only exacerbated the racial divide. Many middle-class and affluent white youth learned how to manipulate the system to avoid the draft or to avoid Vietnam service, so the troops were disproportionately black. But even before the height of the war, racial tensions were at the boiling point. There were riots in Harlem in the summer of 1964, Los Angeles in 1965, Chicago in 1966, and in Detroit and 127 other cities in 1967. The assassination of Martin Luther King in 1968 touched off even more riots around the country. The reasons for the riots were varied and complex, but they marked a turning point in urban American history since they served as an indication that the inner cities were becoming predominantly black, while the system of authority remained predominantly white. The flight of whites from the cities meant a decline in the economic bases of the cities which led to declining services and crumbling infrastructures. The rise of drug use, disproportionately centered in the ghettos, further eroded the fabric of society. The role of television went well beyond the reshaping of American culture; it informed the self-image of American society in a way that no previous art form or medium ever had. Residents of poor urban areas, victims of *de facto* segregation, saw a view of America on television every night that depicted affluent, white, generally suburban life, presented as the epitome of the American dream that was clearly out of reach for a significant portion of the population. Television news also brought images and information about both the war and the riots into homes more graphically and more rapidly than at any previous time in history.

This was the context in which African American drama emerged. Examples of black theatre date to at least the 1820s, although there was little support for – in fact much antagonism toward – serious black playwrights and performers until the twenties, and even then it was minimal. Even during the thirties, when Langston Hughes and others were writing and there were Negro Units of the Federal Theatre Project, the ghost of the minstrel shows hung over black theatre. While white audiences would be sporadically supportive of serious plays about black concerns, especially if written and produced by whites, they were most comfortable with musical revues that showcased singing and dancing and which, if not explicitly degrading, nonetheless seemed to reward black performers for their ability to entertain white audiences, not to make them think. Every seeming advance in black theatre ultimately led to a dead end, the victim of shifts in political or economic climates.

In the postwar era, black concerns with identity, family, and a place in American society were thematically similar to the concerns of white playwrights. The rising prosperity of the era, the beginnings of foundation grants that helped subsidize theatres, and the general spirit of liberal integrationism, all contributed to an atmosphere in which the black theatre could, relatively speaking, experiment and grow. When Lorraine Hansberry's *A Raisin in the Sun*, the first Broadway play both written and directed by African Americans, premiered in 1959 – the director was Lloyd Richards who would later become Dean of the Yale Drama School and the director of August Wilson's plays on Broadway – it seemed reasonable that this would be the first step toward a vigorous black presence in the mainstream theatre. The play, about a black family's decision to move to a white suburb and the emotional upheaval this decision caused within the family, embodied the African American attempt to claim its stake in the American dream and mirrored the first steps toward integration that were then being taken around the country. The chasm between black and white was a given in Hansberry's play – neither white society nor the underlying causes of this gulf were explored. In the best American dramatic tradition, society was encapsulated in the microcosm of the family, and the solution to social problems was seen in questions of identity, self-worth, and personal responsibility and action. If the play broke no new ground dramaturgically, it was certainly a well-crafted drama and its ability to tap into contemporary political liberalism without threatening white audiences contributed to its hit status.

Yet individual successes like this and subsequent ones in the sixties and seventies, such as *The Dream on Monkey Mountain, The River Niger, A Soldier's Play, Ceremonies in Dark Old Men,* and *No Place to Be Somebody,* which had successful runs on and Off-Broadway, winning Tonys and Pulitzers along the way, faced the same problems as commercial drama as a whole, and then some. These plays were being produced during a period of declining audience support for serious drama. Moreover, these productions neither paved the way for a new generation of black producers nor created a coherent theatre movement within black communities. Despite the incredibly dynamic list of black playwrights of the late fifties and sixties – Alice Childress, Loften Mitchell, Lorraine Hansberry, LeRoi Jones/Amiri Baraka, Adrienne Kennedy, Lonne Elder, Charles Gordone, Ed Bullins, Phillip Hayes Dean, Ron Milner –

most of these names remain footnotes in the American canon or are relegated to a separate category. Only in the late eighties did a black playwright, August Wilson, make it into the list of major American playwrights.

Black playwrights and producers in the twentieth century have always confronted the equivalent dilemma as the social and political activists: do they write and produce for a black audience or for a white audience? The idealistic answer, that good drama knows no color line, ignores reality. Given the underlying truth of racial politics in the United States, it is virtually impossible for a black playwright to write serious drama that does not have racial implications. The playwright, then, must implicitly or explicitly envision an audience, and the decision can have significant financial implications. The American Negro Theatre, which spanned the war years, epitomized all these problems. Founded by Abram Hill and Frederick O'Neal in 1939 as an attempt to fill the gap left by the demise of the Federal Theatre Project's Negro Theatre Unit, the ANT sought to create a home for black playwrights while providing an outlet and training for black actors, directors, and technicians. But its focus was never entirely clear. Its greatest success was *Anna Lucasta* by white playwright Philip Yordan. Originally about a Polish working-class family, the play was adapted for the ANT and its success led to a Broadway transfer. The drain on the resources and unity of the company because of this production led to the ultimate demise of the ANT. Their attempt to adapt to white institutions led to temporary success and ultimate failure.

A parallel to Off-Broadway emerged in Harlem in the late forties. Ironically, the very same forces that were reconfiguring the Broadway theatre were also affecting the Harlem theatres. Middle-class blacks who had provided the backbone of the theatregoing audience began moving out of Harlem to the suburbs or to other boroughs. The decline in audience and the general rise in various costs led to a loss of permanent theatre buildings. With no home base, the creation of new work became increasingly difficult. The Off-Broadway Greenwich Mews Theatre in Greenwich Village supported interracial theatre and in the mid-fifties produced William Branch's *In Splendid Error* (1954), Alice Childress's *Trouble in Mind* (1955), and Loften Mitchell's *Land Beyond the River* (1956), all of which dealt directly with racial conflict, though in keeping with the time they tended to see a future society that was integrated and unified. Whatever the success of these latter productions, they were geographically far removed from the black communities of New York.

LeRoi Jones came out of the Beat movement and was a model of the assimilated black intellectual. His early plays, *The Baptism*, *The Toilet*, and *Dutchman* brought the Beat sensibility of raw energy, liminal characters, poetic language infused with the rhythms of jazz, and gritty and violent images to the stage. They all dealt with the inability of language to communicate, a theme that took on extra resonance in confrontations between black and white, as in the 1964 *Dutchman*, in which the young black intellectual character Clay, whose command of language had allowed him to negotiate a white world, was helpless against the verbal gamesmanship of the white temptress Lula. Clay's attempts to master the new language game led to his death. The play was a harbinger of the racial tensions about to erupt in the country as well as Jones's own rejection of assimilation in favor of a radical, militant separatism. Like many black activists of the period, Jones rejected his given name as an oppressive remnant of slavery. As a Marxist-Leninist now known as Amiri Baraka, he abandoned the white theatre institutions and even the conventions of Western literary drama in favor of agit props and dogmatic sociopolitical dramas. In his manifesto for "The Revolutionary Theatre" Baraka declared:

> What we show must cause the blood to rush, so that pre-revolutionary temperaments will be bathed in this blood, and it will cause their deepest souls to move, and they will find themselves tensed and clenched, even ready to die . . . We will scream and cry, murder, run through the streets in agony, if it means some souls will be moved. (Quoted in Gates, "The Chitlin Circuit," 47)

The differing directions of African American theatre were reflected in two theatres formed in the mid-sixties: the New Lafayette Theatre founded by Robert Macbeth (1966) and the Negro Ensemble Company (NEC) founded by Douglas Turner Ward (1967). The former was located in Harlem to work within the community and develop a drama primarily for that audience. A significant and influential body of work was developed by resident playwright and associate producer Ed Bullins who, like Baraka, abandoned Aristotelian form in favor of jazz-inspired and ritualistic structures. The NEC sought to produce plays by black authors and to train African Americans for theatre performance and production but did so in the East Village section of New York, a place of artistic ferment, but far from the black communities of Harlem or Bedford-Stuyvesant.

For critics who bemoaned the perceived decline in American (i.e., white) drama, it appeared as if a vibrant new multifaceted voice was emerging in the theatre. But as the economic constraints grew ever tighter in commercial theatre, as middle-class audiences – black and white – fled the cities, and as racial politics made it increasingly difficult to create seriously engaged drama that would have a broad audience appeal, African American drama retreated to the smaller, black-oriented theatres. Thus, by the late seventies, with a few exceptions such as Ntozake Shange's poetic dance drama, *For Colored Girls Who Have Considered Suicide When the Rainbow Is Enuf*, black theatre was most visible in the form of musicals such as *The Wiz* that had uncomfortable echoes once again of minstrelsy.

The riots in the ghettos and the anti-war demonstrations in the capital and elsewhere raised specters of insurrection – something, most Americans believed, that happened in other parts of the world, but not in the United States. The vision of a decaying society erupting in racial and generational violence, and threatened with nuclear holocaust from frightening political enemies – however inaccurate this vision might have been – led to inevitable and fundamental changes in society and thus art and theatre. Absurdist theatre, which had little success with American audiences in the fifties, despite popularity in much of Europe, began to find a real, if limited niche. The plays of Beckett and Ionesco, in particular, with their characters trapped in bizarre, inexplicable, and frightening worlds in which language either failed them or turned against them, seemed suddenly relevant in the American landscape of the sixties. Political theatre, which had not been seen in any serious way since the thirties, was reborn as performers and audiences alike began to demand that theatre address the social and political problems around them. Alternative methods of staging and acting as well as playwriting were investigated as if in an attempt to find a new means of expression for a new society.

The gulf between theatrical generations could be seen in a 1970 guerilla theatre piece created by New York University students in response to the shooting of Kent State students by the National Guard. Armed with portable tape recorders with recordings of a television statement by the father of one of the victims questioning whether dissent was possible in this country, three groups of demonstrators sneaked into Broadway theatres during intermissions. Richard Schechner described the results of the group that went to *Forty Carats*, a light Broadway comedy.

> About fifteen minutes into the act (at the start of the second scene), the leader of the group rose and went down the aisle. The other members of the group responded to the cue and soon the bases of both aisles were filled with the eight demonstrators. The leader said, "Trina, the girl in this play, is seventeen. Allison Krause was just two years older than Trina when she was shot. Her father wants to speak to you." The tape was played . . . The actors onstage – June Allyson and Tom Poston – froze as the demonstration began. They did not attempt to compete with it. Most of the audience was quiet. About halfway through the tape a woman said, "We didn't spend $8 to hear this kind of thing!" Another woman answered, "This is more important than this trivial play!" Some of the audience joined in the dispute. Tom Poston said, "All right, girls, you've made your point."[10]

The protesters were escorted out peacefully by the house manager, who apologized to the audience, and the performance continued. The artifice of the Broadway fare had been made painfully apparent, yanking the piece into real time; the inconsequentiality of the piece was contrasted with the darker realities of a distant war and a nation in turmoil. It is unlikely that this or numerous similar events changed the politics or actions of many in the audience, but it reinforced a sense of a divided society, divided both culturally and politically, and contributed to the further decay of the Broadway genre.

It was in the midst of the turbulent sixties that Neil Simon, the most commercially successful playwright in American history and possibly the most maligned, emerged. *Come Blow Your Horn* premiered on Broadway in 1961 and he has averaged nearly a play a year ever since. Although his overwhelming success, broad popular appeal, and prolific output earned him the disdain of many keepers of serious theatre, he was, strangely, the epitome of many of the developments of the postwar era. As part of Sid Caesar's brilliant stable of writers he was a product of television's first generation. Though this branded him in some circles at the time as an interloper from an intellectually and culturally deficient enterprise, Caesar's *Your Show of Shows* is now hailed as a high watermark in a golden age of television, and the writers of that show have taken on a mythical status. But Simon, in a certain critical sense, was in the wrong place at the wrong time. His plays were not ostensibly about the radical changes occurring in the American society of the sixties; they did not deal with race, the war in Vietnam, poverty, or even the youth culture (except as a comic reference for baffled members of the over-thirty generation). These were plays about the Broadway theatre audience, that dying contingent of white, upper-middle-class, increasingly suburban theatregoers who were headed toward mid-life crises and for whom the rapid changes in the surrounding world were unfathomable and frightening. As critic John Lahr observed in the early seventies, "This is the theater of the silent majority. In the humor are a moral confusion and spiritual dread which show the foundations of the reactionary wilderness that America is becoming, and the unthinking violence which is condoned as normalcy" (*Astonish Me*, 121). The plays, he suggested, showed "images of impotence."

Though certainly not naturalistic in any conventional sense, these plays – especially the string of hits from the sixties, *Barefoot in the Park*, *The Odd Couple*, *Plaza Suite*, *Promises, Promises*, and *The Last of the Red Hot Lovers* – are photographs of a segment of American society. The protagonists in Simon's plays have lost all sense of identity and have become unmoored from any recognizable landscape of societal codes and mores. The sexes do not know how to communicate, children and parents are enemies separated by radically different understandings of dress and behavior, and even the very rooms in which life is conducted and the furniture and appliances of these abodes take on lives of their own and refuse to yield to the needs and demands of the occupants. And ultimately, language as a means of successful and meaningful communication has deserted them. Husbands and wives, would-be seducers and their intended seducees talk past each other in uncomprehending syntax. When Oscar and Felix of *The Odd Couple* argue over the difference between spaghetti and linguine it is a scene that echoes the language games of Gogo and Didi in *Waiting for Godot* or the argument of Ben and Gus in Harold Pinter's *The Dumb Waiter* over whether one lights the kettle or the stove. Audiences recognized and responded to the rhythms and content made familiar by television. But more careful scrutiny suggests that Simon's comedy was of a piece with the Existential drama of the forties and fifties. Neil Simon's genius was an ability to take the impulses and techniques of Yiddish theatre and vaudeville as filtered through television and meld them with the Broadway comedy-drama. But in the process he grafted – unwittingly one presumes – the themes and strategies of Existentialism and Absurdism onto the television sitcom, thereby creating the quintessential Broadway theatre of the sixties.

American mythology was based, at least in part, on the idea of the rugged individual – the lone cowboy with his gun facing down the bad guys or the savages. But something went wrong. This iconography had contributed to the breakdown of society and transformed the United States into a position as world bully. In seeking new paradigms, alienation and disaffection gave way to a revival of utopianism and even nineteenth-century communitarianism. The alternative to the loner was the ensemble; the alternative to the breakdown of society was communal action. The writings of social critic Paul Goodman and philosopher Herbert Marcuse became the intellectual background of what became known as the "counterculture" – the youthful segment of society that saw itself as a vast community in opposition to the "establishment." Marcuse, in *One-Dimensional Man* (1964), argued that the working class had been neutralized by material goods and that society had lost its ability to speak out against authority, and therefore must make a radical break and regain its voice and its rightful place. The already prevalent tactics of civil disobedience from the Civil Rights Movement coalesced with the student activism of the Free Speech Movement in opposition to the war in Vietnam to generate nearly a decade of mass protests against the war, racism, and the stifling of utopian ideals. Closely related to this was the rejection of societal strictures on sexual conduct and drug use. While the Beats, or "Beatniks" as the media dubbed them, had remained a relatively small and marginal force in the eyes of the general public, the "hippies" who supplanted them by the mid-sixties were ubiquitous. Long hair and flamboyant clothes (inspired by the Beatles), and the loud and public flouting of accepted decorum became the hallmark of the baby-boom generation.

The utopian and communitarian spirit manifested itself in the theatre through ensembles and collectives – groups of performers and writers coming together to create theatre through communal input and creative energy. The ideal and the reality seldom meshed. The most successful of the ensemble groups – the San Francisco Mime Troupe, the Open Theatre, the Bread and

Puppet Theatre, the Performance Group, and the Manhattan Project – were founded and led by strong, even charismatic individuals: R.G. Davis, Joseph Chaikin, Peter Schumann, Richard Schechner, and Andre Gregory. Nonetheless, within these groups, the typical hierarchies of theatrical creation were eliminated or reordered with some success. Ideas for productions were often generated by the company, scripts were evolved through months of improvisation around themes and ideas, the production jobs were democratically divided among group members, and income, meager though it might be, was shared communally. From a stylistic point of view, the major effect of the ensemble companies was to shift the emphasis of drama from the literary and narrative qualities of scripts to an actor-dominated theatre within which thematically structured texts were enacted in a highly physical and emblematic style of performance. In a period in which distrust of language was growing, verbal communication was increasingly problematic, and writers like Norman O. Brown and Wilhelm Reich were celebrating the body, it seemed logical that theatre would begin to abandon its traditional Western role as a place for the enactment of language in favor of physical expression which was seen as more honest and expressive. "The resurrection of the body," Brown wrote in *Life Against Death* in 1959, "is a social project facing mankind as a whole and it will become a practical political problem when the statesmen of the world are called upon to deliver happiness instead of power" (317).

The ensemble theatre movement was most ideally embodied by the Open Theatre, founded as an offshoot of the Living Theatre in 1963. Frustrated with the Living's lack of attention to actor training and technique, the Open Theatre emerged out of the work of Joseph Chaikin and several other Living Theatre actors who began to meet to explore techniques for dealing with non-realistic texts, which, in 1963, meant largely Absurdist material. Chaikin felt that a vibrant theatre could only emerge from the unique vocabulary of an ensemble of actors. Working with theatre games and improvisations based on the work of Viola Spolin and Nola Chilton, they developed new approaches to training that emphasized physical virtuosity. Eventually, inspired by Brecht and working with playwrights such as Jean-Claude Van Itallie, they began to develop scripts that dealt with social and political concerns, including *America Hurrah, Viet Rock,* and, in 1967, *The Serpent,* an exploration of the myths and themes of the Book of Genesis. The work was created through months of improvisation, reading about creation myths with anthropologist Joseph Campbell, and relating the Biblical events to contemporary society through a recreation of the John F. Kennedy assassination. All the action was done simply and expressively in a non-illusionistic way – the presence of the actor behind the character was always apparent and the movement between character and performer was always fluid; there were direct addresses to the audience and personal revelations by the performers. Subsequent productions by the Open Theatre moved further away from language as the primary means of communication; ideas were expressed equally, if not more so, through image and gesture.

The traditional physical arrangement of theatre was designed for audiences to listen and to watch. But if there were to be new paradigms of acting, creation, and production it seemed logical to disrupt the role of the audience as well. Richard Schechner, who as editor of the *Tulane Drama Review* chronicled the emergence of the new experimental theatre, founded the Performance Group in 1967. Drawing heavily on the ideas of Polish director Jerzy Grotowski, Schechner's theatre explored ritual and myth, ensemble-style acting, and environmental staging. Environmental staging took a variety of forms but in its basic form transformed the entire theatre into potential performing space in which actors and spectators shared space or negotiated the use of space during the course of the performance. Schechner's challenge to the conventional staging set off a decade of exploration and experimentation that reached even Broadway in productions such as *Candide* directed by Harold Prince and designed by Eugene Lee.

The first, and most notorious, production of the Performance Group was *Dionysus in '69*, based on Euripides' *The Bacchae* and staged in a converted industrial space in the Soho district of Manhattan. Scaffolding built around the interior walls served as audience area as well as performance space. Audience members were encouraged to move about during the performance to constantly alter their relationship to the piece. The ritual-like action of the production, the nudity of the performers, the scenes suggesting Dionysian orgies, the unorthodox spatial arrangement, and the general sense of sexual freedom and anarchistic behavior that accompanied the rise of the hippie culture in the late sixties contributed to audience participation that often tested the actors' ability to maintain control of the performance. The danger inherent in removing both the physical and psychological barriers between spectators and performers while at the same time emphasizing the presence of the actors as themselves rather than as characters is that it invites the audience to participate in the action without understanding that there is the presence of a text. In the case of *Dionysus in '69*, some spectators literally jumped into the pseudo-rituals and some male spectators took the nudity and sensuality of the female performers as an invitation to physical intimacy. The Group found that it had to re-establish certain boundaries that literally or implicitly told the audience when they could participate and when they had to remain passive spectators.

The Living Theatre encountered a similar response when they returned from Europe in 1968 with four ensemble pieces that had been created abroad.

These productions served as the final catalyst for the destruction of conventional performer–spectator relationships and of traditional literary texts. Their production of *Paradise Now* was an episodic meditation on the war in Vietnam and a virtual catalogue of the ills of society as filtered through the group's anarchist philosophy. The piece began with the actors moving through the auditorium, whispering a series of statements to the spectators, culminating in the declaration, "I am not allowed to take my clothes off in public," whereupon they stripped down to loin cloths. Invariably, members of the audience joined in this action. By the end of the performance actors and audience, some completely naked, had completely intermingled on the stage and auditorium – the normal hierarchy of performer and spectator had been obliterated. For the Living Theatre this was a model for the utopian world order with no hierarchies and no leaders, only communal spirit. The actors led the audience to the doors of the theatre, encouraging them to carry on the revolution in the street. But the audiences attracted to the performances of the newly returned Living Theatre were largely middle-class theatregoers and college students, so the radical message and urge to political action carried only so far. But the total thwarting of dramatic expectations did have a significant effect upon staging and theatrical creation for the next decade, seeming once and for all to destroy any physical and aesthetic barriers to new ideas and new forms of theatre. The down-side to such exercises, however, was that they easily lent themselves to self-indulgent theatre that lacked inspiration or rigor. (For another perspective on acting in alternative theatre, see Hirsch, Chapter 6.)

In the 1970s, the communal movement transformed into spiritual quests for self-fulfillment. The hippies were not a coherent political movement; they were part of an amorphous cultural rebellion. The emphasis on drugs and sex that preoccupied many, and a greater interest in popular music than in left-wing politics, led the country away from utopian idealism toward a more self-centered point of view. As the singularity of purpose of the political movement evaporated the emphasis shifted from changing the "system" to working on the self. In the vacuum created by the collapse of clear-cut ideologies and causes, "new age" movements, groups, and cults ranging from consciousness-raising encounter groups, to yoga-centered ashrams, to the Esalen Institute, sprang up to transform the mind and spirit. Transcendental meditation taught by Indian gurus (first brought to public attention by the Beatles) became popular; complex social, philosophical, and political thought was simplified and popularized by such figures as Alan Watts (Zen), Fritz Perls (gestalt therapy), Wilhelm Reich, R.D. Laing, and Carlos Castaneda (hallucinatory mysticism).

Within a decade, from 1959 to 1969, the combined effect of Happenings and Chance Theatre, and the productions of the Living Theatre, Open Theatre, and Performance Group as well as the ideas of Artaud and Brecht and the productions of Grotowski's Polish Laboratory Theatre along with several other similar groups, served to destroy the grip of narrative theatre, linear structure, language-based scripts, thematic texts, psychological characterization and emotionally-based acting, and the post-Renaissance relationships of performer and spectator. In other words, the entire basis of modern Western theatre was brought into question. It was a heady time, and from the narrow view of the theatre artists experimenting in these new forms it appeared as if the whole structure of theatre was about to change. As with the larger society, however, greater political and economic forces and the inertia of more conservative audiences and artists meant that radical change would be either absorbed into the mainstream or ultimately discarded. (See Carlson, Chapter 2, "Alternative Theatre," for additional coverage of alternative theatres.)

Off-Off Broadway, New Plays, New Musicals

In that moment between the assassination of President Kennedy and the eruptions of racial violence and the massive protests against the war in Vietnam which would galvanize the artistic community into renewed activity, the progressive spirit and adventurousness that had seemingly always typified the American sensibility became confused and unfocused. Even the once dynamic American rock'n'roll had become lifeless and sentimental and was overwhelmed in 1964 by the so-called British invasion of the Beatles, the Rolling Stones, and others, as was the still vigorous rhythm and blues of Motown. A similar fate befell Broadway. The plays of Harold Pinter, John Osborne, Tom Stoppard, Peter Shaffer, Arnold Wesker, Ann Jellicoe, Robert Bolt, and Edward Bond began to appear on and Off-Broadway and in the repertoires of college and regional theatres. And, in 1965, Peter Brook and the Royal Shakespeare Company stunned audiences with their New York production of Peter Weiss's *The Persecution and Assassination of Marat as Performed by the Inmates of the Asylum of Charenton under the Direction of the Marquis de Sade*. In terms of challenging the audience's preconceptions of its relationship to the stage and to performers, the production did little that the Living Theatre's production of *The Connection* or Kenneth Brown's *The Brig* had not already done. But it brought rigorously trained actors and much more highly polished scenography to the production than the Living Theatre ever had done, while finding a mesmerizing form of expression for the ideas of Brecht and Artaud. Three years later, in his book *The Empty Space*, Brook would write, "The Theatre and life are one," and it was true for many spectators that despite the blatant theatricality of this production, the separation of performance and life began to be blurred. Also, in comparison to almost any American play of the period, *Marat/Sade* was sophisticated and complex in its exploration of history, philosophy, politics, and human sociology.

In a season in which the American highlights of the Broadway scene were such mild and unmemorable shows as *Generation*, *The Impossible Years*, and *On A Clear Day You Can See Forever*, *Marat/Sade* was a shocking revelation that, in a sense, did for American theatre what Sputnik did for the American space program: it was a wakeup call that galvanized those concerned about the fate of theatre.

From about 1965 on, as a result of the combined effects of Off-Broadway, the regional theatres, and the British invasion, virtually no play by an American author other than Neil Simon that has received critical acclaim or has made it into the "canon" originated on Broadway. Almost all the major writers of the post-sixties American theatre have originated their work Off-Broadway or outside New York, and the majority of their plays have never been performed on Broadway.

The first wave of new playwrights to arise in the wake of Albee and Kopit came largely from the emergent Off-Off Broadway. The term Off-Off Broadway was coined by *Village Voice* critic Jerry Tallmer in 1960 in an attempt to categorize the increasing amount of new work that was originating beyond the by now well-established and increasingly expensive Off-Broadway. Starting in the late fifties, makeshift theatres were created in the cafés, churches, and lofts of Greenwich Village and its environs. The first of these was Caffe Cino, created by Joe Cino in 1959 in his coffeehouse as a place to present new plays on a minuscule platform that served as a stage. If anything united these early Off-Off Broadway theatres it was their dedication to new plays, their flagrant, even proud disregard of the niceties of commercial production and dramatic precepts, and their lack of concern for financial success (other than, perhaps, the basic need for survival).

Of the original Off-Off Broadway group it was La MaMa that had the most long-lasting and far-reaching impact. Created by the dynamic and enigmatic Ellen Stewart, who came to New York as a fashion designer from Louisiana via Chicago (retaining an accent that was part Cajun, part indeterminate), La MaMa became the home to all the new young playwrights and many of the young directors, actors, and designers of the period. Stewart fought city bureaucracy and indirect censorship to support the work of her "children," as she called them. Leonard Melfi, Julie Bovasso, Sam Shepard, Paul Foster, Tom Eyen, Adrienne Kennedy, Rochelle Owens, Megan Terry, and many more playwrights all had premieres there; Tom O'Horgan, Meredith Monk, Ping Chong, Richard Foreman, and Richard Schechner have directed there; and European directors Andrei Serban, Tadeusz Kantor, and Eugenio Barba, among others, were brought to America by her. Well into the eighties each performance began with Stewart ringing a bell and welcoming spectators to "Café La MaMa, dedicated to the playwright and all aspects of the theatre." She would then pass a basket for donations – the standard method of income production for Off-Off Broadway in the early days. After finding a permanent home on East Fourth Street and changing from a membership club (a ruse to get around various regulations and ordinances) to a regular theatre known as La MaMa Experimental Theatre Club, admission was charged. In 1965, Stewart took a company on the first of several European and world tours. This, plus the presence of the Living Theatre, awakened Europeans to the emergence of a vital American avant-garde, and this in turn had a strong influence on the revitalization of a European avant-garde.

In addition to those mentioned above, the playwrights who came out of these early Off-Off Broadway theatres included Terrence McNally, Israel Horovitz, Rosalyn Drexler, Maria Irene Fornés, Robert Patrick, Ron Tavel, Amiri Baraka, Ed Bullins, Murray Mednick, and Lanford Wilson. Though several of these playwrights went on to critical acclaim – by the seventies, for instance, Sam Shepard was generally considered the successor to Albee – only McNally and Wilson have had commercial success. A few made it into the canon of Off-Broadway and regional theatres, several wrote for Hollywood, but some have never moved past their Off-Off Broadway venues. There has probably been no other period in history in which the divide between critical acceptance and popular and commercial success has been so great. (See Gussow, Chapter 2, "Off- and Off-Off Broadway," for the fuller history of Off-Off Broadway.)

Part of the chasm between the new writers and the traditional theatre institutions can be explained by the frames of reference within which each operated. Both the producers and consumers of mainstream theatre at mid-century were still rooted in essentially nineteenth-century melodrama forms. The linear structure of narrative and the psychological basis of character formed the basis for drama, opera, movies, and even classical ballet. So strong were these influences that the perceptions of the real world were often shaped by these artistic forces. But for the new writers of the sixties, the primary influences were contemporary plastic arts, rock music and jazz, movies, radio, television, comic books, and the burgeoning drug culture. From the visual arts came a familiarity with abstraction and, especially in the wake of Jackson Pollock, an emphasis on process over content. From jazz came ideas of improvisation, dissonance, and an abandonment of traditional structures and even of standard lengths; from rock'n'roll, of course, came an attitude of rebellion and sexuality, an emphasis on volume over subtlety, and the development of an idea or emotion within a simple repetitive structure contained in a three-minute frame. Meanwhile, the vocabulary of film editing – jump cuts, reverse angles, cutaways, and the like – together with radio and television's disruption of narrative flow by commercials, created a comfort and familiarity with non-linear structure. Comic books had a surprisingly similar effect. While many comics were simple narrative sequences of frames, many of the action comics developed a complex page layout that was almost cubistic in its juxtaposition of images, overlapping of time sequences, and unfolding of narrative information. The drug culture also contributed to a greater acceptance of jarring temporal and visual juxtapositions. All these factors created a new vocabulary of popular culture and a referential framework far removed from the high and middle culture that had informed serious theatre through the first half of the century. Popular culture became *the* culture of the United States and thus the basis of much new theatre.

The result was short plays – vignettes to one-acts – which often abandoned any semblance of Aristotelian structure, and placed an emphasis on riff-like flights of language, shocking and grotesque subject matter and imagery, broad references to pop culture, a frequent acknowledgment of the audience or the theatrical nature of the play, and rapid shifts in focus. Production values were limited and the necessity of homemade sets, costumes, and lights were turned into stylistic virtues. Amateur acting was likewise emphasized as preferential to the slickness of commercial theatre. Nudity became a hallmark of the late sixties. Even when the lack of clothing was justified by the script it sometimes seemed as if the script had been written simply to justify the nudity. The daringness of disrobing in public or the supposed freedom it symbolized was exploited, much as it had been in the English Restoration when actresses were first permitted on the stage. Needless to say, it was almost always the women who wound up naked.

The plays and productions of Off-Off Broadway were superficially related to Absurdism – drawing upon the stylistic vocabulary while jettisoning the Existential content. In place of the need for rigorous personal engagement advocated by Sartre and Camus, playwrights like Leonard Melfi, Israel Horovitz, John Ford Noonan, and others seemed to advocate the redemptive power of love as a panacea for all human problems – a philosophy derived from Erich Fromm and propagated via the Beatles and other representatives of pop culture. This meshed well with New Left philosophies woven together from the political ideas of Herbert Marcuse and Norman O. Brown, the social concepts of Erving Goffman and R.D. Laing, and the cultural critiques of Marshall McLuhan and Claude Lévi-Strauss. The plays exhibited a neo-Rousseau-like faith in the innate goodness of natural man while emphasizing spirituality (with a healthy dose of Zen and other Eastern philosophies) and revealing a mistrust of science and the rational mind. The result was ultimately a sentimental theatre that, despite the frequent rejection of Aristotelian structure, was an echo of Romantic drama and often melodramatic in spirit.

The majority of the literally thousands of plays that were produced in the dozens of Off-Off Broadway venues in the sixties and seventies were, in the words of critic and writer Michael Smith, "tentative, lacking in craft, technically crude" (quoted in Berkowitz, *New Broadways*, 97); in reality, most were just bad theatre. But they were a training ground for dozens of playwrights and hundreds of actors, directors, designers, and producers. In earlier times, when theatre was more plentiful and tickets less expensive, young theatre artists could learn by working in various capacities on scores of productions or going to the theatre every night – as Beck and Malina had done as recently as the forties. But by the sixties, there was far less theatre to see, and it was increasingly inaccessible financially to many would-be spectators. Theatre artists had to reinvent the theatre in order to learn from it.

Of all the Off-Off Broadway playwrights, it was Sam Shepard who most successfully wove together new dramatic and theatrical techniques with contemporary American themes. He was one of the first of the new playwrights not merely writing *about* the changing society, but finding a theatrical vocabulary that embodied the new culture. More than any of his contemporaries, Shepard found – through inventive, driving, and poetic language – a vibrant and resonant means of expressing a view of American society. In a certain sense, Shepard's plays – usually set within a western or rural landscape – with their loners and rugged individuals struggling against the numbing forces of faceless institutions and society at large, were well within the American tradition of Clyde Fitch, Eugene O'Neill, Tennessee Williams, William Inge, and even Neil Simon. What separated his works from their thematically related predecessors was a shift to structures more akin to rock, beat poetry, and jazz than to classical narrative. His early plays in particular were filled with long monologues of associative language. They would often incorporate elements of the supernatural and science fiction; time and space would not be presented as obstacles to the interaction of characters or the line of action. Figures from the Old West and Native American culture or their contemporary equivalents would populate the landscape.

By the mid-seventies Shepard seemed to have his finger on the pulse of American culture, and he ultimately won a Pulitzer Prize for *Buried Child* (1978), which, like almost all the acclaimed American dramas of the twentieth century, focused on the family unit as a metaphor for American society and a locus for the failure of communication and human interaction. But many of Shepard's plays gave the impression of having flowed virtually unedited from his fertile imagination, which suggested to some critics a lack of discipline. The non-Aristotelian structure, the narrative and thematic digressions, and occasionally enigmatic symbolism combined to worry producers and alienate audiences more attuned to conventional commercial fare. Despite continued critical praise, intense loyalty from an ever-growing audience, and a significant body of journalistic and academic writing devoted to his prodigious output, no work of his appeared on Broadway until 1996 with a revival of *Buried Child*, and that production was a commercial failure. (For discussions of Shepard and other playwrights mentioned in this chapter, see Chapter 3.)

There was one successful crossover from the Off-Off Broadway sensibility to commercial theatre in the musical *Hair*, the first rock musical and the inaugural offering of Joseph Papp's Public Theater in 1967. It moved for a brief time to a disco before being reworked into a Broadway production under the direction of Tom O'Horgan, who had established a reputation directing many of the new plays at Café LaMaMa, and who here created an imaginative staging derived in part from the neo-Expressionist physical-ensemble work of the Living Theatre and Open Theatre.

The show's lasting success was ultimately a result of the bedrock of musical theatre: good music that was catchy and uplifting. But the producer Michael Butler had the genius to tap into two audiences. Billed as a "Tribal Love-Rock Musical," it appealed to the youthful counterculture movement, many of whom, despite revolutionary rhetoric, had ample disposable cash for Broadway tickets. There was also a contingent of the hippie culture who believed that the performers were part of some communal movement and who came to New York and camped out on the steps of the theatre, sometimes being invited to participate in the finale. On the other hand, the production catered to the prurient interests of the older, traditional Broadway audience. Couching it in terms of the sexual revolution, the first half ended with a notorious nude scene. It was later revealed that some of the performers were paid a bonus if they would take off their clothes. Thus cynical marketing mixed with the apparently naive politics of the flower children. (See Chapter 2, Maslon, "Broadway," and especially Chapter 4.)

Though *Hair* was seen at the time as the harbinger of the rock musical (and thus the revival and future of the musical theatre) only a few abortive musicals followed in its wake. The fundamental three-chord, three-minute structure of traditional rock'n'roll was antithetical to the structures of musical theatre, and as late sixties rock was transformed by drugs into psychedelia and repetitive and unstructured epical formats, the possibilities for a vital rock musical theatre diminished. At the same time, because of venues like the Fillmore Auditorium in San Francisco and the Fillmore East in New York and the rise of discos, theatricality flowed from the legitimate theatre into rock auditoria, and with it, the audience that might have regenerated the theatre. The inventive pyrotechnics that were seen in a nascent form in *Hair* were exploited in the ever larger rock concerts by Alice Cooper, David Bowie, and the later tours of the Rolling Stones, the Who, Kiss, and their progeny.

The massive sums of money generated by rock music, and the perceived need to make the concerts ever more spectacular drove technological developments in lighting, sound, and stage hydraulics. By the mid-seventies, rock concerts had, in fact, become the new musicals. Held together by thematically related visual images, even on occasion by a crude book structure, the concerts were high-tech versions of the seventeenth-century French machine plays, and nineteenth-century pantomimes and spectacles. They would return to haunt theatre in several ways. Audiences grew accustomed to amplified sound and what might be called amplified light. Rock concerts, the lighting of public spaces, outdoor advertising, and even television raised the threshold of visibility so that audiences became dependent on ever increasing amounts of light to render something visible. Computerized control of lighting and stage mechanics led to an expectation of movement and constant change. Traditional theatre lighting seemed dark and crude by comparison.

British composer Andrew Lloyd Webber and producer Cameron Mackintosh seemed to understand the theatrical appeal of rock concerts and were responsible for a string of successful spectacle musicals in the eighties such as *Cats*, *Phantom of the Opera*, and *Miss Saigon*. Lush and pseudo-operatic, and generally lacking the pop tunes of earlier musicals, these productions depended on lavish decor and special effects to support their sweeping and romantic plots. Though frequently decried by critics, they had a broad popular appeal and functioned as tourist attractions, especially for the increasing numbers of non-English-speaking tourists flooding New York, for whom the minimal language of these spectacles was no obstacle.

For the occupants of the spreading suburban landscape, the most spectacular theatre they encountered – though they would never perceive it as such – was the great shopping malls of the eighties and nineties. Like the fantasy-world casinos of Las Vegas and like Disney World, the malls were fantastic stage settings – theatrical facades recalling exotic locales, idyllic home towns, or chic urban centers. Entering into one of these malls was like entering into an elaborate stage or movie setting. The spectator-consumer made a pilgrimage through arid highways and parking lots and was instantly transformed upon entering a world that promised to fulfill desires and meet all possible needs. For the middle-class suburban theatre audience, going into the city to attend the theatre was a similar journey. It was necessary, therefore, that the theatre provide as spectacular and stimulating an experience as going to the mall. Part of the reason for Lloyd Webber's popularity among these suburban audiences (and perhaps the greater disdain from urban dwellers) was that his theatre produced that experience. *Phantom of the Opera* and the Mall of America were, on some level, equivalent.

The New Formalism

A formalist theatre privileges the external form or structure of a piece over specific content. The meaning, as it were, is derived through an experience of the form, not necessarily through a reading of the content. Robert Wilson's opera *Einstein on the Beach*, for example, could be said to be about the threat of nuclear holocaust and the potential power of the atom, since such ideas can be found in the images and text of the opera, yet the "meaning" of the piece resides in the music, the performance, and the repetitive structure of its action and imagery. A primary source for the development of modern formalist theatre was Minimalism, the art world's response to the emotionalism and process-oriented creations of Abstract Expressionism. With roots in Russian Constructivism and Marcel Duchamp's "readymades" from the teens, Minimalist artists placed an emphasis on rationally designed artworks using industrial and other man-made materials. The result was sculptures and paintings that announced the use of real objects in real space. The constructions were conceptually rigorous, simple and literal in presentation, and meant to be appreciated in their own right, not as reference to something else or as an illusion. The predictability of mathematical repetition became a stylistic feature of much of this work. If the unmediated flow of the subconscious as in Pollock's action paintings was one response to the unfathomable horrors of the postwar world, and Absurdism another, then the rigor and rationalism of Minimalism was another possible, if very different, response. Minimalist aesthetics spread in the sixties from painting and sculpture to music, dance, and theatre. The modular structures and repetitive phrasings of the compositions of Philip Glass and Steve Reich were prime examples of Minimalist music; the repetitive use of "found" gestures – that is everyday instead of virtuosic movement – that typified the postmodern dance of Yvonne Rainer, Lucinda Childs, and David Gordon is similarly inspired; and the eighties rock of Brian Eno and David Byrne fits in this category. Even the so-called concept musicals can be seen in the context of Minimalism.

Structured around thematic ideas, the shape and dynamic of the concept musical follows the structures of music and dance or the structures dictated by the concept rather than a traditional narrative. The concept musical reached its peak in 1975 with the Michael Bennett production of *A Chorus Line*. Though this work, about the lives and tribulations of Broadway dancers was, in some ways, the outgrowth of the ensemble theatre movement of the late sixties, with its spirit of collaboration and group creation, its modular structure of a series of monologues and confessions while standing on the stark white line of an otherwise bare stage (in a setting designed by Robin Wagner) indicates a Minimalist influence. Some of the works of composer-lyricist Stephen Sondheim, such as *Company* and *Follies,* can also be seen in this light.

The creators of the new formalist theatre of the seventies rejected the ensemble in favor of the single creator, the cool detachment of formalist aesthetics, and the frequent use of the self as both subject and source. If the ensemble theatre movement had been in some ways an expression of political alternatives to existing societal structures, then the formalist theatre could be seen as a reversion to the American myth of the lone explorer forging new paths in the wilderness. With its rejection of the emotionally cathartic experience, formalist theatre could also be seen as a response to the failure of alternative life styles to transform society in the significantly utopian ways that had been anticipated.

The two major exponents of this theatre were Robert Wilson and Richard Foreman. Although both these artists headed theatre companies – the Byrd Hoffman Foundation and the Ontological-Hysteric Theatre, respectively – their work was a singular inner vision created through total control of the creative and producing process. Despite ultimately differing aesthetics, there were certain stylistic similarities and shared influences in their early works. The excruciatingly slow pace of their early productions, the strong emphasis on striking visual images, the abandonment of not only narrative but even overt thematic structures, and the elimination of conventional emotional expression by the actors that typified their productions in the early seventies were in marked contrast to the energetic, physical, actor-centered ensemble theatre of the time. Critic Bonnie Marranca coined the term "theatre of images" to describe the work of Foreman, Wilson, and Mabou Mines, the latter a collective theatre founded in 1970 by Lee Breuer, JoAnne Akalaitis, and Ruth Maleczech.

A significant influence on both directors was the theories and dramas of Gertrude Stein, particularly her concept of "landscape drama." Stein posited the idea of landscape in opposition to the conventional linear narrative. Narrative drama, she felt, kept the spectator in a kind of syncopation, always being ahead of or behind the action on stage, thus creating a disjointed view. She preferred a theatre that emphasized "sight and sound and its relation to emotion and time, rather than in relation to story and action" ("Plays", 104). She wanted an art that existed in the present moment, a performance which the spectator would experience completely in the present moment.

Wilson took the notion of landscape fairly literally. His work focused on the dream state – what he called the "inner screen." Using his work with autistic and brain-damaged children, he sought to understand how such individuals perceived the world. His pieces were typified by great length (*The Life and Times of Joseph Stalin* was twelve hours; *KA MOUNTAIN AND GUARDenia TERRACE*, created for the Shiraz Festival in Iran in 1972, took place as a continuous performance over seven days on the hills of Haft-tan Mountain), slow movement, bold and startling images, repetitive language, and hypnotic music – they were, in a sense, paintings or landscapes come to life on the stage. At least part of the intention was to alter the consciousness of the spectators, to plunge them into a world in which the distinction between dream and rational vision was blurred, a goal that made him an heir to the Surrealists.

Foreman's work was also inspired by Gertrude Stein, though he focused more on her concept of the continuous present and the idea of "beginning again and again," by which she meant disrupting the linear flow in order to keep the spectator constantly in the present moment. This approach meshed surprisingly well with a vocabulary and stylistic approach derived from Brechtian aesthetics, though lacking the more overt political aspects. Foreman's goal was to disrupt emotional involvement and thus force the spectator into a conscious awareness of the act of watching so that the experience of the performance would lead to a fresh understanding of the world. Though the content of his plays was drawn from readings in science and philosophy, the plays were never "about" such ideas; rather their structure embodied these concepts in a three-dimensional dramatic form. Foreman's primary influence came not from theatre but from avant-garde film known as the New American Cinema. Foreman was impressed with the singular vision, the lack of concern with polished images, and the self-referential nature of these independent films. In them he saw artists pursuing their own ideas, not hampered by the needs of collaboration.

It was in the Wooster Group, created by members of Schechner's Performance Group in the late seventies, that almost every thread of postwar American drama coalesced. Their work combined the impulses of the ensemble movement out of which they had grown, and the formalist theatre, while drawing inspiration from both avant-garde art and classic American drama. Director Elizabeth LeCompte began working with autobiographical material provided by actor Spalding Gray and members of the company to create a performance. The first work was entitled *Sakonnet Point*, which became the first part of a trilogy known as *Three Places in Rhode Island*. The use of autobiography as raw material was, of course, not new and it has been present to varying degrees in much twentieth-century American drama. But here it was essentially unmediated by any fictional context – so much so that ethical and legal questions were raised when Gray used a tape of a conversation with his mother's psychiatrist in *Rumstick Road* that dealt with his mother's suicide. In its use of autobiography it mirrored a new form known as performance art which was developing within the world of conceptual art. In performance art the artist did not create a tangible art object but presented the self as the work of art through autobiographical performance pieces, or by framing aspects of everyday life so that quotidian activity became identified as a work of art. But most such performances were almost always solo pieces. In the work of the Wooster Group, autobiographical material was being shaped by a strong, visionary director, and developed in conjunction with an ensemble of actors. Eventually, Gray went on to develop solo monologues which were not mere story-telling but were carefully configured dramatic pieces. The most fascinating aspect of Gray's monologues was that the central character, Spalding Gray, was not his true, unmediated self, as he appeared to be for most audiences, but a careful theatrical construct based upon himself – a fictional character very closely based on the real performer. LeCompte, meanwhile, began to explore classic texts including *Our Town*, *The Crucible*, and *The Three Sisters*, among others, which became, respectively, *Route 1 & 9*, *L.S.D (. . . Just the High Points)*, and *Brace Up!*. All of these productions represented the unique vision of LeCompte, which would seem to place her in the tradition of Foreman and Wilson, yet the pieces were created by the ensemble. They were, if such a thing is possible, ensemble performance art.

By re-examining plays that had become part of the theatrical canon, the Wooster Group acknowledged the centrality of these texts in contemporary culture. Yet these plays were also rooted in their own time and place. Mere updating through alteration of locale or time period as many productions of classics often did would not, the group believed, be sufficient and could even trivialize the plays. LeCompte and the Wooster Group reframed and recontextualized the plays in a radical way in order to create a contemporary response to the works. As a result of this approach the productions were sometimes identified as deconstructionist. Insofar as the productions dismantled texts for the purpose of exploration they fit the literal definition of the term, but these productions had little to do with Derridean notions of deconstruction, although they correspond to the larger postmodern aesthetic as defined by Jean-François Lyotard and Fredric Jameson. Rather than proving that the text has no inherent authority, as the deconstructionist theoreticians assert, these productions sought to find fresh meanings and reverberations in a contemporary world. The original texts became merely one component in a new and larger performance text that drew upon the particular theatrical world of the Wooster Group. This world included references to past productions, to the panorama of contemporary American culture, to Kabuki theatre, movies, and even racial and gender politics, though the latter was presented as an aspect of contemporary culture rather than as particular sociopolitical tract. The Wooster Group both devoured and re-presented contemporary culture; they had no overt political agenda.

As noted, performance art became, by the late seventies, the most ubiquitous form of avant-garde theatre. With roots in the work of Vladimir Mayakovsky, Marcel Duchamp and the Dadaists, Happenings, the political monologues of comedian Lenny Bruce, and the almost unclassifiable theatrical performances of Jack Smith, performance art began to emerge in the late sixties, first among artists such as Vito Acconci, Carolee Schneeman, Linda Montano, and Chris Burden, and then increasingly among theatre performers. In its rejection of conventional theatrical illusion it can be seen as a logical outgrowth of the work of the Living Theatre. It was also an attack on the commercialization of art, since nothing other than documentation remained of the creative act; there was nothing that could be bought or sold. Its emphasis upon autobiography, and particularly the body, made it the ideal ground for feminist artists and performers to explore concepts of gender. Building on the ideas of the Dadaists and the Living Theatre, early performance art explored the intersection of life and art: the actions of daily life became art and vice versa. Finally, the utter simplicity of much performance art – a single performer on a bare stage, although it could certainly be more complex – seemed an inevitable response to the age of increasing costs. Perhaps because performance art seemed a natural outgrowth of the new age preoccupation with the self, it was not surprising that much of the new performance shifted from New York to California, where so many new age ideas originated.

The Theatre of Identity

Throughout the seventies and eighties, the politics of identity made it increasingly difficult to critique theatre from any universal or absolute viewpoint. Any work of art was seen as representative of the culture that created it, and the diverse culture of the United States was no longer perceived as a vast melting pot as it had been for much of the century, but as a "mosaic" or "salad," to use two of the more colorful metaphors, in which the diverse elements retained their individual identities and characteristics. Thus, one could no longer talk about *the* theatre but about women's theatre, Hispanic theatre, black theatre, gay theatre, and so on. The theatre that grew out of the migrant farm workers' strikes in southern California was Chicano theatre, which was distinctly different from the Latino theatre of New York; theatre by women was seen as separate from theatre by men, but distinct from feminist theatre, which in and of itself might be categorized by differing social and political agendas. These developments allowed voices to be heard that had previously been silent or muted in the American theatre and as a result they began to reach new audiences. While this multivocal, multicultural approach could lead to a revitalization of theatre it could also have the opposite effect. A fragmented theatre is difficult to maintain; a theatre with a limited audience often does not have the resources to sustain itself. On the other hand, many of these identity oriented theatres sprang up in response to a specific need at a particular time and then faded as the needs changed.

Various forms of feminist theatre have had some of the most significant impact on late-century American theatre and drama. The vitality and sheer quantity of women's theatres springing up around the country beginning in the late seventies created an energy and innovation in theatre production similar to that of Off-Off Broadway at its peak. As important was a concurrent development of a significant body of theory that had implications well beyond feminist theatre.

Feminism, which had remained fairly silent since the suffragist movement succeeded in 1920, began to re-emerge in the sixties, stimulated in part by the Civil Rights Movement and the anti-war protests. Although women had been making strides toward social, political, and economic parity with men throughout the century, there was a backlash of sorts following World War II. The women who had necessarily constituted a significant portion of the labor force during the war were now being actively encouraged to return to their "rightful" place in the domestic order. Postwar studies in child psychology suggested that children's happiness depended on the active presence of the mother; the middle-class move to suburbia isolated women in their homes; manufacturers created vast panoplies of "labor-saving" appliances and cleansing products with the clear message that the woman's first task was keeping the home and family clean. Television's situation comedies created a new breed of "supermoms" who were domestic, patient, subservient to husband and children, and always impeccably dressed and coifed even when doing household chores. Television commercials and programs, and to a lesser extent movies, suggested that the major cause of domestic strife was the wrong choice in household products.

In 1963 Betty Friedan published *The Feminine Mystique,* which exploded the myth of domestic bliss and fulfillment and articulated many of the frustrations and anger of women from many sectors of society. This book served as a catalyst for a revitalization of the women's movement, beginning with the National Organization for Women in 1966 and many other, often more radical groups, later. The initial efforts of many of these organizations were aimed at equality and parity in the labor, education, and political arenas, a movement generally known as liberal feminism. But inspired in part by French feminist theorists, several writers began to re-examine the larger situation of women within the society. Radical feminists emphasized differences between men and women while often stressing the superiority of female modes of behavior and thought and, like the militant black movement, advocating separatism; materialist feminists, drawing upon Marxism, looked at the effects of race, class, and gender on women's place in society and advocated the importance of the group over the individual. One aspect of feminist theory was the concept of the "gaze" – who is watching whom and how does the act of watching alter both the observer and the observed? Such a theoretical framework was an ideal approach to theatre and film, both of which are based on the act of watching and the interaction of performer and spectator.

Following the societal trends, the earliest forces in women's theatre were directed largely at providing greater opportunities for women's voices to be heard in the theatre. Prior to the sixties the number of women playwrights whose work received major productions could literally be counted on one hand. In the postwar years this sorority was limited almost entirely to Lillian Hellman and Lorraine Hansberry. While the Off-Off Broadway movement had provided a forum for a significant number of plays by women, and some of these, notably the plays of Megan Terry and Maria Irene Fornés, achieved a recognized place in American drama and significant productions Off-Broadway and in regional and university theatres, none of them was ever accorded a Broadway production or mainstream recognition.

A small group of women playwrights began to emerge in the seventies who were able to achieve a degree of success in the mainstream commercial theatre. The first was Tina Howe, whose Absurdist-inflected and sometimes fantastical plays served as a critique of American culture and mores. Her greatest successes came in the eighties with *Painting Churches* (1983), *Coastal Disturbances* (1986), and *Approaching Zanzibar* (1989), which all dealt in various ways with issues of love and loss. Beth Henley's *Crimes of the Heart* (1981), the first of several of her plays in the Southern gothic tradition, was the first play ever to win the Pulitzer Prize prior to a Broadway production. Marsha Norman also received a Pulitzer Prize for *'night, Mother* (1983), a wrenching play about a mother and daughter and the daughter's suicide. Wendy Wasserstein has been the most successful of the mainstream women playwrights, in part because of her strong characters and fierce wit, and in part because thematically her plays often confront the dilemma faced by many women caught between feminist aspirations and the pressures and appeal of tradition. Her plays such as *Uncommon Women and Others* (1977) and the Pulitzer and Tony Award-winning *The Heidi Chronicles* (1989) dealt with women of the baby-boom generation, with one foot in the world of their mothers and the traditions of the Eisenhower or even prewar years and the other in the feminist ideals of the post seventies. The very things that have made her one of the few commercially viable playwrights of the eighties and nineties – a strong comic sensibility, appealing characters that are derived from social archetypes, easily digestible discussions of contemporary problems – have also brought her condemnation. She has been attacked for many of the same reasons as Neil Simon; critics belittle her seemingly superficial treatment of contemporary society and apparently glib humor. Yet like Simon, she has found an audience which sees in the inevitably simplified world of her plays the complexities of their own lives.

Almost all the women playwrights have suffered to some degree or other at the hands of male critics and producers because of their altered dramatic emphases. The more traditional women playwrights tend to structure their plays around the emotional relationship of characters and place a greater emphasis on mood and language (though precedents can certainly be found in Williams and Inge); the more experimental, including Fornés, Terry, Rosalyn Drexler, and Adrienne Kennedy, have on occasion abandoned Aristotelian structure, discursive language, and even Cartesian time and space. While such strategies are not solely the provenance of women playwrights, they have often baffled male-dominated critiques and rendered some of these writers and their plays virtually invisible. In response, some of these playwrights have abandoned major theatre centers altogether. Jo Ann Schmidman founded the Omaha Magic Theatre in 1968, and since 1974 Megan Terry has been a playwright in residence there.

Some of the energy of the Off-Off Broadway movement of the sixties has been regenerated by the feminist theatres of the late eighties and nineties. Beginning in the wake of the women's liberation movement of the early seventies, radical feminist theatre groups have surfaced around the country. Mostly separatist organizations, their goal has been the restructuring of women's roles in society through a theatre that allowed women to see their lives validated onstage and which raised questions of power and cultural hegemony. To some extent they turned to Brechtian techniques and collective structures to try to free themselves from what has been perceived as a male hierarchical structure. Of those early groups, only a few such as Spiderwoman Theatre, a Native American theatre company, survive. But in the eighties in New York, an active lesbian-feminist theatre began to emerge. Most successful among these has been Split Britches, founded in 1981 by Lois Weaver, Peggy Shaw, and Deborah Margolin at WOW (Women's One World) Café. Their productions confront contemporary social and political issues, but do so by appropriating the vocabulary, style, and content of popular culture to create plays that are both surreal and comic. WOW also gave birth to the performance art of Holly Hughes who has also written for Split Britches and whose autobiographical monologues owe something to the verbal riffs of Sam Shepard, but are also among the more powerful examples of personal writing in the last decade. And it gave rise to the campy performances of the Five Lesbian Brothers, whose sendups of popular culture play with the simultaneous presence and invisibility of lesbians in American society.

Aspects of feminist and African American theatre have been combined in the works of Suzan-Lori Parks in the nineties. Her plays deal in part with themes of racism and feminism, yet they do so by ransacking history and dragging it onto the stage for radical re-evaluation. In *The America Play* (1990), for instance, a black man plays Abraham Lincoln in a side-show setting, allowing paying customers to re-enact the assassination over and over. Parks's discursive and repetitive narrative frameworks and poetic and jazz-like language, which emphasize variations and transformations on a theme rather than linear story-telling, work well for an approach to history that suggests that history is constantly warped and reshaped by the point of view of the viewer and the story-teller. Yet at the core of Parks's plays are characters who long for meaning within an often incomprehensible world and for human connection in a world of loneliness.

Gay theatre underwent a similar evolution. Gay playwrights such as

Williams, Inge, and Albee had virtually dominated postwar theatre, but the homosexual themes in their plays were either masked or non-existent. But the Off-Off Broadway movement, Caffe Cino in particular, gave voice to many openly gay playwrights who placed homosexual characters and themes in their plays and gloried in camp sensibility. In a famous 1964 essay, Susan Sontag explored and defined the world of camp. "To perceive Camp in objects and persons," she explained, "is to understand Being-as-Playing-a-Role. It is the farthest extension, in sensibility, of the metaphor of life as theater." She went on to observe: "Camp taste draws on a mostly unacknowledged truth of taste: the most refined form of sexual attractiveness (as well as the most refined form of sexual pleasure) consists in going against the grain of one's sex" (*Against Interpretation*, 281). Furthermore, camp emphasized "texture, sensuous surface, and style at the expense of content" (280). The plays of H.M. Koutoukas with their combination of "whimsy, speed, camp and insanity" (Poland and Mailman, *The Off-Off Broadway Book*, xvii), Robert Patrick, William M. Hoffman, and Lanford Wilson fit within this definition. Wilson's *The Madness of Lady Bright* (1964), about an aging "screaming preening queen," became the first Off-Off Broadway hit. This sensibility was developed in all its outrageousness in the work of John Vaccaro and the Play-House of the Ridiculous and the plays of Ron Tavel. Flouting sexual and social norms, as well as any semblance of dramatic structure or decorum, these plays out-raged and provoked. The Play-House of the Ridiculous eventually dissolved, but an offshoot, the Ridiculous Theatrical Company, headed by actor Charles Ludlam, eventually transformed from a peripatetic group operating on the perverse edges of the theatrical scene to a respectable company of actors creating travesties of nineteenth-century theatre with a gay and camp sensibility, while elevating the well-made play and other nineteenth-century forms to the sublime. Ludlam's transvestite portrayal of Marguerite Gauthier in *Camille*, his adaptation of Dumas *fils' The Lady of the Camellias*, is generally acknowledged as a piece of *tour de force* acting, while the production remarkably walked an aesthetic tightrope between farce and pathos.

Gay theatre, meanwhile, began to find more mainstream outlets with Mart Crowley's *The Boys in the Band* (1968), which used the context of a party to explore the private loves, longings, emotions and frustrations of a group of gay men. Though in retrospect, the play is stereotypical and even offensive in its depictions of character types, and while there was a somewhat peep-show atmosphere – some straight spectators came to get a view of gay life, much as they did to see the nude scene in *Hair* – it was nonetheless a breakthrough that began to introduce straight audiences to homosexuals as individuals. It also provided gay spectators with gay-created characters – not the humorous or pathetic stereotypes more typical of the mainstream theatre. Just as the Vietnam War aroused many theatre artists into a politically oriented theatre, the Stonewall Riot of 1969 – in which patrons of a gay bar in Greenwich Village actively resisted a police raid, thereby setting off a chain reaction of activism leading to rapidly increased visibility and political presence by gays – was a catalyst in the evolution of gay drama. The number of plays and productions with gay characters and themes increased exponentially, and the plays addressed not only the emotional lives of characters but took on political and social issues. By 1983, Harvey Fierstein's *Torch Song Trilogy* was able to combine elements of sitcom, camp, and tragic irony to win a Tony.

The AIDS epidemic galvanized writers and transformed gay theatre. Just as the disease itself served as a lightning rod for a range of political and social responses to homosexuality both within as well as outside the gay community, the theatre now reflected everything from political-action plays to Arthur Miller-like plays of moral and social conscience. Plays such as Larry Kramer's *The Normal Heart* and William M. Hoffman's *As Is* attacked the mainstream society for its perceived silence and indifference, while trying to come to terms with the enormity of the toll the plague was taking on not only the gay community but society as a whole. The power and success of several of these plays often lay more in their message and passion, which coincided with the mood of the time and helped to transform societal perceptions, than in their dramaturgical excellence. Kramer, through his organization ActUp, brought theatricality to social and political action, somewhat as Abbie Hoffman and the "yippies" had done in the early seventies. Borrowing techniques from guerilla theatre, activists would disrupt social, cultural, and political events to achieve publicity – often on television news – while sending a strong message.

Paula Vogel's *Baltimore Waltz* (1992), however, typified an emerging trend in the nineties toward plays of grief and rage that, by functioning on an allegorical or metaphorical level, removed themselves from the specifics of newspaper headlines and allowed audiences to place the tragedy in a larger historical and, importantly, emotional framework. Tony Kushner's *Angels in America*, more than any other play of the period, was generally regarded as transcending the narrow confines of a single audience or subject while at the same time embodying the themes and ideas of much gay theatre from the previous three decades. Divided into two parts, *Millennium Approaches* and *Perestroika*, each close to four hours long, the play employed an epic structure to observe American society at the end of the twentieth century. With its sweeping overview of history, politics, and culture placed within an apocalyptic yet optimistic vision, and couched in surprising touches of humor, the play cut across lines of gender, sexual preference, and even race to reach a broad audience.

Angels in America has had numerous successful productions at resident theatres across the country as well as an acclaimed London production, and won the Pulitzer Prize. The New York production, directed by George C. Wolfe of the New York Shakespeare Festival, received generally glowing reviews as well as several Tony Awards, yet indicative of the state of commercial theatre in the early nineties, the high cost of producing and running the show combined with less than capacity audiences after the first few months led to a relatively short run. The Broadway theatre of the late twentieth century has had difficulty sustaining dramatic fare.

The sense of loss and existential despair that typified so many of the plays of the fifties and sixties, and the concurrent demise of language as a tool for communication, had transformed over the subsequent decades into desire for human contact and communication and a search for meaning in an often hostile or uncaring world. Loss was no longer vague or recondite in American society: the American dream had been shattered in Vietnam – an inexplicable war that we could not win – and in Watergate where political corruption led to the first presidential resignation in the nation's history; racism, which had briefly appeared solvable, re-emerged as a seemingly incurable cancer eating away at society; materialism, which had been an ever present factor in American society, though always masked beneath the surface of democratic ideals, emerged as a primary social force in the Reagan years; and the AIDS epidemic brought fears and prejudices to the forefront of society while decimating a portion of that society. Perhaps in response to these changes the family, at least in its traditional and historical configuration, dissolved as a workable or relevant metaphor for the drama. *Angels in America*, seen in this context, became a paradigm of *fin de siècle* American drama. A sprawling work, it encompassed history, religion, sexuality, and millennial and apocalyptic visions as each of the characters struggled to find or maintain a human relationship. This struggle for human contact, support, and love emerged as the primary concern of a range of plays.

While it is no longer possible in the last decade of the twentieth century for a single dramatic voice to speak for the cacophony of voices that is the United States, the playwright who may come closest, the one playwright who has a chance of standing in that line of descent from Eugene O'Neill, is August Wilson. Writing in 1997, social and cultural critic Henry Louis Gates, Jr. declared that Wilson "is probably the most celebrated American playwright now writing and is certainly the most accomplished black playwright in this nation's history" ("The Chitlin Circuit," 44). Starting with *Ma Rainey's Black Bottom* (1982) and continuing with such plays as *Fences* (1983; Pulitzer Prize and Tony Award 1987), and *The Piano Lesson* (1989; Pulitzer Prize 1990), Wilson has been creating a chronicle of the African American life. While the characters, locales, situations, and narratives of these plays are drawn specifically from the African American experience, thematically and emotionally they have transcended the narrow confines of identity politics. Wilson has drawn upon the strengths of American drama – the microcosm of the family, fully-dimensional characters with whom an audience can empathize, vernacular language that rises to poetry, touches of symbolism and even magic realism, and an underlying optimism. Nonetheless, Wilson has thrown himself into the midst of the debate on identity politics. He has become a passionate advocate for black-run theatres and has stated unequivocally that black plays should be directed only by black directors and that black actors should act only in specifically black roles by black playwrights. Black actors should not, he argues, play in Shakespeare or Chekhov. Few artists of any race fully support such absolutist views and some have pointed to the contradictions raised by Wilson's own production record. Nonetheless, many are in agreement with Wilson's fundamental point that foundation support for color-blind casting and for supporting African American plays in the repertoires of regional theatres, however well intentioned, have undermined the development of African American theatres by creating an environment of tokenism and draining funds that might be used for the development of new theatres, audiences, and artists.

Conclusion

At the start of the twentieth century, American theatre was centered in a group of magnificent rococo buildings on Forty-second Street near Times Square in New York City, and most cities of any size had at least one theatre that housed either road companies emanating from Broadway or resident companies that would provide the context for productions by touring stars. Theatre was a business and as such it was controlled almost exclusively by two organizations: the so-called Syndicate and the upstart Shubert Brothers. Movies were a new gimmick confined to nickelodeons and as a curiosity in vaudeville shows. As the millennium approaches, to borrow Kushner's title, there are some startling echoes. Despite regular predictions about the imminent death of theatre, it continues to exist, if not exactly thrive. The Syndicate is gone, but the Shubert Organization remains the largest single theatre owner in the country, while its philanthropic arm, the Shubert Foundation, is the largest single supporter of not-for-profit theatre. The theatres along Forty-second Street which had, over the decades, devolved into movie houses, burlesque houses, pornography shops, and boarded-up decaying relics, are being transformed back into legitimate theatres. Interestingly, one of the largest stimuli for the resurgence is the Disney Corporation, which has discovered that live theatre is capable of producing huge profits, and has rapidly become one of the major producers of live theatre in the country. (In a very real sense, Disney has been one of the major producers of live theatre since the mid-fifties: its theme parks produce a wide variety of live entertainment, and the parks as a whole are seen by many cultural observers as a form of theatre. Since the early nineties, however, Disney has moved into legitimate theatres with musicals such as *Beauty and the Beast* and *The Lion King* adapted, interestingly, from its own animated movies.) Another player in the revitalization is a Canadian producing company, Livent, originally headed by producer Garth Drabinsky, who believes that financially independent theatre today depends upon providing huge spectacles for large audiences. Livent has developed a series of 1,500 to 2,000-seat theatres, including a renovation of two of the Forty-second Street houses, and brings in touring large-scale shows.

Serious drama may have little place on contemporary Broadway anymore, but new Off-Broadway theatres are being built for the first time in years to house the large number of productions that are vying for space. Meanwhile, the regional theatres continue to be a major source of original productions and classic theatre, although the ever decreasing public subsidy is threatening the ability of many of these theatres to survive or to produce original contributions. Playwrights, almost none of whom can make an adequate living writing solely for the theatre, have been writing for film and television. While this is hardly a new phenomenon – writers have been devoured by Hollywood almost from the moment moving pictures first "talked" – critics have acknowledged an increasing quality in much television drama. The sort of serious dramatic writing that once was reserved for the stage now shows up more often on television's police and hospital series. Writers for these programs have commented on the greater freedom to develop characters over time and the ability to explore these characters in a variety of situations in ways that the finite shape of a play does not allow.

The fifties was a decade of absolutes: men had jobs while women were housewives; the world was divided into "free" and Communist; one was a Republican or a Democrat, and so on. Shades of gray were suspect. Similarly, theatre was divided into drama, comedy, and musicals; other performance categories included opera and ballet. Popular entertainments such as the circus were not seriously considered as performance by most audiences. But just as the Civil Rights, women's, and gay movements, the counterculture life styles, and the avant-garde all worked to break down barriers and alter assumptions about life and art, theatrical categories evaporated as well. Theatre became performance and included under its umbrella traditional and popular forms, rituals, paratheatrical activities, and even the performative aspects of daily life. Today, many presentations defy simple categorization, training incorporates a wide range of disciplines, and artists work in several genres. On the other hand, identity politics still informs the creation and producing of many theatres and defines the habits of particular audiences.

A great unknown for the future of theatre is the realm referred to as "cyber-space" – the world of computers, virtual reality, and digital communication. Some performance artists such as Laurie Anderson and George Coates have created performance pieces for the World Wide Web that allow "spectators" sitting at their computer terminals to interact with the work of art. There have been primitive attempts at three-dimensional scenery using special goggles and computer-enhanced images. While it seems unlikely that so-called virtual theatre or the gimmickry and wizardry of contemporary technology in and of itself will replace or even seriously alter live theatre, the new technologies are rapidly and subtly transforming the way in which we view and understand the world. Just as perspective painting and scientific thought transformed the art and theatre of the Renaissance, and relativity and quantum physics affected twentieth-century art and theatre, so too will the new digital and electronic technologies transform theatre for the next centuries through the alteration of perceptions in ways that cannot be predicted or even understood.

Spectacle, which has had a central place in American theatre dating back at least to the proto-musical pageant known as *The Black Crook* in 1866, is still to be found in Broadway musicals, especially the British imports of Andrew Lloyd Webber such as *Phantom of the Opera* and *Sunset Boulevard*. But by the mid-nineties, the taste for such spectacle theatre seemed to be declining on Broadway. It found its way instead into the ever increasing technical extrava-ganzas of Las Vegas, into the circus, and, as mentioned, into rock concerts. Ringling Bros. and Barnum & Bailey Circus, for instance, which bills itself as "the greatest show on Earth," has more resemblance to a Las Vegas show than to a traditional nineteenth-century circus. Cirque du Soleil, a Canadian "circus" that employs no animals, has, in fact, found a permanent home in Las Vegas. Its success derives from grafting spectacle and non-verbal narrative onto traditional variety entertainments, all done with consummate showman-ship. Meanwhile, the presidential nominating conventions of the Republican and Democratic parties have borrowed heavily from the technology of rock concerts to provide a theatrical spectacle that is more about impressing a television audience than it is about carrying out the rituals of democracy. These conventions that would undoubtedly seem baffling to a Truman, Eisenhower, Kennedy, or Johnson are perfectly comprehensible to a public familiar with Andrew Lloyd Webber, the Rolling Stones, and the theatrical entertainments of Superbowl halftime shows. Just as historians who study the Renaissance theatre often pay more attention to the court masques, royal entries, public executions, and state pageants than to the written drama of the period, it may be that future historians will find the paratheatrical entertain-ments of American culture in the second half of the twentieth century – sport-ing events, rock concerts, urban street fairs, theme parks, restored historical villages, shopping malls, political campaign rallies and conventions, and Las

Vegas and its clones – more representative of theatre than the conventional drama or musical.

It is clear at the end of the twentieth century that the theatre is far from dead. Statistics suggest a stubborn vitality all across the country. Theatre training programs continue to have ample numbers of applicants; literary offices are swamped with submissions of new plays; almost every city of any size has at least one theatre. What has changed is theatre's place within the society and the means of production. Mainstream theatre is rarely casual entertainment any more. The large commercial theatres and the "official" theatres – the urban or state arts centers – are run by entertainment conglomerates or corporate boards. They have become showcases for culture or tourist destinations. Smaller venues are dedicated to political or artistic agendas aimed at generally narrow but supportive audiences. Those forms that have historically constituted popular theatre have been largely subsumed by television, film, popular music, and perhaps by computers and the Internet. There is a potential danger in this last development. The popular theatre has always been the training ground for performers and writers. Learning to engage an audience, interact with it, and communicate with it is crucial for the continuation of a vital theatre. The loss of that venue will mean the loss of new generations of performers with adequate experience in the give and take of live theatre. Stand-up comedy, one of the last vestiges of variety entertainment, provides some of that experience, but it is not the same as the complex interactions of a narrative structure and several actors.

The human desire for live performance – what Aristotle understood as a human inclination to mimic – will keep theatre alive in the future as it has in the past. But the electronic media are a new factor which makes the future even more unpredictable than ever.

Notes

1 For economic and production figures, see Baumol and Bowen, *Performing Arts – The Economic Dilemma*, and Moore, *The Economics of the American Theater*.
2 Sievers, *Freud on Broadway*.
3 See Peter Stone, "Why Fill the Stage if the Seats Are Empty?" *New York Times*, 10 January 1988: A15.
4 See Bosley Crowther's review of *The Wild One* in the *New York Times*, 31 December 1953.
5 See Ginsberg's "Prologue" in *Beat Culture and the New America 1950–1965*, ed. Phillips.
6 See Kirby, "The Structure of Performance," in *A Formalist Theatre*, 28–29ff.
7 Ginsberg interview on *All Things Considered*, National Public Radio, 31 January 1993.

8 See Brustein's review of *The Connection, The New Republic,* 28 September 1959: 30.
9 The *Tulane Drama Review* initially began as the *Carleton Drama Review* under Robert Corrigan. In 1968 it moved to New York University and became known as *The Drama Review.*
10 Recounted by Schechner in "Guerilla Theatre," *The Drama Review* 14, 3 (T47, 1970): 165.

Bibliography: American Theatre in Context: 1945–Present

While there was once a strong niche in book publishing for theatre history and dramatic literature, the market has shrunk considerably in recent decades. University and small presses have been prolific in areas such as poststructuralist theory and feminist and gay studies, but traditional narrative or analytical histories are less common. There has, however, been a proliferation of journals devoted to aspects of theatre, and any study of contemporary American theatre must look to these as well as newspapers and mainstream periodicals. For the daily and weekly chronicling of events primary sources are the *New York Times,* the *Village Voice, Variety, Backstage, InTheatre* (which replaced *TheatreWeek*), and *Time Out.* The journals and newsletters of professional organizations such as The Dramatists Guild and the Society of Stage Directors and Choreographers (SSD&C) are especially helpful for both current events and long-term issues. The most useful journals and serials include: *American Theatre*; *The Drama Review* (formerly *Tulane Drama Review* – a selected collection of essays can be found in McNamara's and Dolan's *The Drama Review: Thirty Years of Commentary on the Avant-Garde*); *Performing Arts Journal*; *Theater* (formerly *Yale Theater*); *Theatre Crafts*; *Theatre Forum*; and *Theatre Journal* (formerly *Educational Theatre Journal*). For documenting theatre seasons the best source is *The Best Plays* series. John Degen in Chapter 4 provides a lengthy guide to American musical theatre, which should be consulted for those interested in that topic.

The American theatre, of course, must be seen in the cultural history of its time. There are many popular books surveying individual decades, such as Halberstam's *The Fifties*. A superb history of the period 1945–47 is Patterson's *Grand Expectations*. General histories that were of particular use in writing this chapter were Gitlin, *The Sixties*; Miller and Nowak, *The Fifties*; and Morgan and Wynn, *America's Century*. Studies of particular aspects of the postwar society include Bell, *The Cultural Contradictions of Capitalism*; Luce, *The Ideas of Henry Luce*; Brown, *Life Against Death*; Galbraith, *The Affluent Society*; Riesman et al., *The Lonely Crowd*; and Whyte, *The Organization Man*. The intellectual atmosphere and the literary and cultural debates of the era are addressed particularly well in the *Partisan Review*, especially the issue of May–June 1952. For theoretical and analytical underpinnings of the era see Fiedler, *Love and Death in the American Novel*; Huyssen, *After the Great Divide*; Reische, *The Performing Arts in America*; Sontag, *Against Interpretation*; and Trilling, *Beyond Culture.* The emergence of the Beat Generation and the counterculture are documented in Banes, *Greenwich Village 1963*; Holmes, "This Is the Beat Generation"; Knight and Knight, *The Beat Vision*; Kornbluth, *Notes from the New Underground*; Melville, *Communes in the Counter Culture;* Phillips, *Beat Culture and the New America 1950–1965*; and Starr, *Cultural Politics.*

Placing postwar theatre in context requires an understanding of related arts and media, including the visual arts, literature, dance, music, film, and television. The history and theory of postwar visual art could, of course, fill many shelves. Those I found particularly useful include: Duberman, *Black Mountain*; Frascina, *Pollock and After*; Greenberg, *Art and Culture*; Haskell, *Blam! The Explosion of Pop, Minimalism, and Performance*; Guilbaut, *How New York Stole the Idea of Modern Art*; Kaprow, *Assemblage, Environments, and Happenings*, and "The Legacy of Jackson Pollock"; Motherwell, *The Collected Writings of Robert Motherwell*; Rosenberg, *The Tradition of the New*; Seitz, *The Art of Assemblage*; Tomkins, *The Bride and the Bachelors* and *Off the Wall*. For the dance world see Banes, *Terpsichore in Sneakers*; Cunningham, *The Dancer and the Dance;* Copeland and Cohen, *What Is Dance?*. Popular music is dealt with in Goldstein, *The Poetry of Rock*, and Marcus, *Ranters & Crowd Pleasers*. Two classic books on television are Barnouw, *Tube of Plenty*; and Postman, *Amusing Ourselves to Death*. The classic study of media, of course, is McLuhan, *Understanding Media*. A broad look at the trends in performance across disciplines can be seen by reading the catalogues of the *Next Wave Festival* at the Brooklyn Academy of Music from 1983 on. Since the early eighties books on postmodernism have been proliferating. Venturi's *Learning from Las Vegas* is by now a classic; the best collection of essential sources can be found in Docherty, *Postmodernism*.

General histories and overviews of theatre of the period include: Atkinson, *Broadway*; Berkowitz, *New Broadways;* Bigsby, *A Critical Introduction to Twentieth Century American Drama;* Cohn, *New American Dramatists*; Engel, *The American Musical Theatre*; Gottfried, *Broadway Musicals*; Kernan, *The Modern American Theatre;* Harris, *Broadway*; Meserve, *Discussions of Modern American Drama*; and Taubman, *The Making of the American Theatre*.

Useful collections of theory and criticism are Bentley, *The Theatre of Commitment* and *The Theatre of War*; Brustein, *The Third Theatre*; Lahr, *Astonish Me*; Meserve, *Discussions of Modern American Drama*; Reinelt and Roach, *Critical Theory and Performance*; and Rogoff, *Theatre Is Not Safe*.

The economics of the theatre are covered most thoroughly in Baumol and Bowen, *Performing Arts;* Moore, *The Economics of the American Theater*; Poggi, *Theater in America*; and the Rockefeller Panel Report, *The Performing Arts*. A more narrative look at commercial production can be found in Goldman, *The Season*.

Alternative theatre movements (see also sources in Carlson, Chapter 2, "Alternative Theatre") provide great insight into theatre and culture, because they reveal the *status quo* through the reactions against it. The best studies of aspects of the avant-garde are addressed in Battcock and Nickas, *The Art of Performance*; Kirby, *A Formalist Theatre* and *Happenings*; Kostelanetz, *The Theatre of Mixed Means*; Sayre, *The Object of Performance*, while the Off- and Off-Off Broadway movements are covered in Auerbach, *Sam Shepard, Arthur Kopit, and the Off Broadway Theater*; Cordell and Matson, *The Off-Broadway Theatre;* Little, *Off-Broadway*; Orzel and Smith, *Eight Plays from Off-Off Broadway;* Poland and Mailman, *The Off-Off Broadway Book*; Sainer, *The Radical Theatre Notebook*; Schevill, *Break Out! In Search of New Theatrical Environments;* Shank, *American Alternative Theatre*; and Smith, *More Plays from Off-Off Broadway*.

Many individual artists and groups, of course, are covered extensively in the journals mentioned above. Among book-length studies see Beck, *The Life of the Theatre*; Biner, *The Living Theatre;* Blumenthal, *Joseph Chaikin*; Cage, *Silence*; Brecht, *The Theatre of Visions: Robert Wilson*; Chaikin, *The Presence of the Actor*; Davy, *Richard Foreman and the Ontological-Hysteric Theatre;* Foreman, *Unbalancing Acts;* Holmberg, *The Theatre of Robert Wilson*; Kostelanetz, *John Cage (Ex)plain(ed);* Malina, *The*

Diaries of Judith Malina 1947–1957; Pasolli, *A Book on the Open Theatre*; Savran, *The Wooster Group 1975–1985;* Schechner, *Dionysus in '69* and *Environmental Theater.* and Tytell, *The Living Theatre.* Of the great amount written about black theatre I found the following most useful: Abramson, *Negro Playwrights in the American Theatre*; Gates, Jr., "The Chitlin Circuit"; Hill, *The Theatre of Black Americans*; Mitchell, *Black Drama.* The sources on women's theatre and feminist theory are expanding rapidly. Ones I found particularly useful were Case, *Feminism and Theatre* and *Performing Feminisms*; Champagne, *Out from Under*; and Dolan, *The Feminist Spectator as Critic.*

2

A Changing Theatre: Broadway to the Regions

Broadway

Laurence Maslon

Introduction

The object that stands outside the circle usually casts the longest shadow across it. To understand the ever increasingly complicated world of Broadway in the last half of this century, one only has to look at a single event on the evening – midnight to be exact – of 6 April 1947 when, at the Waldorf Astoria, the American Theatre Wing paid tribute to its former executive director, Antoinette Perry, who had died the previous year. The tribute came in the form of awards given for achievements on Broadway in that current season – and they would be called, in respect for Ms. Perry, the Tony Awards.

The evening was a casual affair, by contemporary standards. There were no ranks of nominees from which a winner suspensefully emerged; there were no "bests" – just outstanding achievements; there was some brief entertainment courtesy of several musicals then running, plus performers such as Frank Fay, Ethel Waters, and newcomer David Wayne; the list of awards was broadcast at midnight for fifteen minutes on a local radio station.[1]

What was significant that night is that despite the almost coyly modest affair, the Tony Awards – and the larger enterprise they became – were Broadway's first attempt to model itself after another entertainment industry – the movies – and eventually by the fifties, the selection and presentation of the awards mirrored those of the Academy of Motion Picture Arts and Science's Oscar presentations almost exactly. The television broadcast of the Tony Awards became the apogee of the theatrical season (and occasionally was more provocative than the season itself) and the last, best chance for Broadway to reach a national audience. By replicating the format and the publicity of the film industry with the Tony Awards, Broadway had silently conceded its role as the dominant center for creative achievement in the performing arts.

163

Broadway had survived the advent of Hollywood, the exodus of creative forces moving west, the raids on the talent pool. But, from 1950 on, the challenges were more insidious and more numerous. There were artistic factors, such as the freedom from commercial pressure that could be discovered in the growing Off-Broadway scene; political factors, such as the decay of urban New York in the sixties and seventies; geographic factors, such as the rise of suburbia after the Second World War and the growth of competitive regional theatre outside the New York area; and, of course, technological challenges, such as the rise of television (first broadcast, then cable) and advances in motion picture technology. Even the advent of the credit card had its effect. Broadway had to struggle to find an identity, let alone reclaim a prominence, in an increasingly obstreperous performance culture.

The 1950s: TV and Sympathy

"The stage is a place for ideas, for philosophies, for the most intense discussion of man's fate," wrote Arthur Miller in 1951 (quoted in Atkinson, *Broadway*, 442). For him – and for Tennessee Williams – that stage was to be found on Broadway. Following on an impressive tradition of serious American drama between the wars, Miller and Williams set the terms of the debate for American drama in the fifties and, in many ways, far, far beyond.

Williams's string of accomplishments – *The Rose Tattoo* (1950), *Camino Real* (1953), *Cat on a Hot Tin Roof* (1955), and *Sweet Bird of Youth* (1959), all directed by Elia Kazan, who brought out the best in Williams and Miller – was perfectly in tune with the psychological and sexual issues that postwar audiences were willing to explore (for a discussion of Williams and other playwrights of this period, see Chapter 3). Williams's quest for psychological acuity, sexual frankness, and universal truth in the portrayal of the most neglected of God's creatures provided a model for other playwrights, including William Inge, whose output in the fifties was impressive by any standard, beginning with *Come Back, Little Sheba* in 1950, followed by *Bus Stop, Picnic*, and, to a lesser degree, *The Dark at the Top of the Stairs*. With its fragile frankness, Robert Anderson's *Tea and Sympathy* (1953) – hardly the kind of play that would shock audiences today, let alone engage them – became a major success of the decade. Even this gentle exploration of homosexuality and coming of age was too much for Hollywood to bear; the film version deleted the drama's central conflict.

Arthur Miller – the embodiment of the serious dramatist – was the decade's playwright of ideas and he succeeded admirably with *The Crucible* (1953), his view of the Salem witch trials through the prism of the McCarthy hearings. *The Crucible* had a respectable run (197 performances) on Broadway, tri-

1. Caricatures of (left to right) Tennessee Williams, Elia Kazan, and Arthur Miller, major figures in the Broadway theatre of the 1950s. Illustration by Laurence Maslon.

umphed Off-Broadway four seasons later for 571 performances, became a staple for regional theatres after the seventies, and eventually a Hollywood movie in 1996.

However, these were by no means the only serious dramas. *Inherit the Wind* (1955), a lightly fictionalized version of the Scopes "monkey" trial, by Jerome Lawrence and Robert E. Lee, was a significant work (mounted first at Margo Jones's theatre in Dallas): like *The Crucible*, it provided its own reading of the intellectual and moral retrogression of the blacklisting period. There was some criticism about its synthetic quality, but a star performance by Paul Muni, making his first Broadway appearance in almost a quarter of a century, helped give it a long and successful history in film and revivals.

In a way, the most impressive serious play of the decade was *The Diary of Anne Frank* (1955), adapted by the screenwriting husband-and-wife team of Frances Goodrich and Albert Hackett from Anne Frank's *Diary of A Young Girl*. Ruth Gordon, the actress and wife of the play's director, Garson Kanin, begged him not to do the play, insisting that audiences would be unwilling to watch such a painful work. But it took Broadway by storm, ran for two years, won every award possible, and eventually played to stunned audiences across Europe.

1956 brought two very different and important dramas to Broadway:

Samuel Beckett's *Waiting for Godot* and Eugene O'Neill's *Long Day's Journey Into Night*. *Godot* remains, to this day, the only Broadway presentation of Beckett's work. *Long Day's Journey Into Night* had its first performance in Stockholm, but its eagerly awaited Broadway debut, with Fredric March and Florence Eldridge and directed by José Quintero, met and exceeded all expectations. It ran for over a year, won the Pulitzer, made a star out of Jason Robards, Jr., and paved the way for the production of two more posthumous O'Neill plays – *A Moon for the Misbegotten* and *A Touch of the Poet*.

In 1959, Kenneth Tynan wrote, "There is only one trend in the Broadway theater and its name is Kazan" (quoted in Fehl, *On Broadway*, 334). Moving back and forth from Broadway to Hollywood, with such films as *On the Waterfront* and the adaptation of *Streetcar*, Kazan had a success and fluidity that no other director has matched. He was brilliant in selecting and working on scripts by major writers of the era – Williams, Inge, Miller – and in integrating and recognizing the work of the actors who came from The Actors Studio. There were others of similar drive and integrity, like producer Kermit Bloomgarden. *Salesman* made his career, but he followed it with *Anne Frank*, *The Crucible*, and such varied musicals as *The Most Happy Fella* and *The Music Man*, which, of all shows, several prominent directors and performers were unwilling to take on. Bloomgarden was from the old school of producing, trained in the business, willing to take chances, almost single-handedly, on a difficult project.

Critics and theatregoers would invoke the names of Williams, Miller, and Kazan for decades to come, while lamenting the demise of serious drama, the kind of play where audience members would be shaken and exalted by seeing something never discussed, played out and examined on stage before. The public certainly was not getting that kind of experience from Hollywood or television (and in the years to come, they would not be getting it from Broadway any more either), but in the fifties, because of these artists, Broadway was a forum for national debate.

Comedy on Broadway, however, was almost totally obscured by these achievements. The social satire produced between the wars was almost impossible to find. Even George S. Kaufman's one hit during the decade, *The Solid Gold Cadillac*, written with Howard Teichmann, was less a satire on Wall Street than an excuse for a fine comic performance by Josephine Hull. Sex was the dominant theme in comedy, but was often so coyly presented as to give a minimum of offense. In that respect, George Axelrod's *The Seven Year Itch* (a middle-aged man's flirtations with a beautiful neighbor when his wife is out of town) was paradigmatic. Other hits (*The Tunnel of Love*; *The Marriage-Go-Round*; *Goodbye, Charlie*; *Never Too Late*; and *Take Her She's Mine*) continued the trend into the sixties. Later, television was able to absorb such mildly titillating topics and make them the essence of its daily fare.

For many, the loss of legitimate comedy was more than compensated for by the pizazz and imagination of musical comedy. The fifties were an exhilarating and transitional time with the widest variety of musical styles existing simultaneously. Here, Rodgers and Hammerstein were as dominant in their field as Miller and Williams were in theirs. They ushered in the decade with a resounding success in *The King and I*, a work which displayed their gift for integrating story, songs, dance, and character. It became the model for the next generation of musical theatre artists.

As Rodgers and Hammerstein turned unsuccessfully to more serious subjects, the show for the proverbial "tired businessman" prospered with such gifted concoctions as *Can-Can, Wonderful Town, The Pajama Game*, and *Damn Yankees*, which created or consolidated the reputations of a new generation of artists: dancer Gwen Verdon, director-choreographer Bob Fosse, writers Betty Comden and Adolph Green, and producer Harold Prince. But in 1956, the unlikely musicalization of a 1912 social critique by Bernard Shaw changed the face of the Broadway musical.

Several composers had turned down the task of musicalizing *Pygmalion*, but Alan Jay Lerner and Frederick Loewe accepted the assignment and, under the skilled direction of Moss Hart, the resulting show *My Fair Lady* not only set a standard for elegance in musical theatre, but created a work which ran for a then-record-breaking 2,717 performances.

Although Rosalind Russell, a non-singer, had led *Wonderful Town* four seasons earlier, it was Rex Harrison's musical debut as Henry Higgins that changed producers' perceptions about the kind of actors who could front a musical; from then on, actors as well as musical performers starred in shows. The very improbability of the Shavian source material proved more of an incentive than a warning – the next twenty years would see musical adaptations of the most improbable material. Nevertheless, it was the increasing success of original cast recordings of Broadway musicals that brought in the CBS corporation as a major backer of *My Fair Lady*. The Columbia LP became a recording phenomenon and is now the third longest-selling recording of all time, in any category.[2] Hereafter, record companies and networks were eager to underwrite one of the greatest gambles in modern entertainment – a Broadway musical. With its cast album, successful tours and London production, plus a record-breaking movie sale, *My Fair Lady* made over $800 million (see Lerner, *The Street Where I Live*, 134), proving for this period the accuracy of Robert Anderson's axiom that "in the theatre, you can't make a living, but you can make a killing."

Because of the success of book musicals, such as *My Fair Lady,* the revue became a major casualty of changing theatrical tastes. The engine of Broadway in the twenties and thirties, it had little gas in it by mid-decade. The apparent death of the revue was also abetted by the advent and advance of television. In the fifties, television had a tangled relationship with Broadway. As an industry, it came of age in the late forties in Manhattan, thus giving it easy access to Broadway artists. But, in TV's infancy, it was deemed beneath the dignity of Broadway stars, and became the subject of mockery in musicals like Johnny Mercer's *Top Banana*, starring Phil Silvers (who would forsake Broadway after the 1951 show to become a TV star) and the hit comedy, *Anniversary Waltz*, where a television set was smashed nightly to the amusement of the audience. But gradually theatrical producers saw the appeal of the new medium and the number of prospective ticket buyers it could bring in. Television's early success with variety spectaculars (or "specials") quickly cannibalized the revue talent of comedians, singers, and dancers. Sid Caesar entertained Broadway audiences for a season in 1949 in *Make Mine Manhattan*; by 1954, he was reaching millions nationwide on *Your Show of Shows*.

Television was not only dependent on Broadway for talent, it drew on the Great White Way for a kind of cultural imprimatur. As a way of bolstering its own derided integrity, TV invoked the glamor of the legitimate stage for many of its programs, such as *Texaco Star Theater, All-Star Revue, Broadway Jamboree, Broadway Open House,* even *Stage Show*, a variety series produced by Jackie Gleason, where the show opened with a camera-eye-view of a spectator getting out of a limo, entering a theatre, walking down the aisle, grabbing a program, and sitting in a fifth-row aisle seat (see Brooks and Marsh, *The Complete Directory of Prime Time Network TV Shows*, 787). The most successful of these was Ed Sullivan's *Toast of the Town*, soon to be named after the Broadway columnist who gave Broadway shows a huge amount of publicity; an extended tribute to Lerner and Loewe in 1961 included a twenty-minute clip of their then-ailing new show *Camelot* which, overnight, reversed its fortunes forever after. Television thus, for a while, repaid its debt to theatre.

Dramatic work came out of television, too, as it appropriated the serious side of Broadway with shows like *Kraft Television Theater, Philco/Goodyear TV Playhouse,* and most famously *Playhouse 90*. Several playwrights were "graduated from" television, although critically derided at the time for their "roots," including Paddy Chayevsky, who made his Broadway debut with *The Middle of the Night* in 1956, followed by *The Tenth Man* in 1959. Critics sneered but were then confounded when scripts that began on television were expanded for the legitimate stage, and became hits. William Gibson's *The Miracle Worker*, for example, made a star out of Anne Bancroft, who played Helen Keller's teacher. (This went on to become a successful film, one of the first examples of a property to make the rounds in all three mediums.) Gore Vidal's *A Visit to a Small Planet* (1956) was also derided for its television pedigree, but was one of the few piquant episodes of social comedy during the decade. Vidal produced another successful play in 1960, *The Best Man*, but he grew bored with the theatre and returned to his career as a novelist and essayist.

Television, however, was just one rival for the attention of the Broadway theatregoer. In the fifties, Hollywood bought numerous theatres in the Times Square area and film openings in Times Square became larger events than their legitimate counterparts. A decade after World War II, a new generation with different entertainment habits was emerging. Producers and publicists had to look for new ways of commanding attention and positioning Broadway as the center of cultural life in New York, let alone America.

This required new ideas and new people to have them. Broadway producers came together in the League of New York Theatres and Producers, originally constituted in 1930. They tried to regulate performance schedules in order to accommodate customers; Broadway had to become what, in the nineties, would be called "user-friendly." An earlier (7:00 PM or 7:30 PM) Monday curtain was tried in the fifties to little success. But Sunday matinees were encouraged, box offices were forced to post location charts, fire codes were enforced, and two-for-one vouchers were promoted.

Ticket purchasing was still a cash-and-carry business, utilizing the box office or a ticket broker, but this was not without its problems. In the mid-fifties, a spate of hit shows caused a rash of ticket scalping and box office corruption (known as "ice") that would plague Broadway for two decades. It took until 1965 for the State Assembly to legislate standards for ticket sales, but corrupt practice continued, damaging Broadway's reputation at a time when it could ill afford it. A glimmer of hope in resolving these abuses came in 1958, when four Broadway theatres announced they would take ticket orders directly over the phone. Eventually, in the seventies, credit cards and computerized clearing agencies would take over ticket sales and move the stock out of abusive and illegal hands and into the consumers'.

Enter Merrick, Prince – and Papp in the Wings

Three producers who would have tremendous influence on the American theatre – and who were completely different from one another, except in their tenacity – began their careers in earnest in the mid-fifties: David Merrick, Harold Prince, and later Joseph Papp. The logistics of being a Broadway producer had changed considerably. The days of the gentleman producer, whose word was his bond and who could capitalize a production on his own, were over. Musicals, and even plays, required a consortium of investors, often acquired through a prolonged series of "backers'" auditions. Properties were negotiated with film studios, now frequently up front, and other industries, such as recording studios (especially after *My Fair Lady*'s cast album) and broadcasting networks, underwrote properties for the residual rights. This was also, thanks to producers like Merrick and Prince, the beginning of the long-run smash hit. Conversely, because of increasing labor expenses, shows

2. Caricatures of (left to right) Harold Prince, David Merrick, and Joseph Papp, major Broadway figures of the 1960s and 1970s. Illustration by Laurence Maslon.

became more expensive with considerable losses possible. Seasons were led by a few smash hits, followed by a couple of surprise survivors, trailed by an ever larger number of complete failures.

David Merrick began his career as a lawyer from St. Louis and, after a few initial efforts in the forties, made his mark on Broadway in 1954 by acquiring the musical rights to a series of French films by Marcel Pagnol. The resulting musical, *Fanny*, would never become a classic, but it was a success, due to Merrick's determination and his diabolical talent for publicity. Merrick was a unique combination of cruelty, single-mindedness, self-promotion, ambition, and genius. Five seasons after *Fanny*, he was able to open four productions in less than a month (two were hits). Most of the productions that interested him fell into two categories: the blockbuster musical (usually anchored by a star and a creative staff who had worked with him before, although they usually swore not to repeat the mistake) and a challenging foreign play (usually British). For two decades, these made Broadway a very interesting and robust place to be.

Merrick has been characterized as being neither a creative nor literate producer, often preferring to buy up British plays on shopping trips to England as if they were antiques, rather than read a new script. But the fact is he brought major works to America by John Osborne, Jean Anouilh, Tom Stoppard, as well as Peter Weiss's *Marat/Sade*, directed by Peter Brook. In the 1960–61 season, Merrick had produced six plays, including three musicals, two of which were hits. In the same year he founded the David Merrick Arts Foundation, a kind of not-for-profit subfealty that backed the more serious efforts until they had time to find their audience. It is his combative personality and his shameless audacity that lingers. He infamously publicized a flop musical called *Subways Are For Sleeping*, in 1961, by treating seven citizens to the show, each of whom had the same name as a leading Broadway critic, and writing rave reviews for them to endorse. The intended full page ad only ran in one paper, the *Herald-Tribune*, but it engendered a tremendous amount of publicity (see Kissel, *David Merrick*, 226, 231–34).

Working after the war as an assistant stage manager on *Wonderful Town*, the eager and ambitious Harold Prince joined forces with Robert Griffith (and, for a while, Frederick Brisson) to produce such musicals as *The Pajama Game* and *Damn Yankees*. His early shows were noted for polish and energy, largely because they were overseen by George Abbott, Prince's great personal and artistic mentor. But Prince believed the musical theatre had a journey yet to go. The adventurousness of Prince and Griffith culminated in *Fiorello!*, an unlikely musical biography that won the Pulitzer Prize in 1959 (Griffith died the following year), but the show that set Prince on his path was *West Side Story* in 1957.

At the time, the up-date of *Romeo and Juliet* had been turned down by several writers, abandoned by its initial producer, Cheryl Crawford, and had a cast of complete unknowns. Although director Jerome Robbins's choreography was highly praised by many, to some the subject matter was considered too grim for a musical. It was only with the sale of the property to the movies that the show's reputation and fortune was established. But Prince, watching Robbins work with his collaborators Leonard Bernstein and Stephen Sondheim, knew that the musical had to challenge its audiences if it were to continue to grow as an art form. The next decade, as he began directing, he gave some serious thought to Broadway, and gave it a variety of musicals.

The 1960s: The Age of Precarious

Joseph Papp, who had spent his own herculean battles in the late fifties trying to get the city to allow him to present free Shakespeare in Central Park, drew a line in the sand as the sixties began. On 9 May 1960 in an address to the Women's City Club of New York (trying to raise money, no less), he insisted that Broadway, with its emphasis on commercial hits and long runs, was "barbaric," a "talent-destroyer," and that "Americans have no concept of supporting the theater as an art form. It's 'show business' to them." Papp would spend most of his career trying to battle the barbarity of Broadway, making many enemies along the way.

The same page of the *New York Times* (10 May) that reported on his speech also listed the winners of the 1960 Drama Desk Awards for "outstanding achievement in the Off-Broadway theater." The article included a photograph of the brooding young writer of *The Zoo Story*, Edward Albee. In retrospect, it is an amusing juxtaposition, Papp and Albee, who, from Broadway's point of view in the sixties were, respectively, the Pariah and the Messiah.

The decade opened with some mild shocks and disappointments. The economic and critical momentum of the 1956–57 season, with shows like *Long Day's Journey* and *My Fair Lady*, brought in a record gross box office of $37 million, but this failed to sustain itself. In 1959, for the first time, there were more shows playing Off-Broadway than on Broadway. Actors' Equity went on strike in early June of 1960, shutting down the Broadway theatre for an entire week. That same year the esteemed Brooks Atkinson retired as drama critic for the *New York Times*, to be replaced by Howard Taubman, a music critic, who was considered an outsider and whose reviews were looked upon with some skepticism. (Nor did he help much; in the *New York Times Index*, for his five-year tenure, the word "deplores" follows the name "Taubman" more than any other.) The 1960–61 season produced only forty-six shows on Broadway, an all-time low by a considerable margin. To make matters worse, a 114-day newspaper strike during 1962–63 forced some shows to close and others to preview out-of-town until the dispute was settled.

On the faintly bright side, a 5 percent admission tax on tickets was repealed, with the money going instead to industry pensions and welfare. There were a few hits along the Street. Jean Kerr's divorce comedy *Mary, Mary* ran for 1,572 performances, while the musicals, *Carnival, How to Succeed in Business Without Really Trying, A Funny Thing Happened on the Way to the Forum* came near to or cracked the 1,000-performance mark. But these were the avatars of the "show for the tired businessman": long on professional savvy, high on comedy (probably the last time in the century one would really see "musical comedies"), but offering nothing to take the art form further. The death of Oscar Hammerstein in 1960 ended the triumphant partnership with Richard Rodgers and the eagerly awaited Lerner and Loewe vehicle *Camelot* came into town with the largest advance ever (over $3 million), only to disappoint critics and to end the Lerner and Loewe stage partnership, which had so invigorated the musical stage of the fifties.

The dramatic stage seemed to owe its success to an influx of British plays, a trend which was to continue unabated for the next twenty years. Robert Bolt's *A Man for All Seasons* made its American debut in the 1961–62 season with its star, Paul Scofield, intact and won a record five Tony Awards, while the next season, a meager offering of forty-three shows (the lowest ever) revealed that three-quarters of the hit shows were made abroad and brought to Broadway.

"There was a time when good plays – plays that were not constructed for the mass market only but plays that were honest with themselves and also honest to the historical continuum of the theater . . . could run on Broadway . . . That's no longer true." This is Edward Albee speaking, and one could easily be forgiven for thinking the quote came from the late eighties, when Albee, in critical disrepute, might be speaking elegiacally about the days of his 1962 triumph *Who's Afraid of Virginia Woolf?.* But the quote is from 1963 (see Kolin, *Conversations with Edward Albee*, 29). Albee's standing as a challenger to the conventions of the Broadway scene had been in place for a long time. He was already a triumph Off-Broadway and his work carried, for inquisitive New York audiences, the frisson of the "Absurd," a category Albee rejects for himself, but one that drew more than curiosity, a sense that something new and important was finally being made manifest on the American playwriting scene again.

Who's Afraid of Virginia Woolf?, Albee's first three-act play, was a dissection of marriage and sexual confidences so thorough and coruscating that it ran three-and-one-half hours (a second company had to perform it at matinees), and contained enough frank language and situations to put off several actors and producers. Eventually, Albee's loyal producer Richard Barr improbably teamed up with Billy Rose to open the production, now starring Uta Hagen and Arthur Hill, on 13 October 1962. Mel Gussow wrote, "Edward Albee is clearly the most compelling American playwright to explode upon the Broadway stage since Tennessee Williams and Arthur Miller" (quoted in Harris, *Broadway Theatre*, 82). The play won the Tony, as did its leading actors, ran two years, became a ground-breaking film, and was easily the most talked about play of the decade. At the time, it seemed as if the Messiah had arrived.

But, on Broadway, Messiahs have a way of staying at home. The play did not win the Pulitzer Prize because of its supposed scabrousness, causing two of its judges to quit the panel. Indeed, only two Pulitzers for American drama were awarded during the next six years (ironically, one of them going to Albee for *A Delicate Balance*). Albee himself did not write the wished-for stream of plays that would lead Broadway into understanding the difficult decade ahead; in the sixties, his plays, mostly worthy, some not, both original and adaptations, seemed to baffle his audience, who resented having their visas to the Promised Land canceled. What is most interesting is that the Broadway triumph of *Virginia Woolf* is not completely a Broadway triumph at all; its writer and one of its producers were Off-Broadway talents and the director, Alan Schneider, and co-stars, George Grizzard and Melinda Dillon, started in the resident theatre. There would be more dramatic triumphs on Broadway with similar pedigrees. "Rabbi, wouldn't this be a good time for the Messiah to come?" bewails a dispossessed villager in the 1964 hit *Fiddler on the Roof.* "We'll have to wait for him somewhere else," replies the Rabbi.

Musicals occupied a precarious and rarified place on Broadway mid-decade. They were larger and more expensive to produce (about $500,000 by 1965), they took up to six months to recoup costs (twenty years later, it would take two years), relied on stars and known properties, and only one out of five musicals were hits (although a better average than the straight play). But, for someone with a gambler's instinct, the profits could be enormous. This was the era of the long run: ten musicals that opened in the sixties passed the 1,000-performance mark, three of them passing the 2,000 mark (*Hello, Dolly!*, a Merrick smash, grossed $27 million on Broadway), and one, *Fiddler on the Roof*, passing the 3,000 mark, making back $1,574 for every dollar put into it. Hollywood was also making a new wave of musical adaptations, so that shows that might not prosper on Broadway might make their investments back on a film sale.

Record and film companies became primary investors: MCA, Seven Arts Productions, Capitol, ABC-Paramount were some of the disappointed parties. RCA Victor gave David Merrick $1.5 million in 1966 for the right to record his shows (see the *New York Times*, 19 August 1966, 38). Evidently, the companies were expecting another *My Fair Lady*. What they got in the sixties more often than not was something like *Her First Roman*, an inept attempt to musicalize Shaw again, this time his *Caesar and Cleopatra*. Lightning did not strike twice. With a score by pop composer Ervin Drake and a well regarded British director, inexperienced with musicals, *Her First Roman* had disastrous tryouts in Boston, and the show closed in New York after two weeks, at a $575,000 loss (see Mandelbaum, *Not Since Carrie*, 209–11).

Rising above the tide, and guiding his fleet with an eagle eye, was Harold Prince. He produced *Fiddler*, directed by the extraordinary Jerome Robbins, which became the surprise success of the decade. It had two built-in advantages: it was immediately popular with the influential, largely Jewish, theatre party crowd (who could make or break shows), and it was good theatre. It overcame its one liability, a star role with a star performance by Zero Mostel. When he left after a year, the show continued to run on its own merits, much to the surprise of everyone and, in this, it prefigured the long-running, celebrity-less musicals of the late eighties.

In 1966, Prince, who turned his personal attention to directing as well, brought the musical *Cabaret* to life, displaying some valuable lessons learned from Robbins's approach to integrating musical elements within a dramatic structure around a central idea. This became known as the "concept" musical. Prince was the master of it and, in *Cabaret*, he brought taste and daring to the first Broadway musical to deal with as serious a subject as Nazi Germany. It had much the same effect on the musical as *The Diary of Anne Frank* had by confronting similar material a decade earlier; it raised the standard of the art form. There were serious musicals before and, of course, perfectly silly ones after *Cabaret*, but Prince, to his credit as a producer, never tried to sell the latter to the public as the former.

Broadway found itself further and further outside the mainstream of popular music by the time the decade drew to a close, though that gap seemed to close with *Hair*, "The American Tribal Love Rock Musical," which, after inaugurating Papp's Public Theater, opened on Broadway in 1968 in a considerably different production (there was a brief stop at a discotheque in between). It provided numerous attractions to a Broadway audience inured to formula: a rock score, a disjointed, revue-like format, a diatribe against Vietnam, a young unknown cast, and a fleeting – if provocative – glimpse of its entire cast in the nude. But its charms began to seem as formulaic as what it was rebelling against. Nevertheless, *Hair* ran 1,742 performances. As far as its effect on Broadway's musical scene is concerned, its influence was more selective. An "astute Broadway businessman" summed it up for William Goldman: "Will *Hair* change things?. . . There will now be a spate of shitty rock musicals" (*The Season*, 387). He was right, too. (For an extended analysis of *Hair* and other musicals discussed briefly in this chapter, see Chapter 4.)

For most of the turbulent sixties, American life was in the fast lane and Broadway was puttering along in the service lane. The country was perplexed and those who went to Broadway for some sort of answers were largely disappointed. David Merrick brought the Royal Shakespeare Company's production of *Marat/Sade* to Broadway in 1966, which had an important impact. Broadway audiences who might not venture downtown to see what the Living Theatre was up to, could at least see some of Artaud's theories played out under the guidance of Peter Brook. It was also further evidence of what Goldman coined "the Snob Hit" – a British import that "had" to be seen, whether or not the public understood it. If something like *Marat/Sade* could become a hit, why not equally difficult British material? As American playwriting went into limbo in the seventies, more and more "Snob Hits" sublet Broadway.

The country's racial issues were largely neglected on Broadway. Actors' Equity sponsored an "integration showcase" in 1959 to experiment with what would come to be called "non-traditional casting." As a union, it took increasing interest in providing opportunities for black actors, under its African American President from 1964 to 1970, Frederick O'Neal. But American writing about or by blacks slowed to a crawl after the invigorating promise of Lorraine Hansberry's *A Raisin in the Sun* in 1959. Perhaps there were no writers who could contain and theatricalize the rage in black America and make it palatable to Broadway audiences. This changed in 1967 when Howard Sackler, a white author, wrote *The Great White Hope,* which debuted at Arena Stage. Focusing on Jack Johnson, a black boxer at the beginning of the century, and his relations with his white mistress, Sackler created a slightly fictionalized American epic – raw, unwieldy, potent, and persuasive. The play's critical success in Washington inspired producer Herman Levin to bring the production to Broadway, with most of its original cast and director. After its Broadway opening it made stars out of its leads, James Earl Jones and Jane Alexander, and went on to win the Pulitzer, the Tony, and the New York Drama Critics' Circle Awards.

But its considerable and deserved success could not conceal the fact that *The Great White Hope* was pretty much from top to bottom an import. Broadway had slowly accepted the fact of West End transfers to New York, but now plays and artists were coming to Broadway from all sorts of other places. Walter Kerr, writing for the Sunday *New York Times* on 22 September 1968, admitted as much: "Broadway itself is now a Port Authority Terminal, and the buses from Everywhere leave you standing in the middle of Everywhere without moving a muscle." Off-Broadway flourished during the late sixties, especially when it came to tackling – however haphazardly – the subjects that concerned urban Americans: Vietnam, homosexuality, race relations, drugs. "Happenings" were staged in art galleries and other venues, theatre events were staged in parks and on the street all over New York, and anyone who considered him or herself a member of the cultivated intelligentsia was certainly seeking out some of these attractions. Harold Prince, when asked if "Broadway has had it" by the *New York Times* in 1969, responded defensively, "it depends on your definition of Broadway. More rightly, your question should be, 'Has theater in Manhattan had it?', in which case, the obvious answer is no" (23 April).

Those who wrote about Broadway had come to realize, albeit begrudgingly, that Off-Broadway and regional theatres were there to stay, and they spoke of the shift in the way people talk about their neighborhoods: Kerr wrote in the *New York Times*, "In no time at all, and so imperceptibly we still haven't noticed it, almost everything has changed" (23 April 1969). Broadway also had difficulty entertaining the notion that repertory theatre could exist in its own neighborhood. In 1962, plans for the Repertory Theater of the new Lincoln Center were begun, and they materialized in 1964, when Elia Kazan (the director of the new company, along with producer Robert Whitehead) staged Arthur Miller's new play *After The Fall* in the company's temporary home in Washington Square. Two years later, after a handful of productions in repertory, when the Vivian Beaumont Theater was ready to house the company, Kazan and Whitehead had been inelegantly replaced by Herbert Blau and Jules Irving from San Francisco's Actors' Workshop. This regime (Blau left after two years) specialized in European classics in straight runs.

Perhaps Broadway felt comfortable with something less ambitious. In 1964, the Association for Producing Artists, headed by Ellis Rabb, joined the Off-

Broadway Phoenix Theatre and, a year later, presented their repertory seasons at the Lyceum, on Broadway. This was a company that knew how to work together. Headed by Rabb, Rosemary Harris, Donald Moffat – even Helen Hayes joined them for a season – they made their mark with "American classics" – plays from between the wars, like *You Can't Take It With You*, which sparked that interest in resuscitating American classics with star actors that continues on Broadway to this day. Despite critical acclaim, the APA-Phoenix racked up a $900,000 deficit by 1969, and Rabb departed a year later, but in its time they had quietly achieved the kind of resident theatre company that was flourishing outside of New York.

As the decade ended and the next began, Broadway also had to worry about its own real estate. There are moments when Broadway is rudely awakened to the fact that it sits at the center of the most fractious city in the country, on the most expensive real estate in the free world. This was one of those times. Urban decay had been setting in, strikes – newspaper, transit, taxis, garbage – were rampant, and all of them had hurt business. Mayor John V. Lindsay, who was a theatre enthusiast, attempted a number of civic interventions to make Broadway more relevant to the city, but met with little success.

The 1970s: Naughty, Bawdy, Gaudy, and Sporty

As the seventies began, Broadway was in a state of acute paralysis. The progressive frankness and experimentation of the late sixties had happened very quickly and very intensely and had spread to other art forms. This was most apparent in the movies, which had evolved into a new maturity that appealed to throngs of new audience members. Meanwhile, theatre audiences had to contend with issues on the stage that, even five years earlier, would have been unthinkable. On top of that, New Yorkers could sample every kind of "new theatre": Off-Broadway plays of every style and manner, Sam Shepard at the Vivian Beaumont, the Living Theatre, the Open Theatre, and even Grotowski paid a visit to New York.

What was Broadway to do? Was this the wave of the future? Would all shows have to include nudity, four-letter words, and audience participation? "The audience has got to have more rehearsal time," wrote Walter Kerr. "It is being asked to do so many things these days" (quoted in Guernsey, *Curtain Times*, 184). It was as if the Broadway world was some vast supercollider, with the highly charged particles of the late sixties smashing into the wall of decades of Broadway tradition. No explosion occurred, however; instead there was a kind of implosion where everything settled down into a hiding place, waiting for the all-clear sign, or at least an idea or two that would revitalize the Street.

The early seventies was Broadway's direst period. In the 1970–71 season, there were fifty-six shows, only eight of which were straight plays originating on Broadway. Production and labor costs were growing, necessitating a fifteen-dollar ticket price for weekend musicals, and the rise in costs and ticket prices outpaced inflation. When *Follies*, the Harold Prince–Stephen Sondheim musical, closed in 1972, it had lost, according to Prince, $665,000 (*Contradictions*, 231). This would have been depressing under any circumstance, but the show had run 522 performances – *a year and a half*. When, a year later, *Seesaw*, an infinitely less inspired musical, closed after ten months, its loss was $1.25 million. Shows with reviews that would have put them over the top five years earlier had a tough time of it, plus, by 1972, there were only three newspapers left to supply the reviews. The increase in television theatre critics failed to fill the gap.

There had been other grim times on Broadway, but now there was something new. The city, more specifically the Theatre District in the mid-West Forties, was no longer perceived as safe, let alone glamorous. Prostitution, drugs, pornography, muggings, an extreme night life overran the area. It had a devastating effect on business and, worse, on morale. There was an insidious effect: the fewer the shows, the emptier the Street; the emptier the Street, the fewer the shows. People did not want to come to midtown Manhattan at night and the manifold media portrayals of the decay kept customers away.

Most of the producers' efforts during this time, led by the League, were spent attempting to stem the catastrophic tide. A change in New York City zoning laws provided Broadway with a mixed blessing. A large tax break was given to developers who put theatres in the ground floors of their new buildings. Several new office buildings grew in the Theatre District in the early seventies, housing the Minskoff, the Uris (later renamed the Gershwin) and the revitalized Circle in the Square. Brooks Atkinson called them "theater facilities" rather than theatres, "houses but not homes" (*Broadway*, 471) and the Uris opened with *Via Galactica*, one of the worst bombs in Broadway history, a "shitty rock musical" from the creators of *Hair*.

Among other attempts at Broadway's amelioration were the League's second trial of a 7:30 curtain for the convenience of commuting theatregoers; attempts at a "Middle Theatre" or "Limited Gross" contract for smaller dramatic plays (these never happened); increases in credit card services and other ticket-buying conveniences, such as Ticketron (a computerized ticket service available at department stores); free parking (a short-lived Merrick idea); student rush deals; even a suggestion that unused theatres be turned into gambling casinos. Kerr, in his 3 June 1973 article, fantasized that all of Broadway could move to the Upper East Side to be near residents, just the way movie theatres recently had.

Mayor Lindsay, despite his problems with New York City unions, threw his support into cleaning up Times Square. The most enduring and important change to the Theatre District was the creation of the Theatre Development Fund in 1968. Initially, the Fund used donated money to purchase blocks of tickets to worthy shows and sell them to consumers at reduced rates. By 1972 the Fund suggested the possibility of selling unused tickets to customers on the day of performance at a cut rate. Initially, there was resistance from producers who feared that this would promote the idea that their shows were not hits (well, they weren't), but in the spring of 1973, with the help of the New York City Cultural Council and the Office of Midtown Planning and Development, the Fund opened the Times Square Theatre Center, an open-air booth in Duffy Square. The center, known more affectionately as "the TKTS booth" (for its logo), sold tickets for half-price, plus a small surcharge, and was an instant success. By the end of the nineties, the TKTS sales constituted roughly 11 percent of all sales on and Off-Broadway combined.[3] More importantly, the sight of crowds swarming Broadway and Forty-seventh Street, anxious for tickets, helped Broadway's image immeasurably.

The actual work on stage in the early seventies seemed tentative, with a few notable exceptions. Probably the most exciting and theatrical work on Broadway was done in 1970 by Prince and Sondheim, working for the first time as producer-director and composer-lyricist on *Company*, an original musical about marriage and relationships set in contemporary Manhattan. It was a relief to have a musical which was not set in Victorian England, medieval Spain, or the 1930s (or Ancient Egypt, for that matter), and it was an undeniably adult experience. Prince (working as co-director with choreographer Michael Bennett) and Sondheim worked on *Follies* one season later, another contemporary original musical, this time about a bittersweet reunion of Follies girls. The mordant tone confused audiences who wanted to see the World War II-era cast perform their treasured routines, but the show was one of the most ambitious musicals ever, and, although it garnered much praise and respect for its creators, it was a financial failure. In 1973–74, Prince and Sondheim teamed up again for *A Little Night Music,* a Chekhovian musical of an Ingmar Bergman film. This time, its adult tone resonated with critics and audiences and it went on to become the team's biggest hit and even – *mirabile dictu* – produced a popular song hit in "Send in the Clowns."

In the early seventies, nostalgia also became a major selling item, perhaps as a reaction to the forceful contemporaneity of the late sixties. A revival of the twenties musical *No, No, Nanette,* retrofitted with stars from the thirties, became a huge hit, and gave way to similar revivals that had healthy lives on Broadway and especially on the Road. Revivals found a more than hospitable home on Broadway, a trend that shows little sign of abating in the nineties. In the 1973–74 season, nineteen out of the fifty-four shows on Broadway were revivals. True, some of them were safe repackagings of shows with stars but, in that season, Jason Robards, Jr. and Colleen Dewhurst appeared in a production of O'Neill's *A Moon for the Misbegotten*, which was not only the major event of the season, but a reclamation of an important play. Along with Prince's radical rethink of Leonard Bernstein's *Candide* (which opened at the Brooklyn Academy of Music and moved to Broadway in the 1974–75 season), the O'Neill conferred a new respect on the revival and its potential to infuse Broadway with excitement and box office receipts.

When serious drama appeared, it was almost all from the West End: *Sleuth*, *Home*, *Vivat! Vivat Regina!*, *Butley*, and *The Changing Room* were successful transfers that most often were headed by their British stars. To the rescue came, as if waiting for his cue, Joseph Papp. Papp's relentless activity developing new plays at the Public Theater brought glory to Broadway when he transferred *Sticks and Bones* by David Rabe and, more persuasively, *That Championship Season* by Jason Miller. Miller's play, about a fraught reunion of high-school basketball players, won the 1973 Tony, the Pulitzer, and the New York Critics' Circle Award and ran for an impressive 700 performances. These triumphs, plus Papp's acquisition of the Astor Library from New York City (it became the several-theatre Public) in a sweetheart deal, the transfer of the musical *Two Gentlemen of Verona* to Broadway, and even his aborted arrangement with CBS to broadcast several of his plays, made Papp the one man to inject some energy into the dismal Broadway of the mid-seventies.

He chose to do, as he often did, the impossible: he took over Lincoln Center Theater in 1973. He brought his Public Theater board with him, increased his margin for financial error, and continued to run the Public. For two seasons he produced new plays at the Beaumont and when these were met with insufficient enthusiasm, switched to first-class revivals with major artists (Andrei Serban's *The Cherry Orchard* with Irene Worth and Richard Foreman's *The Threepenny Opera* with Raul Julia were unforgettable events). Meanwhile, he initiated a series of five new plays at Broadway's Booth Theatre, the first formal extended relationship between an Off-Broadway theatre and a Broadway venue, but only one play, *The Leaf People*, opened there (it closed quickly). By 1977, Papp, citing insufficient commitment on the part of his funders (even with the revivals, the Vivian Beaumont was an expensive proposition) and insufficient curiosity on the part of audiences, had pulled out of Lincoln Center completely.

But Papp still ran the Public and it was there, in 1975, amongst the hum of activity, that a workshop he sponsored would change Broadway. Papp had known choreographer and director Michael Bennett slightly and was interested in his directing a musical revival for him. But Bennett preferred to work on an informal project involving the personal stories of chorus dancers that had evolved from taped sessions he had been working on with some colleagues. Papp gave Bennett the space and wrote the checks, and Bennett hired dancers and an artistic team.

Papp's support may have gotten the project started, but it was the skill of Bennett and the raw power and vulnerability of his cast pouring out their lives through the characters of a score of dancers auditioning for a Broadway chorus that ignited the Newman Theater in April of 1975. Word spread throughout New York and by the fall, *A Chorus Line* opened at the Shubert Theatre. It received the best – and most perceptive – reviews of the decade and won every theatre award available. It became the longest-running show on Broadway. It made Bennett's reputation, as well as burnishing the legend of the director-choreographer; it established the workshop as the preferable method of working out costly and complicated Broadway musicals (as opposed to out-of-town tryouts); and it created a modern, dramatic musical that could also, not coincidentally, because of its scale and lack of a star, make millions on the Road. (It also gently paved the way for more intelligent and sympathetic portrayals of gay themes on Broadway, thanks to the revelatory monologue of one of its characters.)

But most of that came later. The immediate effect of *A Chorus Line* was more potent: "[It] came at a time when everybody was predicting the Broadway theatre was dead and would never come back again. Along came *A Chorus Line* and everyone changed their opinion about Broadway. There was a new wave of enthusiasm and hope," recalled producer Bernard B. Jacobs (Mandelbaum, *A Chorus Line and the Musicals of Michael Bennett*, 289). The show certainly gave Jacobs enthusiasm and hope. As the co-Chief Executive Officer of the Shubert Organization with Gerald Schoenfeld, Jacobs profited from the show's long tenancy at the Shubert Theatre. Although Jacobs and Schoenfeld were not descended from the famous Shubert family (former legal employees of the family, they took over the organization in 1972), they became known as the Shuberts and took an increasingly active role in Broadway production in the late seventies. They owned sixteen theatres and a half-share in one more, and began to put money into productions, often bringing shows in from regional theatres, London's West End, or Off-Broadway.

Jacobs was right, up to a point. A hit on Broadway can change things around quickly, but Broadway was on an upswing before *A Chorus Line* opened downtown. The British psychological drama *Equus* created a huge stir in the 1974–75 season, as did Bernard Slade's *Same Time, Next Year*, which was really nothing more than a genteel sex comedy from the sixties, but somehow seemed welcome again, especially with the expert acting of Ellen Burstyn and Charles Grodin. An all-black version of *The Wizard of Oz*, *The Wiz*, became a tremendous hit. Although not the finest hour for black artists, it did have a black producer and artistic staff, and most importantly, brought black audiences to Broadway (as well as families of all kinds, for the first time in about a decade). *The Wiz* built on the achievements of Melvin Van Peebles's *Ain't Supposed to Die a Natural Death* and Vinnette Carroll's *Don't Bother Me, I Can't Cope*, original musicals about the urban African American experience produced in the early seventies, and brought in a new audience, "an audience that the white establishment has for years been saying did not exist" (see "Blacks Gain on Broadway," *New York Times*, 6 June 1975).

Nonetheless, by the time *A Chorus Line* transferred, Broadway was seeing another audience that did not seem to exist: a paying one, and it came in droves. The 1975–76 season's grosses totaled $70.8 million, 20 percent more than the previous record held by the 1967–68 season, especially remarkable, considering an almost month-long musicians' strike in October that closed all the musicals. It was a particularly exciting season musically, with *A Chorus Line*; Prince and Sondheim's most ambitious effort, an all-Asian, mostly male excursion into the perils of empire in *Pacific Overtures*; and Bob Fosse's endearingly malicious look at vaudeville and murder, *Chicago*. Fosse, almost parenthetically, made one of the most important contributions of the decade when he directed the TV commercial for his 1972 musical *Pippin*. The commercial, the first prominent one for a Broadway show, surely did much to extend the four-year life of a mediocre musical and became a model for others.

Although there was not much original drama on stage that season, there were powerful actors, many in the season's twenty-eight revivals (out of sixty-five productions): Shirley MacLaine, Gwen Verdon, Yul Brynner, Katharine Hepburn, George C. Scott, Alfred Drake, Eva Le Gallienne, Vanessa Redgrave, Ruth Gordon, Colleen Dewhurst, and three young actors solidifying their star quality: Sam Waterston, Raul Julia, and Meryl Streep. But no star caught the spotlight quite the way Richard Burton did when he took over the lead in *Equus*, making his first Broadway appearance in twelve years. His fourteen-week engagement sold out and led to his appearance in the film version. More importantly, Burton confounded the unspoken assumption that replacing an original actor was a come-down. From that moment until today, many actors of the first order, such as Liza Minnelli, David Bowie, Mary Tyler Moore, and Whoopi Goldberg, rehabilitated shows and their careers by taking over the leads from lesser known actors in established Broadway shows.

The next season brought in a staggering $93.4 million of total Broadway grosses, proving this comeback was no fluke. A good deal of this success was borne on the backs of musical revivals with their original stars, like *Fiddler on the Roof* and *The King and I*, concert performances by familiar performers like Diana Ross and Debbie Reynolds, and by *Annie*, an unabashedly sentimental musical of the old school, which brought families back to the theatre and, along with *A Chorus Line*, produced the first viable touring shows in years. The Road became an increasing source of theatrical income, thanks to these shows and *Evita*.

Broadway was back as a presence in the New York economy; the *Times* calculated that the upturn in box office produced three times as much additional income for local industry. Ticket prices grew higher; *The Act*, starring Liza Minnelli, went to twenty-five dollars for a top ticket, despite criticism that Minnelli was lip-synching some of her numbers. Broadway had become better able to manage itself as an industry and, largely through its lobbying efforts, the Theatre District was slowly getting cleaned up. A successful ad campaign, sponsored by the New York State Tourism Board, called " I ♥ NY" showed clips of many Broadway musicals, as did the annual, highly polished television broadcasts of the Tony Awards, and these drew the tourist trade in droves.

The Shubert Organization took an increasingly large hand in the industry, establishing a national computerized telephone ticket service for their shows, Tele-charge, and putting more and more money into proven properties from Off-Broadway, the regional theatres, and the West End. This led to an increasing rivalry over theatre bookings with the Nederlander Organization, which made its mark in New York by restoring the Palace in 1965, and owned eight Broadway theatres by the end of the decade. More to the point, these organizations (along with the Jujamacyn Theatres, owners of five Broadway theatres) filled a void by default. There were few producers of the Prince–Merrick school any more (they were both around, but doing less), but, for all the money that the Shuberts and Nederlanders put into Broadway shows, they were real estate people, not artists (though both sponsor philanthropic organizations that fund not-for-profit theatre).

By the late seventies, Broadway had settled into a pattern that would hold, despite a few exceptions, for the next twenty years. There would be an ever decreasing number of productions. In the 1952–53 season, there were fifty-four, which at the time was seen as calamitous. From 1977 on, Broadway rose to that number only once, with the number of productions usually in the mid-forties, or even as low as thirty-six in the 1983–84 season. Conversely, the total box office grosses rose every season from 1975–76 to 1982–83, breaking the $100 million mark in 1978 and breaking the $200 million mark only four seasons later. During the same period, the top ticket price in 1975 was $17.50; the top in 1983 was $45.00. More insidious than the price inflation was the barely mentioned sense that even though business was better, the material on stage was not.

The 1980s: Send in the Clones

In a way, more disheartening than the dwindling number of productions and their high prices by 1980, was the utter predictability of the Broadway menu, season after season, for almost the next two decades. Serious drama would be largely brought in from the regional theatre (*The Shadow Box, Children of a Lesser God, Crimes of the Heart*), Off-Broadway (*Talley's Folly, The Elephant Man*), and the West End (*Whose Life Is It Anyway?* and *Amadeus*). The late seventies and early eighties brought a surprising run of plays about sickness and disability: *The Shadow Box, The Elephant Man, Whose Life, Wings, Bosoms and Neglect, Children of a Lesser God*, and, one might add, *Richard III* (starring Al Pacino). There were interesting plays – *The Fifth of July* by Lanford Wilson (Off-Broadway transfer), *The Real Thing* by Tom Stoppard (West End), David Mamet's *Glengarry Glen Ross* (London and regional) – but nothing to start a movement, or invade the solipsistic cocktail party chatter of the eighties. "These days, the theater is a special interest, occupying a ghetto on the cultural landscape," wrote critic Frank Rich in the *New York Times* (19 February 1984). "Much of what is most loudly acclaimed as serious drama in New York – and then disseminated nationwide through regional and touring productions – isn't really serious at all."

Neil Simon, being cleverer than most playwrights, worked out his strategy for plays in advance. His planned trilogy of memory plays about his youth and growth as a writer was produced throughout the eighties. The first, *Brighton Beach Memoirs*, ran 1,530 performances, after opening in 1983; the second, *Biloxi Blues* (1985), won Simon his first Tony, and, along with the last, *Broadway Bound* (1986), ran over 500 performances. Although no longer quite the comic and economic powerhouse he was in the sixties, Simon, out of a combination of longevity and increased introspection, began to receive the respect of his colleagues and his critics.

Book musicals, on the wane, would be supplemented by a spate of revues: some inspired, like 1977's *Ain't Misbehavin'*, a rediscovery of Fats Waller, and some elegant, like the West End's *Side by Side by Sondheim*. Most of them, however, were of the "And Then I Wrote. . ." school, but, when a book musical like *Shenandoah* could run over 1,000 performances and still lose 80 percent of its investment, a revue looked like a good and economical vehicle. What book musicals remained (often about six per season) usually split their audience in two: the occasional ambitious show like *Sweeney Todd, the Demon Barber of Fleet Street* playing opposite a crowd-pleaser like *They're Playing Our Song* in the 1977–78 season. The dichotomy between *Evita* and *Sugar Babies* fulfilled a similar function the following season, and the 1983–84 season became silly season when Jerry Herman, trumpeting his hit show *La Cage aux Folles* as it swept the 1984 Tonys, said that the "simple, hummable show" was finally having a comeback – a clear swipe at Sondheim's *Sunday in the Park with George*, a demanding, if esoteric, musical that had to content itself with a Pulitzer Prize and a rave review (some said a crusade) from the *New York Times*. The idea of a spat, let alone a duel, would have been welcome the next season, when there were so few musicals that categories of best actor, best actress, and choreography had to be removed from the Tony Awards. The winner by default was *Big River*, a version of *Huckleberry Finn* that did little credit either to its source or Broadway.

Revivals were a permanent powerhouse part of every season, especially musical revivals, which became so prominent in the late 1980s that they received their own Tony Award category. Stars were safe bets to hold down the economic end of things. The eighties opened with the astonishing Broadway debut of Elizabeth Taylor in *The Little Foxes*; she was equal to the part and more than equal, not surprisingly, to the concomitant demands of the enormous publicity that attended her appearance. Actors like Anthony Quinn, Glenda Jackson, Jessica Tandy, Jason Robards, Rex Harrison, and Dustin Hoffman all had commercial revivals built around them (Lena Horne staging a hugely successful comeback concert on Broadway), and the trend only increased into the nineties.

That said, the early eighties had its share of thrills and surprises. No one would think of springing a surprise on Broadway in the dog days of August, except probably David Merrick. After a hiatus of five years, he brought a new musical to Broadway, *42nd Street*, a stage version of the Warner Brothers film. The production was overseen by Gower Champion, the director-choreographer who had delivered Merrick such success in the past. When the opening came on 25 August 1980 at the Winter Garden Theatre, Merrick interrupted the thunderous curtain call applause to announce to a stunned house that Champion had died that afternoon (of complications from a rare blood disease). Some thought he was joking; he was not, and however tactless his tactic was, it brought huge amounts of publicity. The musical ran for 3,486 performances, the longest run for an American show in the eighties, at one point bringing Merrick half a million dollars a week net profit. It was to be his last big success, as he suffered a stroke in 1983.

Merrick had twice brought the Royal Shakespeare Company to Broadway, but no one could have been prepared for their reappearance in the 1981–82 season (under the aegis of another management) in the two-part eight-and-a-half-hour adaptation of Dickens's *The Life & Adventures of Nicholas Nickleby*. The show did not sell well in advance – the unprecedented $100 ticket to both parts had a great deal to do with it, no doubt – and the reviews were not uniformly strong, but word-of-mouth and a cover story for *Time* magazine soon made "Nick Nick" a financial success – and a Snob Hit for people who hated Snob Hits. The superb staging by Trevor Nunn and John Caird brought ensemble work not seen since *Marat/Sade* to Broadway audiences (other companies would attempt this with less success in the decade to come) and Nunn himself would go on to stage some of the biggest musical successes on Broadway.

If, in the early seventies, "massage parlor" was the most frequently heard two-word phrase around the Theatre District, by the early eighties, the phrase had become "John Portman." In 1974, Portman had the unfortunate lot of being the developer for a huge hotel complex on Broadway between Forty-fifth and Forty-sixth streets. His – and Broadway's – troubles began when the building of the hotel necessitated the demolition of the Morosco, Helen Hayes, and Bijou Theatres. Emotions ran extremely high on the subject; the new theatres, which were to replace them, like the Uris, were not popular, and it certainly did not help that one of the endangered theatres – quite a charming one – was named after the First Lady of the American theatre. The next decade was a series of court injunctions and battles, newspaper editorials and demonstrations, but the finale came on 22 March 1982 when, after the United States Supreme Court lifted a temporary stay, the jaws of a backhoe bit into the remaining wall of the Bijou. The hotel, once called the Portman, became the Marriott Marquis and a huge musical theatre was built in its lobby. There was much debate in the ensuing years about whether, in order to avoid a similar battle over expensive midtown real estate, Broadway theatres should be designated landmarks by the New York City Landmarks and Parks Commission, but this, too, caused a rift along Broadway. Some, mostly producers, thought this would inhibit interior changes in the theatre to accommodate productions, and there was also an issue over selling potentially lucrative air rights above the theatres.

Producing became a complicated affair by the mid-eighties. The high costs of production (the musical *My One and Only* cost $4 million in 1983) required a large number of investors to raise the capital for a show and sustain it through rocky times. There was a rash of film corporations entering into production agreements, backing both plays and musicals in order to develop the material and retain the motion picture and residual rights. The advent of cable television in Manhattan brought a number of agreements where cable companies would get the rights to broadcast Broadway shows directly into people's apartments. This helped the prestige of the new cable companies, but not their business; it was a financial disaster, as were most of the film companies' investments. By the 1990s, both media had pulled out of Broadway investment, with the important exception of the Walt Disney Co., and to a lesser degree, independent film producers like David Geffen and Scott Rudin. It fell to a myriad of amateur producers to make up the difference: in the 1993–94 season, ninety individuals were billed over the title as producers for a mere thirty-four productions.

The 1990s: The British Are Humming

If the spread between feast and famine was large in the mid-eighties, it would grow to dangerous proportions from then on. In the dismal days of Broadway in the seventies, when the British play overran American efforts, there was at

3. Caricatures of (left to right) the Shuberts (Gerald Schoenfeld and the late Bernard B. Jacobs), Andrew Lloyd Webber, and Cameron Mackintosh, prominent Broadway figures of the 1980s and 1990s. Illustration by Laurence Maslon.

least the comfort that the American musical was commercial and artistically dominant. All that changed when, in 1982, with distinctly non-cat-like tread, the British musical *Cats* opened at the Winter Garden. Already a surprise sensation in London, it arrived on Broadway with a $6.2 million advance sale. The creative team behind it would go on to wield tremendous power on Broadway. Composer and producer Andrew Lloyd Webber already had two Broadway hits to his credit, *Jesus Christ Superstar* and *Evita*. The director was Trevor Nunn, who would go on to direct several more Webber musicals. The main producer was Cameron Mackintosh, a comparatively young Englishman, who would build a huge empire exporting contemporary British musicals ("pop operas" they would be called, or, simply, "megahits").

Cats was followed by a series of British megahits that involved at least one of these individuals: *Les Misérables* (Mackintosh and Nunn, 1987), *Starlight Express* (Lloyd Webber, 1987), *The Phantom of the Opera* (Lloyd Webber, Mackintosh, directed by Harold Prince, 1988), *Miss Saigon* (Mackintosh, 1991), and *Sunset Boulevard* (Lloyd Webber, Nunn, 1995). They had numerous qualities in common: they were largely through-composed in a pop idiom; they relied on spectacle rather than character or story (not quite fair to say in the case of *Les Miz*, as it was called); they did not require a major star for box office value, nor, in some cases, even a knowledge of the English language. This last was the most crucial part of Mackintosh's genius; the logos for the shows were simple and bold, advertising the experience of the show and therefore continuing to sell it, no matter how many cast changes it might go through.

They also made a great deal of money (or spent it; *Starlight Express* cost $8.8 million and *Sunset Boulevard* $13 million – neither made back its entire investment in New York). As these were essentially produced by the same team (although Mackintosh and Lloyd Webber went their separate ways after *Phantom*), their successes fed on each other, in terms of advertising and perception. They injected vitality into the Broadway box office, and, more impressively, they recreated the economics of the Road; in 1995–96, the gross on the Road was $762 million – nearly double Broadway grosses for that season – largely the result of touring companies of these shows. How much money they brought to Broadway is certainly calculable: *Cats*, as of the night it became the longest running show in Broadway history, 19 June 1997, had grossed $329 million on Broadway (and $2.2 billion worldwide!). Put more boldly, *Cats*, *Phantom*, *Les Misérables*, and *Miss Saigon*, as of June 1998, had run a combined total of forty-five years on Broadway.

There were problems, of course. As the importers of great potential wealth (*Miss Saigon* had a $36 million advance), Lloyd Webber and Mackintosh called the shots, even if their interests and Broadway's were at odds. Casting became an issue. Lloyd Webber wanted to bring his wife, Sarah Brightman, over as the female lead in *Phantom*, despite Equity's objection. Mackintosh wanted to bring over the British female lead of *Miss Saigon*, as well as Jonathan Pryce, its star, to play a Eurasian character, despite Equity's objection on both counts (it insisted on an Asian American actor). Lloyd Webber wanted to bring Glenn Close to Broadway as the lead in *Sunset Boulevard*, breaking his contract with Patti LuPone, who originated the role in London. Lloyd Webber and Mackintosh got what they wanted in all three cases, with only minor compromises. The shows became objects of derision from American producers and artists and there was a xenophobic fear, not entirely unfounded, that these shows were taking over Broadway.

The American musical theatre offered little resistance or competition. Stephen Sondheim and Prince had not worked as a team since 1981; Prince had a long slump before *Phantom*, and Sondheim began working with director-librettist James Lapine on a series of rather inert musicals. More tragically, both Michael Bennett and Bob Fosse died in 1987: Bennett of AIDS, Fosse of a heart attack. Their absence, regrettable at any time, came exactly when Broadway needed their inventiveness and drive. Into the breach high-stepped Tommy Tune, a tall, lanky dancer who had worked with Bennett, and who lent his jolly razzmatazz as director-choreographer to uninspired material like *Grand Hotel* and *The Will Rogers Follies*.

Oddly enough, on the American playwriting scene, at the same time, there began to be heard some unique and invigorating voices, almost exclusively nurtured by regional or not-for-profit organizations. August Wilson made his Broadway debut in 1984 with *Ma Rainey's Black Bottom*, the first in a cycle of plays about the African American experience (six to date), most of which were developed with director Lloyd Richards at the Yale Repertory Theatre. Wendy Wasserstein's work was similarly sponsored and supported, first by Playwrights Horizons and then Lincoln Center Theater, before it moved to Broadway. *The Heidi Chronicles* (1989) and *The Sisters Rosensweig* (1993) were witty and insightful portraits of a new generation of professional women. Writers like Wilson and Wasserstein were finding success in investigating the contemporary zeitgeist and they were matched in their efforts by John Guare's *Six Degrees of Separation* (1990), which captured the social confusion of the 1980s through its use of the true story of a black con man who ensnared an Upper East Side family. After moving to Broadway from Lincoln Center it became that *rara avis* – the talked-about American play.

Lincoln Center Theater had a huge comeback during this period, beginning in 1985, after an interregnum of four years when the Vivian Beaumont was dark or rented out. Under the leadership of Gregory Mosher and Bernard Gerstein, Lincoln Center offered memberships, instead of subscriptions, and soon attracted a large base of customers who enjoyed a wide variety of fare, from revivals of musicals and American classics (*Anything Goes*, *The Front Page*), to South African imports (*Sarafina!*), to new work by authors like Wasserstein and Guare. Although Mosher was succeeded by André Bishop, it was clear that Lincoln Center Theater had finally made a successful transition.

Transition was not immediately as smooth at the Public Theater. Joseph Papp, in ailing health, had passed the reins to JoAnne Akalaitis in 1991, before his own death that year. Akalaitis lasted a year and the Public was taken over by George C. Wolfe, who had contributed his own brand of slightly surreal slick energy to *Jelly's Last Jam*, a 1992 Broadway musical that brought social commentary into a seemingly standard revue of Jelly Roll Morton's life. Wolfe was promptly given the directing assignment of the nineties: staging Tony Kushner's ambitious two-part epic about AIDS and contemporary American life, *Angels in America*. The plays had been done in workshops and various productions around the country, including the Mark Taper Forum. For its Broadway debut, *Angels in America* was taken over by Wolfe, who opened the first part, *Millennium Approaches*, in 1992, and the second part *Perestroika*, in 1993. Rehearsals for the second part required canceling performances of the first, which had gone on to win a Tony Award and a Pulitzer, and when the opening of Part II was delayed, it raised the second play's capitalization to $3 million.

Both parts were equally acclaimed in the press, and they certainly were the kinds of plays Broadway hadn't seen in decades: topical, at times shocking, imaginative, theatrical, controversial. But, both plays together ran less than 600 performances, closing in 1994; what had started so promisingly intellectually and theatrically, was a financial disappointment, only recouping its investment two and one-half years after it closed, thanks to subsequent productions. If the most acclaimed play(s) of the decade couldn't make a go of it, what play could?

Another attempt to ameliorate the situation was the creation of the Broadway Alliance in 1990, an agreement to scale back fees, expenses, and ticket costs, in order to pass the savings on to the consumer. After a series of failures, the Alliance had its first success in 1994 with Terrence McNally's *Love! Valour! Compassion!* and the next year with his *Master Class* (although both plays were transfers from successful engagements). As of June 1997, the League, along with the unions, theatre owners, and business leaders, was examining another program called the "Broadway Initiative" to subsidize and promote serious drama on Broadway, as well as attract a vastly dwindling younger audience. Evidently, drama of any kind on Broadway was in trouble when even Neil Simon moved Off-Broadway for his 1994 comedy *London Suite*.

Still, stars remained capable of drawing audiences on Broadway. In the 1994–95 season, box office names like Kathleen Turner, Matthew Broderick, Glenn Close, and Patrick Stewart helped crack the $400 million mark in total grosses for the first time. Yet no star in recent memory galvanized Broadway in the way Julie Andrews did when she returned in 1995, after a thirty-four-year absence, to carry, Atlas-like (or Sisyphus-like), the musical vehicle *Victor/Victoria*. Unfortunately, her vehicle failed her; when it did not get nominated for a Tony, she withdrew her own nomination, sparking one of the loudest Tony controversies in history. The low-rated 1996 Award ceremony was a particularly sorry affair, as CBS cut back the telecast to two hours and cut off speeches by some of the theatre's giants. This was another sign of Broadway's cultural diminution, as the League seemingly submitted to any humiliation in order to put Broadway on prime time. In 1997, the Tonys regained their glory by giving the extra hour to public broadcasting and having the show hosted by TV personality Rosie O'Donnell, an outspoken supporter of musical comedy on her talk show (her power to help create hit musicals, such as the tepidly received *Titanic* in 1997, gave her clout unmatched since the heyday of Ed Sullivan). Her popularity among television audiences boosted the Tony ratings both in 1997 and 1998.

By the end of the 1997–98 season, a sense of change, rejuvenation, and paradox was easily apparent on the Broadway scene. Two musicals from the 1996–97 season, *Rent* and *Bring in da Noise, Bring in da Funk*, were playing to capacity houses. They were new, raw musicals that owed very little to the pop opera or Tin Pan Alley tradition and they were developed in workshops Off-Broadway. *Rent* received a particularly large amount of attention, as its creator Jonathan Larson died suddenly during its downtown preview. The show drew a new, young audience (the subway ads appealed to customers who "hate musicals"), won the major awards, and seemed on its way to becoming an international phenomenon.

Rent also produced a literal change in the Broadway landscape. It opened on Forty-first Street, formerly a No Man's Land, as was anything south of Forty-second Street. But Forty-second Street, indeed, the entire Theatre District, has changed in a way that would have stupefied the apprehensive urban dwellers of the early seventies. Encouraged by its 1995 success in bringing to Broadway a stage version of its animated film *Beauty and the Beast*, the Walt Disney Company purchased and renovated Ziegfeld's New Amsterdam Theater on Forty-second Street as a house for its own future projects. Its first monumental production there in the fall of 1997 was a stage version of the animated film *The Lion King*, which was capitalized at an all-time high of more than $20 million. On the same block, Canadian producer Garth Drabinsky and his Livent, Inc. paid for a massive renovation of the Lyric and Apollo Theatres, using Ford Motor Company as its corporate sponsor. Its premiere production was a musical based on E.L. Doctorow's novel *Ragtime*, which Drabinsky had tried out in his own theatres in Toronto and Los Angeles. Both new theatres have over 1,300 seats each. In addition, since 1995 the New Victory, also on Forty-second Street, has been a viable and charming space for young audiences. With these renovations has come a plethora of new restaurants, chain stores, neon lights, and coffee boutiques, giving the area a twenty-four-hour sheen that has also driven the prostitutes, pimps, and panhandlers to points beyond.

But with the success of such urban and commercial incentives has come a number of disturbing paradoxes. On 18 June 1997, when *Cats* became the longest running Broadway show of all time, there was little professional enthusiasm for celebrating a landmark that overturned *A Chorus Line*, the quintessential Broadway musical. In marked contrast to that show's extraordinary celebration in 1983, *Cats* merely roped off the street in front of the Winter Garden for some speeches and a small parade. Even this event was trumped by the Disney Company's city-wide "Electrical Parade" to promote the opening of the film *Hercules* only days before. Frank Rich, writing about Andrew Lloyd Webber's declining fortunes on the Op-Ed page of the *New York Times*, 17 June 1997, observed: "The man who Disneyfied the Broadway musical has been downsized by Disneyfication."

The paradoxes continued at the close of the 1998 season: Broadway box office grosses set a record, reaching a total of $557 million. This was an 11.6 percent rise from the previous season's attendance record. However, only two shows that had opened during the 1997–98 season could be called hits. One of them was *Art*, a three-person play imported from London, and a one-man show by performance artist John Leguizamo (*Freak*). Among productions that flopped was a holdover from the previous season called *The Life*, a well-reviewed musical, ironically celebrating the prostitutes, pimps, and panhandlers that used to inhabit Forty-second Street in the seventies. The show lost $6 million.

Even the extraordinary successes of *The Lion King* and *Ragtime* were not without their bleak sides. The Disney Company admitted that their huge success would not show a profit for a long time, although, given its critical success and family appeal, its chances of a long, healthy run are virtually assured. *Ragtime* by the end of 1998 was playing to capacity houses, although Livent, Inc. lost $50 million in other operations over the previous fifteen months, leading to a takeover by Hollywood impresario Michael Ovitz, which relegated Drabinsky to a smaller role in the company.[4] Of the additional $58 million increase in Broadway income from 1997, $44 million came solely from *The Lion King* and *Ragtime*.

Such feast-or-famine economics created a new way of doing business on Broadway. Road productions increased their box office income exponentially. 1997–98 income from the Road was nearly $800 million. In fact, the quality of Road productions has improved so much that producers on the Road charge ticket prices close to those on Broadway. In the wake of increased attention from Hollywood and television shows, Broadway is trying to capture the more sophisticated commericial techniques of those media. "Theatre has been a wonderful cottage industry, but always twenty or thirty years behind the times," says Michael David of Dodger Productions. Into the vacuum of Broadway producers in the David Merrick mode have come large diverse companies like Disney, that have deeper pockets than someone like Merrick could have possibly imagined. Whether this will only widen the gap between shows that struggle to survive and expensive shows that can be run for months at a loss in order to show a profit remains to be seen. What is undeniably true, however, is that everyone on Broadway in the late nineties looks to these corporate experiments with more enthusiasm than skepticism.

Conclusion and Forecast

"When I was growing up," related George Furth, a Broadway actor in the fifties and sixties, and the author of the book to *Company*, "we went to the theater to be enlightened and the movies to be entertained. Now, it's the other way around."[5] Broadway is no longer the place where important topics are tackled and discussed first. That role has been ceded to film, or more accurately, to independent film. True, there isn't much serious drama on Broadway, but there hasn't been for forty years, since the clearly exceptional heyday of

Williams and Miller. Perhaps it is time for Broadway to reimagine itself more realistically. In spite of the lack of serious drama, and the gargantuan size and expense of a few Broadway musicals, Broadway still seems to be the destination for theatre artists at the top of their craft. From all over the world they will eventually come to Broadway. The 1997–98 season hosted, among its thirty-two shows, an all-Irish company performing a new play by Martin McDonagh (*The Beauty Queen of Leenane*); *Art*, written by a French playwright and adapted to English, with an American cast; *Freak* with Leguizamo, an acclaimed Latino actor; and the Broadway debut of director-designer Julie Taymor, one of Off-Broadway's leading avant-garde artists, hired by Disney to reconceive *The Lion King* for the stage. A savvy choice by Disney. The New Amsterdam thus became home for both an avant-garde puppeteer and a multi-million-dollar corporation.

Even a brief stay on Broadway still raises the artistic and commercial profile of a play, artist, or production group. Perhaps the time has come, as Linda Winer wrote in *Newsday*, for Broadway to "embrace its evolved identity as a showcase for works hearty enough to make their way there" (quoted in Guernsey and Sweet, *Best Plays of 1995–1996*, 47). With the massive changes of the information age, the expanding markets and marketing of Hollywood and television will be an ongoing and increasing presence on Broadway. The hermetic world of the theatre can no longer afford to shut out its most obstreperous competitors. It would be a futile struggle in any event. Broadway, as it stretches toward the twenty-first century, has become an unapologetic open-air theatrical market for goods of all kinds. Perhaps it may be hawking more of the "hip hooray and bally-hoo" than more sober critics would prefer, but that has always been the most seductive strain of the lullaby of old Broadway.

Notes

1 See Morrow, *The Tony Award Book*, 23–27, and Atkinson, *Broadway* (revised edition), 530.
2 The tracking of album sales is a tricky one. Unlike producers, who routinely issue box office grosses, record companies are notoriously reticent to make sales units public. *Billboard* magazine, the record industry journal, has kept note of "charts," i.e., a listing of, say, the top twenty-five best-selling albums for a given week, etc. Trying to track the success of the original cast album of *My Fair Lady* requires some extrapolation. According to *Jack Whitburn's Top Pop Albums: '55–'92*, *My Fair Lady* spent 480 weeks on *Billboard's* charts (making it the third longest-selling album). This is an impressive achievement, when one considers that, first of all, the album was competing against pop stars like Elvis Presley and (eventually) The Beatles. Also, until the early sixties, the charts stayed at fifteen, twenty-five, or fifty positions

(there are 200 positions now), so to stay on the charts for *My Fair Lady*'s first five years meant staying in rather select company.

The economic relation of cast albums to Broadway has, to my knowledge, gone completely unexplored. But, again, if one extrapolates, there was not only an original (mono) Broadway cast album for *My Fair Lady*, there was a stereo version, a London cast album, a movie soundtrack, a revival recording from 1977, a "crossover" album with Kiri Te Kanawa, and innumerable cover recordings of the songs. So, perhaps Lerner's numbers are not off the charts, as it were. Nevertheless, it should be apparent to even the most ingenuous reader that there was an immense amount of money to be made with a successful Broadway musical.

3 This is an average of data from the Theatre Development Fund, comparing their gross ticket sales to the gross box office receipts of the last six Broadway seasons (i.e., through 1996–97).

4 Editors' note: after completion of this essay, Drabinsky and Ron Gottlieb, his co-founder of Livent, were ousted from the company in 1998 and indicted on various fraud and conspiracy charges in the U.S. and Canada. As of May 1999 the outcome of these indictments had not been determined.

5 Drawn from Furth's conversation with the author. Although I have seen most of what was interesting of Broadway since 1974, Mr. Furth, along with Anne Kaufman Schneider, and the press agent Robert Ullman, have shared their thoughts and perspectives on all the shows I did not see that they did, which often seemed like every Broadway production since 1940. My thanks to these three great resources.

Bibliography: Broadway

Any attempt to coordinate the multifarious events on Broadway during this period would bring one inevitably – and quickly – to the *Best Plays* series, which has been the chronicle and reference guide to every Broadway season for the past seventy-seven years. All productions that opened on Broadway (eventually Off-Broadway and major regional theatre as well), casts lists, number of performances, and so forth, are in these redoubtable volumes. For this period, the editorship shifted from Burns Mantle (1920–47) to John Chapman (1948–52), Louis Kronenberger (1953–61), and Henry Hewes. With *Best Plays of 1965–1966* Otis L. Guernsey, Jr. took over the editorship and has continued it until the present day (Jeffrey Sweet became associate editor in 1986). Guernsey's prefaces are key for their introduction of financial figures from the industry and "off-stage" news. (These prefaces were anthologized in *Curtain Times* in 1987, which have some new and useful commentary by Guernsey.) I have used box office gross figures from these volumes, which, in turn, are compiled from *Variety*. (Annoyingly, these figures have been dropped from the last three editions.) There are a number of other places from which one can get box office figures – the League of Theatre Producers, the New York State Attorney General's Office – but *Variety* is consistent and relatively non-partisan. The *Best Plays* series can be nicely supplemented by the annual *Theatre World* series, edited by John Willis, which has statistics, minimal text, and many photographs.

The business part of show business during this period has been astonishingly underreported, especially when one considers the plethora of books about the film industry. Erring on the "show" side, Atkinson's *Broadway* is a beautifully written, often elegiac study by one of the greatest critics of the twentieth century, and frequently addresses industry issues. *It's a Hit! The "Back Stage" Book of Longest Running Broadway Shows* by Sheward is an indispensable volume: well-illustrated, temperate in its conclusions, impeccable in its accuracy. Fehl's *On Broadway* is a delightful photographic album of the early part of this period, with many insightful quotes from the shows and their creators. As far as the "business" side goes, one volume towers above the rest: Goldman's *The Season* (the 1984 revised edition has a wonderful introduction by Frank Rich). Goldman's "candid look at Broadway" covers every show on stage and many of the machinations backstage during the 1967–68 season. It reads like a novel, is highly opinionated, and a wonderful barometer of the times. Sad to say, there is no book in its league, nor a sequel. Other books that mix a little commerce into the art are Harris's *Broadway Theatre*, Sponberg's *Broadway Talks*, and Mordden's *The American Theatre*, the last of which blurs the line between idiosyncratic and eccentric prose.

There are a few biographical volumes of note concerning the principals of this period, although there are obviously more to come. David Merrick deserves a more exacting valediction than Kissel's *David Merrick: The Abominable Showman*, but Harold Prince's career is well appraised by Foster Hirsch in *Harold Prince and the American Musical Theatre*, as is Michael Bennett's by Mandelbaum in *A Chorus Line and the Musicals of Michael Bennett*. Mandelbaum also contributed a somewhat recondite but fascinating book, which gives great insight into the industry, the self-explanatory *Not Since Carrie: Forty Years of Broadway Musical Flops*. Among memoirs, recommended are Lerner's fanciful account of his life, *The Street Where I Live*, and Prince's *Contradictions*, which is schematic and abrupt, but a wonderful peregrination through the mind of a producer.

As far as periodicals go, in preparing this chapter I have erred on the side of the *New York Times*, but, certainly since 1965, no paper has been as extensive, thorough, critical (and powerful), especially when Walter Kerr (1966–93) and Frank Rich (1980–93) were writing reviews, editorials, and features. Rich's *New York Times Magazine* article "Exit the Critic" (13 February 1994) is the best overview of the 1980s I have read. *Variety* is also indispensable, especially under the recent editorship of its "Legitimate" section by Jeremy Gerard. *American Theater* magazine seems to regard Broadway, commercialism, and entertainment with some distaste, so is not particularly useful for this subject. *TheaterWeek*, during the brief seven years of its existence (1989–96), was at its best when dealing with Broadway gossip, of which it covered a great deal. The Theatre on Tape and Film Archive at the Performing Arts Library at Lincoln Center has a burgeoning collection of taped Broadway shows from the mid-seventies on, as well as many interviews and documentaries, and is definitely worth a perusal.

Off- and Off-Off Broadway

Mel Gussow

Beginnings

Both Off-Broadway and Off-Off Broadway began with similar intentions, as the antidote to the mainstream and the marketplace. The limitations of Broadway led directly to the creation of Off-Broadway, and the subsequent drift toward commercialism of Off-Broadway led to the creation of Off-Off Broadway, which in a sense was the alternative to the alternative (see Carlson below for more on "Alternative Theatre"). In other words, inaction bred reaction. At some point, this double-barreled dose of non-traditional theatre became the artistic core of the American theatre. As Broadway productions became increasingly expensive and as the megamusical monopolized theatres and curtailed the opportunities for experimentation, the emphasis turned away from Broadway. It was in the other arena (and regional theatre) that almost all the significant events and trends occurred and where new plays, playwrights, directors, and actors were discovered. It is also where there were experimentations with new forms of theatre.

In some cases, the talent moved to Broadway and into films and television and an international spotlight. But Off-Broadway and Off-Off Broadway are not simply a training ground: they are a wellspring for the innovative. Performance art, the use of the artist's self in performance, was born here; as was the idea of environmental theatre, and the merging of theatre, music, dance, and the visual arts (including film and video).

Tennessee Williams and Arthur Miller emerged on Broadway in the forties, but, from the fifties onward the important new American playwrights (Edward Albee, David Mamet, Sam Shepard, Lanford Wilson, David Rabe, John Guare, Wallace Shawn, Terrence McNally, Wendy Wasserstein, David Henry Hwang, Mac Wellman, and others) were nurtured in this arena, as were many of America's finest actors (Geraldine Page, Colleen Dewhurst, George C. Scott, Jason Robards, Al Pacino, Dustin Hoffman, Robert De Niro, Robert Duvall, Kevin Kline, Meryl Streep). It also provided a home for indigenous writers and directors (Richard Foreman, Charles Ludlam) and performers (David Warrilow, Craig Smith, Lola Pashalinski, and Jeff Weiss). Some artists stayed there and others periodically returned, but the effect of Off-Broadway and Off-Off Broadway is inestimable.

196

Off-Broadway, of course, can be traced back to the days of Eugene O'Neill and his residency with the Provincetown Players in Greenwich Village in the early part of the twentieth century. At various times, the Washington Square Players and Eva Le Gallienne's Civic Repertory Theatre also presented plays in this area. But it was not until the fifties that Off-Broadway became a full-scale movement and a permanent part of the theatrical landscape.

Distinctions

Off-Off Broadway was its natural outgrowth. Largely for economic reasons, theatres began in unlikely locations: storefronts, lofts, basements, and coffee-houses. These were not only shoestring operations; often they were thread-bare. Gradually, working conditions improved, seats became more comfortable and public awareness increased (and ticket prices increased). Without regard for critics, a devoted audience sprung up, supporting favored artists and often filling theatres before reviews (if any) were published. Although Off- and Off-Off Broadway were eventually undercut by reductions in support from foundations, both public and private, and by other economic pressures, and by the coopting of talent by other areas of the performing arts, they have managed to remain the heartline of creativity. The primary reason for the continuing vitality of this arena is the dedication of individuals, the people who began and in many cases carried on the mission of art against the marketplace.[1]

Definition remains difficult. Off-Broadway and Off-Off Broadway are states of mind, not rigidly drawn geographic sectors. Although the primary concentration of houses is still in Greenwich Village and the East Village, theatres spread out through Manhattan and into other boroughs. Union regulations, as designated by Actors' Equity, control salaries according to the seating capacity of Off-Broadway theatres (100 to 299 seats), and with Off-Off Broadway also limit the number of performances. In these theatres, profits are seldom made (although there have been some long-running money-making successes Off-Broadway and transfers to more profitable venues). In the earliest days, actors and others passed the hat after performances, soliciting contributions from the audience. As the movement grew, theatres became institutionalized and a network of non-profit companies grew (as it also did around the country with the proliferation of regional theatres; see LoMonaco below).

At the same time, there was movement from one area to the other, as plays originally produced Off-Off shifted into full-fledged Off-Broadway commercial surroundings, just as Off-Broadway plays ended up on Broadway. Some, like Harvey Fierstein's *Torch Song Trilogy*, made the transition all the way from Off-Off Broadway to Broadway, where in 1983 it won a Tony Award as best play.

Similarly, companies like the Manhattan Theatre Club and the Circle Repertory Company began Off-Off Broadway, then with continuing success grew to Off-Broadway status. Subsequently, the Manhattan Theatre Club became even more successful and edged closer to Broadway, while the Circle Rep, fallen on hard times, retreated and then went out of business in October 1996.

The word alternative, often applied to Off- and Off-Off Broadway, should be taken literally: at their best, Off- and Off-Off are for themselves; they are not, or rather should not be, conduits to commercialism, though accidently some ventures there have proven to be profitable. The experimentation in this area had its obvious international influences: Antonin Artaud, Vsevolod Meyerhold, Vladimir Mayakovsky, and, in more recent times, Peter Brook and Jerzy Grotowski. It is where the avant-garde comes to practice its art. (In the last section of this chapter, Carlson discusses in more detail alternative theatre in the United States.)

Many individuals have made significant contributions but two figures, both essentially producers, stand the tallest: Joseph Papp, the godfather of Off-Broadway, and Ellen Stewart, the mother, La Mama of Off-Off Broadway. (See the first section of this chapter for Papp's contributions to Broadway.)

Joseph Papp and Ellen Stewart

Papp did not invent Off-Broadway. Modern Off-Broadway, as we know it, began in 1952 with Theodore Mann and José Quintero and the creation of Circle in the Square. But during his lifetime, Papp (1921–91) was the soul and constantly shifting center of Off-Broadway. Similarly, Stewart did not initiate Off-Off Broadway. As she has always acknowledged, that honor goes to Joe Cino, who opened Caffe Cino in 1959. It was La Mama who became – and as of 1999 still is – the messianic heart of the movement. The American theatre is doubly indebted to Papp and Stewart.

Emerging from television, where he was a stage manager, Papp was the inspirational force behind free Shakespeare. He also strove to liberate theatre from the stranglehold of Broadway producers and theatre owners. Battling with city authorities, in particular Robert Moses, the all-controlling New York parks commissioner, Papp brought the itinerant New York Shakespeare Festival to Central Park, and declared that he was going to stay there. This was not the first location for Papp's apparent pipe dream of bringing classics to the people, but it became its permanent summer setting (eventually in the Delacorte Theatre). A rugged individualist, who challenged authority while assuming his own authority, Papp went from outsider to insider in a very short space of time.

His program of free Shakespeare led directly to his creation of the Public Theater, a multi-theatre structure that he opened in 1967 in the former Astor Library on Astor Place near the Bowery. The Public was soon filled with energy and theatrical life, from *Hair*, the counterculture musical by Gerome Ragni, James Rado, and Galt MacDermot (which opened the new theatre), through plays by David Rabe, Michael Weller, Thomas Babe, Wallace Shawn, and other homegrown talents – and always including Shakespeare. Papp believed wholeheartedly in renegade writers, those who challenged tradition and the political *status quo*. When he brought a playwright into his family, he supported him even to the extent of producing lesser or unfinished work. His investment was more in the playwright than in the play.

Calling upon his youthful background as a political rebel, he favored plays with a social consciousness. More than many producers, he brought in works by black and Hispanic writers (Charles Gordone, Ntozake Shange, Miguel Piñero) that spoke with rage about restrictions they faced in their lives. Rabe, with his anger (and his artistry) about hopeless wars, in plays like *The Basic Training of Pavlo Hummel* (1971), *Sticks and Bones* (1971), and *Streamers* (1976), became his house playwright. If Papp were a playwright, he would have hoped to be Rabe.

Despite a reluctance to produce plays by English writers (with the definite exception of Shakespeare, David Hare, and Caryl Churchill), he consistently presented the work of Vaclav Havel, giving him an American forum even as he was imprisoned in his native Czechoslovakia. At the same time, Papp had a love of theatre for theatre's sake, and for a change of pace would put on works of entertainment, like *The Pirates of Penzance* (1980), one of his many collaborations with Wilford Leach, who for many years was Papp's principal director. British writer Arthur Wing Pinero's *Trelawney of the Wells* (1898), Papp's favorite backstage comedy, shared the theatre with Miguel Piñero's street-smart dramas like *Short Eyes*. The stagestruck Papp himself performed a cabaret show (not at the Public), singing "Brother, Can You Spare a Dime?", which might be considered his signature song: beg, borrow, badger, anything to keep his theatre in business, anything, that is, except compromise what he regarded as his principles. On several occasions, he rejected financial support for what he considered to be ethical reasons.

Although Papp was never able to create an American style of Shakespearean performance or an American Shakespeare company, he did give such individuals as George C. Scott, Colleen Dewhurst, James Earl Jones, Kevin Kline, Meryl Streep, Stacy Keach, and Raul Julia ample opportunity to demonstrate their prowess with Shakespeare. He was a pioneer in what is frequently termed non-traditional casting, freely mixing actors of various races, especially in Shakespeare. Using a variety of directors, including Gerald Freedman and later Wilford Leach – and sometimes himself – he presented productions that ran the gamut from imaginative to negligible, but always emphasizing that his was an open theatre where anything could be tried. Looking back on his time at the Shakespeare Festival as a high point of his professional life, Scott credited Papp with ruthlessness as well as dedication and said that he was devoted to an ideal and would "not let anything stand in his way." He added, "Thank God he's only in the theatre."

Through the years, Papp increased his power, adding Lincoln Center and Broadway to his annexations (after four seasons, he left Lincoln Center, keeping only his Public Theater home base). *A Chorus Line*, which began as a Michael Bennett workshop for dancers at the Public, opened downtown in 1975 and then moved to the Shubert Theatre on Broadway, where it won a Pulitzer Prize and with its unique premise became a turning point in American musical theatre (see Chapter 4). During its long run, it was also the greatest source of income for the Shakespeare Festival. In emulation (and envy) of Papp, other companies began looking for another *A Chorus Line* to free themselves from economic woes. Even Papp looked for another windfall. But *A Chorus Line* was one of a kind. With Bennett's early death in 1987 from AIDS, it also stood as the director's legacy.

Papp himself stirred anger and resentment, for his stubbornness and for closing the door to artists outside of his ken, or at least for not letting other feet in the door. When he died in 1991, Papp's funeral was held at the Public Theater, and, as befitting the producer, it became a theatrical event: a public wailing wall at which people bore witness to his years and, in some cases, to his limitations. Artists he supported begrudged the fact that he had not given them artistic tenure in his house. The Dramatists Guild announced that its members had "sustained a grave loss," and added, "He was impulsive, mercurical [*sic*] and grandiose, but he was a generous and loving promoter of our plays wherever he found them" (*New York Times* obituary, 2 November 1991). Papp was certainly "mercurical." As he said, "I can bend, backtrack, switch directions, do this or that, whatever is necessary – in order to survive. My tactics, out of necessity, keep changing, but my direction has never changed: new plays, new audiences" (Gussow, cover story, *New York Times Magazine*, 9 November 1975). That could in fact serve as his epitaph. Whatever criticism accrued to the Papp years, he made an enormous contribution and was the most powerful and influential man in American theatre.

Reluctantly, Papp had named a successor: JoAnne Akalaitis, one of the founders of the innovative performance art troupe Mabou Mines. After Papp died, Akalaitis took over the Shakespeare Festival, but with only a brief chance to prove her mettle, as she was summarily dismissed in 1993 by her board of directors and replaced by George C. Wolfe. Wolfe, who had worked at the Public as a director and playwright (*The Colored Museum* in 1986), immediately put his own signature on the Festival especially by stressing questions of ethnicity, in the audience as well as the artists. In honor of its founder, the theatre was renamed the Joseph Papp Public Theater, but the spirit of its founder was missing. Papp was, of course, irreplaceable.

At least on a par with Papp in terms of significance was Ellen Stewart, the earth mother of the American theatre, the indomitable, indefatigable – she earned those adjectives – La Mama, the promulgator of pushcart theatre who became a theatrical figure of world importance. While others theorized about the need for a poor theatre, Stewart did something about it. Anyone could have a play done at La MaMa Experimental Theatre Club. With a true sense of democracy, she did not express her artistic taste but simply welcomed everyone, and at first anyone: in this sense she was the direct opposite of Papp and most other artistic directors. With a certain pride, Stewart said that she did not read scripts. She "read" people, she heard "vibes," investing herself and her energy in artists whom she thought were worth encouraging.

A former clothing designer and before that an elevator operator in a department store, she began her first theatre with seeming casualness, as a place to do plays by her brother and Paul Foster, a friend and incipient playwright. Conquering bureaucracy and battling authorities who wanted to close her operation for violating various city ordinances, she survived against all odds. She began in a basement on East Ninth Street in Manhattan, then moved to a loft, and finally, after years of struggle, to her long-term residency on East Fourth Street. Eventually she buttressed her La MaMa theatres with the Annex, a large adaptable space for more epic events, and she also began a cabaret. As the unknown entered and then exited famous, Stewart remained the essence of La MaMa.

A force of nature, she could talk anyone into anything. As she said, "If we were sitting on our tails, waiting for someone to help us, we'd be nothing. We're like gypsies on the front lawn. We're here!" Bargaining and even bullying her way into longevity, she became the surrogate parent and producer to a battalion of domestic and international artists. Sam Shepard, Lanford Wilson, Harvey Fierstein, Tom Eyen, Leonard Melfi, Ed Bullins, and Jean-Claude Van Itallie had their early plays done here, along with those by Harold Pinter, Fernando Arrabal, and Samuel Beckett; the composer Elizabeth Swados, the director Tom O'Horgan, actors like Bette Midler, Robert De Niro, and Diane Lane began their careers at La MaMa. Directors came from abroad: Peter Brook, Jerzy Grotowski, Tadeusz Kantor, and Andrei Serban (and Serban stayed, to become the foundation stone of a La MaMa acting company). Stewart traveled. Her journeys in pursuit of art took her around the world, from Israel to Argentina, where she established satellite La MaMas and spread the word and the talent, and became an unofficial ambassador of the performing arts.

When she was in New York, she would walk on stage before a performance, ring her trademark cowbell, and declare that La MaMa ETC was devoted "to the playwright and all aspects of the theatre." Generally, she would not stay to watch the show, although she sometimes returned for the final performance. Even as she began to stage plays herself, her role remained indefinable. Technically, she was a producer or presenter, but what she did went far deeper than that. La MaMa was the quintessence of the experimental theatre and for her many contributions Stewart was given a so-called genius award by the MacArthur Foundation. In *Who's Who in the Theatre* it says quite plainly that her company had "a profound effect on theatre throughout the world," and that "her own influence probably exceeds that of any other twentieth-century theatre figure."

Development of Off-Broadway

The chronology of the Off-Broadway movement began before Papp and Stewart, with Circle in the Square, which Mann and Quintero, as noted earlier, created in 1951 in Sheridan Square in Greenwich Village. The following year, Circle in the Square began auspiciously with a revival of Tennessee Williams's *Summer and Smoke*, a failure on Broadway in 1948. Quintero's revival, starring a radiant new actress, Geraldine Page, established her, the director, and the theatre, and found a new dimension for the playwright. As with later productions, Quintero's magic was largely one of fidelity and intimacy, of bringing a play back to its roots. Sitting around the stage on four sides – still an innovation in its time – theatregoers eavesdropped on Alma Winemiller and her neighbors. *Summer and Smoke* seeped in.

Something similar could be said about the Circle in the Square's revival of Eugene O'Neill's *The Iceman Cometh* in 1956. It was O'Neill more than anyone else who had been responsible for the birth of the original Off-Broadway, and now, after his death, he became the catalyst in the re-emergence of the Off-Broadway movement. As with *Summer and Smoke, The Iceman Cometh* had failed on Broadway (in 1946) and had been marked as one of a highly regarded playwright's lesser works. Quintero and his astonishing star, Jason Robards, changed all that. Harry Hope's dead end saloon, a landscape of shattered dreams, came seethingly to life at the Circle. Lives and reputations changed, and the success soon encouraged the Circle's move to Broadway with O'Neill's posthumous masterpiece, *Long Day's Journey Into Night*. The company performed similar feats with other writers like Thornton Wilder (with *Plays for Bleecker Street*) and gave Dustin Hoffman one of his earliest showcases (1966) in the English play *Eh?* by Henry Livings.

Circle in the Square moved from its original home in Sheridan Square to a new location on Bleecker Street, and finally to Broadway, in each stop trying to duplicate its first situation, with the audience surrounding the play. Quintero left, and Mann carried on. The company had its failures as well as its successes; its glory time was Off-Broadway in the early eventful years. In those days there was a healthy sense of family throughout Off-Broadway. Actors like George C. Scott and Colleen Dewhurst brought their magnetism to Circle in the Square and to the New York Shakespeare Festival, moving freely from one to the other, as the territory seemed to explode with talent. Similarly, James Earl Jones packed a half dozen roles into a single Off-Broadway season. He never stopped working, along with his peers, brightening many stages. The late fifties and on to the sixties were a halcyon time in the life of the American theatre.

Politics and social awareness always played an important role Off-Broadway, never more so than with the Living Theatre. As invented by Julian Beck and Judith Malina, the Living Theatre ("le Living" as it was known in France) was the radical conscience and agent provocateur of the American theatre. Explaining the choice of name, Malina said the word "living" was meant "not so much in terms of lively, though there certainly is that hope, but more in the sense of being flexible and responsive. We wanted to create a theatre that can say something whether we are playing in an opera house in Italy or in the favelas of Brazil, in prisons when we are prisoners or in the streets."

Repeatedly embroiled in storms of controversy, Beck and Malina refused to compromise their principles. Although the Becks could trace the origins of the Living Theatre back to 1948, it was not until they produced Jack Gelber's *The Connection* in their theatre on West Fourteenth Street in 1959 that they broke through with their message (another perspective on the Living Theatre and *The Connection* is provided by Carlson in the last section of this chapter). Gelber's graphic simulation of reality stirred theatregoers (and dismayed its initial critics) with its Beckettian story of drug addicts waiting for their fix. Gelber was one of a trio of new writers to make their debut Off-Broadway at the time, and to alert the theatrical world to the boldness of their work. The others were Edward Albee, with *The Zoo Story*, and Jack Richardson with *The Prodigal*, both in the 1959–60 season, and they were followed in 1962 by Arthur Kopit with his Absurdist romp, *Oh Dad, Poor Dad, Mamma's Hung You in the Closet and I'm Feelin' So Sad* (starring Jo Van Fleet and Barbara Harris). Although Richardson turned to other pursuits, Gelber and Kopit continued to be active in theatre, and Albee, with his move to Broadway with *Who's Afraid of Virginia Woolf?*, became a seminal force in the new American theatre. Subsequently, he too returned to Off-Broadway.

As for the Living Theatre, it continued its iconoclastic path with Kenneth H. Brown's *The Brig* in 1963, a brutal slice of Marine life (see Carlson below).

Repeatedly, the Living Theatre accosted its patrons. Besieged for non-payment of taxes, it eventually left America to lead a nomadic existence in Europe, returning, in 1968, with the epic *Paradise Now* and then, after another absence, coming back to New York in the mid-eighties. Beck and Malina believed forthrightly that art, in particular, theatre, could alter society. As Beck said on returning to America, "Art opens perception and changes our vision. I think that without art we would all remain blind to reality. We go to the theater to study ourselves. The theater excites the imagination, and it also enters the spirit" (*New York Times*, 15 January 1984). After Beck's death in 1985, the Living Theatre continued under the direction of Malina and Hanon Reznikov.

Other Off-Broadway Pioneers

Equally consequential, in a different way, was the consortium formed by producers Richard Barr and Clinton Wilder and playwright Edward Albee. They began Off-Broadway in 1960 with two one-acts, Samuel Beckett's *Krapp's Last Tape* and Albee's *The Zoo Story*, a seminal moment in contemporary theatre. That was followed by other important innovative work at the Cherry Lane and other theatres (including works by Albee as well as the blistering *Dutchman* by Amiri Baraka, né Leroi Jones). Eventually, Barr and his partners did most of their work on Broadway, but, with profits from their productions, the trio initiated the Playwrights Unit, an invaluable new playwrights' workshop. Through this workshop, Albee was followed by Sam Shepard, Lanford Wilson, Mart Crowley (author of *The Boys in the Band* in 1968, the first commercially successful play about the problems of gay men) and many others.

Under this and other managements, Off-Broadway offered adventurous plays by Beckett, Jean Genet (*The Maids, Deathwatch, The Blacks, The Balcony*), Eugène Ionesco (*The Bald Soprano*), Bertolt Brecht, Harold Pinter, and others.

Furthermore, the openness of Off-Broadway made room for such apparent anomalies as David Ross, who in the late fifties and early sixties created an Off-Broadway outpost for classics in his theatre on East Fourth Street (and, later, on West Fifty-fifth Street). Presenting plays by Chekhov and Ibsen, featuring new and talented actors, Ross educated and uplifted a generation of theatregoers. "My plays have never died," he said. "When I commit myself in terms of my art to Chekhov or Ibsen, it's like Rubinstein committing himself to an all Chopin program." Then turning against what he saw as a craze for newness, he said, "You think greatness can be produced every year? The great ones stand all alone. The classic to me is the newness" (*Newsweek*, 10 October 1962).

Seeking classics, audiences also had the option of the Association of Producing Artists (the APA), Ellis Rabb's touring company of actors (including, most notably, Rosemary Harris, George Grizzard, Nancy Marchand, and Rabb himself). The APA followed what was becoming a standard route, moving from Off-Broadway to Broadway. Similarly, there was the Phoenix Theatre, which Norris Houghton and T. Edward Hambleton began in 1953 with *Madam, Will You Walk?*, starring Hume Cronyn and Jessica Tandy. Emulating European theatres, the Phoenix presented works by Brecht, Pirandello, and O'Casey, among many others. Montgomery Clift did *The Seagull*, Robert Ryan was in *Coriolanus*, Uta Hagen and Zero Mostel did *The Good Woman of Setzuan*, and Irene Worth and Eva Le Gallienne were in *Mary Stuart*. In 1964, the APA and the Phoenix merged, and finally ended their operation in 1970.

Eventually, a network of small classic companies sprang up: the Classic Stage Company (founded by Christopher Martin and continuing through several changes in directors), the Roundabout Theatre Company, the Jean Cocteau (with its leading actor, Craig Smith), and the Pearl Theatre Company. The Roundabout is a good example of the evolutionary aspect of theatre. It began in 1965 in a basement theatre under a supermarket, then moved to a medium size Off-Broadway theatre, and in 1991 transferred to Broadway, where it has two stages (as of 1999 another move is planned). As the Roundabout grew, it also improved. What was once a variety of community theatre was quickly replaced by professionalism: name actors and directors in established classics, and, occasionally, new plays.

Emergence of Off-Off Broadway

For all the José Quinteros and Davis Rosses, Off-Broadway also had its own instincts for commercialism, at least partly because of the lower economic factors. Although Off-Broadway is commonly regarded as an arena for non-profit theatre, that is only a part of the whole. As on Broadway, some theatre buildings (like the Promenade on upper Broadway) became prime real estate properties, and profits are made from long-running shows. A musical could be small yet attract a large audience. Shows like *Little Mary Sunshine* (1959) and *Little Shop of Horrors* (1982) found an enthusiastic public and moved into long runs. *The Fantasticks* (by Tom Jones and Harvey Schmidt) defeated mixed reviews in 1960 to become the longest running musical of all time, while *The Threepenny Opera* opened in 1955 and ran for seven years. Others like *Hair, A Chorus Line, Godspell* (which began at La MaMa), and *Grease*, shifted to Broadway. Drama and comedy, from *Other People's Money* to A. R. Gurney's *Sylvia*, have been successes and encouraged duplication of the plays at regional theatres. As Off-Broadway expanded its role, it became, to a certain degree, a smaller version of Broadway.

As production costs increased, there was a need for forays further into the world of non-profit. The result received the unwieldy label of Off-Off Broadway, representing another step away from Broadway. Despite additional inroads of commercialism, no third "Off" was added to the nomenclature. Although Joe Cino is the recorded progenitor of Off-Off, it was a synchronicity of events that created the movement. While Cino was serving theatre to his patrons in his café on Cornelia Street, Ralph Cook was welcoming artists to Theatre Genesis at St. Mark's in the Bowerie, and Larry Kornfeld and Al Carmines were opening the doors at the Judson Memorial Church. These various groups shared talents. Sam Shepard, Lanford Wilson, Jean-Claude Van Itallie, and others moved from place to place along with actors, directors, and designers. In other words, there was great creative ferment and also a cooperative instinct: a movement was born, and it was one that was to change the face of the American theatre.

Cino, an affable, gregarious man, was the first to put out his shingle, in December 1958, turning Caffe Cino into his own personalized, idiosyncratic coffeehouse theatre. The range of plays was as wide as Cino's smile: from *Dames at Sea*, a nostalgic spoof of the musicals of the thirties (a show that was later to make its way around the world) to early plays by H.M. Koutoukas, Tom Eyen (*Why Hannah's Skirt Won't Stay Down*), Robert Patrick, Robert Heide, and Lanford Wilson. Wilson's *The Madness of Lady Bright* was typical of the adventurous fare on Cino's menu: an empathetic look at the loneliness of an aging homosexual (played by Neil Flanagan).

As described in *The Off-Off Broadway Book* by Albert Poland and Bruce Mailman, Caffe Cino was "dark, smoky, cluttered and dirty. The walls were covered with posters, old photographs, crunched foil, glitter stars and hundreds of pieces of assorted memorabilia" (xvii). There was no admission charge and contributions were solicited from the audience to pay for the actors. With no public or private support, Caffe Cino had "no obligations other than to itself." When Cino killed himself in 1967, it was a tragic loss for his friends and also for Off-Off Broadway.

An equally evocative figure was Al Carmines, the assistant minister (to Howard Moody) at Judson Church. Carmines, an ebullient musical talent, wrote the score to a cornucopia of musicals, some of them based on the work of Gertrude Stein, others, like *A Look at the Fifties*, drawn from his own memory and imagination. In his own way, as composer and lyricist, Carmines became the Rodgers and Hammerstein of Off-Off Broadway. Simultaneously, Ralph Cook made Theatre Genesis a center of experimentation. As he said, "The playwright had complete freedom to offend and to disgust our audiences – but they'll keep coming back. It's only because of this that we're having a renaissance of theatre."

Shepard, Chaikin, Wilson, Mamet

Among Cook's favorites was Sam Shepard, a former busboy at the Village Gate, who entered the theatre in his early twenties and threatened to revolutionize it. "Theater is a big bust," he announced, "so old-fashioned, so steeped in its tradition and its economics." He vowed to "change the areas of reality the audience brings into the theater" (*Newsweek*, 1 May 1967). In plays like *Cowboy Mouth* and *The Tooth of Crime*, he linked theatre with the world of rock'n'roll, while creating his own mythos of an America on the road to self-destruction. Shepard became one of the most American of playwrights, the poet of the outsider, as evoked through legend and a life on the open road. Scores of his plays (*Curse of the Starving Class*, *Fool for Love*, *A Lie of the Mind*) were done in the seventies and eighties Off-Broadway.

True West, a failure in its production at the Public Theater, was redone in 1982 by John Malkovich and Gary Sinise of the Steppenwolf Theatre of Chicago in an electrifying Off-Broadway production that brought acclaim to both the playwright and the Steppenwolf company. As with so many of his contemporaries, Shepard made the transition from renegade to celebrity, winning the Pulitzer Prize for drama for *Buried Child* (through its Off-Off production at Theatre for the New City), and moving on to Hollywood as actor, writer, and director. It was not until Sinise brought the Steppenwolf revival of *Buried Child* to New York in 1996 that Shepard was seen on Broadway. He remains a quintessential Off-Broadway playwright.

Early in his career, Shepard began collaborating with Joseph Chaikin and the Open Theatre (created in 1963 as a laboratory for actors). Shepard and Chaikin continued that collaboration through the years, with plays like *Tongues* and *Savage/Love*. The Open Theatre was itself a cornerstone of the experimental theatre, with its ensemble creations like *The Serpent* (drawn from the Book of Genesis) and *Terminal* (about ways of dying). Other playwrights who worked closely with the Open Theatre included Susan Yankowitz and Jean-Claude Van Itallie, whose *America, Hurrah!* (an enraged look at American consumerism) was widely acclaimed in 1966.

For Chaikin, the Open Theatre was partly a protest against the lack of oxygen in the commercial theatre. As he said, "Training is absolutely the basis of the work"; process was essential (*New York Times*, 12 July 1972). Even as the Open Theatre ended its own run, its influence resonated through the work of others, like Paul Zimet and the Talking Band. Along with other graduates of the Open Theatre, Zimet carried on its goal. As with Chaikin, he blurred the line between actors and authors: the work was genuinely collaborative by nature. In the sixties there was a brief flare-up of political theatre, with Martin Duberman's *In White America* in 1963, Megan Terry's *Viet Rock* in 1966, followed the next year by Barbara Garson's *MacBird*, a vituperative satiric attack on President Lyndon Johnson.

In 1969, Marshall W. Mason, Lanford Wilson, Tanya Berezin, and Rob Thirkield founded the Circle Repertory Company, with high aesthetic principles. Mason, who became the artistic director, said that the company was "for the needs of the artist, based on the relation between the actors and the playwright" (*New York Times*, 12 May 1974). From the beginning, the core of his Off-Off Broadway company was Wilson himself, who emerged from America's heartland with stories of rebellion, families in conflict, and searchers for meanings from the past.

Wilson's first breakthrough came with *The Hot l Baltimore*, about the isolated, sometimes interwoven lives in an ungrand hotel. Wilson's sense of lyrical realism suffused this and other works, three of which centered on the fictional Talley family (the two-hander, *Talley's Folly*, with Judd Hirsch and Trish Hawkins, became a Pulitzer Prize-winner in 1980). As with Shepard, Wilson had a turning point when the Steppenwolf Theatre visited Off-Broadway in 1984 with Malkovich's striking production of an early, neglected Wilson play, *Balm in Gilead* (with Sinise and Glenne Headly heading an ensemble cast). Mason had first staged the play in 1965 at La MaMa.

Later, Shepard and Wilson were followed by Mamet, who came from Chicago with *Sexual Perversity in Chicago* (1975) and *American Buffalo* (1977), winning a deserved reputation for his sharp-sighted observations of wheelers, dealers, and movers. Mamet leaped from Off-Off Broadway to Broadway and then to the movies, while not neglecting his theatrical roots. Later plays like *Oleanna* (1992) became long-running Off-Broadway hits, and a Mamet-inspired company, the Atlantic Theatre, presented plays by him and other writers. (Mamet and other post-World War II writers are discussed in more detail in Chapter 3.)

Long before Mamet came to New York, Chicago had sent its improvisational troupe, the Second City, which, under the direction of Paul Sills, opened Off-Broadway and later was seen on Broadway. With the Second City were such outstanding performers as Barbara Harris, Alan Arkin, Paul Sand, and Anthony Holland, who spread out through the New York theatre. Mike Nichols and Elaine May, who had made their names with Second City's predecessor, the Compass Players, became famous as a double act in nightclubs and then on Broadway. Each began a career as director (and in May's case as a playwright) Off-Broadway.

Charles Ludlam, Richard Foreman, Robert Wilson, Ping Chong, John Kelly[2]

Continuity was established by people like Charles Ludlam and Richard Foreman, each of whom invented an idea and, as author, director, and company leader, created a living legacy.

Ludlam's invention in 1967 was the Ridiculous Theatrical Company. Ridiculous theatre, a step beyond Absurd and a satiric style that mocked itself as well as cultural detritus, was also practiced by John Vaccaro (the founder of the Play-House of the Ridiculous) and the playwright Ronald Tavel, but Ludlam polished it into a performance art. Beginning with plays like *Bluebeard* (1970), and extending through dozens of other works, Ludlam spoofed everything already in an excessive mode: horror movies, opera, farce, melodrama. He often called himself a theatrical ecologist, recycling old material, but he became a true original; his portrait gallery is filled with comic grotesqueries: clowns and emperors, the catarrhic *Camille*, a Promethean puppeteer, and a virtuoso ventriloquist.

He also created actors, giving free rein to Black-Eyed Susan as leading lady, Lola Pashalinski as queens and consorts, John D. Brockmeyer as the creepiest villain never to appear in a Frankenstein movie, and Ethyl Eichelberger, a wizard of cross-dressing. Black-Eyed Susan, née Susan Carlson, could claim the title of diva of Off-Off Broadway. A charming and deliriously amusing actress, she brightened Ludlam's comedies, as well as those by Eichelberger (including *Hamlette*, a version of *Hamlet*, in which she played the title role), John Jesurun, and others. As much as any theatre, the Ridiculous represented the challenge of trying to survive. As Ludlam said, "One year, everyone in our company was on welfare. We were on welfare until we got a Guggenheim" (*New York Times*, 12 July 1972).[3] Ludlam also gave the theatre Everett Quinton, his protégé and co-star, who, after Ludlam's death from AIDS in 1987, carried forward the banner of the Ridiculous and became a first-rate director, playwright, and actor in his own right, while facing the struggle of surviving with limited financial means.

Visionary and voyeur of his dreams and nightmares, Richard Foreman founded the Ontological-Hysteric Theatre (in 1968) in his own image as Off-Off Broadway's poet-philosopher. As he said, "Art is trying to redeem, to learn how to dance with the problematic aspects of the world. It's easy enough to imagine a beautiful world, and to celebrate it, but I would rather learn how to celebrate the fallen world we live in" (*New York Times*, 17 January 1994). After a formal education, which included study at Brown and the Yale School of Drama, Foreman tried writing traditional plays, then drastically altered his perspective. Inspired by underground filmmakers of the sixties, he became one of the first and one of the longest running underground playmakers. With the intricacy of a quantum physicist, he wove patterns on stage, intersecting design elements like string and clocks, and transforming "clouds of language and impulse" into a Caligarian, or rather, Foremanesque universe.

As director and as off-stage narrator with his deep sepulchral voice, Foreman orchestrated his idiographic plays, which often starred Kate Manheim, his favorite leading lady and later his wife. In plays like *Rhoda in*

Potatoland, she played Foreman's muse-like heroine Rhoda, dream woman extraordinaire. Foreman's plays (with devious titles like *Pandering to the Masses: A Misrepresentation*; *Book of Splendours: Part Two*; *Film Is Evil, Radio Is Good*, and *My Head Was a Sledgehammer*) are densely existential and also playful, touched by vaudeville and silent comedy. Later, Foreman was to move out and direct classical plays and operas on major stages, but always came back to his roots. Establishing his Ontological-Hysteric chamber theatre in 1991 at St. Mark's in the Bowerie, he continues to create his own inimitable theatre pieces.

Robert Wilson, a native of Waco, Texas, began his notable career as director, conceptualist, and visual artist with marathon plays like *Deafman Glance* (1970) and the dusk to dawn *The Life and Times of Joseph Stalin* (1973), which encouraged theatregoers to tune in and out. Difficult and demanding, Wilson sought the audience's complicity – and people joined him on his journey, a voyage in time and space. Creating phantasmagoric events, he is a kind of colossus of performance art, influencing other creative artists: choreographers like Jerome Robbins as well as conceptual directors. In his unique fashion, Wilson has explored the worlds of Freud, Lewis Carroll, Einstein, and Stein, and, in his epic *the CIVIL warS*, war through history. Along with Foreman, Lee Breuer, Martha Clarke, Fred Curchack, and others, he became a primary proponent of the Theatre of Images. Some of those images impaled the minds of theatregoers: such as the scene in *Einstein on the Beach* (a 1976 operatic collaboration with Philip Glass) in which a pillar of white light rose from the stage and disappeared into the sky, followed by the landing of a spaceship.

Because of the elaborateness and the expense of most Wilson productions, they are presented for limited runs (at the Brooklyn Academy of Music and elsewhere), and not always in New York. Though he lives in New York, he has found himself, more times than not, staging theatre pieces and his variations on classic operas with great international opera companies or with regional American companies, like the Alley Theatre in Houston.

In a different though related mode was Ping Chong, who at La MaMa and elsewhere took theatregoers on epic excursions into artistic and literary history, at first in tandem with Meredith Monk and subsequently with his own company. With a wry humor and a beguiling sense of theatrics, he covered the spectrum from the origins of man to outer space, often dealing with the subject of the outsider in a society. In the nineties he began looking back at Oriental myths and traditions in *Deshima* and *Chinoiserie*. John Kelly, in contrast, used himself as art object, in solo and group pieces, like *Pass the Blutwurst, Bitte*, his extraordinary incarnation of the world of Egon Schiele. Sometimes he performed in drag. In one play he posed as the Mona Lisa and in another, *Paved Paradise*, he transformed himself into Joni Mitchell. Often in song, always in flight, in common with other avant-garde artists, Kelly was his own invention. Foreman, Wilson, Chong, Kelly, and others are *sui generis*.

Groups and Artists

Taking their names from a town in Nova Scotia, a group of diverse theatre artists (Lee Breuer, JoAnne Akalaitis, Ruth Maleczech, Philip Glass, and David Warrilow) founded a cooperative company, Mabou Mines, in 1970 and quickly became America's foremost avant-garde troupe. Mabou Mines merged aesthetic experimentation with political awareness while creating a series of haunting theatre pieces. Akalaitis took Colette on a fanciful trip in *Dressed Like an Egg*, then looked back with skepticism at the origins of the atomic age in *Dead End Kids* (1982). Breuer, as playful prankster, stir-fried his *Animation* series, a Dadaesque canvas mixing animals and imagery. Together with the composer Bob Telson, he created *The Gospel at Colonus*, a merging of classical Greek tragedy with contemporary gospel music. Restlessly inventive, he presented in 1990 a female *King Lear*, starring Maleczech. Breuer and Maleczech were also responsible for *Haj*, a multidimensional experiment in holographic theatre. Later, Breuer created *Peter and Wendy*, a musical parable with puppets and people, seen most recently at the New Victory Theatre in 1997. In *Cold Harbor*, Bill Raymond and Dale Worsley brought Ulysses S. Grant back to life as an animated museum exhibition, and Warrilow offered his haunting renditions of Samuel Beckett's non-dramatic works. In common with other companies, Mabou Mines was nomadic, finding its longest residency at the Public, where the group was certified as Papp's experimentalists.

In the sixties, Richard Schechner, a critic, academic, and director, founded the Performance Group, inspired by the work of Antonin Artaud and Jerzy Grotowski. *Dionysus in '69*, a collective piece by Schechner and company, a self-proclaimed theatre of ecstasy, brought the audience viscerally into the theatrical event. Schechner took a related approach with Genet's *The Balcony* and Shepard's *The Tooth of Crime*, with in each case artistry subordinated to ritualism. Schechner's successor at the Performing Garage, Elizabeth LeCompte's Wooster Group, specialized in deconstruction, stripping Thornton Wilder, Arthur Miller, and Chekhov from their roots. Actors emerged from this troupe: Willem Dafoe and Spalding Gray, who began to explore the storybook from life, recounting in minute and often hilarious detail his misadventures as man, actor, and author. Without altering his manner or his material, Gray moved from the smallest of stages to the Broadway-scale Vivian Beaumont Theater at Lincoln Center. Only his audience grew.

Through all the changing currents of fashion, André Gregory held fast to his idiosyncratic principles. Committed to the art of process, this director would spend long periods in studio work, which might never be seen by the public. An early piece, his version of *Alice in Wonderland* (1970), performed by his Manhattan Project ensemble, ran Off-Broadway, as did his production of Wallace Shawn's *Our Late Night* (1975). After directing internationally and working as an actor, Gregory reappeared in the nineties with a workshop of

Uncle Vanya, starring Shawn in the title role. Though the play was seen only by a limited invited audience, Louis Malle's 1994 film version of the Gregory production, *Vanya on 42nd Street*, brought the work to a wider public.

Ellen Stewart has the longest list of discoveries; at the top is Andrei Serban, whom she first found at an international theatre festival in Zagreb, Yugoslavia. She sponsored him and brought him to America in the late sixties, a period, as Serban observed with accuracy, when the "avant-garde was in flower" (*New York Times*, 18 March 1984). It was indeed a flourishing time. During a single season, one could see the work of the Open Theatre, Grotowski's Polish Lab Theatre, and Robert Wilson. In 1974, in collaboration with Elizabeth Swados as composer, Serban staged *Fragments of a Trilogy*, a stunning environmental reinterpretation of Greek tragedy, in which theatregoers were made to feel like witnesses to the fall of Troy. Both Serban and Swados, following what was becoming a traditional path, moved on to the New York Shakespeare Festival, where they became exemplars of Papp's own interest in experimentation: Swados with the musical *Runaways* (1978) about young people living on the streets of New York, and Serban with futher adventures in Greek tragedy.

The longer-running companies achieved and maintained an identity. Marshall Mason's partnership with Lanford Wilson at the Circle Rep brought about a rich body of work, and set the tone for others who followed: Mark Medoff with *When You Comin' Back, Red Ryder* (1973), Edward J. Moore with *The Sea Horse* (1973), Jules Feiffer with *Knock Knock* (1976). Within five years, the Circle Rep had become a principal producer of new American plays. Soon it had an Off-Broadway home and presented plays there and on Broadway, including works by Wilson and Albert Innaurato (*Gemini*), and William Hoffman's *As Is* (1985), one of the first plays to deal dramatically with the AIDS epidemic. The company was also notable in giving opportunity to actors like Judd Hirsch, William Hurt, Jeff Daniels, Christopher Reeve, and Demi Moore. Artistic conflicts and a decrease in financial support eventually led to a disruption in the company, and several changes in management. After Mason, Berezin took over the artistic direction and specialized in more Absurdist works by playwrights like Paula Vogel and Craig Lucas. In 1996, the company, then under the direction of Austin Pendleton, went out of business, but its legacy remains.

The Manhattan Theatre Club, under the direction of Lynne Meadow and Barry Grove, also concentrated on new plays, and in a sense became an Off-Broadway version of what might have once been done on Broadway. In common with Broadway's Theatre Guild, the MTC was created as a playwrights' theatre appealing to a mainstream audience. Many of the works produced here, including plays by Terrence McNally, Beth Henley (*Crimes of the Heart*), and Richard Greenberg, went on to have an extended life on or

Off-Broadway. With plays stretching from *Bad Habits* and *It's Only a Play* through *Love! Valor! Compassion!* and numerous others, McNally became the MTC's favorite playwright. Opening its doors, the company also provided a home for new plays from Ireland and England: works by Brian Friel, Alan Ayckbourn, and American-born Timberlake Wertenbaker.

In a relatively short period, MTC grew from a small Off-Off Broadway theatre to become one of New York's largest producing organizations. In contrast to competitors, MTC mastered the art of fund-raising and audience development. It remained Off-Broadway at City Center, where it had two stages, but more and more its eye was on Broadway. "If Ellen Stewart is La Mama of Off-Off Broadway," said Christine Baranski, an actress who has worked frequently at MTC, "Lynne Meadow is La Mère of Midtown" (*New York Times*, 16 June 1994). Meadow's mentor and role model was Papp, and she expressed her own taste in her selection of material.

Through various managements, especially when André Bishop was the artistic director, Playwrights Horizons repeatedly revealed its interest in new American comedies, many with an underlying serious intent. Wendy Wasserstein's Pulitzer Prize-winning *The Heidi Chronicles* (1988) began here along with many other of her plays. Playwrights Horizons also produced work by Jonathan Reynolds, Christopher Durang, Jon Robin Baitz, and A. R. Gurney, among others, as well as experimental musicals by Stephen Sondheim (*Assassins*) and William Finn *(March of the Falsettos).*

In the career of the composer Alan Menken can be seen the arc of the Off-Broadway experience as it opened up and began to reach a broader audience. With his lyricist partner Howard Ashman, Menken wrote small chamber musicals mostly for the WPA Theatre. One show, *The Little Shop of Horrors*, based on a throwaway Grade "B" Hollywood movie, became a huge international success. After Ashman's death from AIDS, Menken made the transition to the Hollywood screen and Broadway itself, as the primary creator of Walt Disney musical epics like *Beauty and the Beast.* For many years, the WPA was a prolific provider of new work by Larry Ketron, Kevin Wade, and other playwrights. The designer, Edward T. Gianfrancesco, carved out a career creating realistically detailed sets for this company, with great resourcefulness using that company's intimate space. Representing the other end of the spectrum, John Arnone perfected his fanciful settings for Off-Off at the Soho Rep and other theatres, before making the inevitable move to Broadway musicals.

The Ensemble Studio Theatre is a wide-ranging ensemble of theatre artists who specialize in studio productions. With Curt Dempster as founder and artistic director, this cooperative nurtures plays from readings to projects and occasionally to full-scale stagings, some of which take place at other theatres. The Ensemble Studio has become a primary progenitor of new one-act plays in its annual "Marathon," freely mixing work by established writers like

Horton Foote, Frank D. Gilroy, David Mamet, Arthur Miller, and Christopher Durang, with newcomers testing themselves in the short dramatic form.

From the first, Off- and Off-Off Broadway emphasized ethnic diversity. Black theatre artists worked everywhere from the New Lafayette Theatre in Harlem to Woodie King, Jr.'s New Federal Theatre on Grand Street. For many years, the Negro Ensemble Company, established in 1967, was a centerpiece of Off-Broadway. Under the leadership of Douglas Turner Ward, the NEC discovered plays by Lonne Elder III (*Ceremonies in Dark Old Men*), Joseph A. Walker (a 1974 Tony winner when his play *The River Niger* moved to Broadway), Samm-Art Williams (*Home*), Charles Fuller (the 1982 Pulitzer Prize-winning *A Soldier's Play*), Leslie Lee, and Gus Edwards. Through the NEC, actors made their initial reputation: Frances Foster, Roxie Roker, Michele Shay, Charles Brown, and Ward himself. At other theatres, Ed Bullins, Amiri Baraka, Richard Wesley, Charles Gordone, Ntozake Shange, and Ron Milner were having their plays produced. Among prominent black writers, August Wilson was a single exception in starting in regional theatre rather than Off- or Off-Off Broadway.

In 1977 Tisa Chang founded the Pan Asian Repertory Theatre at La MaMa, then went off on her own and became the chief New York producer of works by Asian American writers, and at the same time she encouraged Asian American actors and directors. A breakthrough came in 1982 with the Pan Asian production of *Yellow Fever*, a private eye spoof by R. A. Shiomi. René Buch's Repertorio Español, Miriam Colón's Puerto Rico Traveling Theatre, and the Nuyorican Poets' Cafe were among the outstanding Hispanic companies, appealing to a bilingual audience. Irish and Jewish companies asserted their identities, along with gay and lesbian theatres, all of whom entered the mainstream with individual works. The Ubu Repertory Theater filled a vacuum by specializing in contemporary French and other European plays.

Off-Broadway and Off-Off Broadway proved to be extremely hospitable to playwrights from abroad, especially those who would have difficulty in a commercial situation. *Waiting for Godot* was a failure on Broadway, but Samuel Beckett became one of the most produced playwrights away from the mainstream. Eventually a theatre on Theatre Row, on far West Forty-second Street, was named for him, as was one for Group Theatre founder Harold Clurman.

Puppetry, New Vaudevillians, and Solo Performance

Puppetry was among the many forms to make an unusual impact Off-Off Broadway. Paul Zaloom, that irreverent, back-talking critic of cultural and societal Neanderthalism, animated objects in his tabletop theatre. During his brief stops in New York, Bruce D. Schwartz wore a puppet theatre around his body like a hugh greatcoat. Theodora Skipitares told instructional stories about history, science, and food, and Peter Schumann's Vermont-based Bread and Puppet Theatre frequently visited with its totemic figures in political parables.

Julie Taymor began as a puppeteer, in collaboration with Andrei Serban and Elizabeth Swados, but soon moved out on her own as an inventive theatre conceptualist. She continued to use mask and puppetry as an organic adjunct to her brilliantly imaginative tales like *Juan Darién*. Originally presented in a small-scale but widely imaginative Off-Off production, *Juan Darién* reopened in 1996 on a large stage at Lincoln Center. In this and other Taymor pieces, Elliot Goldenthal provided the throbbing musical score. Later, she began exploring Shakespeare (at Theatre for a New Audience) and Carlo Goldoni, among others, and eventually accepted the role of artistic creator for Disney's stage version of *The Lion King*.

At the same time, Stuart Sherman, a solo and very interiorized artist, entertained audiences with postcards and journal jottings from his itinerant life. John Jesurun turned tables on theatregoers. In *Deep Sleep, Black Maria, Everything That Rises Must Converge*, and other works, Jesurun synthesized film and television with live action so that actors sometimes found themselves talking back to themselves on screen. Led by Jesurun, as author, director, and designer, the audience was hurtled into a seemingly chaotic universe; part of the fun in watching one of his unsettling plays was to locate the equilibrium.

Although outwardly it might have seemed that the avant-garde had crested by the eighties, the fact is that like Off-Off Broadway itself it had spread out and fragmented. If anything it had become more experimental and was making freer use of new technology, through the efforts of people like Robert Wilson, Breuer, Chong, and Chris Hardman, who came from California with his walk-through environmental theatre. The experimental had long since left behind psychodrama and was more concerned with questions of art and art in society. The American avant-garde was responding to Peter Brook's statement that "in the theatre the slate is wiped clean all the time" (quoted in the *New York Times*, 18 March 1984).

In the eighties, New Vaudeville was born, springing up in circuses and Renaissance fairs: a converging of old vaudeville comedy with performance art moves. At the height was Bill Irwin, America's genius clown, who polished his art at the Ringling Brothers Clown College and then leaped into the avant-garde. With *The Regard of Flight*, which began at the Dance Theatre Workshop, and then captured a wider appreciative audience, he explored the clown's nightmare, waking up in a bed onstage, and not knowing why he was there. Out of the clown car tumbled Bob Berky, Fred Garbo, the juggler Michael Moschen (a maestro in motion), Geoff Hoyle, the self-satirizing magicians Penn and Teller, and the Flying Karamazov Brothers, who broke through to a Broadway audience with their juggling (of words as well as objects). Dance Theatre Workshop was the home of many New Vaudeville artists, and also other performance specialists like Whoopi Goldberg, who made her solo New York debut there.

The Music-Theatre Group, founded in 1971 by Lyn Austin, became one of the primary producers of innovative musical theatre projects, both at its home in Lenox, Massachusetts, and in various Off-Broadway locations. Among the many artists encouraged by Austin were Richard Foreman, Anne Bogart, and Martha Clarke. Along with Akalaitis and others, Clarke drew from an interest in literary sources and the visual arts. She herself began as a member of the Pilobolus Dance Theatre; dance remained an important element in her theatrical pieces. *The Garden of Earthly Delights* (1984), a free-floating epic inspired by Hieronymous Bosch, with actors performing airs above ground, set the tone for her magical creations, which merged dance, theatre, music, and visual imagery. *Garden* was followed by *Vienna Lusthaus* (1986), *The Hunger Artist*, and *Endangered Species* (1990).

Wynn Handman's American Place Theatre was an early producer of new American plays, focusing on such literary works as Robert Lowell's *The Old Glory* (1964) and plays by Ronald Ribman (*Harry, Noon and Night* [1965] and *The Journey of the Fifth Horse* [1966], both of which starred a newcomer, Dustin Hoffman). Much later, the American Place gave center stage to Eric Bogosian, a sharp-witted monologist (and playwright). For years the American Place collaborated with Julia Miles's Women's Project in presenting new work by female playwrights, whose number included Lavonne Mueller, Marlane Meyers, Kathleen Tolan, and Heather McDonald. Then the Women's Project split off and continued working on its own. The Interart Theatre and New Georges were among other groups committed to expanding opportunities for women in the theatre. As an encourager of new writers, the playwright and director Maria Irene Fornés also played a pivotal role.

In the late sixties Carolee Schneemann used her naked body in performance and told graphic stories while talking about her art work. Counterculture monologists appeared with greater frequency in the late eighties. Of all those who spoke candidly about their life on the line, the most notable was Karen Finley, who achieved celebrity and notoriety when she and Holly Hughes, Tim Miller, and John Fleck were denied grants by the National Endowment for the Arts because of the controversial nature of their material. Although she also wrote plays (and worked as a visual artist) it was in her solo performances (e.g., *We Keep Our Victims Ready*, 1989) that she made the most indelible impression. Using her own body (often unclothed) in her act, she became the medium of her message, blazing new paths in demanding freedom of expression and a liberation of individualism. The censorious attacks misperceived Finley: she was an artist as moralist.

Before this collision with performance art, the National Endowment played a significant but ambiguous role in the development of Off-Broadway and Off-Off Broadway. Through the leadership of Nancy Hanks, the Endowment lent support to worthy individuals and organizations, as did the New York State Council on the Arts (under the direction of Kitty Carlisle Hart). But after attacks by members of Congress, and despite the leadership of Congressman Sidney Yates and others, the NEA became increasingly vulnerable and timid. Private foundations took up some of the slack, but, in time, many of them also decreased their activity. Both the Ford Foundation and the Rockefeller Foundation played pivotal roles in earlier years but changed their direction, leaving many artists in limbo, although individual grants continued to come from the John Simon Guggenheim Foundation and other organizations.

Significantly, the MacArthur "genius" awards in theatre have primarily gone to individuals from Off-Broadway and Off-Off Broadway: Bill Irwin, Martha Clarke, Bruce D. Schwartz, Michael Moschen, Julie Taymor, Ellen Stewart, Richard Foreman, Elizabeth LeCompte, and John Jesurun.

Through the decades, theatre has broken away from traditional surroundings, moving into the streets and other public places. The Happenings of the fifties gave way to the Living Theatre's theatricalized demonstrations in the sixties, and so on. In the eighties Anne Hamburger had the idea of expanding this idea into a company, En Garde Arts, that was devoted to presenting site-specific plays – in other words, plays put on in a specific setting that complements the work itself.

En Garde went from the West Side waterfront to the meat-packing district, from a Harlem street to the facade of a high-rise building in lower Manhattan for a sound, light, and action show. On location, the troupe invented a kind of architectural theatre, as exemplified by the work of Mac Wellman. He wrote plays for En Garde Arts that took place on a lake in Central Park (*Bad Penny*) and in an abandoned former theatre on West Forty-second Street (*Crowbar*). Eventually, in 1996, En Garde returned to Forty-second Street, then in the process of being revitalized and Disneyfied, and offered in late 1996 the United States premiere of Deborah Warner's version of T.S. Eliot's "The Waste Land," a one-woman show for the Irish actress Fiona Shaw.

Wellman himself became a pivotal dramatist of the eighties and nineties, shattering tradition and confronting conservatism (and censorious United States senators) in such provocative plays as *Terminal Hip*, *Sincerity Forever*, and *A Murder of Crows*. His plays were produced Off-Off Broadway (at Primary Stages and the Soho Rep) and in regional theatres, but not at major institutional theatres. Politicians as well as the public at large held Wellman at arm's length. Through stubbornness if not by choice, he remained underground. In common with one of the characters in *The Hyacinth Macaw* (1994), Wellman has "an inescapable penchant for acts that defy convention," and also has a suspicion about the need for naturalism. Surrealism is closer to his mode. At the same time, he performs linguistic acrobatics, bringing a new sense of language into the theatre, combining lexiconic esoterica with street speech.

In this area, he is in company with Eric Overmyer, Len Jenkin, Suzan-Lori Parks, and others. In plays like *On the Verge, Native Speech*, and comic stage noir, like *Dark Rapture*, Overmyer excavates a new American language while taking his audience on fantastical voyages. At the same time, David Ives was writing comic cameos about couples and cultural icons. His one-acts appeared in a variety of places during the nineties and were finally collected as *All in the Timing*, which opened 1 December 1993, a breakthrough work for the author, and one that was to encourage other writers of short plays.

Changes: Seventies Through the Nineties

Off-Broadway spread throughout the boroughs, concentrating, of course, in Manhattan but also becoming a welcome outpost in Brooklyn, with the Brooklyn Academy of Music. By the eighties Harvey Lichtenstein had turned this multi-theatre complex into a home for opera, dance, and drama, inviting major foreign artists like Peter Brook, Ingmar Bergman, Ariane Mnouchkine, Giorgio Strehler, and Robert Lepage, but also presenting work by homegrown talent, including John Kelly, Martha Clarke, Fred Curchack, and Ping Chong. BAM's work continued through the Next Wave Festival (begun in 1983), an annual gathering of experimental artists in various performance disciplines.

For a time in the late sixties and the seventies, BAM also offered a home to the Chelsea Theatre Center. Founded in 1965 by Robert Kalfin and Michael David, the Chelsea made a policy of staging difficult, seldom performed classics, such as plays by Heinrich von Kleist, Jean Genet, and others. Chelsea eventually ended its run, as did the shortlived BAM Theatre Company, an aspiring attempt to create an acting company within the confines of the Brooklyn Academy. These are among the many theatres that made substantial contributions and then curtailed their operations: others include the Hudson Guild (which presented Hugh Leonard's *Da* with Barnard Hughes and Brian Murray), BACA Downtown in Brooklyn, Theatre at St. Clements, and the Manhattan Punch Line. Generally, theatres closed because of financial problems; occasionally it was for artistic reasons, or, simply, that the people in charge felt that the theatre had run its course. For decades, the Equity Library Theatre introduced new actors in worthy revivals, and then fell victim to the economics of play production. As with other areas of the theatre, some of the most impressive talent died of AIDS.

New theatres continued to spring up annually: Naked Angels, Cucaracha, Dixon Place, the New Group, the Drama Department. One with a specific, admirable goal, the Signature Theatre Company, was to make an important impact in the nineties. Founded in 1991 by James Houghton, the Signature had the original idea of devoting an entire season to the work of a single playwright, beginning with Romulus Linney. A revival of Linney's *The Sorrows of Frederick* was followed by the premiere of his *Ambrosio* and other works, giving theatregoers a portrait of the diversity of this underappreciated writer. Linney is in his own way a quintessential Off-Broadway playwright. His plays have also been done in regional theatre and, once, on Broadway, but with a certain regularity they appear in small theatres in New York, including Theater for the New City, each adding to what has become a substantial and rewarding body of work. In common with Lanford Wilson and Sam Shepard, Linney writes about America's heartland.

In subsequent seasons at Signature, Lee Blessing, Edward Albee, Horton Foote, Adrienne Kennedy, and Sam Shepard were all represented, with Signature productions re-establishing the reputations of writers and putting the Signature itself on the theatrical map. Albee won a Pulitzer Prize during his season in residence (1993–94), and Foote won one for a play, *The Young Man from Atlanta*, presented at Signature in 1995. As is typical of the terrain, the company was nomadic, forced to move its location, at one point finding a residency at the Public Theater (a more permanent venue was located in 1998). In Papp's time, that theatre often sheltered visiting troupes.

In its specialization, the Second Stage, founded in 1979, took an admirable, self-limiting approach. The basic premise was that the company would revive plays from the recent past, plays that had been overlooked such as Lanford Wilson's *Serenading Louie* and John Guare's *Landscape of the Body*. But soon the company shifted most of its energies to doing new plays by writers such as Michael Weller, Tina Howe, and Eric Overmyer.

The Theater for the New City is a bastion of theatrical enterprise. Founded in 1971 by Crystal Field, George Bartenieff, and others, it became one of the longest surviving, most prolific companies, in the summers taking its plays out on city streets. Theater for the New City is very much a people's theatre, and theatregoers, clearly oblivious to the press, come out and see their favorites. While TNC continued through lean years, the New York Theatre Workshop quickly became one of the more firmly established of the new theatres, presenting venturesome work by Tony Kushner, Ain Gordon, and Doug Wright. The company's breakthrough show was the 1996 musical *Rent*, Jonathan Larson's transposition of *La Bohème* to New York's Lower East Side. After the death of the author-composer, *Rent* moved to Broadway, gathered the 1996 Pulitzer and other prizes and went on to phenomenal success. More than any other show, this musical demonstrates the outreach of Off-Off Broadway.

Often there has been a connection between theatre and education or professional training. The Juilliard Drama Center gave birth to the Acting

Company, a national touring company that discovered Kevin Kline, Patti LuPone, and others, and made regular stops Off-Broadway. New York University's Tisch School of the Arts opened doors to the public and to theatre artists like Anne Bogart, Richard Foreman, and Robert Wilson (with his seismic production of Heiner Müller's *Hamletmachine*). Off-Broadway companies, like Playwrights Horizons and the Circle Rep, had their own linkage with academia, enlisting artistic associates to teach in collaborative theatre schools. Through his annual Portfolio Review at Lincoln Center, Ming Cho Lee, the dean of scenic designers (and on the faculty of the Yale School of Drama), has encouraged the work of young scenic, costume, and lighting designers, many of whom have begun their careers Off-Broadway.

The International Theatre Institute is a largely unobserved but essential element in the experimental theatre. Headed first by Rosamond Gilder and for many years by Martha Coigney, ITI is a worldwide service organization and clearing-house for foreign artists working in the United States and for American artists wishing to tour abroad. Similarly, the Theatre Communications Group, headquartered in New York, provides an information and networking service among theatres in this country.

When titles were passed around, Lucille Lortel was dubbed the queen of Off-Broadway, a most appropriate appellation for this tireless producer and theatre owner. As other theatres ended their own runs, her Theatre de Lys (on Christopher Street in Greenwich Village), named the Lucille Lortel in 1981, was consistently one of Off-Broadway's most desirable locations. It continues to add cachet to the productions it houses, which have included the long-running *The Threepenny Opera*, David Mamet's *A Life in the Theatre*, Caryl Churchill's *Cloud Nine*, and Larry Kramer's *The Destiny of Me*, and through the fifties and sixties a series of ANTA (American National Theatre and Academy) Matinees of new plays. Her generosity gave playwrights a monetary reward when they won the New York Drama Critics' Circle prize at the end of the season, an award that increasingly went to Off-Broadway plays. Today, the Lucille Lortel Award honors Off-Broadway artists.

Brooks Atkinson's *New York Times* review of Geraldine Page in *Summer and Smoke* at Circle in the Square put that theatre and the actress in the spotlight. But despite his occasional visits to the Circle and Papp's Shakespeare in Central Park and reviews by others of Off-Broadway, the *Times* did not begin covering Off-Off Broadway in depth until Mel Gussow joined the newspaper as a theatre critic. There was pioneering work by Harold Clurman in *The Nation* and Henry Hewes in *Saturday Review*, but in other respects New York critics were slow to recognize the breadth of the work being done Off-Broadway and Off-Off Broadway.

In its early days, *The Village Voice* was both influential and relatively broad-minded. Jerry Tallmer, Michael Smith, and others wrote about a wide range of activity and, through the Obie Awards (created by Tallmer in 1956), the *Voice* honored artists of importance excluded from Broadway's Tony Awards. Beckett's *Endgame*, for example, was given an Obie as Best Play the same year (1958) that Dore Schary's *Sunrise at Campobello* was voted a Tony Award. Julius Novick, Alisa Solomon, Michael Feingold, and others continued this tradition, although in recent years the coverage of the *Village Voice* and the Obies themselves have become increasingly insular. For more comprehensive coverage, theatregoers could turn to Edith Oliver, who for many years made her columns in *The New Yorker* an outpost of sensible Off-Broadway criticism; Bonnie Marranca at *Performing Arts Journal*; and to *American Theatre Magazine* (published by Theatre Communications Group).

Perhaps more than anything, theatre away from Broadway is marked by its fluidity – and the further away from Broadway the more fluid it becomes. Even as individuals like Ellen Stewart and Richard Foreman are icons of survival, the work itself moved with the times, meeting new needs, confronting new and continuing issues and giving a stage or a performance space to emerging talents.

Notes

1 Editors' note: Mel Gussow has had an abiding interest in the areas covered by this chapter since the fifties, and in his capacity as a critic for the *New York Times* (1969–93) he covered many of the events described in this essay. He has also interviewed most of the individuals quoted herein; consequently, unless otherwise indicated, quotes are derived from personal interviews, with specific original sources of quotes, when previously published, noted in the text.
2 For an expanded discussion of these and other alternative theatre artists, see Marvin Carlson's section of this chapter.
3 Guggenheims are only awarded to individuals, yet Ludlam chooses to use the Royal – or rather the Ridiculous – "we" here.

Bibliography: Off- and Off-Off Broadway

There is no complete, authoritative study of Off-Broadway or Off-Off Broadway, but there are books that summarize aspects of each and there are critical works that are helpful in understanding the range of artistic endeavor. Some of the more useful sources are out of print or at least partly out of date.

The Off-Off Broadway Book by Poland and Mailman is basically a collection of early plays by writers such as Ribman, Van Itallie, Guare, Tavel, Horovitz, and Kennedy. As a prelude, there are summaries of the pivotal Off-Off Broadway companies and a valuable listing of all the plays produced by those companies before the publication of the book.

Off-Broadway by Little focuses on major companies and personalities (Theodore Mann and José Quintero at Circle in the Square, Joseph Papp, the Living Theatre; there is a chapter on Off-Broadway award winners from 1955 to 1971). A more recent book on Papp is Epstein's 1994 biography. Foster Hirsch is working on a study of Papp and the New York Shakespeare Festival. The Living Theatre has recently been studied in Tytell's *The Living Theatre*. And the Chelsea Theatre Center has received good coverage by Davi Napoleon, while the first fifteen years of Circle Rep have been chronicled by Mary Ryzuk.

The *Obie Winners*, edited with an introduction by Ross Wetzsteon, brings together many of the best plays, including Jack Gelber's *The Connection*, Samuel Beckett's *Krapp's Last Tape*, and David Mamet's *American Buffalo*. It begins with an introduction by Ross Wetzsteon, a longtime observer of the Off-Broadway scene. *The Best of Off-Off Broadway* is an anthology of seven early plays by Shepard, Tavel, and others. In the introduction, Michael Smith says that Off-Off Broadway was created "for and partly by new playwrights, who have in turn proliferated beyond all expectation."

In *The New American Theatre* (an issue of *Conjunctions,* published by Bard College in 1995 and guest edited by John Guare), there is a sampling of short plays and excerpts from plays by Keith Reddin, Erik Ehn, Doug Wright, and others. The introduction is by Joyce Carol Oates, who is represented by a surrealistic comedy about adoption. Wellman's plays are collected in *The Bad Infinity*, Overmyer's in *Eric Overmyer: Collected Plays*, and Breuer's work is in *Sister Suzie Cinema: The Collected Poems and Performances, 1976–1986.*

Among critical works, *The Collected Works of Harold Clurman* (edited by Loggia and Young) brings together in one hefty, 1,101-page volume the reviews of the most knowledgeable and articulate of American theatre critics, as written over a period of six decades. Many of the reviews are of productions Off-Broadway. Marranca, who with Gautam Dasgupta edits *Performing Arts Journal*, has several books of note, including *Theatrewritings*, a collection of her reviews and essays about Lee Breuer, Sam Shepard, and Richard Foreman, among others; and *The Theatre of Images* (republished with a new afterword in 1996) includes plays by Foreman, Breuer, and Robert Wilson, with commentary by the editor. Gussow's *Theatre on the Edge* is a collection of reviews and essays (1970 to early 1990s) principally of plays Off- and Off-Off Broadway.

American Playwrights Since 1945, edited by Kolin, analyzes the careers of forty playwrights, most of whom began Off-Broadway, and puts each in a biographical, critical, and bibliographical context. Esslin's *The Theatre of the Absurd* deals with the experimental theatre on an international level and is useful in tracing influences and sources, as is Adler's *American Drama 1940–1960* and Roudané's *American Drama Since 1960*, though these are focused on American examples.

Charles Ludlam was one of the most provocative theorizers of the experimental theatre. His essays and critical notations are collected in *Ridiculous Theatre: Scourge of Human Folly*. As edited by Samuels, the book provides a keen insight into the thinking of this multitalented artist. *The Complete Plays of Charles Ludlam* contains twenty-nine plays, preceded by a brief biographical essay by Samuels.

Six plays of Foreman are collected under the title *My Head Was a Sledgehammer* and five others are in *Unbalancing Acts*, an anthology of plays and essays about his theories, philosophy, and methods. An early work, *Richard Foreman: Plays and Manifestos*, edited by Davy, offers a developmental look at Foreman through such plays as *Pain(t)* and *Rhoda in Potatoland*.

Two matching volumes (both published by Theatre Communications Group) let the artists speak for themselves. In *In Their Own Words*, David Savran interviews twenty playwrights, from Lee Breuer to Lanford Wilson (a sequel to this collection is scheduled for publication in 1999), and in *The Director's Voice*, Arthur Bartow talks to twenty-one directors, from JoAnne Akalaitis to Garland Wright. *Speaking on Stage*, edited by Kolin and Kullman, is a collection of twenty-seven interviews with playwrights, ranging from Edward Albee and Jack Gelber to Romulus Linney and Ntozake Shange.

Regional/Resident Theatre

Martha LoMonaco

Definition

In 1951, a theatrical entrepreneur from Dallas, Texas, published a book which would become a manifesto and a source of inspiration for the regional theatre movement. At this early date, however, there was not yet a movement afoot; it was more a nationwide smattering of talented, ambitious, theatre people who were looking for a place to do their work and a community to support it. Margo Jones, her Theatre '47, and her 1951 book, *Theatre-in-the-Round*, inspired a generation of would-be artistic directors. "Every town in America wants theatre!" she wrote. "It is the duty and business of a capable theatre person to go into the communities of this country and create fine theatres" (6). Go out they did, and what had been a handful of theatres in the 1950s grew to sixteen by 1961 and over 300 by 1996. Regional theatre in America was born.

The term "regional" is hotly debated and ultimately eschewed by most theatres, which prefer to be known as resident, repertory, or more comprehensively, resident non-profit professional theatres. Robert Brustein outlines his preference for the word "resident" to "regional" in a 22 May 1988 *New York Times* article in which he states that the resident theatre movement "was originally intended as an alternative to Broadway, not as a provincial tributary." The notion of repertory was also at the heart of the movement, he declares, where the ideal was to develop "a large number of works over the course of a season, preferably in rotation so that in a single week audiences could enjoy a variety of offerings and actors could play a variety of parts." Although a few resident companies have attempted to play in full or partial repertory, it is and has been rare.

All these descriptives have their limitations; ultimately none, alone or even in combinations, provide an adequate umbrella term. Resident non-profit professional is probably the most descriptive, but it encompasses theatres in all U.S. regions including the diverse regions of New York City. There are over thirty such theatres in the borough of Manhattan, including Lincoln Center (uptown), Manhattan Theatre Club (midtown), New York Shakespeare Festival (downtown), and Roundabout Theatre Company, which is resident as of this writing in the heart of the traditional Broadway theatre district. Hence, to describe all those resident non-profit professional theatres outside of New York City, I shall revert, with no disparagement, to the word "regional."

Decentralization

The notions of residency and professionalism were at the heart of Margo Jones's philosophy and thus distinguish the regional houses from amateur ventures. "I say these theatres must be resident," she declared in *Theatre-in-the-Round*, "because they should give the community as well as the staff an assurance of continuity, and they must be professional because, if we insist on the highest standards of production, the actors and staff must spend eight hours a day in the theatre" (6). Jones's directive to establish "resident professional theatre in every city with a population of over one hundred thousand" (4), was an automatic argument for decentralization, another tenet of regional theatre. Brustein combines the basic ingredients – resident, decentralized, and professional as well as the need for subsidy – in his *New York Times* portrait of the movement:

> This movement wished to decentralize American theater in the belief that it was unhealthy to originate so much stage activity in one cultural capital (New York). It sought partial subsidy in an effort to free the theater from undue dependence on the timidity of the box office. And it wished to consolidate itself out of a conviction that permanent ensembles of actors, directors, designers and administrative staff, preserving the classical repertory and developing new plays, created a potentially more enduring theatrical art than pickup casts assembled for a single show and dominated by star personalities.

The desire for resident, decentralized, professional theatres also motivated the movement toward an American national theatre which was a significant forerunner of both Jones and the regional movement she helped to instigate. Robert Porterfield and Robert Breen were the first to formalize these yearnings in an October 1945 article in *Theatre Arts* magazine, "Toward a National Theatre." Buoyed by the recent success of Britain's first arts subsidy, CEMA (Committee for the Encouragement of Music and the Arts), as well as long-established precedents in other nations, these men called for America to catch up. "We have more and better bathtubs, bridges, buildings and machinery than any other country in the world," they argued, "it is time for us to match this leadership in cultural fields as well."

Porterfield and Breen recognized the impracticality of having a single "'shrine' or building, or even ten" representing a national theatre since the United States is simply too large. Hence, they advocated decentralizing the professional theatre as "the only way we can have a truly national theatre:

touring companies, resident companies, civic centre theatres, regional theatres, making available high standard, professional theatre to the 90 percent of our people who have never had the opportunity of seeing it" and presented a plan for a U.S. Public Theater Foundation to subsidize their dream (599–602). Four years later, *Theatre Arts* (April 1949) published a second national theatre proposal bearing the same title but this time presented by two Congressmen, Senator Irving Ives and Representative Jacob K. Javits, who had formalized these desires into a Congressional bill. Their recommendation extended the Porterfield/Breen plan to include a national opera and ballet but they, too, were not concerned with buildings. Their objective was "to make theatre, opera and ballet available to the people everywhere in the United States" simply because "these arts are indispensable to our democratic culture and, consequently, a matter of national concern" (10–13). Neither proposal got off the ground but both established the need for the regional theatres to come and reflected the haphazard state of the national theatre scene prior to 1945.

Whatever terminology is employed, it is a fact that these professional, resident, non-profit, regional theatres (and also those non-commercial venues in New York City) became a national force during the second half of the twentieth century. According to statistics compiled by Theatre Communications Group (TCG), the national organization and principal advocate for America's non-profit professional theatre, these theatres number over 300 and are resident in forty of the fifty states with the highest concentration in New York State, California, and Pennsylvania, with Illinois, Georgia, Massachusetts, and Washington close behind.[1] Collectively, TCG refers to the theatre companies and individual artists as "our national theatre."

Precursors

The principal precursors of the regional theatre movement are contained in Volume 2 of this history, covering the years 1870–1945: "the Road," the Little Theatre movement, summer theatres, the Group Theatre, the Federal Theatre Project, and ANTA. To properly set the stage for the coming regionals, however, a brief review of each follows. Certainly there was a great deal of theatre activity throughout the country prior to 1945 but quantity did not guarantee quality, nor did it satisfy artists or audiences. The two most widespread types were, in fact, at opposite ends of the theatrical spectrum. "The Road," as it is commonly known, was the proliferation of touring companies that crisscrossed the nation beginning in the mid-nineteenth century with the development of the transcontinental railroad. These were strictly commercial operations launched mostly by New York based syndicates whose primary interest was in delivering product – not art – fast and furiously. The second group, known as the Little Theatre movement, evolved nationwide during the first two decades of the century, largely in response to the frequently poor quality of commercial theatre and the excitement generated by the new European art theatres. The Little Theatres, the forerunners of today's community theatres, were founded by groups of serious-minded and ambitious amateurs who considered theatre an ennobling form of self-expression. Although some did very fine work (a few, notably the Cleveland Play House, evolved into professional regional theatres), their work collectively was uneven at best.

Summer theatre, frequently in the form of resident stock companies, sprang up in the blossoming resort areas of the nation, but particularly in the northeastern sector during the twenties and thirties. Unlike the Little Theatres, most were operated by trained artists who saw an opportunity to provide entertainment to vacationers in remote locales. They launched ambitious seasons with weekly changes of bill, mostly of Broadway hits but also some classics and new works being tried for potential Broadway transfers. Several of these, like Virginia's Barter Theatre, also evolved into fully fledged regional theatres with three-quarter or year-round seasons; many others are still active as summer venues. Their limited season and resort milieu naturally attracted a narrow, generally privileged, clientele.

These legitimate theatrical offerings, as well as the proliferation of popular entertainments such as vaudeville, burlesque, and the new mediated entertainments of film and radio, inspired groups of serious theatre people as well as the U.S. government to offer high-quality alternatives. The Theatre Guild, founded in 1919, mounted important, well-produced plays on Broadway and later on tour, thus exposing large numbers of people nationwide to many of the best new European and American dramas. The now legendary Group Theatre, founded in 1931 and active for the next decade, was a theatre collective that emphasized actor training and the development of socially significant American plays. In 1935 the U.S. Congress chartered the American National Theatre and Academy (ANTA) as a non-profit people's theatre designed to disseminate quality drama nationwide. Unfortunately, ANTA was largely inactive until after World War II and then its activities tended to be New York centered. Finally, the ambitious Federal Theatre Project was launched as part of the New Deal's Works Progress Administration in 1935. Under Hallie Flanagan's leadership, it produced innovative and diversified theatre nationwide until dissolved by Congress in 1939. Although hailed by many as the first true national theatre, it really was a temporary relief organization that provided jobs for unemployed theatre artists and administrators.

Amidst this wide array of entertainments and the ever present reign of Broadway as *the* American theatre, there were a few pioneers establishing independent, self-producing theatres outside of New York. The Cleveland Play House, which began as a Little Theatre in 1916, turned professional in 1921 with the hiring of Frederic McConnell as artistic director. By 1927 it had out-grown its old venue and had built a new theatre with two performance spaces that offered a distinguished season of European and American plays by a res-ident company of twenty-five actors. In 1923, eight years before the Group formed what was thought to be the first theatre collective in the United States, Jasper Deeter did the same in the rural community of Moylan-Rose Valley, Pennsylvania, fourteen miles southwest of Philadelphia. Deeter's Hedgerow Theatre began with nine dollars, an old mill which became the playhouse, and a company of players who were dissatisfied with the commercialism of Broadway. They lived communally at the theatre, functioned as a financial cooperative, and became one of the few U.S. theatres to run in full repertory (a policy that continued until 1958) year-round. According to an article in the *Philadelphia Evening Ledger,* in 1934 Hedgerow presented thirty-four plays from its repertoire of 108 for a total of 318 performances operating fifty-one weeks of the year.[2] A similar escape from New York commercialism impelled the founding, in 1933, of the Barter Theatre by Robert Porterfield. Porterfield persuaded a troupe of twenty-two New York actors to come to the remote town of Abingdon in southwestern Virginia with the idea of bringing together hungry actors and farmers with a surplus of produce. He advertised his admission price as "30 cents or the equivalent in rations. Bring us honey, fresh eggs, fresh vegetables, hams and other edibles." Renowned for its fine ensem-ble acting, the company grew from a summer to year-round operation under Porterfield's inspired leadership.

These and other pioneering theatres (including the Pittsburgh Playhouse, Chicago's Goodman Theatre, the Pasadena Playhouse, and San Diego's Old Globe Theatre) were the beginnings of regional theatre in America. Significantly, all were founded and/or operated via the driving force of one person. Whether called the artistic, managing, producing, or executive direc-tor, it was this single individual's energy, artistry, ambition, demands, and vision that gave birth to the theatre and propelled it forward. The director's charisma and sheer force of character attracted fellow artists as well as the local community, which was persuaded to donate time, money, or both to the enterprise. Zelda Fichandler, a founder and the ultimate force behind Washington D.C.'s Arena Stage, describes their shared history:

> In the old days, the theatre *was* its artistic director. It was the artistic direc-tor, propelled by a vision of burning (and blinding; it was not the time of far-sighted five-year plans!) intensity, who brought the theatre into being, assembled the meager economic and physical resources (in our case the theatre was a $1.99 cardboard file-box for many months), persuaded into existence a small board, and collected or already had available a group of artists ready to set out on a journey of undetermined length to a vaguely determined destination.[3]

Since the artistic director was the founder, manager, and self-appointed visionary, there was rarely, in these early days, a contract or other formalized arrangement. As Fichandler contends, the only contract the artistic director had "was one with him/herself and that was unwritten and, therefore, binding, more-or-less until death do us part."[4] In the minds of the community, the theatre was inseparable from the director – their personalities and identities became one. This cult of personality put many of these theatres on the cultural and geographical map and was a source of pride and power to the community that supported it. Difficulties inevitably arose, however, when the director left or died and the theatre had to find an acceptable successor. Fichandler, who spearheaded the Arena for forty years before retiring in 1990, wisely groomed a successor to ensure a smooth transition, yet Douglas Wager subsequently left in 1998 – a sign of the fragile state of non-profit theatres in the late nineties. Fichandler undoubtedly learned from the travails of fellow institutions, many of which struggled for years to redefine their theatres or even folded when boards and artists simply could find no mutually agreeable solution. It is undeniable, however, that these personalities created and nurtured regional theatre in America. The one with the most wide-reaching influence, "the mother of us all," according to Fichandler, was Margo Jones.

Pioneers

Margo Jones

Margo Jones is a prime example of the artistic director with boundless energy, an infectious, messianic personality, and a solid artistic background. She traveled and studied throughout the world and directed in college, community, and professional theatres throughout the United States, including Broadway, thus affording her a broad, sophisticated education upon which to build her new theatre. The Rockefeller Foundation recognized her talent and awarded her a grant to pursue her dream of a permanent, professional, repertory, native theatre in Dallas, Texas, concurrently devoted to showcasing the classics and the best new scripts available. On 3 June 1947, she opened Theatre '47 (the name would change annually on New Year's Eve "in order to remain contemporary at all times") with the first professional production of a play by William Inge, *Farther Off From Heaven* (later revised as *The Dark at the Top of the Stairs*). According to Jones's statistics in *Theatre-in-the-Round*, during its first four seasons Theatres '47–'50 produced eighteen new scripts and eleven classics in repertory fashion on an arena stage. Not only had she proved that she could succeed at such an ambitious project, but she also popularized a new staging configuration to the professional American theatre. Her book, no

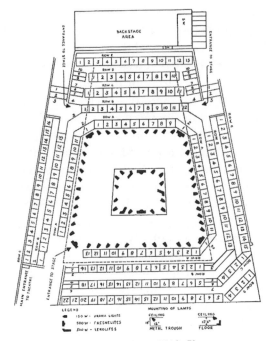

THEATRE '50: Floor and Light Plan
(*Prepared by Marshall Yokelson*)

4. Floor and Light plan of Theatre '50 (Margo Jones Theatre) with sketch of the interior theatre-in-the-round. Don B. Wilmeth Collection.

doubt read by every budding artistic director, provided not only a handbook but a manifesto, compelling the reader to get out and do likewise.

Theatre-in-the-Round was published in 1951 just as Jones was about to launch Theatre '51 for its fifth season. The wide-eyed romanticism of her prose ("Let us stir up the practical realization of a potential, of a dream, of an ideal!") is tempered by the practicality of her method and the documented results. She cites four "absolutely inflexible basic policies":

1. Complete professionalism.
2. Production of only new plays and classics, with an emphasis on the new play.
3. A permanent resident company for the entire season.
4. A minimum of three weeks of rehearsal time for every play. (191)

In order to meet such an ambitious program, Jones offers her economical plan for theatres-in-the-round. She proposes that any space large enough to accommodate both an audience and a playing area can be converted to an arena theatre and provides forty-one pages of "how-to" advice, ranging from structural details, number and placement of lighting instruments, challenges of staging for actors and directors, and perspectives on accommodating a proscenium-trained audience. Throughout, she insists on a completely professional and innovative approach ("we will never rejuvenate the theatre by doing the old things in the same old ways") and warns that just because theatre-in-the-round costs less money, it cannot be artistically less distinguished. Furthermore, she reiterates, this can and should be done in every town in America. "My dream for the future," she proposes, "is a theatre which is a part of everybody's life, just as the railroad and the airplane are, a theatre in every town providing entertainment and enlightenment for the audience and a decent livelihood along with high artistic ideals for the theatre worker" (201). Many heard her call, and eagerly took up the mantle.

Nina Vance

Two of her first disciples were women; the three ultimately became known as the high priestesses of the regional theatre movement. Nina Vance was Margo Jones's assistant at the Houston Community Players where she caught both Jones's enthusiasm and penchant for theatre-in-the-round. After both left the Players, Vance began teaching and directing for Houston's Jewish Community Center and mounting productions in a dance studio in an alley off Main Street. At her instigation, the group of amateurs soon evolved into the Alley Theatre. As the legend goes, Vance had $2.14 in her pocket, so sent out 214 postcards at a penny a piece declaring: "It's Beginning! Do you want a New Theater for Houston? Meeting 3617 Main, Tuesday, October 7, 8 PM, Bring a Friend! Nina

Vance." The hundred people who attended formed the core of that new theatre which premiered 18 November 1947, with Vance's production of Harry Brown's *A Sound of Hunting.*

To borrow Fichandler's characterization, Vance *was* the Alley Theatre from 1947 until her death in 1980. During those thirty-three years, she produced all 245 Alley shows, directed 102 of them, and garnered three major Ford Foundation grants for the theatre. Vance became noted for passionate, unconventional stagings that frequently went beyond the arena into what would become known in the sixties as environmental theatre (see Carlson's discussion below) and was a frequent guest director at other regional houses, notably Fichandler's Arena Stage.

Zelda Fichandler

Zelda Fichandler was Jones's second great disciple and would unofficially take over as a major spokesperson for the regional movement after her death in 1955. Fichandler founded Washington, D.C.'s Arena Stage in 1950 with her husband Thomas, an economist who eventually became the theatre's business manager, and George Washington University theatre professor Edward Magnum, under whose tutelage Fichandler had received her master's degree earlier that year. The triumvirate converted an old movie house into a 247-seat theatre-in-the-round and produced seventeen plays in their first season. Fichandler reprinted the program note for the 16 August 1950 opening production, Oliver Goldsmith's *She Stoops to Conquer,* in "Institution-As-Artwork," as she reconsidered the beginnings of regional theatres:

> Arena Stage plans to bring to its audiences the best of plays both old and new as well as worthwhile original scripts on a permanent year-round repertory basis. Local in origin, it was founded in the belief that if drama-hungry playgoers outside of the ten blocks of Broadway are to have a living stage, they must create it for themselves. Arena Stage was financed by Washingtonians – students, teachers, lawyers, doctors, scientists, government workers, housewives – who love theatre and who want to see it flourish in the city in which they work and live. Its permanent staff of distinguished actors and technicians, many of whom have come to Arena Stage via the stages of other cities, now all call Washington their home.
>
> Arena Stage invites your participation in the excitement of the first production of Washington's playhouse-in-the-round. (1–2)

From a perspective of thirty-five years (she penned this observation in 1985), Fichandler was impressed by how many potentials and pitfalls of the regional movement were embedded in key words and phrases of this first program note, long before anything like a mission statement was ever contemplated: old and new plays, permanent, repertory, local in origin, outside of Broadway, drama-hungry playgoers, create it themselves, permanent staff, home, participation, excitement. These concepts eventually were fleshed out as operating principles for a professional resident theatre:

> The need for artistic control; the need to take responsibility for one's own vision; the value of an ongoing collective; the centrality of an acting company; the fundament of contact between play and playgoer, of a continuing dialogue with the audience; each individual theatre being a part of a whole theatre; the ever-present budgetary tension and the success/failure see-saw; and the primitive yet sophisticated power of selflessness and faith in the dream. (2–3)

Fichandler assumed total artistic control of Arena two years after it opened when Magnum left to take a post at a theatre in Hawaii, and she remained in charge until 1991 when her hand-picked successor took over. In those four decades, she maintained a strong artistic collective while watching several acting companies come and go, moved out of two temporary houses to build what gradually became a three-theatre complex (the 811-seat Arena built in 1961, the thrust-stage Kreeger with a 500-seat fan-shaped auditorium built in 1971, and the Old Vat, a 165-seat cabaret theatre installed in the basement of the Kreeger in 1976), and spearheaded the first regional theatre to send a play to Broadway (*The Great White Hope* in 1968) and be recognized by Broadway with the first Antoinette Perry Award given in recognition of excellence by a regional theatre (April 1976).

Another distinction of Arena was that it operated as a commercial theatre for its first nine years and, even after declaring not-for-profit status in 1959, continued to finance its operations heavily through box office receipts for the next six years. Major grant funding, beginning in 1959, helped develop both the company and the building quickly and Arena, along with the Alley, was among the first regional theatres funded by the Ford and later Rockefeller Foundations.

Irving and Blau

Not all the regional pioneers were women. Two San Francisco State College professors, with actress wives anxious for professional work in what was then the theatre-barren city of San Francisco, launched The Actor's Workshop in 1952. Jules Irving and Herbert Blau, both native New Yorkers, wanted to create a space for individuals to work and experiment (hence the name Actor's Workshop in the singular) in a permanent community of dedicated ensemble players that was as far Off-Broadway as possible. In this respect, it sounded very much like the Alley and Arena; unlike these other theatres, however, the Workshop made little effort to reach out to the larger San Francisco community. The Workshop became a popular in-spot for Bay Area literati, premiering many new American plays and mounting productions of European play-wrights like Beckett, Pinter, and Brecht. A repertoire standard, *Waiting For Godot*, with Irving playing Lucky, when performed at San Quentin penitentiary, inspired the inmates to form the San Quentin Drama Workshop under Actor's Workshop auspices. *Godot* and other productions also traveled to New York and the Brussels and Seattle World's Fairs, all earning positive press notices. The Workshop was also among the pioneer group of regional theatres to obtain Ford Foundation grants.

The Actor's Workshop, ironically, was well respected everywhere except at home. This situation, untenable for any regional theatre, ultimately spelled the Workshop's doom. Joseph Zeigler, who joined the company in 1963 and wrote about it in his book *Regional Theatre*, characterized its thirteen-year residence in San Francisco as a "hate affair with the city" where it always was shabbily housed, radically opinioned, and firmly anti-establishment. Blau and Irving were not interested in playing political games to garner favor and support (hence they frequently were out of money), but remained united in their stand "to be experimental, to embrace blatantly unpopular ideas, to stretch beyond their immediate obvious capabilities, and to speak out against rigidities of form and formality" (Zeigler, *Regional Theatre*, 56). The Workshop in San Francisco disbanded soon after Blau and Irving moved to New York early in 1965 to become joint directors of the ill-fated Repertory Theater of Lincoln Center and took a core of San Francisco actors, technicians and administrators with them. Blau and others left within a year while Irving stayed on for seven years to manage a much changed Repertory Theatre that bore little if any resemblance to The Actor's Workshop that fathered it.

Catalysts

Blau, Irving, Fichandler, Vance, and other regional pioneers, including Joseph Papp, who was working with like-minded fervor in New York City, were brought together for the first time in 1957 under the auspices of W. McNeil Lowry and the Ford Foundation. That year, Ford initiated a program in support of the arts, named Lowry director, and authorized him to commence exploratory fieldwork at once. The first small grants were awarded to artistic directors, principally to allow them to travel and study other theatres at work, and Lowry sponsored the first of many conferences that introduced people working in isolation to a supportive network of artists and companies across America. Zeigler considers this the real beginning of the regional theatre movement in the United States, a movement that flourished during the sixties with major foundation support and with the 1965 establishment of the National Endowment for the Arts, governmental support, the founding of more and more theatres nationwide, and a prevalent belief that a cultural explosion was sweeping the country.

Lowry addresses both the so-called arts explosion and Ford's timely patronage in his 1978 study, *The Performing Arts and American Society*. He dates the new American obsession with culture to the fifties when community leaders argued that the arts were good for society by promoting a strong national image, showcasing American artistry to the world, and by providing liberal education to American citizens, especially the youth for whom art provided "purposeful occupation." More importantly, perhaps, art ensconced in physical institutions (museums, orchestras, ballet companies, and resident theatres) gave communities a source of civic pride and terrific fodder for business and travel brochures that proudly proclaimed "we have culture." Lowry points out that, typically, arguments in favor of art rarely focused on art itself but, rather, art as a means to some other end, and that the so-called culture explosion itself was largely promotional.

Whatever the rationale, there certainly was a lot more money being channeled into the arts during the sixties and regional theatres were prime beneficiaries. But the money providers frequently were more interested in creating cultural institutions than in artists making art. Michael Murray, who resigned as artistic director of Boston's Charles Playhouse in 1968, voiced his concerns on the institutional malaise of regional theatres in a series of articles in the *Boston Sunday Globe*. These theatres "claim an existence and an importance apart from whatever life may be observed on their respective stages," he complained, and "are geared to serving the community in the same way as the public library and the museum . . . as essential ingredients of the cultural life of the cities." Rather than being collectives of actors, playwrights, directors, and designers, he saw these theatres as groups of administrators, boards of directors, ladies' committees, season subscribers, and other non-artists. Furthermore, he found that although a vital part of the city's image of itself, the theatres were patronized by only a small minority of the local citizenry. The citizens, for their part, were happy to have the theatre there so long as they did not have to support it.[5]

Murray's view, although extreme, was not uncommon, and points out the problem shared by directors across the country of balancing the need for funding with the theatre's mission and artistic integrity. Even in enthusiastic communities where people not only attend but also take an active interest in theatre fund-raising and outreach programs, power and money are always factors. Problems inevitably arise as initial subsidies run out and theatres, unable to make ends meet through box office alone, have to solicit the community for what appears to be an endless request for money. Concomitantly, there is the problem of the implied power of patronage; people who feel they are paying for art frequently insist on some degree of control over that art. In the nineties, this has proven a major factor in the attacks on the National Endowment for the Arts and, for regional directors like Zelda Fichandler, it always has posed a problem with civic fund-raising. In an often quoted passage from "Theatres or Institutions," Fichandler contends that while "theatre is a public art and belongs to its public, it is an art before it is public and so it belongs first to itself and its first service must be self-service." Beware the hand that rocks the cradle, she admonishes, "for the hand that rocks the cradle will also want to raise it in a vote" (110).

In 1962, The Ford Foundation declared that the arts constituted one of five key funding areas for the next decade and upped its already sizable support of regional theatre by awarding grants totaling $6.1 million to nine resident theatres; it would supplement this with an additional $10 million over the next ten years. The monies were geared to building the theatres' artistic as well as physical needs, with grants supporting playwright and director collabora-tions, actor ensembles, and audience development as well as funding for architects and stage designers toward conceiving and building new theatres. Ford's support instigated a flurry of philanthropy from other foundations as well as state and local governments, private citizens, and, eventually, the federal government. As such, Ford, wittingly or not, fomented the institution-alization of regional theatres; this continues to be a critical dilemma for man-aging and artistic directors into the end of the twentieth century. The question remains, would many if not most of these theatres ever have begun or have managed to survive without subsidy? And does being institutional automatically imply a loss of artistic integrity?

In *A Theater Divided*, Martin Gottfried simultaneously heralds and blames the totality of funding, what he terms "the American Subsidy," for the boom in regional theatres of the early sixties. He charts a direct line between subsidy and institution, warning that the art theatre rapidly becomes the civic institution and with that assumes all the attendant responsibilities. The artis-tic director who founded a theatre to fulfill a need for personal expression could find her/his desires thwarted by administrative, fund-raising, and public relations obligations. "Institutions are official," he contends. "They are prone to sterility . . . Community stature causes creative obesity. There is a pressure to be inoffensive, an inclination to be sleek, proper and bland. A living theater begins to mummify and decay" (93).

Zeigler in *Regional Theatre* notes the same problem in a slightly different way – by becoming institutionalized, regional theatres officially join the Establishment with a capital "E". Ironically, it was the Establishment theatre of the fifties and sixties – Broadway – that impelled their very existence; in rejecting one establishment, they opted for inclusion in another. Establishment denotes a certain civic responsibility and connotes a rational-ization for existence over and beyond the wish to produce art. Hence, the newly Established regional institutional theatres found themselves increasingly embroiled in community outreach, sophisticated education programs, and season planning around shows that would lend themselves to furthering these high-minded ideals (*Regional Theatre*, 170–4).

As previously noted, one of Zelda Fichandler's principal concerns during her forty-year tenure at Arena was the constant struggle between theatre as an artistic entity and theatre as a corporate institution. In her 1970 article, "Theatres or Institutions?," she ponders the two words, musing that they exist in a "state of uneasy tension." "It seemed to me until quite recently," she says, "that when a theatre finally stopped being on the way to what it was supposed to become and actually became it, then it would be an institution." Institution, she thought, meant a release from the day-to-day struggle for survival, a time for creative rest and re-creation, and an administrative environment that would nurture that creativity. "But it hasn't turned out that way," she laments, "a seduction is what it really was, a leading-from-the-self." Sixteen years later, in "Institution-As-Artwork," she is more accepting of the place of the institution within the context of making art but warns that we not confuse the business of making art with the art of making business. "Unless we get it right," she declares, "this 'institution business' is going to kill us."

In the early sixties, in the flush of sizable funding and seemingly universal enthusiasm for theatre, no one was yet worried about institutionalization; they simply wanted theatres. "I think few artists have any institutional instincts or any but the vaguest sociological impulses," Michael Murray opined in a 1968 *Drama Review* article. "Most of them simply want a place to do their work."[6] If culture-hungry communities wanted to build a theatre, work-hungry artists were only too happy to move in.

Several hundred theatres sprang to life in the sixties and seventies. Many of those survived to become institutions while others never made it that far or, once institutionalized, died because the original artistic impulse had gone. Only one of these theatres actually arrived as an institution, and virtually overnight it became a nationwide sensation that catapulted the regional theatre movement into a new prominence. Unlike other regional theatres, however, this one was founded through the concerted energies of three doyens of the New York stage – Oliver Rea, a Broadway producer, Peter Zeisler, a Broadway stage manager and theatre administrator, and Sir Tyrone Guthrie, an internationally-acclaimed director. Together, they founded the Minnesota Theatre Company, better known as the Tyrone Guthrie Theater.

The Guthrie

Guthrie relates the founding of the company and theatre bearing his name in his book, *A New Theatre*. It all began with Oliver Rea's March 1959 invitation

5. The Guthrie Theater in 1963. Designed by Ralph Rapson and Associates in conjunction with Tyrone Guthrie and Tanya Moiseiwitsch. Pictured on the thrust stage is Guthrie's production of *The Three Sisters.* After more than thirty-five years in this venue, in the late 1990s the Guthrie Theater is contemplating a move to new facilities. Don B. Wilmeth Collection.

to a breakfast at New York's Plaza Hotel, where a mutual dissatisfaction with the commercial theatre persuaded the trio to entertain the idea of creating a resident professional theatre in a major city outside New York. Brooks Atkinson, chief drama critic for the *New York Times,* ran a piece about their quest, inviting interested cities to apply. Seven did and, after visiting each, the triumvirate chose Minneapolis, Minnesota. Besides offering a friendly, welcoming environment, Minneapolis had the right combination of civic-minded young businessmen and their wives who were anxious to make their marks in the public sector and could raise funds quickly to build the theatre structure, its company, and its audience.

Few American theatres have opened with the fanfare that heralded the 7 May 1963 opening of the Guthrie. Critics came from New York and Chicago to see the impressive $2.5 million, 1,400-seat thrust stage theatre built to Guthrie's specifications, as well as the opening productions (*Hamlet* and *The Miser*) of a classical repertory season performed by an acting company featuring the noted husband–wife team of Hume Cronyn and Jessica Tandy. The theatre design, although attributed to Minnesota architect Ralph Rapson, was largely the joint creation of Guthrie and his frequent design collaborator, Tanya Moiseiwitsch, who built the polygonal, stepped stage that jutted deeply into a raked auditorium in emulation of their successful 1957 collaboration for the Shakespeare Festival Theatre in Stratford, Ontario. The star-studded acting company was a first in regional theatre, where companies of well-trained but largely unknown actors were the norm. The classical repertory with occasional American plays that, in Guthrie's view, held promise for classical status, was typical of the regionals, but the praise accorded Minneapolis for its daring to produce such non-commercial playwrights as Molière helped to legitimize other regionals doing the same thing.

Rapid Growth

Legitimacy is, in fact, at the core of the Guthrie's sphere of prestige and influence. Although resident companies not afforded the luxuries of the big names and high finance that propelled the Guthrie may have been jealous or angry, they benefited from the afterglow of the Guthrie's success. National attention finally was being paid to theatre outside of New York; theatres that already existed gained new prominence and new ones began to spring up all over. With communities now feeling they really ought to have a theatre, significant funding coming from prestigious foundations, and models such as the Guthrie that boasted innovative marketing and management techniques (and willing to serve as a resource for fledgling theatres), founding and operating a resident theatre became a slightly easier task during the sixties and seventies. Some, like the Guthrie, were born with full community support and substantial financing – Seattle Repertory Theatre (1963) and the Mark Taper Forum (1967), founded as part of the Center Theatre Group at the Los Angeles Music Center – are two prominent examples. Many others were, like their predecessors, born of the drive and determination of talented young directors who now had the dual advantage of established precedent and a far more welcoming arts climate. This new breed of artistic director, intent on success and survival, was more savvy politically, more ingratiating to the community power structure, and more adept at marketing and advertising than many predecessors. Among the most prominent of the new theatres were Center Stage (Baltimore, 1963), Trinity (Square) Repertory Company (Providence, Rhode Island, 1963), Actors Theatre of Louisville (1964), Hartford Stage Company (1964), South Coast Repertory (Costa Mesa, California, 1964), American Conservatory Theatre (San Francisco, 1965), Long Wharf Theatre (New Haven, Connecticut, 1965), Alliance Theatre Company (Atlanta, 1968),

Berkeley Repertory Theatre (1968), Omaha Magic Theatre (1968), Wisdom Bridge Theatre (Chicago, 1974), Steppenwolf Theatre Company (Chicago, 1976), and Theatre de la Jeune Lune (Minneapolis, 1978). Many others that had been founded earlier either grew to new prominence or transformed from community to professional status during this era: Goodman Theatre (Chicago, 1925), Old Globe Theatre (San Diego, 1937), La Jolla Playhouse (1947), Milwaukee Repertory Theater (1954), Dallas Theater Center (1959), Asolo Center for the Performing Arts (Sarasota, Florida, 1960), and Cincinnati Playhouse in the Park (1960).

Prominent regional houses that are affiliated with university degree programs and receive at least partial funding and/or in-kind support from their host institutions include Yale Repertory Theatre (1966), McCarter Theatre Center for the Performing Arts (Princeton, New Jersey, 1972), Syracuse Stage (1974), PlayMakers Repertory Company (Chapel Hill, North Carolina, 1976), and American Repertory Theatre (Cambridge, Massachusetts, 1979).

In surveying regional theatres, mention must also be made of the Shakespeare Festivals, largely modeled on Tyrone Guthrie's pioneering Stratford Shakespearean Festival, Ontario, which opened in 1953 and was rechristened in 1967 as the Stratford National Theatre of Canada. Although the direct American copy is no longer in operation (American Shakespeare Festival, Stratford, Connecticut, 1955), despite repeated efforts to reactivate it, other major festivals include the U.S. forerunner, Oregon Shakespeare Festival (1935), Utah Shakespearean Festival (1961), The Shakespeare Theatre (Washington, D.C., 1969), and Alabama Shakespeare Festival (1972).

Three Outstanding Regional Theatres and the Personalities that Shaped Them

William Ball and ACT

William Ball founded the American Conservatory Theatre (ACT) as an itinerant company that started in Pittsburgh in 1965 and traveled around the country before settling into its permanent home in San Francisco in January 1967. From its onset, Ball intended ACT to be the American national theatre, producing an enormous, eclectic repertoire of new and classic plays with a permanent company of theatre artists who are in constant training in a Continental-style conservatory. The classes, held not only in acting but in all other facets of theatre from history and literature through design and production, served to provide a continual exchange of knowledge and ideas that ideally would inculcate the young and invigorate the old. The incredible energy, dynamism, and non-stop activity of ACT is a reflection of Ball himself, who spearheaded the company until managerial difficulties forced his resignation in 1986. Invariably described as a mad genius who was both excessive and compulsive, Ball was the prototypical regional artistic director who was his theatre, as his theatre was him. He was an American version of the European regisseur, at once dictator, visionary, teacher, father, and theatre director of enormous talent. ACT experienced the typical readjustment difficulties after Ball's departure, but has continued to be a major force in the American theatre.

Jon Jory and ATL

Jon Jory did not found the Actors Theatre of Louisville (ATL) in 1964 but his arrival in 1969 transformed it from a marginal Kentucky enterprise to an innovative national institution. Jory's quiet dynamism centers on a passion for texts that has been translated into two annual ATL events that attract national and international attention – the Humana Festival of New American Plays and Classics in Context. Jory founded the Humana Festival in 1976 to give visibility to promising new playwrights; later, he expanded that mission to include an emphasis on the development of docudramas and an opportunity for non-theatrical writers to try their hand at playwriting. Playwrights whose careers were either launched or significantly boosted at Humana include A.R. Gurney, Beth Henley, Eduardo Machado, Donald Margulies, and Marsha Norman; non-playwrights who Jory induced to start writing plays include Joyce Carol Oates and William F. Buckley, Jr.

The Classics in Context series began in 1986 as a local outreach program, originally involving thirty of Louisville's arts organizations. Collectively, they investigated classic plays in their historical context to make them relevant for modern audiences. Although it is still a city-wide event, though no longer with universal participation (due to reduced funding), the scope now involves guest experts and audiences from all over the country. Recent investigations include *commedia dell'arte*, Russian masters, and the plays of Ferenc Molnar. Despite his ability to attract national attention, Jory has always maintained ATL as a strongly regional theatre which bespeaks its continuing success. His commitment to his regional audience is first and foremost and is witnessed in the development of new plays reflective of the people and culture of the region.

Robert Brustein and ART

Robert Brustein, the noted theatre director, writer, critic, and teacher, has the distinction of having founded major regional theatres at two of America's most prestigious universities. When Dean of the Yale School of Drama,

Brustein founded the Yale Repertory Theatre in 1966; after being ousted at Yale by a new, largely unsympathetic administration, he went to Harvard, establishing the American Repertory Theatre (ART) in 1979 with at least thirty-five former Yale Rep artists in tow. The two theatres, although similar in their artistic ideology of reinterpreting the classics in sometimes audacious ways, unearthing neglected plays and playwrights, and launching new work, operate quite differently. While Yale Rep is tied to the professional graduate training program it serves as an intensive theatre laboratory, ART is a separately incorporated not-for-profit theatre only tangentially tied to Harvard and until 1987 bearing no academic component (in that year Brustein opened the Institute for Advanced Theater Training as a two-year, non-degree program). Although Yale Rep has thrived under subsequent directorships, Brustein's Yale Rep essentially became ART in 1979. According to a 1989 article in the *Christian Science Monitor*, Brustein brought ART to Harvard to serve "a community of literate, adventurous theatergoers" that lacked a major institutional theatre. His aim was to "establish and maintain a theater that reflects both the contemporary aesthetic and the social, political, and spiritual environment." Brustein's productions tend to provoke controversy and even outrage, but he perseveres with the strength that has made him a godfather of the regional theatre movement. "Any theater that believes and persists in its vision," he insists, "will eventually draw an audience."

Economics

The proliferation of regional theatres and other non-profit performing arts organizations provoked the first serious studies on the economics of art. The 1966 landmark study by two Princeton University economists, William Baumol and William Bowen, *Performing Arts – The Economic Dilemma*, argued unequivocally that performing arts cannot nor should not be expected to pay for themselves. Furthermore, the authors asserted that the arts not only will never make money but will post ever increasing deficits. They make a compelling argument for arts subsidies and outline modes of support by individuals, private institutions such as corporations, labor unions, universities, and foundations, and municipal, state, and federal governments.

Baumol and Bowen's book was published just one year after the U.S. Congress approved a bill establishing a National Foundation on the Arts and the Humanities consisting of the National Endowment for the Arts (NEA), the National Endowment for the Humanities (NEH), and a Federal Council to insure coordination between the two endowments and with related federal programs. Initially, the program was modest, awarding only about $10 million to the arts annually. Although this amount would grow over the years, allocations were at the mercy of Congressional politics. It must also be remembered that theatre comprises a relatively small portion of the arts, which include everything from symphony orchestras and museums to creative writing and media arts. The allocation to the NEA Theatre Program reached an all-time high of $10.8 million in 1981; in fiscal year 1993, theatre received only $8.4 of the total NEA budget of $174.6 million. Most of this money, however, was awarded to professional theatre companies with $7.2 million disseminated among 231 theatres. The 1994 Congressional elections ushered in conservative Republican legislators largely unsympathetic to government subsidies for the arts. For fiscal year 1996, funding for the NEA was reduced to $99.5 million from the 1995 allocation of $162 million and, until 1999, the very continuation of the endowment remained in question.

The significance of NEA grants to regional theatres goes far beyond a dollar amount. Winning a grant means official recognition on a national scale, significantly increasing both a theatre's public reputation and its ability to gain support from other funding sources. The NEA's timely founding in 1965 not only helped solidify and legitimize the existing resident theatres but it paved the way for those to come by saying, in essence, theatre is important to American society.

Despite significant funding and supportive endeavors from the NEA and various foundations from the sixties onward (the Ford Foundation, for instance, in addition to making grants helped the regional theatres to establish such support structures as TCG in 1961), subsidy has always been a debated issue. Despite Bowen and Baumol's report and other major studies, the United States does not acknowledge that resident professional theatre cannot survive on box office receipts and good will. To Europeans and others, where state subsidy of the arts is a long-standing tradition, this is both unbelievable and scandalous. English theatre critic Irving Wardle commented in the London *Times Saturday Review* as early as 24 February 1968 that while Americans are more than willing to provide money for buildings, they are equally willing to allow artists inhabiting the buildings to pay their own way after the first season. While admiring a magnificent theatre such as the Guthrie, he noted, "the European visitor is left gasping at the discovery that [it] is run without any sustaining grant." He discovered that while sustaining grants were acknowledged for orchestras and museums, "the theatre – as a traditional area of profit-making – is treated simply as a business investment." Ruth Mayleas, who was director of the NEA Theatre Program from the late sixties through 1978, concurs, noting in a Summer 1979 article for the journal *Theater* ("Resident Theaters") that not a single theatre in the United States enjoys the resources of the best European and British theatres "because the legacy of the commercial theatre is still with us." Americans seem wedded to the notion that "theatre should pay its own way," and are unable to "comprehend the concept of a theatre institution as an ongoing entity with an artistic point of view, dedicated to the preservation of the past and the exploration of the future." She traces the economic development of regional theatres and the disparity between promise and reality:

> When the resident theater movement began, and through subsequent years of its development, its principal leaders believed that developing along with it would be a support system, public and private resources combined in some miraculous way to make possible the utilization of the country's best artistic resources. Implicit here was a concept of continuity, the development of real theater companies, companies with a full complement of artists and support staff, companies capable of producing the most challenging work in the repertoire . . . We got halfway there, far enough to develop theaters with continuity of artistic leadership, performing lengthy seasons of serious repertoire to larger and increasingly discriminating audiences. But it was the artists themselves who were – and are – subsidizing the theaters. ("Resident Theaters," 8)

Operations

Regional theatre has been – and will continue to be – about the needs of artists to do their work in a nurturing environment. The artists themselves have indeed subsidized the theatres by working long hours for low wages, and many have left. It is rare to achieve fame and fortune in a regional house; if an artist has ambitions for wide exposure and substantial earnings, the lure to film and television is powerful. The theatrical unions, early on, became aware of this dilemma and did their best to combat the problem through ensuring decent wages and benefits for their members working regionally. In response, the largest regional houses formed a collective bargaining alliance, the League of Resident Theatres (LORT), to combat the unions. LORT, which represents approximately one-third of regional theatres (including several in New York City) negotiated its first contract in 1966 with Actors' Equity.

Contracts with the unions are renegotiated every three years with talks generally focused on money, more specifically, the lack of it. In a 1989 salary dispute with the Society of Stage Directors and Choreographers (SSDC), then LORT president Tom Hall, managing director of San Diego's Old Globe Theatre, complained, "the constraints we have are real, not a negotiating posture. But it does throw light on just how underpaid all professionals in the American theater really are," he added, noting, "it's catastrophic that we have to go through this kind of angst just because there aren't enough crumbs on the table."[7]

The joint dilemmas of artists and economics are further exacerbated by the continuing decline of Broadway, which has become increasingly reliant on regional theatres for new shows and talent. Regional theatres always have eschewed being perceived as Broadway tributaries (hence, the discomfort with the term regional), but the lure of Broadway money and fame frequently has led them to compromise artistic principles. As Robert Brustein points out in a 22 May 1988 *New York Times* article entitled "The Siren Song of Broadway Is a Warning," the transfer of a regional production to a Broadway house can provide wider exposure for a playwright, royalties to a financially strapped theatre, and income and celebrity for regionally based artists. He warns, however, that "the co-opting of resident theaters for the sake of Broadway transfers spells the end of a once proud dream of an alternative theater, the abandonment of its animating ideals and the dispersal of its membership" all for the sake of "marketing and merchandising of product." Although many major plays and artists have been introduced via regional-to-Broadway transfers (Marsha Norman's *'night, Mother* from ART, several August Wilson plays including *Fences* and *The Piano Lesson* from Yale Rep, David Mamet's *Glengarry Glen Ross* from the Goodman, and Mark Medoff's *Children of a Lesser God* from the Mark Taper Forum, to name just a few), all have effected varying repercussions – some minimal, some dire – on their originating theatres.

Sadder still is the all too prevalent view of Broadway – by theatre artists and the public alike – as *the* major theatre of America. As Martin Gottfried argues in *A Theater Divided*:

> The relationship of the resident theater people with Broadway is one of love–hate. On the one hand, from the trustees through the artistic director and minor players, they are antagonized by commercialism. *Their* theater is the *real* theater – the *artistic* theater. On the other hand, they are bitterly envious of their Broadway counterparts. Their smugness is defensive and they don't completely believe in their avowed superiority, inwardly giving in to the feeling that the "real" theater is New York's. (110–11)

The Present and the Future

Despite adversities, regional theatres are mostly surviving and many are busy celebrating or preparing for silver plus anniversaries. No one is confidently smug, however; continuing problems with financing, artist attrition to more lucrative jobs, and a steadily aging audience force artistic directors to reassess their theatres' missions and explore ways of attracting a new generation of playgoers. TCG continues to sponsor forums for discussion and debate of shared concerns for keeping theatre alive and vital in the late twentieth century. A landmark series of conferences held across the country in 1987 brought together 120 artistic directors to discuss regional theatres as artistic homes. The results, published by TCG as *The Artistic Home* the following year, underscored key concerns regarding the creative process, artists, repertoire, audiences, structure, and practices. The single most pressing concern for the majority of artistic directors, however, was "to find ways of keeping the most talented artists in the theatre" while recognizing the need "to constantly renew their commitment to making their theatres homes for artists." A follow-up conference held in 1995, "Revisiting the Artistic Home," and reported in the November 1995 issue of *American Theatre,* recognized the economic down-turns since the relatively lucrative eighties and proposed a redefinition of the artistic home as not a place but a community. With the escalating costs of real estate and building maintenance, one artistic director, whose company now tours, suggested, "maybe we should go to the audience and leave the build-ings behind." In response, Lloyd Richards, former artistic director of the Yale Repertory Theatre, revived the continuing dilemma of the institution. "What we have done is develop the institutions without the artists, despite the fact that it was generally the artists who began the theatres," Richards lamented. "How do we make the artist a more integral part of the theatre so that the theatre *means* the artist?"

The original mission and dream of regional theatres, as a place away from Broadway commercialism where theatre artists could exercise imagination and take risks in developing new plays, new forms, and new approaches to the classics and thus reach new audiences, has largely survived. Margo Jones's four original precepts – professionalism, presentation of classics and new plays, permanent resident company, adequate rehearsal time – have been met by most regional theatres, with the largest continuing problem being the maintenance of a company. Consequently, her shared dream of a national theatre has been realized. American regional theatre has become *the* national theatre, collectively representing all areas of the country (including New York City) with its diversity of race, ethnicity, religion, and cultural heritage. In 1995, TCG listed over 300 member theatres nationwide located in major met-ropolitan centers, rural communities, and urban and suburban neighbor-hoods, that presented nearly 60,000 performances of 3,000 productions to a combined annual attendance of over 20 million people.

Notes

1 See Barbara Janowitz, "Theatre Facts 94," *American Theatre* 12 (April 1995): 15. An annual survey is published by Theatre Communications Group.
2 H. T. Murdock, *Philadelphia Evening Ledger,* Hedgerow Theatre, clippings file, Billy Rose Theatre Collection, New York Public Library for the Performing Arts.
3 See Zelda Fichandler, "Institution-As-Artwork," *Theatre Profiles* 7 (New York: Theatre Communications Group, 1986): 11.
4 *Ibid.*

5 Michael Murray, *Boston Sunday Globe*, 11 February 1968, Regional Theatre, Clippings file, Billy Rose Theatre Collection.
6 Quoted in Richard Schechner, ed., "The Regional Theatre: Four Views," *The Drama Review* 13 (Fall 1968): 25–26.
7 Quoted in Richard Hummler, "SSDC Accepts LORT Deal, Avoiding Nonprofit War," *Variety*, 16 August 1989: 73.

Bibliography: Regional/Resident Theatre

There are few general histories of American regional theatre. To glean a comprehensive portrait, a wide range of sources that include monographs, autobiographies, dissertations, pamphlets, economic studies, personal accounts, journals, magazines, and newspapers must be consulted.

The best general history of the regional theatre movement is Zeigler's *Regional Theatre* (1973), which was reprinted in 1977 with a new afterword that marks notable events from 1973–76. Zeigler, who during the sixties worked in regional theatre administration and for TCG, affords an insider's perspective that incorporates a wide cultural and sociological outlook. Berkowitz's *New Broadways* up-dates Zeigler slightly but devotes only one chapter to regional theatre. Novick's *Beyond Broadway*, melds history with critical commentary on the early years of resident theatre by profiling thirty-six regional houses, seven professional theatres in residence at universities, and five summer festivals. New York drama critic Martin Gottfried's incisive critique, *A Theater Divided*, also deals with the beginnings of regional theatre but his views, although fascinating, are far more critical than historical.

Critical and/or historical perspectives of the regional theatre movement and individual theatres abound in newspapers, notably the *New York Times*, particularly in the Sunday "Arts & Leisure" sections, *The Drama Review*, *Performing Arts Journal*, *Theater*, *Theatre* (International Theatre Institute), *Entertainment Design* (formerly *Theatre Crafts*, then *TCI*), and in all TCG publications detailed at the end of this bibliography. Key articles referenced in this chapter are in endnotes or are cited in the text with bibliographical data in the omnibus bibliography; others of note include Edward J. Mendus, ed., "Regional Theatre '67," and the entire issue of *Theater*, Summer 1979, devoted to "Resident Theaters in America."

Historic antecedents are addressed in general histories, such as Taubman's *The Making of the American Theatre*, in specific histories of such enterprises as the Group Theatre (Clurman, *The Fervent Years*) and the Federal Theatre Project (Flanagan, *Arena*), in numerous articles in *Theatre Arts* and *Variety*, especially those covering the development of "Little Theatres" and summer stock; and also in *Theatre Arts* are the two proposals for a national theatre (both are entitled "Toward a National Theatre," the first, by Robert Porterfield and Robert Breen, was published in October 1945, and the second, by Senator Irving Ives and Representative Jacob K. Javits, in April 1949). Of specific interest regarding the forerunners of regional theatre are two grant-funded, enthusiastic surveys of what was then described as hinterland culture: Houghton's *Advance From Broadway*, and Gard's *Grassroots Theater*.

Monographs of individual theatres, many commissioned for or printed by theatre companies as commemorative histories, include Beeson's *Thresholds: The Story of Nina Vance's Alley Theatre*, Maslon's *The Arena*, Dawidziak's *The Barter Theatre Story*, and Danforth's *Cleveland Play House 1915–1990*. The Billy Rose Theatre Collection of the New York Public Library of the Performing Arts at Lincoln Center maintains clipping files for most regional theatres that include articles from local and national newspapers and magazines, press releases, pamphlets, and playbills.

There are numerous autobiographical and biographical accounts of regional theatre artists and their work. First and foremost is Margo Jones's *Theatre-in-the-Round*, which became a veritable manifesto for the regional movement. There also is a good dissertation on Jones, Wilmeth's "A History of the Margo Jones Theatre," and a biography by Sheehy, *Margo: The Life and Theatre of Margo Jones*. Sir Tyrone Guthrie penned a lively account of the founding of the Minnesota Theatre Company in *A New Theatre*, and the artistic and philosophical ideology behind San Francisco's Actor's Workshop is chronicled in Blau's *The Impossible Theatre*. Several regional theatre directors have described their work in book-length studies, notably Schneider's *Entrances* and Vaughan's *A Possible Theatre*. Fichandler has written several important articles, notably "Theatres or Institutions?" and "Institution-As-Artwork."

Business and economic aspects of regional theatre are detailed in Langley's *Theatre Management and Production in America*. Also of interest is the landmark study of arts funding, *Performing Arts – The Economic Dilemma* by Baumol and Bowen, and *The Performing Arts and American Society* edited by Lowry, which gives a good early history of Ford Foundation and NEA subsidies.

By far the best sources on both the artistic and economic aspects of the current regional theatre scene are published by Theatre Communications Group. TCG's serial publications are the biennial *Theatre Profiles*, which began in 1971 as a detailed listing of historical and current data on over 200 regional theatres; *American Theatre* magazine, inaugurated in 1984 and issued monthly ten times a year (May/June and July/August are combined issues), which covers all aspects of theatre nationwide and regularly publishes full-length scripts of new plays; and *Theatre Facts*, published annually since 1974 and now included in the April edition of *American Theatre*, which is a detailed fiscal report resulting from national surveys of non-profit professional theatres. *Theatre Profiles 7*, published in 1986 as a special TCG anniversary issue, contains an historic overview of the regional movement as well as ten retrospective articles. TCG also published *The Artistic Home*, edited by London, a report on the series of nationwide meetings with 120 artistic directors held in 1987 where they explored common artistic and managerial problems. A follow-up discussion, "Revisiting the Artistic Home," was held in March 1995 with a detailed report by Langworthy, "Theatre at the Crossroads," published in the November 1995 issue of *American Theatre*.

Alternative Theatre

Marvin Carlson

Editorial note: In a previous section of this chapter, Mel Gussow provided an overview of Off- and Off-Off Broaday. Although this essay covers much of the same ground, it does so in a more analytic way, reaching beyond New York to other geographical centers of the United States and providing more contextualization. As will become clear, alternative theatre is not limited here to alternatives to Broadway, though anti-commercialism tends to be a common denominator.

Origins and Background

The modern concept of alternative theatre was developed in Europe at the close of the nineteenth century, when a number of amateurs and theatre professionals established small producing organizations outside the existing theatre establishment to evade censorship, to explore new ideas in playwriting and staging, and to seek new or more specialized audiences. Most of the major dramatists of the period, including Ibsen, Shaw, Strindberg, and Chekhov, were closely associated with this alternative theatre, and it was, of course, the theatrical home of the many experimental movements such as Symbolism, Futurism, and Expressionism, that sought to bring new expressive dimensions to the art. Inspiration from the alternative theatres of Europe arrived in America in the closing years of the century, but the major development of an American version of the European alternative theatre did not develop until the years between 1910 and 1920, with the "Little Theatre" movement, the best known examples of which are the Washington Square Players (later the Theatre Guild) and the Provincetown Players (see Volume 2 for coverage of this movement). During the first half of the century the "Little Theatres" and their offshoots provided much of the most exciting and interesting work in American acting, directing, playwriting, and scenic design.

Despite the considerable achievement of the American alternative theatre before 1945, and despite its distinctively American character, most of its practitioners continued to look to Europe for leadership in theatrical experimentation. While this orientation certainly did not disappear after 1945, the postwar American alternative theatre steadily increased in self-assurance and in the respect it was accorded elsewhere, until by the sixties the traditional geography of influence had been reversed and alternative theatres in Europe and indeed around the world frequently looked to American alternative theatre for models and inspiration.

The very concept of alternative theatre necessarily has had a different resonance in America from that in Europe, especially in the early postwar years, since the systems of theatrical production are so different. Any European theatre center will have large commercial theatres corresponding to America's Broadway theatres, but there is also a system of state-supported theatres, with permanent companies and large repertoires centered on the national classics, but usually including major foreign works and important premieres as well. With the exception of the shortlived and quite special Federal Theatre Project, discussed in the previous volume, America has never developed such a system of national theatres, and so the alternative tradition here from the beginning included not only the kind of small experimental ventures more typical of alternative theatre in Europe, but also large and ambitious attempts to establish European-style repertory theatres, which were in fact alternatives to the only well-established American professional theatre, the commercial Broadway-style house.

The hope of establishing a theatre devoted to classic and major contemporary works with a continuing company and relatively modest prices, in imitation of the European state theatres, has been a recurrent dream in America throughout this century, from the early years of the Theatre Guild and Eva Le Gallienne's Civic Repertory Company in the twenties and thirties to Tony Randall's National Actors Theatre in the nineties. The first major postwar attempt to fulfill this dream was the shortlived American Repertory Theatre, founded in 1946 by Eva Le Gallienne with Margaret Webster and Cheryl Crawford, which lasted only until 1948. One of the most successful attempts to establish an American repertory theatre was the Association of Producing Artists (APA) founded in 1960. After four years of touring and of residencies in several cities it joined the Phoenix Theatre in New York, which had been founded in 1953 for the presentation of significant plays at modest prices. Between 1964 and its dissolution in 1970 the Phoenix-APA offered one of the most successful examples of this type of alternative theatre.

During these same years a much more ambitious permanent repertory theatre was planned and launched as a part of the new Lincoln Center for the Performing Arts. Opening in 1965, this consisted of two theatres, the larger thrust-proscenium stage, the Vivian Beaumont, and a smaller experimental stage, originally the Forum, now the Mitzi E. Newhouse. Despite the vision of its founders, Elia Kazan and Robert Whitehead, the Lincoln Center facility was plagued with problems from the beginning, and despite a distinguished succession of directors, has never achieved the original vision of a true alternative to the New York commercial theatre. The large repertory theatres of Europe, whose offerings include many plays per season, some of them remaining in the repertory for years, have no real equivalent in America, though outside of New York many cities, among them Seattle, Milwaukee, Providence, and San Francisco have since 1945 established quite successful repertory houses. Most of these present a "modified" version of repertory, with a fairly small number of plays that change each season. (See the previous section of this chapter for coverage of the regional theatre movement.)

Despite their rather troubled history, regional repertory theatres and even the more troubled repertory experiments in New York have made a considerable contribution to the vigor and the richness of American theatrical life in the late twentieth century and provided a significant alternative to the mainstream commercial theatre. Nevertheless, the term alternative theatre does not for most readers suggest theatre of this kind, but the smaller ventures associated less with accomplished productions of established works than with artistic innovation and experimentation, and it is the theatres of this type that have had the most impact outside America.

The first distinct alternative theatre movement after 1945, as discussed by Gussow, was the Off-Broadway movement, really a postwar extension of the Little Theatre movement, offering a mixture of unusual or neglected classics, new European and American plays, and a variety of experiments in methods of production. The Off-Broadway movement, which sought to escape the commercial pressures of Broadway, had by the early sixties sufficiently fallen prey to those pressures as to generate a felt need for a new non-commercial, experimental theatre in New York, which became known as Off-Off Broadway. Although in a very real sense the Little Theatre movement, the repertory theatres, and the Off-Broadway movement all represented important alternatives to the mainline commercial theatre of America, the actual term "alternative theatre" did not come into popularity until the sixties, and was then used to describe a wide variety of theatrical experiments, some of which were closely related to earlier alternative theatre in the United States and in Europe, and others of which were generated by particular social and political concerns of that turbulent period in American cultural history.

The Living Theatre

Perhaps the best known example of American alternative theatre nationally and internationally has been the Living Theatre of Julian Beck and Judith Malina, and this theatre, in its almost fifty years of existence, has been closely associated with many of the concerns that characterize this movement. Beck and Malina began producing small plays in their own apartment in 1951 and during the next decade closely followed the pattern of many earlier avant-garde theatres in America and Europe, rejecting the prevailing mode of realism and experimenting with abstract and poetic texts. They offered several works by Gertrude Stein, along with, among others, T. S. Eliot, W. H. Auden, Pablo Picasso, Alfred Jarry, Federico García Lorca, Jean Cocteau, and August Strindberg. In these early productions, language was given strong emphasis, but despite a very limited budget, visual experimentation was involved as well. For *Beyond the Mountains,* an adaptation of the *Oresteia* by the poet Kenneth Rexroth, the actors wore oriental masks and choreographer Tei Ko created a sequence based on Noh dances.

One of the most ambitious of these early pieces was Paul Goodman's *Faustina,* presented at the Cherry Lane Theatre in 1952. The play depicted a Roman legend of the period of Marcus Aurelius, and at its conclusion, after the murder of the young hero, the scenery disappeared and the actress playing Faustina, her body splashed with the victim's blood, advanced to the audience on an empty stage and berated them for not stopping the play before this cruel deed had taken place.

Such direct address, challenging traditional theatrical illusion, became in time a central technique in Living Theatre productions. Indeed the tension between theatre and reality clearly led to an interest in Pirandello, whose *Tonight We Improvise* was presented in 1955 and again in 1959, and to an unusual staging of William Carlos Williams's comedy *Many Loves,* where the audience entered the theatre to find the stage bare and actors and technicians in confusion over a blown fuse. Soon the lights were restored, the stage prepared, and the regular play begun. During the Living Theatre's first European tour in 1961, this unconventional opening caused a sensation.

It was Jack Gelber's *The Connection* in 1959, however, that most thoroughly illustrated the Living Theatre's Pirandellian interests at this period and that first brought the group to the attention of a more general public. Here the "reality" suggested by the opening of *Many Loves* extended throughout the evening. The audience entered to find a group of ragged figures on stage. One of them introduced himself as the producer, who claimed that the others were drug addicts who had agreed to come to the theatre and improvise on material he had written in exchange for a fix, to be provided by Cowboy, the "connection." Jazz served as both model and accompaniment, since the addicts listened to a Charlie Parker record and four of them were musicians who do jazz improvisations. Other actors appeared as a film crew documenting these activities. During the intermission the actors panhandled the spectators for drug money, and spectators were truly confused about the borders of reality and illusion. Clearly the musicians were real players of jazz, and it was widely assumed that the company was really using drugs, if not addicted to them, although this was not in fact the case. Later Judith Malina said that it was in *The Connection* that the Living Theatre actors really began to "play themselves." *The Connection* became the signature piece for the Living Theatre in its early years, not only in America, where it remained for several years in the repertoire, but for its first two European tours, in 1961 and 1962 (its frequent pairing with *Many Loves* on the first tour emphasized the playing with reality that the two productions had in common).

The Living Theatre's development was made much more complex by the introduction into their work of two other quite different influences about the time of *The Connection* – those of John Cage and Antonin Artaud. The Living's first new production after *The Connection* was called *The Theatre of Chance,* and was strongly influenced by the theories and practice of John Cage. Cage's revolutionary ideas on music and aesthetics have had a profound influence on modern experimentation in all the arts, but *The Theatre of Chance* was their first significant exploration within the world of the theatre. Cage picked up and developed a concern of the Futurists, that the concept of "music" should be expanded to include all manner of everyday sounds, hitherto dismissed as "noise." This conscious introduction of non-artistic materials into art, which Cage began in the late thirties, paralleled experiments in modern dance by Merce Cunningham, who become a frequent collaborator with Cage, and later, after 1955, in San Francisco's Dance Workshop, where Ann Halprin explored the dance possibilities of everyday activities such as walking, eating, and bathing.

In 1948, after almost ten years of collaboration, Cage and Cunningham were invited to spend the summer working at Black Mountain College in North Carolina, which was emerging as a center for artistic experimentation. With Willem De Kooning, Buckminster Fuller, and others they reconstructed an avant-garde performance from earlier in the century, Eric Satie's *The Ruse of the Medusa.* In 1952, back at Black Mountain, Cage and Cunningham collaborated with Robert Rauschenberg and others in an untitled event that has often been cited as the model for the wave of Happenings and other performance events that became extremely popular in the American art world of the late fifties and early sixties. A variety of activities, each timed to the second, took place in and around an arena audience. Cage read a Dadaist lecture, films were projected on the ceiling, Cunningham danced in the aisles, followed by an unplanned excited dog who was enthusiastically incorporated into the performance. David Tudor, who had worked before with Cage, poured water from one bucket into another.

This event was taken as a model by Cage in the course on experimental music that he began to teach at New York's New School for Social Research in 1956. Many of the pioneers in the New York avant-garde art of the sixties – poets, filmmakers, painters, and musicians – found inspiration in these classes, which stressed the performative nature of art and the process of its creation over the finished product. Typical of the new orientation was an interview with the experimental artist "Woks" in *Art News* in 1959 in which he stated "what counts is no longer the painting but the process of creation" (Pierre Schneider, "Interview with Woks," 62). Among the students in Cage's course was Allan Kaprow, who developed Cage's ideas in his own way in the 1959 presentation at the Reuben Gallery which he called *18 Happenings in 6 Parts,* featuring a number of simple activities simultaneously performed in three different spaces. This event established for the public and the press the "Happening" as a major new avant-garde artistic activity, which it remained throughout the sixties.

John Cage was among those invited to the performances of the Living Theatre in the early fifties, and Merce Cunningham occasionally did choreography there. The interest of both in incorporating into art material of everyday life and in emphasizing process over product clearly related closely to the company whose major works to date had been *Many Loves* and *The Connection.* For *The Theatre of Chance,* the next new work after *The Connection,* John Cage worked out a system to guarantee a highly controlled randomness in the selection of elements to be presented each evening of a script by Jackson MacLow, *The Marrying Maiden.* Such matters as the volume of the voice, the speed of delivery, and the emotional tone of the speech (selected from approximately one hundred terms such as sad, gay, and so forth) were all determined afresh each evening according to the rule of chance derived from the the Oriental *I Ching,* Cage's preferred source of random selection. Rolls of dice determined the order in which lines were read as well as the utilization of the "music" of the piece, created by Cage from distorted tapes of the actors reading their lines.

Although Cage's interest in found material was attractive to the Living Theatre, his rather coldly formal methods were less so, and a deeper and longer-lasting influence provided them with a passionate intensity lacking in this approach. This was the writings of Antonin Artaud. Although Artaud was deeply involved as an actor, director, and theorist in the experimental theatre world of France between the world wars, he was generally regarded as a minor figure at that time. It was only in the sixties that he became widely regarded as one of the central figures of modern avant-garde theatre, and the centrality given to his work by the Living Theatre was one of the major reasons for this. *The Theatre and Its Double,* the first collection of Artaud's writings translated into English, appeared in 1958 and was avidly read by Beck and Malina, who saw in it an expression of many of their own most deeply held beliefs about the power and purpose of theatre. Central to these was a feeling that conventional art and indeed modern civilization erected a barrier between human beings and their deepest and most authentic feelings, desires, and needs, and that ideally theatre should break through that barrier, a painful but liberating process.

The production in which these Artaudian concerns were first strongly articulated was *The Brig*, a slice-of-life depiction of existence in a U.S. Marine Corps brig in Japan, written by a former prisoner, Kenneth Brown. An authentic prison scene was recreated on stage and actors in rehearsal and performance were subjected ruthlessly to its routine and its ugly physical punishments. The preface to the published play, written by Beck, claimed that after 1958 the ghost of Artaud had become their mentor and their goal had become to create the kind of "complusive, plague-ridden" spectacle of which he dreamed, one that would profoundly disturb its audience, shake them out of conventional expectations, and leave them cleansed and with new perspectives.

Despite its close connection with the metaphysical concerns of Artaud, *The Brig* also had clear political implications, about the coercive and violent nature of American society in general and the American military establishment in particular. The Living Theatre had been gradually moving from its initial focus on an alternative theatre to one which united this and an interest in alternative politics. *The Brig* was the clearest illustration of this so far, especially after October 1963, when the Internal Revenue Service closed the theatre for non-payment of taxes. The company resisted, breaking into the padlocked theatre and performing *The Brig* in defiance of the authorities. When they refused to vacate the premises, twenty-five were arrested. The pacifist anarchism manifested in this resistance, and in the theatrical behavior of the accused in the subsequent trial, provided a model and inspiration for the widespread resistance to political authority in the American alternative theatre in the following years. Malina and Beck "paid their debt" to the system with a fine and brief jail terms, but their American career was for the time being completed. The core of the company departed for Europe, where they toured as a kind of exiled artistic commune until 1968, achieving an almost mythic status among devotees of alternative theatre in Europe and America.

The Open Theatre

As reports of the Living Theatre's continued experiments drifted back from Europe, other groups and individuals, many of them building directly upon the Living Theatre's initiatives, began the rapid expansion of alternative theatre that occurred in America in the sixties. One of the most influential of these was Joseph Chaikin, who had been a member of the Living Theatre since

1959 and an actor in most of its productions from *Many Loves* onward. He did not follow the company into exile, however, but remained behind in New York. He and Peter Feldman, another Living Theatre actor, had both been students of Nola Chilton, who also left America at this time to settle in Israel. Chaikin and Feldman gathered a group of writers and other actors, many of them Chilton's students, to establish an ongoing cooperative theatre group which they called the Open Theatre, to distinguish it from the closed theatre of Broadway. This group shared the Living Theatre's dream of a continuing ensemble, and one of their first productions was a theatrical tribute to their forebears, a documentary drama called *The Trial of Judith Malina and Julian Beck*, but ultimately they were less concerned with political matters than with developing the ability of theatre to express individual dreams and feelings in a depersonalized society. Feeling that most existing approaches to acting had become sterile and formulaic, the Open Theatre explored new directions and techniques. Particularly influential were improvisational games based upon the work of Viola Spolin in Chicago. In her home city, Spolin's work in encouraging spontaneous and improvisatory performance was carried on by her son Paul Sills, who co-founded two of the leading improvisatory theatres in modern America, the Compass Players, in 1955, and Second City, in 1959. Kristin Linklater instructed the actors in voice and Joseph Schlichter in sensitivity training based on Gestalt therapy, and in time the Open Theatre developed a strong technique and a distinctive style, but perhaps the group was best known for its collaborative approach. Although Chaikin was the dominant figure, he did not work as a conventional director. The company's most typical productions were painstakingly assembled from the contributions of the individual actors, all given an equal importance. It was the Open Theatre more than any other group that popularized the idea of "collective creations" – group-created works that became one of the favored examples of alternative theatre work in the sixties.

In the early days of the Open Theatre, as its philosophy and technique were developing, a number of playwrights worked closely with it, particularly Megan Terry, Jean-Claude Van Itallie, and Maria Irene Fornés. In 1966, Terry developed a folk-rock collage commentary on the Vietnam War, *Viet Rock*, out of an Open Theatre workshop, their first long work from an improvisational base. Van Itallie composed three short plays, collectively called *America Hurrah*, that were a major Off-Broadway success this same year, but the group became concerned that such work was taking them in a commercial and conventional direction, and their subsequent work was devoted more specifically to collective experimentation. Probably the best known of the Open Theatre productions was *The Serpent*, developed in 1967 from exercises and improvisations based primarily upon the Book of Genesis, but weaving in references to contemporary deeds of violence such as the assassinations of

President Kennedy and of Martin Luther King. *Terminal* (1969) grew out of meditations on human mortality, and, although written by Susan Yankowitz, was derived entirely from the actors' own images. That year the company toured to Paris, London, and Amsterdam, but in the course of the tour already existing divisions concerning the social, political, and artistic goals of the Open Theatre became more serious, and upon their return to America they disbanded. Chaikin re-formed the company with only six actors, who continued to perform *Terminal* and added two further works exploring the actors' individual responses to universal human concerns – *The Mutation Show,* in 1971, concerning the process of adaptation to changing social circumstances, and *Nightwalk,* in 1973, concerned with sleep and consciousness. The group finally disbanded at the end of the 1973 season and Chaikin contined to direct for theatres in New York and California until he suffered aphasia from a stroke in 1984. In the nineties, however, he returned to the stage, first as an actor in plays co-authored by Sam Shepard (*The War in Heaven*) and Van Itallie (*Struck Dumb*) reflecting this experience, and subsequently also as a director of new experimental work, one of the most loved and revered figures in the American experimental theatre.

San Francisco Mime Troupe

Probably the most familiar image of the alternative theatre of the 1960s is that of politically engaged production, and indeed the amount and variety of such activity at this time was unparalleled in American theatre history.

One of the first and longest-lasting of such groups was the San Francisco Mime Troupe, founded in 1959 by R.G. Davis. The early work of this company was focused less on specific political concerns than on exploring an acting approach opposed to traditional psychological realism and drawing upon the more physical tradition of the circus, variety entertainment, and particularly the *commedia dell'arte.* In the early sixties the company favored literary works in the *commedia* tradition by authors such as Molière and Goldoni, but their interest in performing in parks and other non-traditional spaces and in interjecting into the scripts, in the tradition of the *commedia,* references to current news events, gave them a distinct political flavor from the beginning. This became more marked with the growing political radicalism in the mid-sixties within the cultural community of San Francisco and indeed across America. A growing opposition to the U.S. involvement in Vietnam was central to this political climate. The Mime Troupe presented its first commentary on Vietnam in 1965, and two years later, not long after Terry's *Viet Rock* in New York, a full-length work on the subject, a highly contemporary adaptation of Goldoni's *L'Amant militaire.* In 1965 also the Mime Troupe engaged another major political issue, racism in America, with their *Minstrel Show or Civil Rights in a Cracker Barrel.*

In the summer of 1966, R.G. Davis contributed an article entitled "Guerrilla Theatre" to an issue of the *Tulane Drama Review* devoted largely to emerging political concerns in the theatre. In addition to Davis's article, the issue contained a report on a recent *TDR*-sponsored conference on this subject and an article by Saul Gottlieb reporting on the recent activity of the Living Theatre in Europe and stressing their political concerns. Scene 4 of their new work, *Mysteries and Smaller Pieces,* Gottlieb noted, was focused upon protest to the Vietnam War. During the late sixties and early seventies political concerns dominated American alternative theatre. In 1965 Luis Valdez joined the San Francisco Mime Troupe, and that same year Cesar Chavez organized the first strike of migrant workers against the grape growers in California. Valdez, whose parents were such workers, began organizing short comic skits, called *actos,* mixing Spanish and English and using many of the same comic traditions as the San Francisco Mime Troupe to deal with the concerns of the workers. Their short skits were designed to be performed on picket lines and in workers' rallies for the United Farm Workers.

El Teatro Campesino and Chicano Theatre

Valdez's El Teatro Campesino soon became one of America's best-known political theatres. It received an Obie Award in 1968 for its contributions to Workers' Theatre, and performed across the country, even before the Senate Subcommittee on Migratory Labor. It was inspirational in the founding of what eventually amounted to more than a hundred Chicano theatres scattered all across the country. Among the best known of these was Jorge Huerta's Teatro de la Esperanza in Santa Barbara, California, and Joe Rosenberg's Teatro Bilingüe in Kingsville, Texas. In 1971 a national network, TENAZ (El Teatro Nacional de Aztlàn) was established among these groups. The first festival of such theatre was held in Fresno, California, in 1966, and responsibility for such festivals became one of the projects of TENAZ.

In the early seventies the Teatro Campesino began seeking a more spiritual foundation for their social concerns, and they began to introduce Indian and particularly Mayan material into their work and their lives. They formed a community based on Mayan models and sought to develop a performance practice, called Theatre of the Sphere, drawing upon Mayan and Aztec beliefs. The fifth annual festival of Chicano theatre (1974) was held at the pyramids of Teotihuacan, just outside Mexico City, and for this the Teatro created one of their most mystic works, *El Baile de los Gigantes,* recreating an actual Mayan religious ceremony more than a thousand years old. Mayan elements were also important in *El Fin del Mundo* (1975), but these were beginning to be over-taken by elements of a new Campesino style, called the *corrido,* based on the form and stories of traditional narrative folk ballads. Interest also shifted from farm workers to the urban Chicano, leading to Valdez's most widely known work, *Zoot Suit* (1978), premiered in Los Angeles and then moved to New York, where it was advertised as the first Chicano play on Broadway. Valdez, who had been moving toward mainstream theatre for some time, was widely criti-cized for openly joining it here, though he pointed to the poor reception of the play in New York as evidence that on the contrary, mainstream audiences found it too political. In any case the original Teatro was near its end. In 1980 it ceased to exist as a collective ensemble and became a more traditonal pro-duction company, though still, of course, devoted to Chicano theatre.

Although the Chicano theatre has attracted more attention, largely due to the visibility of Luis Valdez, the sixties also saw developing on the East Coast, centered in New York, a Spanish-speaking alternative theatre dedicated to the concerns of this community, made up primarily of Puerto Ricans, Cubans, and the so-called Nuyoricans (New York-born Hispanics). The best known of such groups is probably the Puerto Rican Traveling Theatre, founded in 1967 and led by Miriam Colón, but John C. Miller in the Spring 1978 issue of the *Revista Chicano-Riqueña* discusses an impressive number of similar groups active in New York between 1965 and 1977.

Black Theatres

Another pioneer in modern American ethnic theatre, with goals and concerns very similar to those of El Teatro Campesino, was the Free Southern Theatre. Just as the Campesino was closely associated with organized political action through Chavez's strikes and the United Farm Workers, the Free Southern Theatre was closely tied to the Liberation Movement in the early sixties that sought to produce political, social, and economic changes in the lives of Southern African Americans. John O'Neal, one of the founders of FST, was a field director for the Student Non-Violent Coordinating Committee (SNCC) in Jackson, Mississippi, and Gilbert Moses was a writer for a liberal newspaper in that city. In 1963 they met and began to plan for a theatre to encourage black reflection and social awareness. The following year they sought advice from Richard Schechner, then a professor at Tulane University, and over the next five years Schechner was an influential member of the Board of Directors, eventually editing the major chronicle of this theatre. As Schechner's pres-ence indicates, FST in its early years was an integrated venture in its admin-istration and its company, though this was soon to change with the development of Black Nationalism.

The FST opened in 1964 in New Orleans with Martin Duberman's documentary drama *In White America,* and during the next two seasons they toured through small towns in Mississippi and Tennessee with this and Beckett's *Waiting for Godot.* In 1965 they also toured to New York City, which would during the next few years become the center of the black theatre movement, as Southern California was for the Chicano theatre. Among the pioneers of modern black theatre in New York were Roger Furman, a playwright and director who founded the New Heritage Players in 1965, and Ernie McClintock, an actor who established the Afro-American Studio in 1966. One of the best known black theatres of this period was the New Lafayette, founded in Harlem in 1966 by Robert Macbeth, with Ed Bullins as playwright in residence. In 1971 the Black Theatre Alliance was formed in New York for mutual support and publicity. Its first newsletter (in 1973) listed sixteen member companies, all in New York. By 1977 its membership was national and included fifty-two organizations.

A major tension in the black theatre movement in the mid-sixties concerned integration. Harold Cruse in his 1967 book *The Crisis of the Negro Intellectual* insisted that the entire organizational structure of theatre and other cultural institutions must be controlled by blacks if such institutions had any hope of avoiding the traditional usurpation of power by the Anglo-Saxon majority. The majority of black theatres in the late sixties turned in this direction, and many of them toward the more distinctly radical political position represented most notably by LeRoi Jones, who changed his name to Amiri Baraka when he became the leader of the movement that saw theatre as a weapon in the struggle for black liberation. He founded the Black Arts Repertory Theatre in Harlem in 1965 and Spirit House in Newark, New Jersey, in 1967, which premiered the best known of his revolutionary pieces, the historical pageant *Slave Ship* in 1967. The best-known company that continued in the late sixties to operate with an integrated administration and to avoid distinctly revolutionary plays was New York's Negro Ensemble Company, founded in 1967 by actor Robert Hooks, playwright-director Douglas Turner Ward, and producer-director Gerald Krone. The NEC suffered a good deal of adverse criticism for this moderate position, but its measured and pragmatic approach has paid off in longevity; though it struggles, it is one of the few experimental theatres established in the late sixties that still survives.

Other Minority Theatres

Many minority and disadvantaged groups in America looked to the theatre during the late sixties and early seventies as did these ethnic minorities to provide a forum to articulate their concerns and to encourage a wider public awareness of their situation. The National Theatre of the Deaf was formed in 1967 to provide opportunities for deaf actors and audiences, but their use of mime, music, dance, and narration has also allowed all audiences to appreciate their work. Tale Spinners was formed in San Francisco to respond to the needs and interests of the elderly, and in New York Arthur Strimling founded Roots and Branches to encourage cross-generational communication by mixing very old and very young performers. The Family, formed in New York in 1972, provided ex-prisoners with an opportunity to create theatre for presention both in prisons and outside.

Aside from ethnic theatre, the most important of the many alternative minority theatres have been those concerned with gender and sexual orientation. In 1965 playwright Ronald Tavel and director-performer John Vaccaro founded in New York the Play-House of the Ridiculous, a homosexual transvestite theatre devoted to camp parody of old films and outrageous satire of all aspects of contemporary life and culture. As free-wheeling in their iconoclasm as the earlier Dadaists, the Ridiculous founders prided themselves as being "the only non-academic avant-garde." In 1967 one of the Ridiculous actors, Charles Ludlam, left to form his own troupe, the Ridiculous Theatrical Company, which under his leadership and with his inspired acting and playwriting, brought camp performance to mainstream attention. Ludlam once called his company a "mythic reincarnation" of Molière's use of *commedia dell'arte* and indeed Ludlam himself has been called a "modern Molière." After several sprawling and largely improvisational works in the late sixties, Ludlam turned to more conventionally structured works, often based on a specific well-known play, film, or novel, but liberally sprinkled with wide-ranging references to popular culture, gay culture, and the literary tradition. The first of these was *Bluebeard* (1970), which was also the first Ludlam work to be widely reviewed. *Camille* (1974), with Ludlam in the title role, surprisingly brought audiences from laughter to tears at its conclusion. In 1977 Ludlam further displayed his versatility with a parody of Wagner, *Der Ring Gott Farblonjet*. In 1978 the Company moved into a permanent home in Greenwich Village, where they remained regularly producing until 1996. Ludlam created another memorable female, a Maria Callas look-alike, in the 1983 *Galas*, and in 1984 produced his best-known work, the gothic thriller *The Mystery of Irma Vep*, an acting *tour de force* in which he and his co-star Everett Quinton played all seven roles. His last work before his tragically early death in 1986 was *The Artificial Jungle,* a pet shop parody of Zola's grim tale *Thérèse Raquin*. Ludlam's work was carried on after his death by Quinton with revivals, new plays by other authors, and solo performances by Quinton of such classics as *A Tale of Two Cities* (1989) and *Phaedra* (1996).

During the early seventies performers from the San Francisco Cockettes established a New York version of that anarchic transvestite theatre with such productions as *Razzmatazz* (1974), while other members left behind in San Francisco formed the Angels of Light, offering such camp spectacles as the mock-Indian epic *Holy Cow* (1979). The leading gay–lesbian theatre in the San Francisco area, however, was Rhinoceros, founded in 1977 by Allan Estes. The opening production, inspired by a 1977 workshop at Berkeley by Polish experimental director Jerzy Grotowski, was *Gayhem, a Happening*. By 1980 the company had achieved sufficient visibility to become the first gay company in the United States to receive funding from the National Endowment for the Arts and the first to offer a subscription season. In 1982 the theatre presented its first lesbian play, Jane Chambers's *My Blue Heaven.*

Feminist Groups

An important part of the American alternative theatre from around 1970 onward was individuals and groups exploring feminist concerns. The first such groups were closely related to the women's consciousness-raising groups of the late sixties and early seventies, seeking to provide a voice for women's concerns and a forum for the dreams, memories, hopes, and fantasies of women. Such groups appeared from coast to coast: the Caravan Theatre in Lexington, Massachusetts (1965), The Rhode Island Feminist Theatre in Providence (1973), Lucy Winer's and Claudette Charbonneau's New York Feminist Theatre (1969), the Westbeth Playwrights' Feminist Collective and the It's All Right to be a Woman Theatre (both founded in New York in 1970), the Omaha Magic Theatre (1969), At The Foot of the Mountain (Minneapolis, 1974), Synthaxis Theatre (South Pasadena, California, 1972), Lilith – A Women's Theatre (San Francisco, 1974). Such groups directly and indirectly inspired many others, enough to be listed in 1980 in a substantial volume, *Feminist Theatre Groups,* by Dinah Luise Leavitt, and revisited in a more recent book, *Feminist Theaters in the U.S.A,* by Charlotte Canning.

In 1971 Roberta Sklar, a co-director with Joseph Chaikin at the Open Theatre, attended a performance at the It's All Right to be a Woman Theatre and was inspired to work in a similar direction. She first joined forces with Sondra Segal at the Womanrite Theatre Ensemble, which Segal founded in 1972, then with both Segal and writer Clare Cross to establish in 1976 one of the leading women's theatre collaboratives, The Women's Experimental Theatre (WET). The first and best known work of this ensemble (which Sklar and Segal continued until 1985) was a trilogy of plays, *The Daughters Cycle,* made up of *Daughters, Sister/Sister,* and *Electra Speaks* (produced between 1977 and 1981), exploring the role of women in the Western patriarchal family.

Another member of Chaikin's Open Theatre to establish a feminist theatre was Muriel Miguel, who founded a shortlived consciousness-raising theatre, Womanspace, and then in 1976 a much more long-lasting and influential ensemble, Spiderwoman. Spiderwoman was a Hopi goddess who taught her people designs and weaving, and the group developed a collective improvisational approach which they named "storyweaving." The original group of seven women sought to bring together women of various ethnicities, sexual orientation, and age, and their first production, *Women and Violence*, in 1976, wove together autobiographical material with an historical study of women's oppression even under men battling for ethnic freedom. In 1981, however, the variety of backgrounds in the group, originally seen as a strength, began to create tensions, and the group split into two, both important in the alternative theatre of the next decade – Spiderwoman and Split Britches. The core of Spiderwoman since 1981 has been the three American Indian sisters Lisa Mayo, Gloria Miguel, and Muriel Miguel, who have performed primarily at the alternative theatre showcase Theater for the New City and at the American Indian Community House, both on the Lower East Side of Manhattan. Their *The Three Sisters from Here to There* (1982) was, as its title suggests, primarily a takeoff on Chekhov, but more typically, their productions (*Sun, Moon, Feather*, 1981; *3 Up, 3 Down*, 1987; *Winnetou's Snake Oil Show from Wigwam City*, 1988; *Reverb-ber-ber-ations*, 1990) have mixed autobiography, history, popular culture, and literary references in complex and highly theatrical explorations of Indian identity in America.

The core of Split Britches has been Lois Weaver and Peggy Shaw, who first collaborated on a version of *Split Britches,* based on the lives of Weaver's aunts in the Virginia mountains. It was presented at the first Women's One World Festival of feminist theatre, held in New York in the fall of 1980. The play continued to develop, receiving its final form when playwright-performer Deb Margolin joined Weaver and Shaw in it. This version was presented at the second WOW Festival in 1981, in which Weaver, Shaw, and Margolin appeared as a new company, taking their name from this play. In 1982 Weaver and Shaw founded the WOW Café in New York, dedicated to producing works by and for women, and Split Britches offered its next play, *Beauty and the Beast*. Since that time the members of Split Britches have been an important part of the alternative feminist theatre, performing in a variety of combinations. The original trio have created *Upwardly Mobile Homes* (1984), *Little Women* (1988), and *Lesbians Who Kill* (1992); Shaw and Weaver alone created a celebration of their ongoing relationship, *Anniversary Waltz* in 1989; and during the nineties Deb Margolin has become better know as a solo performer, in such works as *Gestation* (1991), *Of Mice, Bugs, and Women* (1994), and *Oh Wholly Night* (1996).

Shaw and Weaver under the title Split Britches have also created important work with other collaborators. The first of these was Holly Hughes, with whom they created *Dress Suits to Hire* in 1987. Hughes came to the attention of the lesbian community with her darkly erotic *The Lady Dick* at WOW Cafe

6. Peggy Shaw and Lois Weaver in Split Britches' production of *Lust and Comfort*, 1995. Photograph by Tom Brazil. By permission of Peggy Shaw and Split Britches.

in 1985, and *Dress Suits* possesses a similar *noir* tone. Holly Hughes has continued to create new solo performance pieces, such as *World Without End* (1989), *Clit Notes* (1994), and *Cat o' Nine Tails* (1996), but she is probably best known to the general public for being one of the performance artists defunded in 1990 by the then chairman of the National Endowment for the Arts, setting off a controversy about public funding and the relation of art to its surrounding culture that continues to resonate in the work of these four artists, in the alternative theatre world in general, and in the halls of government.

In 1991 Shaw and Weaver collaborated with the British gay company Bloolips in one of their most popular productions, *Belle Reprieve*, a parody gender-exploration of Tennessee Williams's *Streetcar Named Desire*. Such a joint gay and lesbian project was unusual, but Shaw had a connection with Bloolips, having originally performed in the British troupe Hot Peaches with Bette Bourne, Bloolips's founder. Another gay/lesbian project followed, *Lust and Comfort* (1995), with James Neale-Kennedy, of the Gay Sweatshop in London.

Pacifist Groups

While alternative ethnic theatres were developing in the Chicano and African American communities during the sixties, another kind of socially oriented alternative theatre was also rapidly expanding, much of it fueled by the New Left's rejection of the United States' involvement in Vietnam. Probably the best known of the many pacifist theatre companies formed during the sixties was the Bread and Puppet Theatre, founded in 1961 by Peter Schumann, who has remained its central driving force ever since. Although the Bread and Puppet Theatre created many pieces directly condemning the Vietnam War and was a key participant in the Radical Theatre Festival held in San Francisco in 1968, its inspiration drew more upon nineteenth-century Romanticism and early Christianity, stressing the natural goodness of man, the importance of basic needs like bread, and the natural environment, and the corruption of both man and nature by greed and lust for power. Schumann also rejects the intellectual literary tradition of Western theatre, seeking to convey his message by the simplest means – the use of cartoons and puppets, most of these larger than life size, stories drawing upon fairy tales, myths, and the Bible, the inevitable sharing of bread at the end of a performance. The Bread and Puppet has often appeared in outdoor and other non-traditional spaces, as well as in peace marches and parades, causing it to be sometimes classified among examples of street theatre or environmental theatre. Perhaps its best-known production, *The Cry of the People for Meat* (1969), illustrates many of its concerns and strategies. A parable-like mystery play, it begins with the joining of two twenty-foot-high puppets, Mother Earth and a vulgar Uncle Sam representing the forces of greed and imperialism. From their union comes the evil son Cronus, who presides over the fall of Adam and Eve, the killing of Abel, and a whole series of Bible stories. The Virgin Mary appears as a Grey Lady, a sorrowing mother puppet appearing in many Schumann productions. The massacre of the innocents and the death of Jesus after the Last Supper are accompanied by Vietnam style air raids. Other well-known pieces include *The Great Warrior* (1963), *A Man Says Goodbye to His Mother* (1966), and *Domestic Resurrection Circus* (1970). After 1974 and many tours across the United States and to Europe, Bread and Puppet moved to a farm in Vermont where it continued to develop new productions, though less devoted to specific political issues and more to its ongoing message of peace, environmental concerns, and universal brotherhood.

Most of the radical alternative theatres of the sixties and early seventies were more specifically politically focused than the Bread and Puppet. New York's Pageant Players, for example, like Bread and Puppet shunned traditional theatre spaces in favor of schools, parks, and streets. Their first production, *The Paper Tiger Pageant* in 1965, was a condemnation of imperialism designed for presentation at peace rallies. *King Con* (1966) explored the evils of giant corporate power and *Laundromat* (1966) utilized an approach that has since become generally known as "invisible theatre," the term given by the Latin American activist director Augusto Boal to a performance that is staged

7. Bread and Puppet Theatre in *What You Possess*, 1990. Photograph by Tony D'Urso. Courtesy of Marvin Carlson.

to raise political consciousness in an audience that does not know it is watching a performance. In *Laundromat* the actors went to a real laundromat and pretended to be customers, arguing among themselves about Vietnam for the benefit of real customers, who did not presumably know that this was a theatre piece. The Pageant Players did not make a specialty of this kind of work, but other groups did, among them Merc Estrin's American Playground in Washington, which staged invisible theatre at places like the White House and the National Archives; the Guerrilla Theater-Ensemble of Michael Doliner at the University of Chicago in 1967; and Sandra Lowell's staged disruptions of office routines in Los Angeles in 1970. Pageant Players broke up at the end of the decade, but most of its members went on to work in other alternative political theatre, some to Oregon, some to California (to found Moving Men) and some remaining in New York (to form the Painted Women Ritual Theatre, the Burning City Theatre, and the Mass Transit Street Theatre).

Boston's OM-Theatre Workshop mixed amateurs and professionals like Bread and Puppet to explore social issues. Its director Julie Portman encouraged collective creations growing out of the group but developed with serious technical training, both physical and spiritual, with an emphasis on yoga exercises. Their first production, *Riot* in 1967, used a racially and economically mixed cast to create a dramatic exploration of racial tensions in the Boston community.

Guerrilla Theatre

In 1973 John Weisman published a study of guerrilla theatre in the United States which estimated that at the height of such activity, around 1970, there were perhaps 50 such organizations in New York and as many as 400 in the country. Although these naturally varied greatly in organization, strategies, and particular focus, they shared a generally leftist orientation and mobilization against the war in Vietnam, as is clear even from the name of a group like the Haight-Ashbury Vietnam Committee, which began presenting anti-war plays in San Francisco in 1966. The San Francisco Red Theatre, as its name suggests, was closely associated with Marxist, particularly Maoist thought, and with the Progressive Labor Party. They presented cartoon-like agit prop dramas recalling the experimental leftist theatre of the thirties, with such titles as "Lay the Bosses Off – Not the Workers." The 1967 "Week of the Angry Arts" in New York not only gathered anti-war artists and performers, but inspired a number of new companies with this orientation, among them the Sixth Street Theatre, which sought a popular audience for its political message by utilizing masks, mime, puppets, and clown acts for shows in such public locations as Central Park.

A similar orientation could be found in one of the main inspirations for the spread of guerrilla theatre in the United States, the campus-based Students for a Democratic Society (SDS). The SDS established chapters on campuses across America during the sixties, largely in protest to Vietnam and the draft but drawing upon a concern for workers and minorities inherited from the Civil Rights Movement and the socialist old left. SDS developed a network of guerrilla or street theatre organizations under the name of the Radical Arts Troupe (RAT), which presented propagandistic skits on class conflict developed collectively. The model for RAT guerrilla theatre was developed in California, especially on the Berkeley campus, but it soon spread to New York City and Princeton and by 1969 there were RAT troupes on most campuses which had a strong SDS presence. Henry Lesnick's 1973 collection, *Guerilla Street Theatre*, includes pieces not only from Berkeley and Princeton, major centers for such activity, but also from less obvious sources, such as the University of Buffalo and the University of Connecticut.

The term guerrilla theatre was also extended to include a wide variety of unscripted but symbolic actions and demonstrations, contributing to what David Mairowitz in *The Radical Soap Opera*, a 1974 history of leftist politics in

America, characterized as a "Politics of Gesture." Particularly associated with such activities were the Yippies (a conflation of the initials for Youth International Party and the then popular term for bohemian drop-outs from society, hippies) such as Abbie Hoffman or Jerry Rubin. The first Yippie "Action," throwing money onto the floor of the New York Stock Exchange in August of 1967, was described by Hoffman as "pure theatre," which needed no external explanation. Similar subsequent "Actions" continued to express an anti-capitalist, anti-war, and anti-establishment, if not directly anarchist aesthetic: dumping soot and garbage upon high officials of the Consolidated Edison power company, for example, or appearing dressed as revolutionary war patriots at public meetings of the House Un-American Activities Committee.

New York as Center and the Return of the Living Theatre

Although anti-war messages dominated much alternative political theatre of the late sixties and early seventies, other social concerns were also important, as the ethnic theatres already mentioned demonstrate. New York in particular, the traditional center of America's melting pot, saw alongside new ethnic companies concerned with the problems of particular ethnic communities other alternative theatres focused upon breaking down the ghetto walls, upon encouraging representatives of this city's traditionally diverse cultures to recognize and address common social and political concerns. The New York Free Theatre, founded by Stephen Waugh in 1967, sought to gather white, black, and Puerto Rican actors and audiences to examine common neighborhood problems. The Soul and Latin theatre, organized in the New York ghetto of East Harlem by Maryat Lee in 1968, sought to develop plays of the ghetto experience to give voice to the black and Puerto Rican inhabitants. Columbian author and director Enrique Vargas, who had presented *commedia dell'arte* style popular theatre in Bogota before coming to New York, founded the Gut Theatre for East Harlem teenagers the following year with similar goals. Both Soul and Latin and Gut Theatre participated in the Radical Theatre Festival in San Francisco in 1968. On the West Coast, the Inner City Repertory Theatre, organized in Los Angeles in 1966, boasted of being the nation's only professional multiracial theatre company, with African American, Asian American, Hispanic, and Native Americans freely mixed in both its productions and its administration.

The Living Theatre returned to America in the fall of 1968, surrounded by rumors of dazzling new productions and of revolutionary contributions to the student uprisings in France in the spring of that year. The company opened

8. The Living Theatre in *Paradise Now*, c. 1968. Photography by Gianfranco Mantegna. Used by permission of the photographer. From the Collection of the University of California–Davis.

their American tour at Yale University, presenting four new pieces developed in Europe: *Frankenstein, Mysteries – and Smaller Pieces, Antigone*, and *Paradise Now*. Here and at a subsequent four-week run at New York's Brooklyn Academy of Music, now emerging as a center for experimental and avant-garde theatre (see Gussow's essay above), the Living's anarchist message and productions aroused enormous controversy, which continued during their cross-country tour. Many considered them still the leading edge of alternative theatre, while others felt them outdated and self-indulgent. Conservative audiences found their advocacy of anarchy, drugs, and nudity offensive (they were several times arrested), while politically radical groups considered them irrelevant and still too preoccupied with the Establishment. These reactions shook Beck and Malina, who returned to Europe determined to renounce per-forming in traditional venues for Establishment audiences. The company split into four cells, one headed by Beck and Malina, to present free theatre to the disenfranchised. Beck and Malina's cell spent a year in Brazil on this project before they were arrested, imprisoned, and finally deported to the U.S. They continued to work outside the theatrical system, performing in industrial and academic communities until 1974, when a grant from the Mellon Foundation allowed them to settle for two years in Pittsburgh. Here they created two major productions on the conditions of the workers, *Six Public Acts* and *The Money Tower*, both performed out of doors in various symbolic locations.

After the Pittsburgh years, Beck and Malina returned again to Europe, where they continued to perform socially committed drama for unconventional audiences and where they developed an epic collective creation combining myth and modern history, *Prometheus*, in 1978. In 1984 they returned again to New York, where Julian Beck died in 1985. Judith Malina and Hanon Reznikov (who played Prometheus) established a new home for the Living Theatre on the Lower East Side, traditionally a poor working-class and immigrant neighborhood, where they continued to carry on the concerns of this group by developing productions in cooperation with homeless people from the neighborhood.

Spaces and Environments

For a variety of reasons – economic, social, and symbolic – many of the alternative political theatres since 1945 have performed in unconventional or untraditional spaces. An important tradition of modern alternative theatre, however, has explored the use of such spaces as a primary interest, without necessarily having a particular political concern. From the late fifties until the eighties such theatre was often called environmental, while in more recent years the term "site-specific theatre" has become more popular. The nationwide civic pageantry movement in the first quarter of the century staged large, usually outdoor spectacles in sites with strong symbolic or historical ties to the persons or events celebrated by these productions, and a new wave of similar spectacles was launched by Paul Green's *The Lost Colony* at Manteo, North Carolina, in 1937, reaching its peak in the fifties and sixties. This tradition of American site-related theatre, though widespread and popular, had only a minor relationship with what came to be called environmental theatre, whose origins, like those of most American alternative theatre, related more to the art world and the bohemian avant-garde than to popular culture.

Richard Schechner first utilized the term "environmental theatre," in reference to a production of Eugène Ionesco's *Victims of Duty* that he directed for the New Orleans Group in 1967. Schechner was one of the founders of the New Orleans Group in 1965, shortly after his involvement with the Free Southern Theatre. The new group was strongly influenced by contemporary explorations in music, painting, and performance, especially the sort of events called

Happenings, which were at this time an important focus of theatrical experimentation. Schechner and Michael Kirby co-edited a special issue of *The Drama Review* in the winter of 1965 dealing with Happenings and the theatre of chance, and this same year Kirby also published a book on Happenings, and Richard Kostelanetz a related study, *The New American Arts*. In preparing for the special issue, Schechner and Kirby interviewed John Cage about the 1953 Black Mountain Concert and his philosophy of chance and found art, an interview that deeply influenced Schechner's subsequent work. Schechner claims that he took the term "environmental theatre" from Allan Kaprow, the inventor of Happenings, but used it in a somewhat different way. Kaprow always distanced himself and his work from theatre and saw Happenings as evolving not from a performance but from an art background. According to Kaprow's history of the form, cubist collages began introducing non-paint materials into painting. These works became more three-dimensional and gradually left the canvas to exist on their own, eventually filling large spaces and creating "environments," artistic surroundings through which spectators were free to move. Complex environments, with human figures added, and the activities of spectators more regulated, were, according to Kaprow, the first Happenings.

Before discussing Schechner's environmental experimentation, it might be well to mention the importance of *The Drama Review* to both the chronicling of and inspiration for alternative theatre in America, particularly during the years of his first editorship, from 1962 to 1969. During the sixties American theatre entered its richest period of experimentation since the New Stagecraft, and – as in the twenties – one journal in particular served as a sort of clearing-house for the new ideas, seeking out, encouraging, and publicizing new work and new artists. What *Theatre Arts* was to the twenties, *The Drama Review* was to the sixties. *TDR* began in 1955 as the *Carleton Drama Review*, becoming the *Tulane Drama Review* when its editor Robert Corrigan moved to Tulane in 1957. It stressed new voices in the European theatre – Brecht and Artaud, Ionesco, Genet, Ghelderode, and Betti. When Schechner became editor in 1962 he continued for a time this literary orientation, but in 1964, with a special issue on the Living Theatre and a double issue on Stanislavsky in America, he began to look more at production and performance. The Spring 1965 issue contained two articles by Eugenio Barba introducing the work of Polish experimental director Jerzy Grotowski, whose performances and theories became highly influential in the alternative American theatre of the late sixties and seventies. During the following years, individual articles and special numbers of *TDR* focused on other major issues and manifestations of the alternative theatre scene: guerrilla theatre in summer 1966, black theatre in summer 1968, relationships between experimental theatre and the social sciences in the summer of 1967.

Victims of Duty was for Schechner a preliminary experiment in environmental theatre. The entire theatre was converted into the Choubert living room, with the audience scattered about the setting, sometimes directly addressed by the actors and never able to see and hear the entire production because of sight lines and overlapping scenes. These concerns – audience participation, multiple focus, a total performance environment surrounding actors and audience, and the mixing of art and life – were further developed by Schechner with The Performance Group, which he founded in New York in 1967. The best-known work of this group was *Dionysus in '69,* a collective creation growing out of Euripides' *The Bacchae,* staged in a setting designed by Michael Kirby and Schechner's designer from New Orleans, Jerry Rojo, consisting of an open central space surrounded by open scaffold towers, some as high as five stories, for the spectators. Inspired by Grotowski, then giving workshops at New York University, Schechner emphasized physical action, audience involvement, and actor vulnerability. The total nudity in its orgiastic scenes gave this production a particular notoriety even in the free-wheeling late sixties.

Makbeth (1969), the Group's next production, put more emphasis on diverse audience experience, with multiple scenes from Shakespeare being played simultaneously in an environment which allowed audiences to circulate freely and select their focus. *Commune* (1970) had no basic text, but began with two recent events of horror, the My Lai massacre by American soldiers in Vietnam and the murder of film actress Sharon Tate and her friends by members of the Charles Manson commune, and developed improvisations relating these two events to each other and to themes of domination and violence in American history, literary works, the Bible, folk songs, and spirituals. This production was the first involving Elizabeth LeCompte (as assistant director) and Spalding Gray (as an actor), new members who had joined Schechner as a result of their enthusiasm over *Dionysus in '69.*

During the seventies the group continued to explore audience–stage relationships but in a less radical way and with generally more conventional scripts, such as Sam Shepard's *The Tooth of Crime* in 1972 and Brecht's *Mother Courage* in 1974. Their last production was Genet's *The Balcony* in 1979. Certain members of the company, particularly LeCompte and Gray, were interested in taking it in different directions from those which engaged Schechner. The Group disbanded in 1980, but Gray, LeCompte, and several other former members of it formed a new company that continued to perform in the same space, the Performing Garage on Wooster Street in New York's Soho district. From the street they took the name the Wooster Group, and under this name became one of America's leading alternative theatres during the eighties and nineties.

In 1972 Christopher Hardman, who had worked with Peter Schumann of the

Bread and Puppet Theatre, joined Laura Farabough to form The Beggar's Theatre, which utilized the sculptural qualities of Bread and Puppet to create visual spectacles in California that at first suggested social concerns like those of Bread and Puppet, but gradually became more centered on the interplay of the visual elements, often drawn from everyday events and characters, with their environments, usually out of doors. Partly responsible for this shift were Lary Graber and his wife Evelyn Lewis, a composer and dancer with a strong interest in Asian theatre, who joined Hardman and Farabough in 1977, when the venture was renamed Snake Theatre. The found environments of their productions included spectacular natural settings, such as the beachfront Marin headlands near San Francisco for *Somewhere in the Pacific* (1978), and evocative man-made ones, such as an abandoned gas station in Sausalito, California, for *Auto* (1979). After the death of Graber in 1980, Hardman and Farabough formed two separate companies, Antenna and Nightfire.

During the eighties site-specific theatre organizations appeared across the United States. The Vermont Ensemble Theatre, organized as an environmental theatre company in 1984, presented a widely reviewed production of Thornton Wilder's *Our Town* in 1986 with each act presented in a different church or hall around the village green of Middlebury, Vermont, and with staged outdoor vignettes of village life presented to the spectators as they strolled by lantern light from one building to another. Vidlak's Family Café, a functioning diner in Omaha, Nebraska, presented during the mid-eighties a whole series of plays written to be given in the diner, with actors (many of them carried through several of the plays) mixing with the regular patrons of the diner. This was not, however, an example of "invisible theatre," but was known and accepted by the audience as a regular, if unconventional, theatrical performance.

Probably the best-known West Coast example of such theatre was the multimedia spectacles of Lin Hixon, performed with huge casts and crews in the Los Angeles area. Her 1984 *Hey John, Did You Take the Camino Far?* occupied the loading dock of a downtown industrial building, but its song and dance numbers and its teenage gangs and their cars spilled out into the adjacent public streets with no clear division between the performance and the city beyond.

En Garde Arts

In New York, En Garde Arts, devoted to site-specific theatre, was founded in 1985 by Anne Hamburger, and became not only an important producing organization in its own right, but a venue for some of the most innovative alternative theatre artists of the period. The first En Garde Arts production to attract wide attention was *At the Chelsea* in 1988. Several rooms in the Chelsea Hotel, a famous New York architectural and literary landmark, were converted into small spaces for performances and tableaux which audiences could sample as they wished. Various actors, performance artists, and avant-garde artists and composers contributed to this program. One room was devoted to a post-modern version of the popular American TV series *A Little House on the Prairie*, with the youngest sister played by a hay-chomping goat. This was the contribution of the Squat Theatre, a well-known New York experimental company that had made its home nearby on Twenty-third Street from 1977, when they emigrated from Hungary, until 1985.

Squat Theatre shared certain central concerns of environmental theatre, particularly the exploration of the permeable boundary between reality and theatrical presentation. Although they constantly experimented with a wide variety of media and framing devices, they were best known for a basic con-figuration used in most of their Twenty-third Street productions. The audi-ence entered a space originally designed as a shop and was seated at the back of the shop facing the street. The large shopfront window could be curtained off, but it was freqently left open. Performances took place primarily between audience and window, and although the performers themselves sometimes mixed with the street life outside, the unrehearsed reactions of passers-by and the normal passing life of the street provided the major use of this per-spective and a part of the theatre's aesthetic. The occasional nudity in the productions naturally caused particular surprise and occasional protest from passers-by, and in 1978 the mayor's office officially investigated the company following complaints about a nude woman cooking in the window during the production of *Andy Warhol's Last Love*. The Midtown Enforcement Project, however, found Squat a "serious group of artists" engaged in "radical avant-garde theatre," and no charges were filed.

One of En Garde Arts' most ambitious productions took place in 1990, and introduced New York audiences to the work of Iranian-born Reza Abdoh of Los Angeles, who before his death in 1995 (at the age of thirty), was widely con-sidered one of the most innovative and imaginative avant-garde American directors. In California Abdoh assembled a company with whom most of his works were created, but these fragmented, multilayered, multimedia crea-tions, full of pop culture references and Artaudian extremity, were all his own creations. Abdoh was invited to New York by En Garde Arts after his break-through production, *Minamata*, a sprawling, epic dance-theatre work dealing with the mercury poisoning of Japanese fishermen, caused a sensation on the West Coast. For En Garde, Abdoh created *Father Was a Peculiar Man*, loosely based on Dostoevsky's *The Brothers Karamazov*. This production employed sixty actors and was staged in various locations over a four-block area of New York's meatpacking district. Some scenes mixed audience and actors in set-tings taking up entire blocks, others placed the audience on bleachers to

9. En Garde Arts' production of *The Trojan Women a Love Story* (1996) by Charles L. Mee, Jr. Directed by Tina Landau, the production was performed in the ruins of the East River Park Amphitheatre. Pictured are Stephen Webber and Nancy Hume. Photograph by William Rivelli. Courtesy of En Garde Arts.

observe large open theatricalized vistas, still others allowed audience members to wander on their own through the dim recesses of an abandoned packing house, to witness intimate tableaux of torture and ecstasy.

Abdoh returned to the West Coast for his next spectacle, an epic parody in Spanish of television novels, *Pasos en la Obscuridad*, for Peter Sellars's international celebration of multiculturalism in Los Angeles. Abdoh then embarked on his most ambitious project, a trilogy meditation on violence and ecstacy in contemporary America consisting of *The Hip-Hop Waltz of Eurydice*, *Bogeyman*, and *The Law of Remains*. The Los Angeles Theatre Center was to premiere these works, but it went bankrupt before the third, and Abdoh's company, Dar A Luz, presented this instead in New York, in an abandoned hotel, where it was the sensation of the 1992–93 season, compared by some critics in its power and originality to the seminal works of the Living Theatre.

Tight, Right, White (1993) and *Quotations from a Ruined City* (1994) were the final works in Abdoh's tragically brief career.

The next major En Garde Arts production after *Father Was a Peculiar Man* was Charles Mee's *Another Person is a Foreign Country* (1991), directed by Anne Bogart, who had gained a reputation during the eighties for her environmental productions, often with strong political overtones, in university and experimental theatres in America and Europe. *Another Person*, dealing with disabled or "different" persons, was given at the Towers, an abandoned and ruined former hospital and nursing home on Central Park. In 1994 Bogart directed in New York's Masonic Ballroom for En Garde Arts her own *Marathon Dancing*, part of a trilogy she created on American popular entertainment. In 1996 she directed Juliana Francis, the leading actress for Reza Abdoh, in a one-woman multimedia production, *Go Go Go*.

Another director featured by En Garde Arts in the nineties was Tina Landau, who had a strong interest in the work of Abdoh. In 1993 she staged for En Garde Charles L. Mee's *Orestes,* a nightmarish reworking of Euripides, on the ruins of two giant piers in the Hudson River, and in 1994 her own *Stonewall*, also on the Hudson, a carnival musical meditation on Greenwich Village in 1969.

Robert Wilson

Although political and social concerns continued to contribute significantly to American alternative theatre after the peak of interest in such concerns in the late sixties and early seventies, a number of important new artists and groups focused more upon formal and structural concerns, creating a more abstract theatre with artistic connections to minimalism in the visual arts, certain trends in modern and postmodern dance, and the concerns of the creators of events like the happenings. The best known of these formalist theatre artists is Robert Wilson, who began his career as a painter and architect (though with some theatre activities, including designing the larger-than-life-size puppets for Van Itallie's *America Hurrah*) and whose major works, both large and small, have always strongly reflected this visual orientation. Wilson's first productions, in 1965, were essentially modern dance pieces, but he was not interested in working with professional performers. Instead he saw performance as a means to allow all people to develop their potential, and he worked by preference with untrained and handicapped persons, a central interest of the Byrd Hoffman School of Byrds, which he founded to carry on his work in 1969. The same year he presented in New York *The King of Spain*, which like the dance experiments of Ann Halprin encouraged the performers to do everyday activities in a non-theatrical manner.

Wilson became interested in focusing upon the perception of experience, and began utilizing extreme slow motion to induce a kind of dream state of heightened awareness. He also began combining smaller pieces into larger and more complex ones, so that his productions of the early seventies grew to lengths rivaling the classic dance spectacles of Asia. *The King of Spain* became the second act of *The Life and Times of Sigmund Freud,* which in turn became the first three acts of *Deafman Glance,* a spectacle that lasted eight hours, even before Wilson added to it a three-hour prologue. *The Life and Times of Joseph Stalin* (1973), including parts of each of these previous productions, ran for twelve hours.

Sigmund Freud was presented at the Brooklyn Academy of Music in 1969, and it gained Wilson his first wide attention. Many critics were puzzled by the work, but Richard Foreman, who was just beginning his own influential career in the American alternative theatre, wrote a prophetic review of Wilson's work in the *Village Voice,* calling the work a masterpiece of artist's theatre and noting that Wilson was one of the few theatre artists beginning to apply to theatre a new aesthetic, that of many contemporary painters, musicians, dancers, and filmmakers, who created non-manipulative works in which an audience member could explore his or her own perceptions.

Deafman Glance premiered at the University of Iowa in 1970 and was presented at the Brooklyn Academy the following year. It was inspired by Raymond Andrews, an adolescent deaf-mute whom Wilson befriended and who played the leading role in this production. Not a sound occured in this collage-epic, which on one level suggested the fantasy world of a child like Andrews and on another a Western collective unconscious with a dazzling array of images drawn from literature and legend, religion and folklore, high art and popular culture.

After his largest undertaking, the 168-hour epic *KA MOUNTAIN,* staged in Iran for a festival organized by the Shah, Wilson returned to the Brooklyn Academy for the relatively modest twelve-hour *Joseph Stalin,* incorporating material from many of his earlier works and providing a kind of summation of the first phase of his work, which his chronicler Stefan Brecht has called the "theatre of visions" period (*The Theatre of Visions,* 267). During the mid-seventies, Brecht suggested, Wilson did not give up an image-based theatre, but became occupied as well with an assault on discursive language. The opening work in this phase, *A Letter for Queen Victoria,* was Wilson's only Broadway production. Much of its language was derived from Christopher Knowles, a gifted but autistic child who, like Raymond Andrews, provided Wilson with a pathway into another mode of perception. Knowles and Wilson's grandmother had major roles in this production, which offered a kind of apocalyptic deconstruction of both language and history.

Knowles continued to be an inspiration for Wilson and appeared as an actor with him in the 1975 *The $ Value of Man* at the Brooklyn Academy and in two small 1980 plays, *Dialogue* and *Curious George*, but the prolific Wilson was exploring other directions as well. In 1977 he appeared with Lucinda Childs in an abstract piece *I Was Sitting on My Patio this Guy Appeared I Thought I Was Hallucinating*. Childs was one of a group of dancers, including Simone Forti, Yvonne Rainer, Trisha Brown, Steve Paxton, and David Gordon, who under the inspiration of Cage, Cunningham, and the early Happenings, began during the sixties to collaborate with experimental artists like Robert Rauschenberg and Robert Morris to incoporate everyday material and objects into their work. A center for this work in the sixties was the Judson Church, where Childs appeared in Morris's multimedia meditation on Muybridge action photos, *Waterman Switch,* in 1965. In the early seventies Childs, Brown, and others choreographed works by first working out abstract geometrical patterns on paper, somewhat in the manner of a Cage composition. Such was the working method of the 1975 works *Locus* by Brown and *Congeries on Edges for 20 Obliques* by Childs.

After *Patio*, Wilson collaborated with Childs and with avant-garde composer Philip Glass on a much larger work, the five-hour opera, *Einstein on the Beach*, which was toured widely in Europe before being presented at the Metropolitan Opera in 1976 and revived in 1984 at the Brooklyn Academy. *Einstein* is perhaps the best known of Wilson's works and in many ways typical of them – a sequence of striking visual and aural images replace traditional narrative, the only form an abstract mathematical configuration, here based on repeating triads. An even more ambitious work was undertaken by Wilson for performance at the Olympic Arts Festival in 1984, another twelve-hour piece, this one called *the CIVIL warS*. Wilson had now become at least as well known in Europe as in America, and pieces of the new work were developed there and in Tokyo to be assembled in Los Angeles. The text was created by Heiner Müller, the leading German experimental theatre writer of this generation. Funding for the Los Angeles production fell through, and so American audiences were able only to see a touring production of the "knee plays" – short pieces Wilson created as interludes between the major sections of the work – and the Cologne section, which was revived at the Brooklyn Academy.

Wilson continued to work with Müller texts, producing his *Hamletmachine* with students from New York University in 1986 and his *Quartett* at the American Repertory Theatre in Cambridge in 1988. The ART has become one of Wilson's favored venues in America, offering his first staging of a classic, *Alcestis*, in 1986, and his version of Ibsen's last play, *When We Dead Awaken,* in 1992. The Brooklyn Academy has continued to stage most of the larger Wilson works done in America, *The Forest* (based on the Babylonian *Gilgamesh* epic) in 1988, *The Black Rider* (with text by William Burroughs, based on Weber's romantic opera, *Der Freischütz*) in 1993, and *Alice* (based on

10. The interior of the spaceship in Robert Wilson's and Philip Glass's *Einstein on the Beach*, 1976. Photograph: copyright (©) 1976 Babette Mangolte, all rights of reproduction reserved.

Alice in Wonderland) in 1995, though Wilson did return to his home state of Texas to direct Büchner's *Danton's Death* at Houston's Alley Theatre in 1992. More recently, Wilson has presented smaller works as part of the Lincoln Center Serious Fun Festival, an important summer program of experimental work. Here he did his own monologue version of *Hamlet* in 1995 and two stagings of Gertrude Stein works, *Dr. Faustus Lights the Lights* in 1992 and *Four Saints in Three Acts* in 1996.

Richard Foreman

Richard Foreman, an early champion of Wilson, has, like Wilson, been a leader in structural, imagistic alternative theatre in America ever since the late sixties. Foreman has cited Gertrude Stein as an important influence on his work, and like Stein he has been particularly interested in the phenomenology of performance, urging the audience to consider the experience itself and the operations of the mind on that experience rather than follow some discursive narrative. To this end he founded what he called the Ontological-Hysteric

Theatre in 1968. Foreman's early works focused strongly upon phenomenology, placing an object or actor on stage and considering ways of looking at this. Sequences were interrupted by sharp noises, by the appearance of signs commenting on the situation or providing reception suggestions, or by similar miked comments from Foreman himself. Tempo was manipulated, sometimes resulting in extreme slow-motion that suggested the rhythms of Wilson. According to Foreman, his first works, *Angelface* (1968), *Ida-Eyed* (1969) and *Total Recall* (1970), dealt directly with objects, seeking to expose their essence. With *Hotel China* (1971) he became more interested in the effect of objects upon audiences and how objects might be manipulated by the desire of the performer. Fantasy and surrealistic effects began to enter the work, like an airborne house in *Hotel China*. In *Sophia=Wisdom, Part 3* the miked voice of Foreman himself began to be added to the already common signs as another level of commentary, and soon after, the taped voice of actors added another level still. In *The Book of Splendors, Part Two* (1976), Kate Manheim carried on conversations with her own taped voice, which gave lines that usually seemed to be not her own thoughts but those of Foreman. This separation of voice or image from actor by the use of projected images or miked sound has become a common feature not only in the work of Foreman, but in many of the leading alternative theatre artists of the seventies, among them Laurie Anderson, Mabou Mines, and the Wooster Group.

Foreman has credited much of the playfulness and fantasy in his early work to Kate Manheim, who for many years was a leading character in his plays. In the early plays the same names repeatedly appear – Ben, Sophia, Max, Karl, Rhoda – though they are not characters in a conventional sense since they merely exist in Foreman's surrealistic environment, without backgrounds or coherent and ongoing goals or desires. Although a four-play "sequence," *Sophia=Wisdom, Parts 1–4* (1971–74) featured that "character," Manheim (Rhoda) had by *Rhoda in Potatoland (Her Fall-Starts)* (1974) moved to a central position in the group. Manheim was also interested in the shock and playful possibilities of performing in the nude, and included nude scenes in most of the works of this period, adding to their provocative quality.

With *Pandering to the Masses: A Misrepresentation* (1975) Foreman began to move away from his preoccupation with the manipulation of objects toward the manipulation of thought processes, assembling his new works from fragments taken out of jottings in his own notebooks, thoughts triggered by his wide-ranging reading, often in philosophic works. In the late seventies Foreman gave up the loft in Soho which had been his theatre and began appearing in a range of other locations, first with Joseph Papp's Public Theater, which presented several of his works beginning with *Penguin Touquet* in 1981. In 1985 he collaborated with the Wooster Group to present *Miss Universal Happiness*, which Foreman saw as the end of another period in his

11. Richard Foreman's *Rhoda in Potatoland*, 1974. Photograph courtesy of Richard Foreman. Photograph: copyright (©) 1975 Babette Mangolte, all rights of reproduction reserved.

work, one that pushed toward a kind of Dionysian frenzy. His next work, *The Cure* (1986), began moving in a more contemplative direction, seeking within himself and his work mythic and archetypical resonances, a direction that may be traced through his more recent work such as *What Did He See?* (1988), *Eddy Goes to Poetry City* (1991), S*amuel's Major Problems* (1993), and *The Universe* (1996). For Foreman, Wilson, and others discussed in this chapter, see also chapter 5, "Directors and Direction."

Michael Kirby, one of the major chroniclers and theorists of happenings and the turn toward formalism that he called "the new theatre," created what he called The Structuralist Workshop in New York where, in such productions as *Photoanalysis* (1976) and *Double Gothic* (1978), he assembled narrative fragments, sounds, and images in formal patterns that he hoped would approximate the experience of a musical composition, with interpretation, if any, left to the subjective experience of the audience.

Other artists on both coasts during the seventies continued like Kirby to apply the abstract and non-objective strategies of such phenomena as events, environments, and happenings to the creation of highly formal theatrical expressions. One center of such activity was San Francisco, where most such productions developed not out of theatre, but out of related arts. In the early seventies dancer Suzanne Hellmuth began working with sculptor Jock Reynolds. Their first major collaboration, *Hospital* (1977), presented a collage of sounds, images, props, and tasks assembled from lengthy observations of activities in a San Francisco hospital. Similarly, extended observations of the life in San Francisco Bay provided the raw material for their 1979 spectacle *Navigation.* Rather closer to the approach of Wilson in his intuitive assembling of sounds, shapes, and colors is Alan Finneran, a San Francisco sculptor who in 1972 formed Soon 3, for the production of "performance landscapes," involving moving scupture, lighting, sound, and projections. Living persons were added as compositional elements to his 1975 *Desire Circus*, and in *Black Water Echo* (1977) such persons began moving elements about, in the first of what Finneran called "task activated landscapes." Subsequent productions – *A Wall in Venice/3 Women/Wet Shadows* (1978), *Tropical Proxy* (1979), and *The Man in the Nile at Night* (1980) – became increasingly elaborate in their use of movement, costume, fictional references, and finally scraps of language, but these did not move the performances closer to traditional linear and narrative drama. The new elements remained parts of a formal structure, as they are in the work of Foreman.

Meredith Monk

Clearly the formalist alternative theatre significantly overlaps many of the concerns of other art forms, particularly those of the modern visual arts and modern dance. The line between certain aspects of modern alternative theatre and of modern dance is especially fluid and certain major artists of the period since the late sixties have been equally claimed by the worlds of dance and of theatre (though the useful term dance-theatre has never become as well established as *Tanztheater* has in Germany). One of the best known of such artists is Meredith Monk – composer, singer, filmmaker, choreographer, and director. During the mid-sixties Monk was a choreographer and performer at the legendary Judson Dance Theatre, working with Lucinda Childs and others there, but in 1968 she formed her own company, The House, devoted to the crossing of traditional artistic boundaries. She has since carried out more than one hundred interdisciplinary projects. Monk was a pioneer in site-specific performance, creating one of the earliest examples of such work, *Juice* (1969), consisting of three parts performed (with "intermissions" of a week or more) in three different locations, beginning at the Guggenheim Museum and ending in Monk's loft in Soho, and one of the most ambitious, *American Archeology #1*, in several sites on Roosevelt Island in 1994 for a New York based site-specific dance-producing organization, Dancing in the Streets, created in 1984 by Elise Bernhardt.

Monk first achieved wide attention with two choreographed epics, *Vessel* (1971), based on material from the life of Joan of Arc, and *Quarry* (1976), suggesting the devastation of World War II as seen through the images of a feverish child. Movement and dance have always been an important component of Monk's productions, and were central to many of them, as in one of her best-known creations, *Education of a Girl-Child,* premiered in 1973 and revived in 1979 and 1993. This famous work ended with a forty-five-minute solo dance by Monk, a *tour de force* depiction of the stages in a woman's life running backward from extreme old age to childhood. In addition to many smaller compositions and to films and videos, Monk created two more epic dance-theatre pieces in the early eighties, *Speciman Days* (1981), drawing on images from Walt Whitman and the American Civil War, and *The Games*, an exploration of a post-nuclear landscape that she developed in collaboration with Ping Chong. Many of Monk's works integrate film with live movement, from the early *16 Millimeter Earrings* (1966) to the solo work *Volcano Songs* (1990), but perhaps her most original experimentation has been with the exploration of the expressive range and potential of the human voice, a particular concern of the Meredith Monk and Vocal Ensemble, which she founded in 1978. A major expression of this concern was *ATLAS: an opera in three parts* (1991). More recently the Vocal Ensemble presented a non-narrative oratorio, *The Politics of Quiet* (1996), at the Brooklyn Academy.

Ping Chong

Ping Chong was a member of Mededith Monk's company from 1971 to 1978, but he produced his own first work, *Lazarus,* as early as 1972 and formed his own company, the Fiji Theatre Company (later the Ping Chong Company) in 1975. He shares Monk's interests in site-specific and multimedia work, but with his own visual vocabulary and rhythm. His environmental installations have been created in Canada and Europe and in 1988 he developed a triad of site-specific installations called *Plage Concerte* for the Three Rivers Arts Festival in Pittsburgh. Approximately one-third of his more than thirty productions, including *Skiing: A State of Being* (1988) and *Brightness* (1989), have been offered at La MaMa ETC, one of New York's leading venues for experimental theatre since its founding by Ellen Stewart in 1961. Ping Chong derives his material from a wide range of sources – literary, artistic, historical, philosophical, and artistic. His high-tech interests took him in the mid-eighties into the domain of science fiction in such works as *The Angels of Swedenborg* (1985) at the Brooklyn Academy. More recently, he has turned his attention to explorations of East–West relationships in *Deshima* (premiered in Holland in 1990 and first given in America at La MaMa in 1993), and *Chinoiserie,* premiered at the Brooklyn Academy in 1995.

Martha Clarke

Martha Clarke emerged in the mid-eighties as another leader in the creation of dance-theatre, her work grouped by reviewers with that of Robert Wilson, Ping Chong, Mabou Mines, and such European visual artists as Tadeusz Kantor of Poland and Peter Brook of France. Clarke was co-founder of the Pilobolus dance company in 1972. Pilobolus is best known for abstract gymnastic work, but Clarke was more interested in compositions utilizing images from the European painterly and literary tradition like the 1974 *Monkshood's Farewell*, based on medieval illuminations. She left Pilobolus in 1979 and began exploring dance-theatre, achieving her first success in this form with *A Metamorphosis in Miniature* (1982), based on the Kafka story. The two works that established her reputation were *The Garden of Earthly Delights* (1984, revived 1987), inspired by the hallucinatory landscapes of Hieronymus Bosch and the peasants of Pieter Brueghel, and *Vienna Lusthaus* (1986), inspired by the works of Egon Schiele and other artists of turn-of-the-century Vienna.

Clarke returned to Kafka for her 1987 *The Hunger Artist*, woven from Kafka's writings and the biography, and including both sung and spoken material. This excursion into spoken theatre was not well received, however, and Clarke returned to visual and sung material for her 1988 *Miracolo d'Amore*, with images based on Tiepolo's Punchinello drawings and with a Monteverdian score by Richard Peaslee, a frequent collaborator with Clarke. One of Clarke's most ambitious productions was the 1990 *Endangered Species* at the Brooklyn Academy, which drew upon the circus pastels of Toulouse-Lautrec and evocations of the American Civil War and the Holocaust and included a number of live animals. Critical response to this work was highly negative, which may have encouraged Clarke to turn away from the creation of new works to apply her powerful visual imagination to traditional opera, in such productions as *The Magic Flute* in 1992 and *Così fan tutte* in 1993 at the Glimmerglass Summer Opera in upstate New York.

Laurie Anderson

Most of the alternative theatre multimedia formalists have drawn their public largely from those interested in contemporary experimental art and performance, even Robert Wilson, who is surely the most prominent of those so far discussed. One artist working in this general area has, however, enjoyed a more popular success and visibility. This is Laurie Anderson, particularly with *United States* (1983), a seven-hour "performance portrait of the country" which attracted a total audience of over 85,000 to a multimedia production including stories, songs, slide projections, film, and even a percussion solo played on Anderson's amplified skull. Anderson began her career doing small-scale multimedia productions based on autobiographical material such as the 1977 *For Instances,* often at The Kitchen, another important home for experimental performance in New York, but she was inspired by Wilson and Glass's *Einstein on the Beach* to undertake the more elaborate spectacles that, supported by the great recording success she enjoyed with such songs as "Superman," established her reputation.

During the eighties and nineties Anderson contributed to the alternative theatre both as a composer for the work of other avant-garde directors (creating for example the music for Robert Wilson's staging of *Alcestis* in 1986) and as creator of her own new productions exploring political and social concerns of contemporary society, *Empty Places* (1989), a solo piece, and *The Nerve Bible* (1993), with Anderson as the leading performer.

The Wooster Group and Mabou Mines

Two groups have been most prominent in what some have called the "second wave" of Off-Off Broadway experimentation, appearing in the late sixties and early seventies (the first wave having been launched by the Living and Open theatres). These are the Wooster Group and Mabou Mines. The Wooster Group collectively created their first work, *Sakonnet Point,* in 1974. Like subsequent Wooster Group pieces, and unlike the Performance Group creations, *Sakonnet Point* had no coherent narrative, but was woven out of a collection of "found" material contributed by the performers – specific physical objects, autobiographical fragments from Spalding Gray, scraps of text, bits of movement and action.

Among the influences on the developing aesthetic of the Wooster Group Elizabeth LeCompte has cited Robert Wilson's work, especially *Deafman Glance,* with its emphasis on non-linear but geometric form and the visual, and that of Richard Foreman, especially *Pain(t),* which suggested ways of suggesting human actions abstractly. LeCompte was also interested in the dance works of Meredith Monk, especially *Education of a Girl-Child,* and in the one-man performances of Stuart Sherman, who created strange and powerful dramatic effects by manipulating found everyday objects rather in the manner of puppets.

Sakonnet Point became the first work in a trilogy, including *Rumstick Road* (1977) and *Nayatt School* (1979), all beginning with autobiographical material from Gray but rapidly expanding to include material from popular and classical recordings, spoken records, taped telephone conversations (causing a controversy of this use of "private" material), slides and films, and a strange assortment of physical objects. The final piece also included the first extended autobiographical monologue by Gray, a form that would eventually become his favored means of expression, and sections from T. S. Eliot's *The Cocktail Party*, the Wooster Group's first "recycling" of a traditional dramatic text. *Point Judith* (1979) served as a kind of epilogue to this cycle, to the first phase of the Group's work, and to the centrality of Gray. During these years other key members were added to the Group, first Ron Vawter, who soon became a leading actor for the Group, then Libby Howes, who took leading female parts until her departure in 1981. Kate Valk, who arrived in 1979, filled in for her and soon became the Group's new leading woman. Willem Dafoe, the other best-known member of the group, joined in 1977, having previously worked with Theatre X, an experimental group in Milwaukee. The Group's designer and technical director, Jim Clayburgh, has created a unique visual look for Wooster Group performances – partly environmental, partly presentational, partly rough-edged and industrial, partly negotiated by media, and invariably recycling physical material from earlier productions, just as the performances continually recycle and rearrange material from the performers' lives, their previous work, and the surrounding culture.

Gray's autobiographical monologue that began *Nayatt School* may be taken as the first of a continuing series of such monologues that he has created since 1979. These in their totality have amounted to a kind of performance autobiography, beginning with *Terrors of Pleasure, Sex and Death to the Age of 14* (1979) and catching up to the writing of the work being performed in *Monster in a Box* (1988). The best known of this series was *Swimming to Cambodia* (1984), a reflection on a wide variety of contemporary concerns inspired by Gray's work on the film *The Killing Fields.*

As Gray moved into his own performance career, the Wooster Group began a second "trilogy," *The Road to Immortality*, turning to more general cultural explorations, but still exploring collage constructions of found and improvised material. The first two parts of this trilogy proved highly controversial, due to some of the "found" material incorporated, blackface routines in *Route 1 & 9* (1981) which many found racially offensive, and borrowings from Arthur Miller's *The Crucible* in *L.S.D. (. . .Just the High Points. . .)* (1985), inspiring a threatened lawsuit from Miller until the material was rewritten. The third work, *Frank Dell's The Temptation of St. Antony* (1989) aroused less controversy, but was no less complex in its weaving together of sources, which included material from Lenny Bruce, Gustave Flaubert, and Ingmar Bergman. During the nineties the group gradually moved toward the presentation of more conventional dramatic texts, though always with the high-tech yet rough-edged, non-realistic style unique to this company. As an "epilogue" to their second trilogy they offered *Brace Up!* (1990), their first work to follow closely the narrative frame of a traditional play, here Chekhov's *Three Sisters*, though filtered through an electronic web of film, video, and miked passages

12. The Wooster Group in *The Road to Immortality: Part Two (. . . Just the High Points . . .)*, 1985. Pictured (left to right, seated at table): Peyton Smith, Jeff Webster, Norman Frisch; (left to right, in front): Ron Vawter, Kate Valk, Willem Dafoe. Photograph by Bob van Dantzig. Courtesy of Anne Reiss and The Wooster Group.

and with a permeating overlay of reference to Japanese performance traditions. During the early nineties, the Wooster Group developed two productions, *Fish Story 1 and 2*, which began with material from *Brace Up!* and gradually shifted to material focused on Eugene O'Neill's *The Emperor Jones*. O'Neill's *The Hairy Ape*, which followed, was developed during much of 1995, and was the Group's most faithful adaptation to date of a traditional dramatic text, though unquestionably reinvigorated by the Group's distinctive style.

After the departure of Spalding Gray, the Wooster Group has remained fairly cohesive as an ensemble, even though certain of its members also appeared in films or in other performances, as did Ron Vawter (who died in 1994), with his acclaimed one-man recreation of "performances" by recent homosexual men, one open and the other closeted, *Roy Cohn/Jack Smith*, in 1992.

The other best-known alternative theatre company during the eighties, Mabou Mines, was much looser in its organization, with important members sometimes alone, sometimes in varying combinations, pursuing careers that took them in a variety of different directions. The roots of Mabou Mines are in San Francisco, where in the early sixties director/playwright Lee Breuer worked with actress Ruth Maleczech, who had worked earlier with the San Francisco Mime Troupe. In 1965 Breuer and Maleczech went to Paris, where they lived with San Francisco friends JoAnne Akalaitis and composer Philip Glass (later a frequent collaborator with Robert Wilson and other experimental directors and choreographers), and there they met actor David Warrilow.

In 1970 these five artists settled in New York, and began creating pieces based on their exposure to theatre in California and Europe and weaving together popular culture, film, and the emotional autobiography of Breuer, whose psyche provided raw material for this group as Spalding Gray did for the Wooster Group. This was most clearly seen in the early psychic biographical explorations Breuer called "animations," *The Red Horse Animation* (1970), *B. Beaver Animation* (1975), and *The Shaggy Dog Animation* (1978), all premiered at art museums rather than theatres. The group established itself in theatre work, however, with a highly praised trilogy of three short works by Beckett at the Theater for the New City in 1975. During the late seventies David Warrilow left Mabou Mines (though he appeared with Ruth Maleczech in 1987 at the Brooklyn Academy in a production of *Zangezi* by the Russian avant-gardist Velimer Khlebnikov), while actors Bill Raymond and Fred Neumann joined the company. JoAnne Akalaitis also emerged as a major director during this period, with her imagistic productions of Beckett's *Cascando* (1975), the evocation of French novelist Colette, *Dressed Like an Egg* (1977), and a pop culture view of the atomic threat, *Dead-End Kids* (1980).

During the eighties the reputation of Mabou Mines steadily grew, even as its various members also pursued careers outside the group. For the group JoAnne Akalaitis directed *Through the Leaves* by the German neo-naturalist Franz Xaver Kroetz in 1984, but her major work was now at other theatres. She and Glass offered a major production at the Brooklyn Academy, *The Photographer*, in 1983, and they worked together also on a controversial *Endgame* at the American Repertory Theatre in 1984, publicly renounced by Samuel Beckett. At the Minneapolis Guthrie Theater she directed Georg Büchner's *Leonce and Lena* in 1987 and Jean Genet's *The Screens* in 1989. That same year she presented her first Shakespeare, a controversial Victorian gothic version of *Cymbeline* at the New York Public Theater. In 1991 she presented *Henry IV* there and, much to the surprise of New York's theatre world, was named as his successor by Joseph Papp, the founder of this major Off-Broadway cultural establishment. Akalaitis's own productions during her brief directorship, Ford's *'Tis Pity She's a Whore* and Büchner's *Woyzeck* (both 1992) were well received, but her administration of the theatre drew critical attack and she was asked by the trustees to resign in 1993. Since then she has returned to freelance directing, sometimes with former Mabou Mines colleagues, as in the stage adaptation of Jean Genet's novel, *Prisoner of Love* (1995), made into a one-woman show for Ruth Maleczech with music by Philip Glass.

Mabou Mines' *Prologue to Death in Venice* (1979), directed by Breuer, featured music by Bob Telson and a Japanese Bunraku puppet manipulated by actor Bill Raymond. After this, much of Breuer's work used intercultural

13. Mabou Mines' production of *Epidog*, 1996. Courtesy of Ruth Maleczech. Photography by © Beatriz Schiller 1998.

elements – African and Caribbean music, Japanese and Southeast Asian puppets. His best-known production was a Sophoclean adaptation, *The Gospel at Colonus* (1983), set to a gospel score by Bob Telson and performed in New York, Washington, and San Francisco. This same year Bill Raymond directed for Mabou Mines an anti-war meditation based on the career of Ulysses Grant, *Cold Harbor*, but he remained primarily an actor, for this group and for other experimental directors such as Richard Foreman and Joe Chaikin.

Mabou Mines' most ambitious undertaking was the 1990 *Lear*, placed in a Southern U.S. setting and with most of the roles gender-reversed. Breuer directed and Lear was played by Ruth Maleczech. Maleczech directed her own musical theatre piece, *Suenos*, based on the poems of a seventeenth-century nun, in 1989, but she was steadily becoming recognized as one of the leading actresses of the New York experimental scene, frequently used by Breuer and Akalaitis, but increasingly by other directors as well. She often appeared with Fred Neumann, most notably in the continuing autobiographical multicultural epic *Animation*, which involves much of Breuer's work since the mid-seventies and which, if staged in its entirety, would last ten to twelve days. The most ambitious element in this epic was *The Warrior Ant*, presented at the Brooklyn Academy in 1988, with Carribean-based music by Telson and starring a Bunraku puppet. The closely related but much more intimate *MahabharANTa* (1992) was staged as a Balinese shadow play, with Maleczech and Neumann as narrators and with puppets by a Balinese puppet master, I Wayan Wija. Maleczech and Neumann also appeared as narrators in the next section of Breuer's ongoing epic, the more elaborate *Epidog* (1996), which freely mixed living actors, puppets and projections.

Performance Art

In addition to the work of these experimental companies and directors, the 1980s also saw the rise in America of another type of alternative theatre, usually designated as performance or performance art. In the early seventies a group of artists around San Francisco began experimenting with primarily solo actions related to Happenings and involved with the workings of the body. These came to be known as "body art" or "life art," and they ranged from the framing of everyday activity to such extreme actions as Chris Burden's *Shoot* (1971), in which the artist was shot in the arm by a friend, thus fascinating the national media. About the same time Vito Acconci and others began presenting body art in New York.

The term "performance" began to be used in the early seventies to designate a wide variety of such activity, most of it solo and taking place outside of conventional theatres. Indeed, during the seventies it was generally covered not by theatre but by art publications such as *Artweek* and particularly by the journal especially devoted to it, *High Performance*, founded by Linda Burnham in 1978. After 1980, however, performance, now also called performance art, became steadily more visible to the general public and developed steadily closer ties to the theatre world, both in terms of the spaces used and an increasing interest in narrative.

The New Vaudevillians

One group of American performance artists has close ties to the circus and vaudeville traditions, and has sometimes been called the "new vaudevillians." These include both solo performers like Stuart Sherman and Paul Zaloom, who tell stories with junk objects used like puppets, and groups like Seattle's Flying Karamazov Brothers, who intersperse their zany narratives with the astonishing juggling of unconventional objects, or the popular Blue Man Group, whose bizarre collage of percussion, video and live action, and food fights, *Tubes*, has been one of the most durable alternative theatre offerings in New York in the nineties. The best known of these modern entertainers is Bill Irwin, who has engagingly combined traditional clown training with avant-garde and postmodern references in such popular successes as *The Regard of Flight* (1982) and *Largely New York* (1989).

Although much performance art of the seventies tended to emphasize bodily activity and abstract form, since 1980 a growing proportion of such activity has shared with much modern alternative theatre in America an interest in autobiographical exploration, political commentary, or a combination of the two. Women artists were centrally involved with modern performance from its beginnings and, as feminist concerns began to develop during the seventies, leading women performers began to explore these concerns in their work. One important early center of such work was Cal Arts in Los Angeles, where Judy Chicago, Faith Wilding, and Suzanne Lacy were pioneer theorists and practitioners of women's performance art. Each of these artists built their early performances out of their personal experiences, while other artists, such as Eleanor Antin, created and performed alternate personae. A 1976 Los Angeles exhibition of the work of such artists was aptly named "Autobiographical Fantasies." The early seventies saw distinctly less such work on the East Coast, though the dance work of Yvonne Rainer and Simone Forti looked in this direction, as did the performances of Carolee Schneemann, most notably her *Interior Scroll* (1975) in which she read a kind of performance manifesto from a text she pulled from her vagina.

Rachel Rosenthal and Suzanne Lacy

One of the best known of the California-based feminist performist artists is Rachel Rosenthal, who became interested in such issues in the early seventies at Cal Arts. Her first series of pieces were personal explorations, culminating in *The Death Show* in 1978. Later works moved on to social, political, and ecological concerns, and Rosenthal achieved a national and then an international reputation with such performances as *L.O.W. in Gaia* (1986) and *Rachel's Brain* (1987). Suzanne Lacy took political performance in a quite different direction, teaming up with artist Leslie Labowitz and others after 1977 to create a series of projects involving hundreds of women in different communities across the country in exploring their histories and interrelationships. Among the best known of these were *River Meetings* (New Orleans, 1980), *Whisper, the Waves, the Wind* (La Jolla, 1984), and *The Crystal Quilt* (Minneapolis, 1987). Another direction still is represented by Karen Finley, whose abrasive and shocking confrontations with her audience, such as *The Constant State of Desire* (1987), made her one of the most controversial of contemporary performance artists.

Feminist performance artists provided a model for other, primarily solo performers during the eighties and nineties who used this versatile new alternative theatre mode to explore a wide range of personal and social issues. The homosexual explorations such as *Buddy Systems* (1986) or *SEX/LOVE/ STORIES* (1991) of Tim Miller (who, like Holly Hughes and Karen Finley, achieved a certain notoriety by being defunded by the NEA in 1990), are much closer to the monologues of Holly Hughes or Rachel Rosenthal than to the camp homosexual fantasies of The Theatre of the Ridiculous. Performance art dealing with different enthnicities has also contributed to this rich mixture, in the work of such artists as Robbie McCauley, who created a series of performances called *Confessions of a Black Working Class Woman* in the late 1980s, Dan Kwong, whose 1989 *Secrets of a Samuai Centerfielder* explores his tensions as the gay son of Japanese–Chinese parents in California, and perhaps most notably Guillermo Gómez-Peña, whose co-creation with Coco Fusco, *Two Undiscovered Amerindians Visit* (1992), a complex commentary on colonialism, display, ethnic relationships, and modern museum culture, aroused considerable critical attention both in Europe and America.

Bibliography: Alternative Theatre

There are two recommended books devoted specifically to American alternative theatre, both focused on the period from 1965 onward. Shank's *American Alternative Theatre* and Kostelanetz's *On Innovative Performance(s)*. Both cover the main alternative artists and companies. Kostelanetz has the advantage of covering material from the eighties, while Shank includes more California material. Other more general books on modern experimental theatre, both American and European, are Roose-Evans's *Experimental Theatre from Stanislavsky to Today*, Schevill's *Break Out!*, Croyden's *Lunatics, Lovers and Poets*, Goldberg's *Performance Art From Futurism to the Present*, and Weinberg's *Challenging the Hierarchy*.

Schevill's is the most unconventional study, being composed of play texts, essays, interviews, manifestos, and panel discussions. It includes information on a wide variety of primarily political groups. Roose-Evans is least helpful on American work, with chapters only on modern dance and Bread and Puppet. Croyden contains chapters on happenings, the Living Theatre, and the Open Theatre and brief information on several other groups. Goldberg emphasizes the performance art tradition of Cage and Cunningham, happenings, modern experimental dance and conceptual art, and overlaps the other books already mentioned only in dealing with Richard Foreman and Robert Wilson.

Several more theoretical books also provide specific information on American alternative theatre. Wiles's *The Theater Event* deals with such leading artists as the Living Theatre, Wilson, and Foreman as well as with dance theatre. Schmitt's *Actors and Onlookers* looks at modern experimental work through the theories of John Cage, and Heuvel's *Performing Drama/Dramatizing Performance* includes chapters on the Wooster Group and Robert Wilson. Schechner's *Public Domain* contains essays on alternative theatre in the late sixties.

There are countless journal articles on the various groups and individual artists of the American alternative theatre. Almost every issue of the *Tulane Drama Review* (subsequently *The Drama Review*) from the mid-sixties onward contains such material.

American Theatre and *Performing Arts Journal* are also excellent sources and *Theatre Journal* and *Modern Drama* have also often included such material since the late sixties. *High Performance, Avalanche,* and *Artweek* have provided the best chronicles of the development of performance art. In the brief space allocated for this essay, however, only book-length studies can be mentioned.

The best book on the alternative political theatre in America during the sixties and seventies is, rather suprisingly, a German study, Kohtes's *Guerilla Theater.* It deals extensively with Bread and Puppet, San Francisco Mime, El Teatro Campesino, the Pageant Players, the SDS troupes, street theatre, and Yippie actions, and less extensively with more than twenty other political troupes. Sainer's *The New Radical Theatre Notebook* updates the 1965 edition and is primarily made up of scripts from different groups, but has an extended introduction to the subject. Lesnick's *Guerilla Street Theatre* and Weisman's *Guerrilla Theatre* are also anthologies with useful introductory comments (note the varying spellings of "guerrilla").

For the Living Theatre, consult Biner's and Tytell's books with that title and Beck's *The Life of the Theatre.* For Happenings, see Kirby's book with that title as well as Kaprow's *Assemblage, Environments, and Happenings* and Kostelanetz's more general *The Theater of Mixed Means.* For the Open Theatre, see Pasolli's *A Book on the Open Theatre* and Blumenthal's *Joseph Chaikin.* For the San Francisco Mime Troupe, see Davis's book by that title, and for El Teatro Campesino, the book of that name by Broyles-Gonzalez and Elam's *Taking It to the Streets.* For The Free Southern Theater, see the book of that name edited by Dent and Schechner.

There are many books and articles on various artists and theatres in the modern black theatre movement, but the best general introduction is Williams, *Black Theatre in the 1960s and 1970s.* For Split Britches, see the book of that name by Case. For The Performance Group, see Schechner's *Environmental Theater.* Another book concerned with environmental theatre is McNamara, Rojo, and Schechner, *Theatres, Spaces, Environments.* For Squat Theatre, see the book of that name by Buchmuller and Koós. The three basic works on Robert Wilson are Brecht, *The Theatre of Visions,* Shyer, *Robert Wilson and His Collaborators,* and Holmberg, *The Theatre of Robert Wilson.* Sources for plays and essays by Richard Foreman are discussed in Gussow's bibliography. The best general introductions to modern alternative dance and dance-theatre are the two studies by Banes, *Democracy's Body* and *Terpsichore in Sneakers.* For Laurie Anderson see Howell's book of that name. For the Wooster Group see Savran, *Breaking the Rules. The Death of Character* by Fuchs includes useful perspective on many alternative productions of recent years.

In addition to Goldberg's historical survey there are many books on the rapidly developing field of performance art. Good early surveys are Bronson's and Gale's *Performance by Artists* and Loeffler's and Tong's source book of California performance art, *Performance Anthology.* For women's performance art, see Roth, *The Amazing Decade* and Hart's and Phelan's collection of essays *Acting Out.*

3

The Plays and Playwrights

Plays and Playwrights: 1945–1970

June Schlueter

Introduction

Several years after the close of World War II, Joseph Wood Krutch attempted to identify the distinguishing character of modern drama. Focusing on what is now commonly thought of as the first phase of modern drama, from Ibsen through Pirandello (c. 1880–1920), Krutch observed a recurring assumption of European drama: that a cavernous gap lay between the values of previous centuries and the values of our own. Those few who clung to the remnants of moral tradition could only admit, like the despairing old carpenter in Friedrich Hebbel's *Maria Magdalena* (1844), "I do not understand the world anymore."

Such a vision of the twentieth century as fundamentally different from and alien to all previous human history became, in Krutch's assessment, the defining character of "Modernism." Its assimilation into the national character of America, however, and hence of that country's drama, was somewhat delayed. Eugene O'Neill and Maxwell Anderson, he claimed, though responsible for the passage of American drama from childhood to adolescence, were essentially writing classical tragedy at a time when Ibsen, Chekhov, and Strindberg were already dead and Shaw's major work was done.

Krutch acknowledged, of course, the work of those American playwrights who began extending the boundaries of dramatic form in ways that both imitated and anticipated such European experiments as Surrealism, Dadaism, Expressionism, and epic theatre. O'Neill's use of episodic form, Expressionistic techniques, and masks (*The Hairy Ape*, 1922, and *The Great God Brown*, 1926) contributed notably to new dramatic structures, as did Thornton Wilder's fluid treatments of time (*Our Town*, 1938, and *The Skin of Our Teeth*, 1942), Tennessee Williams's memory devices and slide screens (*The Glass Menagerie*, 1945), and Arthur Miller's cinematic reveries (*Death of a Salesman*, 1949). But, for the most part, American dramatists in the period

294

between Pirandello and Beckett, roughly from 1920 to the mid-fifties, were not overly interested in the arbitrary nature of life that so intrigued their European counterparts. Rather, American playwrights, even after the trauma of World War II, reasserted their faith in causality and its attendant moral claims.

Krutch's monograph, published in 1953, may well have been an accurate estimate of modern drama to that point. Indeed, it would be unfair to suggest that Krutch celebrated the conservatism of American drama. For despite his wish to preserve the perception of self as a continuous unity – an assumption on which "all moral systems must rest" – Krutch clearly held American drama in low regard and lamented its more recent tendency to be negative and defeatist.

Admittedly, modern American drama *has* been pessimistic, at least if measured by the work of O'Neill, whose plays clearly set the tone for the American stage. *The Iceman Cometh*, staged immediately after the war (1946), offered Harry Hope's saloon as a metaphor for those whose only hope rests in the refuge and lie of illusion. Alongside the dreariness of O'Neill, however, there was the optimism of Rodgers and Hammerstein's *Carousel*, which ran for 890 performances following its opening in 1945, reminding theatre historians of an American counter-tradition of spirited lightness exemplified by musical comedy.

In the period immediately after World War II, however, even the Broadway musical was at risk. Despite such notable successes as *Street Scene*, *Brigadoon*, *Kiss Me, Kate*, and *South Pacific*, theatre audiences were dwindling, no doubt in part because television was finding its way into the American living room. Visiting companies from England and other European countries booked New York's theatres, and Shakespearean revivals commanded impressive runs. But by 1948, hosts of Broadway actors were unemployed and serious drama needed support.

Obligingly, the two writers who were to take their place alongside O'Neill as major voices in American theatre both appeared. Between 1945 and the end of the decade, Broadway produced major plays by Tennessee Williams – *The Glass Menagerie* (1945) and *A Streetcar Named Desire* (1947) – and by Arthur Miller – *All My Sons* (1947) and *Death of a Salesman* (1949). Together, these two playwrights sustained and revitalized the Broadway theatre as a venue for serious plays.

Arthur Miller and Tennessee Williams in the Forties

Miller, who was born in 1915 in Harlem, had done his apprentice writing at the University of Michigan and in the Federal Theatre Project, which he joined in 1938. His first attempt to capture Broadway audiences, with *The Man Who Had*

All the Luck (1944), failed, but in 1947 he offered the postwar public a play that encouraged memories of the heroism of the war years and provoked thought about the moral responsibility – and losses – of those who remained in the safety of their fenced-in yards.

All My Sons, which opened at the Coronet Theatre in 1947 in a production directed by Elia Kazan and starring Ed Begley, touched the conscience of America: it played to audiences familiar with the Truman Committee's investigation of a scandal involving the manufacture of faulty airplane parts in Ohio. In Miller's play, Joe Keller, owner of a wartime manufacturing plant, allows cracked airplane cylinders to be shipped to the military, an act that results in the deaths of some twenty-one pilots. Keller, who initially claims he will assume responsibility, later allows his partner to take the blame.

Miller sets the play in the suburban backyard, with Keller surrounded by the comfortable domestic routine that characterized the lives of so many following the disruptive war years. Interrupting the veneer of good cheer, however, are a wife haunted by a pilot son missing in action for nearly four years and that son's former girlfriend, who eventually produces a letter that confirms Larry's death: having heard of his father's culpability in the distribution of the cracked cylinders, the pilot committed suicide in a kamikaze flight. In a play that works incrementally to raise the audience's level of awareness, Keller recognizes, finally, that "They were all my sons" and, in a gesture that at once accepts responsibility and acknowledges shame, shoots himself upstairs in the family home. His death, the culmination of a father–son relationship built on lies and denials, both burdens and frees the younger son, Chris, with the lesson of recognition and forgiveness that, Miller hopes, extends beyond the family to society at large.

Though contemporary in its focus on wartime decisions and domestic life following the war, *All My Sons* resurrects the remnants of the nineteenth-century stage, relying on the retrospective technique that Ibsen mastered in *Ghosts*. In such a structure, the past is a continuing presence, and the exposition renews itself at intervals, as each critical piece of information is revealed.

All My Sons ran for 328 performances, won a New York Drama Critics' Circle Award, and was made into a film with Edward G. Robinson in 1948. Its success, which provided Miller with the recognition he needed to pursue a playwriting career, proved a mere prelude to that of his next play, *Death of a Salesman*, which, under Kazan's direction, won both a New York Drama Critics' Circle Award and a Pulitzer Prize, saw a film version in 1951 (with Fredric March), and enjoyed major revivals: in 1975, for example, with George C. Scott as Willy Loman; in 1983, at the Beijing People's Art Theatre, with a Chinese cast; in 1984, with Dustin Hoffman, who also starred in the CBS television production a year later, which was seen by 25 million; and in 1999 with Brian Dennehy. When Lee J. Cobb's 1949 Willy, traveling cases in hand, weighing down the bulky shoulders of the New England salesman, appeared on the Morosco

14. Arthur Miller's *Death of a Salesman*, 1949, with (left to right) Mildred Dunnock (Linda), Lee J. Cobb (Willy), Arthur Kennedy (Biff), and Cameron Mitchell (Happy). Photograph by Fred Fehl. Harry Ransom Humanities Research Center, The University of Texas at Austin.

Theatre stage, it began the public's decades-long devotion to what many consider the quintessential American play.

Clearly this deluded salesman, defeated by self-absorption and misplaced dreams, touched a nerve in the theatregoing public, which had lived through the Depression and World War II and now looked forward to the security and prosperity of the Eisenhower years. In 1949, *Salesman* stood as a symbol of the transition in values that would grip the country. Though nostalgic for the innocence of prewar America, audiences were beginning to concede the chasm that divided the aggressive, success-oriented world that could not accommodate failure and the world of Dave Singleman, the salesman who operated on the strength of friendship and personal style.

Throughout the play, Willy encourages his sons, commending their misdeeds and turning their limitations into promise. Having returned from a New England sales trip that he never completed, the tired salesman turns to his self-sacrificing wife for flattery and support. Assisted by Linda, Willy sustains his dream; in a yard blocked from the sun by high-rise apartments, he plants seeds in a gloomy garden. His suicide stands as final testimony to the persistence and the futility of the American dream: Willy dies expecting that his sons will collect the insurance. An audience is left with a palpable sense of loss and a strong sense of the power of the play to test and tease and withhold.

But the power of *Death of a Salesman* lives less in the plot line than in its interior drama. The playwright who had trusted Ibsenesque drama just two years earlier now constructs a form that combines realism and expressionism in ways that enable an audience both to follow the action and to understand why Willy's dream is so stubborn and grand. A sequence of reveries punctuates the play, consuming Willy at critical moments and providing the audience with privileged insights into a reconstructed or imagined past. Willy slips into daydreams involving the boys as athletes and as willing Simonizers of their father's Chevy; Linda as the patient and frugal wife, mending stockings; a woman in a Boston hotel room, whose affair with Willy is interrupted by an unannounced visit from his older son; and a brother, Ben, who, like his father, left the family to seek adventure and wealth and who, finally, in his endorsement of Willy's commitment to rugged individualism, lures Willy to suicide.

Miller's forties plays are important as well for their focus on family, a theme that came to define serious drama in the postwar years. Willy Loman and Joe Keller are recognizable figures in the American domestic landscape: both fathers to two sons, each wants success for their sake; each wants to pass on the tokens of success, whether wanted or not, to his heirs. Like the families of O'Neill, however, and particularly the Tyrones (*Long Day's Journey Into Night*), Miller's are less than ideal. Joe Keller's leisurely backyard life covers the pain and guilt that trouble relations between wife and husband and father and son and that compel audiences to see what Keller would rather conceal. Willy's lessons in toughness, womanizing, and lying and Linda's quiet nurturing of her husband's illusions suggestively expose the weaknesses of the family that seemed to work in a more innocent time.

Similarly important as dramas of "domestic realism," the form that was to define American theatre immediately after the war, are two major plays by Williams, *The Glass Menagerie* and *A Streetcar Named Desire*. In both, the model of the family that America celebrates is tenuous at best. In *The Glass Menagerie*, a domineering mother, whose husband abandoned her, attempts to hold the family together and assure her children's success even as she constructs romantic illusions of the past and dreams of a future that has little chance of materializing. In *Streetcar*, the now legendary Stanley Kowalski, crude in style and brutal in behavior, claims his masculine prerogative over the pregnant, admiring Stella and her homeless sister through intimidation and force. In the backdrop of Blanche's life is a marriage to a young man who proved to be homosexual and committed suicide; in the foreground is a desperate attempt to marry despite her having violated the womanly ideal. Williams invites his audience to see – and to understand – Blanche's fragility and her promiscuity within the frame of changing values and displaced worlds. But there is little to refresh in his portraits of family life: in Williams's plays, as in Miller's, marriage and family, the nucleus of social organization, is an imperiled institution.

Also like Miller's plays, Williams's two dramas examine the seductive but hurtful lure of illusion. Joe Keller, Willy Loman, Amanda Wingfield, and Blanche DuBois, in designing imaginary, protective worlds, contribute to a view of an emerging America as a country on the cusp of change but unready for it. Though Americans dearly hoped to return to the ordinary after the war, they were inescapably faced with the imperative of including in their experience the personal and mass horrors of World War II; the promise, and the threat, that technology held to transform their lives; and the recognition that the priority of family values was being challenged. In both Miller's and Williams's forties plays, a nostalgia for an older, less conflicted world competes for space with the insistence of a world that is faster, cruder, and crueler than the one remembered.

Williams, who was born in Columbus, Mississippi, in 1911, spent much of his childhood in St. Louis, which became the setting for *The Glass Menagerie*. In a brief run in Chicago in 1944 and an extended run of 561 performances in New York at the Playhouse the following year, that play established the no-longer-young playwright, whose career till then had been unremarkable. Under the direction of Eddie Dowling and Margo Jones, with Laurette Taylor playing Amanda, the play won a New York Drama Critics' Circle Award, a Sidney Howard Memorial Award, a Donaldson Award, and a "Sign" Award; it saw television versions in 1966 and in 1973, the latter with Katharine Hepburn as Amanda, and was made into a film in 1950 and again in 1987. The play is structured as story and re-enactment, with Tom Wingfield, an aspiring poet who works in a shoe factory and dreams of a life free from his nagging mother and gentle but vulnerable sister, narrating the story from a fire escape, then stepping into the family flat to become an actor in their domestic routine.

For Amanda Wingfield, the family matriarch, there is no agenda more important than matching her slightly crippled daughter, Laura, in marriage, and she schemes relentlessly to do so. When her mother fails to make a match with Tom's friend, a young man whose night school course in radio engineering has identified him as a man on the move, Laura retreats into her world of illusion, in which a menagerie of glass animals stands as symbol of her fragility. Poignantly and tenderly drawn, Laura has little chance of a life independent of her overbearing mother, who thrives on memories of a romantic youth in which she was the lady of choice to a gaggle of gentleman callers. The play, which is offered as a memory, is both powerful and sad, capturing the spirit and the longing of one who now lives on the edge of poverty but who has known a finer life.

Amanda Wingfield is one of Williams's powerfully drawn women, who wins

15. Marlon Brando and Jessica Tandy in Tennessee Williams's *A Streetcar Named Desire*, 1947. Museum of the City of New York.

the sympathy, and guarded respect, of an audience that recognizes the futility of her dreams but understands why she needs them. Equally as powerful is Blanche DuBois, of *A Streetcar Named Desire*, an English teacher who is run out of town for her promiscuous behavior but who styles herself "a priestess of Aphrodite." More than any major character in the early postwar years, Blanche embodies the conflicts of a changing world. A lover of poetry and music and ballroom taffeta, Blanche stands as a fading tribute to refined life unable to survive in Stanley Kowalski's crude and raucous world. Herself a complicated woman, Blanche has memories of an ideal she may never herself have known and finds refuge in alcohol and lies.

Williams's presentation of the drama is in eleven scenes, each characterized by the sounds of New Orleans, from blues piano to street vendor cries. Against the ambience, vitality, and decadence of the city, the Kowalskis plan the birth of their first child even as Stanley is given to fits of violence that momentarily alienate an always forgiving wife. Quarrelsome, demanding, and obsessed with his masculine role, Stanley regularly asserts his authority, a misused commemorative to domestic power.

The 1947 production of *A Streetcar Named Desire* at New York's Barrymore Theatre, which ran for 855 performances, was directed by Kazan. The production featured Jessica Tandy as Blanche, Marlon Brando as Stanley, Kim Hunter as Stella, and Karl Malden as Mitch; it won Williams a New York Drama Critics' Circle Award, a Pulitzer Prize, and a Donaldson Award. The play opened two years later in London, with Vivien Leigh as Blanche, and, in 1951, Kazan directed a film version, with Leigh as Blanche and, otherwise, the New York cast. But under pressure to respect both Hollywood's official morality and the Roman Catholic Legion of Decency's objections, Kazan omitted references to Blanche's young husband's homosexuality, dramatized Stanley's rape of Blanche only suggestively, and ended the film with Stella, who embraces her husband in Williams's play, shouting at her husband never to touch her again. (It took until 1984 for a film version of Williams's full text to appear: John Erman directed Ann-Margret and Treat Williams in the remake.)

While able playwrights all have the personal credentials to dramatize illusion and know well the power of imaginative worlds, there is irony in the fact that Miller and Williams became the primary architects of postwar domestic drama. Although Miller was married to Mary Grace Slattery in the forties and added two children to the marriage, by the turn of the decade he had met Marilyn Monroe and begun leading a social life without his wife. Miller was to divorce Slattery in 1956 and marry Monroe, but that marriage would end in 1961 – a year before his third, with Inge Morath, with whom he remains married, would begin. Williams, a homosexual, never married. Nor was early family life for either playwright ideal: Miller's father lost all he owned in the stock market crash, when Arthur was thirteen, and Williams, whose traveling salesman father was frequently absent, grew up in delicate health in an extended family and, at age seven, was uprooted from his southern home and transplanted to St. Louis. Nonetheless, Miller and Williams often dealt with the postwar family as a subject.

Postwar and Fifties Playwrights

The postwar American stage also hosted a number of writers who had established reputations before the war, most notably Lillian Hellman (*Another Part of the Forest*, 1946), Maxwell Anderson (*Truckline Café*, 1946; *Joan of Lorraine*, 1946; *Anne of the Thousand Days*, 1948), Clifford Odets (*The Big Knife*, 1949; *The Country Girl*, 1949), Sidney Kingsley (*Detective Story*, 1949), and Elmer Rice (*Dream Girl*, 1945). O'Neill's major career was also of an earlier era – in 1936, he became the first (and, to date, only) American playwright to win the Nobel Prize for Literature – but in 1946, the first year of the baby boom, *The Iceman Cometh* appeared: *A Moon for the Misbegotten* (written in 1943) received its premiere one year later, and *Long Day's Journey Into Night*, suppressed by the playwright's unwillingness to expose publicly the addictions and deceptions of the Tyrone family – O'Neill's own – was staged in 1956.

As the fifties unfolded, Broadway saw productions of Carson McCullers's *The Member of the Wedding* (1950), Kingsley's *Darkness at Noon* (1951) and *Lunatics and Lovers* (1954), Maxwell Anderson's *Barefoot in Athens* (1951) and *The Bad Seed* (1954), Hellman's *The Autumn Garden* (1951), Robert Anderson's *Tea and Sympathy* (1953), John Patrick's *Teahouse of the August Moon* (1953), Rice's *The Winner* (1954) and *Cue for Passion* (1958), Wilder's *The Matchmaker* (1954), Odets's *The Flowering Peach* (1954), Jerome Lawrence and Robert E. Lee's *Inherit the Wind* (1955), and Frances Goodrich's and Albert Hackett's *The Diary of Anne Frank* (1955).

William Gibson achieved immediate but shortlived fame in 1958 with *Two for the Seesaw* and, a year later, *The Miracle Worker*, which dramatized the relationship between Helen Keller and her tutor. The decade ended on the promise of this new playwright's work and that of another, Lorraine Hansberry, whose *Raisin in the Sun* carved out a place for African Americans in the narrative of family drama. In that play, a black family on the south side of Chicago with ordinary problems and ordinary dreams must make an extraordinary decision when a representative of the all-white neighborhood into which they are about to move pressures them to change their plans. The first African American woman to have a play staged on Broadway, Hansberry held considerable promise. But shortly after her second play, *The Sign in Sidney Brustein's Window* (1964), appeared, cancer claimed her. And Gibson's career never did materialize: subsequent plays dramatized events in the lives of historical figures (John and Abigail Adams, Golda Meir, and, once again, Helen Keller) but failed to have an impact on the American stage.

The lasting contributions of the fifties proved to be those of Miller and Williams. Miller produced *An Enemy of the People* (1951), *The Crucible* (1953), and a double bill of one-acts, *A View from the Bridge* and *A Memory of Two Mondays* (1956). Williams, after *Summer and Smoke* (1948), wrote *The Rose Tattoo* (1951), *Camino Real* (1953), *Cat on a Hot Tin Roof* (1955), *Orpheus Descending* (1957), *The Garden District* (1958), *Sweet Bird of Youth* (1959), and *Period of Adjustment* (1959).

Personally and politically, the fifties were difficult for Miller. These were years of marital transition, with Monroe divorcing Joe DiMaggio, Miller divorcing Slattery, and Monroe and Miller marrying. In 1957, a year into their marriage, Monroe had a miscarriage, which triggered a serious depression that persisted through the 1961 divorce and until her death in 1962.

Politically, Miller, long a leftist, became particularly active. In an environment that was increasingly anti-liberal, Miller watched the House Un-American Activities Committee conduct its investigation and listened as his longtime friend and director Elia Kazan and others named people in the motion picture industry who allegedly had associations with the Communist Party. In 1956, Miller was subpoenaed to appear before HUAC. His testimony was open and candid – until he was asked to name others and refused, an act that resulted in his conviction for contempt of Congress. Though the conviction was subsequently reversed by the U.S. Court of Appeals for the District of Columbia, Miller's experience reaffirmed his insistence on the precedence of the individual moral conscience over a law of society, a commitment that was dramatized with particular force in his fifties plays. In its most assertive form, it appears in the characters of John Proctor (*The Crucible*) and Eddie Carbone (*A View from the Bridge*), who die affirming their personal sense of justice.

Professionally, Miller began the decade with *An Enemy of the People*, which opened at the Broadhurst Theatre in 1950, one month after *Death of a Salesman* completed its 742-performance run. An adaptation of Ibsen's 1882 play, Miller's version speaks with special relevance to the Joseph McCarthy years. The stubbornly insistent Dr. Stockmann (played by Morris Carnovsky), intent on doing what is right regardless of consequences, becomes a recognizable and repeatable character in Miller's plays. Miller's protagonists are ordinary men of uncompromising commitment.

John Proctor in *The Crucible*, a play with suggestive parallels between the Salem witchhunts and the Congressional hearings, asserts his identity and individual conscience in the context of a public terror that finally claims his life. A man of uncommon moral courage, Proctor refuses to yield to those who would hold him guilty of trafficking with the devil. And though he signs a confession on his dying day, and later retracts it, he refuses to name names and, finally, champions as his highest value the honor of his name. By contrast, others in the community who are accused are persuaded that confession offers the only hope of redemption, and each in turn both admits complicity and names others.

Proctor's world is the world of 1692 Puritan Massachusetts, where fire and brimstone sermons assured that residents attended church regularly and knew by heart the Ten Commandments. John's fault is that he has violated – and forgotten – the Commandment prohibiting adultery, having yielded to the sensuous attractions of the young Abigail, who becomes the sustaining power behind the community's obsession with witches. A shrewd opportunist, she names those she does not like and manipulatively tries to reclaim her favor with John.

Miller's dramatizing of the Salem trials reveals society at its tyrannical worst and polarizes good and evil. Clearly, the analogy between the Communist hunt and the Salem witchhunt was fundamental to Miller's purpose. In 1950, Senator McCarthy of Wisconsin, in a devastating gesture characteristic of the Cold War mentality, publicly stated that 205 Communists had infiltrated the State Department: though he could name none, the investigations that ensued ruined the careers and the lives of many. For Miller, the zealous guardians of the public good, in colonial New England and McCarthy's America, led the country into the darkest chapters of its history; the play, which opened at the Martin Beck Theatre in 1953, ran for 197 performances.

In 1955, a one-act version of *A View from the Bridge* shared a 149-performance run with *A Memory of Two Mondays*; the following year, a fuller version, not produced in New York until 1965, had a 220-performance run in London (beginning the relationship between that city and Miller that has since grown into a love affair). It was this version that Sidney Lumet made into a film in 1962. In 1997–98 the fuller version had a very successful Broadway revival.

Genetically linked to Dr. Stockmann and John Proctor, and not unrelated to Joe Keller and Willy Loman, Eddie Carbone completes the family of strong-willed protagonists that were central to the first decade of Miller's highly successful playwriting career. In this play, a narrator, Alfieri, tells the story of the longshoreman's inevitable death, the consequence of Eddie's inability to reconcile the social laws of the Brooklyn community in which he lives with the moral laws that claim him. The family, though important in the two earlier fifties plays, reassumes the primacy of the forties plays in this drama, which involves a daughter's desire to marry a man unacceptable to her father. Catherine, a niece whom Eddie and Bea have raised as a daughter, is attracted to Rudolpho, an illegal immigrant with blond hair, a tenor voice, and pointed shoes. Eddie, who believes in the traditional Sicilian and masculine family values that make his word domestic law, activates his objection by violating the code of the Red Hook community, reporting Rudolpho and his brother to the authorities as "submarines." In part, Eddie is motivated by a fatherly desire to protect a vulnerable young woman from the seductions of the modern world, but Eddie may also have an unacknowledged incestuous attraction to the girl. In breaking faith with both his family and his community, Eddie becomes an object of scorn and, finally, is killed in a knife fight with Rudolpho's brother.

A Memory of Two Mondays, the slighter of the two plays in the double bill, has yet to be appreciated, though in the history of modern drama it might have claimed an important place. Lyrical and sensitive, the piece records the experiences of workers in a warehouse on two successive Mondays, anticipating, in tone and in action, Samuel Beckett's *Waiting for Godot*. Miller's play-world is a warehouse of endless receiving and shipping, of boredom and waiting, of returning the next day to re-experience the routine. At this point in

Miller's life, however, the personal and the political conspired to disincline him to redesign the American theatre. Though he wrote a screenplay of his short story "The Misfits" especially for Monroe and published an occasional short story, he essentially absented himself from the stage until 1964.

Williams, on the other hand, remained a persistent contributor throughout the decade. In the early fifties, he wrote three plays that explored the divide between the spiritual and the physical, a motif he had treated with success in *Streetcar*. Critics thought *Eccentricities of a Nightingale* (1951) (a rewrite of *Summer and Smoke* [1948]) overburdened by symbolism, despite the fact that Geraldine Page, in a production directed by José Quintero, played Alma Winemiller, daughter of a Mississippi minister, with particular sensitivity. They were surprised by the robust comic spirit of *The Rose Tattoo*, staged in New York in 1950 at the Martin Beck Theatre and made into a compelling film with Anna Magnani and Burt Lancaster in 1955. In that play, the Sicilian-born widow, Serafina, given to solitude and prayer until she learns of her husband's infidelity, allows her sensual urges to return, turning the play into a paean to the Dionysian spirit. *Camino Real* (1953), which similarly celebrates the sensuous, but within the insistent presence of death, baffled critics. A series of expressionistic vignettes, the play dramatizes a variety of experiences and an assortment of characters in a raucous and threatening New Orleans street scene.

Following *Camino Real*, Williams returned to the fold of domestic realism with *Cat on a Hot Tin Roof* (1955), a seething drama of a marriage on the brink of disaster. Maggie and Brick Pollitt (played by Elizabeth Taylor and Paul Newman in the film version) muddle through their relationship under the watchful eye of Big Daddy, the quintessential southern patriarch (played by Burl Ives), who, dying of cancer, looks to his favorite son for an heir. Committed to the values of the Mississippi plantation, Big Daddy doesn't realize the extent to which ambivalent sexual identity, sexual frustration, dependency, and mendacity define the couple's life. At the end of the play, Maggie announces that she is pregnant in order to satisfy Big Daddy and provoke her homosexual husband into making the lie come true. Perhaps more powerfully than any drama of the fifties, *Cat* challenged the myths of family and community, offering the uncertain hope of a future constructed on moral paralysis and a mendacious lie. A major achievement, *Cat*, as staged by Kazan at the Morosco Theatre, won a New York Drama Critics' Circle Award and a Pulitzer Prize, became Williams's longest running play, and, in 1958, was made into an MGM film.

Williams closed the decade with three additional plays: *Orpheus Descending* (1957), *Suddenly Last Summer* (1958), and *Sweet Bird of Youth* (1959), all three of which were made into films, testifying to the playwright's continuing appeal. In *Orpheus Descending* (a rewrite of *Battle of Angels* [1940]),

Williams renews the familiar motifs of individual loneliness, sexuality, and bigotry and the collective pains of a Southern community that has succumbed to a degenerate modern world. Heavily symbolic, the play alludes to the myth of Orpheus and Eurydice, with an updated minstrel lover wandering into the hellish city to claim a lady. With its cast of decadent characters, including the figurative lord of the underworld, a promiscuous, alcoholic woman, and a woman at once elated over having conceived a child and disillusioned at having learned of her husband's villainy, the play offers a drama of small achievements and large disappointments, sharing little inclination to endorse the psychological, sexual, or spiritual lives of the individuals and families in this Mississippi town.

Williams's distress was even more emphatically expressed in *Suddenly Last Summer*. The central image of that play – children, armed with tin cans, savagely tearing the flesh of a decadent, homosexual poet, then cannibalizing his body – morbidly memorializes the loss of a world once defined by civility and grace, as well as the fears of the misfit who challenges the natural laws of sexuality or withdraws from society to be the artist. Such a character appears again in *Sweet Bird of Youth*, as Chance Wayne, who begins as an innocent in love with Heavenly Finley but descends into a degenerate life style when Heavenly's father refuses to permit the marriage. A dependent personality, who recalls a host of other Williams characters, Chance teams up with a fading actress and becomes involved in other sexual liaisons as he attempts to establish a career that will impress Heavenly's father. Instead, his behavior results in a dose of venereal disease for Heavenly and an operation that leaves her sterile. Finally, in an unstaged scene reminiscent of the brutal death of the poet in *Suddenly Last Summer* and of the too familiar racial lynchings in the South, a group of townsmen, including Heavenly's brother, castrate Chance, who pleads with the audience to recognize the connection between him and them.

In these and all of Williams's fifties plays, the playwright exploits the myths of the old South and the realities of the new, endowing life below the Mason-Dixon line with a metaphorical authority. For Williams, the inclination toward poetry, kindness, refinement, and grace embodied earlier in a Blanche Dubois fights mightily against the press of time, which insists on a more prosaic world. Yet even as the plays of the fifties reveal an attraction to the myth of an idealized South and a resistance to the threat of its decline, so also do they acknowledge the bigotry, the masculinity, the mendacity that was always there. The site of Williams's drama is clearly postwar, reflecting as it does the disillusionment and the nostalgia of a society wanting to return to the values it once held but unable to do so. Yet it is just as clearly a place where the playwright expresses dissatisfaction with a culture whose values offered little satisfaction in the first place, at least not to those whose imaginations – and sexual orientation – set them apart. At a time when America was pretending that only the evil empire was the enemy, Williams was insightfully acknowledging the beast within and searching for both self- and others' understanding.

William Inge

If there was a playwright who shared the respect of Miller and Williams in the fifties, not for innovation of form but for the sensitivity with which he dramatized the American family, it was William Inge. Born in Independence, Kansas, in 1913, Inge established his credentials as a playwright in 1950 with *Come Back, Little Sheba*, with Shirley Booth and Sidney Blackmer in the leading roles. Set in small-town middle America, as nearly all Inge's plays are, *Come Back, Little Sheba* presents an unhappy marriage twenty years after Doc and Lola had been forced by Lola's pregnancy to marry. Now, Lola is barren, the baby having been stillborn, and Doc is a chiropractor, not having completed his medical degree. The climactic event of the drama is a drunken rampage, in which Doc tries unsuccessfully to kill his wife. Though Inge himself finally succumbed to his own alcoholism and depression, committing suicide in 1973, the playwright characteristically ends this early drama on a note of regeneration, with a chastened Doc and a maturing Lola having recognized their weaknesses and acknowledged their mutual needs.

Picnic (1953) similarly dramatizes the repressiveness of small-town routine through an outsider's appearance at a Labor Day picnic. *Bus Stop*, set in a roadside diner in Kansas, where a busload of passengers is stalled by a snowstorm, introduces an assortment of characters with individual aspirations and destinations that are painfully constrained. And *The Dark at the Top of the Stairs* (1957) follows the lives of a twenties small-town Oklahoma family poised at a point of personal and historical change: Rubin Flood sells harnesses, a commodity that will not survive the transition from an agrarian to an industrial society.

In this important cluster of plays, which had respectable runs on Broadway, Inge examines a large but typical cast of characters and relationships, repeatedly creating situations that dramatize the details of lives anesthetized by habit, dreams suffocated by compromise, and sexuality denied – the stuff of small-town America. The appeal of Inge's plays was recognized by Hollywood, which produced screen versions of each: *Come Back, Little Sheba*, with Burt Lancaster and Shirley Booth (who won an Academy Award for her performance), in 1952; *Picnic*, with William Holden, Kim Novak, and Rosalind Russell, in 1955; *Bus Stop*, with Monroe and Don Murray, in 1956; and *The Dark at the Top of the Stairs*, with Robert Preston, Dorothy McGuire, Angela

Lansbury, and Eve Arden, in 1960. After the unsuccessful *A Loss of Roses* (1959), Inge was to continue writing plays into the sixties, many of them one-acts, and he wrote a well-received screenplay, *Splendor in the Grass* (1961), which won him an Academy Award. Though Inge's plays have not had the staying power of Miller's or Williams's, they enjoy pride of place in the history of drama as examples of the troubled American family at a time when the country was, presumably, in its halcyon years.

Indeed, the collective force of Miller's, Williams's, and Inge's plays extends beyond their analysis of that fundamental but discrete social unit to an analysis of the national condition, which, while marked by optimism and excitement, was showing sure signs of neuroses. The fifties were a time of peace, prosperity, and social progress. This was the decade of color television, credit cards, and the contraceptive pill, of Jackie Robinson, Jonas Salk, Simone de Beauvoir, Rosa Parks, Elvis Presley, and *Playboy*. Yet so also was it the first full decade of the postwar nuclear age. In the fifties, Americans were building bomb shelters and participating in air-raid drills, deluded into thinking that precautionary measures could save them from the devastation of Hiroshima and Nagasaki that had stunned and humbled the world. It is clear in retrospect that in documenting the contradictions and eruptions of families in Kansas or Mississippi or Brooklyn, New York, who failed at domestic coherence, these playwrights were inviting audiences to see that the American way of life, the American character itself, was undergoing change. If the country's central unifying myth – the sanctity and health of the family – was eroding, how would this young, optimistic, no longer innocent nation cohere?

Edward Albee

Even as the major American playwrights of the fifties were approaching this question through the genre that has come to be known as domestic realism, European playwrights were engaged in a more philosophical testing of postwar meaning, one that demanded a radically different dramatic form. In 1956, an American production of Beckett's *Waiting for Godot* left the American theatre reeling. Here was a form of theatre that challenged not only the optimistic vision of a country that still believed in causality, moral responsibility, and the American dream but also the artistic commitment of several generations of realistic playwrights. During the opening run of *Godot*, taxis queued outside the theatre at intermission anticipating fares from those unwilling to sit through a second act in which nothing happens – again. American audiences, unlike their European counterparts, who were familiar by now with the Theatre of the Absurd through the work of Jean Genet, Eugène Ionesco, and Beckett, were not prepared for such radical disruptions of the familiar dramatic paradigm. Careers took unexpected turns after that and, as public sensibilities became more flexible, new American playwrights found themselves more willing to experiment with form, to explore the non-realistic devices that had defined European drama since the period between the wars.

Among the first to react to the Beckett production were Jack Gelber and Edward Albee, who took the lead in redefining – and relocating – the American play. Gelber's *The Connection* drew on Beckett's work both thematically and structurally. A group of heroin addicts, purportedly collected from the streets of New York and asked to improvise while being filmed, wait for Cowboy, their contact with the "connection," who will provide their fix. Like Vladimir and Estragon, the junkies engage in interim activities but consistently direct their energies toward the arrival of that which enables them to endure. Their improvised behavior is complemented by the jazz that accompanies the play, conveying the flux and the intensity of those who need a fix. Acutely conscious of itself as theatre, as was the Beckett play, *The Connection* functions on several levels of illusion, recalling Pirandello's earlier concern with the interplay between the fictive and the real and endorsing that continuing inquiry as central to the contemporary stage. During the intermission, street junkies from Gelber's play ask the audience for handouts, disregarding conventional barriers between spectators and stage. Staged in 1959 by The Living Theatre under Judith Malina's direction, *The Connection* ran for an impressive 768 performances.

Some months later, Albee's *The Zoo Story*, which had been staged first at Berlin's Schillertheater Werkstatt in 1959, appeared Off-Broadway at the Provincetown Playhouse in a double bill with Beckett's *Krapp's Last Tape*. *The Zoo Story* dramatizes a moment in the life – and death – of a lonely New Yorker, whose West Side rooming house features a sexually frustrated landlady, a ferocious gatekeeping dog, a neighboring "queen," and an empty picture frame. On a Sunday afternoon, Jerry claims possession of a Central Park bench from its regular occupant. Jerry spends considerable time winning the attention and irritating the sensibilities of the more conventional Peter, who has an East Side apartment, a job, a wife, two daughters, two parakeets, and a TV. The motifs of isolation, alienation, contingency, and absurdity that had been defining European drama both between the wars and after 1945 graphically found their way into an American play through the park bench drama of Jerry and Peter, which culminates in Jerry's impaling himself on the knife that Peter holds in his outstretched hand.

Albee followed this success with *The American Dream* at the York Playhouse in 1961. Here was a play that frontally challenged the domestic values earlier playwrights had begun to question. *The American Dream* caricatures and distorts the American family, transforming its mendacious and heartless tendencies into grotesque perversities that both shock and amuse.

For adoptive parents Mommy and Daddy, the failure of their infant to become the perfect child, styled in their image, is reason to cut off the offending parts, then demand a refund for the mutilated child. The couple bargain with Mrs. Barker of the Bye-Bye Adoption Agency in a hilarious but sobering display of consumerism gone amok.

Albee's drama acknowledges the values that have been central to American culture but refuses either to lament their demise or to endorse their recovery. Though critics claim Albee's plays hint at the possibility of restoration, both *The Zoo Story* and *The American Dream* support a vision that may best be described as posthumanistic. Grandma, after all, in packing bogus lunches and entering baking contests with day-old cakes, is just as unconscionable as her opportunist daughter, who lets Daddy "bump his uglies" in order to earn her inheritance. And this representative of earlier times is hardly shocked by the commercialism of Mommy and Daddy, who complain of their defective adopted child. Nor does Jerry in *The Zoo Story* have any hope of filling his empty picture frame or of establishing genuine contact with Peter, even after his lessons on the importance of connecting and his analogy of humans with animals in the zoo. As Jerry anticipates the Central Park stabbing on the evening news, he consults his own motive: "could I have planned all this? No – no, no, I couldn't have. But I think I did." Jerry's ultimate purpose may merely have been to communicate through the technology of the evening news, where he will become an electronic image in homes across the nation.

Unlike Gelber, whose subsequent plays – *The Apple* (1961), *Square in the Eye* (1965), *The Cuban Thing* (1968) – received little critical attention, Albee remained a significant figure in American drama and a dominant presence on the 1960s stage.

Albee's first full-length Broadway play, *Who's Afraid of Virginia Woolf?*, which opened at the Billy Rose Theatre in 1962, added layers of illusion to the family drama of O'Neill as it invited audiences into the living room of a New England college professor and his domineering alcoholic wife. George and Martha have managed the failure of their marriage through a ritualized game of one-upmanship involving humiliation and abuse followed by forgiveness and reconciliation. The centerpiece of their lives is an imaginary son for whom they have created a sequence of stories that connect, in provocative and destructive ways, with events that may or may not have marked their own unhealthy and unhappy lives. The "Walpurgisnacht" the audience witnesses is occasioned by a visit from a young couple; he is a new member of the faculty, she a minister's daughter given to hysterical pregnancies and drinking that encourages her to tell tales. During the course of the early morning hours, Martha tells the couple about their son, taunting her husband in the process, until George decides to perform the ultimate act and end their game: in a compelling and heart-rending story, he kills the son in a car crash, hoping to renew the relationship between himself and his wife without the props of illusion.

The play proved a sophisticated foray into the nature of illusion, posing epistemological questions and inviting the kind of postmodern criticism that the work of Sam Shepard would later engender. But critics of Alan Schneider's production, which ran for 644 performances with Uta Hagen and Arthur Hill playing Martha and George, seemed less interested in those questions than in Martha's venomous tongue. Albee won a New York Drama Critics' Circle Award, an Outer Circle Award, and a Tony for this play but did not win a Pulitzer Prize, quite possibly because its language, which was irreverently vulgar, offended Broadway. The play (filmed in 1966 with Elizabeth Taylor and Richard Burton as Martha and George) proved critical in the history of American theatre, for, like John Osborne's *Look Back in Anger* (1956) in England, it reconstituted the idiom of the contemporary stage. Even more important, along with *The Zoo Story* and *The American Dream*, it made clear the need for an alternative New York theatre, one that would not merely comply with conventional public taste and yield to commercial sensibilities but that would stretch and challenge both audiences and writers.

Sam Shepard and Off-Off Broadway

By 1960, playwrights – and the public – were associating Broadway with commercialism, and a number of writers were refusing to take their places on the gravy train. Gibson, who had known modest fame for *Two for the Seesaw*, referred to his success as a hollow achievement, complaining that the contemporary American theatre (meaning the commercial theatre, or Broadway) was primarily a place not to be serious but to be likeable. In the sixties, a generation of playwrights was opting for an alternative. As a consequence, Off-Off Broadway, which came of age in that decade, became the forum for a host of new, often experimental playwrights who found venues for their work in the cafés, lofts, and churches of New York's Greenwich Village and the Lower East Side.

Even as the Off-Off Broadway venues that had hosted Albee's first play began to mature and the Off-Off Broadway theatre went about its business of redefining the American stage, it was becoming clear that that kind of theatre was capturing the ethos of the decade. The sixties were, after all, a decade of political and social contradictions. The Kennedy years were years of progress in the space program: America had a man in space by 1961 and a man on the moon by 1969. But so also did these years see the construction of the Berlin Wall (1961), which made material the political line between West and East, and the Cuban missile crisis (1962), which brought the country perilously close to war with the Soviet Union. If Americans still had a claim to innocence at the beginning of the decade, they surely lost it in 1963 when their Camelot President, John F. Kennedy, was assassinated in Dallas. The shooting proved the first in a sequence that was to claim the lives of Malcolm X (1965), Robert Kennedy (1968), and Martin Luther King (1968). Under Lyndon Johnson, the Great Society Program once again asserted the government's responsibility for the underprivileged masses and for preserving the country's natural resources for its heirs. Yet even as Johnson was humanizing America, he gave the order, in 1964, to send U.S. troops to Vietnam: by 1967 there were 380,000 troops fighting on Vietnamese soil. At home, there were protests, by disenchanted flower children who made marijuana a religion; by angry blacks, who saw their brothers dying in disproportionate numbers; and by citizens concerned with the absurdity of an unpopular and unwinnable war. Meanwhile, the Beatles had made their debut in England, and women in miniskirts, more in control of their reproductive lives than ever before, were assuming positions in the workforce alongside men. The decade closed with its third President, Richard Nixon, in the White House, the nation still stunned by the riots at the 1968 Democratic National Convention in Chicago and the 1970 killings at Kent State University. In such a climate, Sam Shepard, a Southern California transplant, emerged to accelerate the pace and to secure the excitement and the viability of Off-Off Broadway.

Born in Chicago in 1943, Samuel Shepard Rogers III spent the first eleven years of his life moving among the military bases that marked his father's career, then moved with his family to an avocado ranch not far from the freeways and malls of Los Angeles. When he was twenty, Shepard came to New York, where he (temporarily) traded his hopes of becoming an actor for a more practical job as busboy at The Village Gate. At the same time, he began writing plays about contemporary America, which he presented through a mixture of the plastic artifacts of popular culture and the hallowed remains of the legendary West. The young playwright's vision proved one of unrelenting disruption, of an America that perpetuated the forms of its myths without understanding their essence. The Cowboy, the Gangster, the Rock Star, the Millionaire, all part of the American fabric, weave freely in and out of Shepard's plays, creating a sense of surface yet curiously celebrating the persistence of American mythology.

Formally, Shepard used paradox, transformation, juxtaposition, and metaphor, connecting and disconnecting fragmentary moments in a seemingly capricious dramatic design. His characters proved ravaged remnants of the consistency principle that Krutch, some twenty years earlier, had declared essential if characters were to be morally responsible. In place of dramatic dialogue, he offered the monologue, or "aria," an often lyrical – and always fascinating – expression of lonely self-absorption. Particularly in the plays of the sixties, Shepard's attraction to rock music, hallucinogenics, pop culture, and high tech, to John Cage, the Who, and the Rolling Stones found substantive and formal expression. It was almost predictable that Shepard would become America's most original and most exciting playwright of Off-Off Broadway.

Though the sixties plays were not the ones that have emerged as the defining work of Shepard's career – they included *Chicago* (1965), *Icarus's Mother* (1965), *Red Cross* (1966), *La Turista* (1967), *Melodrama Play* (1967), and *Forensic & the Navigators* (1967) – the young playwright was prolific in that decade, and a number of those early contributions exemplify the spirit that this renegade writer delivered to the New York stage. Shepard was to move further east, to London, in the early seventies, where he both secured and extended his reputation as an original theatrical voice. By that time, he had received substantial promotion in Off-Off Broadway venues such as La MaMa and Caffe Cino; six plays had received Obie Awards; Shepard had won two foundation grants, a Rockefeller in 1967 and a Guggenheim in 1968; and Lincoln Center had produced *Operation Sidewinder* (1970).

The first of Shepard's plays to be mounted in New York, *Cowboys*, appeared in 1964 at Theatre Genesis in a double bill with *Rock Garden*. Though the script is no longer extant, *Cowboys #2*, produced in 1967, provides a sense of Shepard's relationship to the concept of the cowboy, which was clearly part of his mythological West, where the free and adventuresome spirit reigns. Shepard compared the bonding among cowboys to his relationship with jazz musician Charlie Mingus, who shared an East Village apartment and a friendship with Shepard and who lent stimulation to the playwright's own sense of unbridled energy in the New York of the sixties. If the rewritten version is representative of the first, then *Cowboys* celebrates the power of language to reclaim a remembered world and to create an imaginative one of unbounded potential. Against a backdrop of sounds that define both an urban setting and the open West, two urban cowboys speak, in successive monologues, of life in the great outdoors even as two city men of pedestrian mind confirm the poverty of the urban landscape and language. Along the way, the cowboys engage in the kind of role-playing that anticipates the transformational drama of the seventies that fascinated Shepard and others in the Open Theatre.

Rock Garden, which Shepard described as a play about his leaving his father and mother, rewrites the American family drama in sixties Off-Off Broadway terms. Here the mythical idea of the garden serves as overlap to a peculiar perspective of rootlessness and desire. Presented in three scenes, the play first provides a silent look at the family at dinner: the father reading a magazine, the teenage daughter and son each sipping milk, and no one speaking. It then moves to a scene in which the mother, in bed, asks the boy, in a rocking chair, to run errands as she offers a complaining monologue about her own father and his. In scene three, father and son, in underwear, engage

in scant conversation and extended monologues, the father about his imagined rock garden, the son about sex, while masturbating.

Given the unorthodox rituals that inform both of the plays in this early
double bill, it is understandable that the reviews were sour. Fortunately,
however, Michael Smith of the *Village Voice* recognized the power and the
potential of this new playwright, providing an appreciation and an analysis
that enabled others to engage his surprising worlds. Shepard stayed in New
York for the remainder of the decade; some seventeen plays later, he had
given shape and form not only to his own career but to Off-Off Broadway. At
the end of the decade, having created a host of characters whose hallmark
was the hallucinogenic monologue, Shepard left New York for London – to get
"clean." (In 1965, he had avoided the draft by claiming heroin addiction.)

The sixties Off-Off Broadway theatre produced the early works of a number
of promising playwrights, including Maria Irene Fornés (*Tango Palace*, 1964;
Promenade, 1965; *A Vietnamese Wedding*, 1967); Michael McClure (*The Beard*,
1967); Rochelle Owens (*Futz*, 1967); Barbara Garson (*MacBird!*, 1967); and
Israel Horovitz (*Line*, 1967; *The Indian Wants the Bronx*, 1968).

Jean-Claude Van Itallie's *America Hurrah*, a trilogy of plays – *Interview, TV*,
and *Motel* – that wryly comments on America in the sixties, emerges from an
inventory of some dozen Off-Off Broadway and Los Angeles plays as his most
compelling. Contemporary in attitude, all three plays regret the impersonal-
ity of experience: in *Interview*, through a series of one-on-one conversations
in which communication fails; in *TV*, through the electronic depersonalizing
of three workers who are seduced by the attractions of television; and, most
conspicuously, in *Motel*, through mechanical dolls serving as desk clerk and
motel guests.

Kopit, Guare, Wilson, and later Albee

Arthur Kopit, after producing several plays in Cambridge, Massachusetts,
while he was a student at Harvard, made his London debut in 1961 and his
New York debut in 1962 with *Oh Dad, Poor Dad, Mamma's Hung You in the
Closet and I'm Feelin' So Sad*, a parodic treatment of the Oedipal impulse. Set
in Havana, with Madame Rosepettle a powerful maternal figure, the play presents a scene of irresistible humor: in it, the babysitter, Rosalie, seduces the
seventeen-year-old Jonathan in his mother's bed, only to be interrupted when
the corpse of his father, stowed in a closet, tumbles down on them. In the
aftermath of the event, Jonathan smothers Rosalie, is grabbed by the animated hand of his father, and, as the sound of harp strings fills the air, floats
out to the balcony to view the sky.

Kopit's irreverent humor also found expression in *The Day the Whores*

Came Out to Play Tennis (1965), in which he satirizes the country club crowd, who are decidedly unprepared for the arrival of eighteen unauthorized female tennis players in unsavory tennis costumes, sans underwear. The other Kopit play of special note (about a dozen were published or staged in the sixties) is *Indians*, which opened in an elaborate Broadway production at the Brooks Atkinson Theatre in 1969, following runs in London and Washington, D.C. In that comic-strip extravaganza, Kopit appropriates the legends of the American West: his Buffalo Bill (played by Stacy Keach) epitomizes the American tendency to romanticize the past and deny its cruelties – a fitting subject at a time when the nation was embroiled in a war in Vietnam and, within its borders, the Civil Rights Movement. Kopit's penchant for absurdity and black comedy, combined with his considerable skill at counterpoint and indirection, mark him as a distinctive voice on the Off-Off Broadway stage. A film version, *Buffalo Bill and the Indians*, appeared in 1976, directed by Robert Altman.

John Guare, whose most respected plays did not appear until 1971, also began his career in the sixties, with *The House of Blue Leaves* and *Two Gentlemen of Verona*, the latter a rock-musical adaptation, by Guare and Mel Shapiro, of the Shakespeare play. A master of the wacky and the weird, Guare surprises and amuses his audience with characters on the extremity of experience and carefully designed worlds that are always willing to yield to the absurd.

Lanford Wilson was among the most prolific of the new writers, with the sixties seeing some fifteen of his plays produced Off-Off Broadway, many of them at Caffe Cino and La MaMa, as well as in regional venues. By the end of the decade, Wilson had been recognized through a Drama Desk Vernon Rice Award (for *The Rimers of Eldritch*) and a Rockefeller Foundation grant and had had a play (*The Gingham Dog*, 1970) produced (unsuccessfully) on Broadway. Saddened by the suicide of Joe Cino, which effectively ended the "theatre of participation," Wilson, director Marshall Mason, and others founded the Circle Repertory Company.

Wilson's major achievement in the 1960s was *Balm in Gilead*, mounted at La MaMa in 1965. In that play, a crowded all-night coffee shop serves as the setting for a large cast of lonely, desperate people, the "riffraff," the drug dealers, the prostitutes of upper Broadway. Through fragments of overlapping, repetitive conversations, in the idiom of the street, Wilson provides a powerful snapshot of the dispossessed underclass and, more obliquely, the urban American family. Gradually, two characters come into focus: Joe, a pusher, and Darlene, a hooker, whose nostalgic monologue, lasting nearly half an hour in production, becomes the centerpiece of a world as bleak but as persistent as those created by Gelber (*The Connection*) and Beckett (*Waiting for Godot*). Through several revivals of this play and through contributions in subsequent decades, Wilson established himself as an important voice on the American stage.

Throughout the development of the Off-Off Broadway theatre, Albee continued to be a powerful force, irrespective of venue. The sixties saw a variety of Albee's dramatic work, including *Fam and Yam* (1960), a short comic sketch that satirizes the Broadway theatre scene; *The Sandbox* (1960), a short dramatic piece that provided Albee with characters for *The American Dream*; *The Death of Bessie Smith* (1960), a one-act play that dramatizes the racially difficult circumstances surrounding the death of the blues singer in Tennessee; four adaptations – *The Ballad of the Sad Café* (1963, based on Carson McCullers's novel), *Malcolm* (1966, based on James Purdy's novel), *Breakfast at Tiffany's* (1966, based on a Truman Capote story), and *Everything in the Garden* (1967, based on Giles Cooper's play) – and several major works, including *Tiny Alice* (1964), *A Delicate Balance* (1965), and *Box* and *Quotations from Chairman Mao Tse-Tung* (1968), all of which connected American drama with the contemporary European style.

Alan Schneider, who directed Broadway productions of all three plays, cast John Gielgud and Irene Worth in *Tiny Alice* at the Billy Rose Theatre. Opaque and symbolic, the play enigmatically explores belief in an abstraction, whether it be illusory or real. Amid allusions to youthful homosexuality, a Lawyer and a Cardinal discuss Miss Alice's huge bequest to the church and appoint Brother Julian to conclude the arrangements. Both the Lawyer and the Butler who welcomes the lay brother into Alice's mansion have had affairs with Miss Alice, and Brother Julian has a story as well: some years earlier, he spent six years in a mental facility suffering a breakdown occasioned by his loss of faith in God. In his interview with Alice, the ancient crone proves an illusion: Alice strips off her disguise to reveal a youthful, beautiful woman, and the two discuss their respective sexual lives and Julian's religious experiences. The meeting ends with the promise of their sexual union and marriage, though it is not clear whether Julian will marry Miss Alice herself or the tiny Alice in the miniature model of Miss Alice's castle – or both.

In fact, little in this play is clear. At the end, the Lawyer shoots Julian, prompting suspicions of a conspiracy among the Cardinal, the Lawyer, the Butler, and Miss Alice that repeats itself with each new victim, Julian having been the unhappy recipient this time. But the role of the miniature model and the replica of Miss Alice's castle preempts such a reading as primary, focusing attention instead on the metaphysical play that aligns Albee's dramatic experiment with those of Genet. For in *Tiny Alice*, as in *The Balcony* and *The Maids*, the palpable presence of the illusion reorients the illusory and the real. For Julian, as for the characters in Genet's plays, there is a moment, or a space, where the two meet to create a purified abstraction. Though Julian, at his death, may or may not understand the metaphysical force of the moment, he understands that the union of Miss Alice and tiny Alice, of the mansion and the model, of the real and the abstract, is what he, in his priesthood, has wanted and insisted on. Though critics were puzzled, and some distressed, over the obscurity of the play, *Tiny Alice* ran for 167 provocative performances.

As though in atonement, Albee countered with a play that returned audiences to the comfort of realism. *A Delicate Balance*, which opened at the Martin Beck Theatre in 1967 and won Albee a Pulitzer Prize, ran for 132 performances, with Jessica Tandy and Hume Cronyn as Agnes and Tobias. Though somewhat elusive, the play may be included among the repertory of domestic drama that dominated the American stage. In it, a middle-aged New England couple are visited by close friends, who seek refuge from an unnamed fear that has enveloped their home. The presence of the second couple provides the occasion for Agnes and Tobias to re-examine their own relationships, upsetting the "delicate balance" that the family, despite insensitivities, power struggles, and failures, has sustained. Intelligent and thoughtful, the play invites a consideration of the larger questions of existence and the careful illusions that keep life in place. (In 1973, it was made into a film, with Katharine Hepburn and Paul Scofield in the leading roles.)

The variety of Albee's art and the intensity of his concern about form are confirmed by his next contributions to the American stage: *Box* and *Quotations from Chairman Mao Tse-Tung*, presented at the Billy Rose Theatre following a run in Buffalo. In these pieces, Albee's theatre becomes, once again, a theatre of the avant-garde, a minimal, provocative theatre that refuses to respect the orthodoxies of the stage. In *Box*, which frames the presentation of *Quotations*, the only actor is in the form of a projected voiceover that meditates and muses while the audience looks at the outline of a cube. Precisely orchestrated, the Voice follows Albee's stage directions, which even specify the length of the pauses. Pervading its pronouncements is a deep sense of loss, encompassing both human experience and art.

In the companion piece, Albee puts four characters on the stage, on the deck of an oceanliner. They are Chairman Mao, a Long-Winded Lady, an Old Woman, and a Minister, the last having no lines. In this play, as in *Box*, Albee creates a musical structure of form and counterpoint, with actors directed to speak their lines rhythmically. The interplay of the Long-Winded Lady's personal past, Mao's predictions of global catastrophe (a recitation from the *Little Red Book* of Chairman Mao), the Old Woman's doggerel poem, and the intruding Voice from *Box* bring together the motif of loss. The box, which appears as prologue and as epilogue to the monologues of *Quotations* (which take place within the outlines of the cube) may be a symbolic coffin, containing the remnants of civilization and art.

Curiously, Albee's plays, though sharp in their challenge to conventional form and contemporary taste, continued to find venues on Broadway. There was an irony in this acceptance, yet there was an appropriateness in it as well, for Broadway had played a significant role in the playwright's youth. Born in 1928, Albee was adopted by a New York theatre owner, Reed Albee, and his wife, Frances. The infant was named for his adoptive grandfather, a well-known vaudeville producer; as a child, he was often taken to Broadway plays. Though Albee was thirty before *The Zoo Story* appeared, he had been an aspiring writer most of his life: at Choate and at Trinity College and for ten years in New York while he was working at odd jobs, including one, for three years, delivering telegrams for Western Union.

Groups and Collectives and Their Performance Pieces

Even as Albee, Shepard, and others were stretching the boundaries of literary form, Off-Off Broadway was playing host to a non-literary theatrical movement that celebrated the primacy of performance (see also Gussow, "Off- and Off-Off Broadway," and Carlson, "Alternative Theatre," Chapter 2). Among the earliest, most applauded, and most maligned of the avant-garde groups that helped create this Off-Off Broadway phenomenon was the Living Theatre, whose productions of Gelber's *The Connection* (1959) and *The Brig* (1963) proved seminal in the experimental theatre movement. The Living's politically radical, pacifist leaders, Judith Malina and Julian Beck, found a theatrical counterpart for their political anarchy in a form of production that insisted on the continuity of theatre and life; that celebrated nudity, sex, and freedom; and that employed provocation, intimidation, seduction, and shock. Its 1968–69 productions of *Mysteries – and Smaller Pieces, Frankenstein, Antigone*, and *Paradise Now* reflected a demolition of conventional forms too irreverent for contemporary critics to endure. The Living thrived on a physical and a verbal freedom so thorough that it was years after the staging of *Paradise Now* before the public knew that, amid the riot of theatrical sex witnessed and participated in by the audience, Malina was raped. The event, ironically, perfectly embodied the absorption of life into theatre, symbolically, though unholily, consummating the marriage between life and art. Even more ironically, the aggression inherent in rape became an operating principle for the experimental theatre, which intruded upon its audience's personal space through verbal and physical assault.

Intent on achieving an audience participation that would obscure the line dividing theatre and life, the experimental theatre of the sixties created performance spaces in places where no one suspected theatre could take place and repealed the law of audience passivity. The Happening, which had its genesis in the plastic arts with Allan Kaprow and soon became theatrically ubiquitous, provided minimal scripts, necessitating abundant improvisation, and freely mixed theatre and life.

In the Open Theatre, established in 1963, Joseph Chaikin and Peter Feldman were developing an aesthetic through which they could present dream, myth, and ritual on stage while breaking out of the rational dictates of mimetic theatre. The Open worked through meditation, developing a non-verbal stage language of gesture, rhythm, sound, and silence that functioned more through instinct than training and that, unlike the work of other groups, reflected passivity, not aggression. Among their important pieces was Van Itallie's *The Serpent*, which ritualistically and therapeutically connects the archetypes of the Garden of Eden and the primal murder with the assassinations of John F. Kennedy and Martin Luther King, and Megan Terry's *Viet Rock*, a fluidly structured satire of the war in Vietnam.

In the late sixties, Richard Schechner and Richard Foreman were redefining theatrical space through designing environments in which to perform the primitive rituals best exemplified by the Performance Group's *Dionysus in '69* (1968). Begun in 1968, Schechner's Performance Group dedicated itself to reacquiring ritual through a celebratory event involving actors, audience, and the free definition of theatrical space. *Dionysus in '69*, based on Euripides' *The Bacchae*, proved an orgiastic rendition of the life cycle, beginning with the ritual birth of Dionysus through the simulated birth passage created by naked actors. Freely sexual, the production invited spectators to partake in the orgy and to help create the portions of the event that did not rely on the Greek text.

At the same time, Peter Schumann's Bread and Puppet Theatre was engaging audiences in the Christian ritual of communion, beginning each of its productions with a bread-breaking ceremony before presenting its New Left activism. John Vaccaro and Charles Ludlam were developing their savagely nihilistic Theatre of the Ridiculous. Robert Wilson was staging his three-hour speechless epic, *Deafman Glance* (1971), in Paris, creating a Theatre of Silence. Jerzy Grotowski was developing his concept of "poor theatre" in Poland, with *Apocalypse cum figuris* (1968), and Peter Brook was experimenting with non-proscenium staging and "the empty space," most notably in his productions of *Marat/Sade* (1964) and *A Midsummer Night's Dream* (1970). In the Shakespeare play, the bare stage offered a whirligig of circus trapezes, conceived not as props but as extensions of the actors' bodies and voices, encouraging contemporary interpretations of the classics that stripped the stage of theatrical cliché.

For the Off-Off Broadway theatre of these performance groups, the dramatic text served as impetus for a range of theatrical experiments. No longer intent on recording the scenarios of daily experience, theatre became an experience in itself. But Off-Off Broadway's commitment to non-literary performance proved to be ephemeral, not only because performance events left only a few scattered scripts behind but also because playwrights with dramatic texts that deserved staging were exceptionally active as well.

Black Theatre

In the sixties African American drama came of age. Sporadically represented until that decade, most notably through Hansberry's *A Raisin in the Sun*, African Americans were now finding venues, in university and regional theatre, Off-Off Broadway, and, occasionally, on the Broadway stage.

The sixties, of course, saw much social action on the part of black Americans. In 1962, the National Guard assisted as James Meredith became the first African American to enroll at the University of Mississippi. In 1965, inner city blacks in Watts, Los Angeles, rioted; it was the same year that 4,000 blacks and civil rights supporters began their march from Selma to Montgomery, Alabama, in a demonstration that was to change the history of race relations.

In the sixties, LeRoi Jones – later Imamu Amiri Baraka – a playwright unwilling to relinquish the identity of black Americans to the national effort to integrate, wrote several assertive plays for the Off-Off Broadway stage: *The Baptism*, *The Dutchman*, *The Toilet*, and *The Slave*, produced in 1964, and *Experimental Death Unit #1* and *J-E-L-L-O*, produced in 1965. In the early years of Baraka's career, it seemed evident that the playwright, in taking a political position on black identity, needed to address some personal identity questions as well. As an undergraduate, Baraka had attended a traditionally black university (Howard), but he did his graduate work at Columbia; in the sixties, he was married to a white woman and was part of a Greenwich Village group of intellectuals for whom creativity was more prominent a priority than race. At a time when the Civil Rights Movement, the killing of black children at a church in Birmingham, and the riots in Watts were pressing men like Jones into action, there appeared to be a disconnection between the angry voice of the plays and Baraka's own life style. Within a short time, however, Baraka had divorced his wife, trained as a Muslim, moved to Harlem, and begun the Black Arts Repertory Theatre. *The Slave*, in fact, may metaphorically have anticipated his own personal conversion: in it, Walker Vessels, leader of a black revolutionary group, kills his former wife's professor husband and watches as a militant black army assaults and destroys their home.

Though Baraka's plays vary in the extent of their violence, all are calls for cultural independence. In *The Toilet*, a relationship between a white and a black that might have been does not find expression. In *Dutchman*, a black man on a subway elects not to kill a white woman who was harassing him, only to be murdered himself. In *Experimental Death Unit #1*, a militant army kills and decapitates two white homosexual men as well as a black prostitute, who, in trafficking with whites, allegedly earned her fate. And in *J-E-L-L-O*, Jack Benny's chauffeur, Rochester, rebels against his abusive and oppressive boss and wins full redress.

Baraka left New York in the mid-sixties to write for black audiences in Newark, where *Slave Ship* (1967), as well as other plays that enable or promote revolution, was performed. His successor Off-Off Broadway was Ed Bullins (b. 1935), whose work profiles the lives of blacks caught in a trap no less forceful and far more immediate than that in *Godot*. Through a cycle of plays that begins with *In the Wine Time* (1968), Bullins expresses frustration and hope over the individual and collective limitations and potential of blacks. Later in the decade, Bullins produced a number of short plays with clearer and angrier political statements about black identity, including *A Son, Come Home, The Electronic Nigger*, and *Clara's Ole Man*, all staged in New York in 1968.

Other African American playwrights of the period include James Baldwin (*Blues for Mister Charlie*, 1963), Douglas Turner Ward (*Day of Absence*, 1965), Alice Childress (*Wedding Band*, 1966, *Wine in the Wilderness*, 1969, and *String*, 1969), Charles Gordone (*No Place To Be Somebody*, 1969), and Lonnie Elder III (*Ceremonies in Dark Old Men*, 1969). Howard Sackler, though white, wrote *The Great White Hope* about the black boxer Jack Johnson, which was produced on Broadway in 1968–69 and won a Pulitzer, a Drama Critics' Circle Award, and a Tony. African Americans were assisted in their work by the Negro Ensemble Group, a Lower East Side theatre company founded in 1967 by Douglas Turner Ward, Robert Hooks, and Gerald S. Krone, and by Joseph Papp, whose New York Shakespeare Festival made a commitment to cross-racial casting and to staging the work of minority playwrights.

Women Playwrights/Feminist Theatre

At the same time, women were just beginning to establish themselves in the American theatre. Though women playwrights had made significant contributions to the theatre in the early part of the century – Susan Glaspell, Zoë Akins, and Sophie Treadwell, for example – and Hellman remained a major figure in American theatre, what is now known as feminist theatre, a phenomenon that has thrived since the seventies, began to emerge in the sixties, particularly in the work of Adrienne Kennedy and Megan Terry. Kennedy's *Funnyhouse of a Negro* (1964) was especially important, both to her career and to the development of a feminist presence on the American stage. Its focus is on Sarah, a young woman of mixed race who tries to find a space where she is secure in her sense of self. The daughter of a black father and a white mother, Sarah lives with a Jewish poet. She is aware of herself as a black with commitments to Africa yet is attracted to the European culture of her white intellectual friends. In the course of this expressionistic play, which generously uses masks, Sarah has fantasies of identity, aligning herself with four historical figures: Queen Victoria, the Duchess of Hapsburg, Patrice Lumumba, and Jesus. Unable to accept her own identity or to reconcile those of Lumumba and Jesus, whom she associates with her abusive father, Sarah commits suicide. In a companion piece, *The Owl Answers* (1965), Clara Passmore similarly attempts to get "rooted" in history and in self: unable to attend her black father's funeral, she seeks out her British heritage through encounters with an unwelcoming trio: Shakespeare, Chaucer, and William the Conqueror. The play culminates in the complicated symbolism of a ritual conflagration on the high altar/bed of St. Paul's.

Terry's *Ex-Miss Copper Queen on a Set of Pills* (1963) presents a similarly confused young woman, caught, without resources, between her sense of herself as a former midwest beauty queen and that of her current drug-addicted life as a prostitute on the streets of New York. *Calm Down Mother*, performed in 1965 at the Open, extends the fantasies and maskings into dramatic transformations, with the three actresses playing eight characters and switching identities on demand. In each of the eight units, women are in circumstances that reveal the range of their limitations as well as their potential as women. The play ends in an affirmation of self as all three celebrate their bellies, their bodies, and their "eggies," the source of both masculine control and feminine power. Five years later, in 1970, Terry wrote a dramatic tribute to the French philosopher Simone Weil called *Approaching Simone*. Clearly, feminist drama was off to a running start.

Broadway in the 1960s: More Miller, Williams, and Albee

Meanwhile, the Broadway theatre endured. In the sixties, Miller returned with *After the Fall* (1964), which opened the Vivian Beaumont Theater's first season at Lincoln Center following a run at the ANTA-Washington Square Theatre. The play is an odyssey of individual anguish, with Quentin, the confessional protagonist, obsessed with trying to understand why he continually searches for hope despite repeated disappointment. Its form, a conversation with a silent off-stage Listener and a dramatization of the landscape of Quentin's mind, enables Miller to range freely between past and present and to explore his protagonist's personal pain as a psychological exercise in memorial reconstruction as well as an investigation into the nature of good and evil – before and after the Fall. Quentin remembers events of his personal and professional life, including an encounter with the House Un-American Activities Committee and a marriage to Maggie, a woman of enormous sexual energy yet undaunted innocence. At the end of a therapeutic two hours, in which a concentration camp tower conspicuously looms, Quentin is closer to understanding guilt and responsibility and prepared to respond to Holga's hopeful hello.

The following year, *Incident at Vichy*, which deals with the public side of guilt and responsibility, documented Miller's continuing preoccupation with the Holocaust. The play, which dramatizes an event in wartime France, when the Vichy government routinely persecuted suspected Jews, is brutally insistent upon a guilt that refuses to discriminate, a guilt suggested by Holga's acknowledgment that, since the concentration camp, no one can be innocent. The event involves eight men and a boy who have been detained; Jews in the group fear that their false identity papers will be discovered, yet they refuse to believe in the death camp. One by one, Miller implicates each of the characters in the conspiracy of silence, self-interest, and delusion that enabled the Nazis to accomplish their barbarity. When only two men are left in the room – Von Berg and Leduc – there are gestures of generosity, even heroism, with the old Austrian Catholic offering the French Jew his pass. One cannot decide with confidence whether Leduc's motives in accepting it are decent or selfish.

In 1968, Broadway's Morosco Theatre became home to *The Price*, a play that collects the motifs and the concerns of Miller's earlier work – guilt, moral debt, self-delusion, choice, and consequence – into a story of two brothers, together for the first time in years. The occasion is the sale of their dead parents' belongings to a shrewd octogenarian dealer, who tries, unsuccessfully, to get them to see the worth of more than just the furniture. Instead, the two brothers, one a physician and one a policeman, invest in moral posturing that, despite revelations and accusations, ends where it began, with neither brother willing to settle the accumulation of moral debt. Solomon gets the furniture, and they the cash, but the differences between the brothers remain unresolved. Their rehearsal of the choices each made and the obligations that ensued once again makes the family the focus of attention, and, as with other Miller families, a framework of self-interest and deception is revealed. Miller's vision of the American family, though packaged in many forms, remained one of suspicion. But with Solomon, whose laughter resonates throughout the attic space at the end of the play, Miller knows the price that life demands.

During the run of *The Price*, which saw 429 performances, the millionth copy of *Death of a Salesman* was sold, leaving no doubt that Miller's reputation if not current influence remained strong. Even as Miller's career seemed to be once more gaining momentum, Williams's, by contrast, was clearly winding down. In addition to an experiment with comedy (*Period of Adjustment*, which opened in Florida in 1958 and New York in 1960) and several one-act plays, the sixties introduced *The Night of the Iguana* (1961, film version

1964), *The Milk Train Doesn't Stop Here Anymore* (1963, film version – *Boom* – 1968), and *In the Bar of a Tokyo Hotel* (1969).

The first of these, *The Night of the Iguana*, is generally seen as a point of punctuation in Williams's career. That play, with its attention to the misfit who struggles to find personal, spiritual, and social space, is thematically of a piece with Williams's earlier work, though its conciliatory tone may suggest a mellowing of Williams's own obsessions. The defrocked minister who is the focus of *Iguana* was locked out of his church after kneeling, then reclining, with a young woman, who, in remorse, tried to commit suicide. Now a tour guide, he visits a resort near Puerto Barrio, Mexico, run by Maxine Faulk. Other hotel guests, including Hannah Jelkes, an artist, and her ninety-seven-year-old poet grandfather, who dies after completing his most lyrical poem; a busload of teachers from the Baptist Female College in Blowing Rock, Texas; and four young Germans form the backdrop for the experience of The Reverend T. Lawrence Shannon, who is removed from his responsibilities as tour guide and dramatically urinates on the ladies' luggage but who apparently pairs off at the end with Maxine. There is a sense of resignation and reconciliation in this Williams play, which still acknowledges the struggle but seems more willing to yield.

Following *Iguana*, which ran for 316 performances at the Royale and was made into a film in 1964 with Richard Burton, Deborah Kerr, and Ava Gardner, Williams's plays became less structured and more philosophically abstract, exploring the culminating moments of life and of art with less of the frustration and anger of the earlier plays. In *The Milk Train Doesn't Stop Here Any More*, he writes a modern-day *Everyman*, with Flora Goforth in search of a way to exit this life with dignity and acceptance. She is assisted in her quest by a man in lederhosen, who is both poet and Angel of Death. Chris Flanders's mission is to give her not what she wants but what she needs: he cryptically does so by presenting her with a mobile called "The Earth is a Wheel in a Great Big Gambling Casino." The withdrawn widow dies behind a screen with Chris escorting her across the bar.

In *In the Bar of a Tokyo Hotel*, Williams insistently explores the artistic imagination, through an American woman, Miriam, who fears the loss of her vitality, and her painter husband Mark, whose style is in a dramatic transition. When the gallery director Leonard arrives from New York, he attempts to convince Miriam not to continue her tour alone. But she has little compassion for her dependent husband, who, faced with her cold refusal, collapses and dies. Though cryptic in purpose, the play invited critics to see the piece as the (autobiographical) profile of an artist at a low point in his career.

The play may have proved prophetic, for in the dozen or so years remaining before the freak occurrence that claimed his life in 1983 (a nasal spray cap suffocated him), the playwright was to enjoy little commercial success. Though theatregoers may recall the titles of some of Williams's seventies and eighties plays – such as *Small Craft Warnings* (1972), *Vieux Carré* (1977), and *Clothes for a Summer Hotel* (1980) – none of these promises to gain prominence in the repertoire of American theatre, and many – *Seven Descents of Myrtle* (1968), *Out Cry* (1971), *This Is (an Entertainment)* (1976), *The Red Devil Battery Sign* (1975), *Demolition Downtown* (1977), *Crève Coeur* (1978), *Something Cloudy, Something Clear* (1981), and *A House Not Meant to Stand* (1982) – have already disappeared from the vocabulary of the stage.

Neither Miller nor Williams left a major mark on the sixties stage. Albee was center stage now, with plays that disturbed complacent audiences and pushed against the boundaries of the realistic form. He shared the spotlight with an unlikely partner: a playwright who thrived on the conventions of the comic form and capitalized on the public's penchant for the one-liner. Born in the Bronx in 1927 (a year before Albee), Neil Simon proved a commercial phenomenon: at one point in the sixties, four of his plays were in simultaneous runs on Broadway.

Broadway's Star: Neil Simon

Neil Simon had begun his writing career doing comedy sketches and revues for radio and television with his brother Danny. His break on Broadway came in 1961, with his first play, *Come Blow Your Horn*, which premiered the previous year at the Bucks County (Pennsylvania) Playhouse and began a sequence of successes that remained uninterrupted until 1970, when *The Gingerbread Lady*, Simon's first effort to mix comedy and tragedy and his first commercial flop, suggested that the public may have had its fill of Simon. (The signal proved false, for Simon, even into the late nineties, though somewhat tempered, continues his appeal.) A master of the running gag, the circular joke, and the witty one-liner, Simon prods his audiences into the kind of unrestrained laughter he himself experienced as a youth at a Charlie Chaplin, Buster Keaton, or Laurel and Hardy movie. Through recognizable characters (often caricatures) and familiar settings – particularly the urban middle-class American living room – Simon, himself the son of a truant father, comically and conservatively upholds the value and the primacy of marriage and family.

In *Come Blow Your Horn*, two brothers, Buddy and Alan, modeled on Neil and Danny, enjoy their independence in New York in the older brother's apartment. Their bachelor exploits, drawn against the backdrop of parents unable to release their sons to the world, prove an education to Alan. By play's end, the profligate older brother has matured into a man who, sounding much like his father, prepares to settle into marriage. Along the way, there are appearances by Peggy, the woman upstairs, with whom Alan has been sexually involved; Connie, who arrives with suitcases in hand, ready to move in with

Alan, with or without marriage; Mr. and Mrs. Baker, parents of the young men; and, finally, Aunt Gussie, who drops in to find Buddy alone, anticipating an evening with a woman named Snow. Mrs. Baker's antics provide much of the humor of the play, which relies on the interrupting doorbell and telephone rings to activate a fresh sequence. Her efforts to be helpful by taking messages even though she cannot find a pencil result in a mêlée of confusions that neutralize some of the crueler behavior of her domineering husband, who has employed both their sons in the family business. It is Mr. Baker who animates the play, however, for, at its heart, *Come Blow Your Horn* is not only an exploration of traditional and newer values but also an inquiry into what manhood and masculinity mean, particularly within the context of family. Though it took the prolific Simon three years to write this first Broadway play, the finished product bears the mark of a craftsman adept at constructing and sustaining a plot, renewing an audience's laughter periodically, and exploring family values at moments of challenge or change. Directed by Stanley Prager, the New York production at the Brooks Atkinson Theatre enjoyed a quite respectable 677-performance run.

At the end of the decade, following the successes of *Barefoot in the Park* (1963), *The Odd Couple* (1965), and *Plaza Suite* (1968), a new Simon play proved once again to be a crowd-pleaser. *Last of the Red Hot Lovers*, which opened at the Eugene O'Neill Theater in late 1969 and ran for 706 performances, is, like *Come Blow Your Horn*, typically Simon. Structured in three parts, the play presents the adventures of Barney Cashman, who is involved sequentially with three women. The setting is Barney's mother's apartment, which he uses during her absences to serve him in his first adulterous affair. Prompted by the boredom of daily life, the middle-aged owner of a fish restaurant, who worries that his fingers smell of fish, invites Elaine Navazio to the apartment; she is a woman given to alcohol, cigarettes, and casual affairs, and her agenda does not include the romantic prologue that Barney imagines. Prevented by their incompatible visions of sexual experience to accomplish the act, Barney is left disappointed and disillusioned.

Eight months later, he tries again, this time with Bobbi Michele, who tells stories of incipient kinky sex that intrigue Barney. Barney joins Bobbi in a joint – his first experience with marijuana – which renders him hopelessly convinced that he is dying and her adamant about her own independence and the viciousness of others.

In the third of his unsuccessful trysts, which occurs one month later, Barney plays host to Jeanette Fisher, who proves to be a deeply depressed woman who clings to her purse, does not enjoy sex, and is married to a long-time friend of the Cashmans. When Jeanette leaves the apartment, Barney has secured from her an admission that some people are decent. Despite his aggressive behavior, however, Barney's sexual appetite and his quest for a beautiful, decent woman have not been satisfied. The play ends with Barney on the phone to his wife, asking the reluctant woman to meet him in his mother's apartment.

In another playwright's hands, such portraits of neurotic people and relationships may well challenge the conventions of marriage and family. In Simon's repertory, however, these institutions, no matter how flawed, survive, if not on the stage then at least in the minds of the audience, who are always made aware of what might have been. It is not surprising that virtually all of Simon's sixties plays – and subsequent ones as well – have been made into films, for they tap into the ordinary lives of middle-class urban Americans struggling to communicate and to understand. Simon's playful humor makes palatable each desperate character and occasion; theatregoers leave Simon's plays feeling good about themselves and comfortably entertained.

The Musical

The Broadway musical, explored in more detail in Chapters 2 (Maslon, "Broadway") and 4, which typically had a goal similar to Simon's, remained a staple of the American theatre during the postwar years. Blockbuster musicals such as *Carousel* (1945), *South Pacific* (1949), *My Fair Lady* (1956), *The Sound of Music* (1959), and *Fiddler on the Roof* (1964) – to name just a few – continued to please the Broadway tourist crowd – and, for many, to define the American theatre.

In 1967, however, a musical of another sort premiered at the Public Theater. Highly theatrical and entertaining, *Hair*, a rock musical, captured the spirit and the conflicts of the sixties, pitting the long-hair generation against the Establishment and celebrating nudity, free love, and rock'n'roll (see Aronson's discussion of these and other factors in Chapter 1). A central character, Claude, finally opts not to burn his draft card, but he winds up a casualty of Vietnam. Galt MacDermot's music and Gerome Ragni and James Rado's lyrics were insistently contemporary, promising the deliverance of the conservative musical theatre into the Age of Aquarius. Though *Hair* ran for 1,844 performances in two venues, first at the Public and then on Broadway, it proved an isolated event, with little lasting influence on the form of the musical stage.

Conclusion

By the end of the sixties, the Broadway theatre's customer base was shrinking, as were its artistic standards. Millions of families across the nation owned television sets, which not only seduced audiences into the effortless evening in the living room armchair but also set a new, diminished standard for drama.

Writers of talent found themselves generating sitcoms, serials, and Westerns in return for handsome financial rewards. At the same time, Broadway was coping with increases in operating costs: by the end of the fifties, a serious play needed a weekly income of $20,000, a musical $40,000, to offset the $250,000–$500,000 it cost to underwrite the show. This situation would only worsen throughout the remainer of the century. To help assure the show's success, producers relied on expensive advertising and star appeal, denying the price of a ticket to all but the elite, for whom seeing a Broadway play became a status game. Discriminating theatregoers with more slender wallets abjured the Broadway stage or selectively invested in a play – after they read the review. For the 1969–70 season, Broadway mounted only sixty-two plays, 200 fewer than had been on its boards forty years earlier. Given the excesses and the mediocrity of Broadway, made palpable in its inhospitality to serious playwrights and its reluctance to revise the musical after *Hair*, it is not surprising that the Off-Off Broadway theatre materialized.

The twenty-five years following the close of World War II saw a number of defining moments in the development of the American theatre. Miller, Williams, Inge, and Albee, whose plays were produced on Broadway, recognized the conventions of culture and theatre that were too stubborn to disappear, yet treated them in original and provocative ways, reconstituting the form of the domestic play and extending America's chronic inquiry into the role of the nuclear family. At the same time, a conservative Broadway theatre, marked by the comedies of Neil Simon, sustained traditional forms and values, as did the ubiquitous musical, a collaboration of song, book, and dance, often bundled into leg shows and lavish entertainments, that continues to attract audiences from around the world and to sustain New York's reputation as the theatre capital. With the rise of regional theatres and the emergence of Off-Off Broadway, however, the focus that Broadway once enjoyed has been diffused, with Broadway increasingly identified as a commercial theatre designed for popular audiences rather than as the venue for the serious play. In the sixties, Shepard and a host of playwrights who might not otherwise have found a stage for their work turned to the developing Off-Off Broadway theatre, which welcomed not only the experimental playwright but a band of new performance groups as well. Mapping the progress of these postwar years reveals a variegated American stage, whose elevations and depressions collectively create a cartography of an art form distinctively our own.

Bibliography: Plays and Playwrights: 1945–1970

Though no survey of American drama precisely dedicates itself exclusively to the twenty-five years immediately following World War II, a number of more comprehensive studies cover the plays and playwrights of this period. Bigsby's work in this area is extensive. In an early analysis, *Confrontation and Commitment*, he offers an assessment of a developing contemporary American theatre. Focusing on the work of Miller, Albee, James Baldwin, Jones (Baraka), Hansberry, and some of the Off-Off Broadway performance groups, including the Living Theatre, Bigsby observes that American audiences, twenty years after World War II, were still attracted to the well-made play and the American theatre had not fully absorbed the lessons of the European stage. From 1982–85, Bigsby published an exceptionally insightful three-volume study of the American drama, with volumes two and three offering coverage of these years. In *A Critical Introduction to Twentieth-Century American Drama, Volume Two: Williams/Miller/Albee*, Bigsby provides information and analyses on the work of these three major playwrights within the social, political, and theatrical contexts of postwar America. In volume three, *Beyond Broadway*, he covers the Off- and Off-Off Broadway theatre movements, critically assessing the patterns and the anomalies of this burgeoning alternative theatre. In yet another study, *Modern American Drama 1945–1990*, he extends his analyses of the work of major playwrights, including Miller, Williams, Albee, and Shepard.

Other valuable studies include Adler, *American Drama, 1940–1960*, which offers a solid overview of the twenty years indicated in its title, with particularly helpful comments on the major writers treated here. Berkowitz's *American Drama of the Twentieth Century* clusters plays chronologically, with the relevant sections running from 1945–60 and 1960–75. Though Cohn's *New American Dramatists* and Roudané's *American Drama Since 1960* include only ten years of the period in focus here, Cohn provides a wide-ranging survey of playwrights and Roudané brings special emphasis to the work of African Americans and women. Krutch, in *"Modernism" in Modern Drama*, a monograph referenced in the early paragraphs of this essay, offers a personal view on modern European theatre, providing a context for his assessment of a modern American theatre in its infant years. And finally, *Realism and the American Dramatic Tradition*, edited by Demastes, though not limited to this twenty-five-year period, includes a number of relevant essays.

Readers interested in a critical overview of Arthur Miller's work may consult any of several introductory books on the plays, including Moss, *Arthur Miller*; Carson, *Arthur Miller*; Welland, *Miller: The Playwright;* Schlueter and Flanagan, *Arthur Miller* – as well as Bigsby's volume on Miller, Williams, and Albee mentioned in the previous paragraph and *The Cambridge Companion to Arthur Miller*, which he edited. Collections of essays worth pursuing are *Arthur Miller: A Collection of Critical Essays* edited by Corrigan; *Critical Essays on Arthur Miller* edited by Martine; and *Arthur Miller: New Perspectives*, edited by Robert A. Martin. Valuable interviews appear in *Conversations with Arthur Miller* edited by Roudané and *Arthur Miller and Company* edited by Bigsby. Essential supplements to any critical reading of Miller's work are *The Theater Essays of Arthur Miller* edited by Robert A. Martin and Miller's autobiography, *Timebends*, in which the playwright offers generous commentary on his life and his writing.

There are a number of introductory studies of Tennessee Williams's work, among them Tischler, *Tennessee Williams*; Jackson, *The Broken World of Tennessee Williams*; Falk, *Tennessee Williams*; Londré, *Tennessee Williams*; and *The Cambridge Companion to Tennessee Williams*, edited by Roudané. Murphy's *Tennessee Williams and Elia Kazan* provides important information on how one of America's most influential directors translated the texts of Williams's plays onto the stage. Readers interested in the film versions of Williams's plays should consult Yacowar, *Tennessee Williams and Film*, which treats fifteen translations of plays to the screen – all released in the fifties and sixties. Two collections of essays worth exploring are *Tennessee Williams: A Collection of Critical Essays* edited by Stanton, and *Tennessee Williams: A Tribute* edited by Tharpe. In 1975, Williams published his *Memoirs*, a volume that joined a number of biographical treatments already in print and anticipated several that were to appear after his death in 1983. The best of these is a critical biography by Spoto, *The Kindness of Strangers*, though the most thorough biography of his early life is Leverich's *Tom*. Interesting interviews with the playwright are collected in *Conversations with Tennessee Williams* edited by Devlin.

Early assessments of Edward Albee's work include Bigsby, *Albee*; Cohn, *Edward Albee*; and Rutenberg, *Edward Albee: Playwright in Protest* – all in 1969. More recent – and confirming – analyses may be found in McCarthy, *Edward Albee*; Roudané, *Understanding Edward Albee*; and Amacher, *Edward Albee*. Two edited volumes that offer focused analyses of particular Albee plays are *Edward Albee: A Collection of Critical Essays* edited by Bigsby, and *Critical Essays on Edward Albee* edited by Kolin and Davis. A stimulating set of interviews may be found in *Conversations with Edward Albee*, edited by Kolin. Those interested in a comprehensive bibliography of primary and secondary works may wish to consult Giantvalley, *Edward Albee: A Reference Guide*.

Insights into Sam Shepard's work may be culled from Tucker, *Sam Shepard;* Mottram, *Inner Landscapes*; Hart, *Sam Shepard's Metaphorical Stages*; DeRose, *Sam Shepard*; and two recent studies: Bottoms, *The Theatre of Sam Shepard*, and Wade, *Sam Shepard and the American Theatre*. Kimball King's *Sam Shepard: A Casebook* is a helpful collection of essays, with several on the sixties plays. *American Dreams: The Imagination of Sam Shepard*, edited by Marranca, offers a compendium of perceptive essays, including several by Shepard. Oumano's biography, *Sam Shepard*, provides a solid analysis of this fascinating figure's life and work. And Bigsby's chapter on Shepard in the *Beyond Broadway* volume mentioned in the opening paragraph is essential reading.

Readers interested in Neil Simon's sixties plays should consult McGovern, *Neil Simon*, or Johnson, *Neil Simon*. Simon's *Rewrites: A Memoir* offers limited insights. Those interested in William Inge would be intrigued by Voss, *A Life of William Inge*, and by Leeson, *William Inge: A Research and Production Sourcebook*. Other full-length studies of individual dramatists who played important roles in the twenty-five years after World War II include Cheney, *Lorraine Hansberry*; Auerbach, *Sam Shepard, Arthur Kopit, and the Off Broadway Theater*; Barnett, *Lanford Wilson*; Brown, *Amiri Baraka*, and Baraka, *The Autobiography of LeRoi Jones; Intersecting Boundaries: The Theatre of Adrienne Kennedy*, edited by Bryant-Jackson and Overbeck, and Kennedy, *People Who Led to My Plays*; and Samuel Hay, *Ed Bullins*.

There are a host of books on the American musical theatre. See Degen, Chapter 4, for suggestions.

Important reference books include Roudané, *Contemporary Authors: Bibliographical Series, Volume Three: American Dramatists*, which offers a primary and secondary bibliography as well as bibliographical essays on a number of playwrights from this period (Albee, Baraka, Hansberry, Kennedy, Kopit, McCullers, Miller, Shepard, Terry, Williams, and Wilson), and Bronner, *The Encyclopedia of the American Theatre 1900–1975*. Methuen's "Writers on File" series is particularly helpful, with compact volumes on many of the playwrights discussed in this chapter. Arnott's *Tennessee Williams on File* offers a representative example: the book catalogues the plays, providing information on publication and production as well as excerpts from critical reviews. Brief biographies of playwrights and entries on many plays from this period can be found in Wilmeth and Miller.

Plays and Playwrights Since 1970

Matthew Roudané

Introduction

American playwrights since 1970 have moved their way toward the center of
the national creative consciousness. The best have done so by making significant contributions to the rhetoric of nationhood, to the languages that define
the "Americanness" of American drama, and to the symbology of the self. Of
the numerous forces affecting the cultural production and reception of texts
and performances, perhaps one of the most distinguishing shifts in recent
American drama concerns its relationship to Broadway. When Eugene O'Neill,
Susan Glaspell, and Alice Gerstenberg first conferred upon the American stage
its modernity, Broadway in New York City was the Great White Way. Then,
Broadway was the site of dramatic originality. Broadway was the launching
site for playwrights who, with uneven achievements, defined the scope and
emphasis of American drama. Broadway somehow mattered. Its stages mirrored the circulation of social *energia*. When O'Neill's *The Hairy Ape* (1922)
premiered, the Mayor of New York City, troubled by the play's themes, tried
to close the show. The public, in response, flocked to see one of the first successful Expressionistic plays staged by an American. When at mid-century
Lillian Hellman, Tennessee Williams, Arthur Miller, and Lorraine Hansberry
extended as they refurbished notions of American theatrical modernity,
Broadway was still a vibrant source of theatrical energy. Four plays in a four-
year span confirm the point: *The Glass Menagerie* (1945), *A Streetcar Named
Desire* (1947), *All My Sons* (1947), and *Death of a Salesman* (1949) together ran
for 2,466 performances. By contrast, Williams's last Broadway play staged
prior to his death, *Something Cloudy, Something Clear* (1981), closed after only
fifty-one showings to indifferent reviews. Miller simply chose to premiere
selected recent plays outside of Broadway, *The Ride Down Mt. Morgan* opening
in London in 1991 and *Broken Glass* premiering in New Haven, then London,
and finally New York City in 1994.

As the twenty-first century begins, Broadway has changed. If the earlier
Broadway was an initiating theatre, where key plays received their premieres,
today many of the best American playwrights open their shows both geographically and symbolically well beyond Broadway. The decentralization
process is unmistakable. Edward Albee opened *Counting the Ways* (1976) in

London and *Marriage Play* (1987) and *Three Tall Women* (1992) in Vienna. David Mamet staged *Glengarry Glen Ross* (1983) and *The Cryptogram* (1994) in London. Sam Shepard waited two decades before staging a play, *A Lie of the Mind,* on Broadway (1985). Further, these three playwrights, along with an increasing number of fellow dramatists, began directing their own works, an exercise of authorial control rarely seen during the mid-century glory days of such directors as Elia Kazan and José Quintero. In some respects, Albee's point in a 1962 article, "Which Theatre Is the Absurd One?" – in which he calls Broadway the true Theatre of the Absurd because of its cultural production of and insistence upon superficial work – remains true today. For the many cultural and ideological reasons suggested throughout this *History,* Broadway now is a receiving theatre. Broadway, a showcase theatre, is a place where musicals, classics, or guaranteed contemporary sensations find their way to the stage. So it is hardly surprising that Tony Kushner's *Angels in America, Part One: Millennium Approaches* was first staged in Los Angeles in 1990, in San Francisco in 1991, in London and then back to Los Angeles (with *Part Two: Perestroika*) in 1992, and – now a profitable play with its moral seriousness left unblemished by commercial pressures – finally opened in New York City in 1993. It is scarcely astonishing that works by "major" playwrights featuring entertainment stars, who ensure packed houses, occasionally open on Broadway, as was the case with Mamet's *Speed-the-Plow* (1988), which starred Madonna, or the 1988 revival of Beckett's *Waiting for Godot* (1952), which featured the comedic talents of Steve Martin and Robin Williams.

If Broadway no longer appears as alluring to actors as it did for Carrie Meeber, Theodore Dreiser's fated star in *Sister Carrie* (1900), the United States today nonetheless continues producing a healthy number of "major" *and* lesser-known but still significant dramatists. Thus this chapter examines selected playwrights who, if not strictly linked to Broadway, have seen their best work staged in New York City and, indeed, throughout the country, and who may be regarded as major shapers of the American stage. Such a selective survey should provide some notion of the aesthetic and cultural power of American drama since 1970, while admittedly, a result of space limitations, omitting many worthy writers from this discussion. As we shall see, the American dramatists' preoccupations with the status of the imagination, the primal family unit, with a Heideggerian *angst,* and with the collapse of physical, mental, and moral space that Christopher Bigsby identified throughout his three-volume *A Critical Introduction to Twentieth-Century American Drama* have become even more pronounced as we approach the next millennium. No wonder Tennessee Williams in the seventies wrote a play called *Small Craft Warnings (1972),* Arthur Kopit in the eighties composed a drama entitled *End of the World* (1984), and Neil Simon in the nineties penned a comedy called *Lost in Yonkers* (1991), fitting titles foretelling the shifts in cultural tastes and theatrical energies.

When in the early sixties, Judith Malina and Julian Beck, leaders of the Living Theatre, were asked to define the artistic vision of the Living Theatre, they replied, "*To increase conscious awareness, to stress the sacredness of life, to break down the walls*" (Beck, "Storming the Barricades," 18). In summarizing the artistic goals of the Living Theatre, they did much more than issue a mere manifesto celebrating their militant, Artaudian stage. More importantly, Malina and Beck did nothing less than distill, in fifteen words, what would evolve into one of the most compelling, distinctive features of American drama since 1970.

Our best dramatists do not compose all of their plays with these three specific ideas in mind. Yet since 1970 America's exemplary playwrights seem emotionally and intellectually to accept Malina and Beck's *pronunciamento*. With the twenty-first century upon us, the idealism, ferocity, and optimism of Malina's "Directing *The Brig*" (1964) and Beck's "Storming the Barricades" (1964) may read more like a dream-glide down memory lane. However, their impassioned belief that the theatre increases consciousness, celebrates the sacred, and, politically as well as existentially, produces change remains as true for Hanay Geiogamah, Tony Kushner, and Holly Hughes as it did for Eugene O'Neill, Susan Glaspell, and Tennessee Williams. If yesterday's revolution has been appropriated by today's mainstream, the pioneering work of Malina and Beck foretold the social confrontations and personal commitments that so characterize recent American drama.

Engaged by the contributions of Eugene O'Neill, Gertrude Stein, and Susan Glaspell, and the subsequent work of Clifford Odets, Robert Anderson, Lillian Hellman, Arthur Miller, Tennessee Williams, and William Inge, American audiences grew increasingly eager to receive new theatre. Despite considerable cultural, financial, and artistic blockades that to this day inhibit the American dramatist, at no time in our cultural history have our playwrights been in a better position to move the American stage from the margins to the center of American cultural life. This generative process is ever on the verge of collapse, of course. Yet American dramatists have learned from their past. They transcended the circus, the carnival, the minstrel show, the farce, and the vaudeville. With an eye toward the future, American dramatists have embedded in their plays a kind of a moral seriousness that the novelists and poets long ago interleaved within their artistry.

The sources of this generative process were many. There was no one single, unifying troupe, movement, or playwright responsible for launching *the* American theatre since 1970. After all, issues of race, gender, tastes, and ideologies in an increasingly heterogeneous universe precluded a unified American dramatic canon. The American dramatic imagination seemed as varied and contradictory as the country itself. Recent American drama emerges as a dizzying amalgam of many voices, many peoples, and few resolutions. The contemporary American playwright, whose conceptions of drama, society, and the individual are as different as any audience could imagine, implicitly shares Malina and Beck's conviction that drama has a unique capacity to produce both social change and individual awareness. The mimetic energy of contemporary American drama reflects a culture seeking to locate its identity through the ritualized action and incantatory language inscribed in live theatre. The playwrights, directors, and players involved in serious theatre in this country presuppose the bewitching power of the theatre to trigger public awareness and private insight, or at least to raise the possibility that the theatre as public laboratory can ask the audience to see and be seen in both a personal and public context. Thus beyond their differing theoretical positions and political strategies, recent American dramatists seem united in their collective quarrel with American history and thought, a quarrel that manifests itself in ideologically and metaphysically diverse scripts.

American drama, for Julian Beck, had the capacity to "involve or touch or engage the audience, not just show them something." He felt that his drama, at once a political and metaphysical gesture, "arose out of a crying need on the part of the authors, and of us, to reach the audience, to awaken them from their passive slumber, to provoke them into attention, shock them if necessary, and, this is also important, to involve the actors with what was happening in the audience" (Beck, "Storming the Barricades," 21). In retrospect, we can now see that Beck really could be speaking with equal force and eloquence about John Guare's *Six Degrees of Separation* (1990), Susan Yankowitz's *Night Sky* (1991), or Anna Deavere Smith's *Fires in the Mirrors* (1993).

Twentieth-century American drama has always been energized by ritualized forms of confrontation and expiation. With the country's ongoing dialogues about the sexes and races, and with the country's past involvement in the Vietnam War and the Persian Gulf War, the playwright's awareness of and uneasiness with American history and politics underscores the notion that, despite the Founding Fathers' claims to democracy, the United States has never in its history experienced cultural hegemony. America's dramatists have always known this. They have narrativized such knowledge in their scripts. Therefore, in a performative and tribal sense, much of contemporary American drama may be regarded as staging myths of rebellion: rebellions against the self, the other, the primal family unit, or the culture itself. The confrontations embodied in contemporary plays reflect the playwright's responses to a culture whose identity radically transformed itself after World War II. The spectacles of Adrienne Kennedy, Christopher Durang, or Megan Terry, like those of their European counterparts, Samuel Beckett, Jean Genet, or Caryl Churchill, not only reflect such transformations but often outline alternative responses that somehow seem more real in their absurdist or alogical textures than surface reality itself. The contemporary dramatist's preoccupation with art, artifice, and theatricality reflects his or her essentially moral impulse to impose some form of order upon an age of uncertainty.

For Tennessee Williams by the seventies, imposing some order seemed problematic at best. Most theatregoers agree that after *Night of the Iguana* (1961), his last major success, Williams entered what he himself called his "stoned age." To be sure, he continued to write until his death in 1983: he composed at least sixty new plays, though most were never published and many seldom if ever performed. Such plays as *The Milk Train Doesn't Stop Here Anymore* (1963), *In the Bar of a Tokyo Hotel* (1969), *Small Craft Warnings* (1972), *Out Cry* (1973), *Vieux Carré* (1977), sparked some popular interest, but the critics became, with each new play, less impressed. Perhaps *The Red Devil Battery Sign* serves as an example of Williams's declining reputation. At the 18 June 1975 preview run of the play at the Shubert Theatre in Boston, Anthony Quinn, who played the lead character, King Del Ray, offered free tickets to any theatregoer who felt he did not get his money's worth. A reviewer in the *Boston Globe* reported that "Director Edwin Sherin appeared on stage and told the capacity house that what it was going to see was a 'working rehearsal . . . Mr. Quinn has asked me to make this explanation to you. If any of you would prefer to come back at some later time during the run, you are welcome to as his guests' . . . No one took up Quinn's offer . . ." (quoted in Arnott, *Tennessee Williams on File*, 61). Indeed, it is difficult to imagine that *Kirche, Kuchen und Kinder* (1979) and *Will Mr. Merriweather Return from Memphis?* (1980) were written by the author of some of America's most brilliant plays. By the time of the last plays staged before his death, *Clothes for a Summer Hotel* (1980) and *Something Cloudy, Something Clear* (1981), Williams was remembered as a playwright whose best works appeared between 1945 and 1961. In all fairness the later Williams is not as bad as the critics tend to think, and recently scholars have argued that the playwright's language and visual and aural experimentations during his last twenty years provide actors and directors with unique materials (see Cohn, "The Last Two Decades," 232–43). Perhaps his *The Notebooks of Trigorin* (1996) will rekindle some critical interest. Still, with such plays as *The Glass Menagerie, A Streetcar Named Desire, Camino Real, Cat on a Hot Tin Roof*, and *The Night of the Iguana*, Williams not only inspired an entire generation of theatregoers but reinvented as he validated the American stage.

Re-enter Albee

While Williams's influence began to fade during and after the sixties, Edward Albee's emerged. Few playwrights in the sixties and seventies influenced

American drama more than Albee. The beneficiary of his American predecessors, O'Neill, Miller, and Williams especially, he also was receptive to European influences, particularly those of Samuel Beckett, Eugène Ionesco, Peter Handke, Jean Genet, and Harold Pinter. Albee would ultimately prove able to move freely, if uncomfortably, between the alternative environs of the Off-Broadway theatrical movement and Broadway. While gaining inspiration from his dramatic forebears here and abroad, Albee also looked ahead, encouraging and supporting a number of then unknown dramatists – Adrienne Kennedy, Amiri Baraka, and Sam Shepard, among others. A playwright more at ease in staging his work on the margins, Albee found himself at the very epicenter of the American dramatic world.

After dropping out of college in his freshman year, Albee worked for ten years at a series of odd jobs before composing *The Zoo Story* (1959), his spectacular first success, as noted in the first section of this chapter. Albee's influence was especially felt during the sixties, though his reputation faded after *A Delicate Balance* (1966) and the inventive companion plays, *Box* and *Quotations from Chairman Mao Tse-Tung* (1968). Despite winning a Pulitzer for *Seascape* (1975), Albee's dramas since 1970, most theatregoers felt, seemed more like unfinished experiments whose scripts fell prey to the mimetic fallacy.

But in the nineties Albee regained his voice in *Three Tall Women,* a work in which he draws much from familial experiences; indeed, it seems to be Albee's most frankly autobiographical work. It first opened at Vienna's English Theatre, Ltd, on 14 June 1991 and, after its 30 July 1992 showing at the Rivers Arts Repertory in Woodstock, New York, had its New York City premiere on 27 January 1994 at the Vineyard Theatre. As in such earlier works as *The Zoo Story* and *The American Dream* (1961), *Three Tall Women* replicates uneasy familial tensions and the playwright's life-long preoccupation with death. A Beckettian play, *Three Tall Women* opens in a well-appointed bedroom in which three women – named A, B, and C – reflect upon and challenge each others' lives. A is the eldest, whose nearness to death seems more pronounced with her props of a sling and walking cane; B appears as a middle-aged and acerbic confidant who tends to A; and C is a young, restless, and hardly supportive attorney.

Clearly approaching her own demise, A launches into a series of verbal reflections, some bordering on vintage Albee verbal assaults, reflections dealing with death and dying. She points out the inevitability of death (or, as B says, "It's downhill from sixteen on!"), but her conception of death extends well beyond the physical. Although A appears as a mean-spirited and bigoted old woman, she also radiates more life than B and C. A recalls a past filled with loss, a sterile marriage, and a son who cannot reciprocate her love. At the end of Act One, A's anguish produces tears and a stroke.

Throughout his career, Albee has subverted audience expectation, and *Three Tall Women* extends this pattern. In Act Two he presents a death watch scenario, reminiscent of *All Over* (1971), in which A, bedridden, lies under an oxygen mask. B, hump-backed and nasty in the first act, appears as a composed and regal woman while C, in pink chiffon, has transformed herself into a gracious, elegant débutante. However, things turn out to be more complicated than ABC in this play. Albee shifts away from realism to non-realism, subverting the theatregoers' sense of objective reality. The three women are really one woman. A reappears, the figure lying in the bed being a dummy, allowing the play to blend the three narratives of A, B, and C into one woman at three different stages of her life – A at ninety, B at fifty-two, and C at twenty-six years of age. Although the three women share the same life experiences, A and B join forces in their opposition to C and in their rejection of illusions. Deception and betrayal form the greatest illusions, they tell C, forewarning that her life will be filled with disappointment. The young boy of Act One appears as the young man now, visiting his dying mother for the last time. All of the characters, representative of various phases of a single woman's life, are haunted by sickness, denials, dying, and ultimately death. Only A accepts her fate, embraces the reality of her death, affirming that the happiest moment is "coming to the end of it." *Three Tall Women* was inspired by the memory of Albee's domineering adoptive mother, with whom he felt little connection. Her arid marriage to a wealthy and submissive father, their marital battles, and the reluctant son mirror Albee's own upbringing. Although Albee claims that he "did not want to write a revenge piece" and "was not interested in 'coming to terms'" with his feelings toward his mother, he calls the writing of the play "an exorcism." The play is his way of putting in perspective his mother (and father), who provided material comfort but little love; he also implies that the play is a reckoning with his own mortality. More tellingly, *Three Tall Women* embodies major philosophical issues that have long been synonymous with each Albee play.

Those issues first surfaced in *The Zoo Story, The American Dream,* and *Who's Afraid of Virginia Woolf?* (1962). After Jerry astonished audiences by impaling himself on a knife in *The Zoo Story* and Grandma reported with appalling specificity the spiritual dismemberment of the child in *The American Dream,* Albee was either lauded or loathed for his dramatization of fatal attractions. Verbal challenges, social confrontations, sudden deaths – real and imagined, physical and psychological – permeate his theatre. From *The Zoo Story* through *Three Tall Women,* his plays address such issues as betrayal, abandonment, sexual tension, the primacy of communication, loss of personal ambition, and withdrawal into a death-in-life existence – hardly issues squaring with the entertainment tastes of a Broadway that beckoned Albee.

Given the militancy of his scripts and his penchant for filling his stage world with self-devouring characters, many critics pigeonhole Albee as a nihilist. It is a curious label. For Albee's world view presupposes the talismanic powers of the theatre to trigger public awareness and private insight. Within the Albee canon, one can locate an affirmative vision of human experience, a vision that questions Albee's reputation as an anger artist. The death-saturated world Albee creates is undeniably a haunting presence in all of his plays. However, the internal action, the subtextual dimension of his plays, reveals the playwright's compassion for his fellow human beings and a deep concern for the social contract. What Albee calls a "dangerous participation" in human relationships is a necessary correlative to living authentically. Albee has long argued, in his plays, essays, and interviews, that through the process of immersing one's self fully, dangerously, and honestly in daily experience the individual may sculpt a better polis. For Albee, the play becomes equipment for living. As The Woman in *Listening* (1976) recalls, "We don't have to live, you know, unless we wish to; the greatest sin, no matter what they *tell* you, the greatest sin in living is doing it badly – stupidly, or as if you weren't really alive." In plays as conceptually different as *A Delicate Balance* (1966) and *Fragments – A Concerto Grosso* (1994), Albee implies that one can choose consciously to mix the intellect and the emotion into a new whole, measured qualitatively, which leads to the heightened awareness for which Judith Malina and Julian Beck yearned during their years with The Living Theatre.

A technically versatile dramatist, Albee demonstrates, often at the cost of commercial if not critical success, a willingness to explore the ontological status of theatricality itself. As he writes in his prefatory remarks to two of his most experimental plays, *Box* and *Quotations from Chairman Mao Tse-Tung*, "Since art must move, or wither – the playwright must try to alter the forms with which his precursors have had to work." Each Albee play demonstrates his ongoing effort to reshape dramatic language and contexts.

One of the qualities of recent American drama concerns the importance of audience participation. Albee remains a leader in asking his audiences to become active participants in the stage experience. He rejects the notion of audience as voyeur. Interestingly, the French actor, director, and aesthetician Antonin Artaud, who described what he called the Theatre of Cruelty, deeply influenced Albee. For Artaud, the dramatic experience should "disturb the senses' repose," should "unleash the repressed unconscious," and should spark "a virtual revolt" (*The Theatre and its Double*, 16). Cruelty, for Artaud, is the key alchemical ingredient that generates an apocalyptic revolt within the audience. Although Artaud and Albee would disagree on many theatrical issues, they share a belief in the use of violence. "All drama goes for blood in one way or another," Albee explains. "If drama succeeds the audience is *bloodied*, but in a different way. And sometimes the act of aggression is direct or indirect, but it is always an act of aggression. And this is why I try very hard to involve the audience . . . I want the audience to participate in the dramatic experience." More significantly, Albee believes that if the audience participates in the play, the violence and death, paradoxically, become positive elements. As Albee suggests, "the theatre is a live and dangerous experience – and therefore a *life-giving force*" (interview with author). His plays embody what the playwright calls "a personal, private yowl" that "has something to do with the anguish of us all" ("Preface," *The American Dream*).

Like Miller and Williams, Albee believes in the powers of the imagination and art to create a liberal humanism. Underneath his characters' public bravado lies an ongoing inner drama, a subtext that presents his characters' quests for awareness. The tragic irony and feeling of loss stem from the characters' inability to understand the regenerative power implicit in self-awareness. If from the perspective of the twenty-first century such a belief seems clichéd or even shrill, it nevertheless appealed to most theatregoers and dramatists when Albee emerged as a genuine force in the American theatre in the sixties and seventies. In brief, Albee's is an affirmative vision of human experience. He underscores the importance of confronting O'Neillean "pipe-dreams," or illusions. In the midst of a dehumanizing society, Albee's heroes, perhaps irrationally, affirm living. If Ionesco's or Beckett's characters seem aware of suffering, they also tend to accept an attitude that precludes any real moral growth. In contrast, Albee's heroes suffer and dwell in an absurd world but realize the opportunity for growth and change. The Albee hero often experiences a coming to consciousness that draws him or her toward "the marrow," to allude to a key metaphor in *Who's Afraid of Virginia Woolf?*, the essence of human relationships. Such awareness, for Albee, is at once a deeply personal as well as a deeply political force.

To regard Albee's use of verbal dueling and death as proof of a nihilistic vision is to overlook the true source of his theatrical largeness. Throughout his career, he has defined, as he argues, "how we lie to ourselves and to each other, how we try to live without the cleansing consciousness of death" (*The Plays*, I, 10). To experience the "cleansing" effects of such self-awareness – as Jerry in *The Zoo Story*, Grandma in *The Sandbox* (1960), Tobias in *A Delicate Balance*, the Wife in *All Over*, Charlie in *Seascape*, Jo in *The Lady from Dubuque* (1980), and Jack and Gillian in *Marriage Play* (1984) discover – has long unified Albee's theatre.

Albee may be regarded as a social constructionist. He sees the playwright as an artist who can destabilize models of communities, expose the inherent weaknesses they harbor, and through catharsis reconstruct a new model of community and citizenship. Subordinating pessimism to the possibility that the individual can communicate honestly with the self and the other, Albee presents that potential for regeneration, a source of optimism which underlies both his sense of social constructionism and his overtly aggressive text and performance. Jerry's death in *The Zoo Story,* for instance, liberates him from an impossible present and also confirms the vitality of the "teaching emotion" he had discovered earlier. Jerry's death gives way, in brief, to nothing less than Peter's rebirth, a recharging of the spirit. Albee even claims that "Peter has become Jerry to a certain extent" (interview with author). Peter and Jerry, like their author, finally have traveled a long distance out of the way to come back a short distance correctly.

Albee does not limit the recuperative spirit of *The Zoo Story* to the actors but extends the benevolent hostility of the play toward the audience. Such a deliberate attempt to diminish the actor/audience barrier, as he would do three decades later in *The Man Who Had Three Arms* (1982), essentializes Albee's dramatic theories. When Jerry dies and an absolved Peter exits, Albee envisions actor and audience as a unified collective, sharing in the emotional intensity of the action. By successfully mixing pity, fear, and recognition in the play's closure, Albee transfers the tragic insight Peter gains to the audience.

Albee emerged at the right place at the right time. His clever dialogues rekindled an excitement in the American theatre, in the process drawing attention to the vitality of Off-Broadway theatre. His finest play, however, *Who's Afraid of Virginia Woolf?*, opened not Off-Broadway but at the Billy Rose Theatre. It was a play that checked, if not halted, Broadway's decline as it ran before packed houses for 664 performances. Whether in praise or scorn, theatregoers responded. The movie version, starring Elizabeth Taylor and Richard Burton, became one of the most lucrative films of 1966 for Warner Bros. and garnered thirteen Oscar nominations that year. The play remained enormously popular in the sixties and seventies, and today is still regarded as one of the key works in American dramatic history. Following his Pulitzer Prize for *A Delicate Balance*, however, his reputation began to slide.

After some forgettable work – *Breakfast at Tiffany's* (1966) and *Everything in the Garden* (1968), an adaptation of Giles Cooper's play, and the inventive companion pieces, *Box* and *Quotations from Chairman Mao Tse-Tung*, plays outlining the collapse of language and human contact itself – Albee entered the seventies with *All Over*, a drama whose subject matter revolves around death. Indeed, the reality of death shapes this play, first performed at Broadway's Martin Beck Theatre on 27 March 1971. Although its working title was simply *Death*, *All Over* reveals the pressures death exerts on the living. Albee reconnoiters the psychic terrain of the survivors. The play extends that interest in death seen in *Quotations from Chairman Mao Tse-Tung*, whose Long-Winded Lady laments, "Death is nothing; there . . . there *is* no death. There is only life and dying."

In terms of plot and action, little happens. The characters congregate around a famous (and never seen) dying man, forming a socially awkward death watch. As the play develops, we see that all of the characters have abrogated their own essential selves; their petty deceits and minor betrayals have grown into death-in-life patterns of behavior. The play ends with the famous man's death, but clearly Albee implies that for the characters life has been "all over" for too long.

Elisabeth Kübler-Ross's theories on the dying process influenced Albee while composing *All Over*. Her *On Death and Dying* (1969), published two years before *All Over*, concerns familial and cultural reactions to death and traces the psychological stresses the living and the dying experience during the various stages of the dying process. Among her complex findings she suggests a simple observation that serves, in dramatic terms, as Albee's point of departure in *All Over* as well as *The Lady from Dubuque* and *Three Tall Women:* the dying patient's problems come to an end, but the family's problems go on. Albee's interest lies well beyond the dying man, for what strikes most forcibly is the other characters' predicaments and their responses toward themselves. Their egocentrism clouds judgment; the dying man remains an afterthought.

In *All Over* the egocentric preoccupations of the characters so infiltrate their motives and language that humane values fade, becoming distant social forces. A special kind of death replaces any humanistic values: not the physical disintegration of the body but the metaphysical dissolution of the individual spirit. Like Bessie in *The Death of Bessie Smith* (1959), who never takes the stage, the dying man in *All Over* remains invisible. Yet, like Bessie Smith, he asserts his presence throughout the play. His dying, ironically, gives definition to the others' lack of vitality. Albee deliberately hides the famous man behind a screen, the symbolic separator of the dying patient from the living family members. The screen represents, for Albee as for Kübler-Ross, a disturbing cultural distancing response, a way to deny an unwanted otherness. Finally, Albee reinforces the inactive spirit of the characters by having them perform as if they were partially anesthetized, sleepwalking through their lives. Throughout the play Albee refers to a dream world, the central problem of *All Over* revolving around the moral sleep that so engaged Thoreau and, later, Bellow. Such a relinquishment of the spirit is, for Albee, unacceptable. The playwright will rethink some of the larger issues embedded in *All Over* in each of his subsequent plays, especially with *Seascape*.

If the collapse of moral nerve forms a central problem in Albee's work through *Box* and *Quotations from Chairman Mao Tse-Tung*, then death has informed his work since *All Over*. *Seascape*, which opened on 26 January 1975 at New York's Sam S. Shubert Theatre, and which won Albee his second Pulitzer Prize, represents the dramatist's persistent concern with the consequences of an attenuated human spirit. Here Albee is not writing merely about the naturalistic evolution of the human and animal species, but about the evolution of human consciousness itself. This sentimental play, a not always convincing mixture of fairy tale, myth, and history, nonetheless appears as one of Albee's more optimistic works.

A companion to *All Over, Seascape* was originally entitled *Life*. The design of the play seems simple enough. Nancy and Charlie are vacationing at the beach, relaxing and contemplating their shrinking future. When two tall green-scaled sea lizards emerge from the sea, conveniently anthropomorphized, Albee joins two distinct worlds, the human and the animal world. Whereas in so many Albee plays such a conjunction leads to violence and death, in *Seascape* the comingling underscores the force of love. Its product is understanding rather than illusion. Things are not "all over" in this play. Albee, if nothing else, implies that through the sweep and play of evolutionary patterns, humankind has aspired to rationality. The danger, however, is that the triumph of rationality may dissipate the primordial life-force, at least in the case of Charlie.

Albee's next plays, *Listening*, commissioned as a radio play for BBC Radio Three in 1976, and *Counting the Ways*, staged at the National Theatre in London in 1976, went largely unnoticed in the United States, as did *Finding the Sun* (1983) and *Marriage Play* (1987). His lackluster adaptation of Nabokov's *Lolita* in 1981 was critically scorned. *The Lady from Dubuque* (1980) and *The Man Who Had Three Arms* drew mainly negative responses and quickly closed after feeble showings at the ticket office while *Fragments – A Concerto Grosso* (1994) received mixed reviews and closed virtually unnoticed.

If his work since *Seascape* lacks the theatricality of the earlier plays, he still ranks as one of the most influential American playwrights since 1960. When he is at his best, Albee produces, in his characters and audience alike, what Robert Frost calls "a momentary stay against confusion" (*Complete Poems*, vi), a still point amidst the confusions of life, a heightened sense of self and moral responsibility. The plays may seem overburdened with death, but it is precisely the presence of death which charges life with significance. Albee received his third Pulitzer Prize for *Three Tall Women* in 1994. The only other dramatist to win more was O'Neill.

Sam Shepard

Albee has always enjoyed helping other artists as they begin their careers. By writing a favorable review of *Icarus's Mother* in a 25 November 1965 issue of the *Village Voice*, Albee, then the most influential theatre voice in New York City, called attention to the then unknown Sam Shepard, whose career immediately took off, though in a direction that differed from Albee's.

If Albee and Arthur Miller ultimately outline a belief in moral optimism,

Shepard reconnoiters a mythic and social terrain touched at first with absurdity if also with humor. *True West* (1980), for instance, a play about family disconnection and illusory impulses, verges at times almost on farce or vaudeville while retaining a sense of menace. Relationships in Shepard's plays are deeply problematic, those between men and women in *Seduced* (1978) and *Fool for Love* (1983), or between parents and children in *Curse of the Starving Class* (1977) or *Buried Child* (1979). A similar pattern reappears in *Simpatico* (1994) and in *States of Shock* (1991), in which a crippled son, a victim of an artillery blast, kills his pro-military father. In Sam Shepard's entropic world, the primal family unit itself becomes a lie of the mind.

Shepard's protagonists struggle to survive in an American landscape warped by its own deflected myths and generational schisms. His career began as American society itself came under pressure with Kennedy's assassination, the escalating war in Southeast Asia, and the emerging Civil Rights Movement. Competing narratives gained increasing authority. Race riots and anti-war marches challenged normative values. American hegemony had disappeared.

Sam Shepard's characters, preoccupied with survival and propelled by an inchoate inertia, seem less concerned with social change than private visions and public myths in a world filled with the iconography of popular culture. Cowboys, rock musicians, Hollywood agents, military personnel, drifters, and mobsters enact their repressed anxieties and depressed lives amidst the alluvia of a postmodernist set and setting. His plays take place in shabby motels and in suburbia, with empty refrigerators, '57 Chevys, nearby shopping malls, or deserts defining an arid world devoid of comfort. Rock'n'roll music or Western films, integral elements to many of his plays, familiar to the audience, become alien and disconcerting in performance. Within such a world his characters struggle, unsuccessfully, to find some authentic force. As Lee says in *True West*, "What I need is somethin' authentic. Somethin' to keep me in touch."

In 1963 Shepard, a nineteen-year-old engaged in an on-the-road adventure from his California home, wound up in New York City where he was working as a busboy at the Village Gate, a popular jazz club, "cleaning up dishes and bringing Nina Simone ice" (quoted in Mottram, *Inner Landscapes*, 8). The young Shepard thrived in New York's East Village. Heavily influenced by the Beat poets, jazz musicians, and an emerging Off-Off Broadway, Shepard turned his energies to playwriting. Indeed, he proved to be an energetic new playwright, one sometimes unable to control his creative energies. Later in his career Shepard would carefully rewrite his scripts, but his early plays seem more like unfinished impressionistic pieces, the product of an imagination that disdained revision. He also proved receptive to international innovations in drama, and his earliest plays, from *The Rock Garden* (1964) to *Back Bog*

Beast Bait (1971), reflect such receptivity. The earlier plays tend to be brief, non-realistic pieces, often filled with fantastic twists of narrative and lacking closure. Traditional versions of plot, character, and linearity find little place. Shepard's plays were rebellions against established notions of dramatic form and structure. From Beckett, whose *Waiting for Godot* influenced his aesthetic principles, Shepard borrowed, for his *Cowboys* (1964) and *The Rock Garden,* a sense of the absurd, an implied futility in any logical connection between words, actions, and deeds. As his career developed, Shepard benefited from other European Absurdists. From Pinter, he inherited a sense of tragicomedic menace. From Handke he derived a sense of the artificiality of the theatre, which in turn allowed him to move more readily from the real to the dream, from the familiar realistic props and settings to a symbolic and even mythic representation. In Pirandello he found a playfulness that darkens as his own postmodern characters search for their identities. From Artaud he drew the power of the sacred, the violent, and the mythic. Although little evidence exists to suggest that these Europeans directly influenced Shepard, as a young, emerging artist, living in the Village, he could hardly help but be caught in international artistic cross-currents.

On native ground, Sam Shepard also learned from the free associative forms of Beat poetry. He embraced the improvisatorial aspects of a free language, a word play liberated from rigid structures of meter and logical coherence. The poetry of Lawrence Ferlinghetti and Allen Ginsberg appealed to his verbal imagination, as did Jack Kerouac's "oceanic" prose in *On the Road* (1957). A rock musician who would later in his career became a film star, Shepard was also drawn to the improvisational forms of jazz music. His association with Joseph Chaikin and Megan Terry, and his involvement in the work of the Open Theatre in the mid-sixties, gave Shepard a chance to move his instinctive experimentalism from the page to the stage.

Shepard began the seventies with *Operation Sidewinder* (1970), his first and ill-fated foray to a mainstream venue, Lincoln Center. He filled the stage with thirty-nine characters and a six-foot electronic snake. A prefatory note to the actors of *Angel City* (1976) captures the metatheatrical quality of his work: "The term 'character' could be thought of in a different way when working on this play. Instead of the idea of a 'whole character' with logical motives behind his behavior which the actor submerges himself into, he should consider instead a fractured whole with bits and pieces of character flying off the central theme. In other words, more in terms of collage construction or jazz improvisation." Even the names of his characters alert audiences to a different kind of theatre: Galactic Jack in *The Tooth of Crime* (1972), Old Oraibi in *Operation Sidewinder,* Slim, Cavale, and Lobster Man in *Cowboy Mouth* (1971), Mazon in *Killer's Head* (1975), Shooter in *Action* (1975), Tympani and Lanx in *Angel City,* and Stubbs in *States of Shock* (1991). Such names indicate the territory in which he works. In *The Mad Dog Blues*, Kosmo and Yahoodi encounter none other than Marlene Dietrich, Mae West, Captain Kidd, Paul Bunyan, Jesse James, and the Ghost Girl, who comes from a South Sea island. These non-traditional plays with alternative settings used a form, language, and timbre that spoke to a newer generation of theatregoers. Shepard provided a fresh alternative. His early success stemmed from his ability to capture the attention of that newer generation of theatregoers, especially those increasingly drawn to the language and music of rock'n'roll.

Within a year of his first works being staged, no fewer than six Shepard plays were performed at various small theatres in New York City, and by the seventies Shepard's career was fully launched. *The Tooth of Crime*, staged at the Open Space Theatre in London on 17 July 1972, pits the aging Hoss, who fancies himself to be a rock'n'roll king, against his youthful nemesis, Crow. One of the best of Shepard's earlier plays, *The Tooth of Crime* presents an age-old conflict in classical mythic form. As Oedipus struggled with the fundamental Sophoclean question, "Who am I?", so Hoss struggles with his own modern version of self-scrutiny and self-revelation. However, whereas Oedipus's pursuit of the truth ultimately leads to self-perception, Shepard's Hoss revels in the ambiguity of the truth/illusion matrix. "You may think every picture you see is a true history of the way things used to be or the way things are," Hoss sings in the play's opening scene, " . . . So here's another illusion to add to your confusion . . ." He finishes the song, a modern-day invocation, a prologue inviting the audience to enter the world of art and artifice, by announcing: "So here's another fantasy/About the way things seem to be to me." That things are not the way they seem quickly becomes clear when Hoss's image of himself clashes with the reality. Obsessed with recording a rock'n'roll hit that will propel him to the top of the music charts, Hoss is a performer of a different sort, a murderer who heads a futuristic interstellar gang. He agonizes throughout the first act over his diminishing musical prowess, determined at all costs to maintain his control, his superiority over all rivals. To dodge a tragic fate, he reasons, he must transcend his suffering and confront Crow, who, like a rival gangster, moves in on his turf to claim his identity.

The second act thus presents Hoss's endgame. He feels compelled to go beyond the "code" of conduct enforced by the Keepers, a group of outsiders functioning as a type of cosmic Mafia gang. Despite warnings from his associates – Becky, Star-Man, Galactic Jack, and Cheyenne – Hoss feels compelled to move from the "inside" to the "outside," from the world confined by strict "codes" of behavior to an outer world in which he may redefine himself musically by breaking the rules, by creating a new music that will ensure his popularity. His associates warn that life "outside" has so changed that Hoss will fail to recognize the perils of this more complex, futuristic world, but Hoss argues, "The game can't contain a true genius . . . We don't have the whole picture."

Hoss is fated to lose the battle with Crow. As he observes, "You tricked me. You wanna trade places with me? You had this planned right from the start." The key to Crow's usurpation lies precisely in the thing Hoss cannot do: adapt. Hoss remains locked, and therefore doomed, in a past image of himself as a rock star. He cannot change. His code of behavior is out of touch with a more contemporary reality. Crow thrives on a capacity to change, to adapt his image to fit the latest trend. Realizing that he no longer harmonizes with either his audience or his music, Hoss performs his final show as the "true killer" he fancies himself to be. Denied the control of self and image that he so craved in life, Hoss concedes defeat. His suicide becomes the ultimate show, the last way for him to live his life outside the "code," a code that long ago left the aging star in its afterwash. Shepard underscores Hoss's impotence when all but Cheyenne embrace the new king, Crow.

Shepard suggests in "Language, Visualization, and the Inner Library" that the emotional impact of myths taps a universal, visceral response with the actor and spectator alike: "Myth speaks to everything all at once, especially the emotions" (217). In *Seduced* the myth he explores is that of the American dream, according to Arthur Miller, a fundamental concern of the American writer.

In *Seduced,* Henry Hackamore is a theatricalized version of Howard Hughes, one of America's more celebrated and enigmatic cultural icons and the ultimate embodiment of wealth, power, and perversity. The opening scene establishes Henry's eccentricities. With Randy Newman's "Sail Away" as background music, he meticulously covers his body with Kleenex. He is deeply paranoid. When Luna, one of Henry's former lovers, comes to his Mexican compound at his summons, she surrenders her purse, lest it conceal weapons with which to murder him.

In his misanthropy, Henry plays out the fractured inner reality of a deranged consciousness, a consciousness not so much aligned with a human being as with an object, with some part belonging to the wreckage of a cultural landscape. The physical geography of the land turns to the inner geography of this dreamer, Henry Hackamore: "Look at it growing! Hotels! Movies! Airplanes! Oil! Las Vegas! Look at Las Vegas, Raul! It's glowing in the dark . . . I'm the demon they invented! Everything they ever aspired to. The nightmare of the nation! It's me, Raul! Only me!" Shepard presents a Hackamore who, as Joan Didion reminds us, slouches toward his Bethlehem, Las Vegas, a fitting symbol of an American wasteland. Despite Henry's enormous wealth and a seemingly regal command of power and action, he lacks true action and energy. Raul, it turns out, will not help Henry. Luna and Miami, seductive dream figures from the past, stand as mere objects, creations of a warped imagination and, as such, incapable of comforting one so disconnected from the self and the other. Thus Henry, billionaire manipulator, exploiter, and recluse, ironically becomes an object subjugated to external forces. The American Dream, in short, seduces, betrays, and rapes Henry: "I was taken by the dream and all the time I thought I was taking it. It was a sudden seduction. Abrupt. Almost like rape. You could call it rape. I gave myself up. Sold it all down the river." Indeed, rape takes on a symbolic energy in the play, as Shepard defines it in terms of sexual, social, and cultural intercourse.

Seduced closes with Raul's betrayal of Henry. Forcing the eccentric billionaire to sign over all assets, he blasts Henry with a pistol, Shepard's last rape symbol. But Henry does not die. Instead, he ends the drama with a haunting monody, "I'm dead to the world but I never been born," a testimony to the illusory resilience of the American Dream myth, destructive or denatured as it may be. With waist-length white hair, five-inch finger nails, and wearing only boxer shorts, Henry's appearance, alone, visually accentuates his freakishness. Even the play's set, with its walls that symbolically entrap the characters, works on the level of theme: they function, like Robert Frost's walls, as dividers, separators that keep Hackamore walled up, sealed from any authentic human exchange. Indeed, unseen presences and felt absences fuel Henry's paranoia throughout the play.

While Shepard's non-realism in many respects reached its apex with *Seduced* in 1978, as early as 1974 he had voiced an interest in developing a more realistic theatre. "I'd like to try a whole different way of writing now, which is very stark and not so flashy and not full of a lot of mythic figures and everything, and try to scrape it down to the bone as much as possible." Shepard's realism, however, was "not the kind of realism where husbands and wives squabble and that kind of stuff" ("Metaphors," 208). His remarks slightly mislead. Husbands and wives "squabble" in most of his later plays, with fighting reaching its height in *A Lie of the Mind*. Yet his comments do indicate a modified realism that informs the later plays. Beginning in 1977 with *Curse of the Starving Class*, and extending through *Fool for Love*, Shepard experimented with that attenuated realism, a form that also informs, but does not define, the 1991 *States of Shock* and the 1994 *Simpatico*. In terms of plot, characterization, and language, these plays were more realistic than the works of the sixties and earlier seventies. Yet for all that the real is still put under pressure, warped by psychological needs, deformed by internal and external pressures.

The changeover to a modified realistic mode may be seen in what Shepard has called his "family trilogy." *Curse of the Starving Class* concerns a family whose members are forever destined, biologically, to remain blood relations, but a "curse" infects this family, a pestilence that goes well beyond heredity and genetics. Economically and socially, psychologically and spiritually,

Weston and Ella and their offspring remain forever doomed, fated to be entrapped in overbearing relationships, dependent on each other even though such dependency leads toward violence and destruction.

Father and son, mother and daughter address one another, but their actions suggest that they exist in their own parallel worlds. The characters live according to their own agendas. They are insular and isolated figures. Each plays a tragic part in the decay of this family. Family life, in this play, is filled with violence and repressed desires. Weston, the father and a drunk, wants to sell the family's home. Ella, the mother, schemes to do the same thing – without telling her husband. Father and mother, separately, seek escape. Near the end the father says to Wesley, his son: "You couldn't be all that starving! We're not that bad off, goddamnit!" He is wrong, of course. This family is so starved of psychological and spiritual sustenance that they have become half-demented figures unaware of their dementia. They often gaze into a refrigerator which contains, like the refrigerator in Marsha Norman's *'night, Mother* (1982), little nourishing food. It becomes yet another symbolic reminder of the "starving class" to which this family belongs. Emma, the daughter who experiences her first period during the play and thus considers herself cursed by her mother, feels so lost that, just before the play ends, she announces, "I'm gone. I'm gone! Never to return"; Wesley assumes the role of the father after Weston, faced with debt and menaced by Emerson and Slater, two hustlers who blow up the family car, abandons his own family. Ella and Wesley at the final curtain reconstruct "that story" Weston "used to tell about that eagle," a story capturing the impossible nature of one-on-one relationships for this family. The eagle and the cat allusion concerns the death of the two animals whose predatory instincts led them to fight to their deaths. Metaphorically, the members of this family remain, like the eagle and the cat, fatally entwined, forever unable to free themselves from their kin.

Shepard followed the Obie Award-winning *Curse of the Starving Class* with the second work in the family trilogy, *Buried Child*, a play also featuring a family whose members are fatally entwined, and which garnered Shepard his first Pulitzer Prize. *Buried Child* is about metaphoric and psychological abuse. First staged at the Magic Theatre in San Francisco on 27 June 1978, *Buried Child* ostensibly charts the life of a "normal" midwestern farm family, with the grandfather and grandmother, Dodge and Halie, presiding over their brood. At the start of Act Two, Shelly, Vince's girlfriend, cannot believe that his family's house seems so normal: "It's like a Norman Rockwell cover or something." Once Shelly enters the home, however, she learns that the exterior facade of the house masks a house of repressed horrors. Despite its realistic trappings, *Buried Child* works within an altogether different, non-realistic atmosphere. When Shelly initially sees Dodge, with butchered, bloody scalp, the abnormality of this family stuns her. Dodge simply glares at her. For most of the play, Dodge, while sneaking sips of whiskey, stares blankly at the television, its flickering blue lights emblematic of the mental vacuity of the entire family. Halie constantly harangues Dodge and is having an affair, it appears, with the local minister. Their sons are terrible extensions of a bizarre family, the genetic lineage carried on with devastating efficiency and symmetry. Tilden, the eldest, a former All-American fullback, now appears mentally unstable. That instability finds its fraternal parallel in Bradley, the younger brother, physically handicapped after accidently cutting off his leg with a chain saw. They talk of their other brother, Ansel, a former high-school basketball star (or so Halie claims), who had died years before in war (not on the battlefield but in a motel room). Vince seems nothing more than a stranger, an intruder into his own home. No wonder many critics have called *Buried Child* an American gothic, for it remains a fable about incest, murder, and the abrogation of individual spirit and social accountability.

Like those in *Curse of the Starving Class*, the family members in *Buried Child* experience the pressures of a dimly perceived "curse." They are victims of what Hemingway in *A Farewell to Arms* (1929) called a "biological trap." The play gains its cultural and theatrical power from several sources, but the most engaging concerns the murdered child, whose very existence and subsequent fate Shepard only slowly reveals. Shelly could hardly realize how bizarre the answer must be to her initial question, "What's happened to this family anyway?" Halie's later comment hints at the tabooed nature of the answer as she refers to "the stench of sin in this house." This pervades every gesture; the "stench of sin," indeed, becomes a palpable force around which Shepard's gothic story revolves.

Shepard works carefully to connect the sins of the past with the crimes of the present and future. Dodge and Halie pass on their curses, their secret, and their sin to their remaining sons, Tilden and Bradley. The Oedipal dimensions of the play are clear. Specifically, Shepard implies that the buried child is the product of an incestuous relationship between Tilden and his mother, Halie. The buried child and the buried truths of the past, repressed through years of denial, rejection, and indifference, are, ironically, the only unifying factors in an otherwise dislocated family. Love is an absent voice in *Buried Child,* isolation the norm. Denial becomes both a source of comfort and anguish. A willed ignorance preserves this family.

The family farm, barren for decades, now mysteriously yields crops, a sign, some critics have suggested, of replenishment. For some, the point seems reinforced by the play's ending, with Vince transforming into the new patriarch of the family, the inheritor of his grandparents' land, which now absorbs a "Good hard rain." This reading remains unconvincing, however, since Shepard ironizes the context: the fertile vegetation, after all, has been fertilized by the corpse of a murdered child whose very birth is the byproduct of an incestuous relationship. In a perverse effort to preserve the family reputation, Dodge has killed and buried the baby. This family is broken, fractured physically, mentally, and morally. The curse must be passed on, symbolized unambiguously when, at the play's end, Vince assumes (literally and figuratively) the father's role after Dodge dies. Dodge has been symbolically buried and spiritually dead throughout the play. Now, after his literal death, his grandson lies on the sofa, a visual replica of Dodge. When the play closes with Tilden carrying the corpse of the buried child, it is clear that, for this family, there can be no escape from their past actions. Shepard offers no neat solution to this gothicized murder mystery. No character atones for his or her sins; no Sophoclean expiation results. Only Shelly, an outsider, escapes this family's tabooed ancestral history.

Shepard continued to examine the American family and its fate in *True West*, the third play of the family trilogy that opened, under the direction of Robert Woodruff, at the Magic Theatre in San Francisco on 10 July 1980. The focus turns to two brothers, Austin and Lee, whose competing narratives converge in a fraternal duel that ends with menace, apocalypse, and possibly a fratricidal endgame as the play's final tableau leaves them trapped in a desert-like landscape, a haunting silhouette of brotherly warring. This final image provides a key to the play. For no resolution is offered at the end of *True West*, simply a family incapable of listening, understanding, or loving. Like the eagle and the cat in *Curse of the Starving Class*, Lee and Austin must both fight to the end if either is to survive.

Shepard energizes the play by contrasting the differing worlds of Austin and Lee. Austin is in his early thirties and dresses conservatively. He has come to his mother's home, located in a suburb near Los Angeles, to get away from the distractions of family life, to concentrate on his latest Hollywood script-writing project and to take care of the house. With an Ivy League education and a natural reserve, Austin appears to be a young professional. Articulate and adjusted, he seems rooted in family and business life. By contrast, Lee, some ten years older, uneducated, and with rotting teeth, wears filthy clothes. Like their never-seen father, he is a wanderer seeking the "true West" beyond civilization. A drifter-turned-thief, Lee, upon an unexpected visit to his mother's house, cases her neighborhood for televisions to steal. Inarticulate, a misfit, he seems as rootless and disconnected from family and social world as Austin is secured to that world. Lee feels abandoned, lost. He has a world-weariness about him. He steals, perhaps, to lay claim to a control otherwise denied him.

As it turns out, Lee steals much more than television sets. The play begins with Austin trying to write and Lee sitting on the kitchen counter, beer in hand. Lee's surprise entrance sets into motion a brotherly conflict; by the play's end the brothers become contestants for each other's very identity.

16. San Francisco's Magic Theatre's 1981 production of Sam Shepard's *True West* with Jim Haynie as Lee and (in background) Ebbe Roe Smith as Austin. Photograph by Allen Nomura. Courtesy of Magic Theatre.

Just as Vince assumes the role of Dodge in *Buried Child*, and Crow of Hoss in *The Tooth of Crime*, so Lee becomes Austin. Austin's identity begins to merge with Lee's, and Lee's with Austin's. The transformation begins when Lee decides to write his own screen play.

Lee's film idea seems outrageous to Austin while his inexperience and ignorance of the Hollywood film industry seem to preclude his participation. Yet when Saul Kimmer, a Hollywood producer, agrees to buy Lee's story of the true West (a story inspired by Lee's love of Hollywood Westerns, no less), the brotherly rivalry takes an ominous turn. Lee has suddenly gained control, but must rely on Austin's writing abilities to articulate his fiction. Austin, needing to maintain Hollywood connections, acquiesces, and types the script for his brother. The play, then, explores the dissolution of individual identity, as the brothers slowly exchange roles. Awkwardly at first, but then with an emerging clarity, the brothers undergo a psychic transplant, their role exchanges animating the stage. As Lee becomes the successful writer, Austin transforms into a successful thief, stealing toasters from the neighbors. As the inarticulate Lee objectifies his Hollywood script, Austin becomes more savage and disheveled, a drunken blathering man. In short, he becomes like his brother. Further, Shepard fills the action of each of the nine scenes of the play with the threat of violence, which begins with the verbal jest, finds its more menacing expression with a physical slap, and culminates in the climactic fight scene. Metaphoric abuse vies with actual abuse. Hence Lee's early remarks about "what kinda' people kill each other the most" intensifies the mood of violence, as it foreshadows the murderous impulses that the audience will presently witness. In Shepard's depleted American family, the "real" finds its authenticity in killing. Resolutions and clarifications may only be found through death or the threat of death.

Shepard works carefully to stage the exchange of the brothers' personalities. At the end of the first act Lee remarks to his brother, "I always wondered what'd be like to be you"; moments later Austin confesses, "I used to say to myself, 'Lee's got the right idea. He's out there in the world and here I am. What am I doing?'" Early in the second act, with tensions building and each brother slowly dissolving into the psychic identity of the other, Lee says, "You sound just like the old man now," to which Austin replies: "Yeah, well we all sound alike when we're sloshed. We just sorta' echo each other." These telling exchanges, staged with a rhythmic, incantatory quality, foreshadow the submerging, merging, and restructuring of filial identities. *True West* concerns much more than two brothers on a fatal encounter. It also raises questions about individual, familial, and cultural identity, as it does about the relationship between art and artifice, fiction and reality, and, ultimately, about the mythicized West versus the "true West."

Buried Child is, at its core, a symbolic homecoming, and much the same may be said of *True West*. The play gains its extraordinary theatrical qualities precisely through the transforming and transfiguring capacities of the imaginative self. Lee and Austin, inadequate creators separately, team up to produce a mythicized script that more closely approximates the true West. Their collective effort is equally an alliance that gives them, together, a creativity that eluded them prior to their merger. Each brother was an artist devoid of artistry. Now they are capable of producing a script that has, for Saul Kimmer at least, a ring of truth about it.

However, Shepard subverts the authority of Austin and Lee's collaborative script. Though Lee thinks he articulates a "true story," and, ironically enough, its authenticity stems from his own gritty experiences of being a societal outcast, he, like his brother before him, panders to the B-movie tastes of Saul Kimmer. Like the Hollywood film men in Mamet's *Speed-the-Plow* (1988) and Arthur Kopit's *Bone-the-Fish* (1989; revised as *Road to Nirvana* in 1990), Saul concerns himself with making serious money, not true art. Shepard ironizes the relationship between life and art to such an extent that apprehending the "true West" remains impossible. The double nature of the brothers' scriptwriting effort (the impulse to make it real, which immediately makes it false) leads to increased divisions within this family, the individual, and creativity itself.

But the nature of the brothers' identities leads to what Shepard calls a divisive "double nature," a split that reveals the fractured and fracturing psyche. Living with this double nature, however, proves nearly impossible for the brothers. They must live in a West denuded of its mythic resonances, drained of its power to nurture the imagination and, by extension, the culture itself. As Austin says, "There's no such thing as the West anymore! It's a dead issue!" Instead, the true West has been supplanted by the freeways, malls, and synthetic green grass ringing Mom's home. If for Lee the true West has its basis in a Kirk Douglas Western, *Lonely Are the Brave,* for Austin it finds its expression in the city life he deals with everyday: "I drive on the freeway everyday. I swallow the smog. I watch the news in color, I shop in the Safeway. I'm the one who's in touch! Not him!"

Austin is both right and wrong. The paradox surfaces when the script Lee constructs, and which his brother dutifully records, strains credibility. Austin claims that Lee's plot falsifies experience. But for Shepard's characters, life imitates art. Lee's film idea not only mirrors *Lonely Are the Brave*, but also echoes the problematic relationship between the brothers.

Shepard accentuates the disconnected state of this family when, near the end, the mother appears. Her entrance is absurdly humorous, underlining Shepard's fondness for mixing realistic sets with surreal behavior. Returning from an Alaska vacation to a home that has been trashed by her sons, she sleepwalks through the house, surveying her dead plants. Her last lines – voiced as she eyes the wreckage that used to be her kitchen and as her sons engage in mortal combat – underscore the absurdity of her homecoming: "I don't recognize it at all." Finding a true home, like finding a true West, remains problematic for Shepard's rootless characters. The absent father appropriately remains in the desert. The brothers turn the kitchen, now filled with broken toasters, burnt toast, shattered bottles, and a smashed typewriter, into a psychological killing field. By the play's end, they come close to fulfilling Lee's earlier prophecy of fratricide. The violence, barely held in check throughout the play, can no longer be contained.

Such physical, psychological, and spiritual violence continues in *Fool for Love,* which opened at the Magic Theatre on 8 February 1983, under Shepard's direction. In this play, Eddie and Mae, half-siblings fathered by the same man, find themselves hopelessly in love with each other. Attraction, however, seems balanced by repulsion. Eddie and Mae's opening dialogue suggests the dizzying give and take of their relationship. Comfort mingles with violence.

These are lovers who one moment indulge in passionate kisses and the next in deadly threats. Mae, indeed, represents a new Shepard female: one who holds her ground. Like Albee's George and Martha, Eddie and Mae emerge as equal competitors. The equality of their strong wills, matched by their equally strong neuroses, creates the tension in this play about relationships. Incestuously united, the two lovers recreate a ritualized courtship, while their father, described as the Old Man, who exists only in their minds, presides over the drama, gradually revealing the details of his own death and his wife's suicide. Eddie, Mae, and the Old Man each voice their own interpretations of the past, offering variants on what may or may not have occurred.

Despite the violence, and beyond the humor, *Fool for Love* differs from the preceding family plays in its hints at the potentially redemptive as well as reifying nature of love. As in *Savage/Love* (1979), *Fool for Love* points toward some guarded hope for the future. That hope, however, seems likely to prove as elusive as the love Eddie and Mae so crave.

Whatever hope might be detectable in *Fool for Love* dissolves in *A Lie of the Mind*, however. Directed by Shepard and first performed at the Promenade Theater in New York City on 5 December 1985, *A Lie of the Mind* returns to a brutalizing world. Connections between men and women prove not only impossible but decidedly treacherous and vicious. Familiar Shepard patterns and motifs resurface. An alcoholic and absent father, spacey mothers, deranged children, surreal atmospheric sets, and the use of music and violence infiltrate the play.

A Lie of the Mind dissects two families. One consists of parents Baylor and Meg, and sister and brother Beth and Mike. After arriving from Montana to care for their savagely beaten daughter, Baylor seems more concerned with his livestock and hunting than with his daughter. He is the frontier man whose frontier spirit long ago dissipated. Meg is the caring and ineffectual mother, while Mike assumes the role of the avenger, hunting down his sister's assailant. The other family seems equally incapable of dealing with objective reality. Lorraine, the abandoned mother, could be the sister of Mom in *True West*, albeit a more articulate and fleshed-out version. After being deserted by her husband (she keeps his remains in a leather box under her son's bed), she formulates her own definition of love: "Love. Whata crock a' shit." Her husband, like the absent father in *True West*, had died in a drunken haze, the victim of his own delusions and, perhaps, patricide. From Sally's viewpoint, "Jake had decided to kill him," although Lorraine claims that he was "run over by a truck in the middle of a Mexican highway." Brothers Jake and Frankie echo Austin and Lee from *True West*. These troubled and troubling families are thus drawn together in *A Lie of the Mind*, Shepard's most savage play.

The most obvious instance of savage love occurs at the beginning of the play. Jake, speaking frantically on the phone, confesses to beating his wife to death. In fact, the brain-damaged Beth survives, although her wounds are so severe that, like Anna in Susan Yankowitz's *Night Sky* (1991), an aphasic patient, she is forced to relearn language. Half-crazed, she convalesces in a hospital in Los Angeles.

A reductive imagery dominates the play. Members of these two families are reduced to infantile states, their regressive patterns of behavior reinforced by illusory rationalizations. Beth's brain injuries diminish her communicative abilities, and she speaks not merely in broken sentences but the tones and language of a young girl. Given Beth's condition, such behavior seems entirely understandable, but the infantile behavior also extends to other members of the family, who are as emotionally maimed as Beth is physically injured. While Frankie and Sally hold out for coherence and resolution, the others revel in their own lies of the mind. Jake, horrified by his murderous impulses, retreats to his boyhood room, complete with model airplanes and a mother who tries to spoon-feed him broccoli soup.

Regression, indeed, seems a central trope as the vestiges of civilization are slowly stripped away. Instinct triumphs over reason, the savage over the civilized. The fundamental tool of communication, language itself, is rendered inadequate, deceptive, lethal. Below the level of rationality, however, beyond the capacity of language to communicate, is a truth about human nature and the relationship between men and women too painful to be acknowledged. Hence the necessary lie of the mind.

During the course of this three-act episodic play, Shepard works with a number of telling images, the most dominating of which concern animals. Indeed, bestial references saturate the performance. Allusions to goats, mules, buffalo, roosters, antelopes, dogs, tigers, rabbits, horses, snakes, and deer abound. More importantly, Shepard presents his characters as hunters, the ones who subjugate or slaughter most of these animals. Shepard, himself an avid hunter, repeatedly links the plight of these various animals with the play's characters. Just as Jake hunts down Beth, so Mike tracks Jake. Just as Jake stalks his father, so Baylor hunts Frankie, and so on. Minutes into the action Frankie reminds Jake that, as a child, he "kicked the shit out of that goat you loved so much when she stepped on your bare feet while you were tryin' to milk her," a pattern born of a personality that erupts again in his assault on Beth, whom he still loves. Baylor, self-appointed "dumb rancher," worries more about getting his mules to the fairgrounds than seeing to his own daughter's needs; near the end, he again refers to his obsession with hunting and animals, a way to keep social or familial duty at arm's length. Though he professes a rugged individualism, he is as immobilized as his daughter. Moments later he cannot even put his own socks over his frozen, bloodied feet.

Shepard often describes the characters as "stray" dogs, or dogs "*with their hackles up.*" In a chilling scene, Lorraine recounts how her husband had been "busted open like a road dog" by a speeding truck; Sally, their daughter, recalls him snarling at her "just like a dog. Just exactly like a crazy dog. I saw it in his eyes. This deep, deep hate that came from somewhere far away. It was pure, black hate with no purpose." Similarly, when Sally recounts Jake's involvement in his father's death, she describes how he "ran like a wild colt and never looked back." As in his earlier plays, the curse of fathers passes to their sons.

A Lie of the Mind is Shepard's most predatory play. It ends while a bewildered Meg, whose husband has just kissed her for the first time in two decades, gazes at a fire that Lorraine has ignited in the house. Just as the woods had been blazing for years in Miller's Loman family home, so the "fire in the snow" has long been smoldering, if not raging, for these characters. They dwell in what Lorraine calls a "Christless world." In such a brutal and mutable environment, individual identities change, mutate, dissolve, and merge with others. Meg insists that "Beth's got male in her" and that "She was like a deer," metaphorically linking the predatory instincts of the male hunters in this play with the ultimate kill, Beth herself. When Mike proudly carries in *"the severed hindquarters of a large buck with the hide still on it,"* the butchered deer stands as a metaphor for Beth's state of being and, by extension, the states of mind of all the play's characters. Within the inverted logic of the action, then, the animal imagery pushes plot and story to its inevitable end.

The love between Jake and Beth continues, but its original binding power fades after Jake's assault. In effect we see the dismemberment of Jake and Beth. The rootless characters gaze, as does Jake, into an "imaginary mirror." They seem scarcely more alive than the dead father and his ashes in the box. Beth's acting talents, her skills at blending pretense and reality succeed so well that she clings, in her final gesture, to a man she barely knows.

When *Simpatico* opened on 14 November 1994, at the Joseph Papp Public Theater in Manhattan, many reviewers detected traces of *True West*. The play concerns Carter and Vinnie, childhood friends from Cucamonga, California. After being involved in a scheme to fix horse-racing bets, they destroyed the former racing commissioner Simms (who now goes by the name of Ames). Thereafter, they went in different directions. Vinnie became a vagabond living in a depressing apartment in his rural home town, barely able to make ends meet. Carter, on the other hand, is a success. Living in Kentucky, he became an influential, wealthy businessman and a happy family man, who pays Vinnie a small sum to keep quiet about their past. To complicate matters, Carter "stole" Vinnie's girlfriend, Rosie, and married her, thus making their present relationship all the more awkward and threatening.

As the action begins, Carter returns to Cucamonga to sever his ties with Vinnie. He wants to pay his former partner a large cash settlement for the negatives of pornographic photographs Vinnie had shot of Rosie and Simms in a motel room years before. However, some of these have apparently fallen into the hands of a woman Vinnie has just met. When Carter finally meets her, however, it seems that the story had been untrue. Once again Shepard raises questions of the nature of the real and how it is to be recuperated. By the end of the play, Carter loses control of Vinnie, and, recognizing the loss of his manipulative powers, begins to break down. Like Lee in *True West*, Vinnie gains a victory of sorts over this play's Austin, Carter.

Shepard symbolizes Carter's uncomfortable alliance with Vinnie through alcohol. Carter abandoned drinking as his professional and private life flourished, but now, back to his roots, reunited with Vinnie, he succumbs to the bottle. By the play's end, he falls ill, the victim less of alcohol than of his own wayward life, a life that symbolically sickens him. Shepard, who directed the play, has explained that "identity is a question for everybody in the play," a point reinforced by characters who drift, search, and desperately try to arrive at the real (Brantley, "Sam Shepard, Storyteller," 26). Ed Harris, whom Shepard directed in the role of Eddie in *Fool for Love* twelve years earlier and who played Carter in *Simpatico*, observed that "'my character is full of guilt and lies. And I was asking Sam, isn't there some place where he admits to all that and gets close to it? He said, 'Sorry Ed, I can't let you off the hook'" (Brantley, "Sam Shepard, Storyteller," 26). Indeed, the play ends with a sense of solitariness permeating the theatre. The mythic illusion of an older, nobler West cannot compete in the age of computers and off-track betting. Simms concurs with Vinnie's contempt for the lawyers who wear "tasseled loafers free of manure." He feels bitter. Once an influential figure in the horse-racing circuit, his involvement in a betting scandal forced him to start a new life under an assumed name. His very identity has been removed. He now survives by virtue of a menial job with the Kentucky Racing Commission. The lawyers are "the ones who'll kill a horse to collect the insurance," he complains. The characters in *Simpatico* seem entrapped in this ruthless world, and their prospects for transcendence are limited. Like so many earlier Shepard heroes, they are victims, of themselves no less than of their circumstances. Although some critics felt that the tensions between Carter and Vinnie failed to rise to those between Austin and Lee in *True West*, a palpable sense of regret, guilt, and loss nonetheless remains. The characters seem haunted by an implied dread, a felt terror. They are caught up in a plot whose very indeterminacy prevents their escape.

The distinguishing marks of Shepard's dramas lie in his distinctive use of language, myth, music, and predatory characters. Victims and victimizers, the pursued and the pursuer vie for a metaphorical, psychological, and spiritual space in his plays. Meanwhile, options slowly diminish.

There are no real survivors, no remissions of pain. Spaces open up which prove unbridgeable. Necessity rules. Irony is constantly reborn from the frustrated desires of those who obey compulsions they would wish to resist. And yet there is "a fire in the snow," there is a fractured poetry, there is an energy and a passion to the lives of those whose demons he stages. There is an intensity, a resonance and a power which lifts them above their social insignificance just as the plays themselves never compromise with the banality of surfaces. Shepard is a myth-maker who deconstructs myths, a story-teller aware of the coercive power of story. He is, finally and incontrovertibly, a poet of the theatre who himself discovers poetry in the broken lives which are the subject of his plays, and in the broken society which they inhabit.

Adrienne Kennedy

If Albee provided Shepard with an artistic boost through his *Village Voice* review of *Icarus's Mother*, his support of Adrienne Kennedy was even more direct. She recalls, in *Deadly Triplets*, her reflections on her life in the theatre and experiences with various artists, a turning point in her career: "When I joined Albee's workshop, January 1962, I submitted my play *Funnyhouse of a Negro* as a writing sample to get into the class." Several weeks later she learned that Albee liked the play and that, indeed, she had been selected to participate in the workshop. Although excited, Kennedy grew apprehensive as the date her play was to be staged approached: "During the winter, I became frightened. My play seemed far too revealing and much to my own shock, I had used the word 'nigger' throughout the text. I decided to drop out of the class." After meeting with Albee, she explained, "'I'm embarrassed to have it done. The other plays so far are not as revealing.'" A supportive Albee replied, "'A playwright is someone who lets his guts out on the stage and that's what you've done in this play.' I didn't know what to say. That was the point. I didn't want my guts let out in front of the whole class. I stepped back and started toward the door." Then Albee added, "'It's your decision' . . . He didn't smile or move but only continued to look at me with his hypnotic eyes" *(Deadly Triplets,* 101).

Adrienne Kennedy quietly established herself as one of the more innovative and important playwrights. Two years before joining Albee's workshop, she experienced another career turning point when she traveled to West Africa in 1960–61, a trip that crystallized in her mind the dilemma blacks face when coming to terms with their racial past and colonized present. In Ghana, at a time when Patrice Lumumba, the Zairean leader, was assassinated and when Ghana had just become a republic, she read the works of Chinua Achebe, Amos Tutuola, and Wole Soyinka, among others, and began conceptualizing her first successful play, *Funnyhouse of a Negro* (1962). Just as Kennedy herself struggled with her double consciousness – as a woman who on a daily basis lived with an awareness of African and American European cultures – so Sarah in *Funnyhouse of a Negro* struggles with a sense of split identity.

After her travels to Africa and her efforts at Albee's playwriting seminars, Kennedy decided to let her "guts out." Through three decades of playwriting she has cultivated an experimental theatre whose non-realistic features have long stood as the shaping principle of her work, her claim to genuine originality. The complexity of her dramaturgy invites charges of obscurity, but hers is an obscurity charged with its own coherence. Her plays are revealing, though their revelatory quality invites audiences to set aside traditional Aristotelian conceptions of unity, place, and time. Her works invite audiences to suspend logical structures and respond to the unexpected. Plot and character, action and theme usually remain in soft focus.

In Kennedy's theatre, action and language emanate not from a realistic character but a surrealistically conceived figure whose subconscious defines her being. Psychological as much as social forces animate her characters, while internal rather than exterior events energize her plays. Perhaps this explains why the playwright calls her dramas "states of mind." It also accounts for her reliance on dream motifs and, indeed, the dream is a key to Kennedy's creativity. Dream motifs, with their disjunctive, associative, and surrealistic textures, unify her unique mimesis. She once noted that "the people I met in the theatre seemed to be dream interludes in my life," and her plays reflect such "dream interludes" (*Deadly Triplets*, viii). Above all, they interweave external experience with a subjectivity whose interiority destabilizes as it informs.

In *Funnyhouse of a Negro*, a woman appears as if in a dream, sleepwalking across the stage. The four locales in which the play takes place – Queen Victoria's chamber, the Duchess of Hapsburg's chamber, a room in a Harlem hotel, and the jungle – further contribute to the non-realistic ethos of the play, a point confirmed when Sarah, the central character, tells the audience that these are her "rooms." Whether these are taken as actual rooms or Sarah's psychologized projections, they define the funnyhouse in which she lives, representing various aspects of her split personality. Other characters – the Mother, the Landlady (Funnylady), Raymond (Funnyman), and Jesus – and the exaggerated props – a huge ebony bed strangely reminiscent of a tomb – only add to the Kafkaesque quality of *Funnyhouse of a Negro*. There is a brittle "funniness" or strangeness to this play, a sinister foreboding that skirts the edges of a repressed hysteria.

Sarah embodies such strangeness. Her very mind represents the funnyhouse of this black woman. Not surprisingly, Sarah is a less than reliable narrator. She appears divided against her self, the two dominant cultures, one black, the other white, affecting her psyche. Feelings of guilt, shame, and loss contribute to her troubled spirit. An alienated and bewildered Sarah possesses four distinct personalities whose narratives no less than cultures intensify her sense of disassociation. Her multiple selves are represented by the Duchess of Hapsburg and Queen Victoria, two white figures from a decidedly Eurocentric culture. Kennedy also includes Patrice Lumumba and Jesus, described as a *"hunchbacked yellow-skinned dwarf."* Meanwhile, a white landlady presides over Sarah's (funny) house, while Sarah must deal with her Jewish boyfriend, Raymond (these two additional characters being the only ones whose identities are separate from Sarah's). Her four selves comingle on stage, revealing her complexity.

Sarah feels emotionally splintered. Her dreams, fantasies, and multiple personalities increasingly make it impossible for her to maintain much grasp on objective reality. She identifies Queen Victoria and the Duchess of Hapsburg with her light-skinned (black) mother, and with her white European sense of self. She associates the other two selves, Patrice Lumumba and Jesus, with her father, whose darkness she emphasizes – "the blackest of them all" – as well as with her African legacies. Kennedy describes Sarah as having "pale-yellow skin" and "no glaring Negroid features," while she agonizes over her hair, which she calls "frizzy" and "kinky." As the play develops, Sarah's four selves verbalize her family's psychohistory, revealing her parents' marriage, her father's insistence that they return to Africa to engage in missionary work, her mother's subsequent descent into madness, and her father's death by hanging in his Harlem apartment, possibly a suicide, possibly victim of a murder. Sarah certainly asserts that she had killed her father, although Raymond insists that he is still alive. "Her father is a doctor, married to a white whore," he announces at the end of the play. "He is a nigger who eats his meals on a white glass table." Raymond indicts her father for succumbing to the dominant white culture, insisting that he now lives "in the city in a room with European antiques, photographs of Roman ruins, walls of books and oriental carpets," obviously a place where blackness is noticeable by its absence. The only theatrical certainty lies in Sarah's final action. Unable to come to terms with her double heritage, with her blackness, with her cross-cultural perspectives, she hangs herself, suicide being the most concrete, definite action she performs during a play defined by its lack of definitions.

Kennedy extended her alogical non-realism in *The Owl Answers* (1965), *A Rat's Mass* (1966), *A Lesson in Dead Language* (1968), *A Beast's Story* (1969), and in *Sun* (1969), a choreopoem, or hybrid of poetry, dance, and drama of a kind that Ntozake Shange would develop five years later with *For Colored Girls Who Have Considered Suicide/When the Rainbow is Enuf* (1974). After her realistic *Evening with Dead Essex* (1973), a play inspired by the murder of African American sniper Mark James Essex, she staged the expressionistic *A Movie Star Has to Star in Black and White* at the Public Theater Workshop in 1976, under the direction of Joseph Chaikin. As she matured as a dramatist,

Kennedy continued to eschew traditional theatrical forms, experimenting instead with a variety of technical styles that placed her in the vanguard of American drama and theatre. Her growing maturity is perhaps best seen in *A Movie Star Has to Star in Black and White*.

Kennedy revives She/Clara from *The Owl Answers*, now transplanting her into yet another white cultural milieu, the American cinema. Whereas the earlier play presented white English literary and historical giants as She's antagonists, *A Movie Star Has to Star in Black and White* replaces them with white film giants who imprison in a more subtle way. This highly inventive play modulates between the reality of the play itself, and the illusions of three black and white movies filmed in the forties and fifties. Dramatic moments in Clara's life intersect with emotional high points in the three films, *Now, Voyager* (the 1942 film featuring Bette Davis and Paul Henreid); *Viva Zapata!* (the 1952 epic starring Marlon Brando as Emiliano Zapata, the Mexican revolutionary, and Jean Peters as his beautiful lover); and, finally, *A Place in the Sun* (the 1951 film version of Theodore Dreiser's classic naturalistic novel, *An American Tragedy* [1925], which starred Montgomery Clift as Clyde Griffiths, Shelley Winters as Roberta Alden, and Elizabeth Taylor as Sondra Finchley). Clara's yearnings and fears complement and conflict with scenes from these film classics, which are now reconstituted in *A Movie Star Has to Star in Black and White* in multiple settings, including a hospital lobby (which also doubles as a ship's deck), her brother Wally's room, and Clara's old room. Theatrical and cinematic illusions meld, creating a montage of compelling narratives that give form and substance to the play.

Kennedy underscores the relation between the cinematic text and the performative script when suggesting that Clara "*has a passive beauty and is totally preoccupied. She pays no attention to anyone, only writing in a notebook. Her movie stars speak for her. Clara lets her movie stars star in her life.*" The melding of the imaginative with the real becomes more pronounced when Clara's husband asks her a question, only to have Bette Davis from *Now, Voyager* reply. Clara, meanwhile, remains fixed on writing throughout the play, her way of reinscribing her own life, of reordering a fictional world so that her real world may make better sense. Thus Kennedy's non-linear strategy perfectly captures the reflections of Clara as she interacts with The Mother, The Father, and The Husband, and with her son, Eddie, Jr., and her brother Wally, who lies near death in a hospital room after an automobile accident. We see Clara in various social and familial roles – mother, wife, writer, sister, and black woman who repeats the lines from *The Owl Answers*, "I call God and the Owl answers."

A Movie Star Has to Star in Black and White is metatheatrical, calling attention to the artificiality of film and play alike. In Scene I, Bette Davis and Paul Henried, on the deck of the ocean liner from *Now Voyager*, narrate Clara's parents' dreams of moving to the North, where they hope to escape "the back woods of Georgia," and where, as The Father continues, "We Negro leaders dream of leading our people out of the wilderness." Of course, historical fact vitiates the parents' heroic ideals, for they discover that racial injustice haunts the North as well.

The action of Scene II occurs in two places simultaneously: in a hospital room where Clara and her mother gather to be together with the brain-damaged Wally, and in the bedroom scene from *Viva Zapata!*. We learn of Clara's marital difficulties, which mirror her parents' own marital break-downs. As The Mother and The Father exchange bitter words, "*Marlon Brando continuously helps Jean Peters change sheets,*" a stylized ceremony prompted by Jean Peters's character bleeding onto the bedside, which in turn triggers Clara's memory of her miscarriage while her husband, Eddie, was in the mili-tary. Clara, moreover, reveals her anxiety of balancing motherhood with career.

The last brief scene, set in Clara's old room, juxtaposes Clara's anxieties about being a creative black woman writer – "Ever since I was twelve I have secretly wanted to be a writer. Everyone says it's unrealistic for a Negro to want to write" – with the climactic murder-by-drowning scene in *A Place in the Sun*. In Dreiser's novel, as in the Hollywood film version, Clyde Griffiths finds himself romantically involved with two women, the working-class Roberta Alden and the socialite Sondra Finchley. When Roberta informs him that she is pregnant and expects his full support, Clyde plots to kill her by rowing her to the middle of the lake and drowning her. Once out on the lake, he panics, horrified that he could ever actually commit murder. The boat overturns, Roberta goes under, and he does nothing to save her. The court finds Clyde guilty, and Dreiser's grim determinism insists on a "no exit" ending in which a sense of helplessness and loss dominates. Kennedy appropriates a similar sense of helplessness and loss in the play's last scene, for Clara's life too closely parallels the tragic lives portrayed by Montgomery Clift and Shelley Winters. Kennedy ends her play at the precise moment when Shelley Winters drowns, and Clara's last lines emphasize the possibility of falling, of collaps-ing: "The doctor said today that my brother will live; he will be brain damaged and paralyzed. After he told us, my mother cried in my arms outside the hos-pital. We were standing on the steps, and she shook so that I thought both of us were going to fall headlong down the steps."

Kennedy remains a vital if lesser-known figure in American drama, though a retrospective of all of her major works staged at the Signature Theatre Company in New York City in 1995 brought fresh attention to her plays. From such dramas as *A Beast's Story* through *The Ohio State Murders* (1992), from her collaboration with John Lennon and Victor Spinetti on *The Lennon Play: In His Own Write* (1967) to *Black Children's Day* (1980), one of her children's plays, Kennedy continues to expand the nature of theatricality with an innovative style whose originality remains as fresh as it is challenging.

Amiri Baraka

Just as Albee had encouraged Shepard and Kennedy, so he helped Amiri Baraka. Baraka's *The Dutchman*, arguably his best play, opened on 12 January 1964 at the Village South Theatre before moving to the Cherry Lane Theatre on 24 March, where Albee's performance workshop, Theatre 1964, produced it. Few dramatists of the sixties and seventies replicate the rebelliousness and incipient days-of-rage ethos of Everett LeRoi Jones (Baraka). His is a theatre of resistance. Prompted by the realities of racial injustice, he moved from his Beat-influenced poetry of the late fifties to a radicalized drama expressive of a new black cultural nationalism in the sixties. Thereafter he became spokesperson for African Americans in the Marxist-Leninist-Maoist tradition. His is a theatre committed to rediscovering and restoring black identity in a white world. (See also Schlueter's discussion.)

His career began in 1958 with *A Good Girl is Hard to Find*, which was followed a year later by an unpublished drama, *Revolt of the Moonflowers*. By 1961 *Dante* had been staged at the Off-Bowery Theatre in New York City, which derived from his novel *The System of Dante's Hell* and was reinvented as *The Eighth Ditch* at the New Bowery Theatre in New York City in 1964. Indeed, 1964 was a watershed year for Baraka. No less than four other plays – *The Baptism, The Toilet, The Dutchman,* and *The Slave* – were staged, with *Dutchman* earning an Obie Award.

Writing twenty years after *The Dutchman*'s debut, he recalled that "when the magazines and electronic media coverage of the play and local word got out, I could see that not only was the play an artistic success, despite my being called 'foul-mouthed,' 'full of hatred,' 'furious,' 'angry,' I could tell that the play had made its mark, that it would not quietly fade away" (*Autobiography*, 188). *The Dutchman* does not fade because in cultural no less than in mythical terms it theatricalizes one of the most divisive public issues of the nation, race relations, and its effect on the individual. The play unwinds in a subway, which Baraka immediately allegorizes through the opening stage directions: Clay, a young middle-class black intellectual, and Lula, a flirtatious young white woman, experience a chance encounter "*In the flying underbelly of the city. Steaming hot, and summer on top, outside. Underground. The subway heaped in modern myth.*" Rather like Albee's *The Zoo Story*, *The Dutchman* presents two characters whose initial light-hearted banter quickly turns to verbal, then physical assault, culminating when Lula, as Edenic temptress taunts, "Come on, Clay. Let's rub bellies on the train Clay." A reticent Clay, pushed by Lula's litany of racial and sexual taunts, lashes back, only to have Lula plunge a knife twice into his chest.

When Albee's *The Zoo Story* ends with a similar murder-by-knifing, the gesture is paradoxically redemptive. Not so with *The Dutchman*. Baraka's ending brooks no epiphanic moment in which Lula or Clay comes to some higher awareness. Instead, Lula instructs her fellow white passengers to throw the body out before eyeing her next victim, yet another young black man who has just entered the subway. The cycle is about to repeat itself.

The Dutchman's virtuosity emanates from its linguistic if not racial ambiguities, and such ambiguities foreground the play's complexity, especially in the context of Lula's anesthetized stance toward murder. The play plainly *is* a social protest drama, but it is something more than that. It transcends its sociopolitical content, germane as it clearly is. Baraka, writer and activist, is drawn in two apparently contradictory directions, so, in *The Dutchman*, Clay must negotiate between conflicting demands. His decision to retreat into language leads to his ritualized murder.

The Slave extends Baraka's moral search for black consciousness and identity. Like *The Dutchman*, it unfolds within a setting that is at once realistic and mythic. Tensions submerged in the subterranean set of *The Dutchman* are exteriorized in *The Slave*. Yet the pressure of personal experience hints at the special significance of the work for a man who, in the fifties, had married "a Jewish girl from Long Island trying to make it in the Village," only to divorce her for ideological reasons. "The play *The Slave*," Baraka wrote, "which shows a black would-be revolutionary who splits from his white wife on the eve of a race war, was what [my wife] called 'Roi's nightmare.' It was so close to our real lives, so full of that living image" (*Autobiography*, 196).

By 1965, months after the debut of *The Slave*, Baraka left Hettie Cohen and the Village, and immersed himself in directing the Black Arts Repertory/School, living in the decidedly African American world of Harlem. The unnamed narrator in Ralph Ellison's *Invisible Man* (1952) concludes "that even an invisible man has a socially responsible role to play" (503). Baraka, flushed from his own invisibility by what he calls "the 'fame' *Dutchman* brought me," felt similarly compelled to wed word and deed in the name of racial justice and cultural autonomy: "I felt, now, some heavy *responsibility*" (*Autobiography*, 189). He met that responsibility with an uneven artistry in the later plays.

In 1967, LeRoi Jones changed his name to Imamu Amiri Baraka, his new name ("blessed prince") bestowed upon him by the same orthodox Muslim who had performed the funeral service for Malcolm X. His plays foreshadowed this personal transfiguration. *Experimental Death Unit #1* (1965) presents Duff and Loco, two white heroine addicts who try to seduce a black whore. Sixties slogans blend with violence as Duff kills Loco. As the chaos proceeds, soldiers from the black rebellion Death Unit #1 appear, a ritualized entrance underscored by drums. The blacks kill Duff while he screams "Niggers! Niggers! Niggers!" and the woman, who assumes her blackness will save her, is summarily shot. Western debauchery, Baraka suggests, must be dealt with if a true spiritual revolution, in the spirit of Kawaida faith, is to become a reality. From such plays as *J-E-L-L-O* (1965), *A Black Mass* (1966), *Madheart* (1967), and *The Death of Malcolm X* (1969) to *S-1* (1976), *The Motion of History* (1977), *Boy & Tarzan Appear in a Clearing* (1981), and *Money* (1982), the playwright increasingly turned his energies to producing agit prop pieces, plays staged at the expense of art. Even the theatrically powerful *Slave Ship* (1967), which chronicles as it celebrates "A Historical Pageant" of black history, from independent Africans to their enslavement in the United States, would soon yield to plays that seemed closer to politicized pamphlets rather than committed art.

Baraka would go on to write some thirty plays, plays whose thematic and political shifts mirror the transformations in his personal life and public politics. He may in the process have too willingly sacrificed art to ideas, but he was never less than committed to those whose dilemmas he acknowledged and whose lives he celebrated in their ambiguities and certainties alike. Baraka's passionate commitment to and immersion in the African American experience registered deeply in the imaginations of many dramatists in the sixties and seventies.

David Mamet

While Albee, Shepard, Kennedy, and Baraka were contributing to an ongoing narrative of American drama in their various and singular ways, David Mamet, beginning in the mid-seventies, appeared at first as a Chicago regionalist. He quickly established his reputation as a writer of national and international significance, however.

A novelist, essayist, poet, Hollywood screenwriter, acting teacher, and director, Mamet remains best known for his plays. But his non-theatre works, too, provide an illuminating point of entry into his world. In *True and False* (1997), he writes about the pressures experienced by young actors. In *The Old Religion* (1997), a novel about a Jewish business manager falsely convicted of rape and murder and lynched by a mob, Mamet explores the past. *The Hero Pony* (1990), a collection of forty-two poems, displays an economy of expression that informs of "the distinction / Between art and decoration" (34). Now a veteran at writing numerous Hollywood scripts, Mamet's recent efforts include the Alec Baldwin–Anthony Hopkins film *The Edge* (1997), the Dustin

Hoffman film *Wag the Dog* (1997), and a projected remake of *The Cincinnati Kid* for actor Al Pacino.

But it was in 1992 that Mamet's career shifted. His brief, autobiographical essay, *The Rake*, reveals his troubled childhood, the tensions stemming from his parents' divorce and a psychologically and physically abusive stepfather. After that stepfather threw Mamet's sister, Lynn Mamet, a California-based writer, across a room – she fractured a vertebra in her back – he never forgave him (his father died in 1992 – the year he published *The Rake*). The anger and silences, the violence and the pauses central to Mamet's theatre, we now learn, stem from his family experiences and the "emotional terrorism" of his upbringing; the vengeance and energy of all of his plays, according to his sister, emanates from their childhood. "They're all familial," Lynn Mamet reports (Weber, "At 50, a mellower David Mamet," 12).

This explains why John, the ten-year-old in *The Cryptogram* (1994), goes up the stairs with a knife – probably to commit suicide; and perhaps this is why *The Cryptogram*, like *The Rake* before, and *The Old Neighborhood* (1997) after it, registers its tonalities in more subtle, muted terms. *The Old Neighborhood*, actually three earlier Mamet plays reformulated as a whole, that opened 17 November 1997 at the Booth Theatre in New York City, is a deeply autobiographical work. Its central figure, Bobby Gould, who Mamet calls his *alter ego*, returns to his old haunting grounds, probably the Chicago of Mamet's youth. Now, in mid-life, Gould engages in three conversations – with a childhood friend, his sister, and a former lover – that plainly reveal that some shared traumatic episodes still haunt all the characters. Mamet's technique of restraint, of pauses, silences, and never fully articulated experiences, forces audiences to speculate on the reality to which they are seemingly exposed.

It is easier to appreciate the 1992 shift in Mamet's career, however, by reference to his earlier plays. The subtle tonalities, the degrees of understatement in *The Cryptogram* and *The Old Neighborhood* are less in evidence there. Instead audiences were confronted by men whose sources of rage elude and baffle them. The rage, in part, comes from the social world in which his heroes find themselves. From the initial plays, *Camel* (1968) and *Lakeboat* (1970), to those pivotal works that first brought him notoriety, *Sexual Perversity in Chicago* (1974) and *American Buffalo* (1975), from *Glengarry Glen Ross* (1983) to *Oleanna* (1992), Mamet appropriates the play space with a singular vision. This unity of vision usually finds its expression in terms of an implicit social critique and sense of a deep ambiguity and inexperience. His wit and comedy seem obvious, but beyond the comedic witticisms lie darker visions. Mamet replicates human commitments and desires in demythicized forms: commodity fetishism, sexual negotiations and exploitations, aborted or botched crimes, brutal physical assaults, fraudulent business transactions enacted by petty thieves masquerading as businessmen, and human relationships whose only shared feature is the presence of physical sex and the absence of authentic love. Within Mamet's theatre, relationships are reductive, women often being marginalized and brutalized, men rendered inarticulate or suspect in their articulateness. Exploitation becomes a normative value.

Through a poetic stage language Mamet explores the relationship between public issues and private desires – and the effects of this relationship on the individual's spirit. Although his plays are varied in terms of plots and themes, he seems at his best when exploring what he feels is a business-as-sacrament mentality that has led to the corruption of both communal decency and individual ethics. His major achievements lie in his use of language, his exploration of private and public betrayals and alienation, his ability to stage the anxieties, the confusions, the self-deceptions, the hypocrisies and the desperate insecurities of the individual.

The mid-seventies were pivotal years for the playwright. In 1975, *American Buffalo* opened at the Goodman and soon moved to the St. Nicholas Theatre. The play won a Joseph Jefferson Award for Outstanding Production, as did *Sexual Perversity in Chicago* that same year. In 1975, Mamet finally saw his work staged in New York City: *Sexual Perversity* and *The Duck Variations* opened at the St. Clement's Theatre and, in 1976, they moved to the Cherry Lane Theatre. In 1976 *American Buffalo* opened at St. Clement's, and Mamet won an Obie for *Sexual Perversity* and *American Buffalo*. No fewer than nine Mamet plays appeared in 1977 in theatres in New Haven, New York, Chicago and, among other cities, London. *American Buffalo*, starring Robert Duvall, premiered on Broadway in 1977, with Mamet receiving the New York Drama Critics' Circle Award. In 1980 Al Pacino starred in a revival at the Long Wharf Theatre in New Haven. Such successes confirmed Mamet's reputation as a new and vital theatrical voice in America.

Mamet has also enjoyed success in reworking older classics, and his adaptations of Chekhov's *The Cherry Orchard* (1987), *Uncle Vanya* (1988), and *Three Sisters* (1991) all received favorable reviews. While first and foremost a playwright, Mamet has gained additional respect for his work in Hollywood. His screenplays – *The Postman Always Rings Twice* (1981), *The Verdict* (1982), *The Untouchables* (1985), *House of Games* (1987), *Things Change* (1988), *We're No Angels* (1989), *Homicide* (1990), *Glengarry Glen Ross* (1992), *The Edge* (1997) and, among others, *Wag the Dog* (1997) – have been praised for their intriguing plots and disturbing monologues. Most scholars point to *House of Games*, with its ritualized forms of expiation, and *Glengarry Glen Ross*, with its dazzling repartee, as his best work in film. Meanwhile, Mamet has demonstrated his skill as an essayist in *Writing in Restaurants* (1986) and *True and False* (1997), collections that spell out the playwright's theory of dramatic art as well as his sense of cultural poetics.

Mamet appears at his best when staging the tensions between his heroes' sense of public responsibility and their definition of private liberties. Mamet often mentions that his views of social boundaries have been greatly influenced by Thorstein Veblen's *Theory of the Leisure Class* (1899), and such indebtedness in part accounts for his preoccupation with business. Veblen's work, like Mamet's, underscores human action and response in terms of "pecuniary emulation," imperialist ownership, and the relationship between self-worth and wealth. Mamet's characters, plots, and themes map out a predatory world in which only the fittest survive. His plays are concerned with charting the moral relationship between the public issues of the nation and the private anxieties of its citizens.

American Buffalo, first produced at the Goodman Theatre Stage Two in Chicago, on 23 November 1975, concerns small-time thieves. They find a buffalo nickel in Don's junk shop, where the play unwinds, a nickel that motivates them to rob the man from whom Don supposedly purchased it. Don orchestrates the robbery plans, which the younger Bob is to undertake. Teach, nervous and unpredictable, insists that he should participate. In a brilliantly modulated conversation, Mamet suggests the extent to which ethics have been devalued and theft elevated to the status of good business practice. Free enterprise, Teach lectures Don, gives one the freedom "To embark on Any Fucking Course that he sees fit . . . In order to secure his honest chance to make a profit." The country, he insists, is "*founded* on this." The robbery never takes place. Indeed, it was never anything more than a fantasy which for a moment had given coherence and purpose to an aimless existence. Whatever friendships exist between the men temporarily dissipate: Teach attacks Bob and trashes the entire junk shop. The play ends as Teach readies himself to take the injured Bob to the hospital.

American Buffalo is a parodic version of the American dream, a social drama, and a metaphysical work of genuine originality. Its characters speak a dislocated language and inhabit a world drained of transcendence. Yet that language is shaped into powerful arias, ironic, humorous, simultaneously evidence of a desperate need for communication and contact and its virtual impossibility. With its echoes of another America, uncontaminated by greed, a product of utopian rhetoric rather than psychotic fear and aggression, it offers a portrait of the Republic in terminal decay, its communal endeavor and individual resilience all but disappeared. The trust and unity invoked on its coinage have now devolved into paranoia, the security and hope it once offered into a frightening violence. Business enterprise has decayed into simple criminality while the play's metaphoric and literal setting – a junk store full of the mementos of Chicago's 1933 Exposition (motto: A Century of Progress) – offers an image of ultimate decline.

Glengarry Glen Ross, which Harold Pinter encouraged Mamet to stage, had its premiere at the Cottesloe Theatre in London, on 21 September 1983, opened in America at the Goodman Theatre in Chicago, on 6 February 1984, and with the Chicago cast intact, moved to its successful Broadway run at the Golden Theatre in the following months. It dramatizes the high-pressure real estate sales profession as seen through the plight of small-time salesmen. Greed lies at the center of the play, for the characters' directing force in life is to secure sales "leads," to buffalo clients to "close" the deal, and rise to the top of the "board," the chart announcing which man in the sales force wins the ultimate prize – the Cadillac. The losers will simply be fired. As in *The Water Engine* (1978), *Mr. Happiness* (1978), and *American Buffalo*, *Glengarry Glen Ross* relies on the myth of the American Dream as its ideological back-drop. The title refers to Florida swamps, not the Scottish highlands, an indication of the extent of irony in this drama. In some ways *Glengarry Glen Ross* revisits that connection between business and criminality implicit in *American Buffalo*. Whereas the characters in *Lakeboat*, *Reunion* (1976), and even *The Shawl* (1985) lead lives of quiet desperation, those in *Glengarry Glen Ross* scream out two hours of obscenity-laced dialogue. The sales team constitute an unappetising team. Levene may be the most desperate figure, for his business failures lead him to crime as he robs his own office to secure precious sales "leads." Moss is the most ruthless salesman, masterminding but not participating in the robbery, while Aaronow simply seems bewildered by his cohorts' sales/conmanship. Williamson is the office manager, whose lack of sales experience and pettiness earn him the scorn of all. Ricky Roma, however, is different.

Roma emerges as the star of the sales team. He also appears as the most complex. Youthful and handsome, he exudes a certain panache that sets him apart from the others. Whereas the others talk about their past conquests and how, with luck (and deception), they will rise to the top of the sales board, Roma produces. If Levene and Moss frenetically pursue customers, Roma appears relaxed. He almost succeeds in swindling the unsuspecting customer, James Lingk, persuading him to buy suspect real estate, only losing out on the deal when Williamson inadvertently reveals the truth. But Roma loses more than his commission. The fact is that he has already lost his ethical perspective. Like Levene and Moss, he has no conscience, no sense of the boundaries of business ethics, and like many Mamet characters uses language to ensnare, deceive, and justify. The play ends with Levene's arrest, but business continues.

In *Glengarry Glen Ross*, entrepreneurial greed has devolved into a vaudevillian leitmotif, with the salesmen as consummate performers. The pursuit of money under the guise of free enterprise becomes a simple excuse to deceive and steal. The real estate salesmen pursue the Deal as their fellow citizens pursue the Dream, a dream now detached from its ethical origins. As Roma

17. Goodman Theatre production of David Mamet's *Glengarry Glen Ross*, 1984, with (left to right) Mike Nussbaum and Joe Montagna. Photograph by Brigitte Lacombe. Courtesy of Goodman Theatre.

remarks to the unsuspecting James Lingk: "I do those things which seem correct to me *today.*" Such rationalizations recur in Mamet's theatre. Thus when Karen, in *Speed-the-Plow* (1988), asks of a movie project, "Is it a good film?", her question is seen as irrelevant. The only legitimate issue, according to her employer, Bobby Gould, is whether it will make money. But Karen, too, is an opportunist, so that money, exchange, and commodity fetishism pervade *Speed-the-Plow* as they do much of Mamet's theatre. Genuine human relationships, moral values, language as a means of communication, society as a model of mutuality, all seem, like the buffalo, on the brink of extinction. Fittingly, the role of Karen, herself prepared to sacrifice personal relationships to ambition, was played by Madonna, the material girl.

Sexuality, meanwhile, is either simply a means of exchange – as it is in *Edmond* (1982) – or an expression of the alienated relations between the genders – as in *The Woods* (1977) and *Oleanna*. Men and women, in Mamet's work, inhabit different worlds, evidence different needs, speak a different language. In his earlier plays, this is an expression of an all but unbridgeable gulf. In *Oleanna*, the failure of communication has a political edge.

Oleanna, a play partially about sexual harassment, represents the playwright's response to the Anita Hill–Clarence Thomas controversy. In Act One, Carol, a female student, comes to the office of a male college professor, John, to sort out her difficulties in understanding his class. John, who is under tenure review, offers to help. The complacent professor, who is married and is negotiating a deal on a house, listens to Carol's confession, "I don't *understand*. I don't understand what it *means.*" He offers Carol advice and a consoling hand. While the audience senses an impending catastrophe, Act One gives little hint of what is to follow as characters and audiences are forced to re-evaluate language and action. Despite the popularity of this play, Mamet's control of language disappoints. Brittle, awkward, unnatural, the repartee never gains theatrical momentum.

In the second act, Carol registers a complaint, accusing the professor of sexism and sexual harassment. A confrontation merely leads to further misunderstandings. Slowly power moves from professor to student, from man to woman, until John faces loss of tenure, the collapse of his marriage, and a charge of rape, as, *in extremis*, he becomes what she accuses him of being. "Right" becomes a function of language, the real a product of interpretation. Only power has authority.

In *Oleanna*, which was originally produced by the Back Bay Theatre Company in association with the American Repertory Theatre in Cambridge, Massachusetts, on 1 May 1992, and moved to its New York City run at the Orpheum Theatre on 25 October 1992, Mamet returns to a world in which the gaps between words and deeds are the source of unease, of fundamental disjunctions, shifting power systems, willful refusals of communication. The play is theatrically powerful precisely because its author never fills in such gaps. Is Carol deliberately framing John? Are her accusations legitimate? Is Carol simply the first to have the courage to challenge a patronizing and, perhaps, womanizing male teacher? Is John so much a part of an inherently misogynistic world that he is blithely unaware that his well-meaning actions are in fact highly sexist? Mamet invites the audience to respond to these and many other issues (questions of censorship, political correctness, a battle of the sexes, representations of women in theatre, among others). This play continues Mamet's exploration of a world which remains a battleground of the sexes, where primal feelings of trust and rational human discourse between women and men remain problematic, if not impossible. The title of the play, taken from a folk song, alludes to a nineteenth-century escapist vision of Utopia. *Oleanna* reminds us of the impossibility of such a vision.

Mamet's theatre, in sum, repeatedly returns to broader social questions about communication and community. Some Mamet dramas do not include verbal tirades, or physical or psychological violence. *The Duck Variations, A Life in the Theatre* (1977), *Reunion* (1976), *The Woods*, and *The Shawl* – to cite plays spanning much of Mamet's career – appear as relatively meditative works whose plots and themes seem more interiorized. On the other hand, the playwright seems most comfortable, and at the height of his aesthetic power, when he explores anger and betrayal, mystery and violence, when private loss is related to social satire. From *Sexual Perversity in Chicago* through *Oleanna* and *The Cryptogram*, relationships are as ephemeral as they are unsatisfying, while a brutalizing language masks primal insecurities. There are no villains in his theatre – just men whose world of diminished possibilities and banalities define and confine them.

In *Reunion*, Bernie tells Carol that, although he comes from a broken home, he is a happy man who works at a good job. But his uneasiness remains, particularly in light of the contemporary world in which he and Carol live: "It's a fucking jungle out there. And you got to learn the rules because *nobody's* going to learn them for you." True knowledge about the soul and the universe comes only at a price: "Always the price. Whatever it is. And you gotta know it and be prepared to pay it if you don't want it to pass you by." There are no epiphanies in Mamet's work, only characters who struggle to survive in an unforgiving world. In *Edmond*, the protagonist is racist, sexist, and homophobic. He leaves his "safe" marriage and embarks on an urban quest to find meaning for his fragmented world. Encountering violence, murder, sexual frustration, and other impediments, he winds up in jail, sodomized by his black cell-mate. What Edmond learns from his quest is the necessity to accept his own role as acquiescent victim. He becomes the compliant partner of his cell-mate.

In *Writing in Restaurants* Mamet writes, "As the Stoics said, either gods exist or they do not exist. If they exist, then, no doubt, things are unfolding as they should; if they do *not* exist, then why should we be reluctant to depart a world in which there are no gods?" (114). This reflection stands as the metaphysical question Mamet raises, and never resolves, in his plays. His characters half believe in a structure of meaning for which they can find no evidence. They display the rhetoric of a civic responsibility which their own lives deny. They acknowledge the need for trust and mutual responsibility while capitalizing on that trust and betraying that responsibility. They fear solitude but distrust the other. As the frightened boy confesses to his mother at the end of *The Cryptogram*, "I hear voices," voices that even an adult, not to mention a ten-year-old, would have difficulty decoding.

Those voices which might be the source of consolation are more likely to be the source of terror. These are people who fail to break the code of their society, fail to acknowledge human necessities. Dimly aware of the values they deny, the social contract which they abrogate, they obey other imperatives, disconnected from their inner lives, inimical to their fundamental needs. Yet, for all that, they are often consummate performers, accomplished storytellers, masters of deceit who implicitly challenge the nature of the real and hence the elaborate structures erected upon it. They may not meet each other in the alienated environment which they inhabit or the sexual encounters to which they are infrequently driven, but they do make momentary contact within the fictions which they deploy with such evident relish as if these constituted the true drama, the stage on which they are to act their lives. In *A Life in the Theatre*, two men perform on and off stage, sometimes reciting lines written by others, sometimes improvising their own existences. There are few of Mamet's characters who do not find themselves living within that same tension between the given and the constructed, the determined and the free. That, indeed, is surely, in part, the basis of their claim on our attention, for in that respect they stand as paradigms of a private, a social, and a metaphysical condition.

Marsha Norman

If Mamet's plays tend to focus on a largely masculine world, often to the exclusion of female characters, the reverse could be said of the world of Marsha Norman, whose work dates from the later seventies. Told by director Jon Jory to "'Go back at least ten years and write about some time when you were really scared,'" she produced the remarkable play, *Getting Out*, which premiered in November 1977 at the Actors Theatre of Louisville under Jory's direction. It was a play which turned on a metaphor that would recur in her work, the isolation of the individual and the attendant struggle to transcend an impossible present: "I know now, all these years and plays later," she has remarked, "that I always write about solitary confinement. But *Getting Out* was my first crack at it" (prefatory note, *Getting Out*, 3).

Her first "crack at it" is her best play to date. *Getting Out* centers upon Arlene Holsclaw, "a thin, drawn woman in her late 20's, who has just served an 8-year prison term for murder." Arlene is divided against herself, sometimes ferociously so. She feels psychologically haunted by her former self, who physically appears on the stage as another woman, Arlie. As Norman suggests in a prefatory note to the play, "Arlie is the violent kid Arlene was until her last stretch in prison." The play gains its theatrical momentum through the dichotomization of Arlene's split selves, whose opposing ambitions and responses to outer experience lie at the drama's philosophical nerve center. With the action modulating between a prison and "a dingy one-room apartment" that Norman specifies "must seemed imprisoned," Arlene wrestles with Arlie, who represents Arlene's "memory of herself, called up by fears, needs and even simple word cues. The memory haunts, attacks, and warns. But mainly, the memory won't go away."

Arlie is a "screechin wildcat." Her opening monologue instantly establishes something of her hardscrabble background and her hard-boiled stance toward life. Her monologue recounts the story of a "creepy little fucker," a young neighbor boy, and how she stole his "stupid frogs," and tossed them on the street where "most of em jus got squashed, you know, runned over?" A speech filled with demonic laughter and violence, it offers a key image that informs the entire production. For *Getting Out* is a play about an Arlie who has been tossed on to the city streets, to live a life of drugs and prostitution, petty thievery and forgery, child abuse and murder. She has been raped by her father while her cab-driving mother has whored around the small Kentucky town. But she is a survivor.

As the play progresses, so we learn that all of the external authority figures with whom she interacts, from her mother and father to the school principal, from the warden to her boyfriend/pimp, remind her of her own insignificance. They torment and tyrannize. She rebels, rejecting the institutions and institutionalization she endures. She becomes, in the playwright's words, "unpredictable and incorrigible," doing time in the state prison for her actions.

Arlene, by contrast, represents a more mature, experienced self. Battle-fatigued by a lifetime of fighting, she appears suspicious and guarded, and Norman indicates that her "withdrawal is always a possibility." Indeed, after a life on the run and years of imprisonment, Arlene, newly released from an Alabama prison, recoils from those interested in using her and her body. The entire play, in fact, charts her new determination to direct her own life on her own terms. When her indifferent mother says, "So, you're callin' yourself Arlene, now?" Arlene's affirmative response functions as more than a simple answer to a question. For *Getting Out* is about "getting out" of Arlie's old self and reclaiming, re-imaging, and renaming herself.

The process of reclaiming, re-imaging, and renaming, however, remains a tortuous one, a process fraught with indecisions, insecurities, and economic hardship. Norman refuses to sentimentalize or sanitize Arlene's struggle for selfhood. Arlene wishes to see Joey, the son she was forced to give up immediately after his birth, but can do so only from a distance and by stealth. She may want to come to terms with her own mother, but when she moves to hug a woman she has not seen in eight years, her mother only stands still, and the disappointed daughter must back away. Arlene, after all, knows she is the product of a sexually abusive father and hooker mother while her siblings are as disjointed as Arlie. Living in a world of few possibilities or pleasures, distanced from her parents, brothers and sisters, and from her own son, she nonetheless perseveres. *Getting Out* presents her struggle to give direction and purpose to her wayward life. While in prison she tried to commit suicide, an attempt to kill her Arlie self; now, on the outside, her freedom will be preserved, not by the killing of her old self nor by the simple blotting out of her past. Rather, during the course of the play, she learns to accept her former self, to grant Arlie her presence, and to push beyond the emotional wreckage of her past. Such an insight becomes the key to Arlene's existence. The act of taking control is itself one of her greatest triumphs.

She confronts, too, the economic realities of being a former prostitute and ex-convict. She knows too well that she re-enters a world that offers her a choice between prostitution and menial work. Her rejections of former prison guard, Bennie, who threatens her with rape, and her former boyfriend and pimp, Carl, who tries to lure her back into hooking, become crucial personal victories. Although she resents having to choose between prostitution or laboring in "some shit job so's you can eat worse than you did in prison," her new friend, Ruby, provides the needed corrective: "Well, you can wash dishes to pay the rent on your 'slum,' or you can spread your legs for any shit that's got the ten dollars." Arlene's resistance to Carl, Bennie, and others becomes her way of reclaiming her body as essential subject. Her resistance signals her incipient transformation from sexual object to independent woman. Arlene comes to understand the necessity for autonomy, the need to escape the male gaze and establish her own female identity.

Like Jessie in *'night, Mother* (1982), she hungers for food, but it must be both psychologically and spiritually nourishing, and served on her own terms. If food, and how it is prepared and eaten, becomes her way of resisting the prison guards and her mother, it is also the source of hope and reconnection. At the end she says to Ruby, "I gotta put my food up first" before she will join her friend upstairs for a card game at the play's end.

Getting Out may be seen as a guarded celebration. Arlie, after all, and for reasons never fully explained, did murder another human being. But its celebratory nature surfaces in the final minutes of the action, a fact confirmed by Arlene's body language. As Arlie and Arlene appear together on stage, exchanging a humorous story about childhood pranks, for the first time in the play Arlene smiles and Arlie's loving laughter fills the stage. As Celie and Shug Avery bond in Alice Walker's *The Color Purple* (1982), so Arlene and Ruby come together. They form a female-centered community of two, which enables Arlene to recover her dignity and draw upon her own courage. She becomes actively involved in her own fate, a central participant in her own life. She succeeds in "getting out" of her angry former self, to take the first steps toward living, honorably, within her own emotional limits. It is a profound change that, significantly, does not involve the killing of her former self. In the final scene "they are enjoyably aware of each other," Norman writes, an awareness that foreshadows a constructive new life.

Arlene's transformation has significance beyond mere self-realization. In some sense it reflects a development in the wider culture, a development reflected in the emergence of women writers. "The appearance of significant women dramatists in significant numbers," Norman commented to an interviewer, "is a reflection of a change in women's attitudes towards themselves. It is a sudden understanding that they can be, indeed are, the central characters in their own lives. That is a notion that's absolutely required for writing for the theatre . . . the notion of an *active* central character is required for the theatre. Not until enough women in society realized that did the voices to express it arrive" (quoted in Betsko and Koenig, *Interviews*, 338). This precisely describes the centrality of Arlene in *Getting Out*.

Norman would return to these larger issues, though would not restrict herself to exploring the relationship between women. Her next play, *Third and Oak* (1978), is made up of a pair of one-act plays. In *The Laundromat*, a woman caught in a sterile marriage and a widow meet by chance at the local laundromat, where they slowly reveal the truth of their lives. Both confess to a feeling of abandonment. *The Pool Hall*, the companion piece, which revolves around the owner of the pool hall and the son of a famous pool player, who exchange tales of frustration and unrealized dreams, explores something of the relationship between men. Like *Getting Out* and *'night, Mother*, *Third and Oak* was made into a successful film, well-received by the critics.

Despite the generally favorable response to *The Laundromat* and *The Pool Hall*, however, these plays have stirred little debate and are seldom produced. So too with *The Holdup* (1983), which concerns cowboys in New Mexico at the start of the twentieth century, *Traveler in the Dark* (1984), and *Circus Valentine* (1979), unsatisfying plays that drew negative reviews. Disturbed by such negative responses, she excluded critics from the Actors Theatre of Louisville production of *Sarah and Abraham* in June of 1988. Despite the popular and critical success of her teleplays *It's the Willingness* (for PBS) and *In Trouble at Fifteen* (for NBC) in 1980, her novel *The Fortune Teller* (1987) remains a footnote to American literature. Her book for the Broadway musical *The Secret Garden* (which received a Tony Award and a Drama Desk Award soon after it opened at the St. James Theatre on 25 April 1991), and *D. Boone*, which premiered a year later at the Actors Theatre Humana Festival to favorable reviews, have made little impact beyond this regional theatre production. However, such was not the case with a play most consider to be her masterpiece, *'night, Mother*.

As Luce Irigaray suggests in *This Sex Which Is Not One* (1985), the mother–daughter relationship is a complex one to sustain in a patriarchal culture. Yet, for Marsha Norman, it is one of the most vital, if mysterious. It certainly plays a crucial role in the psychodynamics of *'night, Mother*. The final night spent together by mother and daughter in this play becomes what Norman calls "a holy object," in that it leads to "the moment of connection between them. Basically, it is a moment when two people are willing to go as far as they can with each other" (quoted in Betsko and Koenig, *Interviews*, 329). That moment of connection, however, comes at a high price.

'night, Mother unsettles theatregoers moments into the action when Jessie Cates announces: "I'm going to kill myself, Mama." During the next ninety minutes, we watch a series of exchanges between mother and daughter that culminate with Jessie's rush to a bedroom, where she kills herself with her father's pistol. For Norman, the contentious relationship between Jessie and

Thelma Cates raises many larger cultural issues regarding the status of women. *'night, Mother* emerges as a play less about suicide and more about the way in which Jessie and Thelma redefine their own individual survival. It is equally a play about choice. Just as Arlene chooses to take control of her life in *Getting Out*, so Jessie elects to assume responsibility for her death. Both women succeed in escaping from what Norman calls their solitary confinement, albeit with one woman saying yes to life and the other embracing death. Unquestionably the play disturbs. Jessie's calmness, meticulous preparation, and inviolable choice unnerves precisely because there remains, as Beckett's Estragon says, "Nothing to be done." Jessie has waited long enough for her Godot to arrive. She tells her mother that she "can get off [the bus] right now if I want to, because if I ride fifty more years and get off then, it's the same place when I step down to it." She is acutely aware that her life is going nowhere, that it is drained of meaning. In this context, the decision to seize control of her life by ending it is simultaneously a decision to give it a direction and purpose. To die for the right reasons is to give her life a shape, a form. As she tells her mother, "Whenever I feel like it, I can get off [the bus]. As soon as I've had enough, it's my stop. I've had enough."

The play makes for engaging theatre not least because of Jessie's courageous struggle to confront her manipulative and controlling mother and her mother's desperate efforts to save her daughter's life. On a quest whose finality is a given, Jessie sorts through a life in which she has endured epilepsy, the death of her father, the collapse of her marriage, unemployment, and a son who has turned into a juvenile delinquent. Forced by illness to return to her mother's home, Jessie hungers for the truth. Meanwhile, her meticulous preparations for her final leavetaking signal yet another shift in the direction of self-responsibility. Indeed, in the course of the play Jessie exchanges places with her mother, comforting, directing, and counseling Thelma, herself increasingly child-like. For Jessie realizes that if she is to succeed, she must both articulate her reasons for self-murder and absolve her mother of responsibility, while she acknowledges her need to end a life of dependency. As Jessie asks, "What if the only way I can get away from you for good is to kill myself? What if it is? I can *still* do it!". Exhausted from a life of disappointment, seeking spiritual sustenance but offered only junk food, Jessie chooses death. In her most eloquent plea to her mother, she outlines the sense of loss that precipitates her suicide: "That's what this is about. It's somebody I lost, all right, it's my own self. Who I never was. Or who I tried to be and never got there. Somebody I waited for who never came. And never will." At last she takes possession of herself. As Norman remarks, *'night, Mother* is "a play of nearly total triumph. Jessie is able to get what she feels she needs. That is not a despairing act" (quoted in Betsko and Koenig, *Interviews*, 339).

After opening at the American Repertory Theatre in Cambridge,

Massachusetts in December 1982, *'night, Mother* played at the John Golden Theatre in New York City from 31 March 1983, and earned a Pulitzer Prize for Drama. Although Norman accepted a 50 percent pay cut to keep the play running during its ten-month engagement, *'night, Mother* grew to be one of the most frequently studied plays by an American woman dramatist. But despite her important and ongoing contributions to the American stage, Marsha Norman has not been fully embraced by the critics. If for some feminist scholars she seems too conservative, resisting a feminist label, she nonetheless feels that *'night, Mother* "came along at the exact moment when a play about two women, written by a woman, could be seen as 'a human play'" (quoted in Brustein, "Conversation," 12). Her less than fulsome embrace of the feminist movement, however, prompted some women scholars to view her skeptically, and Norman despaired over the ambivalent reception she received after her 1984 speech at the Women's Center at Stanford University. Ironically, many of the initial male reviewers of *'night, Mother* reported being frankly bored by the play.

In *'night, Mother,* however, Norman staged one of the first American plays to raise important philosophical and ethical questions about women and their relationships in a provocative and compelling manner. While critics have yet to come fully to terms with her work, Norman herself refuses to compromise her artistic instincts. Much the same could be said of one of her contemporaries, Wendy Wasserstein.

Wendy Wasserstein

Despite some rather obvious differences, Wasserstein and Norman share a crucial belief in creating vital female characters. Like Norman, Wasserstein believes in generating work that appeals to both genders. "I do agree with Marsha Norman in that I think there are stories to tell that haven't been told," Wasserstein has noted. "But you're not only telling them for women, hopefully" (quoted in Betsko and Koenig, *Interviews,* 419). Declining her admission to Columbia University's MBA program and opting instead to enroll at the Yale School of Drama after graduating from Mt. Holyoke, Wendy Wasserstein emerged, with Norman, as one of the more refreshing dramatists since the seventies. Her central characters, plagued with doubt and uncertain about their future, rely on humor to protect themselves from the implications of their existence. She mixes comedy and social criticism, though in a theatrical style that differs greatly from the more radicalized stages of Megan Terry, Laurie Anderson, Karen Finley, or Fiona Templeton. Yet Wasserstein is one of the few women American dramatists to reach a wide audience, albeit a more mainstream one than Terry, Anderson, Finley, or Templeton would care to reach. While Wasserstein's work exudes a moral seriousness, her plays rely on comedy to engage that seriousness. From *Uncommon Women and Others* (1977) to *The Sisters Rosensweig* (1992), Wasserstein creates episodic plays centered on women working through a patriarchal "society [that] is based on cocks," as Rita puts it in *Uncommon Women and Others*, while using humor as a liberating force. Wasserstein, however, steers deftly between the comic and the tragic, as in the Pulitzer Prize-winning *The Heidi Chronicles*, first staged 6 April 1988 in workshop by the Seattle Repertory Theatre before moving to a Broadway production at the Plymouth Theatre on 9 March 1989.

Many of Wasserstein's characters, like Heidi Holland in *The Heidi Chronicles*, feel "stranded." As a feminist art historian and the keynote speaker at the "Women, Where Are We Going" conference, Heidi concludes her speech with a confession of indecision that surprises her audience: "We're all concerned, intelligent, good women. *Pauses.* It's just that I feel stranded. And I thought the whole point was that we wouldn't feel stranded. I thought the point was that we were all in this together. Thank you. *Walks off.*" The play, which moves from scenes set in New York City in the seventies and eighties to Chicago in 1965 and 1974, from Manchester, New Hampshire, in 1968, to Ann Arbor, Michigan, in 1970, centers on the talented Heidi and her friends as they change in relation to a shifting social and political world.

As the play progresses through important moments in Heidi's life from 1964–89, Wasserstein draws upon those issues and people whom Wasserstein saw as shaping the baby-boomer generation. From references to sixties political activism, women's consciousness-raising groups, the death of John Lennon to the *Dinner Party* art of Judy Chicago, and the emergence of AIDS, *The Heidi Chronicles* offers a sweeping account of a generation of women and men struggling to harmonize career ambitions with ideals. Just as Heidi considers her personal fate and the collective trajectory of her generation, so Kate in *Uncommon Women and Others* worries that she will "grow up to be a cold efficient lady in a gray business suit." And what is true of her characters is true, too, of Wasserstein, for whom playwriting is a dialogue with herself and her society.

On the eve of *Isn't It Romantic*'s Los Angeles premiere, Wasserstein remarked that, "You write plays – at least *I* do – for personal emotional reasons, trying to clarify things for myself. Suddenly there was this I-want-it-all-you-should-have-it-all checklist with things that made people feel badly because they *didn't* (have it all) so, as opposed to liberation, it was a reason to feel bad. Now *that's* very disturbing" (quoted in Drake, "Will the Real Wendy," 40). Such concerns lie at the heart of *Isn't It Romantic* (1983) in which Janie Blumberg and Harriet Cornwall, two former college friends, discuss the relative virtues of marriage and careers. The play concludes with Harriet's decision to marry, Janie's decision to remain unencumbered and alone.

There are few certainties in Wasserstein's work, only women improvising their lives, defining their lives by living them, refusing, finally, to accept the authority of convention or the degeneration of the age. No wonder her plays found a ready audience for a generation of theatregoers, especially female, who were, like Wasserstein, living through the feminist movement in the United States. Record-breaking numbers of women were graduating from college and entering the work force in numbers not seen since the days of Rosie the Riveter. That many, male and female, felt the burdens and successes of the women's movement only made Wasserstein's theatre seem all the more relevant and poignant. Just as women struggled to move from the margins to the center of their social and professional lives, so Wasserstein's characters struggle to assert their independence.

Wasserstein stands as one of the few serious women playwrights of our time writing comedies. She differs from many of her contemporaries, women and men, in that she fills her stage with highly educated, privileged, professional white women, many of them Jewish. In *Uncommon Women and Others*, her first major success, we watch several women gather six years after graduating from Mt. Holyoke. In *Isn't It Romantic*, Janie is a talented freelance writer and Harriet, MBA in hand, has long been the successful corporate executive. Heidi Holland, with her undergraduate degree from Vassar and PhD in art history from Yale, is known nationally, thanks to her latest book selling so well that she regularly appears as the keynote speaker at important conventions throughout the country. Sara in *The Sisters Rosensweig* works hard to become a successful international banker. Wasserstein's uncommon women often dine at trendy restaurants, stay at fancy hotels, and enjoy material luxuries. All of them, it seems, are graduates of Ivy League universities, leaders of the yuppie phenomenon of the eighties.

Such characters have left Wasserstein open to charges of writing elitist drama, a drama that hardly addresses the kinds of issues evident, for instance, in Paula Vogel's *The Baltimore Waltz* (1992) or *How I Learned to Drive* (1997), Karen Finley's *The Constant State of Desire* (1986), Henry David Hwang's *F O B* (1979), or Leeny Sack's performance piece, *The Survivor and the Translator* (1980). Unquestionably Wasserstein's plays lack a streetwise grittiness. Perhaps, too, her wealthier characters, beneficiaries of blue-blood educations and the rarified environments they inhabit, provoke an understandable distrust on the part of certain theatregoers and critics. But the women's movement did, indeed, impact first on those, like Wasserstein herself, for whom new possibilities and new responsibilities were proposed.

Wasserstein has suggested that she turned to playwriting precisely because she became aware of an absence at the heart of the drama she studied: "When I was a playwriting student at the Yale Drama School in 1976, my thesis play was a piece I wrote for eight women which was called

Uncommon Women and Others. I wrote the play partly because I'd spent my graduate years reading a great deal of Jacobean drama in which, to put it simply, men kissed the poisoned lips of women and promptly dropped dead. My honest reaction to these works was that although I found the drama compelling, this particular experience was not familiar to me nor to any of my friends." She recalled that, after *Uncommon Women and Others* had its first showing in the basement of the Yale Drama School, a male student remarked, "'I can't get into this. It's about women.'" Wasserstein's response was to object, "'I've spent my life getting into Hamlet and Lawrence of Arabia. Why doesn't he just try it?'" Years later, she queried whether it might not be "the woman playwright who feels the keener urgency to reexamine theatrical traditions and thereby revitalize them" (Wasserstein, "Introduction," in Kilgore, *Contemporary Plays by Women*, xvii, xix).

Wasserstein has herself played a significant role in this revitalization process. She creates, when at her best, sympathetic characters in realistic situations whose intelligence and humor help them remain, in the most positive sense of the term, uncommon women. The private and the public converge. From early work such as *Any Woman Can't* (1973), *Happy Birthday, Montpelier Pizz-zazz* (1974) and *When Dinah Shore Ruled the Earth* (1975), co-authored with Christopher Durang, to *Tender Offer* (1983), her Chekhov short story adaptation *The Man in a Case* (1986), and her collection of essays, *Bachelor Girls* (1990), Wasserstein has constantly extended both her range and her sophistication, as evidenced in the late nineties with *An American Daughter* (1996), her first play to be staged on Broadway without an initial Off-Broadway run. By far her most political play, it was inspired in part by the media harassment felt by Zoe Baird and other prominent women in Washington, D.C. in the mid-nineties. It concerns Lyssa Dent Hughes, freshly nominated as Surgeon General by a Democratic president, who is forced to withdraw her candidacy after a series of news leaks about her failure to respond to a jury notice. A play about an intelligent, dynamic, and powerful woman whose career is cut short by sexism, it ends ironically as the audience sees Lyssa, a descendant of Ulysses S. Grant, denied the basic freedoms her great-grandfather fought to preserve.

Beth Henley

Like Wasserstein, Beth Henley works through comedy. Whereas Wasserstein explores educated, New England women in East Coast settings, however, Henley charts the lives of eccentric figures in small southern towns. Her characters, spiritual descendants of Eudora Welty's or Flannery O'Connor's, fill the stage with the vernacular, mannerisms, and ethos of the South. Enacting their fears and anxieties in realistic sets, her characters skirt the edges of the absurd, the grotesque, and the bizarre. This blend of the real with the absurd, with her characters always one step away from tragedy, redeeming themselves and those they encounter, has proved compelling. Like Wasserstein's, Henley's figures survive through laughter, a laughter which keeps at bay the loneliness, frailty, and loss that would otherwise claim them.

Henley's theatre begins in tragedy and in comedy. Her characters, Henley insists, need not resolve their personal crises; their triumph stems from their merely accepting their often bizarre situations and personalities. And from such acceptance emerges an optimism that propels them into an uncertain future. Henley closes *Crimes of the Heart* with an image of the sisters frozen *"for a moment laughing and catching a cake."* Such laughter protects the sisters as they sort through their troubled past within a small town.

An aspiring actress who, after college, traveled to Los Angeles in 1976 in hopes of becoming a film star, Beth Henley turned to playwriting when she was unable to secure auditions from the Hollywood studios. She began by writing a comedy, based on three eccentric sisters living in Hazlehurst, Mississippi, a small village near Henley's home town of Jackson. After finishing the script, entitled *Crimes of the Heart*, in 1978, she sent it to several regional theatres, only to have it rejected. Unbeknown to her, a friend submitted the play to the Actors Theatre of Louisville, where Marsha Norman launched her career, and her script was not only accepted but became co-winner of the drama festival competition. After successful regional runs, *Crimes of the Heart* was staged in New York, where, after an Off-Broadway run in 1980, it opened at the John Golden Theatre on 4 November 1981. Henley's first major success, it ran for 535 performances and earned her a Pulitzer Prize. She was the first woman to win the award in twenty-three years. Despite her success, however, her other plays – *Am I Blue* (1973), *The Miss Firecracker Contest* (1980), *The Wake of Jamey Foster* (1982), *The Debutante Ball* (1985), *The Lucky Spot* (1986), and *Control Freaks* (1993) – sparked little enthusiasm, repeating, as they largely do, the techniques and concerns of *Crimes of the Heart*. *Abundance* (1990) signaled a shift in style for Henley, dealing, as it did, with the difficult marriages of two mail-order brides in the American West in the 1800s. But ambitious though it was, it drew a lukewarm public response. To date, her reputation rests chiefly on her gothic comedy *Crimes of the Heart*.

The play traces the lives of the Magrath sisters, who have lived through disappointment and solitariness, and now struggle to come to terms with their unusual circumstances. As the play begins, we learn that "Babe shot Zackery Botrelle, the richest and most powerful man in all of Hazlehurst, slap in the gut," soon after he found his wife with a teenage black boy. Thereafter the sisters swap humorous stories about their lives. Babe struggles with her frustrations having, we learn, survived a suicide attempt; Lenny has long ago resigned herself to spinsterhood; while Meg, after an unsuccessful attempt at a singing career, returns home to the comforts afforded by an affair with her former boyfriend, an affair that does not work out. Henley fills her plot with an attorney who courts Babe, a dying grandfather, and the haunting memory of their mother, who hanged the family cat and then herself.

Henley could have easily arranged such story elements into the stuff of a gothic tragedy in the tradition of William Faulkner, as she does with *The Debutante Ball*. But in *Crimes of the Heart*, she deflects the tragic motion of her characters' lives into the protective custody of the comedic. Henley spells out a cautiously affirmative future for her characters. They must, she suggests, progress through the suicide of their mother and other difficult personal experiences. By the end, Meg confronts and accepts her failed singing career and her failed efforts to sustain a relationship with her old flame. Lenny, too, confronts and accepts her personal inhibitions and how they have diminished her life, while Babe comes to terms with her mother's suicide, an understanding whose significance Henley spotlights by describing Babe's explanation as an "*enlightenment.*" The enlightenment affects not only Babe but her older siblings as well. Although their mother could not survive her "real bad day," as Meg puts it, the three sisters bond together and celebrate their resilient lives together, though they can hardly tell if today's event is a harbinger for tomorrow's death or deliverance. Hence the celebration at the play's end represents much more than Lenny's birthday; it also suggests that these sisters will carry on, knowing that for now they can keep at arm's distance the loneliness that drove their mother to the grave.

August Wilson

By the eighties a host of new dramatists emerged, but few with the impact of August Wilson. While becoming interested in literature and the performing arts during the Civil Rights Movement in the sixties, he labored in relative obscurity, though by 1976 had begun work on what would be his breakthrough play, *Ma Rainey's Black Bottom*. The breakthrough, however, did not arrive until the summer of 1982, when Lloyd Richards, then Dean of the Yale Drama School and the artistic director of the Eugene O'Neill Center, picked Wilson's *Ma Rainey's Black Bottom* for a staged reading. Richards, who directed Hansberry's *A Raisin in the Sun* (1959) nearly three decades earlier, has directed Wilson's major works at the Yale Repertory Theatre, plays that have typically gone on to enjoy healthy Broadway runs. Wilson is the first African American to have two plays showing simultaneously on Broadway.

In his introduction to *Fences*, Richards argues that Wilson is "one of the most compelling storytellers to begin writing for the theatre in many years."

Wilson himself has said, "I think black Americans have the most dramatic story of all mankind to tell" (quoted in Jacobus, *Bedford Introduction to Drama*, 1,500). Like Charles Fuller and Ed Bullins, who feel that black history and theatre are inseparable, August Wilson reclaims history for his stage. Like Fuller and Bullins, he has set himself the task of composing a cycle of plays, each one of which is set in a different decade of the twentieth century, each dealing with an aspect of the African American experience. Wilson feels that it is necessary to articulate the past in an effort to reconstitute the present. Past and present, history and myth, music and language blend in his theatre.

After his mother divorced her white husband and moved the family to a slum neighborhood in Pittsburgh, Wilson grew up in a racist school where the white children constantly harassed him and from which he dropped out at age fifteen when his teacher refused to believe that he was the author of an essay on Napoleon. As a young man coming of age during the Black Arts Movement in Pittsburgh, he turned to reading and writing as a way to understand black oppression, struggle, and resistance. In 1968 he assisted in establishing the Black Horizons Theatre Company in Pittsburgh, a liaison that gave him a chance to hear his language in the mouths of actors.

He was not pleased. He admits that at the time he "didn't respect the way blacks talked" and hence falsified their language (Wilson, "August Wilson Interview," 9). In 1978 he moved to Minneapolis and began writing scripts for the Science Museum of Minnesota, and it was in the Twin Cities that he became associated with the Penumbra Theatre in St. Paul. The early plays, *Black Bart and the Sacred Hills* (1981), *Jitney* (1982), and *Fullerton Street* (*c.* 1982), show Wilson struggling, without success, to transmute craft into art. The limitations of these early plays lay in language, in Wilson's unwillingness to tap into the unique rhythms of black language. In effect he denied himself access to the very subjects that would become the greatest resource for his later work: history and the language employed to articulate that history. Their unimpressive debuts notwithstanding, these first plays signaled a turning point for Wilson. For it was during this time that he began to attend to the linguistic and theatrical possibilities implicit in black dialect. Rather than devaluing the black idiom, as he had done in his first compositions, he now celebrated "voices I had been brought up with all my life . . . I realized I didn't have to change it [black dialogue]. I began to respect it" (Wilson, "August Wilson Interview," 9).

Those "voices" are best heard in his major works: *Ma Rainey's Black Bottom, Fences* (1986), *Joe Turner's Come and Gone* (1986), *The Piano Lesson* (1987), and *Two Trains Running* (1990). In *Ma Rainey's Black Bottom*, Wilson refigures the historical past by using as his central character Gertrude (Ma) Rainey who, before her death in 1939, was one of the first black singers to secure a recording contract and went to her grave known as the "Mother of the Blues." In music and in business, she paved the way for Bessie Smith and Billie Holiday. The play, based on an actual recording session at a Paramount recording studio, mixes levity and seriousness as it balances self-achievement and self-betrayal. Like Hansberry's characters, Wilson's pursue a myth, the American Dream, searching for fame and money by working for the white-controlled recording industry. Their pursuit forces them to confront their Americanness, no less than their black identities, identities expressed in and through their music, itself a primary mechanism of Wilson's play. Sturdyvant, the white studio owner, views black musicians as exploitable commodities. The play's real subjects, Wilson writes, are "*these negroes*" that Sturdyvant and, by extension, the whites, exploit. The play provides a partial history of African Americans and, as Wilson describes it, "*Their values, their attitudes, and particularly their music*" (Klaus et al., *Stages of Drama*,158).

If music is central, so too is language, often comic, while the set itself has a metaphoric force. The action takes place in a run-down recording studio, and within this stage(d) world we see the white studio owner and white manager perched over the blacks in a "control room," Wilson's way of dramatizing white appropriation and control of black creativity. For all this the play is not primarily concerned with black–white tensions. At its center is the fragile community of black musicians who come together only in their music, a music, however, which is itself a contested arena as the black artists debate the extent to which they should accommodate the white world.

The action moves between the studio and the warm-up room. As the musicians joke and exchange tales, some harrowing, some comic, they record "Ma Rainey's Black Bottom" and other songs. The play's theatrical impact, however, comes much more from Wilson's staging of black on black tensions. The conflict surfaces in many forms, but is most acute between Ma Rainey and her trumpet player, Levee, a tempestuous figure. Ma Rainey represents an older generation. A singer of traditional blues, she has risen to fame and thus commands respect, at least in the confines of the music hall or the recording studio. Levee is the young impatient man intent on moving beyond the outworn jugband music; he wants to market the novel dance music favored by many northern urban blacks. He is eager to form his own band, to move musically and, hopefully, financially beyond his present circumstances. Impatient and increasingly violent, he emerges as a pivotal figure whose murderous impulses play counterpoint to the drama's celebrative dimensions.

Like Alice Walker's short story *Everyday Use* (1973), Wilson's *Ma Rainey's Black Bottom* contrasts the older generation and its values with the younger generation's. Whereas Walker's fiction ends with familial acceptance and love, Wilson's drama ends in death and feelings of incompletion. Ma Rainey, despite her exuberance, knows her own social limitations. She feels the limits of gender and race. She knows that the whites view her as a commodity whose usefulness will end when she fails to turn a profit for them. "They don't care nothing about me. All they want is my voice. . . . If you colored and can make them some money, then you all right with them. Otherwise you just a dog in the alley."

Levee is fully aware of this. Plagued by the memory of a gang of white men raping his mother years before, he has experienced the effects of capricious victimization. Nonetheless, in his naiveté and ambition, he believes that he can finesse a deal with the white record company. Such hopes prove false and once the company betrays him, he turns his rage on those nearest him: his fellow blacks. Wilson has said that, as a writer, he is attracted to the man who has "a warrior spirit," a strong, ambitious man who, frustrated with outer injustices, seeks to precipitate social change. Levee approximates this warrior image. He also embodies the limitations of one contesting the dominant culture. For Levee is a figure whose flaw lies in his inability to acknowledge reality, his failure to bring about constructive change. Like Walker Vessels in Baraka's *The Slave*, he seems fated to destroy. Frustrated by his inability to secure a recording deal from the record executives, haunted by generations of racial disenfranchisement, he lashes out at those spiritually, musically, and culturally closest to himself. When the play ends with Levee murdering Toledo, the intelligent piano player, it seems clear that Levee has murdered part of himself. Frustrated by the white's designs imposed on him, Levee becomes the architect of his own destruction.

Ma Rainey's Black Bottom is more than a play about black on black generational conflicts. Its logic requires that the characters question the nature of their racial identity. Toledo, in particular, is aware of this. He questions the way his fellow musicians dress and sing, insisting "That ain't African. That's the white man. We trying to be just like him. We done sold who we are in order to become someone else. We's imitation white men." Character analysis thus broadens to social critique. Ma Rainey may sing authentically and insist that singing is a way to understand life, but she allows herself to be assimilated by white culture. Her very celebrity hints at the nature of her compromise. And what is true of her seems true, too, of Levee, whose music is as inventive as it is genuine, but who wishes to see his name in lights. It is within this tension – between a desire for authenticity and a need to survive and prosper within an alien and even hostile culture – that they must live their lives.

Fences, for which he won a Pulitzer Prize, extends Wilson's exploration of the African American experience. Troy Maxon is a former professional baseball player, a talented athlete whose prowess on the field never received the attention or recognition it deserved because blacks were relegated to the Negro League. Now a fifty-three-year-old garbage collector, he has collected his share of dreams deferred and hopes deflected, a truth underscored by the fact that the play is set, in 1957, in the fenced-in yard of the home of Troy and

Rose Maxon, an "*ancient two-story brick house set back off a small alley in a big-city neighborhood.*" Their small yard lacks grass, and the porch "*lacks congruence.*" Troy's life also lacks congruence. The partially completed fence around the yard stands as the play's primary symbol, representing both the industriousness that has characterized Troy's life and the disappointments he has suffered. Like the fence, Troy's life is in a state of disrepair. It lacks completion.

Wilson prefaces the play with copious notes. These chronicle the successful immigration of Europeans whose "*capacity for hard work*" certified their financial and cultural security in the United States. By contrast, "*the descendants of African slaves were offered no such welcome or participation.*" Their lives were filled with "*quiet desperation and vengeful pride,*" a description that fits Troy's own life. Interestingly, Wilson ascribes to Troy many of the terms employed to characterize the Europeans, for he is a large man whose "*honesty, capacity for hard work, and . . . strength*" inspire his friends and family, define his dignity. He has challenged his employer and union about the unfair working conditions under which he and other blacks labor. A lifetime of missed opportunities has plagued him, and he demands a reckoning, insists on his civil rights, and this at a time when the Civil Rights Movement is gathering strength. Troy, a man who had successfully battled pneumonia, is presented as admired and loved by his wife, Rose, and his friend, Bono.

Yet he is at odds with himself and the world. He fences himself in. Like the father–son tension between Willy and Biff Loman, the father–son tension between Troy and Cory emphasizes the nature and extent of his entrapment. Cory yearns to play football; his father wants him to mend fences. Cory exudes youthful enthusiasm; Troy, seeing himself in his son, resents the boy's youth. Cory feels immune from racial injustice; Troy has suffered profoundly from a white world that has fenced him in every way. If Biff Loman saw his father as a fake, Cory sees Troy as a paternal oppressor. Fences do not make good neighbors in this play. They divide. Fences symbolize isolation, otherness, the inability to communicate.

Despite Troy's shortcomings – his strained relationship with his son, the fact that he has fathered an illegitimate child – Wilson mythicizes his protagonist, granting him a status that ultimately defines his dignity. His heroism emerges toward the end of the play when, after he and his son engage in a highly symbolic struggle over a baseball bat, Troy confronts his greatest fear, death, ultimately accepting his own frailties and coming to terms with his own emotional limits.

The final scene of the play, set on the morning of Troy's funeral, unites the family. Despite his physical presence, his vibrancy through the play, he makes that presence felt most acutely in his absence. For during the funeral scene when family members congregate, it becomes clear that the inability of father and son to communicate has yielded to a kind of reconciliation. Gabriel, Troy's brother, whose head injury from the war leaves him believing that he is God's angel, brings the play to a mystical close. Though the horn which he has carried for years emits no music, determined to open the gates of heaven for Troy he breaks into a ritualized dance, pointing toward the sky and singing, "That's the way to go!"

It is Troy's wife Rose, however, who occupies the central role in the action. It is she who sees through Troy's rationalizations and highlights the truth. Where Linda Loman, in *Death of a Salesman*, cannot tell the truth directly to her husband, Rose Maxon can. There is no evasion in her style or her language. When the truth of Troy's affair and illegitimate child becomes clear, she assumes a matriarchal control over her husband and extended family. It is, however, a feminine control borne out of acceptance, although she leaves little doubt about her feelings: "From right now . . . this child got a mother. But you a womanless man."

James Earl Jones and Mary Alice, who played Troy and Rose in the Yale production, recall the cathartic effect acting in *Fences* had on them. "The first time I watched the rehearsal of the last scene," Jones relates, "I was crying – not just for what I should have been crying about. I was crying all the times that I should have been watching it and hadn't. There are three moments that trigger the ending catharsis: the moment when Rose acknowledges Troy has died, Cory's tribute, and Gabe's blowing the trumpet." Mary Alice saw things slightly differently. "Unlike Jimmy, I think I *have* a catharsis. I have mine at the top of the second act. I don't feel it in the evening, but more when I wake up the next morning – then I feel drained." For Jones the emotional demands were as great as any required of him as an actor: "I think this play, this story, demands all of what this man is, and it asks its actors to make a commitment larger than you would make even in a Shakespeare play" (quoted in Henderson, "Building Fences," 70).

The cathartic and celebratory ending, however, is modified by the fact that the Maxons remain entrapped. Indeed, as Wilson explained to David Savran, each major character in *Fences* "is institutionalized. Rose is in a church. Lyons is in a penitentiary. Gabriel's in a mental hospital and Cory's in the Marines. The only free person is the girl, Troy's daughter, the hope for the future. That was conscious on my part because in '57 that's what I saw. Blacks have relied on institutions which are really foreign – except for the black church, which has been our saving grace." This idea, and the logic it provokes, which becomes thematically and racially central to *Fences*, would also prove vital to his next play, *Joe Turner's Come and Gone*. "I would like to see blacks develop their own institutions that respond to their needs" (Savran, "Interview," 1,579).

Joe Turner's Come and Gone is set in 1911, in a Pittsburgh boardinghouse managed by Seth and Bertha, married for a quarter of a century, who play host to a disparate group of characters in search of their individual selves. The off-spring of former slaves, who have drifted to the North in search of work, they appear in transition, forming a human bridge between the past and a brave new world, based on black heritage, rituals, music, and mysticism.

Joe Turner's Come and Gone uses history as its point of departure. Joe Turner, the infamous bounty hunter and brother of the governor of Tennessee, would hunt down and "enslave" blacks for seven years. Bynum, a "rootworker" or conjure man, sings about this travesty in song whose validity finds its source in Herald Loomis. Loomis appears as the mythical central character, who was enslaved by Joe Turner in 1901 and remains so traumatized that he has become a wanderer on the earth, a cosmic waif in his thirties, traveling with his daughter, in search of his wife, alienated from the free world that once so capriciously enslaved him. As he says, "I been wandering a long time in somebody else's world."

Indeed, all the characters have been wandering a long time. From Selig, the white man who searches for lost souls in an effort to reunite them, and Mattie, the young woman searching for her lost love, to Jeremy, the restless young man who searches for any woman, the play presents characters whose dances, songs, and folk tales give shape to their quests and their identities. When the play ends with Loomis reunited with his lost wife, Martha, the audience senses that he has regained part of his essential self. But it is a self defined neither by his wife's return nor by his religious experiences in the play. Rather, he grows into a self-made man, whose song of self-sufficiency maps out his redemption, based on a new identity borne out of African heritage. Separated, now, from the slave identification foisted upon him by Joe Turner, he finds sustenance in his Africanness. As Wilson has said, "Loomis learns that he is responsible for his own salvation and presence in the world" (quoted in DeVries, "The Drama of August Wilson," 54).

The Piano Lesson, the next play in Wilson's projected cycle and winner of the 1990 Pulitzer Prize, extends his exploration of a double world – one black, the other white – and of a double consciousness, in which his characters must make life-defining decisions. A work of competing voices, *The Piano Lesson* centers on the difficult choices African Americans face in terms of past heritage and present exigencies. The piano itself represents the past and the present, the past being a reminder of the white culture that built the piano, but also of Papa Boy Charles, the slave great-grandfather who carved African images onto it. The piano, in other words, bears their ancestral blood on its black and white keys, for the images carved onto it narrate the plight of Boy Willie and Berniece's slave ancestors, slaves who were sold into bondage in exchange for the piano. "On the legs of the piano, carved in the manner of African sculpture," writes Wilson, "are mask-like figures resembling totems."

18. Playwright August Wilson (standing) and director Lloyd Richards photographed on the set of *The Piano Lesson*, 1988. Photograph by Gerry Goodstein. Don B. Wilmeth Collection.

Wilson intensifies the conflict surrounding the instrument when we learn that it is now housed in the northern home of Berniece and her Uncle Doaker. Its presence results from the fact that Boy Willie and Berniece's father died "stealing" it back from white boss Sutter.

The piano becomes a source of contention between brother and sister – Boy Willie and Berniece. Berniece feels haunted by it. She associates it with her father's death, and her mother's subsequent suffering. She wishes to keep it as the symbol of a tragic past, but also as a necessary connection with familial heritage, a heritage that must be honored. With its historical link to slave ancestors, sacrifice, and beauty, the piano must be preserved, even though it is a constant reminder of loss. Fixed on the past, Berniece finds it difficult to conceptualize the future.

Her brother, however, looks to the future. He sees the piano in practical terms. Boy Willie, optimistic, humorous, recognizes the piano's everyday uses. He wishes to use the past family heritage – the piano – to purchase Sutter's land, for with land "you can stand right next to the white man and talk about the price of cotton . . . the weather, and anything else you want to talk about." Securing the land means securing freedom. For Boy Willie, securing the land will also be his way of reconnecting with his familial past: "That's all I'm trying to do with that piano. Trying to put my mark on the road. Like my daddy done. My heart say for me to see that piano and get me some land so I can make a life for myself to live in my own way." The brother–sister tensions over the uses of the piano inform the plot as they shape Wilson's theme.

Such tension manifests itself, too, in the invisible presence of Sutter's ghost. Clearly representative of the legacy of white control, it still haunts the family in 1937. If Berniece seems emotionally paralyzed by this haunting past and felt specter, Boy Willie simply ignores the ghost, thinking its presence is the product of his sister's imagination. Thus Wilson dodges what could be a sentimental or, worse, oversimplified ending by spotlighting the piano's lessons. For Wilson, however, neither sibling is completely wrong or completely right. Boy Willie comes to realize that Sutter's ghost cannot be ignored and that, by implication, the symbolic implications embodied in the piano cannot be glossed over for a quick sale. Indeed, at the end of the play he fights the ghost in "*a life-and-death struggle fraught with perils and faultless terror.*"

Berniece, too, learns an important lesson: she understands now the importance of honoring the past, but a past that is ultimately heroic and that minimizes bitterness and alienation. As her brother fights with the demonized Other, she plays the piano and sings; her music, Wilson writes, "*is intended as an exorcism and a dressing for battle.*" The brother–sister conflict is deliberately left unresolved, thus inviting the audience to participate in the larger moral dilemmas with which the characters themselves struggle.

Wilson's characters, despite themselves and their predicaments, appear determined, resilient, and affirmative. That resiliency is perhaps best seen in *Two Trains Running,* the fifth play in his projected cycle. Although set in 1969, the key date affecting the action is 1936. It was during the Depression that one of the play's main characters, Memphis, traveled north in his efforts to escape white hatred, a migration Memphis recounts at the start of Act Two. The play unwinds in his restaurant, and we learn that the title of the play is a reference to his own experience. He has long wanted to return to the South to reclaim his property. If he is to be successful, he needs to board one of two trains running south daily. In the course of the play he learns how vital this journey is, a journey on which he is to return to his past to reclaim his roots, his land.

The characters in *Two Trains Running* reflect their own form of resiliency and self-determination. Sterling, the other main character, exudes a similar kind of drive, for he seems fixed on finding a home for himself, one in which he hopes to live with Risa, whom he courts. Risa, however, appears as determined as Sterling is driven, cutting her beautiful legs with a razor so that she may appear less attractive to men. She wishes, Wilson suggests in his stage directions, to define herself in terms other than her sexual organs. The razor marks are her red badges of courage, her way of asserting female autonomy. She must not be reduced to a mere sexual object. Nonetheless she appears drawn to Sterling's affirmative stance toward life.

The others, too, radiate a gritty determination. Thus Hambone, driven mad when a butcher failed to reward him for his work with a promised ham, presents himself for payment every day for ten years, refusing to acknowledge defeat. When he dies, Sterling steals a ham and insists that it be buried along with the man whose heroic, if insane, persistence has made him a symbol of resilience.

The ending of *Two Trains Running* is ambiguous. What is not is the spirit of resistance, the determination of character. The question of audience, one black, the other white, that confronted James Weldon Johnson earlier in the twentieth century apparently no longer seems as relevant to Wilson. As he has explained, "I write for an audience of one. For myself. I think I have to satisfy myself as an artist before I write for any particular other audience . . . I don't write for Black people or White people; I write about the Black experience in America. And contained within that experience, because it is a human experience, are all the universalities. I am surprised when people come up to me and say, well, *Fences* is universal. Of course it is! They say that as though the universals existed outside of Black life" ("August Wilson Interview," 9). It is a statement that explains the success of Wilson's work, which regularly finds its way to Broadway, via regional theatre, and which to date has won him two Pulitzer Prizes.

Charles Fuller

Like August Wilson, Charles Fuller is an African American who uses history as the backdrop to his theatre. His best plays reconstruct factual moments from black history and invite the audience to reconsider the relation between fact and imagination. Located against the contours of American history, his plays seek to challenge racial stereotypes while exploring the relationship between personal values and the historical forces, community mores, and familial decisions which have shaped them.

Fuller confirms the point in *We*, an uncompleted play that is part of a projected historical cycle of at least five plays; Fuller plans to follow many of the same group of characters as they progress in time and history from the Civil War to 1900. The history Fuller confronts in *Sally* (1988) is that of the immediate postbellum period. Prince, a former runaway slave, has joined the Union's first black regiment and returns to the South to assist in the freeing of his people. Inspired by his newly celebrated freedom, he discovers that he remains enslaved, at least at a socioeconomic level: the white soldiers in his regiment are paid three dollars more per month than the blacks. Fuller bases part of the play on the actual strike these black soldiers conducted in their protest over the government's policy on black pay. Fuller has explained the imperative behind his historical concerns: "I deal with history because you can't get *here* without going through *there*. You can't change today's myths unless you go all the way and attack them at the point of origin" (quoted in Hulbert, "Black History," 1). In *Sally*, Fuller brings together Prince and a newly liberated black southern woman, the Sally of the title. They meet at the now defunct plantation where she had been held, discovering meaning in and through themselves as well as in the double act of rebellion against the forces of the South and North alike.

Prince (1988), the second of the cycle, traces "the great odyssey of Sally and Prince and other characters as they emerge from slavery into a strange new world. A world that in some ways wasn't much better," Fuller explains (quoted in Hulbert, "Black History," 1, 4). For Fuller, history hurts. But through a theatricalized confrontation with the historical past, he reconstitutes that tragic past while situating contemporary black experience in an historicized present.

Such commitment to revisioning African American history is observable in all Fuller's work. His earliest plays, *Sun Flowers*, *The Rise*, *The Village: A Party* (all 1968), reveal a playwright imbued with the force of history, powerfully influenced by the Civil Rights Movement and an evolving black aesthetic. He was surely also influenced by an unfolding black drama which had seen a number of significant works from Louis Peterson's *Take A Giant Step* (1954), Lorraine Hansberry's *A Raisin in the Sun* and Ossie Davis's *Purlie Victorious* (1961) to Lonne Elder III's *Ceremonies in Dark Old Men* (1965), Charles Gordone's *No Place to Be Somebody* (1969), and the work of Baraka and Ed Bullins. His early work reflects something of the apocalyptical mood of Baraka and, indeed, James Baldwin in *Blues for Mr. Charlie* (1964).

Fuller's continuing engagement with black history and black identity took a further step in 1976 with *The Brownsville Raid*. Again he uses actual historical occurrences to capture the invisibility of the black experience in the dominant discourses of American military and legal culture. The play is an account of a company of black soldiers who were set up, accused, and found guilty of precipitating a riot in Brownsville, Texas, in 1906. Juxtaposing competing voices – the colonialist language ratified by none other than President Theodore Roosevelt against that of the unjustly accused black soldiers – Fuller effectively asks his audience to become a jury. Those black soldiers were dishonorably discharged for a crime they had not committed. Sixty years later, they were vindicated when the courts reinstated the truth. That truth and justice are only honored six decades after the incident only adds to the pathos of *The Brownsville Raid.*

With his long affiliation with the accomplished Negro Ensemble Company and its founding director, Douglas Turner Ward, and with the artistic mentorship provided by his friend, Larry Neal, Fuller effectively came of age with *The Brownsville Raid*. The maturation process continued with *Zooman and the*

Sign (1980), a play about a seventies news account of a black young man slain in his own neighborhood by another black. In Fuller's play, a twelve-year-old girl is accidently killed when caught in a street gang fight. It centers on her devastated parents' effort to bring her killer to justice. The father, frustrated by his neighbors, who fear that coming forward means that they will have to deal with another institutionalized enemy, the police, hangs a sign outside his home proclaiming that, because of neighborhood apathy, his daughter's killers still roam the streets unpunished. Ironically, the neighbors are enraged not by the girl's death but by a sign implicating them in a crime they did not commit. Rage and anger implode as Fuller exposes a form of black on black racism. Zooman, the murderer, rationalizes his actions by arguing that if a black kills a black and is not brought to justice right away, the police drift into apathy, which is not unlike that revealed in this black community. The play ends when the slain girl's uncle accidently shoots and kills Zooman, not real-izing that he is the culprit. The final sense of waste seems confirmed, too, when the girl's parents gaze at the face of the deceased perpetrator only to find that he is not much older than their daughter and that, like their daugh-ter, he is merely another nearly anonymous victim of a capriciously determin-istic, and racist, world.

The critical response to Fuller's other works has been mixed. *In My Many Names and Days* (1972), *Candidate* (1974), *In the Deepest Part of Sleep* (1974), *Sparrow in Flight* (1978), and *Burner's Frolic* (1990) reveal a playwright who has not always successfully balanced cultural and theatrical concerns. He has also been criticized by some fellow blacks for supposedly pandering to a white theatre establishment. Of the dissenting voices who felt Fuller was com-promising his art, Amiri Baraka's stands out. He directed his attack at Fuller's best work, *A Soldier's Play*, which won the Pulitzer Prize in 1982. Baraka feels that Fuller's close association with the Negro Ensemble Company betrayed the black cause: "The Negro Ensemble has been, in the main, a skin theatre, offering only colored complexion but not sustained thrust in concert with the whole of the BLM [Black Liberation Movement] to liberate ourselves. It has been fundamentally a house slave's theatre, eschewing struggle for the same reason that the house niggers did – because they didn't have it so bad" (Baraka, "Descent," 53). Baraka's is a curious attack, for his argument would seem to promote rather than ameliorate racial division. Fuller's *A Soldier's Play*, Baraka's comments notwithstanding, stands as a major contribution to the communal debate regarding black experience in the United States.

A Soldier's Play is in part about a murder. It begins when Sgt. Waters, the leader of a black platoon, cries out, "They still hate you!" to an unseen man who blasts him with a .45 caliber pistol, killing him instantly. Suddenly the stage transforms into a barracks, and the murder mystery unfolds. As the play begins, Cobb, a soldier Waters demoted for insubordination, insists to Taylor, the white colonel, that "nobody colored killed the man!" Henson, a private, agrees: "You know the Klan did it, sir . . . They lynched Jefferson the week I got here, sir!" Taylor's response is to insist that the men must keep their opinions to themselves. He is less concerned with identifying the murderer than with preventing black soldiers seeking revenge in the nearby white town.

A Soldier's Play, set in Fort Neal, Louisiana, in 1944, depicts a segregated society in microcosm, the black regiment serving as an ironic reminder that while these men are preparing to fight Hitler in the name of freedom, they themselves remain entrapped in their own country. No wonder Fuller describes the set, and those who perform in it, as being in a state of *"limbo."* These are men conscious of living in a white world, with its network of values, while simultaneously living in a black one, with all its traditions, customs, foods, and music. For Fuller, such divisions lead to a profound moral choice. As soldiers, they must obey orders and serve their country. As black men, they must serve their larger African American community. Himself a former Army lab technician who served during the fifties in Korea and Japan, Fuller sees in the military an ideal model for exploring racism and the kinds of dilemmas faced by black Americans in the trenches of Europe as in the streets of America. Black life in the military, Fuller has said, "crystallizes, in a powerful dramatic way, the dilemma so many blacks face. Are you loyal to your country, or your people?" (quoted in Hulbert, *Black History,* 4).

Sgt. Waters seems right to insist that soldiers remain loyal and obedient. His murder is doubly senseless because, in addition to being a good family man, he genuinely wants his fellow blacks to succeed. Such ambiguities abound. When Davenport, the black lawyer, is sent from Washington to investigate the murder, we are led to believe, with Cobb, Henson, and the others, that the Klan murdered Waters. As the play proceeds, however, such assumptions prove unreliable. The more we learn about Waters the less honorable he appears. By degrees it becomes apparent that he appropriates the law rather than obeys it. He is contemptuous of those blacks who, like C. J. Memphis, act in ways that he believes disgrace the black race. Indeed, he emerges as a neo-Nazi. He even orchestrates his own form of racial genocide. He terrorizes the country bumpkin C. J., imprisoning him and provoking his suicide, insisting that "Them Nazis ain't all crazy – a whole lot of people just can't fit into where things seem to be goin' – like you, C. J. The black race can't afford you no more . . . The day of the geechy is gone, boy. . ." Peterson, outraged by Waters's complicity in C. J.'s death, reverts to frontier justice and, we learn at the play's end, is Waters's murderer. There is a sense of poetic justice to the murder but it seems clear that Peterson falls prey to the same myopic strategies that prefigure Waters's doom. Like Waters, he becomes a victim of his own rage. Both Waters and Peterson, indeed, are victims of their own victimization. The final irony lies in the fact that the entire outfit is later killed in the European war.

Whatever insight they might have gained is rendered meaningless. *A Soldier's Play*, which premiered at New York's Theatre Four on 10 November 1981, won the Pulitzer Prize for Drama in 1982.

Arthur Kopit, Lanford Wilson, David Rabe

In an essay, "The Vital Matter of Environment" (1961), Arthur Kopit suggested that American dramatists, lacking a rich theatrical tradition, were by necessity drawn to European dramatic styles. Indeed, from *The Questioning of Nick* (1957) through *Discovery in America* (1992), his own plays reflect the force of European experimentation, even though his plays are located in unmistakable American social and historical contexts. It would be misleading to align Kopit too directly with the Theatre of the Absurd, but, technically, his work does bear traces of the great European writers – Jean Giraudoux, Jean Anouilh, and Eugène Ionesco – who held court over the theatrical avant-garde in Europe in the late fifties. Kopit, like Albee, not only absorbed the works of his contemporaries but also looked back to the great Modernists in Italy and Germany. As a result, Pirandellian maneuverers and Brechtian social textures animate his plays.

Beginning with *The Questioning of Nick* and *Gemini* (both 1957) and, among other early plays, *Sing to Me Through Open Windows* (1959), Kopit borrowed from his European forebears in ways that reached an apex on 26 February 1962. On this date the funny and disturbing *Oh Dad, Poor Dad, Mamma's Hung You in the Closet and I'm Feelin' So Sad* had its premiere at the Phoenix Theatre in New York City. The play, subtitled *A Pseudoclassical Tragifarce in a Bastard French Tradition*, ran for 454 performances and brought Jo Van Fleet (as Madame Rosepettle) and Barbara Harris (as Rosalie) Obie Awards for their performances.

His most significant play, however, opened in 1968. *Indians* is concerned with war between differing peoples, cultures, and values. Beyond its ostensible subject it engages with a principal issue of the day – Vietnam. Kopit transposed the exact words of General William Westmoreland, the Commander-in-Chief of the American military in Southeast Asia, to Colonel Forsyth, a character in his play, who, surveying the scene of a massacre of Indians, says: "Of course innocent people have been killed. In war they always are. And of course our hearts go out to the innocent victims of this." By juxtaposing the war in Vietnam with the butchering of Native American Indians, Kopit offers an interpretation of American values. The gulf in understanding between an Indian Chief – Chief Joseph – and Buffalo Bill stands for a fundamental breach in communication with political and ontological implications. For Buffalo Bill the government displays a "benevolent attitude toward these savages." For Chief Joseph – militarily but not spiritually defeated – it displays a brutal disregard for those whose values and lives remain a mystery. It is a lesson whose contemporary no less than historical significance seemed evident in the most significant of years.

In *Wings* (1977), for which Kopit earned a Pulitzer Prize, communication was again a central concern. Focusing on the plight of Emily Stilson, the play revolves around what happens to someone who suffers a debilitating brain stroke, as Kopit's own father did in 1976. What happens, Kopit's play asks, when language disappears? Kopit breaks the play into four parts: Prelude, Catastrophe, Awakening, and Explorations. In each part Emily slowly reconstructs her shattered identity, in doing so gaining a renewed appreciation and understanding of both self and reality. Kopit's reputation was further enhanced by the black humor play, *End of the World* (1984), about the threat of nuclear Armageddon.

While Kopit continued to write engaging plays, Lanford Wilson had also staged compelling works since the sixties, though as a clear inhabitant of the Off- Off Broadway movement. In such early plays as *Home Free!* (1964), which traces the incestuous relationship between brother and sister, Lawrence and Joanna, and *The Madness of Lady Bright* (1964), which revolves around a homosexual "preening queen" who worries openly about his age and fading sexual prowess, Wilson's characters seem philosophically related to Stephen Crane's Maggie or O'Neill's Yank. That is, they are societal misfits and victims of a naturalistic universe in which, as Joe discovers in *Balm in Gilead* (1965) (see Schlueter's section), betrayal and death make for deadly bedfellows. Pessimistic and pathetic characters energize *The Rimers of Eldritch* (1966), *The Gingham Dog* (1968), and the autobiographical *Lemon Sky* (1970). The typical Wilson protagonist is one whose hopes for fulfillment, social purpose, or simple human acceptance occupy that ambiguous space between dreams and desires. His characters often yearn for an idealized past because their present seems minimal, unfulfilling, and baffling. As Carl, in *Serenading Louie* (1970), says before killing his wife and himself, "We're all telling each other every minute how important all the things we believe in are, how the world would collapse if we let up for a minute believing all the things we believe and doing all the things we do and, hell, nobody believes it." Many of his characters seem incapable of believing in a future that has been tainted by depressing present circumstances. This, in turn, threatens the primal family unit in Wilson's theatre as it does, by extension, the very essence of the social musculature of the country. In Wilson's plays characters have difficulty harmonizing private passions with public convictions, as April Green remarks to Jamie in *The Hot l Baltimore* (1973). Thus, at least in the plays preceding this warmly comedic play, Wilson, as a naturalistic writer, presents tragic legacies of an indifferent world in which the prostitutes, pimps, addicts, crooks, and destitute hold court in shabby rooms. Like Dreiser's Carrie, they dream of happiness that they will probably never know.

Some critics feel that the playwright vitiates his effectiveness with a sentimentality that betrays the plays' gritty bleakness. While charges of sentimentality ring true, his plays have evolved from the early defeatist plays to a decidedly more accepting and optimistic kind of theatre, one based on true comedy. Since the tragic and the comic share the same psychological border, Wilson seems at his best in his effort to limn the disenfranchised with a sense of compassionate humor, as he did in *The Hot l Baltimore*. Wilson's best-known work, the play ran for 1,166 performances and inspired a popular television series of the same title.

If, as William Dean Howells once said, Americans want tragedies with happy endings, *The Hot l Baltimore* may approximate that paradoxical mixture of tragedy and comedy. When theatregoers watched the first performance on 4 February 1973 at the Circle Theatre Company (later Circle Rep) in New York, they were taken by Wilson's realistic set and the way in which the front desk of the Hotel Baltimore, and the fifteen characters congregating around it, complemented the subsequent action. The hotel, Wilson writes, was constructed toward the end of the nineteenth century, a time during which railroads and gracious hotels flourished. A once grand structure, the Hotel Baltimore, like its current residents, has seen better days: "*Its history has mirrored the rails' decline.*" Wilson also writes about the "*impermanence of our architecture*," a reference that finds its human corollaries in the prostitutes, retired waitresses, and hotel clerks who fill the stage.

Yet Wilson balances the impermanence of Jackie, Jamie, Mr. Moore, Millie, and the others with resiliency that is hard-earned. On the one hand, these characters look backward to a past that once made Baltimore and the railroads, like the hotel, models of civic eloquence and vibrancy. On the other hand, Wilson calls attention to a decline, a slippage: "Every city in America used to be one of the most beautiful cities in America," April says. By glancing backward at history and in surveying their present circumstances, the group of misfits in *Hot l Baltimore* learn, and celebrate, their own sense of community. Although April correctly identifies her fellow hooker Suzy as "a professional trampoline," Suzy also accurately locates the importance of human relationship – "I need love!", not derision, she says. These characters know that the demolition ball will destroy their home, but, Wilson implies, they are survivors whose sense of charity will ensure their sanity and, perhaps, their happiness. Their spiritual balm comes from their ability to laugh.

Like Christopher Durang, Wilson in his later plays uses a guarded comedy as a way to come to terms with the schisms within the family and the United States. For example, in the Pulitzer Prize-winning *Talley's Folly* (1979), Sally and Matt forge a love relationship despite ostracism, racism, and small town bigotry. The humor becomes more rarified in *5th of July* (1978). This play concerns a reunion of old friends who forged their social values during the free-speech days in Berkeley and the Vietnam War. Together on the Talley farm near Lebanon, Missouri, during the summer of 1977, the characters exchange stories about their deferred and deflected dreams, about their sixties idealism that clashed with the Vietnam débâcle, and about how they might now be able to push beyond a war that left Kenneth Talley, Jr. wounded, both legs amputated. *Angels Fall* (1982) again calls attention to the primacy of community and a sense of purpose. As Niles Harris says, "We'll look at the map and see if we can find some semblance of a decent highway." All the highways, however, have been closed in this desolate part of New Mexico because of a nuclear accident. Father Doherty and a young Indian, Don Tabaha, become models of decency, revealing both their humanity and warmth while acknowledging that, as Doherty says, "The only good thing that can come from these silly emergencies, these rehearsals for the end of the world is that it makes us get our act together." He flatly states that "This is the end of the world" but also talks with the others about "a remarkable sense of self-preservation." This point is precisely the one Pale and Anna discover in *Burn This* (1987). Their sense of self-preservation gives them an opportunity to forge a new relationship, based on love, that just may endure.

American dramatists, to borrow Julia Kristeva's words, interweave history and geography, but the *mise-en-scène* of such an interweaving process varies considerably. Whether in Albee's suburban living room of a white upper class, or in Bullins's black urban ghetto, or among Fornés's troubled protagonists, America's dramatists record how that outer history and geography impinge on the individual. This interweaving may manifest itself in terms of the Civil Rights Movement or the American feminist movement, or in one of the most divisive wars in United States history: the Vietnam War. This last issue, touched on by Lanford Wilson, lies at the heart of the work of David Rabe.

Near the end of Act One of Rabe's *Streamers* (1976), two soldiers in their army barracks sing a song about "streamers," the term used to refer to a parachute that never deploys properly. The central image of the lyrics – a paratrooper hurtling toward the earth, parachute unopened, shouting to God for a salvation that will not come during the last thirteen seconds of his life – functions not merely as an arresting title but as an image that informs all of Rabe's plays. For Rabe fills the stage with characters who seem helplessly and hopelessly out of control. Like the doomed paratrooper, they can neither alter the trajectory nor rapidity of their fall. They know that their lives, like the fated paratrooper's, will end in a bone-crushing impact whose inevitability is the only sure thing in their lives. The characters, raised in a Rabean America dominated by racism, sexism, and ignorance, are whipped into a personal dementia. Death by suicide or a fellow soldier's knife is, for most of these characters, both a predictable end and a welcome relief from a hurlyburly world.

Cokes's and Rooney's song about streamers, sung to the music of Stephen Foster's "Beautiful Dreamer," defines Rabe's theatrical vision. Denied either individual choice or self-knowledge, his figures try to survive a Vietnam skyline filled with streamers. If they succeed, however, they still face death in non-combat by "some mean motherfucker, you don't even see, [who will] blow you away" – the fate of Pavlo in *The Basic Training of Pavlo Hummel* (1971). Or they might survive the Vietnam War, only to return home – blinded, like David in *Sticks and Bones* (1972) – to a family that encourages and participates in his suicide. Yet it is not enough, it seems, for Rabe to consign his heroes to death; many of his protagonists die without coming to terms with their misspent or shattered lives. David dies, his ignoble end sparking little self-knowledge on the part of either himself or his family.

In *The Orphan* (1973), Rabe saturates the stage with murderous rampages from the past – Aeschylus' *Oresteia* providing one pole, the My Lai massacre and the Charles Manson murders the other. Indeed, all of Rabe's characters find themselves orphaned. Theirs is a life of misery. Bereft, their desultory lives are often the end-products of war. For Arthur Miller, whom Rabe claims deeply influenced his own moral vision, charity remains a central part of the social contract. Love, Miller insists, must find its expression, must define its presence daily. But for Rabe, charity and love remain distant forces.

In *Sticks and Bones*, for example, David loves Zung, his Vietnamese girl-friend, but deserts her. When she appears as a spectral presence, Harriet berates Zung and Ozzie strangles her. In *Streamers*, Carlyle and Richie establish a sexual relationship, which outrages Billy, who can neither understand nor tolerate homosexuality in the military. Carlyle responds by stabbing Billy to death. Rabe even reduces language, like the human relationships he depicts, to its barest forms. Hence Carlyle's all but inarticulate response to killing Billy: "FUCK IT, FUCK IT, I STUCK HIM. I TURNED IT." Some of Rabe's characters struggle desperately to latch onto the force of charity or love, but brutalizing characters, like Al in *In the Boom Boom Room* (1974), subvert such a gesture. Pavlo's life, in *The Basic Training of Pavlo Hummel,* is inglorious. He is wounded when someone tosses a hand grenade into a Saigon whorehouse, blowing out his entrails. "It hit you in the stomach, man, like a ten-ton truck and it hit you in the balls, blew 'em away," Ardell says. A well-meaning but ignorant ne'er-do-well, Pavlo, like the psychologist's "Pavlov's dog," merely reacts to external stimuli. External experience, not internal choice, commands Rabe's Pavlo. Only after experiencing combat first-hand, surviving his third serious wound, and realizing that he desperately wants to return home, does Pavlo understand the reality of an infantry soldier's life in the trenches. Armed with such insight, he travels with Yen, not to his home but to the whorehouse, where a hand grenade explosion ends his life.

Yet for all his fascination with the Vietnam War, Rabe is more than the pre-eminent chronicler of the war in Southeast Asia. He is, to be sure, a Vietnam veteran himself (he did not see actual combat), and he knows about the post-traumatic stress syndrome that Emily Mann dramatizes in *Still Life* (1979), a subject that also occupies a central place in Steve Metcalfe's *Strange Snow* (1983). He also shares that distrust of abstractions that informs Tom Cole's *Medal of Honor Rag* (1977), and, like Amlin Gray, in *How I Got That Story* (1979), and Terrence McNally, in *Botticelli* (1968), Rabe repeatedly addresses the absurdity of that war. But he declines to be seen as merely an anti-war play-wright, and indeed here and in his later work his critique of American values goes beyond a concern with the events in Southeast Asia.

The themes of his war plays – lack of communication, sexism, racism, ignor-ance, and brutality – manifest themselves equally in his other work. Nor does Rabe merely shift the geography from the army barracks in Virginia or the whorehouse in Saigon to an American city. *In the Boom Boom Room*, which Rabe situates in a rough, decadent section of Philadelphia in the 1960s, becomes, like the Vietnam plays, a deeper emblem for a wayward America. In the play, featuring Rabe's only female protagonist, Chrissy longs to become a successful go-go dancer in New York City. But she finds herself, like her Vietnam counterparts, ambushed. Her own family, boyfriends, neighbors, and supervisors exploit her, mainly for sex. By the play's end, Al, her latest lover, reduces her to a husk. At the final curtain, she has finally made it to New York but as a masked topless dancer, drained of all individuality, a sexual object completely alienated from the self and the other.

In Rabe's *Goose and Tomtom* (1982) Tomtom keeps his girl, Lulu, in a closet, where she hangs, blindfolded, gagged, and bound. Whenever he feels like it, Tomtom takes her out to "pump her and put her back." As he tells the audi-ence, "There's somethin' very unfuckin' natural about broads . . . I love to bang 'em, man." *Hurlyburly* (1984) takes place in Hollywood. Eddie and Mickey, two directors, live in a drug-filled world in which men compete with men and hate women. A play concerned with fear, alienation, and violence, *Hurlyburly* extends Rabe's singular vision of male–female relationships. One woman, Bonnie, limps across the stage in torn clothes after being thrown from a speeding car. Another, a fifteen-year-old girl, is offered to them for sex. A third offers herself. In *Those the River Keeps* (1991), the invitations and seductions of past crimes haunt Phil, the ex-convict protagonist (who also was seen in the earlier *Hurlyburly*). All of Rabe's figures are, in effect, *Casualties of War*, the title of his 1989 screen play, whether they struggle in the jungles of Vietnam or in the urban warfare in American cities. The geographical location of Rabe's plays may change, but he circles around the same motifs of betrayal, exploitation, and ignorance.

Neil Simon and Tony Kushner

While such dramatists as Kopit, Lanford Wilson, and Rabe stage harrowing plays filled with disturbing moments, Neil Simon has for a half a century, as noted in the first section of this chapter, leavened the Broadway stage with comedies appealing, it seems, to vacationers traveling to the Big Apple who need to see such musicals as *Cats* or *Rent* – and, pocket books permitting, perhaps a Broadway play. While most serious scholars of American drama ignore Simon, the fact is he has been one of the most prolific and popular "mainstream" playwrights. If we remember that American theatre has its roots as a popular rather than elitist art form, that its origins and evolvement prior to the twentieth century were largely entertainment-based, then it is hardly surprising that Simon has reached a wide audience through his numerous domestic comedies, musicals, and screenplays.

After serving in the Second World War, Simon, with his brother, Danny, supplied comedic scripts for Tallulah Bankhead, Jackie Gleason, Carl Reiner, and Red Skelton, then enormously popular television comedians in the fifties, and honed his skills as comedian when he wrote lines for Phil Silvers's *Sergeant Bilko* and Sid Caesar's *Your Show of Shows*. By the early sixties, however, he set his sights on Broadway, where he quickly established his reputation for writing funny plays that celebrate family and marriage; his plays typically address issues concerning divorce, sibling rivalry, sexual awakening, and adultery. *Come Blow Your Horn* (1960), *Barefoot in the Park* (1963), *The Odd Couple* (1965), *Last of the Red Hot Lovers* (1969), *The Gingerbread Lady* (1970), *The Sunshine Boys* (1972), *California Suite* (1976), *I Ought to Be in Pictures* (1980), *Brighton Beach Memoirs* (1982), *Biloxi Blues* (1984), *Broadway Bound* (1986), and his Pulitzer Prize-winning *Lost in Yonkers* (1991) have become household titles for most Americans. Despite an over-reliance on gag one-liners and problems with plot structure, his work is popular with audiences whose idea of theatre may be better reflected in his *The Star-Spangled Girl* (1966) than in John Guare's *House of Blue Leaves* (1971), Maria Irene Fornés's *Fefu and Her Friends* (1977), or Terrence McNally's *Lips Together, Teeth Apart* (1991).

While Neil Simon, veteran of the American stage and screen, entertained playgoers with well-crafted comedies, a newcomer has captured the imagination of the country with dramas of a most serious kind. Tony Kushner, for many, has emerged as one of the most refreshing dramatists in the nineties.

19. Trinity Repertory Company's (Providence, R.I.) climax moment from *Angels in America, Part I: Millenium Approaches* (Jennifer Madge Tucker as the Angel and Brian McEleney as Prior Walter). Photograph by T. Charles Erickson.

While his children's play *Yes, Yes, No, No* (1985) remains largely unknown, and *A Bright Room Called Day* (1987), a politicized drama concerning Nazi Germany, drew mainly poor reviews, his *Angels in America: A Gay Fantasia on National Themes* became a Broadway hit and won the Pulitzer Prize in 1993. *Angels in America*, its two parts *Millennium Approaches* (1991) and *Perestroika* (1992) totaling some seven hours to perform, has played to appreciative audiences throughout the country and in London. Appealing to a wide cross-section of theatregoers – gay, lesbian, straight, black, WASP, and so on – both parts of *Angels in America* are epic in scope, cosmic in spirit, and grounded in both the fantastic and the real. The play's broad-based appeal "is even more remarkable when one considers the fact that all five of its leading actors are gay" (Savran, "Tony Kushner," 291). Clearly the play locates itself in a world of gay anxiety and celebration, the reality of AIDS informing its theatrical text and cultural context. Yet *Angels in America* is much more than "an AIDS play," for AIDS becomes, for Kushner, a larger metaphor for an undeniable sense of vulnerability and collapse; as one character in Part One laments, "everywhere, things are collapsing, lies surfacing, systems of defense giving way." The play captures the anxieties of a nation in a sweeping way that speaks to individuals of varying ages, ideologies, and life styles. From the perspective of a narrative history of American theatre, Kushner's work is noteworthy in that its homosexual concerns are no longer closeted subjects that can only be staged in Off-Off Broadway venues but are part of a national dialogue, a dialogue staged in the major "Broadway" theatres in most major cities in the United States. American plays, and the ways in which the public receives them, have changed noticeably since Mart Crowley's *The Boys in the Band* (1968), generally considered the first gay play staged on Broadway.

Millennium Approaches, whose Broadway productions were directed by George C. Wolfe, takes place in 1985, when Ronald Reagan was President, and when the general public was only beginning to become aware of AIDS. It involves a host of characters from various walks of life. The action and multilayered plots take place in Washington, New York City, Salt Lake City, and Antarctica. In the play Roy Cohn, modeled on the gay-bashing attorney of the same name who succumbed to AIDS in 1986, tries to conceal his own homosexuality and disease. As the play develops, he offers to help Joe Pitt, a Mormon from Utah, find a position with the Justice Department. Cohn, it turns out, wants Pitt to eavesdrop on the disbarment deliberations underway against him. The idealistic Pitt and the racist Cohn, however, despite coming from such differing backgrounds, have the same secret: they are both gay. Kushner works carefully in establishing a commonality within characters who share little in common. Prior Walter, the sensitive man who carries utopian hopes as well as the despairing knowledge that humankind will never be able to reconcile the gaps between the ideal and the real, is also as different from Cohn as one might imagine, but they, too, share something in common: the same disease, AIDS. Pitt's conservative and agoraphobic wife, Harper, plays counterpoint to the liberal Prior Walter, but they share the same emotional pain of loss: both have been abandoned by their lovers, the right-wing Joe Pitt and liberal Louis Ironson. When Joe and Louis, political opposites, fall in love, however, they learn the beauties and truths about their differing values and beliefs. Kushner's theatrics, the blending and sharing of opposing value systems as reflected through these various relationships, gives *Millennium Approaches* its larger-than-life quality, a quality felt more acutely by audiences when they see the play's historical figures, ghosts, and, finally, the stunning appearance of The Angel at the end.

The characters' intersecting lives and Kushner's resolutions to their plights are played out on a cosmic scale in *Perestroika*, whose Hannah Pitt, Joe's mother from Salt Lake City, talks about the strange, sprawling "interconnectedness" of life. As The Angel closes Part One with the admonishment to Prior, "Greetings, Prophet; The Great Work Begins: The Messenger has arrived," so Prior ends Part Two with a kind of valediction:

> I'm almost done . . .This disease will be the end of many of us, but not nearly all, and the dead will be commemorated and will struggle on with the living, and we are not going away. We won't die secret deaths anymore. The world only spins forward. We will be citizens. The time has come. Bye now. You are fabulous creatures, each and every one. And I bless you: *More Life.* The Great Work Begins.

Angels in America, Part One and Part Two, then, joins European Americans, African Americans, Jews, Mormons, reactionaries and leftists, straights and gays in a celebration of and lament for American citizens and their history. This deeply political play descends into Hell, reaches into Heaven, and, above all, invites audiences to rethink what precisely constitutes reality in a play that Kushner calls a contribution to the "Theatre of the Fabulous." As one critic has suggested, "Spanning the earth and reaching into the heavens, interviewing multiple plots, mixing metaphysics and drag, the sacred and the profane, vengeful ghosts and Reagan's vicious henchmen, *Angels* demonstrates conclusively that what passes for reality is in fact deeply inflected by fantasy and dreams" (Savran, "Tony Kushner," 292). A play mixing myth, history, sexual identity, and the queering of America, *Angels in America* undermines traditional binaries, blurring the differences, and the distances, between sexual identities and cultural politics, and how they affect the definition of "America" and "Americans." Kushner implies that there are angels in the country, but as the images remind us in a painting that inspired Walter Benjamin and Kushner himself – Paul Klee's painting *Angelus Novus* – there are also monsters lurking. As Jonathan Freedman concludes, "The beauty and brilliance of *Angels* is that the play points beyond itself – and so imposes hard questions about the nature of identities, Jewish and queer alike, that a less insistent, more troubled vision of utopia would leave in its wake" ("Angels, Monsters, and Jews," 101). The play may announce the Queer Nation chant, "We're here. We're queer. We're fabulous. Get used to it," but, to its credit, it also announces much more to all people, regardless of racial, sexual, religious, or political preferences and affiliations. *Angels in America* is ultimately sad yet uplifting, compassionate and humorous, a play that delights and instructs theatregoers as we approach the next millennium.

Coda: Arthur Miller

It seems fitting to end this selected survey of recent American playwrights with a consideration of one born on the eve of World War I, who came of age during the Great Depression, was a major voice in postwar theatre, and remains a significant force as we near the twenty-first century. Now the elder statesman of the American stage, Arthur Miller may rightfully be regarded as one of America's most inventive and exemplary playwrights. The vitality of Miller's theatre is particularly evident in his plays of the nineties.

In the opening moments of *The Last Yankee* (1993), the audience listens to a seemingly realistic exchange between John Frick and Leroy Hamilton, strangers who come together when visiting their wives at a state psychiatric hospital. The dialogue sounds and, on one important level, is, exceedingly realistic. Yet the nervous friction of the ensuing exchange, a mix of comedy and anxiety, betrays the bland surface realism of *The Last Yankee*. Indeed, in a theatre essay, "About Theatre Language" (1994), Miller alludes to both realistic and non-realistic qualities in the characters' dialogue, what the playwright calls "a conversation bordering on the absurd. I would call this realism," he writes, "but it is far from the tape-recorded kind." He cites Frick's and Leroy's lines, arguing that:

> the play is made of such direct blows aimed at the thematic center; there is a vast parking space because crowds of stricken citizens converge on this place to visit mothers, fathers, brothers, and sisters. So that the two patients we may be about to meet are not at all unique. This is in accord with the vision of the play, which is intended to be both close up and wide, psychological and social, subjective and objective, and manifestly so. To be sure, there is a realistic tone to this exchange – people do indeed talk this way – but an inch below is the thematic selectivity which drives the whole tale. Perhaps it needs to be said that this split vision has informed all the plays I have written. ("Theatre Language," 94)

This methodology provides a key to understanding every Miller play. From *The Golden Years* (1939–40) through *Broken Glass* (1994), Miller creates a duality that defines the private condition of the individual and outlines the collective anxieties of a nation. The private and the public, combined, lend clarity to Miller's split vision. This fact remains as true for Leroy and Patricia Hamilton in *The Last Yankee* and Phillip and Sylvia Gellburg in *Broken Glass* as it does for Joe and Kate Keller in *All My Sons* (1947), Willy and Linda Loman in *Death of a Salesman* (1949), John and Elizabeth Proctor in *The Crucible* (1953), and Quentin and Maggie in *After the Fall* (1964). For five decades Miller has shown an unwavering search for a poetic language and style that complements his particular vision for each play, a language designed so that its rhythms seem to deny its artifice and its poetry, to simulate realism. Yet at times it is undeniable that Willy Loman's clichés rise to the level of pure poetry.

Miller brings a linguistic richness to the American stage previously matched only by O'Neill and Williams, and subsequently by Albee, Mamet, and August Wilson. Miller, with Tennessee Williams, is one of the most radical sculptors of poetic language in American drama. He came of age as a young dramatist when the realism of Broadway, which Miller found unchallenging in its "simpleminded linear middle-class conformist view of life," was dominant ("Theatre Language," 81). And so during his apprenticeship years, an apprenticeship that lasted from his college days at the University of Michigan (1934–38) and included his first plays produced in 1936, *No Villain* and *Honors at Dawn*, and would extend until 1944 with the flawed *The Man Who Had All the Luck*, which closed on Broadway after only five shows, Miller struggled with both the social power and aesthetic limitations of realism. Ironically, his first Broadway success, *All My Sons* (1947), a play that edged out O'Neill's *The Iceman Cometh* for that year's Drama Critics' Circle Award, was a realistic work. The award was a great inspiration for the young and relatively unknown Miller, especially since *The Iceman Cometh* was O'Neill's first produced play since earning the Nobel Prize a decade earlier. Despite the success of *All My Sons*, however, Miller began his life-long project of discovering new dramatic formulas. He wished to transcend the limits of realism. The result was *Death of a Salesman*.

While Miller concedes the power of realism, his central concern lies elsewhere, with authenticity and the logic of style. "So that the question I bring to a play," he explains in "About Theatre Language,"

> is not whether its form and style are new or old, experimental or traditional, but first, whether it brings news, something truly felt by its author, something thought through to its conclusion and its significance; and second, whether its form is beautiful, or wasteful, whether it is aberrant for aberrancy's sake, full of surprises that discover little, and so on. (96)

Miller's own inventiveness reveals itself in three plays staged in the 1990s: *The Ride Down Mt. Morgan*, *The Last Yankee*, and *Broken Glass*. These plays signal the return of the playwright's dramatic powers, for they are arguably his best works since *The Price* (1968). *The Ride Down Mt. Morgan*, which opened in October 1991, at Wyndham's Theatre, London, recalls *Death of a Salesman* in many intriguing respects. Its protagonist, like Willy Loman, involves himself in insurance, though Willy does so at the expense of his very life in the climactic automobile crash while Lyman Felt is an executive insurance tycoon who survives a car accident on Mt. Morgan. Ted Colby, commander of the state police, thinks that Lyman's accident is a suicide attempt, but the question remains unresolved. Structurally, the play bends time more than *Death of a Salesman*. Like its more famous antecedent, it modulates between past and present action while its action takes place within "the inside of Lyman's head," as events filter through his sensibility and consciousness. Shades of *Death of a Salesman* appear in the form of Lyman's father, a spectral presence who even talks like Ben, Willy's brother and surrogate father figure. Finally, references to Africa, wealth, lost offspring who become cosmic waifs after their fathers betray their mothers, and the problem of guilt inform both plays.

The Ride Down Mt. Morgan charts Lyman's attempts to address the "split vision" of his past, a past in which he has been bigamously married, first to Theodora, who bore their daughter, Bessie, and subsequently to the younger Leah, who bore his son, Benny. The two wives and daughter, none of whom has any inkling of Lyman's double life, are brought together in the hospital after his car accident. For the first time, Lyman, bedridden with a broken leg and medication, cannot escape the responsibility for his actions. Although he symbolically elevates out of his cast, he must sort through his past with no exit in sight.

Lyman Felt is not unlike Tom Wolfe's Sherman McCoy, the self-fashioned and selfish anti-hero of the novel *The Bonfire of the Vanities* (1987), whose bungled affair with Maria and numerous other falls from grace belie an egocentric conception of himself as, in Wolfe's phrase, "the Master of the Universe." Lyman thinks he, too, is the master of his universe, and so he is. Yet what he has "mastered" leads him from poetry-making to insurance-dealing, from monogamy to bigamy. An amoral man, whose egotism makes him function as a black hole, sucking up everything and everyone who comes within his orbit, Felt tries mastering his universe to such an extent that Bessie screams to her father near the end of the play, "Will you once in your life think of another human being?" Miller himself calls Lyman "the quintessential Eighties Man, the man who has everything, but there's no end to his appetite" (quoted in Lewis, "Change of Scene," 6).

The Ride Down Mt. Morgan extends the central themes Miller has explored for some fifty years. Feelings of guilt, betrayal, deception, and the misguided cravings of the ego dominate the play, issues that saturate Miller's entire theatre. Lyman believes he tells the truth, but the interactions with his two wives suggest otherwise. Unquestionably Lyman exudes a zest for living *carpe diem*. However, having caressed and, one supposes, even loved Theo and Leah for years, the lover's eyes of the fifty-four-year-old Lyman have turned inward. A poet turned wealthy businessman, he searches for an ideal through practical solutions. Self-interests motivate Lyman, who shows little ability to celebrate anything external to the self.

Throughout the play, the audience is never sure of Lyman's truthfulness. Truth and illusion collide. It is not even clear whether the two women really

meet in the hospital room with their shared husband, or if they exist as projections of Lyman's troubled mind. The play's certainties, however, are the
issues that divide the lovers: the vainglory; the self-absorption; and the
bonfire of Lyman's vanities. Still, viewed in the context of their past relationships – when presumably the force of love brought Theo and Lyman, and then
Leah and Lyman together – all now emerge as essentially tragic figures. Too
introspective and too inveterately aware of reconstructing his life for the
service of his own private needs, Lyman, especially, is a tragic figure, whose
focus on greed, envy, guilt, and the self leave him incapacitated well beyond
the injuries sustained while crashing down the mountain. For Miller's tragic
hero, this burden is the one he bears. At the play's end, he contemplates his
aloneness and increasing sense of dread.

Miller does not have his anti-hero commit suicide (although some think he
tried), as Willy Loman does, or be executed by public hanging, as John Proctor
is in *The Crucible*, and the playwright certainly does not have the character
perform some canonizing gesture, as Von Berg does in *Incident at Vichy* (1964).
Still, at the end of the play, Lyman emerges as an oddly understandable, if not
forgivable, figure, whose search for his own humanity, despite his *hubris* and
womanizing, hints at some form of redemption. The saving force of grace,
however, remains in soft focus. There is hope in this play, but who will receive
the benefits of grace remains a mystery.

At the very end of the performance, Lyman wears a shroud, a richly
encoded symbolic garment. The audience, with the characters, may associate
the shroud with a burial cloth. But, like Lyman himself, the shroud has multiple definitions: the word "shroud" also means something that protects,
screens, hides, or shelters. Just as the garment he wears has multiple definitions, so too does Lyman's life define itself on multiple levels – through his
marriages, relationships, and divided selves. Lyman flings off the shroud,
Miller's stage notes read, only to reveal a baffled Lyman left to ponder his
aloneness and suffering.

The Last Yankee, which opened at the Manhattan Theatre Club on 21
January 1993, and which had its premiere five days later, at the Young Vic
Theatre in London, was largely dismissed by the New York critics, although
the British reception was more favorable. Regardless of the balkanized critical responses the play evoked, *The Last Yankee* is a significant achievement.
It is also one of Miller's more affirmative plays, one that emerges as a poignant, genuine piece of theatre that has not yet received the critical attention
it deserves. A brief play of two scenes, *The Last Yankee* concerns Leroy and
Patricia Hamilton, the central figures in the play, and John and Karen Frick,
who act as foils to the other couple. As mentioned earlier, all are drawn
together by chance, the wives while undergoing treatment for nervous break-
downs, the husbands while waiting in the visitors' room of a mental hospital.

The unfolding action gains its momentum from a clash of competing values, particularly evident in the first scene, which involves only the two husbands. Leroy Hamilton, a forty-eight-year-old father of seven, has not followed in his father's footsteps as a lawyer but instead has chosen to follow his true vocation, carpentry. A skilled craftsman and talented banjo player, he appears as a man who can deal with pressure. A faithful husband who is a direct descendant of one of the Founding Fathers, Alexander Hamilton, Leroy is a prideful, but in no way an arrogant, figure who has learned to live within his own emotional speed limits.

Although Leroy emerges as an optimistic man by the final curtain, Miller works assiduously not to sentimentalize the role. Accordingly, Leroy readily admits his flaws. The sources of his human frailty come from multiple past experiences, experiences that prompted his withdrawal from the messy business of dealing with others. He is, he reveals, repressed, depressed, a withdrawn man who is, perhaps in an allusion to a shaping metaphor in Williams's *Night of the Iguana*, "at the end of my rope." Although he is content with his profession as a carpenter, he fights against feelings of inadequacy or lack of ambition, which become a source of contention throughout the play. As his wife tells him, "you're scared of people, you really don't trust anyone, and that's incidentally why you never made any money." She is right. To his credit, however, he recognizes his culpability in contributing to his own and his wife's psychological conditions. Leroy, a sensitive, caring man whose genuine love of Patricia is undeniable, meets the brash, arrogant John Frick. Frick, by contrast, is a shallow, unfeeling, wealthy lumber businessman who encourages Leroy to charge as much as he can get for his labors: "if they'll pay it, grab it." Like Lyman Felt, Frick has no capacity to celebrate anyone outside of his own limited and egocentric concerns. A racist who is unaware of his insensitivity, he can never reciprocate his wife's love. Indeed, as Karen Frick desperately clings to a distant hope that her husband will provide some nurturing sustenance to help her leave the asylum, John Frick remains enameled within what William Faulkner calls the "secret self." Whereas Lyman Felt ultimately tries to repair the ruins of the past in *The Ride Down Mt. Morgan*, in *The Last Yankee* at the final curtain, when Karen's emotional paralysis reaches its zenith, John Frick abandons his wife. While Leroy and Patricia celebrate their togetherness, Karen is destined to be alone.

In spotlighting the clash of values between the two men, Miller contrasts the bonding of the two women. Although Karen Frick appears comedic, even shallow, she craves the one deeper thing her sixty-year-old husband refuses to share: love. Haunted by the kind of terror that emotionally plagues Harry and Edna in Albee's *A Delicate Balance*, oscillating between hope and despair, love and indifference, Karen warms to her relationship with Patricia, and the two women exchange absurdist lines that hint at the play's comedic dimensions.

Patricia is a humorous, caring woman. Just as Leroy on this day nurtures his wife, so Patricia nurtures Karen. A beautiful women of Swedish descent, a mother of seven now forty-four years of age, Patricia has for the last twenty-one days weaned herself from the paralyzing drugs that have haunted her for some fifteen years. Whereas Mary Tyrone in O'Neill's *Long Day's Journey into Night* remains addicted to drugs, retreating into a self-induced fog, Patricia Hamilton transcends her addictions, while accepting that a relapse remains a distinct possibility. However, her frailties still haunt her, just as Leroy's plague him.

Patricia is on a quest. She remains as unsure of the final destination of her quest as she is of the precise direction it will take. Perhaps, she reflects, hers is a quest for God, for a clarity that will banish her mental instabilities, or for some ordering principle that will fulfill a spiritual void that emotionally paralyzes her. "My problem is spiritual," she confides to her husband. Her spiritual search, which complements Leroy's own, leads her to survey her life. She recalls an overbearing father, who absorbed and deflected the racism of the "Yankees" against the Swedish in this country a century earlier, and who pressed his children to succeed. That pressure led to tragic results. Patricia's attractive and successful brothers both committed suicide. Ever since, Patricia has quietly struggled to come to terms with her familial past. She utters the word "disappointment" at least a dozen times in the second scene, a word that hints at the issue with which Leroy and Patricia wrestle. Both have contributed to their own disappointments, and both yearn for stability.

The Last Yankee is a homecoming. The play reaches its climax with Patricia's decision to return home. Hers is a conscious decision, made with conviction and lucidity, and inspired by the unifying force of love that bonds Leroy's and Patricia's marriage. Music and dance fill the stage at the end, a guarded celebration underscoring Patricia's willingness to struggle against self-doubt. Miller unambiguously emphasizes the saving grace of their love. Body gestures complement words, which, together, become a therapeutic force, a healing moment that paves the way for their homecoming. Leroy may be the stubborn last Yankee, but through his relationship with Patricia he also acknowledges that in his role of the last Yankee, he, and all people, "can start living today instead of a hundred years ago." In other words, a collective sense exists that suffering and stubbornness have for too long plagued the body politic.

If *The Last Yankee* spotlights the recovering self, Miller's next play, *Broken Glass*, addresses a similar motif, but in more problematic terms. The cautious humor and bonding that restore Leroy and Patricia are not to be found in

Phillip and Sylvia Gellburg's relationship. Whereas he never situates the former drama in any specific time, Miller locates the latter in Brooklyn in November 1938. The date is anything but arbitrary. As the title underlines, at the heart of the play is *Kristallnacht*, when the Nazis fomented riots that led, among other acts of violence, to the shattering of glass in many Jewish storefronts.

At the nerve center of the play lies the Jewish Sylvia Gellburg. Before the action begins, she has been afflicted by some mysterious disorder that leaves her unable to walk. While Dr. Harry Hyman attempts to diagnose the medical cause of her malady, she feels haunted by newspaper accounts and photographs of Germans forcing elderly Jewish men to scrub sidewalks with toothbrushes. The images especially bother her because one of the Jews reminds her of her grandfather, an early explanation for her intense personal identification with the persecution of all Jews in Europe. Transfixed by the Nazis' inexorable rise to power and their notorious treatment of Jews, Sylvia's malady, we see, has nothing to do with her physical health, and everything to do with her spiritual well-being. The embodiment of emotional paralysis, she interiorizes the plight of all Jews. Living in the Depression, Sylvia is herself immeasurably depressed.

Revealing her innermost feelings to Dr. Hyman, she recounts a recurring dream in which the Germans chase her. One of them catches and molests her. He then begins to mutilate her. By linking the appalling newspaper accounts of Nazi persecution and Sylvia's equally horrifying dreams, Miller interfolds the public catastrophe, events that occur across an entire ocean, with the private struggles of his heroine. The public and the private, for Miller, define the pressing issues of the republic and the tensions of its citizens.

Sylvia's husband, Phillip Gellburg, is an eager-to-please businessman in his late forties who works for a Gentile real estate firm. He seems nervously passionate about his work. Indeed, the audience cannot help but notice the discrepancy between his stance toward his commitment to business and his relationship with his wife. Aroused by his work, he has for twenty years been flaccid within his marriage. When the curtain rises at the start of the play, Gellburg waits motionless, legs crossed, reflecting his sexual stillness. When the final curtain falls, Sylvia grasps her dying husband's "limp" hand. Although Phillip insists to Dr. Hyman that he and Sylvia have an active sexual life, she discloses that they have not had relations for over twenty years. In both text and performance, this is a stunning revelation. Gellburg has embarked on a lifetime of evasion and repression, denial and control, manipulation and deception. Their marriage is filled with tensions that lead Phillip and Sylvia into a terrible decline: from engagement to habit, and from habit to indifference. Worse, although he professes love for his wife, Gellburg resents her. She may battle what was then called "hysterical paralysis," but Gellburg radiates repressed hysteria.

His hysteria contributes to the suspense of *Broken Glass*, which slowly probes into the various mysteries at its heart. With Dr. Hyman, the spectator begins piecing together the psychohistory of Gellburg. After the birth of Jerome, he had become unwilling or unable to engage in sexual intercourse with Sylvia. Sexually impotent, he repressed his condition, a condition which seems irreversible.

The calcification of Gellburg's private world has its parallels in the public world as well. While he exudes pride in the fact that his son, a Jew, makes a mark for himself in the largely Gentile U.S. military, at other times he denies his Jewishness. Just as he represses his sexual self, so he does his heritage. Much to his discomfort, Margaret, Dr. Hyman's wife, calls him "Goldberg" rather than "Gellburg," a mistake that reflects the extent to which he denies his religious and cultural alliances. While his wife submerges herself in the accounts of German militancy, Gellburg admits that his eleven-hour business days have not allowed him much time to follow news of Hitler in the papers. In his first meeting with Dr. Hyman, he is even inclined to indict the attitudes and manners of German Jews, suggesting that they may have brought their sufferings upon themselves. As Dr. Hyman suggests to him on the verge of his heart attack, "You hate yourself, that's what's scaring her to death. That's my opinion. How it's possible I don't know, but I think you helped paralyze her with this 'Jew, Jew, Jew' coming out of your mouth and the same time she reads it in the paper and it's coming out of the radio day and night." Phillip, indeed, becomes so overbearing and fascist in his personal politics that in her dreams his wife associates him with her German tormentors. She sleeps with the enemy.

Perhaps at the end Gellburg gains some deeper understanding of himself. Perhaps he learns from Dr. Hyman, who nurtures the very thing Sylvia craves: love. Hyman has his own considerable faults, the most notable of which involves his unfaithfulness to Margaret. While Miller skirts dangerously with sentimentality, he steers deftly between the maudlin and the authentic in dramatizing the warming, and then loving, relationship that unites patient and doctor. The sexual imagery in both characters' body language works. Hyman knows that Sylvia's condition comes from within, an insight that helps her to begin her spiritual recuperative process.

A lone cellist opens all but one scene in the play. Like the cellist, Sylvia has been also playing for time. At the end, Sylvia moves beyond her hysteria. Initially, Dr. Hyman explains to Gellburg that "Hysteria comes from the Greek word for the womb because it was thought to be a symptom of female anxiety." Later Sylvia attempts to name her paralysis, but she is unable to articulate its sources or identify its etiology. She simply calls it a terrible aching. In an earlier published version, the play ends with Phillip's descent to the floor (and return to the womb, to his own form of hysteria), where he lies dying. In the later version that Miller favored and republished, Phillip falls dead. Sylvia, however, rises from her wheelchair, and she takes her first symbolic steps toward wholeness, completion. She has progressed from the hysteria, and from the womb, and experiences nothing short of a transfiguration, a rebirth. She stands. Mixing grief and guilt, hope and celebration, by the final curtain Miller pieces together some of the shards of broken glass.

During the play's initial run, Miller told a reporter for *The New Yorker* that the production unfortunately had its contemporary corollaries.

> I sense people withdrawing into all kinds of sub-societies, whether it be gays or women or religions. It's destructive, because, in their extreme wings, they all adopt the idea that any method of securing their aims or protecting themselves is legitimate. Just yesterday, I heard on the radio of an anti-abortion organization that declares that it has the right to murder a doctor who commits an abortion. Assassination, they claim, is right. It's what Hitler believed.

If he oversimplifies, Miller still pinpoints divided loyalties that lead to public anomie. It is scarcely surprising that he has said that *Broken Glass* is "dealing with ethnic nationalism in a way" ("Miller's Tales," 35–36).

All My Sons (1947), *Death of a Salesman* (1949), *The Crucible* (1953), *A View from the Bridge* (1955), *After the Fall* (1964), *Incident at Vichy* (1964), and *The Price* (1968) remain important plays within the Miller canon, but his subsequent works have met with smaller and more indifferent audiences in the U.S. In 1970, two one-act pieces, *Fame* and *The Reason Why,* faded after a twenty-show performance at the New Theatre Workshop in New York. *The Creation of the World and Other Business* (1972), his fable of Adam and Eve, and Cain and Abel, received poor reviews, while *The Archbishop's Ceiling* (1977) proved successful only in Britain. Set in a small Eastern-European town, this drama presents a group of writers gathered in a room, which may or may not be bugged with hidden microphones. They try to persuade Sigmund, a dissident and well-respected writer, to defect. He has been working on a novel for five years, but the police have confiscated his manuscript. Marcus, a writer whom the state tolerates, argues that Sigmund should go – so that he and others can continue to enjoy what eclipsed freedoms they have. A visiting American novelist, Adrian, suggests that Sigmund travel West, where surely he will enjoy celebrityhood on college campuses; Maya, a former mistress of all three men, wishes to protect Sigmund from prosecution from the authorities. All urge the dissident writer to exile himself, but he refuses on moral principle, for to leave would be to turn his revolutionary back on all that he fights for. A powerful play, with metaphysical no less than political implications, *The Archbishop's Ceiling* remains largely undervalued, and even unknown, by American audiences.

So, too, with *The American Clock* (1980), a play set in familiar Miller territory, the Great Depression, but which came and went with little critical notice, though again successfully produced by Britain's National Theatre. Even the inventive *Elegy for a Lady* and its companion play, *Some Kind of Love Story* (both 1982 and published as *Two-Way Mirror* in 1984) as well as *I Can't Remember Anything* (1987) and *Clara* (both published as *Danger: Memory!* in 1987) were greeted mainly with critical and popular indifference. Yet, in the 1990s Miller experienced notable revivals (including award-winning productions of *A View from the Bridge* and *Death of a Salesman*) and a season of plays by the Signature Theatre (1997–98), including the premiere of *Mr. Peters' Connections*. Unquestionably, Miller more than any contemporary American playwright occupies a central place in American theatrical history.

Death of a Salesman is, for many, the quintessential American play, while *The Crucible*, whose paperback sales exceed those of *Salesman,* occupies a central place in any narrative history of American drama. Miller elevates the civic function of drama in ways that define the ethical landscape of the United States. His is a morally serious and theatrically dynamic corpus, one informed with a profound sense of charity and love for his fellow human beings. A playwright of an older generation, Miller remains a timeless pioneer who keeps his, and the audience's, eye on the future.

Bibliography: Plays and Playwrights Since 1970

Several narrative histories of recent American drama chart in varying degrees of specificity the accomplishments of both major and lesser known but still important playwrights. For years, it seemed, such works as Weales's *American Drama Since World War II*, Lahr's *Up Against the Fourth Wall*, Allan Lewis's *American Plays and Playwrights of the Contemporary Theatre*, Porter's *Myth and Modern American Drama*, Morris Freedman's *American Drama in Social Context*, and, among many other possible examples, Cohn's *Dialogue in American Drama*, were standard reading for scholars and students interested in the serious study of the contemporary American stage. But it was Bigsby's authoritative three-volume *A Critical Introduction to Twentieth-Century American Drama* that did nothing less than change our fundamental way of seeing and reading American drama. Although the first volume covers the earlier twentieth century, it nonetheless provides an essential context for understanding the aesthetic experiments that were to gain force during the mid-twentieth century, with Williams, Miller, and Albee, the subjects of Volume II. *Beyond Broadway*, the subtitle of the third volume, moves from the more textual-oriented works of Williams, Miller, and Albee to the more performance-centered contributions of so many current Off-Broadway and Off-Off Broadway playwrights and performance artists. Central to Bigsby's analyses are the dominant images of physical, emotional, and moral loss, the increasing unreliability of language, and the confluence of the public issues of a nation as those issues are reflected through the private anxieties of the individual. Bigsby revisits such issues in his equally rewarding *Modern American Drama, 1945–1990*. Authoritative and original, Bigsby's excellent studies remain essential reading, especially for those interested in such "major" figures as Williams, Miller, Albee, Mamet, August Wilson, or Shepard.

Other valuable narrative histories or books concentrating on the contemporary period include Cohn's *New American Dramatists 1960–1980*, whose attention to theatre language informs this balanced overview of some thirty-four playwrights, Berkowitz's *American Drama of the Twentieth Century*, which provides a chronologically arranged assessment, and Thomas P. Adler's *American Drama 1940–1960*, whose study, despite its 1960 cut-off date, discusses all of Williams's theatre. Roudané's *American Drama Since 1960* surveys over thirty playwrights, including both a sampling of canonized playwrights and many who have consciously eschewed Broadway and traditional definitions of canonicity.

Several other books are rewarding. Demastes's *Beyond Naturalism* examines the American preoccupation with realistic forms and demonstrates the various ways in which Beth Henley, David Rabe, Marsha Norman, Sam Shepard, and others refigure the realistic image. Susan Harris Smith's *American Drama* chronicles the numerous cultural and curricular barriers that have inhibited the development of the American stage, and Walter A. Davis, in *Get the Guests*, gives fresh readings of five classics: O'Neill's *The Iceman Cometh* and *Long Day's Journey into Night*, Williams's *A Streetcar Named Desire*, Miller's *Death of a Salesman*, and Albee's *Who's Afraid of Virginia Woolf?* Marc Robinson's *The Other American Drama* charts the theatrical achievements not only of such major figures as Williams and Shepard, but also of Gertrude Stein, Maria Irene Fornés, Adrienne Kennedy, and Richard Foreman, whom Robinson sees as essential, not marginalized, figures of the American stage. Kintz's *The Subject's Tragedy*, Vorlicky's *Act Like a Man*, and Carla J. McDonough's *Staging Masculinity* explore the nature of gendered subjectivity in the theatre.

Numerous collections of critical essays devoted to recent American drama – only a few of which I mention – remain useful. Kernan's *The Modern American Theatre*, Downer's *The American Theater Today*, Parker's *Essays on Modern American Drama*, Debusscher and Schvey's *New Essays on American Drama*, Bruce King's *Contemporary American Theatre*, Roudané's *Public Issues, Private Tensions*, Engle and Miller's *The American Stage*, and Demastes's *Realism and the American Dramatic Tradition* (1996) are but a few noteworthy volumes that address contemporary American drama.

For more focused readings of American theatre, readers may wish to consult Thomas P. Adler's *Mirror on the Stage*, Cohn's *Anglo-American Interplay in Recent American Drama*, Watson's *The History of Southern Drama*, and Kimball King's *Hollywood on Stage*. Of some interest, too, is Oliphant's editing of *Twentieth-Century American Playwrights*, an exhibition catalogue compiled by Cathy Henderson that features draft versions, working papers, poster work, and so on of eight dramatists, including Williams, Miller, Lillian Hellman, and Adrienne Kennedy, that are held in the library at the University of Texas at Austin.

One of the more refreshing developments in dramatic critical discourse concerns its attention to women and American drama. For too long a male-dominated genre, American drama now attracts a wide variety of critical and theoretical perspectives critiquing such issues as constructions of gender, race, sexuality, class, and cultural politics. The following excellent collections of critical essays suggest something of the scope and range of studies devoted to women and the theatre, collections that complement such provocative studies as Dolan's *The Feminist Spectator as Critic* and Schroeder's *The Feminist Possibilities of Dramatic Realism*; Brater's *Feminine Focus*, Hart's *Making A Spectacle*; Schlueter's *Feminist Rereadings of Modern American Drama* and her *Modern American Drama: The Female Canon*; Case's *Performing Feminisms*, Hart and Phelan's *Acting Out*; Burke's *American Feminist Playwrights;* Murphy's *The Cambridge Companion to American Women Playwrights*; and Keyssar's *Feminist Theatre and Theory.* Of related interest is Betsko and Koenig's *Interviews with Contemporary Women Playwrights*, which contains thirty conversations with leading women playwrights.

Several important collections of interviews with playwrights often reveal the relevant dramatist's theory of art, the nature of his or her imagination, and something of the person behind the art. Wager's *The Playwrights Speak*, Savran's *In Their Own Words* (a second volume to be published 1999), Bryer's *The Playwright's Art*, which contains interviews with, among others, Alice Childress, Beth Henley, Ntozake Shange, and Wendy Wasserstein, and Kolin and Kullman's *Speaking on Stage*, which features twenty-seven interviews with such key figures as Maria Irene Fornés, Tina Howe, David Henry Hwang, Tony Kushner, and Megan Terry, are all thoughtfully conceived volumes.

Several reference works stand out as particularly sensible resources that, in turn, point toward many more specific articles, monographs, collections, and books on recent American drama. Wilmeth and Miller's *Cambridge Guide to American Theatre* is exemplary and encyclopedic: with entries on playwrights and their plays from the colonial period to the present, this guide, with its attention to the contemporary, helps readers better understand the range and depth of American theatre. This work remains the best of its kind. For a guide to the major theatre companies in the United States, scholars may turn to Kullman and Young's *Theatre Companies of the World,* which contains the history of fourteen leading companies throughout the country. Two valuable bibliographic volumes are by Kolin, whose *American Playwrights Since 1945* covers forty dramatists, and Roudané's *American Dramatists: Contemporary Authors Bibliographic Series*, which evaluates seventeen playwrights.

So many playwrights have long since built upon the achievements of Williams, Miller, and Albee – Sam Shepard, David Mamet, Megan Terry, Marsha Norman, August Wilson, Adrienne Kennedy, and Tony Kushner – and so many scholars have written books on them that I spotlight only a selected few that merely hint at the rich variety of scholarship now available. Sam Shepard has attracted the most critical interest. Since Marranca's *American Dreams*, the first collection of critical essays published on the playwright, many books have been written on Shepard, from Hart's *Sam Shepard's Metaphorical Stages* to Wade's *Sam Shepard and the American Theatre* and Bottoms's *The Theatre of Sam Shepard.* Much, too, has been written on David Mamet, from Bigsby's *David Mamet*, the first sustained examination of the playwright, to Dean's *David Mamet*, Jones and Dykes's *File on Mamet*, and Kane's *David Mamet.*

New work on Tennessee Williams and Arthur Miller, not surprisingly, continues to appear. Schlueter and Flanagan's *Arthur Miller;* Bigsby's *Arthur Miller and Company;* Savran's *Communists, Cowboys, and Queers*; Murphy's *Tennessee Williams and Elia Kazan*; Griffin's *Understanding Tennessee Williams* and *Understanding Arthur Miller;* Crandell's *Tennessee Williams*; Roudané's *The Cambridge Companion to Tennessee Williams*, Centola's *The Achievement of Arthur Miller;* and Bigsby's *The Cambridge Companion to Arthur Miller* are but a few new studies that provide fresh rereadings of these playwrights' works. Perhaps it is fitting, too, to cite a recent collection of critical essays on Broadway's most prolific mainstream playwright, one who continues to be largely ignored in the scholarship, Neil Simon. Konas's *Neil Simon* is a sensible resource to consult for those interested in Simon. Since Tony Kushner, for many, has emerged as one of the key playwrights in recent American theatre, readers may wish to consult Geis and Kruger's *Approaching the Millennium* and Vorlicky's *Tony Kushner in Conversation*.

Important studies to recently appear concerning African American theatre include Brown-Guillory's *Their Place on the Stage*; Hay's *African-American Theatre*; and such more focused studies as Nadel's collection, *May All Your Fences Have Gates: Essays on the Drama of August Wilson*; Jackson and Overbeck's *Intersecting Boundaries: The Theatre of Adrienne Kennedy*; Benston's *Baraka*; and Carter's *Hansberry's Drama*. August Wilson has long said that African Americans have some of the most dramatic stories to tell, and the above studies highlight the inherent drama and struggle implicit in Wilson's remarks.

Just as American drama since 1970 has experienced unprecedented growth, so, too, has the scholarly response. Hundreds of individual books and essays not mentioned here add to our better understanding of the American stage, and, obviously, I mention only a few above that spotlight the rich variety of critical resources available to scholars, students, and the general theatregoer.

4

Musical Theatre Since World War II

John Degen

Prelude

World War II was the crucible from which most of the trends of the twenty years following the war developed. The post-Depression economic boom, and the fact that New York was a major point of both embarkation and recreational leave for American servicemen, pumped much-needed dollars into the theatre and gave rise to long runs that surpassed all earlier eras, as well as a rebirth of that most topical of music-theatre forms, the revue. Indeed, the seeds of virtually all of the major trends in the musical theatre after the war can be seen in the attractions offered during 1943 and 1944. Rodgers and Hammerstein's *Oklahoma!*, often heralded as the beginning of the modern "musical play," opened in 1943 (see Volume 2's coverage of pre-1945 Rodgers and Hammerstein). At the same time, such unabashedly old-fashioned musicals as Cole Porter's *Mexican Hayride* and the vaudeville-burlesque-flavored *Follow the Girls*, both major hits of 1944, showed that there was plenty of life in the old forms. 1944 also saw the first of the major choreographer-conceived dance musicals, *On the Town*, and the dawning of a new social consciousness in *Bloomer Girl*. Nostalgia for an earlier, more simple era also led to revivals of older operettas (*The Student Prince, The Merry Widow*), as well as the rise of such "new" old-fashioned operettas as 1944's *Song of Norway*. This was the picture as the musical theatre entered the postwar period in 1945.

The 1940s

Rodgers and Hammerstein

The most commonly heralded aspect of the postwar theatre is the collaboration of Richard Rodgers (1902–79) and Oscar Hammerstein II (1895–1960).

Both had been major figures in the musical theatre for nearly twenty years when they first collaborated on *Oklahoma!*, the framework of which they repeated in many regards in their next musical, *Carousel* (1945). Like *Oklahoma!*, *Carousel* was produced by the Theatre Guild and, again like *Oklahoma!*, it was based on a non-musical play which the Theatre Guild had produced some years earlier. In this case, the original was *Liliom*, a 1909 Hungarian play by Ferenc Molnár, which had been a great success in 1921 in an English version by Benjamin Glazer. As he had done before, Hammerstein hewed closely to the original, taking lines and whole scenes directly from Glazer's script while using others as springboards for his lyrics. Much of the *Oklahoma!* production team was reassembled, including director Rouben Mamoulian and choreographer Agnes de Mille, and again the cast consisted of virtual unknowns.

There were structural similarities as well. Both shows were examples of period Americana, rejecting wit and sophistication in favor of a wistful, senti-mental look at a bygone era. Both were "serious" in many regards, including the death of a major character, and both abjured the contemporary musical idiom for a more appropriate "old-fashioned" sound. Both made a strong use of dance, including a "dream ballet" of the sort that would remain a dominant element in musical theatre for more than fifteen years. And both were char-acter-driven shows, diminishing the role of the chorus and certainly doing without the traditional female "kick-line." Both, in short, recalled Hammerstein's and Kern's *Show Boat* (1927) more than the more familiar musical comedies of Cole Porter or Rodgers and Hart.

But *Carousel* was by no means *Oklahoma! Liliom* was a much darker piece than *Green Grow the Lilacs*, and the original (set in Budapest) required more adaptation to make it American. While the dark quality of the play appealed to Hammerstein, the original ending – in which Liliom is hustled off to hell after slapping his daughter – had to be softened to make it more palatable to American music-theatre audiences. But more important was that with more time, money, and experience together than they had had in preparing *Oklahoma!*, both Rodgers and Hammerstein took chances in adapting the form of musical theatre. Rodgers wrote the most inherently dramatic score of his sixty-year career. Where the score of *Oklahoma!* has been an attractive col-lection of songs, the score of *Carousel* is through-composed in the manner of serious operetta. The dramatic universes of Carrie and Julie, or of Snow and Jigger, are established and distinguished through their music as much as their dialogue. From their opening number, we are aware that the chirpy Carrie is not as deep as the more contemplative and grounded Julie, and while Carrie and Snow belong to the same musical universe, so do Julie and Billy. The score also features two of Rodgers's greatest achievements. The ten-minute "If I

Loved You" musical scene is not simply a song illustrative of the preceding dialogue; it constitutes the entire development of the romantic relationship between Billy and Julie, as well as showing us the softer side of Billy that he can express only in music. The eight-minute "Soliloquy" in which Billy contemplates his impending fatherhood is a masterpiece of music-theatre writing, in which key changes, time signatures, and intervals are as expressive as words. Music, in a sense, gives expression to what for Billy would otherwise be inexpressible.

There are other notable innovations in *Carousel*. While it features the dream ballet in which Billy perceives his daughter's unhappiness and longing, it also begins with "The Carousel Waltz," a wordless opening number in which characters and situations are introduced; this device will later be taken up by such other major musicals as *Guys and Dolls* and *West Side Story*. It also introduces in "You'll Never Walk Alone" the characteristic Rodgers and Hammerstein hymn, an anthem to hope that will recur in other works and which climaxes with "Climb Every Mountain" in *The Sound of Music*. But even more important, *Carousel* – far more than *Oklahoma!* – defines the model of the modern musical play, wrapping a dark, even sordid story in expressive, glorious music. It is, in many ways, the true heir to *Show Boat*.

Although *Carousel* won numerous awards and ran on Broadway for two years, it was never as popular as *Oklahoma!*, which opened two years before *Carousel* and closed a year after it. But its success encouraged the experimental artistic aims of Rodgers and Hammerstein sufficiently for them to become even more experimental in their next effort. *Allegro* (1947) defied virtually all musical theatre conventions. It took place on a virtually bare stage, using light not only to define space but to illustrate moods. It followed the life of a young doctor from the moment of his birth to his mid-thirties, tracing his hopes and disappointments, his idealism and his sell-outs, all to the accompaniment of a pseudo-Greek chorus which both narrates and expresses the inner thoughts of characters. Despite a record presale, this novel musical play did not do well. This can in part be explained by the extent of its novelty, but there were other major problems. For one thing, Hammerstein was not working with an existing play, but rather with an entirely original libretto – never his strength. For another, choreographer Agnes de Mille, so influential in Rodgers and Hammerstein's earlier shows, was assigned to direct as well as choreograph, despite the fact that she had little experience working with actors. Her answer to most problems was to add another dance, so that, by the time *Allegro* opened, it featured four extended "ballet" sequences. Although it turned a mild profit on the strength of its presale, it did not please and has been relegated to cult status among music-theatre afficionados. The lesson for Rodgers and Hammerstein was that if they were to continue in the "musical play" vein, there was such a thing as too much novelty. In *South Pacific* (1949) they would continue to break new ground, but they would return to an existing source and a more realistic framework.

Social Issues

South Pacific mines another of the new trends of the 1940s – an interest in serious social issues of politics and race. Such issues had historically been the province of the revue more than of the book musical, and of course the revue continued to deal in topicality. The most successful revue of the late forties was *Call Me Mister* (1946), with songs by revue veteran Harold Rome (1908–93), the theme of which was mustering out of the army and adjusting to civilian life. In addition to skits involving the inevitable red tape, there were also jibes at such things as the unenlightened views of prehistoric Southern senators. But such social concerns were creeping more and more into traditional musical comedy, too, during the postwar era. This was certainly true in the last two stage works of Kurt Weill (1900–50). *Street Scene* (1947) was Weill's semi-operatic version of Elmer Rice's 1929 play dealing with a day in the life of the inhabitants of a New York tenement, fitted with lyrics by poet Langston Hughes. It was even more notable in *Lost in the Stars* (1949), Weill's stirring musicalization (with words by Maxwell Anderson) of Alan Paton's novel of racial turmoil in South Africa, *Cry, The Beloved Country*. Staged by Rouben Mamoulian, *Lost in the Stars*, like *Allegro*, had a quasi-Greek chorus which commented on the action, carried out by a predominantly black cast headed by Todd Duncan, the original Porgy of *Porgy and Bess*.

But probably no figure was more consistently concerned with social relevance than E.Y. ("Yip") Harburg (1898–1981). Harburg, frequently in collaboration with composer Harold Arlen (1905–86), began writing for revues; indeed, it was for the *New Americana* revue in 1932 that Harburg (with composer Jay Gorney) wrote the anthem of the Depression, "Brother, Can You Spare a Dime." Harburg and Arlen then wrote an anti-war musical for Ed Wynn before moving to Hollywood (where they wrote the score for *The Wizard of Oz* in 1938). They returned to Broadway in 1944 with *Bloomer Girl*. Although in many ways it sought to imitate *Oklahoma!* (period Americana, Agnes de Mille dances, even the original Ado Annie, Celeste Holm, as star), this story of a Civil War suffragette and abolitionist dealt with such issues as women's rights, the misery of slavery, and the horrors of war. Arlen moved to Hollywood, although he would return to Broadway to write several less politically pointed musicals for black casts, notably *St. Louis Woman* (1946) with Johnny Mercer and *House of Flowers* (1954) with Truman Capote. Harburg, with *Bloomer Girl* librettist Fred Saidy (1907–) and composer Burton Lane (1912–97), continued to pursue his political agenda in the highly successful

20. *Finian's Rainbow* (1947) by E.Y. "Yip" Harburg and Fred Saidy with music by Burton Lane. In this famous scene, Senator Billboard Rawkins is turned black by a magical bolt of lightning. Culver Pictures, Inc.

Finian's Rainbow (1947). Essentially a love story fantasy that combined leprechauns and sharecroppers in the American South, it nonetheless managed to comment on labor exploitation, socialism, and race relations. Particularly notable was the character of racist Senator Billboard Rawkins (a composite of two real Southern senators), who is temporarily turned into a black man by Og the leprechaun. Gentle rather than angry in its satire, *Finian's Rainbow* was a major hit, running nearly two years.

In this climate, Rodgers and Hammerstein again sought to expand the boundaries of the musical play in *South Pacific*. Adapted from James Michener's stories, *South Pacific* deals with prejudice, both social and racial, in a story of colliding cultures. Nellie Forbush's naive love is tested when she must come to grips with the fact that Emile has fathered children by a native woman, but more notable was the tragic interracial love affair between Liat and Lt. Cable. Indeed, there was great pressure to cut Cable's song telling Liat that in America she would have to be "carefully taught" to hate and fear, "to be afraid of people whose eyes are oddly made and people whose skin is a different shade," though Hammerstein insisted that it remain. As with *Finian's Rainbow*, the "message" was couched in warm, good-natured fun, and the show, with Mary Martin and opera singer Ezio Pinza in the leads, was a triumphant success, running more than twice as long as *Carousel*. After *Allegro*, Rodgers's and Hammerstein's changes in the form were not so drastic, but *South Pacific* did have its share of novelties. There was no slick Broadway chorus, as the production numbers were, in the context of the show, performed by amateurs – and there was no credit for choreography. Director and co-author Joshua Logan also staged the action continuously, with no blackouts for scene changes, which were made part of the action. The latest Rodgers and Hammerstein "musical play" won the Pulitzer Prize for Drama.

Other Forties Musicals

In addition to Rodgers and Hammerstein, the forties also saw the beginning of the other major music-theatre writing team of the forties and fifties. The careers of Alan Jay Lerner (1918–86) and Frederick Loewe (1901–88) and of Rodgers and Hammerstein are chronologically parallel, as they wrote their first three musicals in the same years. But where Rodgers and Hammerstein were music-theatre veterans, Lerner and Loewe were relative music-theatre novices, and their development was slower. Lerner, a native New Yorker trained in American universities, and Loewe, a Viennese-influenced immigrant who learned the American musical idiom playing piano in clubs, took a while to find their stride. Their first show, the unsuccessful *What's Up?* (1943), was an old-fashioned musical farce, even though it did have the requisite post-*Oklahoma!* dream ballet. Their second, *The Day Before Spring* (1945), was more ambitious, bridging contemporary realism and nostalgic fantasy in a psychological study illustrated by several dream ballets. But their third show, informed by the results of the earlier efforts, was a major success. *Brigadoon* defines Lerner and Loewe's style much as *Carousel* does Rodgers and Hammerstein's – and it shows the influence of *Carousel*. Like *Carousel*, it is a fantasy with a darker side, and it evokes an exotic period charm, albeit through a 200-year-old Scottish village that appears for one day each century. And once again, Agnes de Mille was on hand to provide evocative dances, including several "ballet" sequences, and the cast was made up of unknowns. But what distinguishes Lerner and Loewe is a greater sense of charm, which cuts through the bittersweet quality. This is enhanced by the Viennese lilt which invariably flavors Loewe's music, even when it is ostensibly Scottish. Lerner and Loewe's most popular musicals do not really try to expand the musical theatre form, but rather vary a successful formula, as we will see.

It was with other collaborators that Lerner could experiment, as he did in *Love Life* (1948), written with composer Kurt Weill. *Love Life* took the form of a vaudeville, interspersing olio-type numbers that served to comment on the central story, the chronicling of a marriage in which the principals moved without aging from 1800 to 1948. Daringly novel and endlessly fascinating, it (like *Allegro*) had a modest run and was relegated to cult status. Lerner would next collaborate with Loewe in 1951, and when he did it was with many of the same production team that produced *Brigadoon*. Once again, *Paint Your Wagon* was a period fantasy, this time mining the popular vein of period Americana with a story set in the California Gold Rush of the 1850s. Loewe, unfamiliar with writing American folk music, turned to the real thing, as he did in adapting the western ballad "Cool Water" into "They Called the Wind Maria." Agnes de Mille, in her element, produced some rousing dance numbers, but this time there was too little charm and too much sentimentality, and the production lost money. This lesson would not be lost on Lerner and Loewe.

While the new teams and new trends were becoming established, several of the old guard were continuing in the old style. Indeed, both Irving Berlin (1888–1990) and Cole Porter (1891–1964) had the biggest hits of their careers in the forties, and the success of these old masters with old-style musical comedies proved that not all audiences were thirsting for modern serious "musical plays." Berlin's huge hit was *Annie Get Your Gun* (1946), a shamelessly old-fashioned star vehicle for Ethel Merman that fitted precisely her talents. The show business setting of Annie Oakley in Buffalo Bill's Wild West exhibition provided the occasion for spectacle, gaudy costumes, and production numbers, while the simple romantic story served as little more than a frame for the songs and dances. So successful was this formula that after Berlin's sentimental *Miss Liberty* (1949) failed, he returned with yet another formula vehicle for Merman, *Call Me Madam* (1950), a political satire which received an eighteen-month run.

Cole Porter, after an unbroken string of hits from 1939 to 1944, had a few overproduced flops before he hit gold with *Kiss Me, Kate* (1948), yet another old-fashioned "show-within-a-show" musical. The "show-within-a-show" context allows a wide range of numbers which can be excused by the "performance" context, although *Kiss Me, Kate* is still Porter's most integrated score. While most of the songs within the musical version of *The Taming of the Shrew* build cleverly on situations established in the dialogue, a number, in framing plot, actually advance the story, although Porter still finds room to include such suggestive lyric-focused numbers as "Always True to You in My Fashion" and "Brush Up Your Shakespeare." The two-and-a-half-year run of *Kiss Me, Kate* encouraged Porter to mine the old vein, which he continued to do in the fifties.

Not all of the new faces of the forties were breaking new ground. Indeed, one of the most successful was Jule Styne (1905–94), who made his mark with a number of old-fashioned star vehicles whose only concession to the newer trends was that they were period pieces. Styne's first success was *High Button Shoes* (1947), written with veteran lyricist Sammy Cahn and directed by the master director of prewar musicals, George Abbott. Set in 1913 New Jersey, it followed the exploits of a fast-talking con-man, played by veteran burlesque comic Phil Silvers. The same old-fashioned spirit infused *Gentlemen Prefer Blondes* (1949), written with veteran lyricist Leo Robin and veteran librettist Joseph Field. Set in the twenties, it focused on lovable gold-digger Lorelei Lee, whose motto is "Diamonds are a Girl's Best Friend," as she travels to Paris amid flappers and athletes of the 1924 U.S. Olympic team. The only novelty was that instead of using a familiar star, *Gentlemen Prefer Blondes* established a new star, long-legged, deep-voiced Carol Channing.

The 1950s

As the musical theatre entered the fifties, there were two clear trends – the developing "musical play" and the traditional "musical comedy" – although each typically used elements associated with the other. Most of the familiar names continued in their familiar styles. Irving Berlin sat out the decade after *Call Me Madam*, but Cole Porter closed out his career with three more conventional formula musical comedies: *Out of This World* (1950), mixing ancient Greek deities and present-day mortals, was an underappreciated failure, but two other shows set in Paris – the period, dance-driven *Can-Can* (1953) and the cold-war political romance *Silk Stockings* (1955) – were successful. Jule Styne tried to repeat *Gentlemen Prefer Blondes* with another period musical to showcase a rising star, but *Hazel Flagg* (1953) failed, despite the use of the still-requisite dream ballet, to do for Helen Gallagher what *Gentlemen* had done for Carol Channing. He would have far more luck with his next specially tailored star vehicle, *Bells Are Ringing* (1956), which showcased the remarkable Judy Holliday. But perhaps the oddest traditional hit was the work of librettist-director Joshua Logan and songwriter Harold Rome. *Wish You Were Here* (1952) was a triumph of press agentry in one of the leanest years the musical theatre has ever known. A romance set in a summer camp for adults, its chief attraction was a swimming pool – a technical marvel which caused the show to forego out-of-town tryouts. Despite clever publicity (Bloomingdale's department store sold "official" audition swimsuits), the show was greeted poorly by the critics. Logan rewrote and restaged it, but most effective was a popular recording of the title song, which endlessly repeated the title of the show. Curious audiences came, and a 600-performance run ultimately turned a profit for investors.

Rodgers and Hammerstein continued their pattern. Given the success of

South Pacific, they attempted to clone it with another exotic musical about cultural collision based on an existing literary work, *The King and I* (1951), which featured yet another tragic romantic subplot – and added, as in *Carousel*, the death of the central male character. The success of *The King and I* led Hammerstein to again attempt a wholly original libretto. *Me and Juliet* (1953), like *Kiss Me, Kate*, featured a show-within-a-show, but it was in many ways a love letter to the theatre, complete with a number called "Intermission Talk" in which ostensible audience members debate the question of whether or not "the theatre is dying." Spurred by the popularity of one song, a tango called "No Other Love" (which Rodgers took from his television score for the naval documentary *Victory at Sea*), the show ran for nearly a year and turned a small profit, but its success was far less than its immediate predecessors'. For their next effort, Rodgers and Hammerstein reverted to a gimmick from *South Pacific*, using a superannuated opera singer for the leading role. But *Pipe Dream* (1955), adapted from John Steinbeck and set among the losers of California's Cannery Row, ran barely six months and lost money.

After writing a musical version of *Cinderella* for television, the team returned to the tried and true theme of cultural collision in *Flower Drum Song* (1958), again adapted from a novel. Set in San Francisco's Chinatown, the show dealt with the conflict between tradition and assimilation, as well as the rift between generations. *Flower Drum Song* ran for 600 performances, enough to be profitable, but half the run of *The King and I*. Returning again to the traditional, the team now produced a show that pundits might call "*The King and I* Goes to the Alps." *The Sound of Music* (1959), based on the true story of Maria van Trapp, again showed a governess arriving at the home of a despotic but rather distant father to tend to his rather large brood of adorable children. In addition to bringing back Mary Martin, the star of *South Pacific*, and including the subplot of doomed love, it added nuns and a melodramatic escape from the Nazis. The critics were not particularly enthusiastic – some found it cloyingly sugary – but the public loved it, and the show ran for nearly four years. It was to be their last success. Hammerstein died the following year, ending the fruitful partnership of Rodgers and Hammerstein.

The career of Lerner and Loewe during the fifties was hardly as prolific. Lerner, who came from a wealthy family, liked to work. Loewe, who had never known wealth, liked to take money when he earned it, go to Europe, and gamble. Following the failure of *Paint Your Wagon* in 1951, the team would (apart from the film *Gigi*) produce only one new title in the fifties, but that one would be sufficient. It was *My Fair Lady* (1956). As with so many musicals of the time, *My Fair Lady* is a period piece, set in 1912 London. Unlike the Western setting of *Paint Your Wagon*, this locale played right into Loewe's strength; it suited his continental Viennese background, and instead of seeming oddly old-fashioned, it proved entirely successful. Swirling waltzes were what

21. Julie Andrews in Lerner's and Loewe's *My Fair Lady*, 1956. Fred Fehl photograph. Harry Ransom Humanities Research Center, The University of Texas at Austin.

Loewe did best, and when he needed lower-class songs to contrast with the upper crust, he simply borrowed traditional pub tunes ("With a Little Bit of Luck" is, essentially, "Listen to the Mockingbird"). Lerner did not have to write an original libretto (never his strength), and he was extremely faithful to his model, borrowing freely from Bernard Shaw's *Pygmalion*. There were some changes, such as the toning down of Doolittle's political philosophizing and the addition of the Ascot scene, but the only major change is having Eliza come back to Higgins at the end of the play, an ending which Shaw had authorized for the film version. Director Moss Hart seamlessly staged his prominently British cast (Rex Harrison, Julie Andrews, Stanley Holloway), and Lerner and Loewe allowed the non-singing Harrison essentially to speak his songs in rhythm. There was nothing innovative about *My Fair Lady*, basically an old-fashioned scene-song show wrapped in gorgeous spectacle, but everything about it was of a piece, and it was a goldmine. The show won one-third of the year's Tony Awards and with 2,717 performances surpassed *Oklahoma!* for the musical long-run record. In an early instance of corporate financing, CBS provided much of the production cost in exchange for the recording rights, a bargain for which they were repaid handsomely. (See also Maslon's discussion in Chapter 2, "Broadway".)

The repression of the McCarthy years cut down on the social relevance that marked the late forties. Harburg and Saidy continued their topical comment wrapped in romantic fantasy in *Flahooley* (1951), with music by Sammy Fain. *Flahooley* was, in many ways, an embarrassment of riches. In addition to Fain's attractive score, two wordless numbers were interpolated for the exotic Yma Sumac, playing an Arabian princess, to show off her three-octave range and exotic trills. The story, satirizing big business and public gullibility, concerns dolls (represented by the Bil Baird marionettes) who are ultimately brought to life by a genie (a clear imitation of *Finian's* leprechaun). Without the cohesion and clarity that marked *Finian's Rainbow*, the show fell under its own weight and is now remembered for introducing soprano Barbara Cook. Harburg and Saidy would next rejoin Harold Arlen for *Jamaica* (1957), an odd story about Caribbean pearl divers that was supposed to feature an all-black cast until Ricardo Montalban was rushed in to replace Harry Belafonte. Even in this calypso-flavored piece, there was plenty of social comment on such things as the atomic bomb, capitalist greed, automation, and American advertising. Unlike *Flahooley*, *Jamaica* found an audience and ran for a year and a half.

Another trend of the fifties that continued from the late forties was the rebirth of interest in the operetta, a form that had fallen from favor since the twenties. During the Depression, the opulent staging and large orchestras and choruses required by operetta were generally out of reach, while the old-fashioned music and the fascination with the long ago and far away seemed somewhat irrelevant. During the war, however, the longing for escapism helped several revivals of operettas to succeed, as did the success of *Oklahoma!*, which some have, in fact, styled a folk operetta. As older operettas began to be revived, there was a movement to produce new "old-fashioned operettas," inspired by the success in 1944 of *Song of Norway*, for which George Forrest (1914–) and Robert Wright (1915–) borrowed Edvard Grieg's music for a fictionalized biography of Grieg, in much the same way as Sigmund Romberg had done in the twenties with Franz Schubert and *Blossom Time*. *Song of Norway's* two-year run led to a profusion of shows which borrowed the work of classical composers to set new stories, most of them unsuccessful. But Forrest and Wright used this formula with striking success in 1953 for *Kismet*, which used the nineteenth-century romantic music of Alexander Borodin to recast an old Arabian Nights play from 1911. Energized with a memorable performance by

Alfred Drake, *Kismet* was a major hit, opening the way for other ambitious efforts at serious new operettas.

Two of the most ambitious efforts in this tradition both appeared in 1956. One, Frank Loesser's *The Most Happy Fella*, was quite successful. A musical adaptation of Sidney Howard's *They Knew What They Wanted*, it features nearly twice the amount of music one expects in a standard musical, with the result that there is much less dialogue. The music, which ranges from conventional Broadway writing to complex, almost grand-operatic dimensions, is often extremely demanding, and it was sung by a cast that included singers from both the opera and the Broadway stage. This was also true of Leonard Bernstein's *Candide*, which opened later that same year and became one of Broadway's most famous failures. Smacking more of comic opera than of operetta, Bernstein's clever neo-classical score framed an adaptation by Lillian Hellman of Voltaire's famous satire, bogged down (some said) in Tyrone Guthrie's stolid production. *The Most Happy Fella*, which touched the heart, ran for 676 performances; *Candide*, which challenged the intellect, closed in nine weeks.

Of the new figures to appear around 1950, the most significant is probably Frank Loesser (1910–69). Loesser had actually begun as a lyricist before starting to write his own music during World War II. In 1948, he first hit Broadway with a musical adaptation of the old farce *Charley's Aunt*, with a libretto by old pro George Abbott. *Where's Charley?* (1948) was a straightforward star vehicle tailored for Ray Bolger. Staged by the veteran Rodgers and Hart team of director Abbott and choreographer George Balanchine, it was a great training ground for Loesser – and proved his first hit, running for two years. For his next musical, Loesser turned to the stories of Damon Runyon and produced one of the enduring masterpieces of the musical theatre, *Guys and Dolls* (1950). Armed with an expert, character-driven book by Abe Burrows, Loesser dressed this story of Times Square gangsters, nightclub floozies and the Salvation Army with a string of standards in styles ranging from Tin Pan Alley pop for the love songs and artful mock trashiness for the club numbers to complex part-writing and contrapuntal numbers. Dance, too, played a huge part, from the opening "Runyonland," which set the mood, to the exotic Havana dance and athletic crapshooters' "ballet." This use of dance, so unlike the ballet in *Oklahoma!*, characterizes another major aspect of the fifties musical theatre – the rise of the modern dance musical.

Dance, West Side Story, *and Jerome Robbins*

The narrative importance of dance began to grow during the thirties, especially in a series of musicals by Rodgers and Hart, typically directed by George Abbott and choreographed by George Balanchine (such as *On Your Toes*) or

Robert Alton (such as *Pal Joey*). After Agnes de Mille's contributions to both *Oklahoma!* and *One Touch of Venus* in 1943, the dream ballet, as we have seen, became a regular element of Broadway musicals. But also of note during World War II was *On the Town* (1944), which introduced choreographer Jerome Robbins (1918–98) as well as composer Leonard Bernstein (1918–90) and lyricists Betty Comden (1915–) and Adolph Green (1915–) to Broadway. In expanding the Bernstein-Robbins ballet *Fancy Free* into a Broadway musical, the novices realized that they needed a theatre veteran and recruited George Abbott to direct. This successful musical, an early instance of a musical conceived by a choreographer, set in motion the rise of the conceptual director-choreographer. After *On the Town*, Bernstein turned his attention to his symphonic career, while Comden and Green, after a few failures, turned theirs to Hollywood. Robbins and Abbott, however, continued to work together.

Robbins's next major success was with Jule Styne's *High Button Shoes* in 1947, which Abbott directed. Ever the researcher, Robbins watched innumerable Mack Sennett films in preparation for his classic "Keystone Kops" ballet in this show, a show-stopping masterpiece of pratfalls, takes, and slamming cabana doors in the Atlantic City scene. Robbins had now become Abbott's protégé, and on their next project, *Look Ma, I'm Dancing* (1948), a musical with a ballet context based on an idea of Robbins's, Abbott billed Robbins as his co-director. Robbins would next choreograph for Abbott on *Call Me Madam* in 1950, while he also worked for other directors, as in the case of *The King and I*, for which he staged the memorable "Small House of Uncle Thomas" ballet (which has been preserved in the film version). But Robbins was interested in directing as well as choreographing. He would co-direct (but not choreograph) *The Pajama Game* in 1954 before assuming sole director status for *Peter Pan* (1954) and *Bells Are Ringing* (1956). For his next project, he was reunited with Leonard Bernstein for the creation of one of the musical theatre's greatest masterpieces: *West Side Story* (1957).

West Side Story is important not only because it is in essence a musical tragedy rather than a musical comedy, but because it shows how expertly the elements of musical theatre – music, words, dance – can be blended in the hands of masters. The show also introduced to the Broadway musical two new figures who would be of enduring importance: librettist Arthur Laurents (1918–) and lyricist Stephen Sondheim (1930–). In transferring *Romeo and Juliet* to the upper West Side of Manhattan, Robbins and his colleagues set the tone from the very beginning of the evening. The opening notes of Bernstein's masterful score introduce the dissonant tritone that will be the unifying basis of the entire work; tension is further reinforced by the juxtaposition of major against minor. In the opening dance, as in *Carousel*'s opening number, the basic circumstances are established without words, as Robbins's choreography displays not only events and characters, but the conflicting vocabulary

22. Gym scene from *West Side Story* (1957). This was the first musical to include the credit: "conceived, choreographed, and directed" by one person, in this instance the late Jerome Robbins. Fred Fehl photograph. Harry Ransom Humanities Research Center, The University of Texas at Austin.

of gesture that differentiates the two gangs. Musical numbers do not merely illustrate or ornament the story; they are vital in moving the story along. From the prologue to the dance at the gym, where Tony and Maria meet, from the rumble to the still inescapable dream ballet that shows the characters' hopes for a better world, it is in the musical numbers as much as the scenes that the story unfolds. As in *Carousel*, music enables essentially inarticulate characters to express their higher longings, while Bernstein's score ties everything together. The same notes that begin the show will, through inversions and variations, become Tony's "could be / who knows?" in "Something's Coming," his statement of his beloved's name in "Maria," the opening notes of both "Cool" and "Somewhere," and the end of the show. Even the most presentational of the show's numbers, the comic "Officer Krupke," serves a dramatic purpose in showing the Jets after the rumble as essentially frightened boys. While *West Side Story* was not fully appreciated during its initial run of nearly two years, it has subsequently earned the status of one of our greatest musicals.

Kidd and Fosse

While Robbins was perhaps the most important of the early conceptual director-choreographers, he was not the only one. Two other major figures also emerged during this period: Michael Kidd and Bob Fosse. Kidd (1919–), like Robbins, came to Broadway from ballet. Kidd first drew attention as a choreographer in *Finian's Rainbow* in 1947, staging not only the energetic production numbers, but also the dances through which the mute Susan expresses herself. After a few other shows, he was again successful with *Guys and Dolls*, notably in the pyrotechnical Havana dance and the athletic crap-shooters' "ballet." Kidd's choreography was always marked by an extreme athleticism, so demanding that he had his own stable of dancers capable of executing it. This was again evident in his dances for *Can-Can*, notably in the frenzied apache dance and the comic Garden of Eden ballet. Following the tradition of Robbins, Kidd became a director as well as a choreographer, crafting entire productions around his preferred dance style. His first directorial effort, the Gene de Paul–Johnny Mercer *Li'l Abner* (1956), which was highlighted by a lengthy comic dance sequence called the "Sadie Hawkins Day Ballet," was a hit, but Kidd never had as much success with his own productions as did Robbins and Fosse.

Bob Fosse (1927–87), Robbins's protégé as Robbins had been Abbott's, came not from ballet but the nightclub tradition, beginning his performance career in strip clubs. His dance is less in the tradition of de Mille and Robbins than in that of Jack Cole (1914–74), whose Oriental-flavored jazz dancing made him the choreographer of choice for such exotic musicals as *Kismet* and *Jamaica*. From this tradition, Fosse borrowed many of the devices that would become hallmarks of his style – the preference for small groups, the angular isolations, the knee work, and the use of sound effects produced by the dancers. Indeed, two of his favorite dancers, Carol Haney and Gwen Verdon, had been partners of Cole. Fosse began as a performer, but when Robbins told Abbott that he wanted to co-direct but not choreograph *The Pajama Game* in 1954, Fosse applied for the job. *The Pajama Game*, the first musical by the short-lived team of Richard Adler (1921–) and Jerry Ross (1926–55), featured a considerable amount of dance, much of it quite frenetic in keeping with Abbott's pace. But one number in particular, a song called "Steam Heat" in a show-within-a-show, became the seminal statement of Fosse's style. Danced by two men and a woman moving in close unison, it featured the other major attributes of Fosse's style: physical contortions; striking isolations stressing shoulders, hips, and elbows; slides on the knees; hats used as physical props; and such sound effects as the clicking of teeth and tongues and the snapping of fingers. The show was a success, and Fosse went on to choreograph the

23. Gwen Verdon, the prototypical dancer/singer/actress of 1950s musical comedy, as Lola, Satan's sexy assistant, in Adler's and Ross's *Damn Yankees* (1955), successfully revived in 1994–95. Fred Fehl photograph. Harry Ransom Humanities Research Center, The University of Texas at Austin.

next Adler–Ross show, *Damn Yankees* (1955), and Bob Merrill's *New Girl in Town* (1957) – the latter a musical version of O'Neill's *Anna Christie* featuring a notorious dream ballet set in a whorehouse – for Abbott, as well as *Bells Are Ringing* for Robbins. In both *Damn Yankees* and *New Girl in Town*, the star was Gwen Verdon, a dancer-actress who had made her name in *Can-Can* and who would later marry Fosse. Chafing under the needs of collaboration, Fosse too yearned to direct as well as choreograph. His first such assignment came with *Redhead* (1959), a Victorian music-hall mystery crafted as a vehicle for Verdon. Thus Fosse had joined Robbins and Kidd in the ranks of director-choreographers.

The end of the decade essentially followed the trends already established. In the wake of *My Fair Lady*, for instance, there was a glut of period pieces set early in the century that set out to charm their audiences. Of all of these (including *Goldilocks* and *Take Me Along*), easily the most successful was *The Music Man* (1957), the first stage musical of Meredith Willson (1902–84), who wrote book, music, and lyrics. Set in the American Midwest in 1912, *The Music Man* was shamelessly sentimental and old-fashioned, offering something to please everyone, with music ranging from barbershop to marches to Broadway ballads – and even an adorable child rhapsodizing about "Gary, Indiana." Again evoking *My Fair Lady*, the leading role was played by a non-singer, Robert Preston, who talked as much as sang his songs. Folksy, nostalgic, and patriotic, it charmed its audience for three and a half years, and it won virtually all the awards over *West Side Story*.

One last trend of the final year of the decade was a string of musical biographies, which included *The Sound of Music* and Bock and Harnick's *Fiorello*. Of these, the most notable was certainly *Gypsy* (1959), the next effort of the team that had produced *West Side Story*, except that Jule Styne (always adept at writing for stars) replaced Leonard Bernstein. Ostensibly the life story of stripper Gypsy Rose Lee, *Gypsy* actually was a star turn for Ethel Merman as Gypsy's mother Rose. Originally conceived by Robbins as an historic tribute to burlesque, *Gypsy* became the *Pal Joey* of the fifties, a tribute to sleaziness focusing on a highly unsympathetic central character. Oddly for a show conceived by a choreographer, the dance is essentially confined to the vaudeville sequences, and there is no traditional chorus. Another innovation is that the show begins and ends with dialogue scenes. Styne pulled many of the songs from his trunk, but he crafted an excellent score; while no Bernstein, he still added certain leitmotifs, like the four-note "I had a dream" theme that opens the overture and recurs throughout the show. Much of the show's daring originality, however, was masked by Ethel Merman's memorable performance, her final original role and one of her greatest triumphs.

The 1960s

As the sixties dawned, new blood was clearly needed. The old guard was continuing to work, but their ranks were progressively thinned. The two most successful partnerships since the war were both finished early in the decade. Oscar Hammerstein died, and Lerner and Loewe were effectively finished after *Camelot* (1960). This musical adaptation of T. H. White's *The Once and Future King* was troubled from beginning to end. Lerner struggled with the libretto, and there were unmistakable suggestions of an attempt to echo *My Fair Lady*. Once again, here was Julie Andrews playing opposite a non-singing

British actor, in this case Welshman Richard Burton as King Arthur. Production difficulties abounded, and both Lerner and director Moss Hart were hospitalized. The ultimate irony was that the two-year run of *Camelot*, helped by its association with the new Kennedy administration, enabled Frederick Loewe to retire, leaving Lerner, along with Rodgers, searching for a new collaborator.

Other figures of the earlier years faded away as well. Cole Porter died without having written a new show in the sixties, while Irving Berlin retired after writing his last show, the failed *Mr. President*, in 1962. Meredith Willson wrote two more shows in the sixties before he died – *The Unsinkable Molly Brown* (1960) and *Here's Love* (1963), the latter an adaptation of the film *Miracle on 34th St.* – and neither approached the popularity of *The Music Man*. Richard Adler, having lost partner Jerry Ross, tried to strike out on his own with *Kwamina* (1961), an interracial love story set in Africa, which failed. Indeed, the only figure who continued with business as usual through and beyond the sixties was Jule Styne, who generated a number of well-crafted star vehicles with a variety of collaborators (most commonly Comden and Green); most were financial failures, although another musical biography, *Funny Girl* (1964), written with Bob Merrill (1921–98), was a major success starring Barbra Streisand.

Most interesting among the older figures in the sixties was Frank Loesser, who continued to defy classification after having written the conventional *Guys and Dolls* and the unconventional *Most Happy Fella* in the fifties. Loesser began the sixties with a gentle rural fable, *Greenwillow* (1960), based on B. J. Chute's novel, which found a cult following but not a broad audience. The following year, however, he again broke type with a successful blockbuster, *How to Succeed in Business Without Really Trying*. This cartoon depiction of the world of big business, focusing on a charming but immoral hero, was a major success, running for three and a half years and winning a Pulitzer Prize. So successful was it that it inspired a string of musicals with anti-heroes dealing with the business world – Harold Rome's *I Can Get it for You Wholesale* (1962), Ervin Drake's *What Makes Sammy Run?* (1964), Elmer Bernstein's *How Now, Dow Jones* (1967) – but it marked the end for Loesser, who died in 1969.

Happily for the musical theatre, new talent was at hand. The first new team of writers appeared in the form of composer Charles Strouse (1928–) and lyricist Lee Adams (1924–). Teaming with young librettist Michael Stewart (1929–87), they brought to Broadway *Bye Bye Birdie* (1960), the story surrounding a rock'n'roll idol drafted into the army (clearly a reference to Elvis Presley, although the name and singing style referred to Conway Twitty). Considering the Broadway audience, however, Strouse and Adams used the rock idiom only to mock it, focusing their story on an older couple (played by Dick Van Dyke and Chita Rivera) and the score on a traditional Broadway sound. The show was an enduring success, in part due to the contribution of director-choreographer Gower Champion (1921–80), at the helm of his first Broadway show. The importance of Champion's contribution is suggested by the fact that his next show, the sugary *Carnival* (1961) with score by Bob Merrill and book by Michael Stewart, was an even bigger hit, while Strouse's and Adams's next, *All-American* (1962), with a book by Mel Brooks and Ray Bolger as the star, was a failure. Indeed, Champion would over the next two decades prove himself the king of the glitz-and-glitter style of production. Strouse and Adams meanwhile continued to work throughout the sixties in a range of styles, from the rich musical texture of the underappreciated *Golden Boy* (1964), a vehicle for Sammy Davis, Jr., with masterful rhythmic choreography by Donald McKayle, to the camp musical *It's a Bird, It's a Plane – It's SUPERMAN* (1966). Their association culminated in their biggest hit, *Applause* (1970), an exciting musicalization of the classic film *All About Eve*, before Strouse turned to other collaborators and Adams all but disappeared.

Another new face in the musical theatre of the sixties was pop composer Cy Coleman (1929–), who with his lyricist partner Carolyn Leigh (1926–) produced *Wildcat* (1960), a vehicle for Lucille Ball that had a modest run but proved that they could write for a star. This led to their engagement to write the score for a vehicle for Sid Caesar, *Little Me* (1962), with a book by Neil Simon. This was far more successful but, more importantly, it teamed Coleman with Bob Fosse, who choreographed and co-directed *Little Me*. Fosse created a new vehicle for Gwen Verdon, and Coleman, now writing with veteran lyricist Dorothy Fields, was asked to provide the score. The result was *Sweet Charity* (1966), which featured Verdon in her classic naughty but nice persona as a hopeless romantic in a dog eat dog world. The show was a major success and produced several popular hits ("If My Friends Could See Me Now," "Big Spender"). Coleman, though he would not be heard from again until the seventies, was now firmly established and had suggested that he (like Frank Loesser) could be a musical chameleon, shifting styles adeptly according to circumstance.

Even more important was another new team which had actually debuted in the late fifties. Composer Jerry Bock (1925–) and lyricist Sheldon Harnick (1924–) first collaborated in 1959 on *Fiorello*, a musical biography of former New York mayor La Guardia's early career. Subscribing in some ways to the trends of the time (a non-singer in the title role), *Fiorello*, directed and co-written by George Abbott, was in many ways highly novel. The leading character sang only when campaigning, and many of the other numbers were less popular songs than musicalized scenes, although there was also occasion for some period production numbers. With a two-year run and a Pulitzer Prize, *Fiorello* firmly established the team of Bock and Harnick, though they failed with their next effort, *Tenderloin* (1960), in large measure because they tried to clone *Fiorello* in another period New York show by practically the same production team with a non-singing leading man. But in *She Loves Me* (1963), they turned in a completely new direction and began a string of highly innovative musicals. *She Loves Me* is essentially a romantic operetta on a small scale, with a familiar story told with style and grace. Bock and Harnick's producer, Harold Prince, was now their director, and they were joined by a new librettist, Joe Masteroff (1919–), who essentially wrote a play leaving room for musicalization, with the result that many of the songs seem conversational in nature. The score was eclectic – it includes a beguine, a tango, and even a bolero – and there was so much music that the cast album required two LP discs. Although the show lost money, it earned a devoted following and has been consistently revived over the years.

Bock and Harnick's next musical was *Fiddler on the Roof* (1964), in which they were joined by a new librettist, Joseph Stein (1912–) and, more important, Jerome Robbins. Bock, Harnick, and Stein had asked producer Prince to direct, but he preferred Robbins for the project, which really took shape under Robbins's conception. Drawing his inspiration from a picture by Marc Chagall, Robbins viewed the show as an affirmation of the persistence of faith in the face of adversity, and the story became less a narrative of a dairyman and his family than a story of a village – and of the importance of tradition. Robbins threw himself into the project (his last for the musical theatre), drawing the cast through an investigation of Jewish heritage and of racial persecution in general. Bock's and Harnick's score served Robbins's purpose well, and *Fiddler on the Roof* set a new record of 3,242 performances.

Bock and Harnick's next project, this time for producer Stuart Ostrow rather than Prince, was *The Apple Tree* (1966). It was a bold departure, as it was not one story, but rather three, all adapted by Bock and Harnick from different authors. Tying the story together were consistent themes, a few recurrent images and musical motifs, and the fact that the central roles in all three stories were played by the same actors. But each story, constituting an act, was written in a completely different style, each with different orchestrations. Such experimentation could not last, however, as big money pleaded for a clone of *Fiddler*. The result was Bock and Harnick's final musical, *The Rothschilds* (1970), which was described by some as "Fiddler on the Continent." It was not, because the context of urban European sophistication was hardly rural Russia, and, instead of dealing with a village, the show traced the rise to power of a family from the German Jewish ghetto. The show was expensive and, despite a 500-performance run, lost money. After *The Rothschilds*, Bock and Harnick dissolved their partnership and have not worked together again.

The other major team to appear in the sixties was that of composer John Kander (1927–) and lyricist Fred Ebb (1932–). They first teamed in 1965 for a

George Abbott-directed period musical, *Flora, the Red Menace*. Set in the thirties, it was designed as a vehicle for Liza Minelli. Despite her personal success, it closed in eleven weeks. But producer Harold Prince admired their work and engaged them to write the score for his next project, *Cabaret* (1966). With *Cabaret*, Kander and Ebb were teamed with *She Loves Me* librettist Joe Masteroff, and the team produced a landmark show. Although based on Christopher Isherwood's *Berlin Stories*, *Cabaret* went beyond its source in investigating the decadence of Berlin and the capacity for good people to do nothing in the face of a disintegrating world. Fred Ebb would later claim that the key to *Cabaret* was the idea of the Master of Ceremonies, who became the central thread, as events in the book are viewed and commented on, in an almost Brechtian way, through the scenes in the cabaret, which serve not to advance the narrative but to enhance the air of danger and decadence. Prince emphasized this dual nature by having denizens of the cabaret watch the book scenes from the periphery of the stage, while the stage was topped with a large mirror that could tilt so as to force the audience to confront themselves. The music, evoking the dissident quality of Kurt Weill's early music, was rarely aesthetically pleasing – which only made the exquisite melody of the Nazi anthem "Tomorrow Belongs to Me" ironically seductive. Here was a distressing show with a horrific theme, and with often gross, abrasive humor – and yet it was a commercial success running nearly three years. *Cabaret*, like *Fiddler*, actually looks forward to the "concept" musical of the seventies in its concern for theme rather than linear narrative, and it was certainly a milestone of the sixties.

Kander and Ebb, now commercially established, would go on to write several other musicals in the sixties – *The Happy Time* (1968), directed by Gower Champion, and *Zorba* (1968), directed by Prince – but none would achieve the success or the power of *Cabaret*.

Off-Broadway Musicals

Beyond the novelty of new faces, other trends in the sixties were breaking new ground. One was the development of Off-Broadway as an alternative venue for the American musical. Off-Broadway had developed as an alternative to Broadway commercialism (see Gussow, Chapter 2, "Off- and Off-Off Broadway"). With smaller theatres and less financial pressure, it sought to encourage experimentation. Some of the first to appear Off-Broadway were productions of the innovative Phoenix Theatre on Second Avenue, which produced a number of experimental musicals of potentially limited appeal, two of which (*The Golden Apple* in 1954 and *Once Upon a Mattress* in 1959) had actually transferred to Broadway. But the granddaddy of Off-Broadway musical hits was the Marc Blitzstein adaptation of Brecht's and Weill's 1928

The Threepenny Opera. An international hit in the twenties, it had been a Broadway failure in 1933, but the 1954 Off-Broadway production ran for six years and grossed millions of dollars. This encouraged other Off-Broadway revivals of earlier shows that, along with small-scale revues, were the staples of Off-Broadway musicals during the early years. Then, late in 1959, came the first original Off-Broadway musical to achieve major success. Rick Besoyan's *Little Mary Sunshine*, a tongue-in-cheek takeoff on earlier American operetta and musical theatre, was produced on a shoestring in the Orpheum Theatre, a former movie theatre in the East Village. Rather than trying to hide its minimal production values, it sought to emphasize them, from the small cast to the threadbare sets to the two-piano accompaniment. *Little Mary Sunshine* ran for three years, but that achievement would soon pale next to another original Off-Broadway musical.

Composer Harvey Schmidt (1929–) and librettist-lyricist Tom Jones (1928–) had conceived *The Fantasticks*, their whimsical musicalization of an old Edmond Rostand play, when they were college students. With a cast of eight and an "orchestra" of piano and harp, it was the perfect Off-Broadway show, in that it asked the audience to use their imaginations, to "try to remember." When it opened in 1960 in a 153-seat Greenwich Village theatre, it cost roughly $15,000 to produce. Again, restrictions to opulence were made a virtue; at the intermission, the lights were regelled to permit night-time to give way to day. The whimsy of the piece found an audience, and almost forty years later, *The Fantasticks* is still running at the same theatre.

Off-Broadway had now shown that it could be a goldmine, and it grew exponentially in numbers. The fare was generally consistent. There were, in the tradition of *The Fantasticks*, original musicals based on classic plays; there were, in the tradition of *The Threepenny Opera*, revivals of earlier shows – *Anything Goes* (1962), *The Boys from Syracuse* (1963); and there were small revues. Off-Broadway also provided a venue for new figures and others who were often shut out from Broadway, notably black authors and performers. As such, it became a launching pad for new talent.

Another phenomenon of the sixties was what might be called the British invasion. American musicals had long been popular in London but, in the sixties, London musicals began to be imported wholesale to New York. The key figure here was producer David Merrick, who, in addition to his home-grown efforts (like *Gypsy*), had begun to import English plays. Typically he brought over not only the plays, but the productions, assuming that what made them hits in London would make them hits in New York. Merrick's first major import was *Irma La Douce* (1960), actually a French musical imported via London. He brought over director Peter Brook's entire production, including sets, costumes, and the three leading actors; the show reaped a profit. In the following years, Merrick imported still more London hits – Anthony Newley and Leslie Bricusse's inventive *Stop the World, I Want to Get Off* (1962), Lionel Bart's *Oliver!* (1963) – with similar success. But then the trend began a downturn. Joan Littlewood's *Oh, What a Lovely War!*, a big hit in England, was a failure in America in 1964, and Merrick's attempt to debut a London musical in New York died when Newley and Bricusse's *The Roar of the Greasepaint, The Smell of the Crowd* was unsuccessful in 1965.

But Merrick was not relying solely on London for his Broadway novelties. It was Merrick who brought the writers of *The Fantasticks* to Broadway. Their first effort was fairly conventional, a musicalization of N. Richard Nash's play *The Rainmaker*, now called *110 in the Shade* (1963), with Nash writing the libretto. Schmidt and Jones showed that they were comfortable with a large cast and a full pit orchestra, and Agnes de Mille returned to choreograph the prairie as she had in *Oklahoma!*, but the results were encouraging rather than electrifying. A much greater experimental spirit marked Schmidt and Jones's next show for Merrick, *I Do! I Do!* (1966). A major musical with a cast of two, given an imaginative staging by Gower Champion, it told, like its source, the story of fifty years of a couple's married life. With Mary Martin and Robert Preston as the entire cast (Howard Keel and Carol Lawrence at matinees), the show ran for nearly 600 performances.

Other new faces were providing novelty to Broadway as well. Stephen Sondheim, who had been the lyricist for *West Side Story* and *Gypsy*, turned in his first complete score with *A Funny Thing Happened on the Way to the Forum* (1962), a manic romp through the plays of Plautus for which Bert Shevelove and Larry Gelbart provided a book so hysterical that the songs seemed almost "serious relief." *Forum* is also notable as the last "hit" of director George Abbott, although, when the show was in trouble, Jerome Robbins came in to pay back his old mentor by doctoring the production without taking program credit, adding (among other things) the opening "Comedy Tonight" sequence. Sondheim would return to Broadway in 1964 with *Anyone Can Whistle* to a libretto by his *West Side Story* and *Gypsy* collaborator Arthur Laurents, but despite a cult following and the impressive musical debut of Angela Lansbury, the show lasted only nine performances.

Other novelty came from Richard Rodgers who, after finding he could not work with Alan Jay Lerner, became his own lyricist for *No Strings* (1962). The book by Samuel Taylor chronicled a failed interracial love affair in Paris, and the imaginative production by director-choreographer Joe Layton (1931–94) featured onstage musicians who played instruments characterizing each of the principals and mannequins to flesh out scenes in combination with live actors. Another inventive production was Mitch Leigh, Joe Darion, and Dale Wasserstein's *Man of La Mancha* (1965), staged (on Broadway contracts) in a large three-quarter-round theatre in Greenwich Village whose seats rose in arena style well above the stage. Designer Howard Bay used a long staircase descending from the ceiling to separate the world of the prisoners from the outside world, and producer-director Albert Marre's inventive staging led to a run of over 2,300 performances.

Not all of sixties Broadway was innovative, of course. Indeed, one new face helped reinforce the traditional blockbuster, with its huge casts and lavish scenery. Composer-lyricist Jerry Herman (1932–) began in the theatre by writing Off-Broadway revues in the fifties. He was brought to Broadway in 1961 with *Milk and Honey*, a musical set in Israel that featured an exciting score, romance, folk-dancing, and a paean to the Jewish spirit. It also focused, as would most of Herman's shows, on older characters, particularly older women. *Milk and Honey* ran for nearly 550 performances, but this was nothing compared to the next Herman–Merrick collaboration. *Hello, Dolly!* (1964), adapted by Michael Stewart from Thornton Wilder's *The Matchmaker*, virtually defined the traditional blockbuster. It was in every way old-fashioned, save perhaps in its focus on a middle-aged leading lady, a role written for Ethel Merman but created memorably by Carol Channing. Given a stunningly opulent production by Gower Champion, the show featured many of Herman's standard traits. Perhaps most notable is the almost irrelevant title number (the occasion is Dolly's return to the restaurant, hardly worthy of such fireworks). The number consists of a simple melody repeated until it is unforgettable, which also endlessly repeats the show's title. Once established, the melody gives way to a major dance interlude of increasing tempo, climaxing in a full choral restatement of the central melody that modulates upward, until the first sopranos are wailing in the stratosphere, all to a rhythm that evokes a cakewalk. It is a device designed to pull an audience to their feet. *Hello, Dolly!*, cleverly managed by producer Merrick, would remain on Broadway for seven years. Herman's next show, *Mame* (1966), built along the same lines with no innovation, once again focused on an older woman and gave a traditional audience everything it could want. Perhaps because it was neither produced by Merrick nor directed by Champion, it ran for "only" 1,500 performances. Encouraged, Herman became more ambitious with his next show, *Dear World* (1969). Returning *Mame*'s librettists, Jerome Lawrence and Robert E. Lee, and its star, Angela Lansbury, *Dear World* was a musical version of Jean Giraudoux's *The Madwoman of Chaillot*. While Herman was careful to repeat the formula for his title song, his music was often much more ambitious than in the last two shows. Whether because he had varied the model or because the times were changing, *Dear World* was Herman's first failure.

By the late sixties, a new spirit was infusing the country. It was a great age of protest, social division, and generational hostility. This division was reflected in the musical theatre. The late sixties on Broadway produced what Gerald Bordman terms "a parade of mediocrities" in the traditional mold, and as production costs increased toward the million-dollar mark, the failures spelled financial suicide. Few new faces appeared on Broadway, and the hits during the last years of the decade could be counted on the fingers of one hand. *Promises, Promises* (1968) had the virtues of an attractive pop score, a clever book by Neil Simon, and choreography by a young Michael Bennett. Sherman Edwards's *1776* (1969) was arrestingly novel in its form, but it also had enduring patriotism in a divisive age to recommend it. For the most part, the successes of the late sixties – *You're a Good Man, Charlie Brown* (1967), *Jacques Brel is Alive and Well and Living in Paris* (1968), *Dames at Sea* (1968) – were warm, unpretentious, small-scale Off-Broadway shows. But also brewing Off-Broadway was a new type of musical – the countercultural rock musical.

Hair

The seminal event in this movement was James Rado's and Gerome Ragni's *Hair* (1967), the "American tribal love-rock musical" which opened at Joseph Papp's Public Theater. Set to an appealing but undramatic pop-rock score by Galt MacDermot (1928–), *Hair* was a plea for understanding from the young, protest-oriented, drop-out counterculture. It sought to present its life style, albeit a sanitized version in which no one died of exposure or drug overdoses, and it reveled in its naughtiness. *Hair* was a "concept" musical in that it did not attempt to tell a story, but rather to present a way of life, somewhat as *Fiddler* had done. Its use of rock music brought amplification into the theatre, and its use of nudity attracted much notice. Director Gerald Freedman's original production at the Public had an unfinished, almost improvisational quality to it that made *Hair* as much an event as a play. At the end of its downtown run, Papp sold the rights to *Hair* to Michael Butler, who brought it to Broadway in a far more tightly staged, reorchestrated version by maverick director Tom O'Horgan which would be produced around the world. When *Hair* came to Broadway with its rock music, its naughty words, and its nudity, counterculture met traditional culture with a bang. Some came to it to learn; others came to it as to a freak show. But *Hair* brought a new audience into the mainstream musical theatre, and its success spawned a long series of other non-narrative musical depictions of minority segments of society, accompanied by rock music and its attendant amplification. (See also Maslon, chapter 2, "Broadway.")

The 1970s

The first half of the seventies saw a number of significant new trends, virtually all of them in some way encouraged by the success of *Hair*. And while conventional musical comedies continued to be written, only a handful were solid

24. The infamous "nude" scene from the rock musical *Hair*. Though controversial at the time, this moment lasted only a few seconds and, as this photograph from *The New York Times Magazine* (1 September 1968) suggests, in dim and subtle lighting. Photograph by William Sauro. *New York Times* Permissions.

successes. Richard Rodgers, now writing with lyricist Martin Charnin (1934–), had a success with a musical about Noah and the ark, *Two by Two* (1970), which owed much of its success to the antics of Danny Kaye. Jule Styne and Bob Merrill had a hit with *Sugar* (1972), a musical version of the film *Some Like It Hot*, while Cy Coleman and Dorothy Fields, in combination with Michael Bennett, had a mild hit with *Seesaw* (1973), a musicalization of William Gibson's *Two for the Seesaw*. But the period also saw crashing failures by Styne, Kander and Ebb, and Jerry Herman, while the only one-thousand-performance run of a traditional musical was that of Gary Geld's and Peter Udell's *Shenandoah* (1975), a sentimental Civil War musical so old-fashioned that it seemed to defy all of the trends and so found a conservative audience.

Rock Musicals and Other *Hair* Offshoots

The legacy of *Hair* essentially lies in three areas: rock musicals, nude musicals, and minority musicals. Like *Hair*, many of these were non-narrative. In some ways, *Hair* might also be held responsible for the nostalgia movement, if only by provoking a reaction. The most immediate legacy was certainly the procession of imitators, a series of "bookless" shows, pastiches of songs and scenes dealing with a way of life or a social-political issue. They were aggressively counterculture, often angry in tone, invariably young, and unstintingly amplified. The Off-Broadway musical in the post-*Hair* years teemed with *Hair* clones, usually with one-word names like *Stomp* (1969, against all conventional values), *Sambo* (1969, on black alienation), and *Mod Donna* (1970, on the exploitation of women). The authors of *Hair* were, of course, accepted on Broadway, although the only one to have a major success was Galt MacDermot, who composed an eclectic pop-rock score for the John Guare–Mel Shapiro musical version of Shakespeare's *Two Gentlemen of Verona* (1971). Recast in term of blacks and Hispanics, the show was a success, winning the major awards in a lean season. Success breeds imitation, but the imitations – like Cliff Jones's *Rockabye Hamlet* (1976), staged by Gower Champion – were quick failures.

Other attempts were legendary disasters. Gerome Ragni's *Dude* (1972), again with music by Galt MacDermot, for which the huge Broadway Theatre was gutted and an arena stage covered with dirt erected in the middle of its auditorium, consisted of an incoherent rambling about a young crusader against environmental pollution. As confusing to its cast as to its audience, it closed in two weeks and lost nearly a million dollars. A similar disaster was Christopher Gore's *Via Galactica* (1972), again with music by MacDermot, which was "conceived" and overseen by British director Peter Hall. Set in 2971, it featured Raul Julia as the leader of a group of pilgrims who, leaving behind a hopelessly conformist Earth, set out into space to found a new Eden. Entirely sung in operatic fashion, it was performed on a stage covered with trampolines, which simulated weightlessness. This expensive flop, which opened the huge Uris (now Gershwin) Theatre, lasted only seven performances. The third *Hair* collaborator, James Rado, stayed Off-Broadway to produce *Rainbow* (1972), a rock fantasy taking place in the mind of a young man killed in Vietnam that ran for six weeks.

The major rock-music success of the period was actually British in origin. *Jesus Christ Superstar* (1971), by composer Andrew Lloyd Webber (1948–) and lyricist Tim Rice (1944–), had started life as a record album. When it caught on, it began to receive concert versions, so it was extremely familiar, especially with young audiences, when Tom O'Horgan brought it to the stage in one of his typically outrageous, overblown productions. As with *Hair*, *Superstar* was helped along by controversy. Some condemned it as blasphemous, while others praised it for glorifying and humanizing Jesus. It also suited the political climate of the moment, as Jesus was shown as a long-haired rebel preaching peace and love who was denounced as a dangerous radical by repressive, paranoid authorities. In keeping with this theme, Lloyd

Webber's score really is not exclusively rock. Indeed, it reflects the generation gap both in its use of orchestration (rock band for the young, orchestra for the establishment) and its songs (rock for the young, older music-hall style for the elders). *Jesus Christ Superstar* ran for nearly two years, encouraging other "rock operas," all of which failed. By the middle of the decade, the rock musical in the *Hair* mold was already somewhat passé.

Another legacy of *Hair* was the arrival of a couple of highly successful "shock" musicals, revelling in nudity and sexual naughtiness. The first and most successful was *Oh! Calcutta!* (1969), a series of skits and fragments by famous writers assembled by critic Kenneth Tynan and director Jacques Levy, set to a forgettable score by Peter Schickele. But what *Oh! Calcutta!* really offered was sexual humor and full nudity, including a nude *pas de deux* choreographed by Margo Sappington. Neither particularly witty (the title is a pun from the French: *Oh, quel cul tu as* – oh, what an ass you've got) nor musically distinguished, *Oh! Calcutta!* originally ran for more than 1,300 performances. A 1976 revival ran until 1989, almost 6,000 performances, making it at that time the second longest-running musical in Broadway history (it now ranks third after *A Chorus Line* and *Cats*). A similar show was Earl Wilson, Jr.'s *Let My People Come* (1974), which made no pretension to sophistication, but rather traded in sophomoric locker-room humor. Its nudity and sniggering sexuality earned it a run of nearly three and a half years.

Far more enduring than the early rock operas was another new type of sound that entered the theatre in the seventies – the more melodic, less drivingly aggressive and thus more widely palatable sound known as "soft rock." Like other forms of the rock musical, the soft rock shows first appeared Off-Broadway, gaining acceptance and moving uptown, where they became more elaborate. Like *Hair* and its ilk, they also had their roots in the youthful, protest-oriented school of "relevance." But unlike their hard-rock cousins, soft-rock musicals were not loud and aggressive. Their rock beat was easy, supporting a melodic line and letting words be understood without excessive repetition. This quieter, less strident expression of a new generation's thoughts was what really served to establish and popularize rock music in the theatre.

Some of the earliest soft-rock shows came from the only all-female team to write for the musical theatre: composer Nancy Ford (1935–) and librettist-lyricist Gretchen Cryer (1935–). They were championed by *Fantasticks* director Word Baker, who staged their first two Off-Broadway successes. *Now Is the Time for All Good Men* (1967) was a gentle story of a conscientious objector who is pilloried in a conservative Indiana town for teaching such "radical" ideas as those of Thoreau. Combining a traditional show-music sound with a folk-rock idiom (and even a fifties rock sound for some older characters), the show was a mild success. More successful was the futuristic *The Last Sweet*

Days of Isaac (1970), two interrelated one-act musicals whose trendy theme was a search for identity in an ever more mechanized society. A similar theme in *Shelter* (1973) died a quick death on Broadway, but the autobiographical *I'm Getting My Act Together and Taking it on the Road* (1978), which dealt with an older female performer trying to assert her independence, was a major success that ran Off-Broadway for nearly five years.

The most successful soft-rock composer of the seventies was composer-lyricist Stephen Schwartz (1948–). Trained in both music and theatre, Schwartz and a college classmate, John-Michael Tebelak, hit it big their first time out with *Godspell* (1971), a child-like celebration of the Gospel with a gentle soft-rock score, some of it based on old hymns. Essentially a clown show on a sacred theme, performed by a young cast in jeans and T-shirts, it did not inspire controversy like *Jesus Christ Superstar*, and it ran for five years Off-Broadway before transferring to Broadway, where it ran for another 500 performances.

Schwartz's next show was *Pippin* (1972), written with librettist Roger Hirson but in reality shaped by Bob Fosse, who used the original show only as a point of departure for his directorial creativity. Fosse, for instance, developed the figure of the Leading Player as a parallel to the Master of Ceremonies in *Cabaret* (the movie of which he had just directed) and turned Schwartz and Hirson's conventional tale about a disillusioned youth looking for the meaning of life into a gaudy vaudeville-cum-magic show, a morality tale drenched in sex and infused with an electrifying theatricality. So furious was Schwartz with Fosse's liberties that Fosse finally barred Schwartz from the theatre, and the final product was far more Fosse's vision than that of its creators, who were nonetheless rewarded with a five-year run. Ironically for someone who had objected to Fosse's magic-show motif for *Pippin*, Schwartz's next musical was, in fact, *The Magic Show* (1974), designed to frame the talents of Canadian magician Doug Henning. It became Schwartz's third five-year run in three tries. Ironically, success brought certain expectations, and when in Schwartz's next show he went beyond soft rock to produce a rich, ambitious score for *The Baker's Wife* (1976), the show closed out of town.

Concept Musicals

The circumstances of *Pippin* bring us to another trend of the seventies – what has been called the "concept musical." Actually, the precise meaning of the term is rather vague. It has been used to describe shows which are "conceived" by a master director-choreographer, either before the fact (as had been the case with Jerome Robbins's *On the Town* or *West Side Story*) or after the fact (as in Robbins's *Fiddler on the Roof* or Fosse's *Pippin*). In either case, the director-choreographer becomes the major shaping element of the show and the major creative force behind it. Another view of the "concept musical" is part of the legacy of *Hair* – an essentially non-narrative musical that investigates a theme rather than telling a story. In this sense, shows like *Fiddler* and *Cabaret* are clear antecedents, but after *Hair* this sort of concept show tended to consist of plotless ensemble pieces that sought to give faces and voices to groups that were often ignored. *Hair* and its immediate ancestors certainly sought to do this, as did another string of seventies musicals. *The Me Nobody Knows* (1970), for example, was based on the writings of ghetto children. Something similar marked shows like Elizabeth Swados's *Runaways* (1978) or *Working* (1978), which Stephen Schwartz crafted from Studs Terkel's book to a score by half a dozen songwriters. But the show that perhaps best defined both types of concept musical was *A Chorus Line* (1975), which was not only meant to give expression to the faceless, but was entirely the conception and execution of director-choreographer Michael Bennett (1943–87).

A Chorus Line

As conceived by Bennett, *A Chorus Line* sought to give identities to Broadway's "gypsies," who dance as members of the ensemble. Based on hours of interviews with actual career dancers (several of whom appeared in the show), the book assembled by James Kirkwood and Nicholas Dante took the guise of an audition. As part of the audition process, the auditioners are asked about their lives, thus letting the individual stories be told. It also enabled Bennett to use dance, executed to composer Marvin Hamlisch's (1944–) and lyricist Edward Kleban's potpourri score, not merely to demonstrate the auditioners' skill, but to express their deepest feelings. At the end of the evening, eight dancers are chosen. The evening ends with a huge production number, "One," by the entire company, in which, ironically, the individuals fade back into obscurity. Like *Hair*, *A Chorus Line* began life at Joseph Papp's Public Theater before moving to Broadway, where it won the Pulitzer Prize and ran for fifteen years, setting the then long-run record of 6,137 performances.

Bennett's next musical, the failed *Ballroom* (1978), reverted to a traditional narrative, although Bennett's conceptual touch was apparent throughout. This was always the style of Bob Fosse, whose concept musicals generally stemmed from his distaste for collaboration. In Fosse's next show, Kander's and Ebb's *Chicago* (1975), he was not merely the driving creative force, but took bookwriting credit as well. Like *Pippin*, *Chicago* was crafted as a vaudeville show, with a procession of specialty acts serving to comment on the central theme – the public's glamorization of certain criminals and the showmanship with which their deeds are packaged. *Chicago* was a success, but

25. Costume sketch by Theoni Aldredge for the final moments of *A Chorus Line*. Photo: Don B. Wilmeth Collection.

Fosse, still frustrated by the concessions necessary in collaboration, did away with collaborators completely on his next project, *Dancin'* (1978), an evening-long dance concert to existing music.

The Black Musical

Another phenomenon of the seventies that fits into both the thematic concept musical and the arrival of rock in the musical theatre is the re-emergence of the black musical. While the postwar musical had seen black shows, they were few and far between. *Bloomer Girl* and *Finian's Rainbow* had had racially mixed casts, but the focus was squarely on the whites. Harold Arlen had written some shows for black casts, and we had *Lost in the Stars*, *Kwamina*, and *Golden Boy*. But the beginning of the return of the black musical dates from 1967. In that year, *Hello, Dolly*'s popularity was beginning to wind down; David Merrick revivified it by recasting it entirely with black performers, notably Pearl Bailey in the leading role. It was still a white show with black actors, however, so one must also view *Hallelujah, Baby!* (1967) as of equal significance. Written by the all-white team of Jule Styne, Betty Comden, Adolph Green, and Arthur Laurents (with the help of black arranger Luther Henderson), *Hallelujah, Baby!* traced the career of a black singer and the two men in her life (one black, one white) as they move through time without aging from the twenties through the sixties. It was a satirical musical in which blacks received top billing, but this was clearly a show in the white musical-comedy tradition. More authentic in its sound was *Purlie* (1970), a musical version of Ossie Davis's play with a score by white songwriters Gary Geld and Peter Udell, again helped by Luther Henderson. *Purlie* was one of the first shows aggressively marketed to a black audience, and, helped by the stunning achievement of Melba Moore, this mixed-race show ran for nearly 700 performances.

Still more important was a series of non-narrative evocations of black life written as well as performed by blacks. The first truly all-black Broadway show of the seventies was Melvin Van Peebles's *Ain't Supposed to Die a Natural Death* (1971), directed by Gilbert Moses, which brought ghetto life to Broadway. Like so many rock-oriented, post-*Hair* shows, it was a series of vignettes, subtitled "Tunes from Blackness." The show was aggressively confrontational (it ended with a woman singing "Put a Curse on You" to the white audience), and its view of life in the ghetto was often hard to take, but the show ran for nine months. More popular was a similar, much less angry if no less serious show by Vinnette Carroll and Micki Grant called *Don't Bother Me, I Can't Cope* (1972), which ran for more than a thousand performances. Black "book musicals" were still frequently written by whites – as in the case of the highly successful *Raisin* (1973), energized by director-choreographer Donald McKayle – although some, notably *The Wiz* (1975), a black retelling of *The Wizard of Oz* with a rock score by black songwriter Charlie Smalls, used mostly black production teams. Given a stunning theatrical production by Geoffrey Holder and George Faison, *The Wiz* ran for four years.

Nostalgia and Revivals

Another trend of the seventies stemmed from a reaction to the novel elements invading the musical theatre. This was a heavy dose of nostalgia, perhaps generated by the tumultuous social-political climate, perhaps by a distaste on the part of traditional theatregoers for the new sounds and subjects. The nostalgia movement took two major guises: revivals of older musicals, and new musicals written to celebrate an earlier age. The nostalgia craze really began in 1971 with a revival of Vincent Youmans's classic musical of the twenties, *No, No, Nanette*. Few theatregoers remembered the fifty-year-old original, but they remembered the songs, and the producers even went so far as to advertise the production as "supervised by Busby Berkeley" (a familiar name, though he had had nothing to do with the original *Nanette*). With a book revised by Bert Shevelove, but the score left more or less intact, the revival ran for two years, turned a huge profit, and prompted many imitations. The same producers returned two years later with an even older vintage musical, the 1919

Irene. As *Irene* was less familiar, however, they retained only five songs from the original, interpolating others (both old and new). Starring Debbie Reynolds, *Irene* still ran for more than 600 performances. Thus began a whole profusion of revivals of old musicals from the teens and twenties.

At the same time, more recent musicals began to be revived in profusion. As costs were continuing to rise and new old-fashioned musicals were failing wholesale, it made more economic sense to offer a tried and true product to audiences reluctant to risk twenty-five or thirty dollars a ticket on an unknown title. The more recent musicals, which were more familiar, were generally not adapted; indeed, every effort was made to resurrect the original production, complete with stars if possible. Occasionally, as in the case of *Lorelei, or Gentlemen Still Prefer Blondes* (1974), updatings and new songs were added, but this was a rare novelty, as were an all-black *Guys and Dolls* (1976) or a *Kismet* set in Africa and retitled *Timbuktu* (1978), both of which were effectively "re-rhythmed." More common were revivals like Rex Harrison in *My Fair Lady* (1976), Zero Mostel in *Fiddler* (1976), or Yul Brynner in *The King and I* (1977). Soon the revival tendency assumed the proportions of an epidemic.

For those who liked their nostalgia original, there were such attractions as *Grease* (1972), a *Happy Days*-style view of a fifties that never really existed, with songs written in imitation of specific period hits, or *Over Here* (1974), a forties musical that unearthed two of the Andrews Sisters. For those who preferred their old-style songs without the encumbrance of a story, there were a number of highly successful retrospective Broadway revues, such as *Bubbling Brown Sugar* (1976) or *Ain't Misbehavin'* (1978) – and even an oddity called *Beatlemania* (1977), which ran for more than 900 performances.

Stephen Sondheim

Amid this profusion of the new and the old, only one enduring figure consistently broke new ground in the seventies. Composer-lyricist Stephen Sondheim produced five major musicals which make up the decade's most substantial body of work. All of them were produced and directed by Harold Prince, without whom most of the shows would never have seen the light of day. Sondheim began the decade with *Company* (1970), written with George Furth. *Company* is essentially a concept musical in its focus on theme over narrative, and that theme is personal relationships (particularly marriage) within contemporary New York. Various couples and single women are brought together by their association with Robert, an unmarried man entering middle age. Sondheim has said that he looks for the musical pulse of a show, and in *Company* that pulse is defined by a telephone busy signal and a clock, two manifestations of the impersonal, frantic pace of the city, the coldness of which was visually represented by Boris Aronson's metallic set, which used elevators to connect isolated segments of a skeletal structure. The songs do not attempt to advance the "plot," but rather are used (in Sondheim's words) "in a Brechtian way, as comment and counterpoint." Although not to everyone's taste, *Company* still ran for 700 performances and turned a small profit.

Such was not the case with the next Sondheim–Prince collaboration, the ambitious *Follies* (1971), which sought to examine memories and actuality, dreams and reality, hopes and disappointments. Set at a party for veterans of old revue series on the eve of their theatre's demolition, *Follies* juxtaposed past and present, confronting older characters with their younger selves on a set through which walked huge ghostly figures of a dead glamorous past. William Goldman's libretto examined the various senses of "follies" – the revue, yes, but also the folly of youthful hopes and the folly of dependence on a dead past. Prince assembled actual celebrities from forty or fifty years before, whose age contrasted with the audience memories of them. Sondheim's score combined a disillusioned contemporary lyricism ("The Road You Didn't Take," "Too Many Mornings") and a clever upbeat evocation of the sounds of yesteryear which could become ironic, as when Ethel Shutta, a former beauty now in her seventies, sang "Broadway Baby." The ultimate folly was the opulent "Loveland" sequence, a fantasy in which each of the four principals saw their disappointments in terms of a "follies" number in a gingerbread setting that dissolved as reality reasserted itself. This extraordinary show ran for nearly sixteen months, but still lost its entire investment.

As a result of *Follies'* failure, Prince had to hold backers' auditions for his next project, and both he and Sondheim pulled back their experimental impulses to produce *A Little Night Music* (1973), a bittersweet romance with book by Hugh Wheeler, set in turn-of-the-century Sweden. Based on a film by Ingmar Bergman, the musical took the shape of an elaborate dance of interchanging romantic partners, all set to music that is mostly in variations of three-four waltz time. Musical commentary was again provided, in this instance by an onstage *Liebeslieder* quintet. Popular with audiences and critics alike, it put Sondheim and Prince back on a firm financial footing – and took them back to experimentation.

Pacific Overtures (1976), Sondheim and Prince's "bicentennial" show with a libretto by John Weidman (1946–), was perhaps their most daringly innovative. It told the story of the opening of Japan by the West, but from the Japanese point of view, so that Americans and Europeans were viewed as devils. Within the Japanese culture, the focus lay on the tension between tradition and modernism. To emphasize the point of view, the cast was entirely Asian and, until the last scene, entirely male, in keeping with traditional Japanese theatre. Prince's staging made use of a wide range of staging devices, particularly Kabuki, enhanced by Boris Aronson's brilliant scenery.

26. Construction of the elaborate iron-foundry superstructure (requiring the shoring up of the Uris Theatre's stage) for *Sweeney Todd*, scenery by Eugene Lee, unique among America designers, with his predilection for environmental settings. Courtesy of Eugene Lee.

Similarly, Sondheim's score drew from a wide range of Japanese theatre music, becoming more and more Westernized as the evening progressed. Although the show was highly admired, it was not commercially successful, running less than six months.

Undaunted, Sondheim and Prince returned with another unlikely topic for a musical, *Sweeney Todd, The Demon Barber of Fleet Street* (1979), a musical adaptation by Hugh Wheeler of a Victorian thriller about a demented barber who slaughters Londoners while pursuing the judge who ruined his life. The grotesqueness is furthered by his partnership with a woman who makes meat pies from the bodies of his victims. Prince turned the show into a Grand Guignol parable of the dehumanization of the Industrial Revolution, with a Brechtian chorus narrating the action amid an iron-foundry superstructure. The show is almost entirely sung, and Sondheim's score, incorporating a strong use of leitmotifs, often sets gruesome events and imagery against an ironic lyricism, undercut by dissonant accompaniment (as when a song about cannibalism is scored as a playful waltz). This quirky show horrified some but caught the fancy of many others, and it ran for a year and a half.

Were it not for Sondheim's contribution, the spotty record of the other music-theatre veterans would be even more alarming. The failures of the old guard continued apace in the second half of the decade. Still looking for new partners, both Richard Rodgers – *Rex* (1976) with Sheldon Harnick, *I Remember Mama* (1979) with Martin Charnin – and Alan Jay Lerner – *1600 Pennsylvania Avenue* (1976) with Leonard Bernstein, *Carmelina* (1979) with Burton Lane – had multiple failures. So did Jerry Herman (*The Grand Tour* [1979]) and Charles Strouse and Lee Adams (*A Broadway Musical* [1978]). Marvin Hamlisch, helped by a witty book by Neil Simon, did have a hit with an autobiographical pop-rock show about songwriters, *They're Playing Our Song* (1979), and Cy Coleman, as always a musical chameleon, had two popular shows of wildly different styles: the opulent operetta *On the Twentieth Century* (1978) with Comden and Green, and the inventive *I Love My Wife* (1977), a small show with four actors and four onstage musicians who had to act as well as play, on which Michael Stewart proved himself as excellent a lyricist as a librettist. But the outstanding late-decade conventional hit was Strouse's and Charnin's sentimental *Annie* (1977), a show that pointedly defied the trend toward modernism and sophistication. Advances in the musical notwithstanding, there was life in the old style yet.

The 1980s

After the intense formal experimentation of the seventies, the eighties were a period of retrenchment. Much of this was the result of economics, as ticket prices rose to fifty-five dollars by the end of the decade, and the average cost of mounting even a modest musical on Broadway passed $2 million, while gaudier shows could cost more than $10 million. The trend of revivals continued apace, as did other efforts in nostalgia. A huge hit at the start of the decade was *42nd Street* (1980), an opulent David Merrick stage production of the old movie musical and the last production of director-choreographer Gower Champion, who died on the day of the opening. The success of *42nd Street* led to other attempts to stage movie musicals – *Seven Brides for Seven Brothers* (1982), *Singin' in the Rain* (1985), *Meet Me in St. Louis* (1989) – though none of them approached the success of *42nd Street*. In all instances, the movies had an insufficient number of songs for a stage show, and so the song-writers' catalogues were plundered for extra musical material.

Sequels, More Nostalgia, and Tradition

Other manifestations of the continuing taste for nostalgia were a number of sequels to earlier musicals, like Strouse and Adams's disastrous *Bring Back Birdie* (1981) and *Snoopy* (1982), Larry Grossman's attempt to clone *You're a*

Good Man, Charlie Brown. Another example of a new "old" musical was *My One and Only* (1983), which began as a revival of the Gershwins' *Funny Face* (1927) and ended as a completely new book laden with familiar Gershwin tunes. Both Jerry Herman, in *Jerry's Girls* (1985), and Jerome Robbins, in *Jerome Robbins' Broadway* (1989), crafted Broadway revues of their earlier work.

The old guard continued to falter when attempting new musicals. Charles Strouse had two failures, one with Alan Jay Lerner (*Dance a Little Closer* [1983], Lerner's final show) and another with Stephen Schwartz and Joseph Stein (*Rags* [1986]). Kander and Ebb, with librettist Peter Stone, had a hit in 1981 with *Woman of the Year*, another musicalization of an old film, now made a vehicle for Lauren Bacall, but they also had an underappreciated failure with *The Rink* (1984), a vehicle for Chita Rivera and Liza Minelli. Jerry Herman did have his first hit in over a decade with *La Cage aux Folles* (1983), with a book by Harvey Fierstein. *La Cage* was in many ways a formula Herman musical, but it was notable because it was the first blockbuster musical to deal with gay characters. Audiences were also kept amused by trying to pick the few actual women in the chorus line of men in drag. Of the traditional figures, only Cy Coleman had two hits in the 1980s. *Barnum* (1980), written with Michael Stewart, was blessed with a brilliant production by director-choreographer Joe Layton, who turned the theatre into a circus, and a memorable performance by Jim Dale in the title role. At the end of the decade, now writing with lyricist David Zippel and librettist Larry Gelbart, Coleman had another hit with the jazz-flavored film noir musical *City of Angels* (1989).

Perhaps the most shocking event among the familiar faces was the dissolution of the Stephen Sondheim–Harold Prince collaboration after the failure of *Merrily We Roll Along* (1981). Sondheim's score for George Furth's adaptation of Kaufman's and Hart's play of hope and disillusion told in reverse chronology was masterful. In effect, he deconstructed the score, beginning with restatements of themes not yet heard, so that one heard the fullest development of motifs before their initial statements. The production was cast with unknowns, and Prince's decision to dispense with most scenery and costumes (replaced by labeled T-shirts) gave the show an amateurish look. *Merrily* closed within a week.

After the divorce from Sondheim, Prince's career went into temporary decline. He had two ambitious failures with large musicals composed by Larry Grossman. *A Doll's Life* (1982), with words by Comden and Green, was a complex, operetta-like continuation of Ibsen's *A Doll's House*, narrated by an omniscient chorus. While the score had much to recommend it, the show confused just about everyone and closed quickly at an enormous loss. Prince's next effort was *Grind* (1985), a parable of racial hostility in the thirties set in an interracial burlesque house. Critics noted the parallels to *Cabaret*, and the comparison was not flattering. *Grind* ground to a halt after ten weeks.

Sondheim, on the other hand, moved on successfully. Joining forces with librettist-director James Lapine (1949–), he wrote *Sunday in the Park with George* (1984), a challenging musical on the unlikely subject of the nature of artistic creation. Though Pointillistic music was inappropriate to the story of Pointillist painter Georges Seurat, Sondheim and Lapine effectively created, with the help of Tony Straiges's brilliant design, a Pointillist production, in which melodic phrases, words, and visuals were all seen in isolation before being assembled into a whole. Virtually without dance, the show still flowed seamlessly in Lapine's production, and it won the Pulitzer Prize for Drama. Sondheim and Lapine next turned to the deconstruction of fairy tales in *Into the Woods* (1987). Combining several tales, both traditional and original, in the first act, the second act (as in *Show Boat* and *The Fantasticks*) showed what happens after happily-ever-after, when characters must become accountable for their naive actions. The show ran for nearly two years, six months longer than *Sunday in the Park*.

Michael Bennett returned to form as a master director/choreographer with *Dreamgirls* (1981), a Motown musical centering around the rise of a black singing group amid the cutthroat world of the music business. Written by composer Henry Krieger and author Tom Eyen, both white, the score was electrified by black arranger Harold Wheeler, who gave it its soul. Like *Gypsy*, *Dreamgirls* is a backstage musical, but it is far more complex in its writing. Reflecting the "pop versus soul" division in the music world, songs are introduced and then go through progressive stylistic permutations according to dramatic circumstances. Concentrating on the overall production, Bennett turned the few major dance numbers over to associate choreographer Michael Peters. Bennett choreographed the overall movement, which included several massive light towers which moved like dancers to establish the various locations. With very little spoken dialogue, *Dreamgirls* moved cinematically and showed the art of a master director. But this was to be Bennett's last major show. Although he did work on the London production of *Chess*, he died of AIDS before completing another project. If any evidence of Bennett's importance in shaping *Dreamgirls* were needed, one could note that Krieger's next musical, *The Tap Dance Kid* (1983), was, while pleasant, only a shadow of *Dreamgirls*.

Bennett's mantle as the major conceptualist director-choreographer fell to Tommy Tune (1939–). Tune had first made his mark as a performer, and he has continued to perform over the years. But he began to make his mark as a director in the seventies, culminating in his inventive production of Carol Hall's *The Best Little Whorehouse in Texas* (1978), in which he added such clever devices as using cut-outs to supplement numbers of performers. He entered the eighties with the highly inventive *A Day in Hollywood/A Night in the Ukraine* (1980), including a show-stopping tap-dance number, "Doing the Production Code." But he achieved the top rank of director-choreographers in 1982 with *Nine*, composer-lyricist Maury Yeston's (1945–) and librettist

Arthur Kopit's musicalization of the Fellini film *8½*. In a unit setting of a white spa, a visual tapestry of light and costume served to change the background in a nightmarish way, illustrating the creative and emotional decline of a womanizing film director trying to retain his control of his life and the women in it. Tune showed an endlessly imaginative visual sense in a show that is entirely about vision, while Yeston's ethereal score and clever lyrics suggested an important new voice. Tune would soon fulfill his promise; Yeston would not until he garnered some success in 1997 with *Titanic*.

Tune's next original project was *Grand Hotel* (1989). The show was originally a pre-Broadway failure for Forrest and Wright on the West coast in the fifties. When Tune became interested in a musical of *Grand Hotel*, he sought out their version but decided that he wanted to workshop it. With pianist-arranger Wally Harper at the piano, the cast and Tune evolved *Grand Hotel* in an actual hotel ballroom. When he was not getting what he needed from Forrest and Wright, Tune called in Maury Yeston to amplify the score. The result was a seamless spectacle performed on a unit set with a large orchestra suspended above the action. Chairs were used to define space and barriers, and, evoking *Follies*, a pair of ghostly dancers reflected the action visually. As with *Nine*, *Grand Hotel* became a sumptuous visual feast, its physical production both clarifying and commenting on events.

Another, and Bigger, British Invasion

While Tune and Bennett produced native extravaganzas, the most popular Broadway musicals of the eighties tended to come from London. None were more successful than a series of musicals by Andrew Lloyd Webber. The series began with *Evita* (1979), Webber's final effort with Tim Rice, another story which, like *Jesus Christ Superstar*, examined the price of celebrity. While Lloyd Webber's scores tended to repeat musical motifs without dramatic logic, his melodies were invariably popular, and *Evita*, given a striking production by Harold Prince, had a four-year run. Its success paled next to that of Lloyd Webber's next extravaganza, *Cats* (1982), based on T.S. Eliot's poems. Though the score was, aside from the popular "Memory," undistinguished and the narrative non-existent, director Trevor Nunn and choreographer Gillian Lynne led their actors to a remarkable creation of feline movement, which, wrapped in spectacular scenery by John Napier, has run for almost eighteen years, becoming in June 1997 Broadway's longest running musical. Although a small-cast show called *Song and Dance* (1985), with a one-year run, and a spectacular roller-skating musical, *Starlight Express* (1987), with a two-year run, were less successful, *The Phantom of the Opera* (1988) shows signs of running forever. Once again, the score tends to be musically repetitive and not particularly dramatic, but the production, by Prince and Lynne, is spectacular. While Lloyd Webber has often been accused of a lack of originality ("Memory" is reminiscent of Ravel's "Bolero," while *Phantom*'s "Music of the Night" seems to quote *Brigadoon*'s "Come to Me, Bend to Me"), his power as a popular melodist compensates for a lack of dramatic sense in his music.

Lloyd Webber was certainly not the only British import. Some, like Tim Rice's *Chess* (1988) with a score by ABBA's Benny Andersson and Bjorn Ulvaeus were quick failures. On the other hand, a British production of *Les Misérables* (1987), a semi-operatic French musical by composer Claude-Michel Schonberg and lyricist Alain Boublil, has shown signs of competing with *Phantom of the Opera* for long-run honors.

The development of new American talent has been inhibited by the economic circumstances of the musical theatre. Most have been developed in the insular atmosphere of non-profit theatres and professional seminars. As both *Hair* and *A Chorus Line* were nurtured in Joseph Papp's Public Theater, other musicals have come from regional theatre. The Goodspeed Opera House in East Haddam, Connecticut, has sent fourteen productions to Broadway, among them *Man of La Mancha, Shenandoah*, and *Annie*, while the American Repertory Theatre in Cambridge, Massachusetts, first presented Roger Miller's popular country musical, *Big River: The Adventures of Huckleberry Finn* (1985). Tiny, non-profit Playwrights Horizons in New York developed *Sunday in the Park with George* and all three of the "Marvin" plays of William Finn (1952–) – *In Trousers* (1979), *March of the Falsettos* (1981), and *Falsettoland* (1990) – chamber musicals that chronicle the life and times of a gay man, culminating in the horror of AIDS. Perhaps most characteristic of the development process was composer Alan Menken and author Howard Ashman's *Little Shop of Horrors* (1982). It was originally developed in the BMI Musical Theatre Workshop before being produced at the tiny WPA Theatre in New York. From there it moved to a commercial Off-Broadway production, where it ran for more than five years.

The 1990s

The patterns that took shape in the late eighties persisted into the nineties. Costs continued to rise, and ticket prices by the late nineties had reached seventy-five dollars for Broadway musicals. As a result, only the familiar had much chance of reaching Broadway. This was, to some extent, a boon for the Off-Broadway musical, but there too rising costs and ticket prices (forty-five dollars or even more) precluded much experimentation. Indeed, only the non-profit theatres with healthy subscriber lists could afford to take chances on new writers and daring material. Even then, the results could be catastrophic.

As of this writing, more and more of Broadway's offering are revivals of familiar musicals as old as *Show Boat* (1994) or as recent as *Annie* (1997). In addition to actual revivals, there have been new book shows recycling old songs, like the "new Gershwin musical" *Crazy for You* (1992); new revues recycling old pop-hits, like the Mike Leiber–Jerry Stoller *Smokey Joe's Café* (1995); and sequels to old musicals, like Carol Hall's *The Best Little Whorehouse Goes Public* (1994). The trend of staging familiar movie musicals has continued as well, with Disney's *Beauty and the Beast* (1994), Henry Mancini's *Victor/Victoria* (1995), and Rodgers's and Hammerstein's *State Fair* (1996), typically with scores fleshed out either by new songs or recycled songs from other sources. Familiar non-musical movies continue to be musicalized, like Jule Styne's last musical *The Red Shoes* (1993), with lyrics by Marsha Norman, or Neil Simon's adaptation of his own *The Goodbye Girl* (1993), with a score by Marvin Hamlisch and David Zippel. Yet another nostalgic Broadway success, albeit imported from the La Jolla Playhouse in California, was a staging of Pete Townshend's sixties "rock opera" *Tommy* (1993), already familiar from the original recording and the Ken Russell movie.

British imports continue at a similarly torrid pace. Andrew Lloyd Webber had a failure with *Aspects of Love* (1990), but also what appeared to be a hit with his own adaptation of a familiar film, *Sunset Boulevard* (1994), both with lyrics by Don Black, though the latter closed in 1997 without breaking even. Some British imports have been a disappointment – like the nostalgia-laden *Buddy* (1990), a musical biography of Buddy Holly, or Willy Russell's *Blood Brothers* (1993) – but Schonberg's and Boublil's *Miss Saigon* (1991), a modern pop-rock retelling of *Madama Butterfly* set in Vietnam, proved a major success, if not so great a success as *Les Misérables*. One of the most curious London imports was Kander's and Ebb's *Kiss of the Spider Woman* (1993), with a book by Terrence McNally. The show was originally produced in 1990 at the State University of New York at Purchase, in what was to be the first of a series of developmental musicals (a series that was intended to workshop several other titles which eventually found their way to Broadway). Directed by Harold Prince, it drew a great deal of attention, but against the wishes of the producers, it was reviewed and shortly closed, the only show of the intended series to be mounted. Unable to find a producer in New York, the show then went to London, where its success led to a New York production. Even American musicals, it seemed, sometimes had to come from London.

Much of commercial Off-Broadway followed the example of Broadway. There was a string of nostalgic evenings built around familiar popular tunes, like the fifties era *Forever Plaid* (1990) – and even an oldies-filled import from London, *Return to the Forbidden Planet* (1991). But lower costs were also drawing Broadway veterans. *Annie Warbucks* (1993), the second attempt by the creators of *Annie* to produce a sequel, was intended for Broadway, but finances ultimately led to its production Off-Broadway, with smaller cast, scenery, and orchestra. A particularly notable Off-Broadway production was Stephen Sondheim's *Assassins* (1990), with a book by John Weidman, which was produced at Playwrights Horizons. This ambitious musical chronicle of presidential assassins, melding historical melodies with original music, sold out the tiny theatre, but no commercial transfer was forthcoming.

As fewer new musicals opened on Broadway, only rarely were new faces introduced there. A rare successful exception was composer Lucy Simon's *The Secret Garden* (1991) with a book by Marsha Norman, which featured an all-female production team (authors, director, choreographer, and designers). Even established faces often met with failure, including Stephen Sondheim and James Lapine, whose dark, moody *Passion* (1994) lasted barely six months. Of particular note was *Nick and Nora* (1991), with a score by Charles Strouse and Richard Maltby and a book by Arthur Laurents. The opening was repeatedly delayed while changes were made during nine weeks of "previews" at full prices, leading to action by the Consumer Affairs office of New York; there were only nine official performances.

Two original musicals that succeeded in the early nineties were ostensibly biographies of historical figures. In *The Will Rogers Follies* (1991), with a book by Comden and Green, Cy Coleman tried to repeat the formula that had worked in *Barnum*, depicting the life of a showman in the context of the medium in which he worked. Despite a lesser score and historical inaccuracies, the show ran for two and a half years in a gaudy production by Tommy Tune. More substantial if less successful (a fifteen-month run) was *Jelly's Last Jam* (1992), a musical biography of jazz composer "Jelly Roll" Morton, whose music was arranged and augmented by Luther Henderson with lyrics by Susan Birkenhead. In an excellent book by director George C. Wolfe, Morton, on the occasion of his death, is forced to look back over his life and ultimately admit the black roots of his music which he had always denied. Energized by the performance of Gregory Hines, Morton's sordid life became a transcendent experience.

With new voices virtually denied a Broadway debut, the developmental venues assumed ever increasing importance. The strongest new voices in the field were all developed in non-profit Broadway theatre companies. The Public Theater, for instance, workshopped and premiered *Bring in da Noise, Bring in da Funk* (1995), a choreographic tribute to the importance of rhythm and dance throughout African American history conceived and directed by the Public's artistic director, George C. Wolfe, which moved to Broadway the following year. Playwrights Horizons, which had earlier discovered William Finn, also nurtured composer Stephen Flaherty (1960–) and lyricist Lynn Ahrens (1948–), first in *Lucky Stiff* (1988) and then with the successful calypso-flavored *Once on this Island* (1990), which moved to Broadway. When

Playwrights Horizons artistic director André Bishop moved to Lincoln Center, he gave Ahrens and Flaherty their large-scale Broadway debut with *My Favorite Year* (1992), a pedestrian blockbuster that failed. Lincoln Center (which has also produced such successful major revivals as *Anything Goes* [1987] and *Carousel* [1994]) and the Public have also been among the non-profit venues that have produced the work of another major new figure, composer-lyricist Michael John LaChiusa (1962–). In such challenging works as *Hello Again* and *The Petrified Prince* (both 1994), LaChiusa has shown the musical talent, the dramatic skill, and the daring to suggest a young Sondheim, but he has yet to have a Broadway production, aside from having provided some "additional material" to Bob Telson's score for Graciela Daniele's production of *Chronicle of a Death Foretold* (1995), another unsuccessful Lincoln Center production. The great Broadway success of 1996, Jonathan Larson's Pulitzer Prize-winning *Rent*, an East Village recrafting of *La Bohème* with an amplified pop-rock score, also began in a non-profit venue, the New York Theatre Workshop. While *Rent* introduced a new voice, that voice was silenced when composer-lyricist Larson (1960–96) died on the eve of the show's original Off-Broadway production.

While *Rent* and *Bring in da Noise* were bringing new audiences into the theatre, the old patterns were persisting. As the 1995–96 season ended, there were fifteen musicals playing on Broadway. Five were British imports by Lloyd Webber or Schonberg and Boublil; three were revivals; three were stage versions of movie musicals; and one was a nostalgic revue. Apart from *Rent* and *Noise*, the only original American musical was *Big* (1996), a musicalization by composer David Shire, lyricist Richard Maltby, Jr., and librettist John Weidman of another popular movie. Despite (or perhaps because of) little or no originality, *Big* closed in only six months (late 1996) with a $10.3 million loss.

As the end of the century approaches, the American musical theatre stands at a crossroads. Broadway has, for some time, only rarely produced original material, relying instead on revivals, British imports, and properties developed in New York's non-profit theatres. The spring of 1997 brought some encouragement. Amid several attempts to recycle familiar music (like *Play On!*, a short-lived adaptation by Cheryl L. West of *Twelfth Night* using Duke Ellington standards, and *Dream*, a revue of songs with lyrics by Johnny Mercer) and yet more revivals (*Annie*, *Candide*), four new musicals opened on Broadway, despite the closing of Andrew Lloyd Webber's latest, *Whistle Down the Wind*, before its Broadway opening. One, Frank Wildhorn and Leslie Bricusse's *Jekyll and Hyde*, had been produced regionally for several years and was familiar through two recordings, but the other three were major new works by old hands. Kander and Ebb's *Steel Pier* died a quick death, but Cy

27. One of the few successful original musicals of the late 1990s created by U.S. artists, though it premiered in Canada and was developed by Canadian producer Garth Drabinsky and Livent, Inc., *Ragtime* was notable for its music by Stephen Flaherty, lyrics by Lynn Ahrens, book by Terrence McNally, direction by Frank Galati and choreography by Graciela Daniele, and spectacular scenery by Eugene Lee, lighting by Jules Fisher and Peggy Eisenhauer, and costumes by Santo Loquasto. "The People of New Rochelle," photograph by Michael Cooper. Courtesy of Livent, Inc.

Coleman's *The Life* (a musical view of the Times Square sex industry with lyrics by Ira Gasman and book by Coleman, Gasman, and David Newman) and Maury Yeston's *Titanic* (book by Peter Stone) won awards and showed staying power.

The 1997–98 season promised even more new musicals. Disney scheduled a live version of their animated film *The Lion King* at the newly restored New Amsterdam Theater, while the Canadian producing giant, Livent, planned to inaugurate Forty-second Street's new Ford Center for the Performing Arts with the highly anticipated *Ragtime*, with music by Stephen Flaherty, lyrics by Lynn Ahrens, and book by Terrence McNally.[1] Four other new musicals were scheduled. Such a flurry of activity defies the recent drought of originality. But with tickets costing as much as seventy-five dollars, only time will tell whether the American musical theatre will move forward into the new millennium – or became a staid museum, looking backward to a hallowed past.

Notes

1 Editor's note: Although this chapter anticipated the 1997–98 season, its coverage ended with the 1996–97 season. As predicted, however, both *The Lion King* and *Ragtime* proved to be mammoth hits. The former won the Tony for best musical, while the latter won Tonys for music, lyrics, and book. The director of *The Lion King*, Julie Taymor, was the first woman in history to win a Tony for the direction of a musical.

Bibliography: Musical Theatre Since World War II

The literature on the American musical theatre is both vast and erratic, ranging from chatty biography to scholarly academic discourse. Given the volume of material and the limitations of space, this bibliography, which makes no pretense of exhaustiveness, is limited to books, although there is also a wealth of valuable articles on the subject. Space limitations force a number of omissions, notably biographies of performers and a number of reference works. For organizational purposes, this essay will be divided into overviews of the field, structural studies of musical theatre form, biographies of important figures, and histories of individual shows.

There is no definitive analytical history of the American musical theatre. Perhaps the most thorough is Bordman's *American Musical Theatre*, a chronological survey of every Broadway season since 1866 which necessarily sacrifices depth for breadth. More discursive but far less inclusive are Bordman's three narrative histories of the primary subgenres – *American Operetta*, *American Musical Comedy*, and *American Musical Revue* – which, although they consider the present, focus more on the pre-1945 musical theatre. Another indispensable history is Stanley Green's *The World of Musical Comedy*, organized by composer and lyricist. For illustrations as well as text, no serious student can ignore Gottfried's two coffee-table volumes, *Broadway Musicals* and *More Broadway Musicals*. Other useful general histories include two works by the iconoclastic, acid-tongued, and insightful Mordden: *Better Foot Forward* and *Broadway Babies*. A depressing but essential examination of the economics of the musical theatre is provided by Rosenberg's and Harburg's *The Broadway Musical*, which, despite occasional flaws, is an effective look at the state of the musical theatre today.

Several lesser general histories could be added to the list. Ewen's *New Complete Book of the American Musical Theater* offers a wealth of information on individual shows but suffers from chaotic organization. Litton's idiosyncratic 1981 updating of Cecil Smith's classic *Musical Comedy in America* is of interest to those already versed in the field. Suskin's *Opening Nights on Broadway* and *More Opening Nights* quote reviews of practically all Broadway musicals opening between 1943 and 1981 and offer fascinating reading, though the first volume suffers from a lack of analytical commentary by the editor. Splendidly illustrated but textually lightweight are Jackson's *The Best Musicals from Show Boat to A Chorus Line* and Gänzl's *Song and Dance*, both of which devote a good deal of space to British musicals. Mast's *Can't Help Singin'* attempts a study of the interrelationship of stage and screen musicals, but the result is not particularly coherent.

Among more specialized histories, one cannot ignore Woll's *Black Musical Theatre*;

although less than a third of the text deals with the post-1945 musical, the book is invaluable and includes an impressive bibliography. Another essential specialized history is Mandelbaum's *Not Since Carrie: Forty Years of Broadway Musical Flops*. A substantial history of music-theatre choreography is sorely needed; probably the best to date is Kislan's *Hoofing on Broadway*.

The first and still among the best analyses of music-theatre form is Engel's *The American Musical Theatre*, which he followed up with *Words with Music*. Both examine the structure of the musical and ways in which the elements interrelate, although the former is more objective and the latter, while perhaps more far-reaching, is more concerned with pursuing Engel's personal critical agenda. Subsequent analyses of musical theatre form include Frankel's approach to structural analysis, *Writing the Broadway Musical*, which is far more useful than Kislan's *The Musical*, which cannot decide if it wants to deal with history or with structure. Far more effective in combining history with structural analysis is Citron's *The Musical from the Inside Out*, a practical study in the making of a musical with extensive reference to specific examples. Swain's *The Broadway Musical* should be used with caution; it offers extensive musical analysis, but Swain's conclusions are sometimes open to question.

Biographical and autobiographical literature on modern musical theatre figures tends to consist of one or two works on most figures and a virtual library on others. Rodgers and Hammerstein, for instance, are widely represented, from Rodgers's illuminating but at times splenetic and self-serving autobiography *Musical Stages* and Fordin's definitive biography of Hammerstein, *Getting to Know Him,* to several joint biographies, the most recent of which are Nolan's readable *The Sound of Their Music* and Mordden's opulently illustrated coffee-table *Rodgers and Hammerstein*. Lerner and Loewe are represented by Lerner's autobiography *The Street Where I Live*, Lees's joint biographical-critical study *Inventing Champagne*, and Jablonski's recent *Alan Jay Lerner*. An interesting crossover between these two partnerships is provided by Citron's *The Wordsmiths: Oscar Hammerstein 2nd & Alan Jay Lerner*, comparing the two lyricists.

Among the old guard of writers-composers who continued into the postwar era, Cole Porter has probably received the most attention, with Schwartz's *Cole Porter* perhaps the best single source. Bergreen's compendious *As Thousands Cheer* has surpassed all earlier critical biographies of Irving Berlin. No book-length studies of Frank Loesser existed until Susan Loesser's excellent *A Most Remarkable Fella*. Jablonski's *Harold Arlen* supersedes his earlier biography as the only major work on Arlen, and Harold Meyerson's and Ernie Harburg's *Who Put the Rainbow in The Wizard Of Oz?* is the definitive treatment of E.Y. Harburg. Composers' autobiographies include Richard Adler's *"You Gotta Have Heart,"* Jerry Herman's *Showtune*, and Marvin Hamlisch's *The Way I Was*. Theodore Taylor's *Jule* remains the only full-length study of Jule Styne, while McKnight's unreliable *Andrew Lloyd Webber* has been surpassed by Walsh's substantial, lavishly illustrated *Andrew Lloyd Webber*. Stephen Sondheim's work has been well covered. Zadan's *Sondheim and Co.* remains the best popular source, followed by Gottfried's *Sondheim*; both are splendidly illustrated. Among scholarly works, Banfield's remarkable critical analysis *Sondheim's Broadway Musicals*, while less accessible to a non-musician, is far more substantial than Gordon's *Art Isn't Easy*.

Apart from the shocking lack of a monograph on Jerome Robbins's music-theatre contributions, directors and choreographers have been better represented in print. Loney's *Unsung Genius* is the sole book devoted to Jack Cole, but it is definitive. In the healthy list of books by and about Agnes de Mille, a good starting point would be

Easton's *No Intermissions*, despite some irritating errors. George Abbott is represented by his entertaining autobiography *Mister Abbott*. Harold Prince's early autobiography *Contradictions* is indispensable, while his entire career is covered in Ilson's scholarly *Harold Prince* and Hirsch's less "academic" *Harold Prince and the American Musical Theatre*. Of the biographies of Bob Fosse, Gottfried's definitive *All His Jazz* is vastly superior to Grubb's *Razzle Dazzle*, though the latter has its merits, notably some excellent photographs. Apart from books devoted to *A Chorus Line*, Michael Bennett's work is covered by Mandelbaum's *A Chorus Line and the Musicals of Michael Bennett* and Kelly's *One Singular Sensation*.

Among books chronicling the making of *A Chorus Line*, based on interviews with company members, *On the Line* by Robert Viagas and others is superior to Flinn's *What They Did for Love*. Other specific shows have been the subjects of individual books, some by major participants, including Willson's *But He Doesn't Know the Territory* on *The Music Man*, Charnin's *Annie*, and Larry L. King's *The Whorehouse Papers*. Among secondary works are Farber's and Viagas's *The Amazing Story of The Fantasticks*, Nassour's and Broderick's *Rock Opera* on *Jesus Christ Superstar*, Altman's and Kaufman's *The Making of a Musical* on *Fiddler on the Roof*, Dunn's *The Making of No, No, Nanette* (1972, dealing with the revival), Isenberg's *Making it BIG*, and a series by Garebian including *The Making of My Fair Lady*, *The Making of Gypsy*, and *The Making of West Side Story*. Christopher Davis's *The Producer* chronicles the productions of *Oh! Calcutta!* and *The Rothschilds* from the perspective of producer Hillard Elkins. On the seminal *Hair*, cast member Lorrie Davis's *Letting Down my HAIR* is far superior to Horn's utterly inadequate, error-filled *The Age of Hair*. Virtually all of Broadway's most recent extravaganzas have generated coffee-table books, among them Behr's *The Complete Book of Les Misérables* and (with Steyn) *The Story of Miss Saigon*, Perry's *The Complete Phantom of the Opera* and *Sunset Boulevard*, and Jacobs's *The Who's Tommy*. A less in-depth but broader look at the making of successful shows can be found in Laufe's *Broadway's Greatest Musicals*.

5

Directors and Direction

Samuel L. Leiter

Introduction

The end of World War II did not instantly create a revolution in American stage direction, but it would not be long before radical new developments began to affect the field. During the early postwar years Broadway remained the principal source of all important American theatre activity, but it would soon find its eminence threatened. The major directors of the day were, for the most part, veterans with established track records, although several were younger men and women who would quickly assume command in the staging of both straight plays and musicals. Before long, realism – the dramatic theatre's mainstay in 1945 – would be countered by various forms of theatricalism, choreographers would assume the director's mantle, the invisible director would be rivaled by the auteur, and the director's white male hegemony would be challenged.

This chapter looks at these developments in a roughly chronological order. In most – not all – cases, directors are mentioned or discussed in sections covering the period during which they first began to make their mark, even though their work continued into later decades. In the 1945–1960 section, the names of new postwar directors mentioned, but not discussed, are accompanied by the year of their first Broadway production (see also Kliewer, Chapter 9, Volume 2).

1945–1960: The Shifting Landscape

Although advances continued in the integration of effects in musical theatre, few unusual steps were being made in the progress of dramatic staging, still largely confined to the theory that the best direction is invisible, an approach that works best in realism. Experimental theatre generally meant experimental (chiefly European) dramaturgy, not directing. During the immediate

466

postwar years avant-gardism usually suggested poetic drama with coterie appeal, as in the plays staged during the fifties by Judith Malina and Julian Beck (discussed below; also in Carlson, Chapter 2, "Alternative Theatre"). Their Living Theatre, and other progressive groups and individuals, found their roots, not on Broadway, but in the alternative, non-commercial (at first) concept of Off-Broadway, and in smaller venues elsewhere that, under the pressure of architectural and economic circumstances, began to abandon the proscenium for innovative audience–actor relationships. Furthermore, American cities that had long been denied live theatre started to make a home for it again.

As before, some commercial directors focused on straight plays, others on musicals, and a few were at home in both. New plays continued to benefit from the direction of old guard members, who were joined by several substantial postwar competitors, including Martin Ritt (1946),[1] Joseph Anthony (1948), Alan Schneider (1948), Daniel Mann (1950), Arthur Penn (1956), and Lloyd Richards, who became the first black mainstream director when he debuted with Lorraine Hansberry's *Raisin in the Sun* (1959).

Although some tended to do serious plays, and others comedy, most were unconfined to any genre. There were those (Morton DaCosta [1948] and Abe Burrows [1951] among newcomers), who also included musicals in their bailiwick. Few choreographers also directed, although the future was foreshadowed when Agnes de Mille took on both the dances and the book for *Allegro* (1948).[2] A number of popular directors were also playwrights, although most were from the prewar period. Several were leading actors: joining them were Hume Cronyn (1949) and Burgess Meredith (1950). Only rarely would a director also be his own designer. Several powerhouses produced as well as directed.

The best classical revivals could usually be attributed to British-born actor-directors, but a new generation of American-born classicists would shortly dash onto the scene. England's Peter Brook (b.1925) began his influential American career in 1951, and would regularly return with plays old and new, usually in remarkable interpretations. Also joining their more experienced countrymen (like Noël Coward and Tyrone Guthrie) in placing their English feet in the New World were frequent visitors such as Peter Glenville (1949), Tony Richardson (1957), Peter Hall (1957), and Australian-born Cyril Ritchard (1952). Most continentals regularly directing in New York were working there before 1945.

Margaret Webster, one of the few prominent prewar female directors, very slowly began to see more of her gender challenge the patriarchal system. The greatest impact of women directors in the early postwar years was in reviving the regional theatre: The pathblazers, whose contributions are discussed in LoMonaco, Chapter 2, "Regional/Resident Theatre," were Margo Jones in

Dallas (1947), Nina Vance in Houston (1947), and Zelda Fichlander in Washington, D.C. (1950).

In 1959, the acceptance of directing as an established profession was recognized when, largely through the efforts of Shepard Straube, the directors' union, the Society of Stage Directors and Choreographers, was founded.

The Realistic Director

The dominant mode of postwar acting and directing, known as "the Method," was based on the American adaptation of Konstantin Stanislavsky's actor-training system, filtered through the lens of the Group Theatre of the thirties. In 1947, this system was enshrined at The Actors Studio. The Method's focus on inner truth, discussed in more detail in Chapter 6, became a lodestone for American actors. The Studio eventually created a Directors' Unit in 1959, but it was an intermittent affair, secondary to the Studio's concerns with actors.

The Method's outstanding directorial exemplar was Studio co-founder Elia Kazan (b. 1909). This Group alumnus[3] climbed to success in the late forties with emotionally powerful, psychologically incisive stagings of the most exciting new dramatists, Arthur Miller and Tennessee Williams. Kazan, an Anatolian Greek born in Turkey, gained acclaim for several pre-1945 stagings, but his true fame was postwar, when he presented a remarkable string of preeminent dramas, including Miller's *Death of a Salesman* (1949) and Williams's *A Streetcar Named Desire* (1947), as well as major works by other contemporaries. These were linguistically rich plays touching on compelling issues. Tiring of the Broadway rat race, Kazan joined Robert Whitehead as co-artistic director of the new non-profit Lincoln Center Repertory Company, where he began by staging Miller's *After the Fall* (1964). At Lincoln Center, as noted in the "Broadway" section of Chapter 2, Kazan proved incapable of mastering either premodern drama or the institution's bureaucracy. He departed to make films and write fiction.

Kazan gained a reputation for urgency, rapid pace, and psychological depth. Although his actors were still essentially realistic, he began to move the theatre toward a more theatricalist expressiveness by placing them within impressionist settings, combining external realism and psychological symbolism. A good example is Jo Mielziner's skeletal setting of a Brooklyn house, combined with scrims and dramatic lighting, to evoke Willy's state of mind in *Death of a Salesman*. Music, sounds, light, and thematically pregnant staging united to create emotional, atmospheric potency.

Kazan normally demanded considerable revision from his writers, most notoriously when he had Williams completely rewrite the third act of *Cat on a Hot Tin Roof*. This led the initially complacent, but later annoyed, dramatist to eventually publish both versions so that the reading public could judge the differences for themselves.

Stanislavsky influenced most young directors of the day, some, like Joshua Logan (1908–88), actually having met the Russian master. Logan's postwar career pushed him to the top of the commercial ladder, with comedic, dramatic, and musical hits. One of his outstanding achievements came in Richard Rodgers's and Oscar Hammerstein II's musical *South Pacific* (1949), where Logan's revolutionary staging employed almost no dancing and demonstrated a then novel scenic continuity suggestive of cinematic technique. If dramatic theatre direction like Kazan's was inching toward the theatricality of musicals, musical productions like Logan's were slowly moving toward the seriousness of dramatic theatre. Logan was often criticized for gilding the lily by overproduction, yet, no matter how theatrical his work, he always believed in making his directorial presence undetectable. Elaborate settings that used real water for rain or on-stage pools conveyed his taste for the spectacular, a Broadway tendency which only increased as technology improved.

New Directors and Arena Staging

Crowd-pleasing, Method-despising conservatives like George Abbott watched warily as a new school, led by men like Alan Schneider and José Quintero, took control. These recruits saw their mission from a deeply personal artistic point of view, and viewed Broadway and its prosceniums as only one of several possibilities. Schneider (1917–84), born in Russia, made his first Broadway impact in 1953 with a commercial potboiler, but would become the preeminent American director of the plays of Samuel Beckett, and would be as closely linked with Harold Pinter and Edward Albee. Schneider was the thinking spectator's director, preferring elusive, poetically ambiguous work to the instantly accessible. Directors like Schneider were in growing demand as a result of plays associated with the so-called "Theatre of the Absurd," which employed non-rational dialogue, non-linear plots, abstract characters, and other Surrealistic touches. Still, Schneider insisted on the mantle of invisibility, referring scornfully to the opposite type as the "colored lights" school of directing.

Much of Schneider's work was linked with Fichander's Arena Stage. Fichander (b.1924) was one of the forward-looking postwar leaders who realized the exciting possibilities of theatre viewed by an audience surrounding the action. Fichander and Margo Jones, who began using an arena in Dallas in 1947, proved that spaces originally designed for other, non-theatrical purposes, could, with a relative minimum of expenditure, be converted into a new and, in this country, rarely tried, type of staging, requiring minimal scenery and focusing on the actors and the play.

Off-Broadway was equally congenial to Schneider, who first directed there in 1958, and who worked at other regionals as well. His career epitomized the peripatetic mixture of commercial and non-commercial, New York and regional, that would become the mark of an ever increasing number of postwar directors, making their careers in the face of dwindling Broadway opportunities and the simultaneous burgeoning of other venues.

Panama-born Quintero (1924–99) also made his first impression as an arena director, his opportunity coming in a Greenwich Village nightclub converted to the 270-seat Circle in the Square Theatre, which he co-founded in 1951. Quintero – and the newly reborn Off-Broadway – came to wide attention in 1952, when he directed the unknown Geraldine Page in a revelatory revival of Williams's previously unsuccessful *Summer and Smoke*. The playwright with whom he came to be most closely associated, Eugene O'Neill, was already dead when Quintero produced his powerful revival of *The Iceman Cometh* (1956), only moderately well received in its 1946 premiere. So effective was Quintero's evocation of O'Neill's goals that the playwright's widow gave Quintero the rights to commence a series of brilliant O'Neill revivals (and the Broadway premiere of the posthumous *Long Day's Journey into Night* [1956]) that resuscitated the late dramatist's reputation. The director felt a spiritual and emotional bond with the dramatist that allowed him, he believed, to experience much of O'Neill's own pain.

The Shakespearean Revival

The fifties witnessed other forms of theatre that would entice directors and further shift the national theatre landscape. One was the Shakespeare festival, an idea with two successful amateur antecedents dating from the thirties. The concept was jolted to professional distinction in the mid-fifties when Joseph Papp (1917–91), soon aided by the perceptive Shakespearean staging talents of Stuart Vaughan (b.1925), started what became the New York Shakespeare Festival (NYSF, 1954), ultimately a multipurpose enterprise providing outlets for all types of theatre, on and Off-Broadway. It was followed a year later by the American Shakespeare Theatre, in Stratford, Connecticut, one of whose first artistic directors was Bucharest-born John Houseman (1902–88). By the nineties there were over eighty such companies, summertime and all year round, with numerous directors specializing in or devoting large portions of their careers to classical revivals. The productions were often radicalized versions of Shakespeare that attempted to fill the plays with contemporary relevance or directorial ingenuity, while others were more traditional, emphasizing fundamentals such as good acting, unified ensembles and design, and the communication of the author's (not the director's) story.[4] Shakespearean revivals were increasingly on the menus of more eclectic regionals, while periodic infusions of the Bard on Broadway, usually with twenty-one-gun star power in the leads, continued.

The type of Shakespeare production that was evolving was likely to gain attention by the transposition of periods, or by the abandonment of "pictorial" staging in favor of simplified methods designed not only to move the scenes along swiftly, but to bring the action closer to the audience, as when John Houseman had Donald Oenslager build ramps and platforms into the orchestra pit for his 1954 Phoenix staging of *Coriolanus*. Soon, this return to minimalist Shakespeare would include a rough-hewn, politically charged quality encouraged by the style pioneered at the Berliner Ensemble, which made an influential visit to England in 1956. Directors who could provide resourceful revivals were soon in great demand, and visiting Britons, like Guthrie, Douglas Seale, and Michael Benthall, joined American specialists like Jack Landau, Allen Fletcher, Papp, Vaughan, and Houseman.

One of the most theatricalist – and internationalist – of Shakespeareans, England's Guthrie (1900–71) often brought his idiosyncratic perspectives to America. In 1963, he founded Minneapolis's Tyrone Guthrie Theater, still among the most distinguished of resident theatres, which opened with a striking modern-dress staging of *Hamlet*. At both Stratford, Ontario, and Minneapolis, Guthrie and designer Tanya Moiseiwitsch created architecturally challenging stages that provided thrust stages with permanent scenic facades that could be decoratively adapted for most plays. As with the arena, such stages forced directors to learn entirely new ways to handle the movement of actors and scenery. Guthrie was the master of such stages, filling them with boldly choreographed movement, dynamic activity, and spectacle, being particularly adept at the handling of crowds. His productions were known for their unexpected bits of business, rapid pacing, and the textual liberties he took to wrestle the classics into shape for a contemporary audience.

The Director-Choreographer Appears

One of the most momentous postwar developments took place in the musical theatre, where choreographers began to direct. Major musical directors now contended with geniuses like Jerome Robbins, Gower Champion, Bob Fosse, and Michael Kidd (1956). As Ethan Mordden notes in *Broadway Babies*, "By putting the dancers and actors together, under one hand, a musical could try for a unity it too seldom had in the past, in which everyone on stage would do everything as if in one feint, one profile" (165). The creations of these new superstars – whose power was such that they even claimed partial royalties for the libretto, to which they may not have contributed a word – eventually overshadowed those of the writers, and their names drew audiences as readily as once had Rodgers and Hammerstein. Dance, incorporated into situational acting as well as into production numbers, was on view almost continually, and dancers were given more individualized personalities than before.

Jerome Robbins (1918–98), originally a dancer, had been a pathbreaking choreographer of both musicals and ballet. He first joined directing to his art in *Peter Pan* (1954) and, when he staged *West Side Story* (1957), the program carried the phrase, "Conceived, Directed and Choreographed by Jerome Robbins." With this success, in which the family rivalries of *Romeo and Juliet* were metamorphosed into urban gang warfare, Robbins trailblazed the "concept" musical, in which the director's vision tied all elements together in a unified style supportive of the theme, both in musical and non-musical parts. Dance became essential as a means of textual elucidation and character revelation, and good dancers had to be good actors. Robbins did only two more major musicals before he returned in the mid-sixties to the world of ballet.

His most immediate successor was Bob Fosse (1927–87), who, like Robbins, had revealed brilliant choreography in George Abbott-directed shows. Fosse brought his razzle dazzle style, evolved as a way of making the best of his own physical limitations, to the total staging of *Redhead* (1959), starring his then wife and frequent collaborator, Gwen Verdon. The slouching, angular, loose-jointed, knock-kneed, derby-topped, splay-fingered Fosse manner, with vividly sensual female dancers, enlivened some of Broadway's most memorable concept musicals, many of them dealing with social outcasts, such as *Chicago* (1975).[5]

Dancer-choreographer Gower Champion (1918–80) arrived as a director-choreographer in 1960, when he charmed with *Bye Bye Birdie*. Less stylistically distinctive than Fosse or Robbins, his various flops were outweighed by the wide popularity of such light – but inventive – shows as *42nd Street* (1980), on the afternoon of whose premiere he died of a rare disease (see Maslon, Chapter 2, "Broadway," for details).

1960–1970: The Fragmented Landscape

Broadway continued to produce worthwhile theatre despite rapidly rising expenses and an ever more alienated youth culture that was turning its back on the bourgeois traditions associated with the Great White Way. Some new directors, like Gene Saks (b.1921) – adept at both musicals and Neil Simon comedies – could still make a career as purveyors of populist fare. The theatre's energies, however, were expanding in numerous other directions. The regional movement, given a blast of energy by the huge sums now being dispensed by the Ford Foundation (from 1959) and the National Endowment for the Arts (from 1965), as well as by state and local arts councils and private and corporate philanthropy, saw magnificent playhouses springing up nationwide, sometimes before there was a policy to guide them. Less financially blessed enterprises were arising in unexplored corners, especially in Off-Off Broadway, located mainly in the Lower East Side, or East Village, of New York. Here, hundreds of new artists began to remake the American theatre in their own image. As the experimental theatre bloomed, many directors who would not be caught dead on Broadway rose to prominence.

Off-Broadway

Off-Broadway – gradually becoming a less expensive Broadway – offered additional opportunities. Method-influenced, Belgian-born Ulu Grosbard (b.1929) was one of the few important directors to leap from Off-Broadway to Broadway without a company affiliation. On the other hand, German-born Mike Nichols (b. 1931), originally part of a famous comedy act, began his rise to commercial directing success by staging Simon's *Barefoot in the Park* (1963) on Broadway, and then switching to Off-Broadway for his follow-up hit, *The Knack.*

Off-Broadway became as much a participant in the non-profit movement as did cities in the heartland. It had gained celebrity as a congenial home for non-commercial companies dedicated to an artistic ideal. (The notion quickly caught on in other cities.) Of those new Off-Broadway companies devoted to the work of the playwright, the most conspicuous was the Circle Repertory Company, co-founded in 1969 by director Marshall W. Mason (b.1940), who, aided by the dramas of another founder, Lanford Wilson, established a reputation for a style of "lyrical naturalism" that gave the Circle Rep a special distinction.

The Non-profit Regional Theatre

Off- and Off-Off Broadway became principal starting places for most state-of-the-art directing careers, many of which then became the bedrock of the non-profit regionals. One of the major directorial notions for which the non-profits became a testing ground was the idea of playing freely with theatrical space and audience placement, so that the arrangements varied according to the needs of each play. This "environmental theatre" approach, pioneered in the experimental theatre by directors like Richard Schechner[6] (discussed below), became part of the artistic arsenal of several resident directors, especially Robert Kalfin (b.1933) at the Chelsea Theatre Center (1965) – located for a period in Brooklyn, New York – and Adrian Hall (b.1928), first artistic director of Providence, Rhode Island's Trinity (Square) Repertory Company (1965). At

Trinity, Hall developed a permanent troupe and created a number of innovative stagings, not only of established fare and classics, but of controversial new works on then generally taboo subjects, such as homosexuality and abortion. Projects developed from literary sources – a growing practice in resident companies – also joined his repertoire. For a brief period, Hall ran, with minimal success, two geographically distant regional theatres, Trinity and the Dallas Theater Center. Understandably, no other director has attempted this.

With their growing success, the non-profits began to see their better productions optioned for Broadway or other commercial venues. This created an ongoing debate concerning the potential compromising of artistic integrity when directors chose material showing potential for profit-making exploitation. Still, some companies might not have survived had this course not been followed, especially as outside funding began to diminish.

With companies appearing everywhere, residencies as "artistic directors," for varying durations, were established. Although most artistic directors move on, by their own or board of directors' choice, these can be lifetime jobs: Hall remained at Trinity until 1989; Arvin Brown (b.1940) ran New Haven's Long Wharf Theatre from 1965 to 1996; Jon Jory (b.1938), famed for his development of new plays when most regionals were focusing on revivals, has been at the Actors Theatre of Louisville since 1969; and Gordon Davidson (b.1933), whose sometimes documentary-style productions often have revealed a commitment to social and political problems, has overseen Los Angeles's Mark Taper Forum since 1967. Freelancers – many of whom held occasional leadership posts at regionals – spent nearly as much time traveling as plying their trade.

Ethnic Diversity

The more traditional theatre also benefited from the experiences provided by Off-Off Broadway (which spawned similarly oriented communities and groups nationwide), both in terms of the directors nurtured there, as well as in the ideas appropriated from it. Thus Paul Sills's Story Theatre, developed improvisationally by a collaborative group under Paul Sills's (b.1927) eye, became a Broadway hit in 1970. At the same time, the politically sensitive era provoked the growth of ethnically diverse theatre activity, and national focus came, for example, to Asian American groups, like East West Players, founded in 1965 in Los Angeles, and to African American companies, such as the Negro Ensemble Company, founded in New York in 1967.

Important directors emerged from these companies, especially the black ones. Most have focused on African American subjects. Douglas Turner Ward (b.1930), for example, a writer as well as actor and director, was intimately associated with the Negro Ensemble Company, of which he was a co-founder. Woodie King, Jr. (b.1937), also multitalented, founded the New Federal

Theatre (1970) at New York's Henry Street Settlement House, which continues to produce plays reflecting local audiences' concerns. Leading a phalanx of black women directors was Vinnette Carroll (b.1922), whose career took off with her creation of the "song play," vibrantly theatricalist works combining uplifting African American subjects with rousing gospel music. Her work as head of New York's Urban Arts Corps from 1968 helped nurture the talents of many black artists and, with composer Micki Grant, she created two Broadway musical hits of the seventies. Lloyd Richards (b.1923) has been artistic director of Connecticut's National Playwrights Conference – where new plays are developed – since 1968, headed the Yale Repertory Theatre from 1979 to 1991, and is the premier regional and Broadway director of August Wilson's plays of African American life.

Hispanic American theatre and its directors also began to gain notice with the establishment in 1966 of the Puerto Rican Traveling Theatre, still run by Miriam Colón (b.1935); the Repertorio Español, co-founded in 1968 by René Buch (b.1925); and El Teatro Campesino, an activist political group founded in 1965 by Luis Valdez (b.1940) among the Chicano farm workers of California – and discussed by Carlson in Chapter 2, "Alternative Theatre."

New Trends

During the sixties, directors of all races began to struggle not only with issues of ethnicity, sexuality and gender, and political beliefs, but to handle challenging techniques, profanity, nudity, audience participation, sexual behavior, and cross-gender and cross-racial casting.[7] Female directors were still struggling for recognition, and would have to wait a bit before substantial numbers grabbed the limelight.

Classical staging was not immune from the new trends, and American directors like Gerald Freedman, Stephen Porter, Ellis Rabb, Jack O'Brien, William Ball, and Michael Kahn, and frequently visiting British directors, such as Brook and Michael Langham, offered new insights into Shakespeare and other standard dramatists (most of these men also worked with important modern material). Most were often active in the non-profit sector, frequently making their niche as artistic directors of leading companies. Although not yet noticed for the classics, England's Jonathan Miller and John Dexter joined already mentioned compatriots in becoming mainstays of the serious American theatre.

Musicals

The American musical continued to blossom under the ministrations of the director-choreographers. The only non-choreographing director able to match their brilliance was Harold Prince (b.1928). A successful producer at an early age, Prince moved into directing with *She Loves Me* (1963), and thereby furthered the cause of the concept musical. Although he has staged straight plays and operas, he is indelibly associated with musicals. Beginning in the seventies he gained acclaim for a series of outstanding collaborations with lyricist-composer Stephen Sondheim – dealt with in Chapter 4 – and then with England's Andrew Lloyd Webber. In addition to these works, wherein song and story were ever more intimately blended, he offered landmark revivals, often bringing to the commercial stage the innovations of experimental theatre. His 1974 *Candide*, for example, was staged in Brooklyn's intimate Chelsea, with an environment that mingled audience and actors. Transferred to Broadway, the uptown playhouse's interior had to be thoroughly reconfigured to allow for the same audience–actor relationship. The range of Prince's styles and the depth of his material was untouched by any other musical director of his time.

Experimentalists and Ensembles

The influence of French theorist Antonin Artaud and his "Theatre of Cruelty"[8] was being felt in avant-garde quarters, but made its first great impact in Brook's explosive version of Peter Weiss's *Marat/Sade* (1964), a visiting production which employed many methods soon to be familiar in American experimental work. With the freedom from commercial constraints allowed by the birth of Off-Off Broadway, where plays could be put on in basements, coffeehouses, lofts, and factories, some directorial creations challenged the very definition of what was generally considered theatre. The "Happenings" movement of the sixties, for example, dispensed with a prearranged script and allowed chance to govern the outcome of what was more a theatre "event," "piece," or "project" than a scripted play. Similarly, numerous cutting-edge artists felt that the traditional theatre hierarchy was too redolent of out-moded thinking, and chose to abandon the conventional role distribution of actor, writer, designer, and director, preferring instead the collaborative or collective approach of the "ensemble." However, specialized skills could not always be hidden and, for all the ensemble input, the work was normally associated with some individual's directorial talent. For many, the rehearsal process was even more important than the final product – some plays began with actors doing warm-up exercises – and theatre often became the search by a band of devotees for a holy artistic grail.

Directors, sometimes driven by political and social concerns, sometimes by aesthetic ones, sought new methods of communicating states of consciousness, new ways to work collectively, new ways of configuring space, and new ways to remind the audience that they were part of a theatrical, not illusionistic, experience. Directorial "invisibility" was being replaced by works bearing the unmistakable signature of a group or individual style.

The Living Theatre's founders, Julian Beck (1925–85) and the German-born Judith Malina (b. 1926), created a theatre that, throughout the fifties, epitomized the bohemian avant-garde (their work, along with other alternative groups, is discussed in more detail earlier in this history). The Becks, pacifist anarchists and political activists, had focused at first on low-budget stagings of poetic plays by Gertrude Stein, García Lorca, Jean Cocteau, and the like. The company, influenced by Artaud, had an Off-Broadway hit with Jack Gelber's *The Connection* (1959), in which the audience was made to feel that the event was not a play but an actual occurrence in which drug addicts were waiting for their fix. In 1964, the communally organized company, consistently harassed by government agencies, moved to Europe. It returned in 1968, when student radicalism and anti-war fervor were at fever pitch and stirred enormous controversy with such company-developed pieces as *Paradise Now* (1968), using minimalist settings in which actors wore next to nothing, confronted spectators in the auditorium, mixed improvisational with scripted portions, and allowed the audience to mingle with it physically on stage and even to dictate the course of the action.

The Open Theatre was also organized on collective principles but its output during its 1963–73 existence was widely regarded as due to the inspiration of actor-director Joseph Chaikin (b.1935),[9] formerly a Living Theatre member. The company, begun with only the intention of exploring its mutual acting interests, had to be persuaded to show its work publicly. Under Chaikin's guidance, the actors, usually working in an improvisational fashion to develop their material with a resident dramatist, created a number of remarkable, non-linear, thematically rich works in which they played multiple roles through a process called "transformation," based on rigorous training exercises and improvisation.

Also inspired by Artaud, as well as by the "poor theatre" ideas of the late Polish director Jerzy Grotowski[10] (a Beck influence, as well), was Richard Schechner (b.1934) – critic, scholar, and editor of *The Drama Review*. Schechner moved to the forefront of the sixties' experimental theatre after he founded The Performance Group, a company ensconced in a garage in lower Manhattan until it dissolved in 1980. Spokesman for theories about the nature of the theatrical event – especially its relation to ritual – Schechner advocated environmental theatre. Actors were free to mingle with the spectators, and the latter were sometimes encouraged by Schechner himself to move around and view the action from different perspectives. Probably the best known of Schechner's collectively created works was his radical updating of *The Bacchae*, *Dionysus in '69* (1968). Schechner propounded his ideas while teaching at New York University, where other important experimentalists also were fostered, including Andre Gregory, associated with the Manhattan Project, and Leonardo Shapiro, of the Shaliko Company.

A prime objective of most experimentalists was increased focus on the actors' contributions, but German-born Peter Schumann (b.1934) moved in a different direction by putting his unique combination of small and oversized, naively crude yet beautiful archetypal masks and puppets – built by the company itself – at the center of his art. Schumann – producer, director, designer, writer, composer, and puppet- and mask-maker – considers theatre a religious or ritualistic event, yet an entertaining one, and uses his folk art-like productions to promote ideas of peace, good will, and sharing, signified by the act of passing home-baked bread around among actors and spectators. The company shares a commitment to a simple life style mirrored in the deceptively simple, yet emotionally powerful, morality play-like stagings it often does mainly in public venues like parks and streets.

Most of the work – often called Theatre of Images or Theatre of Visions – for which auteurs Robert Wilson and Richard Foreman are famous uses the actor as only one element in an inscrutable, personalized vision of reality. The usually apolitical Wilson (b.1941), considered by some the greatest living American director, began creating theatre in 1968. He has spent most of his career in Europe because his expensive productions have been unable to generate appropriate financial support at home. His work since the eighties has included exceptional rethinkings of well-known classics and moderns, but he is best known for conceptually unified, dream-like creations stemming from his own teeming visual and aural imagination (he often serves as his own designer). Wilson combines interests in painting and psychotherapy to develop often lengthy (twelve hours, in one case), phantasmagoric events using hallucinatory lighting, visionary sets and costumes, extraordinarily slow motion, whirling dances, mechanical scenic devices, both small and huge casts, enigmatic images linked by some thematic core (such as Albert Einstein in *Einstein on the Beach* [1975]), and unconventional music (often by Philip Glass or Tom Waits) and sounds (including language as sound rather than meaning). Much of the work, in which the director himself sometimes appears, has sought to express the special perceptions of the deaf or brain-damaged.

Richard Foreman (b. 1937), who has staged traditional works and several original musicals, is best known for his non-narrative, autobiographically derived works – which he writes, stages, composes, and designs – created under the auspices of Off-Off Broadway's Ontological-Hysteric Theatre (1968). At the sixty-seat loft theatre he opened on downtown Broadway in 1975, he offered spectacles set on a raked, tunnel-like stage. Foreman creates tableaux of actors and scenery in surrealistic images, using props and people to play perspective tricks on the eye. A standard Foreman work includes Alice in Wonderland effects using well-drilled, almost robotic, actors (originally, most were amateurs) who assume odd, cubistic, gravity-defying tableaux, often staring directly at the audience; inanimate objects take on a life of their own;

unexpected sound effects (including a loud buzzer) surprise the audience; the director remains visible and audible at one side, narrating and manipulating the events, surrounded by sound and lighting equipment; taped speech and effects interrupt the actors; written comments are viewed on projections; the lighting is mostly ungelled; tautly drawn strings break up the picture into tension-laden force fields and geometrics; and nudity is prevalent. All is intended as a reflection of Foreman's internal creative states, and, as in Wilson's projects, the audience must sift out meanings and feelings (often jarred by Brechtian estrangement devices) for itself, although his later work has proved increasingly accessible.

Tom O'Horgan (b.1926), at home with musicals and plays, epitomized the conceptualism of the sixties avant-garde as translated to the work of others. Hoping to create a communal atmosphere similar to a religious experience, he stressed fourth-wall smashing, imaginative, closely choreographed, sometimes acrobatic action over text and verbal expression. First given the opportunity to make waves Off-Off Broadway, O'Horgan brought his taste for exaggerated theatricality to Broadway when he reconceived Gerald Freedman's production of the rock-musical *Hair* (1968), and converted it into a Broadway hit that introduced uptown audiences not only to the radical life style of its characters but to a revolutionary way of doing musicals. It was played on an essentially bare stage with actors singing into handheld mikes, and with the songs (O'Horgan had jettisoned the script in favor of having the entire show sung) tied together more by theme and character types than by story. O'Horgan's production, with its trap door entries, in-the-aisle and on-the-proscenium numbers, and dimly lit nudity, made conventional musicals look like something from another planet. No other major experimentalist of the period was in as steady demand on Broadway, that is, until O'Horgan's commercial career – which at one time saw four of his shows on Broadway simultaneously – slackened following the extravaganza-like rock opera *Jesus Christ Superstar* (1971).

Although he had a definite theatrical agenda, Charles Ludlam (1943–87) was unlike others in that his aim was to debunk artistic pretension and to create laughter. He founded Off-Broadway's Ridiculous Theatrical Company in 1967 after breaking with the similarly inclined Playhouse of the Ridiculous. Serving as playwright, director, and leading actor, Ludlam provided many parodistic, high camp, gay-oriented, pop culture-based romps in which gender confusion was a frequent theme, made palpable by cross-gender casting in which he himself often dressed in drag. For all the exaggerations, the staging and acting were conventional, if exaggeratedly broad, for here was theatre of laughter that did not pretend to expand the boundaries of performative aesthetics. Unlike the practice in other troupes, Ludlam considered words highly, although the source for much of his language stemmed from actors' improvisations.

1970–1980: The Multicultural Landscape

During the seventies, most of the trends established in the previous decade intensified, and many directors who by then had begun to make their mark blossomed into leading figures. Avant-garde breakthroughs were gradually absorbed into the commercial mainstream. The nation's shifting political and demographic changes led to an explosion of interest in theatre's multicultural possibilities, with directors presenting not only black and Hispanic, but Native American, gay, feminist, Asian American, and other "marginal" viewpoints. Within this maelstrom of social change, women finally began to firmly establish their directorial presence. Forced by economics to diversify, most mainstream directors – male and female – became surprisingly eclectic, but some leaned more toward new plays, while others were best known for the classics. Although classical stagings were occasionally noted for their postmodernism, directors by and large adhered to a policy of serving the playwright's intentions more than their own, at least in the treatment of new plays. Several directors remained predominantly commercial, and, with their clout, could earn millions from a Broadway hit. A few vital new black directors gained notice – Harold Scott, Oz Scott, Michael Gates, and Claude Purdy among them – but most did not gain the far-reaching acclaim of their predecessors in the sixties.

The majority of new plays were subjected to workshop development, including staged readings, and the director's work was augmented by the expanded employment of dramaturgs, a European practice that stimulated renewed attention to the text and to new play development in non-profit theatres.[11] Although some playwrights found the process abusive, workshops were generally considered an important way for directors to link up with playwrights, and several director–dramatist alliances became significant. There were fewer new nationally prominent avant-gardists than in the sixties, but several did reach the level of that decade's great experimentalists, all of whom reached new heights in the seventies.

Women Directors

The unprecedented surge in women directors, some of them founding and/or running their own companies, was primarily Off-Broadway and in the regionals. This group, representing an ethnic rainbow, included Lynne Meadow (artistic director of the Manhattan Theatre Club since 1972), Julianne Boyd (former President of the directors' union), Elizabeth LeCompte (artistic director of the Wooster Group since 1975), Susan Einhorn, Elizabeth Swados, Shauneille Perry, Tisa Chang (artistic director of the Pan Asian Repertory

Theatre since 1977), Linda Mussman (artistic director of Time and Space Limited), Elinor Renfield, JoAnne Akalaitis, Maria Irene Fornés (also a renowned dramatist), and star actresses Geraldine Fitzgerald and the late Colleen Dewhurst.

Each made stunning contributions, especially those with strongly conceptualist tendencies, such as Akalaitis (b.1937). A co-founder of Mabou Mines, the renowned avant-garde collective, she provided often controversial, sometimes politically slanted productions ranging from her hyperrealist version of Franz Xaver Kroetz's *Request Concert* (1980), to her anti-nuclear power, multimedia collage *Dead End Kids* (1980). In her postmodern classical revivals, multiple, often anachronistic, visual and auditory effects create a non-integrated impression from which each spectator may draw different conclusions. Her rejection of Beckett's wishes for *Endgame* (1984), which she set in an abandoned subway, at Cambridge, Massachusetts's American Repertory Theatre, landed her in the thick of the decade's most talked-of director–author dispute. Akalaitis briefly succeeded Joseph Papp at the NYSF.

Foreign Directors

Great foreign directors appeared with regularity. The most influential of the new English directors regularly showing their wares locally was Trevor Nunn (b.1940), whose eight-hour staging of *Nicholas Nickleby* (1980) sparked a surge of dramatized novels. Eventually, he would provide New York (and elswhere) with blockbusters that helped move Broadway musicals toward over-reliance on scenic gigantism and technological wizardry. (Such operatic effects, including hundreds of lighting cues, have infected even regional revivals of Shakespeare.)

Meanwhile, a group of Romanians came to the U.S. during the decade, most noticeably Andrei Serban, Liviu Ciulei, and Lucien Pintilié, each of whom displayed an inventiveness that helped further jar the American theatre loose from its realistic preoccupations. Serban (b.1943), beginning Off-Off Broadway, staged a series of extraordinary classical revisionings, including a version of Chekhov's *The Cherry Orchard* (1977) at Lincoln Center that dispensed entirely with interior walls and set the play – indoors scenes and out – on a vast, white carpeted space, with highly selective pieces of furniture, so that the play's human relationships, which proved highly comic, could stand out in sharp relief. In assuming the leadership of the graduate acting program at Columbia University in 1992, he represented a trend that has touched many top American directors: partly because of the instability of the profession, they have accepted professorial positions at important universities and conservatories, directing only when their schedules allow.

Broadway Careers/Regional Masters

The other leading new directors were – like many already mentioned – a varied group, who went wherever the work was, sometimes stopping to run a theatre for several years, and bringing outstanding work to audiences throughout the nation.

Some would be inextricably associated with Broadway, where opportunities continued to shrink. Michael Bennett (1943–87) and Tommy Tune (b.1939), for example, continued the director-choreographer revolution begun by Robbins and Bennett, the latter most notably with *A Chorus Line* (1975), the best example of a production developed from a non-existent script during months of workshops. Tune became the first director to win Tonys for both direction and choreography in two consecutive years (*Grand Hotel*, 1989; *Will Rogers Follies*, 1991). Doing both plays (mostly comedies) and musical revivals to Broadway applause is Jerry Zaks (b.1946), a director in the fast-paced, gag-filled Abbott tradition.

Many new directors dominated because of their distinguished guidance of a regional theatre: for example, Robert Falls (b.1954) at Chicago's Wisdom Bridge (until 1985) and Goodman Theatres; Garland Wright (1946–98) at the Guthrie until the end of 1995; Des McAnuff (b.1952) at the La Jolla Playhouse; and Mark Lamos (b.1946) at the Hartford Stage Company until 1998 (the departure of several of these and others indicates a trend of the nineties, with regional directors becoming freelance artists, often working more frequently in New York). Most ranged freely through the repertoire, moving easily from the classics to the moderns. Wright, for example, was as successful staging a musical comedy as a play about the Holocaust or a classic by Molière. Critic Don Shewey praises these eclectics – especially Robert Woodruff, Lamos, Wright, McAnuff, and Adrian Hall – for their ability to "see text-oriented naturalism and visual-oriented non-naturalism as aesthetic choices rather than ideologies – who patch up the rift between Stanislavsky and Meyerhold, so to speak" ("A Boot in Two Camps," 14). Interestingly, conceptualist Elizabeth LeCompte argues that these directors are not really "inventing new work. They're just rehashing old plays . . . The problem begins with how you stage it, and ends with how you stage it." She contrasts this with the open-ended creativity of work such as hers. "We're making art, not just interpreting it" (quoted in Berson, "Keeping Company," 71).

New Visions

While certain avant-gardists already described continued to test new ideas, while auteurs like Akalaitis moved into the non-profit mainstream, and while advanced ideas never stopped influencing the great eclectics, there was still room for innovators, perhaps the most renowned being Lee Breuer, Elizabeth LeCompte, and Ping Chong. All are responsible for multimedia, interculturally rich, intellectually provocative presentations.

Breuer (b.1937), another co-founder of Mabou Mines, draws influences from various international sources, such as Grotowski. He has studied in India and Japan, and regularly employs ideas from these countries' traditional theatres. Breuer's work includes startlingly novel versions of classics such as *Oedipus at Colonus*, which he adapted as *The Gospel at Colonus* (1988) in the context of a rousing black Pentecostal Church service. He is also famed for the multileveled works he has either created collaboratively or written himself, such as the epic-sized *The Warrior Ant* (1989).

LeCompte (b.1944), heading the small Wooster Group since 1979, began her work with the introspective, autobiographical ruminations of Spalding Gray. Her controversial company offended many and lost funding when their use of blackface – an attempt to force the audience at *Route 1 & 9* (1981) to confront its own racism – was misinterpreted, and they upset Arthur Miller when they subverted the text of *The Crucible* in their *L.S.D.* (1983). LeCompte develops the company's work over lengthy rehearsal periods, and the material remains in a constant state of evolution before the troupe takes on a new project. These non-linear, non-representational, densely textured works make use of found objects, pornography, electronic media, and various other intriguingly manipulated elements.

Ping Chong (b.1946), the first Asian American (he was actually born in Canada) to become nationally known as a director, also makes considerable use of media effects in futuristic, non-narrative works that typically confront the theme of "otherness" and the "outsider," in terms of both individuals and cultures. He has often collaborated with dance-theatre conceptualist Meredith Monk, but is best known for his work with the Fiji Company (now the Ping Chong Company), founded in 1975. His beautiful, thoughtful stagings are, like those of his fellow avant-gardists, considered postmodern because, among other things, they allow each element to express its own discrete point of view rather than to be merged in a conventionally unified artwork.

1980–1996: The Theatricalist Landscape

During the century's closing decades, numerous talented new directors achieved eminence, though space allows for the mention of only a few here. Most deepened and enriched the traditions they inherited, while a handful gained recognition for bending the theatre into ever new and surprising shapes. Some playwrights, such as Edward Albee, Romulus Linney, Sam Shepard, and David Mamet frequently handled their own plays – sometimes openly revealing their distrust of other directors – and stars like Kevin Kline, Gary Sinise, Estelle Parsons, and Joanne Woodward expanded their horizons by guiding other players. A few important writers, like James Lapine and George C. Wolfe, made waves not only by staging their own literary creations, but by directing the work of others. As before, certain directors – at least for several years – became joined at the hip to specific playwrights. One of the only such partnerships in which a director allows the writer to communicate with the actors or to "co-direct" is the long-existing one between Marshall W. Mason and Lanford Wilson. Such collaborations would appear to muddy the current debate concerning whether directors should be entitled to the same copyright protection for their ideas as playwrights enjoy for theirs.

The national push for diversity and multiculturalism continued to bear fruit for women and racial minorities. A new generation of female directors joined their already present sisters to effectively challenge the profession's male dominance, many of them – like Sharon Ott, Anne Bogart, Elizabeth Huddle, Carole Rothman, Carey Perloff, Josephine Abady, Tina Packer, and playwright-director Emily Mann – leading the nation's principal non-profits. Other women who gained recognition included Liz Diamond, Martha Clarke, Pamela Berlin, Argentina-born Graciela Daniele (one of the few emerging director-choreographers in commercial musicals), Gloria Muzio, Tina Landau, Pat Brown, Julie Taymor, Amy Saltz, Susan H. Schulman, and Mary Zimmerman. This unparalleled burst of female artistry even produced a body of theory focused on "feminist directing" (see Donkin and Clement, eds., *Unstaging Big Daddy*).

Meanwhile, important directors from non-white constituencies appeared, including Benny Sato Ambush, Ricardo Kahn, Tony Curiel, Tazewell Thompson, Kenny Leon, and George C. Wolfe. Yet racial diversity did not lead to racial equanimity. Some, like dramatist August Wilson, argued that whites could not direct black plays, and the number of blacks staging non-black plays remains small. Still, Ambush has asked, "Why not hire competent ethnic directors to direct not just ethnic plays at white theatres, but also the sacred cows from the traditional Euro-American repertoire?" ("Pluralism to the Bone," 5).

The New Revolutionaries

Attention must be paid to a handful of revolutionaries who have burst the theatre's seams. Like almost every other contemporary theatricalist, African American director-dramatist George C. Wolfe (1955) has borrowed Asian techniques, most notably his Japanese Noh-influenced adaptation of Zora Neale Hurston stories, *Spunk* (1990). Wolfe's meteoric rise as a director is attributable to his magnificent staging of black-oriented material, hit Broadway musicals, and mainstream white drama, modern and classical, including Brecht and Shakespeare. He acknowledged his role in the production of Tony

Kushner's monumental, two-part *Angels in America* (1993): "I think it was the first time in the history of Broadway that a black director had directed a major play that was not about people of color on Broadway." Yet he believes that his ethnicity helped him to bring a racial "signal" to a play that was "very much about sexual orientation" (quoted in Morales, "Theatre and the Wolfe," 20).

Iranian-born, London-educated Reza Abdoh (1963–95), who, like a number of other brilliant directors, died of AIDS, also brought to his productions a sense of who he was in American society, but, while Wolfe appeals to a broad audience, Abdoh's anger erupted in out-of-the-way, environmental spaces for risk-taking audiences. His multilayered, abstract, dream-like plays, such as *The Law of Remains* (1992), which he himself largely wrote for his Los Angeles-originated Dar a Luz ensemble, combined raucous, live and electronic images, and sounds of death, sex, and violence in fragmented, environmentally conceived, non-linear multimedia collages that raged at various topics on the post-AIDS American landscape. John Bell notes that, for all Abdoh's postmodernist tendencies, the ferocity of his convictions removed him from the cool neutrality considered a postmodernist marker ("AIDS and Avantgarde Classicism," 21).

Martha Clarke (b.1944) and Julie Taymor (b.1952) have an equally visionary view of theatre, although theirs, despite a layer of subversive intent, is generally more benign and principally devoted to aesthetic values. Clarke is a dancer-choreographer who has put her movement skills to unusual use in crafting abstract, often lyrical, music-dance-theatre pieces of rare beauty, in works such as *The Garden of Earthly Delights* (1984), inspired by Bosch's painting, in which actors in nude bodysuits and flying gear floated about the space. These works are evolved by Clarke and her company over long periods of intense but constantly changing collaboration.

Taymor is at the forefront of interculturalists whose work is pervaded by the influence of Asian theatre. A trained mime, she spent years studying and working in Indonesia, and developed a unique style – using actors and grotesque or recognizably human puppets and masks – that led to her designing for others as well as co-designing her own projects, which may be originals or classics, staged with methods ranging from realism to ideographic acting using mime and dance, and employing music in abundance. A master puppeteer and craftswoman, she is a total theatre artist, and, with works such as *Juan Darién* (1988, restaged 1996) and *The Lion King* (Tony for Best Direction, 1998), created some of the most exceptional works of the era.

Anne Bogart (b.1951) has compiled an impressive record of postmodern revivals and ensemble-style, often dance-inclined, creations. She, too, has felt the influence of the East. In fact, she and Japanese director Tadashi Suzuki run the Saratoga Theatre Institute, in Saratoga, New York. Her deconstructed versions of familiar works, frequently used to touch on politically oriented themes, are typified by her approach to the musical *South Pacific* (1984),

28. *The Adding Machine* (Elmer Rice) as directed by Anne Bogart at Actors Theatre of Louisville (January 1995). With William McNulty and Ellen Lauren. Photograph by Richard Trigg. Courtesy of Actors Theatre.

which she used to comment on war and racism by framing the action within a veterans' mental institution where the patients perform for therapy. She is a devotee of site-specific performances, often using unusual spaces (including apartments or the street) to test the boundaries of the audience–actor relationship. Bogart combines music, song, speech, choreographic movement, and gesture in frequently epic-scale productions that require immersion in her singular, collaborative rehearsal methods, called the "Viewpoints." Among Bogart's impressive re-examinations of standard plays are Clare Booth Luce's *The Women* (1992), while her premieres include Charles L. Mee, Jr.'s *Another Person Is a Foreign Country* (1991), staged in an abandoned gothic-style nursing home.

Equally at home with old plays deconstructed from a postmodern, multicultural vantage point, and Asian-influenced, anti-realistic techniques, is Peter Sellars (b.1957), once American theatre's *enfant terrible.* Sellars is always capable of disturbing audiences, especially with the most familiar materials. For example, his *The Count of Monte Cristo* (1985), at Washingon, D.C.'s short-lived American National Theatre, mingled Brechtian and expressionistic styles with Wooster Group techniques, playing a duel in darkness with the audience hearing only whispered words, mining the text for hidden political or social themes, and, via deliberate anachronisms, upsetting those hoping for a more conventionally melodramatic presentation.

Conclusion

Mike Nichols once said that "Directing . . . is one of the few professions you can practice without knowing what it is. Fifty percent of the job is just showing up" (quoted in "Briefly Noted," *American Theatre* 8 [December 1984], 32). This facetious remark has been belied by many American directors who know precisely what they are doing, and have moved onto a plateau – often equal to or surpassing that shared by the great figures of world theatre. Each new generation brings new types of theatre, and new kinds of artists. Many in the current generation may not share racial or gender similarities with those of earlier decades, but they have demonstrated how much America has lost by waiting so long to embrace them.

What the best of these directors all seem to be working toward is a way to move the theatre away from the realism it was mired in forty years ago and in the direction of a way to embrace an intense theatricality that is, perhaps, captured by Liz Diamond's description of her goals: "We're constantly shifting back and forth in rehearsal from explorations of meaning and sense to explorations of formal presentation and how we can make our reading of it *pop* – visually, gesturally, orally" (quoted in Pearce, "Liz Diamond," 39). American directing of the future will surely continue searching for that "pop."

Notes

1 Ritt actually directed a revival of Sidney Howard's *Yellow Jack* in New York in 1944, but it was more in the manner of a workshop production, staged for a single performance with fellow military personnel then appearing on Broadway in *Winged Victory.*

2 Louis Jeriel Summers, Jr., claims that the task became so daunting that, in actuality, librettist-lyricist Oscar Hammerstein II ended up directing the book, composer Richard Rodgers the songs, and de Mille only the dances. See "The Rise of the Director-Choreographer in the American Musical Theatre," Ph.D. Diss., University of Missouri-Columbia, 1976.

3 The Group produced three other major postwar directors, Harold Clurman, Robert Lewis, and Lee Strasberg, all of them introduced in Warren Kliewer's chapter on directors and direction in Volume 2.

4 For an excellent account of American approaches to the classics, especially during the seventies and eighties, see Amy S. Green, *The Revisionist Stage.*

5 In 1972, Fosse became the first director to win the triple crown: Oscar, Emmy, and Tony.

6 Environmental stagings were influenced most strongly by the work of Poland's Jerzy Grotowski, whose book *Towards a Poor Theatre* was widely read.

7 Such casting, usually called "non-traditional" or "color-blind," has become one of the modern director's most controversial tools.

8 The seminal work for directors was Artaud's *The Theatre and its Double*. Artaud's ideas inspired experimentation with environmental uses of space, sound as text, use of all the actor's physical resources, deconstruction of texts, the destruction of social taboos, and the use of theatre as a means of affecting the spectator's consciousness.

9 Roberta Sklar claims to have shared much of the directorial credit for the company's work, and believes that the Open Theatre was even infected with a patriarchal attitude that denied a female artist her due. See Brunner, "Roberta Sklar: Toward Creating a Women's Theatre."

10 Grotowski was associated with intimate spaces using varying actor–audience relationships, ritualism, non-verbalism, physical and vocal expressivity, total artistic commitment, and a de-emphasis on technical supporting elements such as costumes, lights, and scenery. See also Chapter 6, *Actors and Acting.*

11 The process of new play development for directors (and the recent drop-off in such activity) is described in Kahn and Breed, *Scriptwork*. There have been several recent attempts to create developmental workshops for directors as well as writers, such as one at Lincoln Center described in Gener, "Put 92 Directors in a Room."

Bibliography: Directors and Direction

One of the signs of increased directorial activity and of interest in the art of directing has been the eruption of books and articles on the subject, especially since the eighties. The standard, albeit dated, collection of documents remains Cole's and Chinoy's *Directors on Directing*, which includes comments by a number of postwar American directors. Other collections, such as Wills's *The Director in a Changing Theatre* and Schevill's *Break Out!*, cover experimental work of the sixties and early seventies. Books with essays on the avant-garde of roughly the same era include Croyden, *Lunatics, Lovers and Poets* and Shank, *American Alternative Theatre*. American postmodernist directing of world classics is the focus of Amy S. Green, *The Revisionist Stage*. Among significant works with narrow directing-related focuses are Schechner, *Environmental Theater*, Donkin and Clement, eds., *Upstaging Big Daddy*, Kahn and Breed, *Scriptwork*, and Whitmore, *Directing Postmodern Theater*.

Works providing essays on famous directors include Leiter, *From Belasco to Brook* and *The Great Stage Directors*, Frick and Vallillo, eds., *Theatrical Directors*, and Bradby and Williams, *Directors' Theatre*. A survey of directors (European as well as American) and techniques is in Albert and Bertha Johnson, *Directing Methods*. Important women directors are described in Robinson, Roberts, and Barranger, eds., *Notable Women in the American Theatre*. Many careers are capsulized in Wilmeth and Miller, eds., *Cambridge Guide to American Theatre* and Bordman, *The Oxford Companion to American Theatre*.

Interviews with directors appear frequently in periodicals, but two interview books are Bartow's *The Director's Voice* and Morrow's and Pike's *Creating Theater*.

Rehearsal methods of selected American directors are examined in Cole, *Directors in Rehearsal*. There is only one American covered in David Richard Jones, *Great Directors at Work*. There is excellent insight into the Broadway domain in Goldman, *The Season*. Much about contemporary American directing may also be gleaned from the essay collections of critics such as Robert Brustein, Walter Kerr, Harold Clurman, Richard Gilman, Eric Bentley, Herbert Blau, Gordon Rogoff, John Lahr, John Gassner, Charles Marowitz, Richard Hornby, and Martin Gottfried, a list of resources too extensive to include here with detailed citations. Gottfried provides material on the great musical directors in *Broadway Musicals* and *More Broadway Musicals*.

Among the many – sometimes biographical or autobiographical – books by and about specific directors whose major work was in the postwar period are Vaughan, *A Possible Theatre*; Clurman, *On Directing*; Brecht, *The Theatre of Visions: Robert Wilson*, the anonymous *Robert Wilson: The Theatre of Images*, Shyer, *Robert Wilson and His Collaborators*, and Holmberg, *The Theatre of Robert Wilson*; Quintero, *If You Don't Dance They Beat You* and Edwin J. McDonough, *Quintero Directs O'Neill*; Logan, *Josh*; Forsyth, *Tyrone Guthrie* and Guthrie's own *A Life in the Theatre*; Davy's *Richard Foreman* and Foreman's own *Unbalancing Acts*; Woods, *Theatre to Change Men's Souls: The Artistry of Adrian Hall*; Kazan, *Elia Kazan: A Life* and Murphy, *Tennessee Williams and Elia Kazan*; Margo Jones, *Theatre-in-the-Round* and Sheehy, *Margo*; Ball, *A Sense of Direction*; Napoleon's look at Robert Kalfin, *Chelsea on the Edge*; Savran's examination of Elizabeth LeCompte, *The Wooster Group*; Schneider, *Entrances: An American Director's Journey*; Robert Lewis, *Slings and Arrows*; Blumenthal, *Joseph Chaikin*; and Blumenthal and Taymor, *Julie Taymor*; Gottfried, *All His Jazz: The Life and Death of Bob Fosse* and Grubb, *Razzle Dazzle: The Life and Work of Bob Fosse*; Kelly, *One Singular Sensation: The Michael Bennett Story*; Hirsch, *Harold Prince and the American Musical Theatre* and Ilson, *Harold Prince*, as well as Prince's *Contradictions*; Epstein, *Joe Papp*; Tytell's study of Julian Beck and Judith Malina, *The Living Theatre*; Dixon and Smith, *Anne Bogart*; and Menta, *The Magic World Behind the Curtain: Andrei Serban in the American Theatre*.

There are several surveys covering narrow periods: see Carra, "The Influence of the Director – for Good or Bad," and Leiter, "Actors, Directors, and Critics." Berkowitz, *New Broadways: Theatre Across America 1950–1980* pays attention to advances over three decades. The overall history of American directing is surveyed in Henderson, *Theater in America*, and major Tony Award-winning directors are treated in Morrow, *The Tony Award Book*.

The most helpful periodicals for director-related articles and interviews include *The Journal of the Society of Stage Directors and Choreographers, Theatre Journal* (formerly *Educational Theatre Journal*), *American Theatre* (cited several times in this chapter), *The Village Voice, Performing Arts Journal, Theatre, Dramatists Quarterly, Theatre Topics, The Drama Review, Studies in Theatre History, In Theater,* and the defunct *Theatre Arts, Players,* and *Theater Week,* although important material often appears in other periodicals, general and academic.

6

Actors and Acting

Foster Hirsch

Background

In the beginning was the Group Theatre. Co-founded in 1931 by Harold Clurman, Lee Strasberg, and Cheryl Crawford, the Group was a young people's theatre dedicated to producing new American plays which illuminated the troubled spirit of the times. Defecting from the Theatre Guild, the Group's leaders designed their new theatre on native grounds. In the twenties the Guild had been America's leading art theatre, but with the advent of the Depression the Group's firebrands had begun to regard it as an elitist, outdated producer of mostly foreign plays. And unlike the Theatre Guild, which claimed the no-stars policy of a repertory company but nonetheless frequently featured the Lunts as headliners, its leaders envisioned the Group as a true company united by political convictions and molded into an ensemble through the common study of a specific acting technique. In its approach to actor training the Group has had a profound and enduring impact on the formation of what has come to be known as the American style.

For Clurman and Strasberg the concept of an ensemble tightly bound by its immersion in a particular approach to actor training was sparked by the visit to New York in 1923 of Stanislavsky's renowned Moscow Art Theatre. Having been instructed in his system by Stanislavsky himself and having worked together over long rehearsal periods on plays, like those by Chekhov, which had been written especially for them, the troupe performed in a radiant style: realism lit by a remarkable depth and unity. When two members of Stanislavsky's company, Richard Boleslavski and Maria Ouspenskaya, remained behind to teach the principles of Stanislavsky's system, Strasberg, Clurman, and others who were to join the Group attended their courses at the American Laboratory Theatre. It was the wisdom of Stanislavsky, as filtered through the instruction (and the accented English) of Boleslavski and Ouspenskaya, which the Group's leaders wanted to impart to their new company.

Before the Group convened in 1931, it is fair to say, as Watermeier notes in Volume 2 (Chapter 7, *Actors and Acting*), that actor training in America had been random. Actors might have been schooled in a local stock company, or attended an acting institute such as Steele MacKaye's Lyceum Theatre School or Franklin Sargent's American Academy of Dramatic Arts, or simply depended on intuition and luck. No teacher or school before the Group brought to the study of acting the rigor, the passion, and the idealistic commitment the Group's fired-up young performers were to demonstrate. In the end, Harold Clurman's call for American plays of political and literary distinction elicited a disappointing yield: *Waiting for Lefty, Awake and Sing!*, and *Paradise Lost*, all written by Group member Clifford Odets in a vivid vernacular poetry, were the theatre's most significant contribution to American drama (see Murphy, Volume 2, Chapter 3, "Plays and Playwrights: 1915–1945"). But in its intense focus on actor training the Group was the single most important institution in the history of acting in America.

How do actors act? How can actors induce a creative mood? How can they summon and recreate "true" emotion? How can actors make their roles real to themselves and thereby inspire the spectator's belief? What kind of creative contribution can actors make to the playwright's dialogue and characters? In pursuing answers to these questions – the great primary questions first formally posed by Stanislavsky – the Group had seismic rows. At the center of the arguments was Lee Strasberg, the company's self-appointed coach. Stubborn, prickly, authoritarian, and emotionally masked, Strasberg was a scientist of acting, fascinated by the mysteries of the actor's quest for true emotion. And in a technique called affective memory, which Boleslavski had demonstrated at the American Laboratory Theatre, Strasberg believed he had found a reliable aid for achieving it.

At a certain point in his role an actor, for example, must respond to the death of a loved one, yet the actor remains unmoved: how can he arouse the feelings he needs to play the scene? Using the affective memory technique he focuses on an analogous experience from his own life, but instead of trying to force the emotion directly the actor is trained to reconstruct for himself details of place, time of day, weather, dress, and smells – the sensory reality which framed the charged event. Strasberg claimed that if properly recreated the memory would evoke the emotion – grief at the death of a family member – which the actor could then channel directly into the scene. What Strasberg prized about the technique was that the actor would be using true emotion – his own reawakened real-life feelings – to color and deepen his performance.

Strasberg cautioned Group actors to turn to past rather than recent events and to rely on the technique sparingly and only when the play's circumstances failed to ignite their response. But he assured the actors – it was a promise he continued to make for the rest of his life – that if they had chosen well the memories they had used, the technique to recreate would always produce the reaction they needed. (He also claimed that with practice emotions could be ignited in a minute.) Maintaining that the technique was the surest way of achieving the style of psychological realism the Group was searching for, Strasberg placed it as the foundation of his work. When some of the actors resisted, arguing that the exercise was painful, that it encouraged a potentially dangerous narcissism and introspection, and that it stole the focus away from work on their characters and the play, Strasberg became more insistent. There were frequent clashes, but the first major challenge came in 1934 when Group member Stella Adler returned from Paris after having studied with Stanislavsky.

Adler had told Stanislavsky that his system, at least as it was being interpreted by Strasberg, wasn't helping her. She worked with Stanislavsky intensely for six weeks and by the time she returned to New York, she announced to the Group in her forthright manner that she had the Master's word that they weren't using his system properly. "Stanislavsky doesn't know, I know!" Strasberg bellowed.[1] With this impassioned legendary exchange the Great Divide over affective memory, a debate which continues up to the present, was formally inaugurated. On one side were Strasberg and his adherents, on the other were gathered the naysayers led by Adler. To Strasberg's increasingly strident claims for the efficacy of the technique, Adler answered with a corresponding fervor that it was "poisoned water."

The fractious atmosphere continued to escalate until Strasberg departed in 1937. Members began to drift away to pursue individual careers, and, although Clurman did not formally disband the company until 1941, much of its initial resolve had long since eroded. Regardless of their differing opinions of Strasberg, however, Group actors were united in their commitment to developing a performing style of psychological revelation based in a secure and systematic technique. And from the crucible of the Group's debates over how to achieve truth in acting emerged America's most influential teachers.

The Actors Studio

In the fall of 1947 three Group alumni – Elia Kazan, Robert Lewis, and Cheryl Crawford, who once again assumed fund-raising responsibilities – founded The Actors Studio. Unlike the Group, the Studio was not intended to produce plays; nor was it to be, strictly speaking, a school or an institute. Rather, it was to be (and has remained) a workshop, a place where actors could tinker with their instruments (that is, themselves) apart from the pressures of the commercial theatre.[2] The Studio was set up to be a protected environment where specially selected actors could work on craft problems.

29. Acting teacher/guru Lee Strasberg conducting a class at The Actors Studio. Courtesy of the Private Collection of Anna Strasberg.

In the first year Robert Lewis taught an advanced class while Kazan worked with a hand-picked group of younger, less experienced actors. In both classes actors were instructed in elements of the Stanislavsky system which had been dissected and fought over in the Group. (Admission to the Studio's first season was by invitation; thereafter, membership has been granted through auditions. General auditions are open to anyone; those who pass the general audition then appear before a council of elders who make a final selection. Once admitted, actors are members for life and never have to pay any fees.)

Absent from the Studio's initial roster was Lee Strasberg, who since his departure from the Group had had a spotty career as a director and coach. A would-be theatrical lawgiver without a throne, he had become a marginal figure. At the time the Studio was founded, Kazan by contrast was the most successful director in America, sought after on Broadway and in Hollywood, who had already acquired a reputation for his extraordinarily skillful work with actors. Kazan, in fact, was far too busy to be able to meet his classes at the Studio on a regular basis. When Robert Lewis resigned at the end of the first year, Kazan needed to hire a teacher who did not have the demands of a successful career to contend with, and he turned to the man he had overlooked in the first place.

Strasberg began to work at the Studio in 1949 and remained on the job until his death in 1982. As the guru of West Forty-fourth Street, where the Studio has been located, in a former Quaker meeting hall, since 1955, Strasberg shaped an ensemble of exercises which formed the basis of the Method. The heart of the Studio became the two-hour sessions on Tuesday and Friday when actors would bring in work which Strasberg would comment on. Speaking in a flat, untrained voice, Strasberg was prolix and pontifical, a most unlikely orator who nonetheless for nearly forty years captured the attention of some of the best actors in America.

Strasberg's abiding, indeed obsessive concern was with the actor's impediments to arousing and expressing emotion. Theoretically, it was his position that if an actor was not blocked in creating a fluid emotional expressiveness, then he or she did not need the Method; but in fact Strasberg never seemed to encounter an untrammeled actor. His focus on extracting emotion may well have sprung from his own chilly temperament: with his masked face, his narrow, suspicious eyes, and his toneless voice, he was forbiddingly unyielding. Actors struggled to elicit the trace of a response from him, and rarely succeeded. Assisting actors, decade after decade, to break through their emotional impasses may have been a way for Strasberg to avoid confronting his own.

Over the years Strasberg devised a series of exercises to unleash the actor's creative spirit. In addition to the controversial affective memory, Strasberg worked with actors on improvisations, private moments, animal and song and dance exercises. In the private moment, along with affective memory the most criticized element of Strasberg's approach, the actor is charged with recreating an activity he would perform at home, in private, behaving as if he were still at home rather than at the Studio. Training actors to be private in public, the exercise may have aroused expectations of impropriety, but in fact neither the moderator, professorial as ever, nor the actors used the private moment as a chance to shock or transgress. The animal exercise requires actors to substitute an animal for the character they are working on, and then to explore its movements and gestures. In the song and dance exercise, which became a way of identifying sources of physical tension, an actor delivers a song with no extraneous movement permitted. In improvisations actors find their own words, departing from the scene as the playwright wrote it in order to navigate subtext or to create scenes of their own which might have occurred at some point in their characters' past or future.

Concentrating on the actor's creativity, Strasberg had little interest in the playwright's and spent little time in character interpretation or analyzing a play's given circumstances. His exercises constituted a series of warm-ups, of work on self which prepared the actor for his or her ultimate encounter with a script. Because the Studio was expressly designed as a lab where actors worked on themselves apart from the pressures – and the realities – of actual production, Strasberg discouraged members from playing for results: scene work at the Studio was not supposed to be tidy and polished. In coaching actors to be private in public and in helping them to investigate their inner lives, Strasberg focused actors' attention on themselves, on what was happening inside them on stage from moment to moment, rather than on the audience. Working with and for Strasberg it did not matter if actors mumbled or failed to project – not projecting even within the intimate playing space of the Studio was a possible indication that actors were doing the work "correctly," as Lee wanted.

Strasberg did not tell actors to mumble and slouch, and though his critics claimed that he never said it enough Strasberg maintained that in production *of course* actors had to be audible – he regarded matters like volume and diction as technical "adjustments" unworthy of his scrutiny. Strasberg's perfectly reasonable defense was that, at the Studio, actors were not in production and were not working toward professional performance, but quite to the contrary were in a lab where they were examining, adjusting, fine-tuning their instruments.

Studio work was not intended to be a blueprint for a rehearsal technique: this was homework, the kind of preparation actors would undertake on their own. The Strasberg-trained actors who did not adjust their approach from workshop to a rehearsal helped to establish the cliché of the slow-moving, solipsistic Method actor who worries about subtext and motivation and who improvises lines and behavior throughout the rehearsal period and even sometimes during performances.

Training actors to rekindle emotional and sensory memories and to liberate their expressiveness, Strasberg endowed them with a heady sense of their own inner resources, the potential riches within. He taught actors to regard their own lives as a library of experiences, impressions, and feelings that could be reformulated as the raw material of their art. Against a chorus of opposition Strasberg defended the affective memory technique as the surest route to vibrant and truthful acting; the great actors of the past had used affective memory by instinct, he claimed, and he cited its use by Wordsworth and Proust, among others, to substantiate his belief in its universal validity. Some opponents concede that well-trained actors should at least know how to use the technique; other skeptics accept its possible utility as a class or studio exercise while deploring it as a device for revving up actors during a performance. Adamant atheists, however, decry affective memory as a trap, a breeding ground for neurosis. Even some true believers question its relevance as an approach to the classics, pointing to the probable gulf between an actor's life experiences and those, say, of Oedipus or Medea or Hamlet as being too vast to be bridged by an affective memory exercise.

In his search for true emotion Strasberg remained cognizant of the fact that no matter how real it may seem acting is always the construction of an illusion. As his keenest critics are reluctant to admit, Strasberg did acknowledge that acting is a form of trickery, a skillful sleight of hand, in which the performer's materials are always approximate rather than actual. It was his intention to narrow the margin between real life and its theatrical recreation rather than to erase the seams altogether, an impossible task in any case but one he is sometimes accused of undertaking. As Strasberg warned, once actors dredge up their own true emotions they must then monitor and control them: "Hysteria is hysteria," he announced, "and acting is acting."

Other "Schools"

Stella Adler and Sanford Meisner, veterans of the Group's internal conflicts over technique, developed their own systems in response to Strasberg's emphasis on inner work. Adler founded her conservatory in 1949 and continued to be a vigorous teacher until her death at ninety-one in 1992. Meisner directed the Neighborhood Playhouse School for the Theatre for over sixty years and continued to teach until his death, also at ninety-one, in 1996. Both have had a deep impact on generations of students and, perhaps just as significant, on scores of acting teachers who have spread the gospel according to Stella and Sandy. Like Strasberg, Adler and Meisner cultivated an oracular style and leavened their comments with heavy doses of Jewish wit, irony, and sarcasm. All three could be brutal to lazy or untalented students yet to those who had seen, or who they felt were capable of seeing, the light, they offered warm encouragement.

Where Lee Strasberg appeared closed-off, a magisterial *tabula rasa*, Adler was a live wire. Where Strasberg rarely stopped actors working on a scene or exercise, Adler interrupted as soon as she detected a false note. "No, no, no," she would wail as students crumbled under the weight of her disapproval. If Strasberg was a remote patriarch, Adler was an overbearing mother. Personally as well as philosophically at odds, they had always disliked each other; Strasberg rarely referred to his archrival while Adler remained vocal in her opposition. "I don't ever want to see another Method actor: give it all to Lee," she hissed at actors who imitated the scratch and mumble style associated with Actors Studio naturalism. "Don't slouch; sit up; I can't teach you if you sit in such a collapsed way," she'd berate students with slovenly or merely casual deportment. Where Strasberg welcomed the common touch,

Adler bristled when she saw it. "Everything's Hoboken to you," she chided an actor sidling up to a scene in Shaw by being casual and contemporary. "It will take one hundred years to undo the damage this man has caused," she announced to her classes on the day of Strasberg's death.

"Strasberg's continuing belief in affective memory has made him a laughingstock," Adler declared – and she seemed to construct her own method as a riposte to his. "Your talent is in your imagination: the rest is lice!" she would remind her students regularly. Adler had little patience for self-analysis and she urged students to transcend rather than to fixate upon or limit themselves to their own life experiences. "The stage is a platform," she warned, reminding students that the personae they display in this arena are to be built out of their imaginations rather than the scrutiny and "regurgitation" of their own experiences. For Adler the watchword was "size." "The stage is not to be confused with the street," she declaimed, as always aiming an arrow through Strasberg's naturalist aesthetic.

Unlike Strasberg, Adler focused on the text, urging actors to explore the play's given circumstances rather than their own. Her courses on script analysis, like Strasberg's work with actors on an affective memory exercise, became a legendary part of the New York acting scene. Adler was not a scholar and historical accuracy was decidedly not her strength (she maintained, indeed, that theatre scholars know more about the plays than "we do"); her approach was grounded in the actor's point of view, what the actor needs to know about the characters, the world the playwright has created, and the style of the language, in order to play the role. She honored the writer in ways Strasberg never did. "Shakespeare is God!" she intoned, a claim Strasberg would never have made. And in her classes, students were exposed to classic plays and poetic drama as well as to the contemporary realists.

Unlike Strasberg, who himself had an intellectual interest in the history and literature of the theatre but who sternly warned actors against a "mental" approach, Adler did not fear that a little cerebration would blunt or corrupt an actor's instincts. Where Strasberg trained actors to become sensory and emotional wizards, Adler encouraged a knowledge of theatre history and of a playwright's life and world view. At The Actors Studio actors typically confronted a writer's words only after a lengthy preparatory period of inner work, but Adler forced students to honor a writer's language right from the start. At the Studio a frequent, perhaps inevitable, question asked of working actors was what they were trying to accomplish for themselves, whereas with Adler the essential question was how the actor's intentions fused with and served the writer's.

At the Studio "style" has always been a forbidden word. Studio code for an external, lacquered kind of performing, "style" is for the British. Adler, in contrast, often talked about style, warning students that style was applicable not only to the classics but to their own vaunted realism as well. "Realism is the largest, most demanding style of all," she insisted, preaching to students who may have been told otherwise. Regardless of the "style" of the piece the actor was working on, Adler promoted clear speech, projection, and size as unvarying criteria. Quite unlike Strasberg, with his common man way of speaking ("good speech" sounded false to him), Adler spoke (and moved) like American aristocracy. The daughter of renowned Yiddish actor Jacob Adler, Stella was born into theatrical royalty and she exuded the hauteur of a social as well as theatrical *grande dame*. She spoke in a rich, deep, clearly trained voice; she had immaculate diction of the kind that used to be called mid-Atlantic, and she had little patience with actors who sounded like thugs.

Strasberg rarely did any acting for his actors, but Adler frequently got up from her throne to demonstrate. The acting teacher as great performer, she sawed the air with her oversized gestures and her booming voice penetrated into the waiting area and offices outside her classroom. Adler's classes were circumscribed by rituals: there was wild applause on her entrances and exits, which Adler would acknowledge by blowing kisses; periodically she would ask rhetorical questions, as if checking to see that the house was awake, and students would respond with a resounding chorus of appropriate "yesses" or "nos." For a fee anyone could sit in on an Adler class, whereas sessions at The Actors Studio were strictly off-limits to civilians – protocol defined a revealing distinction between these two brilliant, manipulative master teachers.

A regular criticism of Strasberg's sessions at The Actors Studio as well as of Adler's scene classes was their lack of apparent structure: actors would bring in work, at various levels of preparation, to elicit a response from the experts. Sessions were valuable, or not, depending on how Lee or Stella was "performing" that day. Sanford Meisner, the third great acting teacher to emerge from the Group, responded to the need for a more systematic approach by developing a two-year program that has come to be known as (what else?) the Meisner technique. At least in its initial phases, in which actors' concentration is taken off themselves and trained on their partners or their props instead, the technique is staunchly anti-Strasberg. In the crucial repetition exercise, as actors mimic each other's words and phrases over and over, they are forced to make eye contact with their partners and to react to minute changes of mood and inflection. "Don't think, just behave," Meisner admonished. In another early exercise actors are required to work on a demanding physical activity – having to concentrate on putting together the pieces of a smashed plate, for instance, is supposed to elicit the kind of specific, truthful, spontaneous behavior which Meisner considered essential for all good acting.

In Meisner's training actors work on exercises and activities for many months before embarking on scene study. Critics of his method question why scene work is delayed, but Meisner insisted that only after a prolonged period do the exercises become second nature and therefore reliably useful to the working actor. Meisner students are trained to break down scenes into a sequence of actions – to threaten, to warn, to plead, to arouse, to hurt. "Play the action," Meisner urged, "and never, never be cerebral."

Like his Group Theatre colleagues, Meisner was a vivid presence in class. A Zen master who could be ruthless, he was also a wit who could work the room, extracting laughter and applause in the Adler mode. After the removal of a cancerous lung Meisner was forced to speak through a voice box; the effort it took to produce sounds caused him to measure his words carefully, and though he had never been as prolix as Strasberg, infirmity necessitated a terseness which increased his reputation as a legendary teacher who persevered against great odds.

Strasberg often complained that he was misunderstood, and in dark moods he declared that no one fully understood his method; Meisner wasn't so imperious. He was clearer, more direct, than Strasberg, and he was less hesitant in training successors. The Meisner technique is routinely taught in acting schools in New York and across the country. More second and third generation teachers use Meisner's technique than Strasberg's Method, although often enough their training (sensibly) combines elements from both, along with aspects of Adler's approach. Non-partisans recognize that, of course, there are significant areas of overlap among the Big Three and that, while particular elements of their systems differ, they were in pursuit of a similar result: lustrous realistic acting. The legacies of Strasberg, Adler, and Meisner continue to dominate actor training in America.

Uta Hagen, who has conducted classes at the HB Studio in New York (named after her husband, the late actor Herbert Berghof) for five decades, is the one major acting teacher who did not emerge from the Group Theatre. Unlike her predecessors Hagen in class pays no attention to her own iconography. She has a potent presence, but her focus is on the actors rather than herself. As her students work on scenes and monologues she smiles, snorts, guffaws, gasps, frowns, as the case may be; takes notes in the pauses between her full-hearted, uncensored responses; and once the work is completed offers comments in a remarkably succinct straightforward manner. In her clear, wonderfully husky voice she appraises the work using the language of the trade. "You were off circumstances," she might say; "you didn't personalize the objects." She never translates terms and she makes each point one time only. Unlike the Group maestros she doesn't season her comments with quips and barbs; in the best sense, she is impersonal.

Much closer to Strasberg's method than to either Adler's or Meisner's, Hagen regularly enjoins students to work on substitutions from their own lives as a way to fuse with their characters. Any analogous personal event, object, sense memory, feeling from the actor's own experience constitutes an appropriate Hagen substitution – her students are urged to draw on their own lives in a more extensive way than even Strasberg permitted. Hagen students haul bags, cartons, sometimes wagon loads of props to class, and they are expected to have "endowed" their relationship to each and every object with a suitable personalization or substitution. A fervent realist, Hagen frequently asks students to prepare elaborate prior lives for their characters: what is the history of their character's relationships with each character in the play? What is their character's emotional history beginning from early childhood right up through the moment before they enter the play?

Stern but accessible, Hagen communicates an aura of absolute dedication and professionalism. Her presence "endows" acting with significance. It becomes an important labor in which creativity depends on technique and artistry arises from a mastery of craft.

In addition to her high reputation as a teacher, Hagen continues to attract students because of her acting resumé, which includes some of the most notable stage performances of the last half century; among other achievements Hagen succeeded Jessica Tandy as Blanche DuBois in *A Streetcar Named Desire* (1948) and created the title role in Clifford Odets's *The Country Girl* (1950) and Martha in *Who's Afraid of Virginia Woolf?* (1962). As performers, Meisner, Adler, and Strasberg (until his appearance in *The Godfather, Part II* in 1974) were more or less unknown commodities. None had had important roles since their appearances with the Group Theatre, and for generations of students the question of whether their teachers could actually act remained a matter of speculation and myth. Students in Adler's classes would sometimes refer to her performances as the Jewish matriarch in Odets's plays like *Awake and Sing!* and *Paradise Lost*, but of course none of them had seen her work. Meisner and Strasberg could not claim any famous roles they had created and Strasberg had a stronger reputation as a director than as an actor. Acting was something they had done in the past and whether they had been disappointed in their work or had failed outright (as rumor suggested) no longer mattered in light of their dynamic performances in class.

Adler and Meisner seemed at peace with their lackluster resumés, but for Strasberg the tension between coaching and acting, between the protected world of The Actors Studio and the temptations of the commercial theatre a few blocks to the east, remained unresolved. When he appeared in *The Godfather, Part II*, anonymity as an actor was ended. To have accepted the role was in a sense to go public – spectators who knew who he was would regard his performance as a demonstration of the Method delivered by the master himself. Playing a gangster, a man of reptilian cunning, as a benign-seeming Jewish grandfather, he creates a pulsing inner life. His wary eyes and his hushed, guarded voice contain potent suggestions of the menace his

Machiavellian character could unleash. On the strength of his performance – so effective in part because at the time Strasberg was an unfamiliar actor – he became a late-in-life film star. He never again had so rich a role in so strong a film; however, in front of the camera Strasberg was consistently natural. It seemed oddly fitting that this particular acting teacher, America's most famous coach, should also become a famous movie actor.[3]

Art Versus Commerce

Studio members perhaps initially sensed the contradictions in Strasberg's temperament – the pull between art and commerce, between idealistic attention to craft and the pursuit of fame – when Marilyn Monroe first began to attend sessions at The Actors Studio in 1955. For Monroe, the biggest movie star in the world, Strasberg suspended all the rules, allowing a non-member the rights and privileges of full-fledged membership. Lee and his wife Paula attached themselves to Monroe, who was desperately insecure about her talent; they became her acting mentors and, in effect, her surrogate parents. Strasberg told skeptics at the Studio that Monroe had a great natural talent and that with proper training she could play a variety of rich roles in classic and contemporary works. Many members were unconvinced. "Strasberg sometimes confused a disturbance with a gift," as Estelle Parsons has said.

Strasberg had always talked to Studio members in idealistic terms about the actor's responsibility to the art of the stage. Now he was upholding a movie star as the real goods – a movie star who may indeed have been talented but one who had no technique and whose career choices represented the commercialism and self-exploitation Strasberg had traditionally warned against. Many began to feel their leader had feet of clay. Monroe's association with the Studio was tenuous – she worked on only one scene, the opening of *Anna Christie* with Maureen Stapleton, an event which has passed into Studio legend – but her fame catapulted the Studio and its artistic director into a national and even international spotlight. For an acting lab which was off limits to outsiders, which was not involved in production, and which shunned publicity, by the mid-fifties the place and its Method had achieved a fame the most zealous press agentry would have been unlikely to purchase.

The split in Strasberg between disavowing and embracing popular acclaim never healed. On the one hand, he remained a tireless student of the actor's creative process; on the other, he began to favor those members who had achieved recognition in the marketplace over against those who had not. At the same time that he courted movie stars he advised Studio actors to remain in New York to devote their art to the theatre. The schism set up in the Studio between theatre and film acting was a legacy from the Group, whose members made at least one reluctant visit to Hollywood. Only a few found regular work in films and only one, John Garfield, became a star, though Franchot Tone had a credible film career. All of them, including Garfield, felt bruised, exploited, and undervalued by the Hollywood system. The lingering prejudice against films that was in the air in the Studio's early history was misplaced because the Studio's Method is at heart a technique for the screen rather than the stage. In the theatre acting must be larger than life; on film it can be a much closer approximation of the real thing. Films, typically, are set in the real world or a convincing facsimile; plays unfold in an artificial *mise-en-scène*. The close-up welcomes, indeed demands, the introspection and the sense of privacy Strasberg sought from actors, and the illusion of spontaneity which he prized is easier to capture when the actor doesn't have to keep on capturing it eight times a week month after month. On stage actors can in fact more easily fake feeling, and if their eyes are dead only their fellow performers are likely to know, whereas in probing close-up an actor's eyes must be alight with a continuous flicker of thoughts and emotions. While acting, the film actor is much less protected than his stage counterpart, and the isolation and discontinuities of constructing a performance on film provide ripe circumstances for an affective memory exercise. Shooting his role in fragments and out of sequence, and acting to the camera, with the director and a corps of technicians as the only likely audience, an actor might well need an emotional or sensory memory to help propel him into the proper moods which he must be able to summon at short notice.

In the event, it was film acting which put the Method and The Actors Studio on the cultural map. And once again, as in the Group, it was not Lee Strasberg who won most of the recognition but this time the man who had hired him, Elia Kazan. As a Group alumnus and a co-founder of The Actors Studio, Kazan was steeped in the Method, and unlike Strasberg, Adler, or Meisner, he was at his best working with actors on a stage or a film set rather than in a classroom or lab. Kazan understood the actor's creative process and more, he knew, at a deep intuitive level, how to talk to actors. Typically, Kazan would take an actor off to the side for a private conference, his arm around the actor's shoulder. He would whisper into the actor's ear, offering suggestions which would trigger the imagination. "When Kazan talked to you, you couldn't wait to get up on stage and try things out," Geraldine Page said.

Among other major performances which became a showcase for the Method Kazan directed Marlon Brando in both the stage and screen versions of *A Streetcar Named Desire* (1947; 1951) and in *On the Waterfront* (1954) and James Dean in *East of Eden* (1955). Along with Montgomery Clift in *A Place in the Sun* (directed in 1951 by George Stevens, who did not know about the Method but who certainly knew what good screen acting demanded), these performances defined a new and vibrant approach which has been widely imitated. In the annals of Method acting Brando, Dean, and Clift comprise an inescapable trio, their names recited together in the same kind of litany that links Tennessee Williams, Arthur Miller, and William Inge as the leading postwar American dramatists.

To what degree were the actors' performances shaped by the work Strasberg was encouraging at the Studio? All three were Studio members; all three sat in on a number of Studio sessions. None attended regularly and none worked there consistently, although Clift did return, to observe, even after he became a film star. Until his death in 1955, Dean had attended sporadically, and might have continued, like Clift, to drop in on sessions. Brando, on the other hand, has denounced Strasberg, denying that Strasberg made any contribution to his artistic development. As Brando writes in *Brando: Songs My Mother Taught Me*,

> After I had some success, Lee Strasberg tried to take credit for teaching me how to act. He never taught me anything. He would have claimed credit for the sun and the moon if he believed he could get away with it. He was an ambitious, selfish man who exploited the people who attended the [*sic*] Actors Studio, and he tried to project himself as an acting oracle and guru . . . I sometimes went to the [*sic*] Actors Studio . . . because Elia Kazan was teaching. . . But Strasberg never taught me acting. Stella did – and later Kazan. (85)

As on practically every other matter, Stella and Lee also fought over Brando, each claiming credit for developing America's greatest postwar actor. But in a larger sense it does not matter who "invented" Marlon Brando, or how regularly or faithfully he, Dean, or Clift attended the Studio or studied the Method at the feet of Lee Strasberg. Seemingly spontaneous, intuitive, brooding, "private," lit with potent vibrations from an inner life of conflict and contradiction, their work exemplified the style of heightened naturalism which (whether Brando agrees or not) Lee Strasberg devoted his life to exploring and promoting.

With Brando, Clift, and Dean a new idea seemed to be introduced into American acting, the same idea that became associated, and properly so, with The Actors Studio. In their signature roles – the most influential performances in the history of American films – these three performers revealed new kinds of body language and new ways of delivering dialogue. In the pauses between words, in the language "spoken" by their eyes and faces, they gave psychological realism an unprecedented charge. Verbally inarticulate, they were eloquent "speakers" of emotion. Far less protective of their masculinity than earlier film actors, they enacted emotionally wounded and vulnerable outsiders struggling for self-understanding, and their work shimmered with a mercurial neuroticism. The realism they pioneered was "new" in degree rather than kind. Indeed, in a famous statement in the mid-fifties Strasberg created a furor among Studio members when he announced that movie stars like Gary Cooper, James Stewart, and Spencer Tracy used the Method instinctively, achieving a level of conviction, relaxation, and truth for which the Method prepares actors. To the solid realist tradition built by precisely the kind of actors Strasberg cited, the Method-trained performers in films of the fifties added an enhanced verbal and gestural naturalism and a more vivid inner life.

In the opening shot of *A Place in the Sun*, a version of Theodore Dreiser's *An American Tragedy*, the camera moves in for a tight closeup on Montgomery Clift's face. The gaze that Clift returns to the prying camera is, tantalizingly, both open and closed, inviting as well as resisting exposure. As in the other seminal Method performances, the real drama is played out across the actor's face. As George Eastman, Clift plays a poor relative enticed by money, power, and beauty as exemplified by débutante Angela Vickers (played by the exquisite young Elizabeth Taylor) but held back by a forlorn, possessive girlfriend, fellow factory worker Alice Tripp (Shelley Winters). Tempted by a world of riches that, unexpectedly, seems to be in reach, George contemplates drowning his nagging, pregnant girlfriend who is trapping him into a marriage which will insure that Angela and her world will be forever lost to him.

The drama is an inner one, the character's debate with himself, his intense moral and ethical conflict. Raised in an impoverished religious atmosphere – his mother runs a mission – George is not a hustler; as Clift plays him, he is in fact "one of us," decent, aching for love and acceptance, deeply wounded by a past which is not detailed but which Clift's presence richly alludes to – in true Method fashion, the actor supplies an aroma of the character's prior circumstances. As George's temptation intensifies, Clift becomes increasingly veiled and distracted, and as if weighed down by some powerful existential sorrow his head and shoulders slump. The pauses, stammerings, repetitions, and backtrackings of Clift's delivery – the first full-scale demonstration of the Method actor's detonating way with words – suggest his character's inner battle. "What are you thinking?" Angela asks repeatedly, responding, as the audience is, to the palpable aura of torment radiating from the actor's body language, his face, and voice.

When George takes Alice rowing, he has murder in his heart. As he looks at her with an ambiguous mixture of contempt and compassion, which seems aimed also at himself, Clift visibly shakes with the force of his character's struggle with his inner demons. Suddenly rising up in the boat, Alice upsets its balance, topples over, and drowns. George, who tried to stop her from getting up, runs like a criminal. Is he guilty? A jury finds him to be, and the Production Code mandated that the character be punished. But Clift subverts the screenplay's conservative but not full-hearted endorsement of a conventional scenario of crime and punishment. "In my heart I don't feel I'm guilty; I wish I knew, I'm not sure," George says on the eve of his execution, and it is a measure of Clift's skillful "rewriting" that most viewers will not be certain about the character's guilt either.

Playing a character with a hidden life Clift may well have used memories drawn from his own double life. Clift was a bisexual who had to conceal his relationships with men for the sake of his career, a masquerade the actor found excruciating. Already at the time of *A Place in the Sun*, the scars of the actor's own travails – his sexual conflicts and his struggles with alcohol and drugs – were engrained in his face and voice. Clift's performances came from a deep inner source, from a fund of personal suffering which actors who disapprove of Strasberg's Method claim to be both a damaging and unnecessary way to create emotion. Nonetheless, acting from a genuinely personal core Clift endows his role in *A Place in the Sun*, as well as his portraits of other victims and outsiders in *From Here to Eternity* (1953), *The Young Lions* (1957), and *Judgment at Nuremberg* (1961) with an extraordinary sensitivity that marked a new level in acting as an imitation of life.

Probably never before, and certainly not since, has there been such a cadre of fresh and intense actors as in the late forties and fifties, at the time when The Actors Studio was in its heyday and the studio system in Hollywood was in its twilight. Complementing the work of Brando, Clift, and Dean on film was a trio of brilliant actresses – Julie Harris, Geraldine Page, and Kim Stanley – who made their greatest impression in the theatre. Harris as the odd and lonely adolescent in *The Member of the Wedding* (1950); Page as the passionate spinster Alma Winemiller in Tennessee Williams's *Summer and Smoke* (1952); and Kim Stanley oozing sex and vulnerability as the no-talent torch singer in William Inge's *Bus Stop* (1955) were luminous, high-strung performances gilded with Method insignia. Harris's quivering voice, Page's fluttering hands, and Stanley's illuminated silences invited charges of mannerism and eccentricity, but at their best, as in their star-making roles, they exhibited the keen psychological revelation which was the Studio's byword.

Surely it is no coincidence that virtually all of the most original, zealous, and sheerly interesting performers of the era, on both stage and screen, were members of The Actors Studio. In addition to the sextet already cited the roster includes Shelley Winters, Paul Newman, Carroll Baker, Ben Gazzara, Eva Marie Saint, Eli Wallach, Karl Malden, Kim Hunter, Maureen Stapleton, and Jo Van Fleet, among others. These performers in turn have influenced a second generation of Actors Studio members including Jack Nicholson, Dustin Hoffman, Robert De Niro, the late Sandy Dennis, Al Pacino, Sally Field, Jane Fonda, Estelle Parsons, and Ellen Burstyn.

In following Strasberg's injunction to examine themselves, they act and re-enact a set of limited variations on the inner being the Method releases and artistically shapes. Shunning versatility or elaborate self-transformations, Strasberg's Method thus conforms to the demands of the star system which has always dominated acting in America. In popular discourse, stars are believed to play themselves – the star is an icon who maintains a more or less stable persona from role to role – while "real" actors create a variety of parts; but as Strasberg insisted, the projection of self requires technique, a mastery of the self and of craft.

In Hollywood films, as at The Actors Studio, versatility has been an all but useless commodity: who would have wanted to see Marilyn Monroe cast as a decrepit old woman, despite the ingenuity which such a makeover would have entailed? It has long been axiomatic at the Studio that elaborate disguise and alterations in voice and style of movement (the kind of experiments which Brando has often conducted, in fact) are external "adjustments" which interfere with the purity of an actor's work. "Disguise is for the British," Strasberg declared, and cited Laurence Olivier's often virtuoso physical and vocal transformations as mere stunts, hollow tricks of the trade rather than the real thing. At the Studio, James Dean playing "James Dean" rather than Meryl Streep with an accent (die-hard Methodists tend to regard Streep as too technical) continues to provide the dominant model. As if underlining the continuities between the Method and (the best kind of) star acting, Strasberg announced that "our most famous members are not necessarily our least talented."

Broadway and the Hollywood studio system which, until the advent of television provided the showcases for most of the acting in America, were set up to promote and indeed were financially dependent on, star acting. In 1945 both institutions were flourishing. Over the past half century, however, both have withstood seismic economic shifts which as a result have altered the status of the star and of star acting.

Although Hollywood has been a lure to stage actors for nearly a century, a corps of performers remained loyal to the theatre when it was still a bustling industry. Great stage stars like the Lunts, Katharine Cornell, Ethel Merman, Mary Martin, and Helen Hayes made only sporadic film appearances (Cornell avoided the medium altogether). Sometimes stage performers – Ethel Merman is a prime example – could not adjust their style for the camera, but more often they simply preferred live acting. They supported the theatre and, equally important, the theatre supported them. There are no Ethel Mermans or Katharine Cornells on Broadway anymore; there is hardly any Broadway, at least as Merman and Cornell knew it. Plays are produced too rarely to sustain entire careers – Zoe Caldwell may be the only latter day stage star who has remained exclusively devoted to the theatre, and Caldwell appears much less frequently than stars of the Cornell era did. Musicals comprise the majority of offerings both in New York and what is left of the Road, but stars no longer necessarily provide the box office bait.

The Musical Stage and Changing Star Status

Historically, the musical theatre had always been a star-driven form, and from 1945 at least through the mid-sixties a series of memorable performances were by stars headlining tailor-made vehicles: Mary Martin in *South Pacific* (1949) and *The Sound of Music* (1951); Ethel Merman in *Annie Get Your Gun* (1946), *Call Me Madam* (1950), and *Gypsy* (1959); Zero Mostel in *Fiddler on the Roof* (1964); Carol Channing in *Hello, Dolly!* (1964); Rex Harrison and Julie Andrews in *My Fair Lady* (1956); John Raitt in *Carousel* (1945) and *The Pajama Game* (1954); Barbra Streisand in *Funny Girl* (1964); Alfred Drake in *Kiss Me, Kate* (1948) and *Kismet* (1953); Robert Preston in *The Music Man* (1955); Richard Kiley in *Man of La Mancha* (1965). Regardless of the quality of their material these stars performed with the outsized energy, the vivid projection of personality, which the musical form demands.

The star vehicle is no longer the dominant mold for musicals. Contemporary Broadway divas like Bernadette Peters or Patti LuPone, who have had to supplement their stage appearances with work in other media, are rare. Typically, there were only a few star-oriented vehicles during the 1996–97 season. Julie Andrews headlined *Victor/Victoria,* a lackluster rendition of an old-fashioned star vehicle which gives a bad name to the form. *Sunset Boulevard* foundered at the box office once the original star, Glenn Close, left to return to making movies – star replacements could not be found to keep a star vehicle afloat. Nathan Lane, followed by Whoopi Goldberg, starred in *A Funny Thing Happened on the Way to the Forum*, a revival of a 1962 show. Without stars, the musical theatre has continued to reinvent itself. A composer like Andrew Lloyd Webber or Stephen Sondheim, or a show's concept, is now more likely than a headliner to be a musical's financial ace in the hole. *Hair* (1967), *Company* (1970), *A Chorus Line* (1975), *Rent* (1996) – in landmark musicals like these the ensemble has the "starring" role. Year after year, audiences are drawn to shows like *Cats* (1982), *Les Misérables* (1987), *The Phantom of the Opera* (1988), and *Miss Saigon* (1992) not because of a star or any individual actor but because of the score, the subject matter, or the spectacle – the sound and light show in which the music is embedded. As the staging of musicals has grown increasingly fluent, cinematic, and technically sophisticated, the need for the larger-than-life stars of the past has decreased. Musical demands have escalated – the leads in pop operas like *Miss Saigon* or

Phantom of the Opera or *Evita* (1979) have to sustain longer musical passages than in the old-style musicals with their separable numbers; and as subject matter has become darker acting standards have also risen. But today's singing actors do not have to be stars.

In Hollywood's Golden Age actors typically signed seven-year contracts with one of the major studios. During that period the studios offered coaching, assigned roles, nurtured promising performers into stars, orchestrated publicity campaigns, and even stage-managed private lives. Contract players regularly complained about being forced to act in unsuitable films and being underpaid. But the studios were in business to promote and protect their stars and more often than not they molded careers shrewdly, presenting their stars in roles that, in effect, comprised chapters of an ongoing novel: The Musical Adventures of Judy Garland, say, or The Western Heroics of John Wayne.

After the system broke down by the end of the fifties and studios became distributors rather than producers, stars negotiated salaries for each picture. And in today's free-market system star performers can command figures undreamed of by actors, no matter how popular, who were bound by the terms of a seven-year contract. But so far few careers in the post-studio era have achieved the continuity or demonstrated the commonsensical judgment of those the studios constructed. Stars now appear much less frequently, and their own choice of material is often less astute than under the old regime, when they acted on assignment. Bette Davis, for instance, grumbled about the roles Warner Brothers handed to her, but she was almost always well cast, in marked comparison to contemporary "stars" like Kevin Costner, Jim Carrey, Julia Roberts, Sandra Bullock, and Alec Baldwin, among others, who on their own have made career-threatening choices. At present Tom Cruise and Harrison Ford may be the only film stars who negotiate their projects with the steady sense that studios regularly demonstrated in overseeing the portfolios of their valued star properties.

There are notably fewer stars in the post-studio era, and fewer star performers can sustain careers, or redesign their iconography, as cunningly as in the past. But actors on the whole are better trained now than in the studio years: having studied the Meisner technique, or having explored the Strasberg Method, at an acting conservatory or in a college program, they have a grounding in craft that is deeper and more systematic than the superficial "grooming" (which often meant voice lessons to erase a regional accent or lessons in posture and general deportment) the studios regularly provided. Indeed, for the formulaic action or event pictures which are Hollywood's current primary commodities and in which explosions, car chases, gunfights, fragmented editing, and THX sound do much of the "acting," many of today's film actors are pointedly overtrained.

Non-realistic Traditions

Films and realistic plays require an invisible style in which not to be caught acting is traditionally the first and often the ultimate criterion. The experimental theatre, in contrast, has fostered a counter-tradition which rejects the seamless realist approach. Invoking Antonin Artaud rather than Stanislavsky, and emphasizing body language rather than the spoken word, leading avant-garde practitioners to varying degrees have attempted to redefine the theatrical functions of the actor and acting. Fusing aesthetics with ideology they have indicted realism in writing, staging, and performance as a way of maintaining the *status quo*, and thereby reaffirming patriarchal capitalism. In this scheme, realism enchains spectacle and spectator in an endless circuit of imitation and repetition. The avatars of non-traditional theatre have thus worked to deconstruct the regnant model of performance as a mirror of realistic behavior.

The first major postwar alternative theatre was the Living Theatre founded by Julian Beck and Judith Malina in 1947. In its original format the Living Theatre had a literary emphasis and produced classic and modern plays likely to be ignored by the commercial theatre. With their famous productions of *The Connection* (1959) and *The Brig* (1963) the theatre attempted to be more real than the realistic commercial theatre, to abolish the gap between acting and being. Seated around a central playing area enclosed by a barbed wire fence, audiences at *The Brig*, where soldiers are imprisoned for having committed military infractions and submitted to a grueling regime of deprivation and punishment, became eavesdroppers offered the illusion of watching a real action in real time. Refusing to pay taxes to support government policies it detested, the company left America in 1964 and during many years as theatrical vagabonds in exile they developed a new kind of performance art. Assuming the role of sexual and political anarchists, Beck and Malina, together with their actors, devised productions such as *Paradise Now* (1968) and *Frankenstein* (1965), which assaulted the manifold repressions of life under capitalism. Choreography, ritual, choral declamation replaced naturalistic movement and dialogue – aiming for "the truth," the Living Theatre cultivated a raw style, as if to contest the "lies" of the finished performances valued by the bourgeois realist theatre. In their work, conceived as spectacles of propaganda, Brechtian alienation mingled promiscuously and sometimes contradictorily with their paraphrase of some of Artaud's prescriptions for a theatre of cruelty. When the Living Theatre returned to America in the late sixties, offering performances which climaxed with Dionysian interactions between actors and spectators, it became a preliminary emblem of the era's counter-culture. (See also Carlson, Chapter 2, "Alternative Theatre," for additional discussion of the Living Theatre and other such groups discussed here.)

In exile and then in their notorious return the Living Theatre was a paradigm for other radical groups of the sixties. At the Performing Garage Richard Schechner continued the Living Theatre's attempts to challenge the safe, detached actor–audience relationship of the proscenium stage. Collaborating with a brilliant conceptual artist, Jerry Rojo, Schechner created a series of environments for his productions – as the arrangement of space changed so did the kind and level of interaction between performers and spectators. In *Dionysus in '69*, as in the Living Theatre pieces, the audience was invited to become part of the actors' orgiastic revels.

Joseph Chaikin, a refugee from the Living Theatre, founded the Open Theatre in 1963. Although he had a far less aggressive agenda than Beck and Malina, Chaikin also based his theatre on an ideal of a group of actors working together to write and perform material in a new, anti-naturalist style. The group's most famous piece, *Terminal* (1969), carries the name of its dramatist-in-residence, Susan Yankowitz, who in fact collated the memories, dreams, and feelings of actor-members on the subject of death and dying. Performing their piece as a mosaic of choreographed rituals, the actors changed identities in a continuously fluid pattern.

Acting in performance pieces like those devised by the Living Theatre, the Performing Garage, and the Open Theatre demanded a charged, kinetic style, but for all their theatrical audacity these groups did not provide a model for an alternative acting technique. In their in-house training the groups stressed body work, as if heeding the examples of Meyerhold and Grotowski rather than Stanislavsky, and in performance they often acted with a liberating physical expressiveness. But vocally the actors seemed unequal to the lyrical, declamatory style their pieces required – often enough they sounded like Method actors who could not speak well and who had been corrupted by partially digested infusions of Brecht's and Artaud's theories about the function of the actor in anti-bourgeois theatre. Despite their radical aspirations, at some level these groups remained attached to the centripetal pull of realism.

Since the sixties, significant alternative performing styles have been explored by Robert Wilson, Richard Foreman, and Elizabeth LeCompte, directors who more decisively than their avant-garde predecessors eschew the realist mandate. In their theatre, movement, sound, gesture, intonation, all organized and superintended by directorial ingenuity, typically replace dialogue as the actor's primary material. As realistic acting is mocked, "quoted," and deconstructed, it is the directors' conception rather than the actors' which becomes the real show.

Working with her Wooster Group actors on *The Hairy Ape* (developed during much of 1995), Elizabeth LeCompte daringly dismantles O'Neill's tragedy. An essay on the play rather than the play performed straight, the Wooster Group's performance is a kind of extended jazz improvisation, a series of sound riffs in which shards of the original text are occasionally overheard. The multilayered sound design is projected through a system of elaborate amplification, and the voices of actors who are only a few feet away from the audience in the Group's intimate performing space are strangely remote, eerily disembodied. Actors not only act, they become part of the crew, manipulating the technical gadgetry that projects their voices: in a sense the audience is privileged to witness the actors construct (and then deconstruct) their own performances. Like the play itself, the acting is aurally and visually detonated.

Directors like LeCompte, who take a possessive approach to text and performance, are theatrical termites. Audiences at her version of *The Hairy Ape* are allowed to savor neither O'Neill's vision nor the contribution of individual actors (despite the fact that the mainstay of the Wooster Group is film star Willem Dafoe) – what is principally on display is the director's redaction. In these circumstances truth to life is only a fleeting part of the actor's labor. Fragments of psychological realism are rapidly cross-cut with tricks culled from the director's anti-mimetic arsenal. As both Stanislavsky and Brecht are parodied and interbred, a *mise-en-scène* of maximum instability is created, and in the dense aural mix the focus of traditional, character-centered theatre cannot, and is not allowed to, hold.[4]

Acting styles in experimental theatre have challenged the realist tradition without dislodging it and without evolving a comprehensive counter system code. Actor training, like the performances, has tended to be haphazard and scattershot, consisting varyingly of doses of Artaud, Meyerhold, Grotowski, Brecht, of rituals borrowed from ancient Greek drama and the Christian mass, of encounter therapy, and, however reluctantly, of the precepts of Stanislavsky. No alternate system of actor training has secured the same currency or influence as Stanislavsky's, and perhaps none ever can. Intended to flourish only at the margins, in the negative space surrounding realism, avant-garde performance comprises a shadow history which only confirms the centrality and inescapability of the questions about creating truthful characters which the actors in the Group Theatre, inspired by the great quest Stanislavsky had embarked on, began to pursue over six decades ago.

Notes

1 Unless otherwise cited, all quotations are from the author's interviews or from class observations.

2 In 1994 The Actors Studio initiated with New York's New School a three-year master's program, providing training in acting, directing, and playwriting.

3 Meisner did reaffirm his personal abilities as an actor with his final role as a patient in the television series *ER* (February 1995), though this one appearance did not establish his credentials in the way Strasberg did in films.

4 When LeCompte moved her production of *The Hairy Ape* uptown in Spring 1997, she made more of O'Neill's dialogue accessible and allowed Defoe's performance to become more pivotal than it had been in the company's Soho workshop.

Bibliography: Actors and Acting

When the Group Theatre began its systematic examination of Stanislavsky's ideas, his works had yet to appear in English translation. Strasberg based his instruction on notes taken during Boleslavski's lectures at the American Laboratory Theatre, published in serial form in 1933 and as *Acting: The First Six Lessons* in book form in 1949. *An Actor Prepares,* Stanislavsky's first book, did not appear until 1936 and, remarkably, since Stanislavsky thought of his work as a unit, his second and third books, *Building a Character* and *Creating a Role*, were not published in America until 1949 and 1961, respectively. Despite criticized translations the books have become standard acting reference tools. (A newly translated collection of Stanislavsky's complete works was announced several years ago but as yet no volume has appeared.)

At the time of his death in 1938 Stanislavsky did not regard his published work as either final or sacred but as suggestions for further study. Surely he would have welcomed the many books which have expanded on and reinterpreted elements of the immense subject he had undertaken.

Fittingly, the first sustained discussion in print of the Method, the American adaptation of the Stanislavsky system, was by Group alumnus Robert Lewis. His *Method – or Madness?* collects Lewis's lectures to theatre professionals given at the Playhouse Theatre on Broadway. Lewis attempts to separate the Method from its notorious reputation – by the time of his lectures the Method had become a code term among theatregoers and journalists as well as working actors for the proletarian slouch and mumble school of acting. In his remarks, as in his own theatre practice, Lewis argues for the Method's applicability to the classics, poetic drama, and the musical theatre in addition to contemporary realism. Lewis touches lightly on the inflammable subject of affective memory, unwilling to enjoin Strasberg in heated battle.

Confusion about the Method, and curiosity about what actually takes place at The Actors Studio, continued because of the public silence of Lee Strasberg. For many years the only sustained account of his Method was *Strasberg at the Actors Studio*, a collection of taped sessions edited by Hethmon. A series of closeups of Strasberg on the job, the book lacks an explanatory guide or "map" against which to gauge the details.

Strasberg and the other legendary teachers from the Group Theatre waited until near the end of their careers to publish accounts of their life-long studies. Strasberg's *A Dream of Passion* (published in 1987, five years after Strasberg's death); Stella Adler's *The Technique of Acting*, and *Sanford Meisner on Acting* (with Dennis Longwell) fail to capture the personalities of the teachers on *terra firma*, in the studio or classroom. On the page their voices are curiously inert.

To a fault, Adler in her book keeps herself offstage, and this strangely impersonal volume, indicating all the signs of a rushed job, degenerates into a series of baldly outlined exercises. Strasberg's book is more thorough but also dull: in the transition from speech to writing, the flavor and sting of Strasberg's tireless passion for his subject have been mislaid. Presented in his book from the point of view of an eyewitness who observes him working with students and occasionally relaxing offstage, Meisner too is disembodied. And without an explication of how the Meisner technique resembles and departs from the articles of faith of Strasberg's method, the book, like *Strasberg at the Actors Studio*, suffers from a surfeit of closeups. It is likely to be puzzling to anyone who has not actually studied the Meisner technique, but for that core audience the book has become a steady seller.

Uta Hagen's wonderfully titled *Respect for Acting* is the best-selling book by an American acting teacher. Hagen's brisk, no-nonsense manner is faithfully transcribed. Her well-organized approach is offset by examples of how she solved some of her own acting problems, and in recounting how she applied her technique to creating Martha in *Who's Afraid of Virginia Woolf?*, for instance, she adds a personal note largely absent from the books of the other master teachers. In *A Challenge for the Actor*, Hagen touches up points in her earlier book; notably, "substitution" is now called "transference."

Among the numerous books which contest the Method the most persuasive is Hornby's *The End of Acting*. Bemoaning Strasberg's stranglehold on American acting, Hornby discounts affective memory and berates Strasberg and his followers for encouraging an anti-intellectual approach and for making students work on exercises and scenes rather than allowing them the chance to develop parts in plays. Hornby calls for a new regime in actor training in which actors study the history of the theatre and its literature; work on full-length plays in a variety of styles and from a variety of periods; and are encouraged to develop their imaginations rather than to focus on past wounds and traumas.

For accounts of acting in experimental theatre, books by Julian Beck, Judith Malina, Joseph Chaikin, and Richard Schechner are noteworthy. Beck's *The Life of the Theatre* and *The Diaries of Judith Malina* are primarily concerned with the vision of the ways radical theatre can help to create a radical society, but they offer parenthetical comments about actor training within the Living Theatre and about the aura of the acting style they were trying to achieve in their communally created pieces. In *The Presence of the Actor* Chaikin stresses acting as a group enterprise rather than a showcase for the individual actor; despite its title, however, the book is more concerned with the inner life of the Open Theatre, its coming together and its gradual dissolution, than with constructing a theory of acting. Schechner's *Environmental Theater* is a stimulating discussion of the elemental ways in which environmental staging realigns all aspects of the theatrical occasion from acting and set design to audience reception.

Like Artaud's prescriptions for an anti-realistic acting style developed in *The Theatre and Its Double*, Grotowski's investigations of the nature of acting in *Towards a Poor Theatre* seem destined to be more read about than practiced. Citing the actor's use of his body and voice as the essential, irreducible theatrical element, Grotowski has developed rigorous exercises designed to unchain and to integrate the actor's mental, physical, emotional, and spiritual processes. Borrowing elements from disparate acting traditions, including Peking Opera, Japanese Noh theatre, Indian theatre, Meyerhold, Brecht, Artaud, and Stanislavsky, Grotowski has erected a *via negativa* intended to remove an actor's impediments to a fluent, dynamic, irradiated use of his physical and vocal capacities. *Towards a Poor Theatre* has become a standard text in any serious actor's library, but its tenets have not taken root on native grounds, and are never likely to in a society in which star acting has always been the dominant performing tradition. Finally, Zarrilli's collection of essays, *Acting (Re) Considered*, provides useful inclusions on most major approaches to acting, other than realism, in the nineteenth and twentieth centuries.

7

American Theatre Design Since 1945

Ronn Smith

Introduction

The history of contemporary American theatre design, that is, the design of scenery, costumes, and lighting in the United States after World War II, can actually be traced back to the 1915 production of *The Man Who Married a Dumb Wife*, directed by British director Harley Granville-Barker and designed by Robert Edmond Jones (see Volume 2, Chapter 8 for a discussion of this event and its context). Jones's flat, monochromatic set presented a stark contrast to the popular, realistic productions produced by David Belasco, and it is often cited as the first important domestic example of what would eventually be known as the New Stagecraft, which some recent scholars and critics have claimed to be the most significant development in twentieth-century American theatre.

In comparison to "Belascan realism," the New Stagecraft presented a "simplified realism." Primarily inspired by Edward Gordon Craig and Adolphe Appia, it promoted a visual stage picture that often bordered on the abstract. European designers associated with the New Stagecraft style included Max Reinhardt, Oskar Strnad, Georg Fuchs, and Joseph Urban, who began his American career working at the Boston Opera in 1912. In the United States, Samuel Hume's 1914 exhibition of new designs from Europe (seen in Boston, New York, Detroit, Chicago, and Cleveland), Boston's Toy Theatre, Chicago's Little Theatre, and the design work of Livingston Platt also played an important part in introducing this style to American production.

While *The Man Who Married a Dumb Wife* occupies a critical position in the history of American theatre design, it was Jones's other designs – for *The Devil's Garden*, directed by Arthur Hopkins in 1915; for the John Barrymore Shakespeare productions (also directed by Hopkins) during the following decade; and his work on the major plays of Eugene O'Neill for the Provincetown Players – that actually popularized the New Stagecraft. Design styles go in and out of fashion with some regularity (particularly in the second half of the twentieth century), and often as the result of economic realities. These realities are reflected in the New Stagecraft, for the simplicity of the style provided economic benefits that, at the time, could not be ignored by those working in the Little Theatre movement.

Besides being closely identified with the New Stagecraft movement in the United States, it is also Robert Edmond Jones who can be credited with introducing another significant innovation, one which has had a far greater impact on the evolution of American theatre and theatre design than is commonly recognized. Jones insisted that the scenic designer be present as an active participant at the beginning of the production process, thus changing the practice of design by giving the designer an opportunity to contribute to the interpretation of the script. The importance of this can be more fully appreciated when one considers the original productions of Tennessee Williams's *A Streetcar Named Desire* (1947) or Arthur Miller's *Death of a Salesman* (1949), both of which were designed by Jo Mielziner, or, more recently, *A Chorus Line* (1975), designed by Robin Wagner. The pivotal position each of these productions holds in the history of American theatre can be attributed not only to the work of the individual playwrights, directors, and actors, but to the scenic designers as well.

Of those designers working during the twenties and thirties, Lee Simonson and Norman Bel Geddes have been the most influential. Simonson, who, like Jones and Hume, studied in Europe, designed for the Washington Square Players and, during the twenties, for the Theatre Guild. His work is characterized by the unit set, which was often surrounded by open space and backed with a cyclorama, on which additional scenic elements were projected. In comparison, Bel Geddes's style was far more abstract, but it also established a bolder, more theatrical image that became the hallmark of the so-called American style. Although many other significant designers can be linked to the New Stagecraft movement and its various permutations throughout the rest of the twentieth century, it was Jones and Simonson, and then Donald Oenslager, Jo Mielziner, Oliver Smith, and Boris Aronson who dominated American theatre design between 1920 and 1960.

Scenic Designers: Forties to Sixties

Donald Oenslager, who assisted Robert Edmond Jones at the Provincetown Playhouse in the early twenties, designed over 250 productions in his career, including Broadway musicals (for example, *Anything Goes*), operas for both the Metropolitan Opera and the New York City Opera, and productions for regional theatres. Although he used a variety of styles, depending on the needs of the script, his work is often cited for its detailed elegance. His greatest influence, however, may be on the many design students he trained at Yale School of Drama between 1925 and 1971, many of whom went on to establish their own careers as designers.

Jo Mielziner was both a production designer (with an impeccable control of color and light) and a theatre consultant, and is therefore considered by many to be the single most important figure in American theatre from the time he started working, in the mid-twenties, until 1976, when he died. His atmospheric, painterly work, sometimes referred to as "theatrical realism" or "poetic realism," usually combined scrims, scenic units, and intricate lighting plots (which he also designed) that allowed scenes to flow from one to the next with remarkable ease. In addition, Mielziner had a tremendous impact on the plays themselves (especially those produced in the thirties, forties, and fifties), and distinguishing between the success of the play and the success of the design can sometimes be difficult. Best known for his lyrical work on Tennessee Williams's *A Streetcar Named Desire* (1947) and Arthur Miller's *Death of a Salesman* (1949), both of which were directed by Elia Kazan, Mielziner could also design astonishingly realistic sets, like that for *Street Scene* (1929), as well as Broadway musicals, like *Guys and Dolls* (1950) and *Gypsy* (1959).

In contrast to the design work of Mielziner, Oliver Smith's sets were bright, bold, and in themselves often entertaining. Although trained as an architect, Smith began his design career in dance, with Agnes de Mille's *Rodeo* and *Fall River Legend*. He also had an extensive career as a producer of both theatre and dance – he was the co-director of American Ballet Theatre from 1945 to 1981 – and taught at New York University. Of the 400 theatre, dance, opera, and film productions he designed, Smith's name is indelibly linked to musicals of the forties, fifties, and early sixties, including *My Fair Lady* (1956), *Candide* (1956), *West Side Story* (1957), and *Hello, Dolly!* (1964).

Russian-born Boris Aronson was a painter, sculptor, and set designer, whose career as a designer nearly divides into two parts. The first, from 1923, when he emigrated to the United States by way of Berlin, to the late fifties, exhibits the strong influence of Aleksandra Ekster, a constructivist designer with the Kamerny Theatre, and painter Marc Chagall. His "second" career, characterized by a stronger sense of line and a more subtle use of color, dates from 1964, when he began collaborating with Harold Prince on a series of musicals, including *Fiddler on the Roof* (1964), *Cabaret* (1966), *Company* (1970), *A Little Night Music* (1973), and *Pacific Overtures* (1976).

The painterly, atmospheric sets of the post-World War II era eventually gave way, in the early to mid-sixties, to a style that emphasized sculptural, textured, and symbolic qualities. Although elements of this new approach to set design were already apparent in the work of Boris Aronson and Rouben Ter-Arutunian, it is Ming Cho Lee's set for the New York Shakespeare Festival's production of *Electra* in 1964 that is considered to mark the beginning of this new design aesthetic. In general, new materials and technologies, the symbolic use of color, and a sculptural use of space characterize the design of this period. Major designers associated with this style include David Mitchell, Robin Wagner, John Conklin, Douglas Schmidt, Santo Loquasto, and Marjorie Bradley Kellogg. While space limitations prohibit a detailed analysis of the work of these designers, a few words about Ming Cho Lee are in order here.

Born in Shanghai and educated at Occidental College and UCLA, Lee began assisting Jo Mielziner in 1954. His signature use of pipes, scaffolding, and collage-like images can be seen, in part, as a direct response to the poetic realism of Mielziner. Even the more recent work, which often reveals an acute attention to realistic detail, can be described as spare, efficient, or almost minimal in the way it supports the needs of a script. Although Lee's work is seldom seen on Broadway, he does design regularly for regional theatres and opera companies, plus the New York Shakespeare Festival and New York City Opera. But Lee also teaches, and has been the head of the design program at Yale School of Drama since the mid-eighties. When considering the number of professional designers who have studied with Lee at Yale, it is apparent that his influence on American scenography is substantial, and will remain so well into the next century.

Costume and Lighting Design

Costume design, as a separate discipline of the production process, is a relatively recent phenomenon. During the early part of the twentieth century, one designer typically assumed full responsibility for the entire production, with assistants overseeing the various elements through the construction phase. As the process grew more complicated, however, the assistants were given more design responsibility, until ultimately each element had its own designer. Significant figures in the gradual evolution of design credits – and thus the development of each discipline as a legitimate field of endeavor – include Aline Bernstein, Robert Edmond Jones, and Jo Mielziner, all of whom were actively engaged in advancing the careers of their assistants in this manner.

Another critical event in the history of costume design was the actors' strike in 1919 for better wages and improved working conditions. As a result of the strike, costumes (including wigs, shoes, and stockings) had to be provided by the producer for all women in principal and chorus roles. (Up until this time, principal performers appeared in their own costumes.) It was only when the producers were contractually required to purchase costumes for their productions that they began consulting designers, or "specialists" as they were identified at the time, about the design of the clothes. By 1936, costume designers were admitted into the United Scenic Artists Association, a union originally established for stage painters but which began accepting scenic designers in the early twenties. It was not until 1966, however, that costume designers were allowed to vote on union issues. According to one recent source, almost 50 percent of the programs for New York productions at the end of the forties included a credit for costume design, as compared to 1 percent around the turn of the century.

Names associated with the early history of costume design include Irene Sharaff, who at one time was a costume assistant for Aline Bernstein and who eventually became known primarily for her stylish designs and use of color on stage and in films; Raoul Pene Du Bois, who also designed scenery; Charles LeMaire; Lucinda Ballard, who designed for theatre, film, and ballet; and, as the profession progressed into the forties, Miles White, Freddy Wittop, and Alvin Colt.

Although the history of stage lighting is considerably older than that of costume design, the initial attempt consciously to determine how light illuminates the scenery and actors to complete an integrated stage picture can be linked to David Belasco and his electrician, Louis Hartmann, who worked together during the first three decades of the twentieth century. Not surprisingly, given Belasco's devotion to theatrical realism, Belasco and Hartmann are acknowledged to have brought a more realistic look to the lighting of theatre productions. For their 1900 production of *Madame Butterfly*, for example, they used silk color rolls behind the set's translucent screens to replicate a slow fade from day to night. According to the critics of the time, the result was astonishingly lifelike.

Not unlike the gradual emergence of the costume designer, the role of the lighting designer also evolved over a period of time (that is, it wasn't until 1962 that the United Scenic Artists Association expanded its membership to include lighting designers). However, advancements in the professional practice of lighting design can be more directly related to the developing technology. As the technology developed, so too did the profession. For example, the introduction of ductile-tungsten filament lamps (which replaced carbon-filament lamps) in 1910; their improved efficiency over the next five years; the elimination of footlights and the increased use of spotlights between 1915 and 1920; new suspension devices, developed in the early twenties (which meant that lighting units could be hung where appropriate rather than where dictated by a theatre's permanent mounts); the use of ground glass slides in planoconvex lens spotlights; the installation of reactance dimmers and the ability to preset those dimmers; the round Fresnel lens of the early thirties; and the ellipsoidal-reflector spotlights, demonstrated by Kliegl Bros. Lighting in 1933 – all of these advances had (and in some cases continue to have) a vast impact on lighting design.

One of the key figures in the early history of lighting design is Stanley R. McCandless. Trained as an architect, McCandless taught the first academic course in stage lighting at Yale University in 1926. The syllabus for the course was published the following year, and in 1932 he published *A Method of Lighting the Stage*, which is still used in the teaching of lighting design. Theodore Fuchs, author of *Stage Lighting* (1929), was one of McCandless's students, as were Jean Rosenthal and Peggy Clark, who, along with Abe Feder, were the first to be given program credit as "lighting designers" on Broadway.

Jean Rosenthal designed lighting for both theatre and architectural projects and is often credited, along with Feder (for whom she worked as an assistant), with inventing the field of lighting design. It was Rosenthal who devised symbols to represent lighting instruments, plotted her designs on paper, and insisted on lighting rehearsals as part of the production process. Although she had worked in the Federal Theatre Project with Orson Welles and John Houseman, it was her position as lighting and production supervisor for choreographer Martha Graham from 1938 until her death in 1969 that informed nearly all of her work, which was often noted for the mood it precisely evoked. Rosenthal's major Broadway productions included *West Side Story* (1957) and *The Sound of Music* (1959).

Peggy Clark began her career in theatre as a costume and set designer, but eventually, while working for Oliver Smith, decided to focus on lighting design. Although she lit theatre, dance, and opera, she is best known for her work on musicals, on many of which she collaborated with Smith. She was, in 1968, the first woman to serve as President of the United Scenic Artists.

Abe Feder is a seminal figure in the history of lighting design, and he was as well known for his architectural lighting as he was for his stage lighting. In both areas he established standards that other designers, for many years, would attempt to emulate. Often identified as "a genius with light," Feder was also described as being obsessed with light and how it enhanced an object, whether it was a stage set or the exterior of a building or the building's interior. The "Lighting by Feder" credit appeared in more than 300 Broadway programs, including *My Fair Lady* (1956) and *Camelot* (1960), and is forever linked with the illumination of the 1964 New York World's Fair and the RCA Building (and Prometheus Fountain) in Rockefeller Center.

Another significant development in lighting design occurred in 1947, when George C. Izenour introduced a lighting control system that incorporated a main lighting console and a preset panel, which had the ability to hold ten full presets. Not only could the system be run by one or two electricians, but because it was small, it could be located in the auditorium with an unhampered view of the stage. It was one of the more popular of the flexible control systems installed in theatres throughout the United States during the fifties.

Additional progress was made in the sixties when the control system's thyrathon tube was replaced by the silicon-controlled rectifier. This allowed for smaller dimmer banks, which meant that more dimmers could fit in the equivalent space. By the mid-sixties, stage lighting was also utilizing new computer devices to store data, although it wasn't until the opening of *A Chorus Line* in 1975 that a lighting "memory" system was used on Broadway. Shortly thereafter, the control of a large number of dimmers through the use of memory computers and miniature consoles became standard practice, allowing designers to include more lighting instruments in their shows. The number of lighting units used in Broadway productions leaped from between 300 and 400 in 1950 to frequently over 1,000 in the early nineties.

Globalization of Design

While many of the technical and professional advances mentioned above continued to influence the design of American theatre throughout the rest of the twentieth century, forces of a profoundly different kind began to influence theatre production around the late sixties and early seventies. It would require a great deal of space to analyze in depth these various phenomena and their effect on the design of theatre, but collectively they produced what might best be described as a "globalization" of design, which can be seen both vertically and horizontally throughout the theatre industry. (As used here, "theatre industry" is understood to include the production of commercial, non-profit, and "public" theatre – that is, rock concerts, industrial shows, theme parks, and so forth.

In other words, while the introduction and popularization of a new style or design trend during the last quarter of the twentieth century could be linked to a specific individual, production, or technical innovation, it was in actuality a broader constellation of cultural, social, political, and economic factors that produced the more significant changes in the design of scenery, costumes, and lighting. In addition, these factors affected all aspects of theatre production, from what was happening *within* clearly defined segments of the theatre community (hence "vertically") to what was happening *between* various theatre communities (hence "horizontally").

One of the major factors in this globalization process was the proliferation of theatre activity that occurred between 1965, when the National Endowment for the Arts was founded, and the mid-eighties. Although primarily associated with resident non-profit professional theatres, the impetus for this extraordinary growth – from 35 regional companies in 1966 to 230 theatres mounting 3,400-plus annual productions twenty years later – can be located in the Off- and Off-Off Broadway movements of the fifties and early sixties, discussed in more detail elsewhere in this history.

For the purposes of this chapter, Off-Broadway refers to New York City theatres, either commercial or non-profit, not located in the immediate vicinity of Times Square.[1] Compared to what was being produced on the Broadway stages, these theatres presented less well-known plays or experimental productions on very small budgets.

While Off-Off Broadway could be defined along similar lines, the resolutely non-commercial productions in this category were often produced, on even smaller budgets, in coffeehouses, churches, lofts, garages, and storefronts throughout Greenwich Village and the Lower East Side.[2] Both Off-Broadway and Off-Off Broadway were viewed as alternative theatre movements, the former to what was happening in the commercial theatre on Broadway, and the latter to what was happening in the Off-Broadway sector.

Also referred to as the regional, repertory, or simply the resident theatre movement, the resident non-profit professional theatre movement established an alternative theatre network outside of New York. These non-profit institutions, which presented both classical and innovative contemporary work, received a great deal of support initially from the Ford Foundation, the Rockefeller Foundation, and the National Endowment for the Arts. They also provided a kind of training ground for professional actors, directors, administrators, and, of course, designers.[3] Support services for this network, now including many of the non-profit theatres in New York City, continue to be the focus of the Theatre Communications Group (or TCG), which was founded in 1961 to serve as the national organization of these theatres.

The increased number of Off-Broadway, Off-Off Broadway, and resident theatres naturally provided more opportunities for designers, but the growth in numbers also suggests that theatre was assuming a more important position in the cultural life of the entire country. Whether or not this was in response to the increased number of hours Americans devoted to leisure-time activities, or to some other reason, may be difficult to determine, yet the fact remains theatres were attracting larger audiences and, simultaneously, more individuals began seeing the theatre as a place where they could build careers.

Consequently, as the number of professional theatres grew during this period, so too did the opportunities to study design in undergraduate or graduate programs. Previously, would-be designers apprenticed themselves to someone already working in the field; and eventually, if they were lucky, they would be asked to design a show. However, with the escalating cost of productions, fewer and fewer theatres could provide on-the-job training for designers with little or no experience. As a consequence, many individuals turned to academic programs to learn their trade and build portfolios. According to a survey conducted by the National Endowment for the Arts, an estimated 9 million people saw 30,000 productions at approximately 2,500 universities and colleges in 1977. This staggering number of productions suggests an explosion of theatre activity at universities and colleges across the country, but it also suggests that the academic theatre community could provide viable career opportunities if, for whatever reason, the designer chose not to work in either commercial or non-profit theatres.

Much of the academic training was conducted on the graduate level, in what are commonly referred to as pre-professional programs that, after two or three years, award Master of Fine Arts degrees. Although no two MFA programs were exactly alike, many are or were focused on practical ability and studio experience. Such programs were offered by such institutions of higher education as Boston University, Brandeis University, California Institute of the Arts, California State University–Long Beach, Carnegie Mellon University, DePaul University, Florida State University, Indiana University, Ithaca College, New York University, North Carolina School of the Arts, Rutgers, Southern Methodist University, State University of New York–Purchase, Temple University, University of Missouri–Kansas City, University of California–San Diego, University of Southern California, University of Texas–Austin, University of Washington, University of Wisconsin–Madison, and the Yale School of Drama. Many a professional career has been built and sustained through the relationships established while attending one of these academic programs.

Another aspect worth considering as it relates to the history of theatre design is the professional networks that were established as a result of attending one of these programs. In an environment where future professionals are learning their craft, whether it be designing, directing, acting, or producing, certain alliances were bound to occur, and these alliances often provide expanded opportunities for building a career after graduation. For example, directors would hire designers and actors they had worked with at college, or a designer, when available to work on a particular production, would recommend another designer with whom he or she had studied. Such "networking" is a part of many industries, but the effect it has had on theatre design at the end of the twentieth century cannot be underestimated.

There was one other significant training program for designers that needs to be mentioned here, but it was not affiliated with a college or university. The Polakov Studio and Forum of Stage Design, begun in New York City in 1958 by Lester Polakov, trained many important designers during its thirty-five-year history. Besides being an esteemed teacher, Polakov designed on and Off-Broadway as well as for opera, film, and industrial shows. Many of the designers of the last forty years of the twentieth century were trained either at the Polakov Studio or at one of the educational institutions listed in a previous paragraph.

Another major influence affecting American theatre design since 1945 includes a complicated set of economic factors, some of which were no less powerful for being less apparent than those most frequently mentioned in discussions on this issue. How American theatre as a business has evolved over the course of its history is beyond the scope of this particular chapter, but certain points are worth mentioning. Although never completely dormant during the Great Depression of the thirties, theatre did experience a gradual decline throughout the period. It was not until the early forties, with the arrival of the musical, that this trend was reversed, but by then investment in professional theatre had become a highly speculative business. As a result, capitalization through corporate financing was replaced by limited partnerships, a process in which several individuals (or a group of individuals acting as a single unit) would invest in a production and share the financial consequence, whether good or bad.

Another alternative to the high cost of commercial productions can be seen in the formation of non-profit theatres, especially those founded in the sixties (see note 3, and LoMonaco, "Regional/Resident Theatre," in Chapter 2). The rapid expansion of this national network was a result, in part, of support received from the newly established National Endowment for the Arts, but also from changes in the tax laws, which made it easier for individuals to make tax-deductible donations to non-profit institutions. Thirty years later many of these theatres – for some have already closed due to mounting and unmanageable deficits – now face new financial challenges as certain members of the Congress call for the complete elimination of the NEA. Concurrently, the commercial theatre in the United States, which in the nineties is still found primarily in New York, is also wrestling with the reality of escalating production costs, ticket prices beyond the budget of many individuals who would otherwise support the theatre, and an amorphous audience base.

What all of this means in terms of design and designers is worth considering, even though briefly. When public and private support for the arts is being radically reduced, those administrators who are responsible for an institution's annual budget will understandably look for ways to trim their costs. Certain operating expenses, however, cannot be cut without seriously compromising the effectiveness of the organization, so other line items, like the design of a specific production, are looked at for a quick fix. Good designers know how to stretch a dollar, as it were, but the dollar can be stretched only so far before it snaps back to reality.

This factor does present one reasonable explanation for the prevalence of minimalist or fragmented sets (in which an entire environment is suggested by just a few objects) and the eclectic use of period and contemporary costumes (often pulled from the institution's stock) throughout the eighties and

30. Model (exterior of Palmer House in Act II) for *Show Boat* as designed and executed by Eugene Lee. Unlike many designers, Lee prefers to work with models rather than set renderings. Courtesy of Eugene Lee.

into the nineties as a response to this economic situation. More than one resident theatre with a serious cash flow problem has addressed its deficit by performing much of its season in the round, thus completely avoiding the more expensive sets that otherwise would be required to fill its stage space. Other theatres have made different choices, including producing plays that use one set instead of two or three, the producing of plays with relatively small casts, or co-producing productions with another theatre, thus sharing expenses. The full and long-range effects of these cost-cutting measures have yet to be determined, but they clearly influence the work of the designers and, by extension, the theatregoer's experience.

But the health of the theatre community and the quality of the work of its designers is also a product of other financial issues, some of which relate to the theatre only tangentially. For example, the costume shops in New York originally served Broadway, Off-Broadway, opera, and ballet, and more recently both film and television. However, as money became tighter, one noticed in New York fewer productions, fewer lavish period extravaganzas, and an increased number of "modern dress" shows. With fewer and fewer shows being "built," each of the costume shops had to find new ways to stay afloat financially. Some of them diversified their services by working for film and television, which fortunately was moving back into the city, while others simply closed.

Additional economic challenges surfaced as the result of a booming real estate market in New York City during the eighties, which affected many small businesses, including costume shops (but not scene shops, which for various reasons could operate competitively within a 100-mile radius of Manhattan). Astronomical increases in rents forced some of the shops to seek smaller spaces, others to purchase a building cooperatively, and still others to close completely. Some of the costume shops dealing with the financial situation of the times include Accu-Costumes (formerly Schnoz and Schnoz), Eaves Brooks Costume Co., Grace Costumes, Barbara Matera, Michael-Jon Costumes Inc., Jimmy Meyer, Ltd., Parsons-Meares Ltd., John Reid Costumes, Inc., Studio, and Vincent's.

As more and more set, costume, and lighting designers found, for some of the reasons discussed above, fewer and fewer opportunities to work in the theatre, they began seeking employment in other areas. Although the resumés of select older designers do contain a mix of theatre, opera, and ballet, the younger designers began patching together careers by working for resident theatres, accepting full- or part-time teaching positions, or designing the occasional film or television show (which became easier when film and television production returned to New York in the eighties). Some designers, like Eugene Lee and Santo Loquasto, successfully combined work in the theatre with work, respectively, in television and film. (Lee has designed *Saturday Night Live!* since its inception; Loquasto has been the production designer on many of Woody Allen's films.) Others, however, like Patrizia von Brandenstein and David Chapman, went into film and rarely returned to the stage.

Another group of designers sought work in what is not traditionally thought of as theatre, but could be described as a kind of "public theater," by which is meant rock concerts, industrial shows (also referred to as "business theatre" or "industrial theatre"), and theme parks (such as Disney World and Universal Studios). Given the demanding schedules associated with productions for these, few designers could maintain a career that included one of them plus theatre, but they did provide a late-twentieth-century alternative for talented individuals who wished to find a major outlet for their creative and technical skills.

The design of rock concerts – and how the design of rock concert lighting consequently influenced theatre design – is a fascinating phenomenon, but far too complex and technical for this overview. Suffice it to say that an entire moving light industry was developed to accommodate the concert tours of David Bowie, Michael Jackson, Mick Jagger and the Rolling Stones, Kiss, Madonna, Queen, and Tina Turner, to name a few of the more popular performers. In addition, the design of these shows, as well as the accompanying music videos that promoted the performers, also had a profound effect on the design of theatre, film, and television. Given the economic reality of the time, a designer could not afford to specialize in one theatre form. Nor could the designer remain competitive if he or she were unaware of what was occurring in other theatrical forms, whether or not they choose to work in those forms.

Cross-fertilization

As designers move between theatre, opera, ballet, film, and television, between rock concerts, industrial shows, and theme parks, between commercial, non-profit, and academic institutions; as the definition of theatre continues to expand to include all kinds of performances and public presentations; as interest in theatre and the financial health of its major institutions fluctuates from year to year, one notices a kind of movement within the industry that can, at first glance, appear unsettling. While some may consider this movement to be the symptom of an unhealthy industry, others view it as an opportunity for the industry to renew itself, which it must do if it is to remain a vital part of the culture in which it is found. It is this rich and various process of cross-fertilization that ultimately characterizes much of what is happening in the design of American theatre at the end of the twentieth century.

For example, the physical staging of *Dreamgirls* (1981) and the opening sequence of *La Cage Aux Folles* (1983) were lavishly praised for their cinematic qualities, and, in fact, the set designers of these productions (Robin Wagner and David Mitchell, respectively) did find a theatrical equivalent for replicating cinematic conventions on the stage. Or for another example, a Russian architecture student by the name of George Tsypin moved to New York, studied stage design at New York University, and then produced settings, like those he designed for productions directed by Peter Sellars or JoAnne Akalaitis, that exhibited a remarkable understanding of the plasticity of architectural space, an understanding that had not been part of the theatrical vocabulary up until that point.

For better or for worse, Las Vegas, MTV, and Walt Disney also generated new approaches and methods that called into question the traditional assumptions about design and the creative process. And although the theatre industry has never suffered from a glut of professional publications, such magazines as *Theatre Design & Technology*, *Theatre Crafts*, and *American Theatre* participated in the process by publishing articles and illustrating them with production photographs, which subsequently informed the work of many American designers who otherwise would not have known about the productions. Patrice Chereau's 1976 production of Wagner's *Ring* cycle for the Bayreuth Festival, for instance, had an enormous impact on subsequent design not only because of its radical interpretation but because photographs and video documentation of the production were available worldwide.

This last example brings up one more topic for consideration, one which directly addresses the relationship between movement across geographical

31 and 32. Designs by two of the most prominent and active designers in the American theatre during the last quarter of the twentieth century. John Lee Beatty's set design (top) for Lanford Wilson's *Burn This* (he has designed virtually all of Wilson's premieres) reflects a kind of lyric realism, typical of one of his many styles. Courtesy of John Lee Beatty. The model (below) of the revival of the musical *A Funny Thing Happened on the Way to the Forum* (1996) as designed by Tony Walton (designer of the original 1963 production as well) is a good example of his witty and playful style. Courtesy of Tony Walton.

boundaries and the design process. Not everyone could travel to Europe to see the ground-breaking, visually stunning productions of directors such as Peter Brook, Ariane Mnouchkine, or Giorgio Strehler, or the many productions presented as part of the Festival d'Avignon, the Edinburgh International Festival (and Festival Fringe), or Italy's Spoleto Festival. Productions from Europe, as well as from Africa, Asia, and South America, however, appeared somewhat regularly on American soil after the mid-seventies, either as independent productions or under the auspices of various festival umbrellas, including the Brooklyn Academy of Music's Next Wave Festival, PepsiCo Summerfare and the Spoleto Festival in Charleston, South Carolina. The work of German choreographer Pina Bausch was virtually unknown in the United States until her company, the Tanztheater Wuppertal, was presented in the Next Wave Festival of 1984. Designers and general theatregoers alike were in awe of her work, much of which depended on meticulously crafted stage pictures that bordered on the surrealistic. In the previous year, Giorgio Strehler's ravishing production of William Shakespeare's *The Tempest*, presented as part of PepsiCo Summerfare on the campus of State University of New York–Purchase, was also lauded for its visual effects. While it is difficult to determine precisely how these and other foreign productions informed the work of American designers, it is safe to assume that on some level, whether seen in person or in photographs, they did in fact influence the quality and approach of the work by designers working in America, even if only indirectly. What is undeniable is that the process by which American theatre design is influenced by both internal and exterior forces is a complex one, and one which cannot be reduced to a simple discussion of cause-and-effect or the identification of various stylistic trends.

Conclusion

At the end of the twentieth century it is ever more difficult to suggest what theatre will look like, both figuratively and literally, in the twenty-first century. In the time it will take this chapter to move from the editor's desk to the printed page, the death of Broadway will be announced yet again, exciting new theatre companies will receive rave reviews in their local newspapers, and any number of young, talented individuals will be hired to design their first professional productions. With near-instant access to almost anything almost anywhere in the world, tracing influences and making predictions becomes an exercise in futility.

The theatre, in other words, is constantly reinventing itself, and designers play a pivotal role in this process. With rare exceptions, however, their work is seldom acknowledged in reviews with any more than a sentence or two.

And while a handful of designers might be known to the general public who regularly attend theatre performances, there is little evidence to indicate that many of these theatregoers fully understand the important role set, lighting, sound and costume designers often play in the productions they attend, especially in the productions of new work. Playwrights, directors, and actors receive a fair amount of coverage, although even in the trade press these articles almost always tend to be personality-based. Designers, except for the award-winners, get noticeably less coverage. Even in the specialized publications that focus on contemporary art and design, the feature article that takes an informed, critical look at theatre design is a rarity.

Part of the problem lies with the press, of course, but equal responsibility for the situation must be shared by those academic communities that train future theatre professionals and by the practicing theatre professionals themselves. A program that includes a course, or even part of a course, in which students are taught how to look at, analyze, and write about contemporary theatre design is a rarity. This is unfortunate for several reasons. First, it implies that theatre design is less important, less valuable than some other forms of design. Second, it fails to document a rich legacy of interesting and innovative work now being done by a large number of very talented artists. And third, the lack of such documentation affects the quality of work to come not only from designers, but from everyone involved in the production or study of professional theatre.

Granted, the ephemeral nature of theatre and the challenges involved in mounting a production cannot be discounted, but better documentation is necessary if the art form is to develop and grow. As David Cockayne, a British theatre designer and educator, writes at the end of "Documenting Design" (*TD&T*, Spring 1989): "We are known by the works we carry out. But we may be forgotten and fail to make our proper mark on the development of theatre and the people we serve through it if we simply neglect to make a record that truly does our work justice." Without a proper record, and without the proper scholarly writing about "the record," the future of theatre may be more precarious, certainly more allusive, than even the most cynical practitioner could imagine.

The following is a selective, short list of the significant set, costume, and lighting designers working in the United States at the end of the twentieth century. For every name that appears on the list, three to five others could be added. The designers included, however, have made immeasurable contributions to American theatre design, and their work is worth studying for what it contributed to a particular production as well as for how it advances theatre history in general and theatre design in particular.

Set designers, some of whom also design costumes (c) or lighting (l), include: Loy Arcenas, John Arnone, Chris Barreca, Mark Beard, John Lee

Beatty, Maria Bjorson (c), Scott Bradley, Zack Brown (c), David Chapman, Jim Clayburgh, John Conklin (c), Clarke Dunham (l), Ben Edwards (l), Dex Edwards, Karl Eigsti, Eldon Elder (l), Heidi Ettinger (previously Landesman), Richard Foreman, Ralph Funicello, Edward T. Gianfrancesco, David Gropman, David Hays (l), Desmond Heeley (c), Riccardo Hernandez, Robert Israel (c), Andrew Jackness, Neil Peter Jampolis (c), David Jenkins, Marjorie Bradley Kellogg, Hugh Landwehr, Peter Larkin, Eugene Lee, Ming Cho Lee, Adrianne Lobel, Santo Loquasto (c), Thomas Lynch, Charles McClennahan, Michael McGarty, Derek McLane, David Mitchell, John Napier (c), Paul Palazzo, Russell Parkman, Neil Patel, Kevin Rigdon (l), Douglas W. Schmidt, Ann Sheffield, Loren Sherman, Sharon Sprague, Douglas Stein, Anita Stewart, Tony Straiges, Rouben Ter-Arutunian (c), James Tilton (l), George Tsypin, Robin Wagner, Tony Walton (c), Robert Wilson (l), Paul Wonsek (l), Michael Yeargan (c), and James Youmans.

Costume designers include: Theoni V. Aldredge, Joseph G. Aulisi, Whitney Blausen, Jeanne Button, Patton Campbell, Judy Dearing, Judith Dolan, Deborah Dryden, Ann Emonts, Christina Giannini, Jess Goldstein, Jane Greenwood, Susan Hilferty, Ann Hould-Ward, Willa Kim, Florence Klotz, Franne Lee, William Ivey Long, Carol Luiken, David Murin, Jennifer von Mayrhauser, Patricia McGourty, Robert Morgan, Ruth Morley, Carol Oditz, Martin Pakledinaz, Nancy Potts, Dunya Ramicova, Carrie Robbins, Melina Root, Ann Roth, Rita Ryack, James Scott, David Toser, Susan Tsu, Ann Waugh, Robert Wojewodski, Albert Wolsky, Patricia Zipprodt, and Catherine Zuber.

Lighting designers: Frances Aronson, Martin Aronstein, Brenda Berry, Ken Billington, John Boesche (projections), Dawn Chiang, Peggy Clark, Pat Collins, Peggy Eisenhauser, Beverly Emmons, Arden Fingerhut, Jules Fisher, Paul Gallo, John Gleason, David Grill, Wendall Harrington (projections), David Hersey, Ralph Holmes, Allen Lee Hughes, James I. Ingalls, Peter Kaczorowski, Kevin Lamotte, Kirby Malone (projections), Anne Militello, Craig Miller, Robby Monk, Roger Morgan, Tharon Musser, Richard Nelson, Dennis Parichy, Richard Pilbrow, Richard Riddell, Leni Schwendinger (projections), Jerome Sirlin (projections), Thomas Skelton, Stephen Strawbridge, Howard Thies, Jennifer Tipton, Gil Wechsler, Marc B. Weiss, and Scott Zielinski.

The twentieth century has witnessed great advances in the way theatre productions have been designed. Some of these advances, as suggested in the beginning of this chapter, are based on developing technology and changing professional practices. Other advances, occurring later in the century, are more closely connected to public and private support for the arts, the broader entertainment industry, popular culture, mass media, the proliferation of academic and professional training programs, and economic factors. What any of this means for theatre in the twenty-first century remains to be seen, of course, but we can be sure that future changes will be both rapid and exciting, and that new influences are likely to emerge from the unlikeliest of places.

Notes

1 A list of such theatres would include American Place Theatre, Chelsea Theatre Center, Circle Repertory, Hudson Guild, Jewish Repertory, Lincoln Center Theater Company, Manhattan Theatre Club, Negro Ensemble Company, New York Shakespeare Festival, Pan Asian Repertory, Phoenix Theatre, Roundabout Theatre Company, and Second Stage.
2 Included in this list would have to be Caffe Cino, Ellen Stewart's La MaMa ETC, Judson Poets' Theatre, and Theatre Genesis, followed by such companies, usually associated with a particular individual, as the Byrd Hoffman School for Byrds (Robert Wilson), Mabou Mines (JoAnne Akalaitis, Lee Breuer, Ruth Maleczech), Manhattan Project (Andre Gregory), The Performance Group (Richard Schechner), Ontological-Hysteric Theatre Company (Richard Foreman), The Open Theatre (Joseph Chaikin), the Ridiculous Theatrical Company (Charles Ludlum), The Wooster Group (Elizabeth LeCompte), and, in California, George Coates Performance Works. For more specific coverage of many of these, see Carlson's and Gussow's essays in chapter 2.
3 Theatre institutions associated with this movement include Actors Theatre of Louisville, the Alley Theatre (Houston), Alliance Theatre (Atlanta), American Conservatory Theatre (San Francisco), Arena Stage (Washington, D.C.), Center Stage (Baltimore), Dallas Theater Center, The Guthrie Theater (Minneapolis), Hartford Stage Company (Connecticut), Long Wharf Theatre (New Haven), Magic Theatre (San Francisco), Mark Taper Forum (Los Angeles), Milwaukee Repertory Theater, Seattle Repertory Theatre, South Coast Repertory (Costa Mesa, California), and Trinity Repertory Company (Providence, R.I.). See LoMonaco's discussion in Chapter 2.

Bibliography: American Theatre Design Since 1945

The history of American theatre design must be patched together from a variety of sources, as there are no comprehensive, scholarly studies of the field. Of the design books that do exist, the majority can more accurately be described as "how-to" manuals (that is, how to construct a set or build a costume or illuminate the stage), and, therefore, with one or two exceptions, are not included here. Brief historical entries for each of the disciplines can be found in the *Cambridge Guide to American Theatre*, edited by Don B. Wilmeth and Tice L. Miller, from which came much of the pre-1945 information in the beginning of this chapter (see "Costume," "Scenic design," and "Stage lighting"). The important topic of theatre architecture, omitted from this chapter, is given a useful survey as well (additional sources on architecture are suggested in this bibliographical essay). General histories of theatre that include significant amounts of historical information on the design of scenery, costumes, and lighting include Bordman's *The Oxford Companion to American Theatre*; Brockett's *History of the Theatre*; and Mary C. Henderson's *Theater in America*, which contains an extensive bibliography. Bigsby's *A Critical Introduction to Twentieth-Century American Drama* is also very helpful in the piecing together of a comprehensive history.

Although ostensively a "how-to" manual, *Designing and Drawing for the Theatre*, by Pecktal, is included here because it is lavishly illustrated with many photographs of contemporary sets, set models, and sketches for sets and costumes. Unlike other "how-to" books, it also includes commentary from those working in the profession as well as lengthy, very informative "conversations" with Tony Walton, Robert O'Hearn, Douglas W. Schmidt, Ming Cho Lee, Tony Straiges, David Mitchell, Robin Wagner, Santo Loquasto, David Jenkins, John Conklin, John Lee Beatty, and John Napier. Two other books, both by George C. Izenour, provide a detailed, historical analysis of theatre architecture and technology: *Theater Design* and *Theater Technology*. While both books are intended primarily for professional architects, theatre consultants, and technicians, they each contain much useful information for the evaluation of theatre practice in the second half of the twentieth century.

Books specifically about scenic design include Appelbaum's *The New York Stage*; Aronson's *American Set Design*; Blum's *A Pictorial History of the American Theatre, 1860–1976*; Burdick's (et al.) *Contemporary Stage Design, USA*; Hainaux's *Stage Design Throughout the World Since 1950*; Kienzle's *Modern World Theatre*; Larson's *Scene Design in the American Theatre from 1915 to 1960*; Owen's *Scenic Design on Broadway*; Rischbieter's *Art and the Stage in the Twentieth Century*; and Ronn Smith's *American Set Design 2*. Aronson's *American Set Design* contains critical essays on the work of John Lee Beatty, John Conklin, Karl Eigsti, Ralph Funicello, Marjorie Bradley Kellogg, Eugene Lee, Ming Cho Lee, Santo Loquasto, David Mitchell, Douglas Schmidt, and Robin Wagner. Smith's *American Set Design 2* contains interviews with Loy Arcenas, John Arnone, David Gropman, Robert Israel, Heidi Landesman (who changed her name to Heidi Ettinger in 1997), Hugh Landwehr, Adrianne Lobel, Charles McClennahan, Tony Straiges, George Tsypin, and Michael Yeargan. Both books contain many photographs. Unfortunately, no comparable books for either costume or lighting designers exist, so interviews with – as well as essays about – these designers must be searched for in various magazines (see below).

There are also a number of books by (or about) designers and design that can be very useful when studying American theatre production. These include Appia's *Music and the Art of the Theatre*; Craig's *On the Art of the Theatre, Scene, The Theatre Advancing*, and *Towards a New Theatre*, the latter two providing excellent introductions to the New Stagecraft; Bay's *Stage Design*; Robert Edmond Jones's *The Dramatic Imagination*; Mielziner's *Designing for the Theatre* (Mary C. Henderson has completed a yet unpublished biography of Mielziner); Oenslager's *Scenery Then and Now, Stage Design*, and *The Theatre of Donald Oenslager*; Pendleton's *The Theatre of Robert Edmond Jones*; Polakov's *We Live to Paint Again*; Rich's (with Lisa Aronson) *The Theatre Art of Boris Aronson*; and Simonson's *The Art of Scenic Design: A Pictorial Analysis of Stage Setting and its Relation to Theatrical Productions* and *Part of a Lifetime*.

Other books that provide useful information relating to theatre design include Goldberg's *Performance: Live Art Since 1960*; McNamara, Rojo, and Schechner's *Theatres, Spaces, Environments*, which provides a very good introduction to environmental theatre; Morrow's *The Tony Award Book*; and Zeigler's *Regional Theatre*.

There are far fewer books about costume design, lighting design, and the designers who work in these disciplines. Even the general theatre histories listed above tend to devote more space to set design than to costume or lighting design. (There is much good, critical work to be found in theses and dissertations, of course, but space limitations prevent them from being listed here.) Books about costume design include the Andersons' *Costume Design*; Corey's *The Mask of Reality*; Owen's *Costume Design on Broadway: Designers and Their Credits, 1915–1985*; and Russell's *Stage Costume Design, Theory, Technique and Style*.

Books about lighting design include Bergman's *Lighting in the Theatre*; Hartmann's *Theatre Lighting*, useful as an historical record of early practice; Hay's *Light on the*

Subject; McCandless's *Method of Lighting the Stage* and *A Syllabus of Stage Lighting*; McCandless and Rubin's *Illuminating Engineering*; Owen's *Lighting Design on Broadway*; Palmer's *The Lighting Art*; Rosenthal and Wertenbaker's *The Magic of Light*; Rubin and Watson's *Theatrical Lighting Practice*; Selden and Sellman's *Stage Scenery and Lighting*; Sellman and Lesley's *Essentials of Stage Lighting*; and Lee Watson's *Lighting Design Handbook*.

The dissemination and documentation of new ideas about design through magazines cannot be overestimated. While some of the following publications are devoted exclusively to design, others may run only the occasional design article, which may (or not) be accompanied with one or two production shots. However, each magazine, in its own way, documents an art form that is, by definition, ephemeral, and thus provides a valuable service to future designers and scholars. Principal design publications include *Theatre Arts Magazine* (published between 1916 and 1948; also known as *Theatre Arts Monthly*); *Theatre Crafts* (which began publishing in 1967, and then in 1992 changed its name to *TCI*, for *Theatre Crafts International*); and *Theatre Design & Technology* (which the United States Institute for Theatre Technology began publishing in 1965). Other publications that occasionally cover design, but to a lesser extent, include *American Theatre* (published by Theatre Communications Group), *Back Stage*, *The Drama Review* (*TDR*), *Dramatists Quarterly*, *Lighting Dimensions*, *Other Stages*, *Performing Arts Journal* (*PAJ*), *Playbill*, *Studies in American Drama 1945–Present*, *Theater*, *Theatre Annual*, *Theatre Profiles* (published annually by Theatre Communications Group), *Theatre Guild Magazine*, *Theatre Journal* (and *Educational Theatre Journal*), *Theatre Survey*, *TheatreWeek* (succeeded by *InTheatre*), *Theatre World* (published annually since 1943), and *Variety*.

Finally, coverage of theatre architecture, in addition to Wilmeth and Miller, *Cambridge Guide to American Theatre*, McNamara, Rojo and Schechner, *Theatres, Spaces, Environments*, Izenour's *Theater Design,* and Mary C. Henderson's *Theater in America*, can be found in Young's *Famous American Playhouses*, as well as standard histories of the theatre building, such as Mullin's *The Development of the Playhouse*. A fascinating recent study, providing some insight into American theatres (such as Lincoln Center) but more specifically suggesting ways to look at theatres as semiotic objects, is Carlson's *Places of Performance*. Lincoln Center, along with general ideas of theatre architecture, is discussed in Mielziner's *The Shapes of Our Theatre,* in Mary C. Henderson's forthcoming biography of Mielziner, and in Ralph Martin's *Lincoln Center for the Performing Arts*. Visionary ideas from the early sixties can be seen in *The Ideal Theater*, edited by Cogswell, while actual design of the period is covered in Silverman's *Contemporary Theatre Architecture*; design of the seventies is dealt with in *Theatre Design 75*, edited by Frink. The possibilities of reclaiming older theatres today as seen through the history and total restoration of The New Amsterdam on New York's Forty-Second Street (part of the mammoth restoration of this theatre district in the nineties) is beautifully told and illustrated in Mary C. Henderson's *The New Amsterdam*. Sources on both architecture and design, though now dated, can be found in the recommended annotated lists by Stoddard, *Theatre and Cinema Architecture*, as well as in Silvester's *United States Theatre*. Frequently, the best coverage of theatre architecture can be found in technical theatre journals, mentioned above, as well as such architectural journals as *Architectural Record* (see, for example, the November 1969 issue on the Milwaukee Center for the Performing Arts and the Krannert Center for the Performing Arts at the University of Illinois), *Architectural Design*, and *Journal of the American Institute of American Architecture*.

Bibliography

(The sources below include those mentioned in the text, in notes, and in bibliographical essays at the conclusion of each chapter.)

Abbott, George. *Mister Abbott*. New York: Random House, 1963.

Abramson, Doris E. *Negro Playwrights in the American Theatre 1925–1959*. New York: Columbia University Press, 1969.

Adler, Richard, with Lee Davis. *"You Gotta Have Heart": An Autobiography*. New York: Donald I. Fine, 1990.

Adler, Stella. *The Technique of Acting*. New York: Bantam Books, 1988.

Adler, Thomas P. *American Drama 1940–1960: A Critical History*. New York: Twayne Publishers, 1994.

　Mirror on the Stage: The Pulitzer Plays as an Approach to American Drama. West Lafayette, Ind.: Purdue University Press, 1997.

Albee, Edward. "Which Theatre is the Absurd One?" *New York Times Magazine* 25 February 1962. In Walter Merserve, ed., *Discussions of Modern Drama*. Boston: D.C. Heath, 1966.

　The Plays, I. New York: Coward, McCann, Geohegan, 1981.

Altman, Richard, and Mervyn D. Kaufman. *The Making of a Musical: Fiddler on the Roof*. New York: Crown, 1971.

Amacher, Richard E. *Edward Albee*. Rev. edn. Boston: Twayne, 1982.

Ambush, Benny Sato. "Pluralism to the Bone." *American Theatre* 6 (April 1989): 5.

Anderson, Barbara and Cletus. *Costume Design*. New York: Holt, Rinehart, and Winston, 1984.

Appelbaum, Stanley. *The New York Stage: Famous Productions in Photographs*. New York: Dover Publications, 1976.

Appia, Adolphe. *Music and the Art of the Theatre*. Coral Gables, Fla.: University of Miami Press, 1962.

Arnott, Catherine, comp. *Tennessee Williams on File*. London and New York: Methuen, 1985.

Aronson, Arnold. *American Set Design*. New York: Theatre Communications Group, 1985.

　The History and Theory of Environmental Scenography. Ann Arbor, Mich.: UMI Research Press, 1981.

Artaud, Antonin. *The Theatre and Its Double*. Trans. Mary Caroline Richards. New York: Grove Press, 1958.

Atkinson, Brooks. *Broadway*. New York: The Macmillan Company, 1970.

Auerbach, Doris. *Sam Shepard, Arthur Kopit, and the Off Broadway Theater*. Boston: Twayne Publishers, 1982.

Ball, William. *A Sense of Direction*. New York: Drama Book Publishers, 1984.

Banes, Sally. *Democracy's Body*. Ann Arbor: University of Michigan Press, 1983.

Terpsichore in Sneakers: Postmodern Dance. 3rd edn. Middletown, Conn.: Wesleyan University Press, 1987.

Greenwich Village 1963: Avant-Garde Performance and the Effervescent Body. Durham, N.C.: Duke University Press, 1993.

Banfield, Stephen. *Sondheim's Broadway Musicals*. Ann Arbor: University of Michigan Press, 1993.

Baraka, Amiri. "The Descent of Charles Fuller into Pulitzerland and the Need for African-American Institutions." *Black American Literature Forum* 17 (1983): 53.

The Autobiography of LeRoi Jones. New York: Freundlich Books, 1984.

Barnett, Gene A. *Lanford Wilson*. Boston: Twayne Publishers, 1987.

Barnouw, Erik. *Tube of Plenty: The Evolution of American Television*. New York: Oxford University Press, 1990.

Bartow, Arthur. *The Director's Voice: Twenty-one Interviews*. New York: Theatre Communications Group, 1988.

Battcock, Gregory and Robert Nickas. *The Art of Performance*. New York: E.P. Dutton, 1984.

Baumol, William J., and William G. Bowen. *Performing Arts – The Economic Dilemma*. New York: The Twentieth Century Fund, 1966.

Bay, Howard. *Scene Design*. New York: Drama Books Specialists,1974.

Beck, Julian. *The Life of the Theatre*. San Francisco: City Lights Books, 1972.

"Storming the Barricades." In Kenneth H. Brown, *The Brig*. New York: Hill and Wang, 1965.

Beeson, William. *Thresholds: The Story of Nina Vance's Alley Theatre*. Houston: Alley Theatre, 1969.

Behr, Edward. *The Complete Book of Les Misérables*. New York: Arcade-Little, 1989.

Behr, Edward and Mark Steyn. *The Story of Miss Saigon*. New York: Arcade-Little, 1991.

Bell, Daniel. *The End of Ideology: On the Exhaustion of Political Ideas in the Fifties*. New York: The Free Press, 1962.

The Coming of Post-Industrial Society: A Venture in Social Forecasting. London: Heinemann, 1974.

The Cultural Contradictions of Capitalism. New York: Basic Books, Inc.,1976.

Bell, John. "AIDS and Avantgarde Classicism." *The Drama Review* 39, T148 (Fall 1993): 21–47.

Benston, Kimberly W. *Baraka: The Renegade and the Mask*. New Haven, Conn.: Yale University Press, 1976.

Bentley, Eric. *The Theatre of Commitment*. New York: Atheneum, 1967.

The Theatre of War; Comments on 32 Occasions. New York: The Viking Press, 1972.

Bergman, Gösta M. *Lighting in the Theatre*. Totowa, N.J.: Rowman and Littlefield, 1977.

Bergreen, Laurence. *As Thousands Cheer: The Life of Irving Berlin*. New York: Viking-Penguin, 1990.

Berkowitz, Gerald M. *New Broadways: Theatre Across America 1950–1980*. Totowa, N.J.: Rowman and Littlefield, 1982; rev. edn., New York: Applause Books, 1997.

American Drama of the Twentieth Century. London and New York: Longman Group, 1992.

Berson, Misha. "Keeping Company." *American Theatre* 7 (April 1990): 6–23, 70–73.

Best Plays series. Various editors. New York: Dodd, Mead, 1920–1987; Applause Books, 1988–present.

Betsko, Kathleen, and Rachel Koenig, eds. *Interviews with Contemporary Women Playwrights.* New York: Beechtree Books, 1987.

Bigsby, C.W.E. *Confrontation and Commitment: A Study of Contemporary American Drama, 1959–1966.* Columbia: University of Missouri Press, 1968.

Albee. Edinburgh: Oliver & Boyd, 1969.

David Mamet. London: Methuen, 1985.

A Critical Introduction to Twentieth Century American Drama, Vols. II (Williams/Miller/Albee) and III (Beyond Broadway). New York and Cambridge: Cambridge University Press, 1984 and 1985.

Modern American Drama 1945–1990. Cambridge and New York: Cambridge University Press, 1992.

Bigsby, C.W.E., ed. *Edward Albee: A Collection of Critical Essays.* Englewood Cliffs, N.J.: Prentice-Hall, 1975.

Bigsby, Christopher, ed. *Arthur Miller and Company.* London: Methuen Drama, 1990.

The Cambridge Companion to Arthur Miller. Cambridge and New York: Cambridge University Press, 1997.

Biner, Pierre. *The Living Theatre.* New York: Horizon Press, 1972.

Blau, Herbert. *The Impossible Theatre: A Manifesto.* New York: Macmillan, 1964.

Block, Geoffrey. *Enchanted Evenings: The Broadway Musical from Show Boat to Sondheim.* New York: Oxford University Press, 1997.

Blum, Daniel. *A Pictorial History of the American Theatre, 1860–1976.* New York: Crown, 1977.

Blumenthal, Eileen. *Joseph Chaikin: Exploring the Boundaries of Theatre.* Cambridge: Cambridge University Press, 1984.

Blumenthal, Eileen, and Julie Taymor. *Julie Taymor: Playing with Fire.* New York: Harry N. Abrams, 1996.

Boleslavski, Richard. *Acting: The First Six Lessons.* New York: Theatre Arts Books, 1949.

Bordman, Gerald. *American Musical Theatre: A Chronicle.* New York: Oxford University Press, 1978.

The Oxford Companion to American Theatre. 2nd edn. New York: Oxford University Press, 1992.

American Musical Comedy: From Adonis to Dreamgirls. New York: Oxford University Press, 1982.

American Musical Revue: From The Passing Show to Sugar Babies. New York: Oxford University Press, 1985.

American Operetta: From H.M.S. Pinafore to Sweeney Todd. New York: Oxford University Press, 1981.

Bottoms, Steven J. *The Theatre of Sam Shepard: States of Crisis.* New York and Cambridge: Cambridge University Press, 1998.

Bradby, David, and David Williams. *Directors' Theatre.* New York and London: St. Martin's Press, 1988.

Brando, Marlon, with Robert Lindsey. *Brando: Songs My Mother Taught Me.* New York: Random House, 1994.

Brantley, Ben. "Sam Shepard, Storyteller." *New York Times* 13 November 1994: Sec. 2, 26.

Brater, Enoch, ed. *Feminine Focus: The New Women Playwrights.* Oxford and New York: Oxford University Press, 1989.

Brecht, Stefan. *The Theatre of Visions: Robert Wilson.* Frankfurt am Main: Suhrkamp Verlag, 1978.

Breuer, Lee. *Sister Suzie Cinema: The Collected Poems and Performances, 1976–1986.* New York: Theatre Communications Group, 1987.

Brockett, Oscar G. *History of the Theatre.* 7th edn. Boston: Allyn and Bacon, 1994.

Bronner, Edwin. *The Encyclopedia of the American Theatre 1900–1975.* San Diego and New York: A. S. Barnes; London: The Tantivy Press, 1980.

Bronson, A.A., and Peggy Gale. *Performance by Artists.* Toronto: Art Metropole, 1978.

Brooks, Tim, and Earle Marsh. *The Complete Directory of Prime Time Network TV Shows (1946–1985).* New York: Ballantine Books, 1985.

Brown, Lloyd W. *Amiri Baraka.* Boston: Twayne Publishers, 1980.

Brown, Norman O. *Life Against Death: The Psychoanalytical Meaning of History.* Middletown, Conn.: Wesleyan University Press, 1959.

Brown-Guillory, Elizabeth. *Their Place on the Stage: Black Women Playwrights in America.* New York: Greenwood Press, 1988.

Broyles-Gonzalez, Yolanda. *El Teatro Campesino.* Austin: University of Texas Press, 1994.

Brunner, Cornelia. "Roberta Sklar: Toward Creating a Women's Theatre." *The Drama Review* 24 T86 (June 1980): 23–40.

Brustein, Robert. *The Third Theatre.* New York: Alfred A. Knopf, 1969.

"Conversation with Marsha Norman." *Dramatists Guild Quarterly* 21 (1984): 9–21.

"The Siren Song of Broadway is a Warning." *New York Times* 22 May 1988: Sec. 2, 5.

Bryant-Jackson, Paul K., and Lois More Overbeck, eds. *Intersecting Boundaries: The Theatre of Adrienne Kennedy.* Minneapolis: University of Minnesota Press, 1973.

Bryer, Jackson, ed. *The Playwright's Art: Conversations with Contemporary American Dramatists.* New Brunswick, N.J.: Rutgers University Press, 1995.

Buchmuller, Eva, and Anna Koós. *Squat Theatre.* New York: Artists Space, 1996.

Burdick, Elizabeth B., Peggy C. Hansen, and Brenda Zanger. *Contemporary Stage Design, USA.* New York: International Theatre Institute of the United States, 1974.

Burke, Sally F. *American Feminist Playwrights: A Critical History.* New York: Twayne Publishers, 1996.

Cage, John. *John Cage.* Ed. Richard Kostelanetz. London: Allen Lane – Penguin Books, 1974.

Silence. Cambridge, Mass.: The MIT Press, 1961.

Camus, Albert. "Art and Revolt." *Partisan Review* 19.3 (May–June 1952): 268–81.

Carlson, Marvin. *Places of Performance: The Semiotics of Theatre Architecture.* Ithaca: Cornell University Press, 1989.

Carra, Lawrence. "The Influence of the Director – for Good or Bad." In Henry B. Williams, ed., *The American Theatre: A Sum of its Parts.* New York: Samuel French, 1971.

Carson, Neil. *Arthur Miller.* New York: Grove Press, 1982.

Carter, Steven R. *Hansberry's Drama: Commitment and Complexity.* Urbana: University of Illinois Press, 1991.

Case, Sue-Ellen. *Feminism and Theatre.* New York: Methuen, 1988.

Split Britches. London and New York: Routledge, 1996.

Case, Sue-Ellen, ed. *Performing Feminisms: Feminist Critical Theory and Theatre.* Baltimore: Johns Hopkins University Press, 1990.

Centola, Steven R., ed. *The Achievement of Arthur Miller: New Essays.* Dallas: Contemporary Research Press, 1995.

Chaikin, Joseph. *The Presence of the Actor*. New York: Atheneum, 1972.

Champagne, Lenora. *Out from Under: Texts by Women Performance Artists*. New York: Theatre Communications Group, 1990.

Chapman, John, ed. *Best Plays of 1950–1951*. New York: Dodd, Mead, 1951.

Charnin, Martin. *Annie: A Theatre Memoir*. New York: Dutton, 1977.

Cheney, Anne. *Lorraine Hansberry*. Boston: Twayne Publishers, 1984.

Citron, Stephen. *The Musical from the Inside Out*. London: Hodder & Stoughton, 1991.

   The Wordsmiths: Oscar Hammerstein 2nd & Alan Jay Lerner. New York: Oxford University Press, 1995.

Clurman, Harold. *On Directing*. New York: Macmillan,1974.

   The Fervent Years. New York: Alfred A. Knopf, 1945.

   The Collected Works of Harold Clurman. Ed. Marjorie Loggia and Glenn Young. New York: Applause Books, 1994.

Cogswell, Margaret, ed. *The Ideal Theater: Eight Concepts*. New York: American Federation of Arts and October House, 1962.

Cohn, Ruby. *Edward Albee*. Minneapolis: University of Minnesota Press, 1969.

   Dialogue in American Drama. Bloomington: Indiana University Press, 1971.

   New American Dramatists: 1960–1980. New York: Grove Press, 1982.

   American Drama, 1960–1990. New York: St. Martin's Press, 1991.

   Anglo-American Interplay in Recent Drama. Cambridge: Cambridge University Press, 1995.

   "Tennessee Williams: The Last Two Decades." In Matthew C. Roudané, ed., *The Cambridge Companion to Tennessee Williams*. Cambridge: Cambridge University Press, 1997.

Cole, Susan Letzler. *Directors in Rehearsal: A Hidden World*. New York: Routledge, 1992.

Cole, Toby, and Helen Krich Chinoy. *Directors on Directing*. Indianapolis: Bobbs-Merrill, 1953.

Coming to Terms: American Plays and the Vietnam War. Intro. by James Reston, Jr. New York: Theatre Communications Group, 1985.

Copeland, Roger, and Marshall Cohen, eds., *What Is Dance? Readings in Theory and Criticism*. New York: Oxford University Press, 1983.

Cordell, Richard A., and Lowell Matson, eds. *The Off-Broadway Theatre: Seven Plays*. New York: Random House, Inc., 1959.

Corey, Irene. *The Mask of Reality: An Approach to Design for Theatre*. Anchorage, Ky.: Anchorage Press, 1968.

Corrigan, Robert W., ed. *Arthur Miller: A Collection of Critical Essays*. Englewood Cliffs, N.J.: Prentice-Hall, 1982.

Craig, Edward Gordon. *On the Art of the Theatre*. New York: Theatre Arts Books, 1980.

   Scene. Rpt. New York: Benjamin Blom, 1968.

   The Theatre Advancing. Rpt. New York: Benjamin Blom, 1963.

   Towards a New Theatre: Forty Designs for Stage Scenes with Critical Notes by the Inventor. Rpt. New York: Benjamin Blom, 1969.

Crandell, George. *Tennessee Williams: A Descriptive Bibliography*. Pittsburgh: University of Pittsburgh Press, 1996.

Croyden, Margaret. *Lunatics, Lovers and Poets: The Contemporary Experimental Theatre*. New York: McGraw-Hill, 1974.

Cunningham, Merce, in conversation with Jacqueline Lesschaeve. *The Dancer and the Dance*. New York and London: Marion Boyars Publishers, 1991.

Danforth, Roger. *Cleveland Play House 1915–1990*. Cleveland: Cleveland Play House, 1990.

Davis, Christopher. *The Producer.* New York: Harper & Row, 1972.

Davis, Lorrie, with Rachel Gallagher. *Letting Down my HAIR: Two Years with the Love Rock Tribe – From Dawning to Downing of Aquarius.* New York: Arthur Fields Books, 1973.

Davis, R.G. *The San Francisco Mime Troupe.* Palo Alto, Calif.: Ramparts Press, 1975.

Davis, Walter A. *Get the Guests: Psychoanalysis, Modern American Drama, and the Audience.* Madison: University of Wisconsin Press, 1994.

Davy, Kate. *Richard Foreman: Plays and Manifestos.* Ann Arbor, Mich.: UMI Research Press, 1981.

Dawidziak, Mark. *The Barter Theatre Story: Love Made Visible.* Boone, N.C.: Appalachian Consortium Press, 1982.

Dean, Ann. *David Mamet: Language As Dramatic Action.* Rutherford, N.J.: Fairleigh Dickinson University Press, 1990.

Debusscher, Gilbert, and Henry I. Schvey, eds. *New Essays on American Drama.* Amsterdam: Rodopi, 1989.

Demastes, William W. *Beyond Naturalism: A New Realism in American Theatre.* Westport, Conn.: Greenwood Press, 1988.

Demastes, William W., ed. *Realism and the American Dramatic Tradition.* Tuscaloosa: University of Alabama Press, 1996.

Dent, Thomas C., and Richard Schechner. *The Free Southern Theater.* Indianapolis: Bobbs-Merrill, 1969.

DeRose, David J. *Sam Shepard.* New York: Twayne Publishers, 1992.

Devlin, Albert J., ed. *Conversations with Tennessee Williams.* Jackson: University Press of Mississippi, 1986.

DeVries, Hillary. "The Drama of August Wilson." *Dialogue* 83 (1989): 54.

Dixon, Michael Bigelow, and Joel A. Smith. *Anne Bogart: Viewpoints.* Lyme, N.H.: Smith and Kraus, 1995.

Docherty, Thomas. *Postmodernism: A Reader.* New York: Columbia University Press, 1993.

Dolan, Jill. *The Feminist Spectator as Critic.* Ann Arbor, Mich.: UMI Research Press, 1988.

Donkin, Ellen, and Susan Clement, eds. *Upstaging Big Daddy: Directing Theater as if Gender and Race Matter.* Ann Arbor: University of Michigan Press, 1993.

Downer, Alan S., ed. *The American Theater Today.* New York: Basic Books, 1967.

Drake, Sylvie. "Will the Real Wendy Please Stand Up?" *Los Angeles Times* 28 October 1984: 40.

Duberman, Martin. *Black Mountain: An Exploration in Community.* New York: E.P. Dutton & Co., 1972.

Dunn, Don. *The Making of No, No, Nanette.* Secaucus, N.J.: Citadel Press, 1972.

Easton, Carol. *No Intermissions: The Life of Agnes de Mille.* Boston: Little, Brown, 1996.

Elam, Harry J., Jr. *Taking It to the Streets: The Social Protest Theater of Luis Valdez & Amiri Baraka.* Ann Arbor: University of Michigan Press, 1997.

Ellison, Ralph. *Invisible Man.* New York: Random House, 1952.

Engel, Lehman. *The American Musical Theatre: A Consideration.* Rev. edn. New York: Collier Books, 1975.

Words with Music: The Broadway Musical Libretto. New York: Schirmer-Macmillan, 1972.

Engle, Ron, and Tice L. Miller, eds. *The American Stage: Social and Economic Forces from the Colonial Period to the Present.* Cambridge and New York: Cambridge University Press, 1993.

Epstein, Helen. *Joe Papp: An American Life.* Boston: Little, Brown, 1994.

Esslin, Martin. *The Theatre of the Absurd*. Rev. edn. Garden City, N.Y.: Doubleday, 1969.

Ewen, David. *New Complete Book of the American Musical Theater*. New York: Holt, 1970.

Falk, Signi. *Tennessee Williams*. 2nd edn. New York: Twayne Publishers, 1978.

Farber, Donald C., and Robert Viagas. *The Amazing Story of The Fantasticks: America's Longest Running Play*. Secaucus, N.J.: Citadel Press, 1991.

Fehl, Fred. Text by William Stott with Jane Stott. *On Broadway: Performance Photographs by Fred Fehl*. Austin: University of Texas Press, 1978.

Fichandler, Zelda. "Theatres or Institutions?" *Theatre 3*. New York: International Theatre Institute, 1970: 104–17.

"Institution-As-Artwork." in *Theatre Profiles 7*. New York: Theatre Communications Group, 1986: 1–18.

Fiedler, Leslie A. *Love and Death in the American Novel*. Cleveland: Meridian Books – The World Publishing Company, 1962.

Flanagan, Hallie. *Arena*. New York: Duell, Sloan & Pearce, 1940.

Flinn, Denny Martin. *What They Did for Love: The Untold Story Behind the Making of A Chorus Line*. New York: Bantam, 1989.

Musical! A Grand Tour. New York: Schirmer, 1997.

Fordin, Hugh. *Getting to Know Him: A Biography of Oscar Hammerstein II*. New York: Random House, 1977.

Foreman, Richard. *Unbalancing Acts: Foundations for a Theatre*. Ed. Ken Jordan. New York: Pantheon Books, 1992.

My Head Was a Sledgehammer. Woodstock, N.Y.: The Overlook Press, 1995.

Forsyth, James. *Tyrone Guthrie: A Biography*. London: Hamish Hamilton, 1976.

Frankel, Aaron. *Writing the Broadway Musical*. New York: Drama Book Specialists, 1977.

Frascina, Francis, ed. *Pollock and After: The Critical Debate*. New York: Harper & Row, 1985.

Freedman, Jonathan. "Angels, Monsters, and Jews: Intersections of Queer and Jewish Identity in Kushner's *Angels in America.*" *PMLA* (113) 1998: 90–102.

Freedman, Morris. *American Drama in Social Context*. Carbondale: Southern Illinois University Press, 1971.

Frick, John W., and Stephen M. Vallillo. *Theatrical Directors: A Biographical Dictionary*. Westport, Conn.: Greenwood Press, 1994.

Frink, Peter H., ed. *Theatre Design 75*. New York: The United States Institute for Theatre Technology, 1975.

Fromm, Erich. *The Art of Loving*. 1957. London: Unwin, 1975.

Frost, Robert. *Complete Poems of Robert Frost*. New York: Holt, Rinehart, 1964.

Fuchs, Elinor. *The Death of Character: Perspectives on Theatre after Modernism*. Bloomington: Indiana University Press, 1996.

Galbraith, John Kenneth. *The Affluent Society*. Boston: Houghton Mifflin, 1958.

Gänzl, Kurt. *Song & Dance: The Complete Story of Stage Musicals*. New York: Smithmark, 1995.

The Musical: A Concise History. Boston: Northeastern University Press, 1997.

Gard, Robert. *Grassroots Theater: A Search for Regional Arts in America*. Madison: University of Wisconsin Press, 1955.

Garebian, Keith. *The Making of Gypsy*. Toronto: ECW Press, 1994.

The Making of My Fair Lady. Toronto: ECW Press, 1993.

The Making of West Side Story. Toronto: ECW Press, 1995.

Gates, Henry Louis, Jr. "The Chitlin Circuit." *New Yorker*. 3 February 1997: 44–55.

Geis, Deborah R., and Steven F. Kruger, eds. *Approaching the Millennium: Essays on Angels in America.* Ann Arbor: University of Michigan Press, 1998.

Gener, Randy. "Put 92 Directors in a Room." *American Theatre* 12 (September 1995): 50–51.

Giantvalley, Scott. *Edward Albee: A Reference Guide.* Boston: G.K. Hall & Co., 1987.

Ginsberg, Allen. *Howl and Other Poems.* San Francisco: City Lights Books, 1959.

Gitlin, Todd. *The Sixties: Years of Hope, Days of Rage.* New York: Bantam, 1987.

Goldberg, Rose Lee. *Performance: Live Art Since 1960.* New York: Harry N. Abrams,1998.

Goldman, William. *The Season: A Candid Look at Broadway.* New York: Bantam, 1970; New York: Limelight, 1994.

Goldstein, Richard. *The Poetry of Rock.* New York: Bantam, 1969.

Gordon, Joanne. *Art Isn't Easy: The Theater of Stephen Sondheim.* Updated edn. New York: Da Capo, 1992.

Gottfried, Martin. *A Theater Divided: The Postwar American Stage.* Boston: Little, Brown, 1967.

Broadway Musicals. New York: Abradale Press/Harry N. Abrams, 1984.

More Broadway Musicals: Since 1980. New York: Harry N. Abrams, 1991.

All His Jazz: The Life and Death of Bob Fosse. New York: Bantam, 1990.

Sondheim. New York: Harry N. Abrams, 1993.

Green, Amy S. *The Revisionist Stage: American Directors Reinvent the Classics.* New York and Cambridge: Cambridge University Press, 1994.

Green, Stanley. *The Rodgers and Hammerstein Story.* New York: John Day, 1963.

The World of Musical Comedy. 4th edn., revised and enlarged. San Diego: A. S. Barnes, 1980. Rpt. New York: Da Capo, 1983.

Greenberg, Clement. "Avant-Garde and Kitsch." *Partisan Review* 6.5 (Fall 1939): 34–49.

Art and Culture: Critical Essays. Boston: Beacon Press, 1961.

Griffin, Alice. *Understanding Tennessee Williams.* Columbia: University of South Carolina Press, 1995.

Understanding Arthur Miller. Columbia: University of South Carolina Press, 1996.

Grotowski, Jerzy. *Towards a Poor Theatre.* New York: Simon and Schuster, 1968.

Grubb, Kevin Boyd. *Razzle Dazzle: The Life and Work of Bob Fosse.* New York and London: St. Martin's Press, 1989.

Guare, John, ed. *The New American Theatre (Conjunctions #25).* Annandale-on-Hudson, N.Y.: Bard College, 1995.

Guernsey, Otis L., Jr. *Curtain Times: The New York Theater 1965–1987.* New York: Applause Books, 1987.

Guilbaut, Serge. *How New York Stole the Idea of Modern Art: Abstract Expressionism, Freedom, and the Cold War.* Trans. Arthur Goldhammer. Chicago and London: University of Chicago Press, 1983.

Gussow, Mel. *Theatre on the Edge: New Visions, New Voices.* New York: Applause, 1997.

Guthrie, Tyrone. *A Life in the Theatre.* New York: McGraw-Hill, 1959.

A New Theatre. New York: McGraw-Hill, 1964.

Hagen, Uta, with Haskel Frankel. *Respect for Acting.* New York: Macmillan, 1973.

A Challenge for the Actor. New York: Scribner's, 1991.

Hainaux, René. *Stage Design Throughout the World Since 1950.* New York: Theatre Arts Books, 1964.

Halberstam, David. *The Fifties.* New York: Villard Books, 1993.

Hamlisch, Marvin, with Girard Gardner. *The Way I Was.* New York: Scribner's, 1992.

Harris, Andrew B. *Broadway Theatre.* New York: Routledge, 1994.

Hart, Lynda. *Sam Shepard's Metaphorical Stages*. Westport, Conn. and New York: Greenwood Press, 1987.

Hart, Lynda, ed. *Making a Spectacle: Feminist Essays on Contemporary Women's Theatre*. Ann Arbor: University of Michigan Press, 1989.

Hart, Lynda, and Peggy Phelan. *Acting Out: Feminist Performances*. Ann Arbor: University of Michigan Press, 1993.

Hartmann, Louis. *Theatre Lighting: A Manual of the Stage Switchboard*. Rpt. New York: DBS Books,1964.

Haskell, Barbara. *Blam! The Explosion of Pop, Minimalism, and Performance 1958–1964*. New York: Whitney Museum of American Art, 1984.

Hay, David. *Light on the Subject*. New York: Limelight Editions, 1989.

Hay, Samuel A. *African-American Theatre: An Historical and Critical Analysis*. Cambridge and New York: Cambridge University Press, 1995.

Ed Bullins: A Literary Biography. Detroit: Wayne State University Press, 1997.

Henderson, Heather. "Building Fences: An Interview with Mary Alice and James Earl Jones." *Theater* 16 (Summer/Fall 1985): 67–70.

Henderson, Mary C. *Theater in America: 200 Years of Plays, Players, and Productions*. Rev. edn. New York: Harry N. Abrams, 1996.

The New Amsterdam: The Biography of a Broadway Theatre. New York: Hyperion, 1997.

Herman, Jerry, with Marilyn Stasio. *Showtune: A Memoir*. New York: Donald I. Fine, 1996.

Hethmon, Robert H., ed. *Strasberg at the Actors Studio*. New York: Viking, 1965.

Heuvel, Michael Vanden. *Performing Drama/Dramatizing Performance*. Ann Arbor: University of Michigan Press, 1991.

Hill, Errol. *The Theatre of Black Americans*. Englewood Cliffs, N.J.: Prentice-Hall, 1980.

Hill, Patricia Liggins, gen. ed. *Call and Response: The Riverside Anthology of the African American Literary Tradition*. Boston: Houghton Mifflin, 1998.

Hirsch, Foster. *Harold Prince and the American Musical Theatre*. New York and Cambridge: Cambridge University Press, 1989.

Holmberg, Arthur. *The Theatre of Robert Wilson*. Cambridge and New York: Cambridge University Press, 1997.

Holmes, John Clellon. "This Is the Beat Generation." *New York Times Magazine*. 16 November 1952.

Horn, Barbara Lee. *The Age of Hair: Evolution and Impact of Broadway's First Rock Musical*. Westport, Conn.: Greenwood Press, 1991.

Hornby, Richard. *The End of Acting: A Radical View*. New York: Applause Books, 1992.

Houghton, Norris. *Advance From Broadway*. New York: Harcourt, Brace, 1941.

Howell, John. *Laurie Anderson* (American Originals series). New York: Thunder's Mouth Press, 1992.

Hulbert, Dan. "Black History in the Spotlight." *Atlanta Journal-Constitution* 24 July 1988: Sec. M, 1.

Huyssen, Andreas. *After the Great Divide: Modernism, Mass Culture, Postmodernism*. Bloomington and Indianapolis: Indiana University Press, 1986.

Ilson, Carol. *Harold Prince: From Pajama Game to Phantom of the Opera*. Ann Arbor, Mich.: UMI Research Press, 1989.

Isenberg, Barbara. *Making it BIG: The Diary of a Broadway Musical*. New York: Limelight, 1996.

Ives, Irving, and Jacob K. Javits. "Toward a National Theatre." *Theatre Arts* (April 1949): 10–13.

Izenour, George C. *Theater Design.* 2nd edn. New Haven: Yale University Press, 1997.
Theater Technology. 2nd edn. New Haven: Yale University Press, 1997.
Jablonski, Edward. *Alan Jay Lerner: A Biography.* New York: Henry Holt, 1996.
Harold Arlen: Rhythm, Rainbows, and Blues. Boston: Northeastern University Press, 1996.
Jackson, Arthur. *The Best Musicals from "Show Boat" to "A Chorus Line": Broadway, Off-Broadway, London.* New York: Crown, 1977.
Jackson, Esther Merle. *The Broken World of Tennessee Williams.* Madison: University of Wisconsin Press, 1965.
Jackson, Paul K., and Lois More Overbeck, eds. *Intersecting Boundaries: The Theatre of Adrienne Kennedy.* Minneapolis: University of Minnesota Press, 1992.
Jacobs, Rita D., ed. *The Who's "Tommy": The Musical.* New York: Pantheon, 1993.
Jacobus, Lee A., ed. *The Longman Anthology of American Drama.* New York: Longman, 1982.
The Bedford Introduction to Drama. 3rd edn. Boston: Bedford Press, 1997.
Johnson, Albert and Bertha. *Directing Methods.* South Brunswick, N.J.: A.S. Barnes, 1970.
Johnson, Robert K. *Neil Simon.* Boston: Twayne Publishers, 1983.
Jones, David Richard. *Great Directors at Work: Stanislavsky, Brecht, Kazan, Brook.* Berkeley, Calif.: University of California Press, 1986.
Jones, Margo. *Theatre-in-the-Round.* New York: Rinehart & Co., 1951.
Jones, Nesta Wyn, and Steven Dykes, eds. *File on Mamet.* London: Methuen, 1991.
Jones, Robert Edmond. *The Dramatic Imagination: Reflections and Speculations on the Art of the Theatre.* New York: Theatre Arts Books, 1941.
Kahn, David, and Donna Breed. *Scriptwork: A Director's Approach to New Play Development.* Carbondale and Edwardsville: Southern Illinois University Press, 1994.
Kane, Leslie, ed. *David Mamet: A Casebook.* New York: Garland, 1992.
Kaprow, Allan. *Assemblage, Environments, and Happenings.* New York: Harry N. Abrams, 1966.
"The Legacy of Jackson Pollock." *Art News* (October 1958): 24–26, 55–57.
Kazan, Elia. *Elia Kazan: A Life.* New York: Alfred A. Knopf, 1988.
Kelly, Kevin. *One Singular Sensation: The Michael Bennett Story.* New York: Doubleday, 1990.
Keniston, Kenneth. *The Uncommitted: Alienated Youth in American Society.* New York: Dell, 1970.
Kennedy, Adrienne. *People Who Led to My Plays.* New York: Alfred A. Knopf, 1987.
Adrienne Kennedy in One Act. Minneapolis: University of Minnesota Press, 1988.
Deadly Triplets: A Theatre Mystery and Journal. Minneapolis: University of Minnesota Press, 1990.
Kernan, Alvin B., ed. *The Modern American Theatre.* Englewood Cliffs, N.J.: Prentice Hall, Inc., 1967.
Keyssar, Helene, ed. *Feminist Theatre and Theory: Contemporary Critical Essays.* New York: St. Martin's Press, 1996.
Kienzle, Siegfried. *Modern World Theatre: A Guide to Productions in Europe and the United States since 1945.* New York: Ungar, 1970.
Kilgore, Emilie S., ed. *Contemporary Plays by Women.* New York: Prentice Hall, 1991.
King, Bruce, ed. *Contemporary American Theatre.* New York: St. Martin's Press, 1991.
King, Kimball. *Sam Shepard: A Casebook.* New York: Garland Publishing, 1988.

King, Kimball, ed. *Hollywood on Stage: Playwrights Evaluate the Culture Industry.* Hamden, Conn.: Garland, 1997.

King, Larry L. *The Whorehouse Papers.* New York: Viking, 1982.

Kintz, Linda. *The Subject's Tragedy: Political Poetics, Feminist Theory, and Drama.* Ann Arbor: University of Michigan Press, 1992.

Kirby, Michael. *A Formalist Theatre.* Philadelphia: University of Pennsylvania Press, 1987.

   Happenings. New York: E.P. Dutton, 1966.

Kislan, Richard. *Hoofing on Broadway: A History of Show Dancing.* New York: Prentice-Hall, 1987.

   The Musical: A Look at the American Musical Theatre. Revised edn. New York: Applause, 1995.

Kissel, Howard. *David Merrick: The Abominable Showman.* New York: Applause Books, 1993.

Klaus, Carl H., Miriam Gilbert, and Bradford S. Field, Jr., eds. *Stages of Drama: Classical to Contemporary.* 2nd edn. New York: St. Martin's Press, 1991.

Knight, Arthur, and Kit Knight, eds. *The Beat Vision: A Primary Sourcebook.* New York: Paragon House Publishers, 1987.

Kohtes, Martin Maria. *Guerilla Theater.* Tübingen, 1990.

Kolin, Philip C., ed. *Conversations with Edward Albee.* Jackson: University Press of Mississippi, 1988.

   American Playrights Since 1945: A Guide to Scholarship, Criticism, and Performance. Westport, Conn.: Greenwood Press, 1989.

Kolin, Philip C., and J. Madison Davis, eds. *Critical Essays on Edward Albee.* Boston: G. K. Hall & Co., 1986.

Kolin, Philip C., and Colby H. Kullman, eds. *Speaking on Stage: Interviews with Contemporary American Playwrights.* Tuscaloosa: University of Alabama Press, 1996.

Konas, Gary, ed. *Neil Simon: A Casebook.* Hamden, Conn.: Garland, 1997.

Kornbluth, Jesse, ed. *Notes from the New Underground.* New York: Viking, 1968.

Kostelanetz, Richard. *The Theater of Mixed Means.* 1968. New York: RK Editions, 1980.

   On Innovative Performance(s). Jefferson, N.C.: McFarland & Co., 1994.

   John Cage (Ex)plain(ed): New York: Schirmer, 1996.

Krutch, Joseph Wood. *"Modernism" in Modern Drama: A Definition and an Estimate.* 1953. Rpt. New York: Russell & Russell, Inc., 1962.

Kullman, Colby H., and William C. Young, eds. *Theatre Companies of the World, Vols. I and II.* Westport, Conn.: Greenwood Press, 1986.

Lahr, John. *Up Against the Fourth Wall: Essays on Modern Theater.* New York: Grove Press, 1968.

   Astonish Me. New York: Viking, 1973.

Langley, Stephen. *Theatre Management and Production in America.* New York: Drama Book Publishers, 1990.

Langworthy, Douglas. "Theatre at the Crossroads." *American Theatre* 12 (November 1995).

Larson, Orville K. *Scene Design in the American Theatre from 1915 to 1960.* Fayetteville: University of Arkansas Press, 1989.

Laufe, Abe. *Broadway's Greatest Musicals.* Revised edn. New York: Funk & Wagnalls, 1977.

Lees, Gene. *Inventing Champagne: The Worlds of Lerner and Loewe.* New York: St. Martin's Press, 1990.

Leeson, Richard M. *William Inge: A Research and Production Sourcebook.* Westport, Conn.: Greenwood Press, 1994.

Leiter, Samuel L. *From Belasco to Brook: Representative Directors of the English-Speaking Stage.* Westport, Conn.: Greenwood Press, 1991.

The Great Stage Directors: 100 Distinguished Careers of the Theater. New York: Facts on File, 1994.

"Actors, Directors, and Critics." In *Ten Seasons: New York Theatre in the Seventies.* Westport, Conn.: Greenwood Press, 1986.

Lerner, Alan Jay. *The Street Where I Live.* New York: W.W. Norton, 1978.

Lesnick, Henry. *Guerilla Street Theatre.* New York: Bard Books, 1973.

Leverich, Lyle. *Tom: The Unknown Tennessee Williams.* New York: Crown, 1995.

Lewis, Allan. *American Plays and Playwrights of the Contemporary Theatre.* New York: Crown, 1965.

Lewis, Peter. "Change of Scene for a Mellow Miller." *Sunday Times* 3 November 1991: 6.

Lewis, Robert. *Method – or Madness?* New York: Samuel French, 1958.

Slings and Arrows: Theatre in My Life. New York: Stein and Day, 1984.

Little, Stuart W. *Off-Broadway: The Prophetic Theatre.* New York: Coward, McCann & Geoghegan, Inc., 1972.

"The Living Theatre." Special issue of *Yale/Theatre* 2.1 (Spring 1969).

Loeffler, Carl, and Darlene Tong. *Performance Anthology.* San Francisco: Contemporary Arts Press, 1980.

Loesser, Susan. *A Most Remarkable Fella: Frank Loesser and the Guys and Dolls in his Life.* New York: Donald I. Fine, 1993.

Logan, Joshua. *Josh: My Up and Down, In and Out Life.* New York: Delacorte Press, 1976.

London, Todd, ed. *The Artistic Home.* New York: Theatre Communications Group, 1988.

Londré, Felicia Hardison. *Tennessee Williams.* New York: Frederick Ungar, 1983.

Loney, Glenn. *Unsung Genius: The Passion of Dancer-Choreographer Jack Cole.* New York: Franklin Watts, 1984.

Lowell, Robert. "Memories of West Street and Lepke." In *Life Stories.* New York: Farrar, Straus, Giroux, 1959.

Lowry, W. McNeil, ed. *The Performing Arts and American Society.* Englewood Cliffs, N.J.: Prentice Hall, 1978.

Luce, Henry. *The Ideas of Henry Luce.* New York: Atheneum, 1969.

Ludlam, Charles. *The Complete Plays of Charles Ludlam.* New York: Harper & Row (Perennia Library), 1989.

Ridiculous Theatre: Scourge of Human Folly. Ed. Steven Samuels. New York: Theatre Communications Group, 1992.

Malina, Judith. *The Diaries of Judith Malina 1947–1957.* New York: Grove Press, 1984.

"Directing *The Brig.*" In Kenneth H. Brown, *The Brig.* New York: Hill and Wang, 1965.

Mamet, David. *The Hero Pony.* New York: Grove Press, 1990.

Writing in Restaurants. New York: Viking, 1986.

Mandelbaum, Ken. *A Chorus Line and the Musicals of Michael Bennett.* New York: St. Martin's Press, 1989.

Not Since Carrie: Forty Years of Broadway Musical Flops. New York: St. Martin's Press, 1991.

Marcus, Greil. *Ranters & Crowd Pleasers: Punk in Pop Music, 1977–1992.* New York: Doubleday, 1993.

Marranca, Bonnie. *Theatrewritings.* New York: Performing Arts Journal, 1984.

The Theatre of Images. Rpt. with new afterword. Baltimore: Johns Hopkins University Press, 1996.

Marranca, Bonnie, ed. *American Dreams: The Imagination of Sam Shepard.* New York: Performing Arts Journal Publications, 1981.

Martin, Ralph. *Lincoln Center for the Performing Arts.* Englewood Cliffs, N.J.: Prentice Hall, 1971.

Martin, Robert A., ed. *The Theater Essays of Arthur Miller.* New York: Viking, 1978.

Arthur Miller: New Perspectives. Englewood Cliffs, N.J.: Prentice Hall, 1982.

Martine, James J., ed. *Critical Essays on Arthur Miller.* Boston: G.K. Hall & Co., 1979.

Maslon, Laurence. *The Arena: The First Forty Years.* Washington, D.C.: Arena Stage, 1991.

Mast, Gerald. *Can't Help Singin': The American Musical on Stage and Screen.* Woodstock, N.Y.: Overlook Press, 1987.

Mayleas, Ruth. "Resident Theaters and National Theaters." *Theater* 10. 3 (Summer 1979).

McCandless, Stanley. *Method of Lighting the Stage.* New York: Theatre Arts Books, 1958.

A Syllabus of Stage Lighting. New York: Drama Book Specialists, 1964.

McCandless, Stanley R., and Joel E. Rubin. *Illuminating Engineering: Significant Developments for the Past Fifty Years.* New York, 1956.

McCarthy, Gerry. *Edward Albee.* New York: St. Martin's Press, 1987.

McDonough, Carla J. *Staging Masculinity: Male Identity in Contemporary American Drama.* New York: Garland, 1997.

McDonough, Edwin J. *Quintero Directs O'Neill.* San Francisco: a capella press, 1991.

McGovern, Edythe M. *Neil Simon: A Critical Study.* New York: Frederick Ungar, 1979.

McKnight, Gerald. *Andrew Lloyd Webber.* New York: St. Martin's Press, 1984.

McLuhan, Marshall. *Understanding Media.* New York: McGraw-Hill, 1964.

McNamara, Brooks, Jerry Rojo, and Richard Schechner. *Theatres, Spaces, Environments.* New York: Drama Book Specialists, 1975.

McNamara, Brooks, and Jill Dolan, eds. *The Drama Review: Thirty Years of Commentary on the Avant-Garde.* Ann Arbor, Mich.: UMI Research Press, 1986.

Meisner, Sanford, with Dennis Longwell. *Sanford Meisner on Acting.* New York: Vintage Books, 1987.

Melville, Keith. *Communes in the Counter Culture.* New York: William Morrow & Co., 1972.

Mendus, Edward J., ed. "Regional Theatre '67." *New York State Community Theatre Journal* (1967).

Menta, Ed. *The Magic World Behind the Curtain: Andrei Serban in the American Theatre.* New York: Peter Lang, 1995.

Meserve, Walter, ed. *Discussions of Modern American Drama.* Boston: D.C. Heath, 1966.

Meyerson, Harold, and Ernie Harburg. *Who Put the Rainbow in The Wizard of Oz? Yip Harburg, Lyricist.* Ann Arbor: University of Michigan Press, 1993.

Mielziner, Jo. *Designing for the Theatre: A Memoir and a Portfolio.* New York: Atheneum, 1965.

The Shapes of Our Theatre. New York: Clarkson N. Potter, 1970.

Miller, Arthur. *Timebends: A Life.* New York: Grove Press, 1987.

"Miller's Tales." *New Yorker* 11 April 1994: 35–36.

The Portable Arthur Miller. Ed. and Introduction Christopher Bigsby. New York: Viking, 1995.

"About Theatre Language." In *The Last Yankee.* New York: Penguin, 1994.

Miller, Douglas T., and Marion Nowak. *The Fifties: The Way We Really Were.* New York: Doubleday, 1977.

Miller, Judith. "Future of Arts Agency Unclear." *New York Times* 14 March 1996.

Mitchell, Loften. *Black Drama: The Story of the American Negro in the Theatre.* New York: Hawthorn, 1967.

Moore, Thomas Gale. *The Economics of the American Theater.* Durham, N.C.: Duke University Press, 1968.

Morales, Ed. "Theatre and the Wolfe." *American Theatre* 10 (Dec. 1994): 15–20.

Mordden, Ethan. *The American Theatre.* New York: Oxford University Press, 1981.

    Better Foot Forward: The History of American Musical Theatre. New York: Grossman-Viking, 1976.

    Broadway Babies: The People Who Made the American Musical. New York: Oxford University Press, 1983.

    Rodgers & Hammerstein. New York: Harry N. Abrams, 1992.

Morgan, Iwan W., and Neil A. Wynn, eds. *America's Century: Perspectives on U.S. History Since 1900.* New York: Holms and Meier, 1993.

Morrow, Lee Alan. *The Tony Award Book: Four Decades of Great American Theater.* New York: Abbeville, 1987.

Morrow, Lee Alan, and Frank Pike. *Creating Theater.* New York: Vintage, 1986.

Moss, Leonard. *Arthur Miller.* 1967. New York: Twayne Publishers, 1980.

Motherwell, Robert. *The Collected Writings of Robert Motherwell.* Ed. Stephanie Terenzio. New York: Oxford University Press, 1992.

Mottram, Ron. *Inner Landscapes: The Theater of Sam Shepard.* Columbia: University of Missouri Press, 1984.

Mullin, Donald C. *The Development of the Playhouse.* Berkeley: University of California Press, 1970.

Murphy, Brenda. *Tennessee Williams and Elia Kazan: A Collaboration in the Theatre.* New York and Cambridge: Cambridge University Press, 1992.

Murphy, Brenda, ed. *The Cambridge Companion to American Women Playwrights.* Cambridge: Cambridge University Press, 1999.

Nadel, Alan, ed. *May All Your Fences Have Gates: Essays on the Drama of August Wilson.* Iowa City: University of Iowa Press, 1994.

Napoleon, Davi. *Chelsea on the Edge: The Adventures of an American Theatre.* Ames, Iowa: Iowa State University Press, 1991.

Nassour, Ellis, and Richard Broderick. *Rock Opera: The Creation of Jesus Christ Superstar from Record Album to Broadway Show and Motion Picture.* New York: Hawthorn Books, 1973.

Nolan, Frederick. *The Sound of Their Music: The Story of Rodgers and Hammerstein.* New York: Walker, 1978.

Novick, Julius. *Beyond Broadway: The Quest for Permanent Theatres.* New York: Hill & Wang, 1968.

Oenslager, Donald. *Scenery Then and Now.* New York: Russell & Russell, 1966.

    Stage Design: Four Centuries of Scenic Invention. New York: Viking, 1975.

    The Theatre of Donald Oenslager. Middletown, Conn.: Wesleyan University Press, 1978.

Oliphant, Dave, ed. *Twentieth-Century American Playwrights: Views of a Changing Culture.* Austin: Harry Ransom Humanities Research Center, 1994.

Orzel, Nick, and Michael Smith. *Eight Plays from Off-Off Broadway.* Indianapolis: The Bobbs-Merrill Company, 1966.

Oumano, Ellen. *Sam Shepard: The Life and Work of an American Dreamer.* New York: St. Martin's Press, 1986.

Overmyer, Eric. *Collected Plays.* Lyme, N.H.: Smith and Kraus, 1993.

Owen, Bobbi. *Costume Design on Broadway: Designers and Their Credits, 1915–1985.* Westport, Conn.: Greenwood Press, 1987.

Lighting Design on Broadway: Designers and Their Credits, 1915–1990. Westport, Conn.: Greenwood Press, 1991.

Scenic Design on Broadway: Designers and Their Credits, 1915–1990. Westport, Conn.: Greenwood Press, 1991.

Palmer, Richard H. *The Lighting Art: The Aesthetics of Stage Lighting Design.* Englewood Cliffs, N.J.: Prentice Hall, 1985.

Parker, Dorothy, ed. *Essays on Modern American Drama: Williams, Miller, Albee, and Shepard.* Toronto: University of Toronto Press, 1987.

Partisan Review. "Our Country and Our Culture." 19.3 (May–June 1952): 282–326.

Pasolli, Robert. *A Book on the Open Theatre.* Indianapolis: The Bobbs-Merrill Company, 1970.

Patterson, James. *Grand Expectations: The United States, 1945–1974.* New York: Oxford University Press, 1996.

Pearce, Michele. "Liz Diamond: She's a Director with Obsessions, on the Verge of a Sea Change." *American Theatre* 9 (September 1992): 38–41.

Pecktal, Lynn. *Designing and Drawing for the Theatre.* New York: McGraw-Hill, 1995.

Pendleton, Ralph. *The Theatre of Robert Edmond Jones.* Middletown, Conn.: Wesleyan University Press, 1958.

Perry, George C. *The Complete Phantom of the Opera.* New York: Holt, 1988.

Sunset Boulevard: From Movie to Musical. London: Pavilion, 1993; New York: Holt, 1993.

Phillips, Lisa, ed. *Beat Culture and the New America 1950–1965.* New York: Whitney Museum of American Art, 1995.

Poggi, Jack, *Theater in America: The Impact of Economic Forces, 1870–1967.* Ithaca, N.Y.: Cornell University Press, 1968.

Polakov, Lester. *We Live to Paint Again.* New York: Logbooks Press, 1993.

Poland, Albert, and Bruce Mailman. *The Off-Off Broadway Book: The Plays, People, Theatre.* Indianapolis: Bobbs-Merrill, 1972.

Porter, Thomas E. *Myth and Modern American Drama.* Detroit: Wayne State University Press, 1969.

Porterfield, Robert, and Robert Breen. "Toward a National Theatre." *Theatre Arts* (October 1945): 599–602.

Postman, Neil. *Amusing Ourselves to Death.* New York: Penguin Books, 1985.

Prince, Harold. *Contradictions: Notes on Twenty-Six Years in the Theatre.* New York: Dodd, Mead, 1974.

Quintero, José. *If You Don't Dance They Beat You.* Boston: Little, Brown, 1974.

Reinelt, Janelle G., and Joseph R. Roach, eds. *Critical Theory and Performance.* Ann Arbor: University of Michigan Press, 1992.

Reische, Diana, L., ed. *The Performing Arts in America.* New York: The H.W. Wilson Company, 1973.

"Resident Theaters in America." *Theater* 10, no. 3 (Summer 1979): entire issue.

Rich, Frank. "Exit the Critic." *New York Times Magazine* 13 February 1994.

Rich, Frank, with Lisa Aronson. *The Theatre Art of Boris Aronson.* New York: Alfred Knopf, 1987.

Riesman, David, et al. *The Lonely Crowd: A Study in the Changing American Character.* New Haven, Conn.: Yale University Press, 1950.

Rischbeiter, Henning. *Art and the Stage in the Twentieth Century.* Greenwich, Conn.: New York Graphic Society, 1968.

Robert Wilson: The Theatre of Images. New York: Harper and Row, 1978.

Robinson, Marc. *The Other American Drama.* Cambridge and New York: Cambridge University Press, 1994.

Robinson, Mary C., Vera Roberts, and Millie Barranger, eds. *Notable Women in the American Theatre.* Westport, Conn.: Greenwood Press, 1989.

Rockefeller Panel Report. *The Performing Arts: Problems and Prospects.* New York: McGraw-Hill, 1965.

Rodgers, Richard. *Musical Stages: An Autobiography.* New York: Random House, 1975.

Rogoff, Gordon. *Theatre Is Not Safe.* Evanston, Ill.: Northwestern University Press, 1987.

Roose-Evans, James. *Experimental Theatre from Stanislavsky to Today.* New York: Universe Books, 1971.

Rosenberg, Bernard, and Ernest Harburg. *The Broadway Musical: Collaboration in Commerce and Art.* New York: New York University Press, 1993.

Rosenberg, Harold. *The Tradition of the New.* New York: McGraw-Hill, 1965.

Rosenthal, Jean, and Lael Wertenbaker. *The Magic of Light.* Boston: Little, Brown, 1972.

Roth, Moira. *The Amazing Decade: Women and Performance.* Los Angeles: Art in America. Astro Artz, 1983.

Roth, Philip. *American Pastoral.* London: Jonathan Cape, 1997.

Roudané, Matthew C. *Contemporary Authors Bibliographical Series, Volume Three: American Dramatists.* Detroit: Gale Research, 1989.

Roudané, Matthew C. *Understanding Edward Albee.* Columbia: University of South Carolina Press, 1987.

Roudané, Matthew C., ed. *American Drama Since 1960: A Critical History.* New York: Twayne Publishers, 1996.

Public Issues, Private Tensions: Contemporary American Drama. New York: AMS Press, 1993.

Conversations with Arthur Miller. Jackson: University Press of Mississippi, 1987.

The Cambridge Companion to Tennessee Williams. Cambridge and New York: Cambridge University Press, 1997.

Rubin, Joel, and Lee Watson. *Theatrical Lighting Practice.* New York: Theatre Arts Books, 1954.

Russell, Douglas A. *Stage Costume Design, Theory, Technique and Style.* Englewood Cliffs, N.J.: Prentice Hall, 1985.

Rutenberg, Michael E. *Edward Albee: Playwright in Protest.* New York: Avon Books, 1969.

Ryzuk, Mary S. *The Circle Repertory Company: The First Fifteen Years.* Ames: Iowa State University Press, 1989.

Sainer, Arthur. *The New Radical Theatre Notebook.* New York: Applause Books, 1997.

Savran, David. *The Wooster Group 1975–1985: Breaking the Rules.* Ann Arbor, Mich.: UMI Research Press, 1986.

In Their Own Words: Contemporary American Playwrights. New York: Theatre Communications Group, 1988.

Communists, Cowboys, and Queers: The Politics of Masculinity in the Works of Arthur Miller and Tennessee Williams. Minneapolis: University of Minnesota Press, 1992.

"An Interview with August Wilson." In Jacobus, *Introduction to Drama.* 1, 576–79.

"Tony Kushner [Interview]." In Kolin and Kullman, *Speaking on Stage.* 291–313.

Sayre, Henry M. *The Object of Performance: The American Avant-Garde Since 1970.* Chicago: The University of Chicago Press, 1992.

Schechner, Richard. *Public Domain.* Indianapolis: Bobbs-Merrill, 1969.

Environmental Theater. New York: Hawthorn Books, 1973; new edn. New York: Applause Books, 1994.

Schechner, Richard, ed. "The Regional Theatre: Four Views." *The Drama Review* 13 (Fall 1968): 25–26.

Schevill, James. *Break Out! In Search of New Theatrical Environments.* Chicago: The Swallow Press, Inc., 1973.

Schlueter, June. *Modern American Drama: The Female Canon.* Cranbury, N.J.: Fairleigh Dickinson University Press, 1990.

Schlueter, June, ed. *Feminist Rereadings of Modern American Drama.* Cranbury, N.J.: Fairleigh Dickinson University Press, 1989.

Schlueter, June, and James K. Flanagan. *Arthur Miller.* New York: The Ungar Publishing Co., 1987.

Schmitt, Natalie Crohn. *Actors and Onlookers.* Evanston, Ill.: Northwestern University Press, 1990.

Schneider, Alan. *Entrances: An American Director's Journey.* New York: Viking, 1986.

Schneider, Pierre. "Interview with Woks." *Art News* 58 (March 1959).

Schroeder, Patricia R. *The Feminist Possibilities of Dramatic Realism.* Madison, N.J.: Fairleigh Dickinson University Press, 1996.

Schwartz, Charles. *Cole Porter: A Biography.* New York: Da Capo, 1979.

Seitz, William C. *The Art of Assemblage.* New York: The Museum of Modern Art, 1961.

Selden, Samuel, and Hunton D. Sellman. *Stage Scenery and Lighting.* New York: Appleton-Century-Crofts, 1959.

Sellman, Hunton D., and Merrill Lesley. *Essentials of Stage Lighting.* Englewood Cliffs, N.J.: Prentice-Hall, 1982.

Shank, Theodore. *American Alternative Theatre.* New York: Grove Press, 1982.

Sheehy, Helen. *Margo: The Life and Theatre of Margo Jones.* Dallas: Southern Methodist University Press, 1990.

Shepard, Sam. "Language, Visualization, and the Inner Library." In Marranca, *American Dreams.* 214–19.

"Metaphors, Mad Dogs and Old Time Cowboys: Interview with Sam Shepard." In Marranca, *American Dreams.* 187–209.

Sheward, David. *It's a Hit! The Back Stage Book of Longest Running Broadway Shows 1884 to the Present.* New York: Back Stage Books (Watson-Guptill), 1994.

Shewey, Don, "A Boot in Two Camps." *American Theatre* 3 (October 1986): 12–17, 46.

Shyer, Laurence. *Robert Wilson and His Collaborators.* New York: Theatre Communications Group, 1989.

Sievers, W. David. *Freud on Broadway.* New York: Hermitage House, 1955.

Silverman, Maxwell. *Contemporary Theatre Architecture: An Illustrated Survey.* New York: The New York Public Library, 1965.

Silvester, Robert. *United States Theatre: A Bibliography from the Beginning to 1990.* Romsey, UK: Motley Press, 1993; New York: G.K. Hall & Co., 1993.

Simon, Neil. *Rewrites: A Memoir.* New York: Simon & Schuster, 1996.

Simonson, Lee. *Part of a Lifetime: Drawings and Designs, 1919–1940.* New York: Duell, Sloan and Pearce, 1943.

The Art of Scenic Design: A Pictorial Analysis of Stage Setting and its Relation to Theatrical Productions. New York: Harper, 1950.

Smith, Cecil, and Glenn Litton. *Musical Comedy in America*. New York: Theatre Arts Books, 1981.

Smith, Michael. *The Best of Off-Off Broadway*. New York: E.P. Dutton, 1969.

More Plays from Off-Off Broadway. Indianapolis: The Bobbs-Merrill Company, 1972.

Smith, Ronn. *American Set Design 2*. New York: Theatre Communications Group,1991.

Smith, Susan Harris. *American Drama: The Bastard Art*. New York and Cambridge: Cambridge University Press, 1997.

Sontag, Susan. *Against Interpretation*. New York: Dell, 1966.

Sponberg, Arvid F. *Broadway Talks: What Professionals Think about Commercial Theatre in America*. Westport, Conn.: Greenwood Press, 1991.

Spoto, Donald. *The Kindness of Strangers: The Life of Tennessee Williams*. Boston: Little, Brown and Co., 1985.

Stanislavski, Constantin. *An Actor Prepares*. Trans. E.R. Hapgood. New York: Theatre Arts Books, 1936.

Building a Character. Trans. E.R. Hapgood. New York: Theatre Arts Books, 1949.

Creating a Role. Trans. E.R. Hapgood. New York: Theatre Arts Books, 1961.

Stanton, Stephen S., ed. *Tennessee Williams: A Collection of Critical Essays*. Englewood Cliffs, N.J.: Prentice Hall, 1977.

Starr, Jerold M., ed. *Cultural Politics: Radical Movements in Modern History*. New York: Praeger Publishers, 1985.

Stein, Gertrude. "Plays." In *Lectures in America*. Boston: Beacon Press, 1985.

Stoddard, Richard. *Theatre and Cinema Architecture: A Guide to Information Sources*. Detroit: Gale Research Company, 1978.

Strasberg, Lee. *A Dream of Passion: The Development of the Method*. Boston: Little, Brown, 1987.

Summers, Louis Jeriel, Jr. "The Rise of the Director-Choreographer in the American Musical Theatre." Diss., University of Missouri–Columbia, 1976.

Suskin, Steven. *Opening Nights on Broadway: A Critical Quotebook of the Golden Era of the Musical Theatre*. New York: Schirmer-Macmillan, 1990.

More Opening Nights on Broadway: A Critical Quotebook of the Musical Theatre, 1965 through 1981. New York: Schirmer-Simon and Schuster Macmillan, 1997.

Swain, Joseph P. *The Broadway Musical: A Critical and Musical Survey*. New York: Oxford University Press, 1990.

Taubman, Howard. *The Making of the American Theatre*. New York: Coward McCann, 1965.

Taylor, Deems. *Some Enchanted Evenings: The Story of Rodgers and Hammerstein*. New York: Harper, 1953.

Taylor, Theodore. *Jule: The Story of Composer Jule Styne*. New York: Random House, 1979.

Tharpe, Jac, ed. *Tennessee Williams: A Tribute*. Jackson: University Press of Mississippi, 1977.

Tischler, Nancy M. *Tennessee Williams: Rebellious Puritan*. 1961. New York: The Citadel Press, 1965.

Tomkins, Calvin. *The Bride and the Bachelors*. New York: Viking, 1968.

Off the Wall: Robert Rauschenberg and the Art World of Our Time. New York: Penguin Books, 1981.

Trilling, Lionel. *Beyond Culture: Essays on Literature and Learning*. New York and London: Harcourt, Brace, Jovanovich, 1965.

Tucker, Martin. *Sam Shepard*. New York: The Continuum Publishing Co., 1992.

Tytell, John. *The Living Theatre: Art, Exile, and Outrage.* New York: Grove Press, 1995.

Updike, John. *Museums and Women.* New York: Alfred A. Knopf, 1972.

Vaughan, Stuart. *A Possible Theatre: The Experience of a Pioneer Director in America's Resident Theatre.* New York: McGraw-Hill, 1969.

Venturi, Robert, D. Scott-Brown, and S. Izenour. *Learning from Las Vegas.* Cambridge, Mass.: MIT Press, 1977.

Viagas, Robert, Baayork Lee, and Thommie Walsh. *On the Line: The Creation of A Chorus Line.* New York: William Morrow, 1990.

Vorlicky, Robert. *Act Like a Man: Challenging Masculinities in American Drama.* Ann Arbor: University of Michigan Press, 1995.

Vorlicky, Robert, ed: *Tony Kushner in Conversation.* Ann Arbor: University of Michigan Press, 1998.

Voss, Ralph F. *A Life of William Inge: The Strains of Triumph.* Lawrence: University Press of Kansas, 1989.

Wade, Leslie A. *Sam Shepard and the American Theatre.* Westport, Conn.: Praeger Publishers, 1997.

Wager, Walter, ed. *The Playwrights Speak.* New York: Delta Books, 1967.

Walsh, Michael. *Andrew Lloyd Webber, His Life and Works: A Critical Biography.* London: Viking-Penguin, 1989; New York: Harry N. Abrams, 1989.

Wardle, Irving. "America's Cultural Supermarkets." *The London Times Saturday Review* 24 February 1968.

Watson, Charles S. *The History of Southern Drama.* Lexington: University Press of Kentucky, 1997.

Watson, Lee. *Lighting Design Handbook.* New York: McGraw-Hill, 1990.

Watt, Stephen, and Gary A. Richardson, eds. *American Drama: Colonial to Contemporary.* Fort Worth: Harcourt Brace, 1995.

Weales, Gerald. *American Drama since World War II.* New York: Harcourt Brace, 1962.

Weber, Bruce. "At 50, a Mellower David Mamet May Be Ready to Tell His Story." *The New York Times.* 16 November 1997: Arts Sec.: 7, 12.

Weinberg, Mark S. *Challenging the Hierarchy: Collective Theatre in the United States.* Westport, Conn.: Greenwood Press, 1992.

Weisman, John. *Guerrilla Theatre: Scenarios for a Revolution.* Garden City, N.Y.: Anchor Press/Doubleday, 1973.

Welland, Dennis. *Miller: The Playwright.* 1979. London and New York: Methuen, 1983.

Wellman, Mac. *The Bad Infinity: Eight Plays by Mac Wellman.* Baltimore: Johns Hopkins University Press, 1994.

Wetzsteon, Ross, ed. *The Obie Winners: The Best of Off-Broadway.* Garden City, N.Y.: Doubleday, 1980.

Whitmore, Jon. *Directing Postmodern Theater.* Ann Arbor: University of Michigan Press, 1994.

Whyte, William H. *The Organization Man.* New York: Simon and Schuster, 1956.

Wiles, Timothy. *The Theater Event: Modern Theories of Performance.* Chicago: University of Chicago Press, 1980.

Williams, Mance. *Black Theatre in the 1960s and 1970s.* Westport, Conn.: Greenwood Press, 1985.

Williams, Tennessee. *Memoirs.* Garden City, N.Y.: Doubleday, 1975.

Wills, J. Robert. *The Director in a Changing Theatre.* Palo Alto, Calif.: Mayfield, 1976.

Willson, Meredith. *"But He Doesn't Know the Territory."* New York: Putman, 1959.

Wilmeth, Don B. "A History of the Margo Jones Theatre." Diss., University of Illinois, 1964.

Wilmeth, Don B. and Tice L. Miller, eds. *Cambridge Guide to American Theatre.* New York and Cambridge: Cambridge University Press, 1993; updated/corrected, 1996.

Willis, John, ed. *Theatre World.* New York: Crown, 1945–89; Applause, 1990–present.

Wilson, August. "August Wilson Interview." *Dialogue* (Summer 1990): 9.

Woll, Allen. *Black Musical Theatre: From Coontown to Dreamgirls.* Baton Rouge: Lousiana State University Press, 1989.

Woods, Jeannie Marlin. *Theatre to Change Men's Souls: The Artistry of Adrian Hall.* Newark: University of Delaware Press, 1993.

Yacowar, Maurice. *Tennessee Williams and Film.* New York: Frederick Ungar, 1977.

Young, William C. *Famous American Playhouses.* 2 vols. Chicago: American Library Association, 1973.

Zadan, Craig. *Sondheim & Co.* 2nd edn., updated. New York: Harper & Row, 1989.

Zarrilli, Phillip B., ed. *Acting (Re) Considered.* New York: Routledge, 1995.

Zeigler, Joseph Wesley. *Regional Theatre: The Revolutionary Stage.* Minneapolis: University of Minnesota Press, 1973; rpt. with with new afterword, New York: Da Capo Press, 1977.

Index